Heinrich Schliemann, Archibald Henry Sayce

Troja

Results of the Latest Researches and Discoveries on the Site of Homer's Troy

Heinrich Schliemann, Archibald Henry Sayce

Troja
Results of the Latest Researches and Discoveries on the Site of Homer's Troy

ISBN/EAN: 9783744798525

Printed in Europe, USA, Canada, Australia, Japan

Cover: Foto ©ninafisch / pixelio.de

More available books at **www.hansebooks.com**

TROJA

RESULTS OF THE LATEST
RESEARCHES AND DISCOVERIES ON THE SITE OF HOMER'S TROY

AND IN THE HEROIC TUMULI AND OTHER SITES
MADE IN THE YEAR 1882

AND A NARRATIVE OF A JOURNEY IN THE TROAD IN 1881

BY

DR. HENRY SCHLIEMANN

HON. D.C.L., OXON., AND HON. FELLOW OF QUEEN'S COLLEGE, OXFORD
F.S.A., F.R.I.B.A.
AUTHOR OF "ILIOS," "TROY AND ITS REMAINS," AND "MYCENAE AND TIRYNS"

PREFACE BY PROFESSOR A. H. SAYCE

WITH 150 WOODCUTS AND 4 MAPS AND PLANS

"Die Oertlichkeit ist das von einer längst vergangenen Begebenheit übriggebliebene Stück Wirklichkeit. Sie ist sehr oft der fossile Knochenrest, aus dem das Gerippe der Begebenheit sich herstellen lässt, und das Bild, welches die Geschichte in halbverwischten Zügen überliefert, tritt durch sie in klarer Anschauung hervor."—
MOLTKE: *Wanderbuch*, p. 19, Berlin, 1879

NEW YORK
HARPER & BROTHERS, FRANKLIN SQUARE
1884

MAP OF THE TROAD

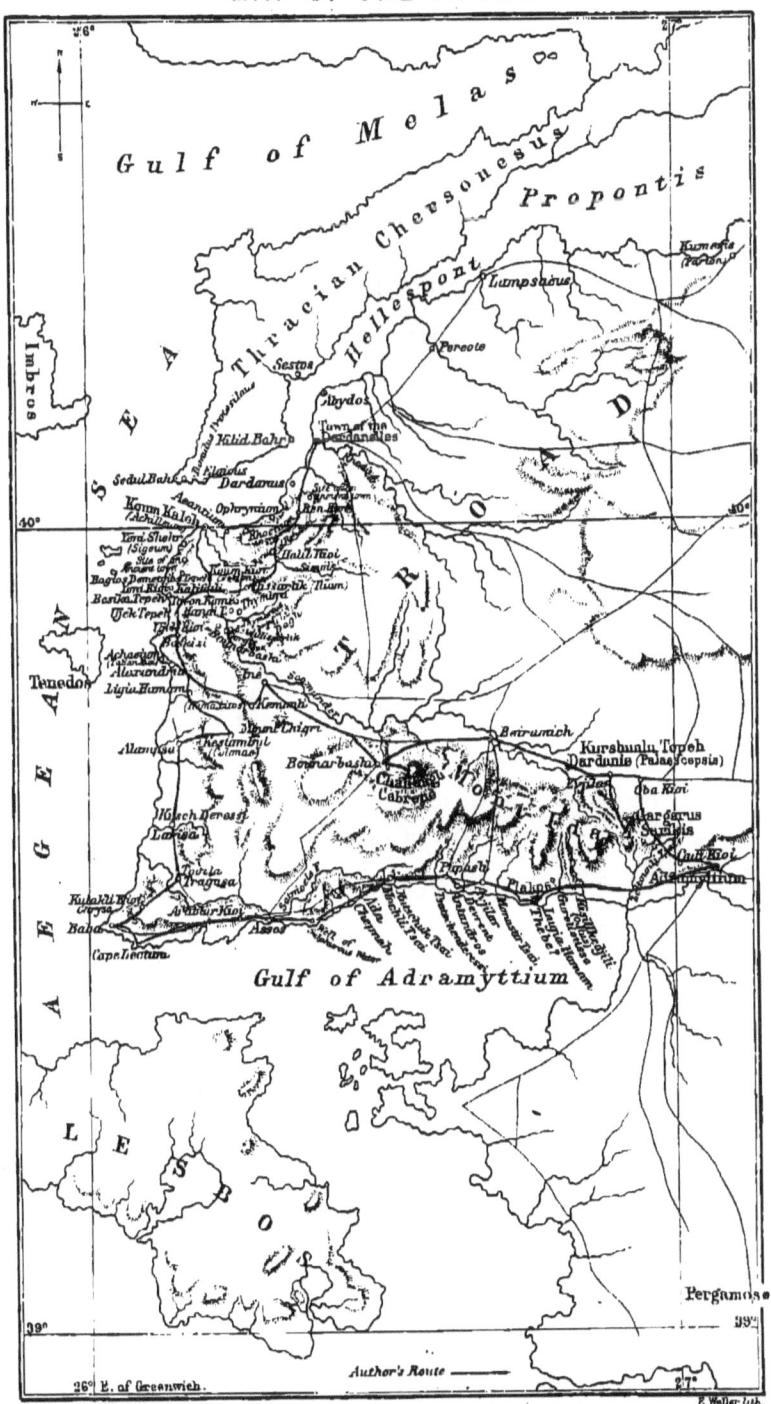

HAVING INSCRIBED HIS FORMER WORKS
WITH THE NAMES OF
GREAT SCHOLARS AND EXPLORERS,
THE AUTHOR
DEDICATES THIS TO ALL WHO LOVE
THE POETRY OF HOMER,
AND TO ALL WHO ARE SEARCHING FOR
THE LIGHT THROWN ON HISTORY
BY THE
SCIENCE OF ARCHÆOLOGY.

PREFACE.

HARDLY ten years have passed since the veil of an impenetrable night seemed to hang over the beginnings of Greek history Wolf and his followers had torn in pieces the body of Homer; the school of Niebuhr had criticized the legends of pre-literary Hellas until it had left none of them remaining; and the science of comparative mythology had determined that "the tale of Troy divine," like that of the beleaguerment of Kadmeian Thebes, was but a form of the immemorial story which told how the battlements of the sky were stormed day after day by the bright powers of heaven. The earlier portion of the "History" of Grote marks the close and summing-up of this period of destructive criticism. We have no authorities, the great historian showed, which reach back to that heroic epoch of Greece, between which and the literary epoch lies a deep unchronicled chasm, while the legends turned into history by rationalizing annalists cannot be distinguished from those that related to the gods. Our evidence for the so-called heroic or prehistoric period had been tried and found wanting; the myths told of the ancient heroes might indeed contain some elements of truth, but it was impossible for us now to discover them. All parts of a myth hang closely together, it was pointed out with inexorable logic, and we cannot arbitrarily separate and distinguish them one from another.

The work of destruction necessarily precedes the work of reconstruction. It is not until our existing authorities have been sifted and judged, until all that is false and uncertain has been swept out of the way, that the ground is cleared for building up the edifice of fact with new and better materials. Even while the decisions of Grote were still ruling our conceptions of primaeval Greece, Professor Ernst Curtius had perceived with the eye of genius that they were not, and could not be, final. The ethnology of Greece at the dawn of literary history presupposes the ethnology of the heroic age, and ancient myths could not have been attached to certain events and been localized in certain regions, unless there had been some reason for their being so. Cyrus and Charlemagne are heroes of romance only because they were first of all heroes of reality. But Professor Ernst Curtius perceived more than this. The discoveries of Botta and Layard in Nineveh and of Renan in Phoenicia had revealed to him that the germs of the art, and therewith of the culture, of primitive Greece, must have come from the East. The discredited theories which had connected the East and West together were revived, but in a new and scientific form; no longer based on wild speculations, but on the sure foundations of ascertained facts. Curtius even saw already that Oriental influence must have flowed to Greece through two channels, not through the Phoenicians only, but along the high roads of Asia Minor as well.

But what Curtius had divined he was not in a position to prove. The conclusions of Grote still held almost undisputed sway, and the 6th or 7th century B.C. was fixed upon by classical scholars as the mystical period beyond which neither civilization nor history was possible. Even now we are still under the influence of the spirit of scepticism which has resulted from the destructive criticism of the last half-century. The natural tendency of the student of to-day is to post-date rather than to ante-date, and to bring everything down to the latest period that is possible. The same reluctance which the scientific world felt in admitting the antiquity of man, when first asserted by Boucher de Perthes, has been felt by modern scholars in admitting the antiquity of civilization. First, however, the

Egyptologists, then more recently the decipherers of the monuments of Assyria and Babylonia, have been forced to yield to the stubborn evidence of facts. It is now the turn of the students of Greek and Asianic archaeology to do so too. For here, also, the hand of the explorer and excavator has been at work, and the history of the remote past has been literally dug out of the earth in which it has so long lain buried.

The problem, from which the scholars of Europe had turned away in despair, has been solved by the skill, the energy, and the perseverance, of Dr. Schliemann. At Troy, at Mykênae, and at Orkhomenos, he has recovered a past which had already become but a shadowy memory in the age of Peisistratos. We can measure the civilization and knowledge of the peoples who inhabited those old cities, can handle the implements they used and the weapons they carried, can map out the chambers of the houses where they lived, can admire the pious care with which they tended their dead, can even trace the limits of their intercourse with other nations, and the successive stages of culture through which they passed. The heroes of the Iliad and Odyssey have become to us men of flesh and blood; we can watch both them, and older heroes still, in almost every act of their daily life, and even determine their nature and the capacity of their skulls. It is little wonder if so marvellous a recovery of a past in which we had ceased to believe, should have awakened many controversies, and wrought a silent revolution in our conceptions of Greek history. It is little wonder if at first the discoverer who had so rudely shocked the settled prejudices of the historian should have met with a storm of indignant opposition or covert attack. But in this case what was new was also what was true, and, as fact after fact has accumulated and excavation after excavation been systematically carried out, the storm has slowly died away, to be followed by warm acknowledgment and unreserved acquiescence. To-day no trained archaeologist in Greece or Western Europe doubts the main facts which Dr. Schliemann's excavations have established; we can never again return to the ideas of ten years ago.

Excavation probably seems at first sight a very simple matter. This is not the case, however, if it is to be of any real use to science. The excavator must know where and how to dig; above all, he must know the value of what he finds. The broken sherds which ignorance flings away are often in the archaeologist's eyes the most precious relics bequeathed to us by the past. To be a successful excavator, a combination of qualities is necessary which are seldom found together. It is to this combination that we owe the recovery of Troy and Mykênae, and the reconstruction of ancient history that has resulted therefrom. Dr. Schliemann's enthusiasm and devotion to his work has been matched only by his knowledge of ancient Greek literature, by his power of conversing freely in the languages of his workmen, by the strength of body which enabled him to withstand the piercing winds, the blinding dust, the scanty food, and all the other hardships he has had to undergo, and above all by that scientific spirit which has led him in pilgrimage through the museums of Europe, has made him seek the help of archaeologists and architects, and has caused him to relinquish his most cherished theories as soon as the evidence bade him do so. And his reward has come at last. The dreams of his childhood have been realized; he has made it clear as the daylight that, if the Troy of Greek story had any earthly habitation at all, it could only have been on the mound of Hissarlik.

This, as he himself has told us, was the supreme goal of the labour of his life. But in arriving at it he has enriched the world of science with what many would regard as of even greater importance. He has introduced a new era into the study of classical antiquity, has revolutionized our conceptions of the past, has given the impulse to that "research with the spade" which is producing such marvellous results throughout the Orient, and nowhere more than in Greece itself. The light has broken over the peaks of Ida, and the long-forgotten ages of prehistoric Hellas and Asia Minor are lying bathed in it before us. We now begin to know how Greece came to have the strength and will for that mission of culture to which we of this modern world are still indebted. We can penetrate into a past, of which Greek tradition had forgotten the very existence. By the side of one of the jade axes which Dr. Schliemann has uncovered at Hissarlik, the Iliad itself is but a thing of yesterday. We are carried back to a time when the empires of the Assyrians and the Hittites did not as yet exist, when the Aryan forefathers of the Greeks had not as yet, perhaps, reached their new home in the south, but when the rude tribes of the neolithic age had already begun to traffic and barter, and travelling caravans conveyed the precious stone of the Kuen-lûn from one extremity of Asia to the other. Prehistoric archaeology in general owes as much to Dr. Schliemann's discoveries, as the study of Greek history and Greek art.

Why is it that Dr. Schliemann's example has not been followed by some of the rich men of whom England is full? Why cannot they spare for science a little of the wealth that is now lavished upon the breeding of racers or the maintenance of a dog-kennel? There are few, it is true, who can be expected to emulate him in his profuse generosity, and freely bestow on their mother country the vast and inestimable store of archaeological treasure which it had cost so much to procure; still fewer who would be ready to expend upon science one-half of their yearly income. But surely England must contain one or two, at least, who would be willing to help in recovering the earlier history of our civilization, and thereby to earn for themselves a place in the grateful annals of science. Dr. Schliemann, indeed, has created for himself a name that can never be forgotten,

Slavs on the north; in other words, in the very country which was known to classical geography as Thraké.

Thanks to Dr. Schliemann's discoveries, accordingly, we now know who the Trojans originally were. They were Europeans of Thraké, speaking a dialect which closely resembled the dialects of Thraké and Phrygia. And since the dialect was one which belonged to the Aryan family of speech, the probability is that the speakers of it also belonged to the Aryan race. If so, we, as well as the Greeks of the age of Agamemnôn, can hail the subjects of Priam as brethren in blood and speech.

The antiquities, therefore, unearthed by Dr. Schliemann at Troy acquire for us a double interest. They carry us back to the later Stone-age of the Aryan race, an age of which memories have been preserved in the enduring records of language, but of which tradition and history are alike silent. They will serve to settle the question, which is at present perplexing the minds of archaeologists and ethnologists, as to whether the people of the later Stone-age in Western Europe can be regarded as Aryans, or as representatives only of the races which inhabited this part of the globe before any Aryans arrived here. If the objects of stone and bronze, of earthenware and bone, found at Hissarlik, agree with those found in Britain and Gaul, a strong presumption arises that the latter also were made and used by tribes of the Aryan race

But the discoveries that have resulted from Dr. Schliemann's excavations of 1882 do not end here. He has found that the second prehistoric city, and probably the first also, was not confined, as he formerly believed, to the narrow limits of the hill of Hissarlik. Hissarlik, in fact, was only the Pergamos or citadel, crowned with six public edifices, which to the men of that time must have seemed large and stately. Below it stretched a lower city, the foundations of which have been now laid bare. Like the Pergamos, it was surrounded by a wall, the stones of which, as Dr. Schliemann has acutely noticed, must have been those which, according to Strabo, were carried away by Arkhaianax the Mitylênaean, who built with them the walls of Sigeion. To those who know the size and character of early settlements in the Levant, the city which is now disclosed to our view will appear to be one of great importance and power. There is no longer any difficulty in understanding how treasures of gold came to be discovered in its ruins, or how objects of foreign industry like Egyptian porcelain and Asiatic ivory were imported into it. The prince whose palace stood on the citadel of Hissarlik must have been a powerful potentate, with the rich Trojan plain in his possession, and the entrance to the Hellespont at his command.

Can we venture to call him the king of Ilion? The best answer to this question will be found in the final result of the operations in 1882, which I have left till now unnoticed. More extended excavations, and a closer attention to the architectural details of the site, have proved that the burnt city was not the third, as Dr. Schliemann still believed in *Ilios*, but the second, and that the vast mass of ruin and *débris*, which lie on the foundations of the second city, belong to it and not to the third. What is more, two distinct periods can be traced in the life and history of this second city; an older period, when its walls and edifices were first erected, and a later one, when they were enlarged and partially rebuilt. It is clear that the second city must have existed for a long space of time.

Now it is impossible to enumerate these facts without observing how strangely they agree with what tradition and legend have told us of the city of Priam. The city brought to light by Dr. Schliemann lasted for a long while; its walls and edifices underwent at one time a partial restoration; it was large and wealthy, with an acropolis that overlooked the plain, and was crowned with temples and other large buildings; its walls were massive and guarded by towers; its ruler

two or three centuries. Even the masses of potsherds with which the ground is filled must have required a long period to collect, while an interval of some length seems to have intervened between the decay of the third city and the rise of the fourth.

But we have more certain evidences of the age to which Ilion reaches back, in the objects which have been discovered in its ruins. As I pointed out five years ago,* we find no traces among them of Phoenician trade in the Aegean Sea. Objects of Egyptian porcelain and oriental ivory, indeed, are met with, but they must have been brought by other hands than those of the Phoenicians. Along with them nothing is found which bears upon it what we now know to be the stamp of Phoenician workmanship. In this respect Hissarlik differs strikingly from Mykênae. There we can point to numerous objects, and even to pottery, which testify to Phoenician art and intercourse. Ilion must have been overthrown before the busy traders of Canaan had visited the shores of the Troad, bringing with them articles of luxury and the influence of a particular style of art. This carries us back to the twelfth century before our era, perhaps to a still earlier epoch.

But not only has the Phoenician left no trace of himself at Hissarlik, the influence of Assyrian art which began to spread through Western Asia about 1200 B.C. is equally absent. Among the multitudes of objects which Dr. Schliemann has uncovered there is none in which we can discover the slightest evidence of an Assyrian origin.

Nevertheless, among the antiquities of Ilion there is a good deal which is neither of home production nor of European importation. Apart from the porcelain and the ivory, we find many objects which exhibit the influence of archaic Babylonian art modified in a peculiar way. We now know what this means. Tribes, called Hittite by their neighbours, made their way in early days from the uplands

---

* *Contemporary Review*, December, 1878.

of Kappadokia into northern Syria, and there developed a powerful and wide-reaching empire. From their capital at Carchemish, now Jerablûs, on the Euphrates, their armies went forth to contend on equal terms with the soldiers of the Egyptian Sesostris, or to carry the name and dominion of the Hittite to the very shores of the Aegean Sea. The rock-cut figures in the pass of Karabel, near Smyrna, in which Hêrodotos saw the trophies of Sesostris, were really memorials of Hittite conquest, and the hieroglyphics that accompanied them were those of Carchemish and not of Thebes. The image on the cliff of Sipylos, which the Greeks of the age of Homer had fabled to be that of the weeping Niobê, now turns out to be the likeness of the great goddess of Carchemish, and the cartouches engraved by the side of it, partly in Hittite and partly in Egyptian characters, show that it was carved in the time of Ramses-Sesostris himself. We can now understand how it was that, when the Hittites warred with the Egyptian Pharaoh in the 14th century B.C., they were able to summon to their aid, among their other subject allies, Dardanians and Mysians and Maeonians, while a century later the place of the Dardanians was taken by the Tekkri or Teukrians. The empire, and therewith the art and culture, of the Hittites already extended as far as the Hellespont.

Now Hittite art was a modification of archaic Babylonian art. It was, in fact, that peculiar form of early art which has long been known to have characterized Asia Minor. And along with this art came the worship of the great Babylonian goddess in the special form it assumed at Carchemish, as well as the institution of armed priestesses —the Amazons, as the Greeks called them—who served the goddess with shield and lance. The goddess was represented in a curious and peculiar fashion, which we first find on the cylinders of primaeval Chaldea. She was nude, full-faced, with the arms laid upon the breasts, and the pelvis marked by a triangle, as well as by a round knob

B

below two others which represented the breasts. At times she was furnished with wings on either side, but this seems to have been a comparatively late modification.

A leaden image of this goddess, exactly modelled after her form in archaic Babylonian and Hittite art, and adorned with the *swastika* (卐), has been found by Dr. Schliemann among the ruins of Ilion, that is to say, the second of the prehistoric cities on the mound of Hissarlik (see *Ilios*, fig. 226). Precisely the same figure, with ringlets on either side of the head, but with the pelvis ornamented with dots instead of with the *swastika* (卐), is sculptured on a piece of serpentine, recently found in Maeonia and published by M. Salomon Reinach in the *Revue archéologique*. Here by the side of the goddess stands the Babylonian Bel, and among the Babylonian symbols that surround them is the representation of one of the very terra-cotta "whorls" of which Dr. Schliemann has found such multitudes at Troy. No better proof could be desired of the truth of his hypothesis, which sees in them votive offerings to the supreme goddess of Ilion. Mr. Ramsay has procured a similar "whorl" from Kaisarieh in Kappadokia, along with clay tablets inscribed in the undeciphered Kappadokian cuneiform. Até, as Dr. Schliemann has pointed out in *Ilios*, was the native name of the Trojan goddess whom the Greeks identified with their Athêna, and 'Athi was also the name of the great goddess of Carchemish.*

The " owl-headed " vases, again, exhibit under a slightly varying form the likeness of the same deity. The owl-like face is common in the representations of the goddess upon the cylinders of primitive Chaldea, as well as the three protuberances below it which are arranged in the shape of an inverted triangle, while the wings which distinguish the vases find their parallel, not only on the engraved stones of Babylonia, but also in the extended arms

---

* See my Paper on "The Monuments of the Hittites" in the *Transactions of the Society of Biblical Archaeology*, VII. 2, p. 259.

of the Mykenaean goddess. The rude idols, moreover, of which Dr. Schliemann has found so many at Hissarlik, belong to the same type as the sacred vases; on these, however, the ringlets of the goddess are sometimes represented, while the wings at the sides are absent. These idols re-appear in a somewhat developed form at Mykênae, as well as in Cyprus and on other sites of archaic Greek civilization, where they testify to the humanizing influence that spread across to the Greek world from the shores of Asia Minor. Thanks to the discoveries of Dr. Schliemann, we can now trace the artistic type of the old Chaldean goddess as it passed from Babylonia to Carchemish, and from thence to the Troad and to the Peloponnêsos itself.

As might have been expected, the same type is met with on the peculiar cylinders which are found in Cyprus, on the southern coast of Asia Minor, and in the neighbourhood of Aleppo and Carchemish, and which I have shown elsewhere to be of Hittite origin.* Here it is frequently combined with the symbol of an ox-head, like that which occurs so often at Mykênae, where it is found times without number associated with the double-headed axe, the well-known characteristic of Asianic art. A similar axe of green jade has been unearthed on the site of the ancient Hêraion near Mykênae, along with the foot of a small statue in whose hand it must once have been held. The foot is shod with a boot

---

* *Academy*, November 27, 1881 (p. 384); see also Major di Cesnola's *Salaminia*, pp. 118 *sq.*, and Fr. Lenormant in the *Journal des Savans*, June, 1883, and the *Gazette archéologique*, VIII. 5-6, (1883). The art of the engraved stones of the Hittite class, which is based on an archaic Babylonian model, must be carefully distinguished from that of the rude gems occasionally met with at Tyre, Sidon, and other places on the Syrian coast, as well as from that of the so-called lentoid gems so plentifully found on prehistoric sites in Krêtê, the Peloponnêsos, and the islands of the Aegean. The origin of the latter is cleared up by a seal of rock-crystal found near Beyrût, and now in Mr. R. P. Greg's collection, which has the same design engraved upon it as that on the lentoid gem from Mykênae figured under No. 175 in Schliemann's *Mycenae*. This fact disposes of the theory so elaborately worked out in Milchhoefer's

with a turned-up toe, now known to be the sure mark of Hittite and Asianic sculpture. The double-headed axe is also engraved on the famous chaton of the ring discovered by Dr. Schliemann at Mykênae, the figures below it having boots with turned-up ends, and wearing the flounced robes of Babylonian priests. The whole design upon the chaton has manifestly been copied from the Asianic modification of some early Babylonian cylinder.*

The presence, in fact, of small stone cylinders points unmistakeably, wherever they occur, to the influence of primaeval Chaldea. When Assyria and Phoenicia took the place of Babylonia in Western Asia as civilizing powers, the cylinder made way for the lentoid or cone-like seal. Hence the discovery of cylinders at Ilion is one more proof of the age to which the prehistoric ruins of Hissarlik reach back, as well as of the foreign culture with which its inhabitants were in contact. The cylinder figured under No. 1522 in *Ilios* is especially important to the archaeologist. Its ornamentation is that of the class of cylinders which may now be classed as Hittite, and, in its combination of the Egyptian cartouche with the Babylonian form of seal, it displays the same artistic tendency as that which meets us in indubitably Hittite work. A cartouche of precisely the same peculiar shape is engraved on a copper

---

Anfänge der Kunst in Griechenland. The art of the lentoid gems must be of Phoenician importation. Whether, however, it may not have owed its original inspiration to the Hittites at the time when they bordered upon Phoenicia, must be left to future research to decide. Some of the designs upon these gems seem clearly to refer to subjects of Accadian or archaic Babylonian mythology, but this may be due to direct Babylonian influence, since Sargon I. of Accad (whose date has been fixed by a recent discovery as early as 3750 B.C.) not only set up a monument of victory on the shores of the Mediterranean, but even crossed over into Cyprus. The rudely-cut stones from Syria, to which I have alluded above, may have been the work of the same aboriginal population as that which carved the curious sculptures in the Wadis of el-'Akkab and Kânah, near Tyre.

* Schliemann's *Mycenae*, fig. 530. See *Academy*, Aug. 25, 1883, p. 135.

ring which has recently been discovered by Dr. Max Ohnefalsch-Richter in Cyprus. Here the interior of the cartouche is filled with the rude drawing of the Trojan goddess, as she appears in the Hissarlik idols, excepting only that the Cyprian artist has provided her with wings similar to those on the owl-headed vases. In the case of the Hissarlik cylinder, on the other hand, a figure is drawn inside the cartouche, which is curiously like a rudely-designed scarab or beetle on a Hittite seal now in the possession of Mr. R. P. Greg. The flower placed by the side of the cartouche may be compared with one upon the Mykenaean ring to which I have before alluded, as well as with others on Cyprian cylinders of the "Hittite" class. I have already referred to the fact that the so-called *swastika* (卍) is figured upon the pelvis of the leaden image of the Asiatic goddess found among the ruins of Ilion. This would seem to stamp that mysterious symbol as of Hittite origin, at least as regards its use at Ilion. That it really was so, seems to have been proved by a discovery made last year by Mr. W. M. Ramsay at Ibreez or Ivris in Lykaonia. Here a king, in the act of adoring the god Sandon, is sculptured upon a rock in the characteristic style of Hittite art, and accompanied by Hittite inscriptions. His robe is richly ornamented, and along it runs a long line of Trojan *swastikas*. The same symbol, as is well known, occurs on the archaic pottery of Cyprus, where it seems to have originally represented a bird in flight, as well as upon the prehistoric antiquities of Athens and Mykênae, but it was entirely unknown to Babylonia, to Assyria, to Phoenicia and to Egypt. It must, therefore, either have originated in Europe and spread eastward through Asia Minor, or have been disseminated westward from the primitive home of the Hittites. The latter alternative is the more probable, but whether it is so or not, the presence of the symbol in the lands of the Aegean indicates a particular epoch, and the influence of a pre-Phoenician culture.

The gold-work of Ilion may be expected to exhibit traces of having been affected to some degree by the foreign art to which the idols and cylinders owed their ultimate origin. And this I believe to be the case. The ornamentation of the gold knob given in this volume under No. 38 exactly resembles that of the solar disk on the Maeonian plaque of serpentine of which I have before spoken. The solar disk is depicted in the same way on a haematite cylinder from Kappadokia now in my possession, and the ornamentation may be traced back through the Hittite monuments to the early cylinders of Chaldea. But, simple as it seems, we look for it almost in vain at Mykênae; the only patterns found there which can be connected with it being the complicated ones reproduced in Dr. Schliemann's *Mycenae*, fig. 417 and 419. Here the old Asianic design has been made to subserve the Phoenician ornamentation of the sea-shell.

The foregoing considerations establish pretty clearly the latest limit of age to which we can assign the fall of the second prehistoric city of Hissarlik. It cannot be later than the tenth century before the Christian era; it is not likely to be later than the 12th. Already before the 10th century, the Phoenicians had planted flourishing colonies in Théra and Mélos, and had begun to work the mines of Thasos, and it is therefore by no means probable that the Troad and the important city which stood there could have remained unknown to them. The date (1183 B.C.) fixed for the destruction of Troy by Eratosthenês—though on evidence, it is true, which we cannot accept—would agree wonderfully well with the archaeological indications with which Dr. Schliemann's excavations have furnished us, as well as with the testimony of the Egyptian records.

But it is difficult for me to believe that it could have happened at a period earlier than this. The inscriptions which I have discussed in the third Appendix to *Ilios* seem to make such a supposition impossible. I have there shown that the so-called Cypriote syllabary is but a branch of a system of writing once used throughout the greater part of Asia Minor before the introduction of the Phoenico-Greek alphabet, which I have accordingly proposed to call the Asianic syllabary. The palaeographic genius of Lenormant and Deecke had already made them perceive that several of the later local alphabets of Asia Minor contained Cypriote characters, added in order to express sounds which were not provided for in the Phoenician alphabet; but Dr. Deecke was prevented by his theory as to the derivation and age of the Cypriote syllabary from discovering the full significance of the fact. It was left for me to point out, firstly, that these characters were more numerous than had been supposed, secondly, that many of them were not modifications but sister-forms of corresponding Cypriote letters, and thirdly, that they were survivals from an earlier mode of writing which had been superseded by the Phoenico-Greek alphabet. I also pointed out—herein following in the steps of Haug and Gomperz—that on three at least of the objects discovered by Dr. Schliemann at Hissarlik, and possibly on others also, written characters were found belonging, not indeed to the Cypriote form of the Asianic syllabary, but to what may be termed the Trojan form of it. Up to this point the facts and inferences were clear.

But I then attempted to go further, and to make it probable that the origin of the Asianic syllabary itself is to be sought in the Hittite hieroglyphics. Since the Appendix was published, this latter hypothesis of mine has received a striking confirmation. A year and a half ago I presented a memoir to the Society of Biblical Archaeology, in which I endeavoured by the help of a bilingual inscription to determine the values of certain of the Hittite characters. Among these there were eight which, if my method of decipherment were correct, denoted either vowels, or single consonants each followed by a single vowel. A few months afterwards, at Dr. Isaac Taylor's suggestion, I compared the forms of these eight characters with the forms of those characters of the Cypriote syllabary which possessed the same values. The result was most unexpectedly confirmatory of my conclusions; the forms in each case being almost identical. Those who wish to test the truth of this assertion can do so by referring to Dr. Taylor's recently-published work on *The Alphabet*, where the corresponding Hittite and Cypriote characters are given side by side (vol. ii. p. 123).*

If, now, the Hittite hieroglyphics may be definitively regarded as the source of the Asianic syllabary, it is evident that Lydians or Trojans could not have come to employ it till some time, at all events, after the period when the conquerors of Carchemish carved their legends on the cliff of Sipylos and the rocks of Karabel. The cartouche of Ramses II., lately discovered by Dr. Gollob, by the side of the so-called image of Niobé, as well as the fact that the latter is an obvious imitation of the sitting figure of Nofretari, the wife of Ramses II., which is sculptured in the cliff near Abu Simbel, indicates that this period was that of the 14th century B.C. Between this date and that at which the inscriptions of Hissarlik were written, a full century at least must be allowed to have elapsed.

I have little to add or change in the Appendix in *Ilios* on the Trojan Inscriptions. The reading, however, of the legend on the terra-cotta seal reproduced on p. 693 (Nos. 1519, 1520) of *Ilios* has now been rendered certain by two deeply-cut and large-sized inscriptions on a terra-cotta weight in the possession of Mr. R. P. Greg, which is alleged to have come from Hissarlik. The characters, at any rate, resemble those of the Hissarlik inscriptions, and before the

---

* It is particularly gratifying to me to find that Dr. Deecke in his latest work on the Cypriote inscriptions (in Collitz's *Sammlung der griechischen Dialekt-Inschriften*, I. p. 12) has renounced his theory of the cuneiform origin of the Cypriote syllabary in favour of my Hittite one.

weight passed into Mr. Greg's hands were invisible through dirt. They establish that the inscription upon the seal must be read *E-si-re* or *Re-si-e*, the name, probably, of the original owner. The word, moreover, on the patera found in the necropolis of Thymbra, which I had doubtfully made *Levon* or *Revon*, is now read ῥέζω by Dr. Deecke, no doubt rightly.

The alphabet of Kappadokia I am no longer inclined to include among those that preserved some of the characters of the old Asianic syllabary. Mr. Ramsay has copied an inscription at Eyuk, which goes far to show that the one given by Hamilton is badly copied, and that the characters in it which resemble those of the Cypriote syllabary had probably no existence in the original text. In fact, Mr. Ramsay's inscription makes it clear that the Kappadokian alphabet was the same as the Phrygian, both being derived, as he has pointed out, from an early Ionic alphabet of the 8th century B.C., used by the traders of Sinôpê.* As I now feel doubtful also about the alphabet of Kilikia, the alphabets of Asia Minor, which indubitably contain characters of the Asianic syllabary, will be reduced to those of Pamphylia, Lykia, Karia, Lydia, and Mysia. These, it will be noticed, form a continuous chain round the western and south-western shores of Asia Minor, the chain being further continued into Cyprus. The Karian alphabet, though still in the main undeciphered, has been determined with greater exactness during the last two or three years in consequence of the discovery of new inscriptions, and I have recently made a discovery in regard to it which may lead to interesting results. A peculiar class of scarabs is met with in Northern Egypt, on which certain curious figures are scratched in the rudest possible way, reminding us of nothing so much as the figures on some of the Hissarlik "whorls." The art, if art it can be called, is quite different from that of the "Hittite" cylinders of Cyprus or of the

---

* *Journal of the Royal Asiatic Society*, XV. 1 (1883).

excessively rude seals that are found on the coast of Syria, and even as far west as the Lydian stratum of Sardes. On one of these scarabs belonging to Mr. Greg's collection I have found a long inscription in well-cut Karian letters, and an examination of another of the same class has brought to light some more letters of frequent occurrence in the Karian texts. Something at last, therefore, is now known of the native art of the south-western corner of Asia Minor; and a comparison of it with the scratchings on the Trojan "whorls" may hereafter help us to distinguish better than we can at present between the European, the Hittite, and the native Asianic elements, in the art and culture of Ilion.

One of the most curious facts, which Dr. Schliemann's excavations have made clear, is that even the destruction of the second city did not bring with it a break in the continuity of religion and art among the successive settlers upon Hissarlik. The idols and owl-headed vases, as well as the "whorls," all continued to be made and used by the inhabitants of the third, the fourth, and the fifth settlements. Even apart from the geological indications, it is evident from this that the site could never have long lain deserted. The old traditions lingered around it, and though new peoples came to dwell there, there must have been among them some relics of the older population. It could only have been the lower city, not the Pergamos itself, which even an orator in the full flow of his eloquence could have described as "uninhabited." It is not until we come to what Dr. Schliemann has called the Lydian stratum that the first break occurs. The second and more important break is naturally that of the Greek city.

 The Greek city itself passed through more than one vicissitude of growth and decay. In the lower part of its remains, which do not extend for more than six feet below the present surface of the hill, excepting of course at the sides, we find that archaic Hellenic pottery which always marks the site of an early Greek town. Mixed with it is another species of pottery, which seems of native manufacture, but cannot be of earlier date than the 9th century before our era. At the time when this pottery was in use, the Aeolic Ilion, like the four villages that had preceded it, was still confined to the old Pergamos. Those who have visited the sites of early Greek cities in Asia Minor will readily understand that this was almost necessarily the case. Like the Aeolians of Old Smyrna or Kymê, the Aeolian colonists at Hissarlik were few in number and scanty in resources, while their position among a hostile population, or within reach of sea-faring pirates, made them choose the most isolated and defensible summit in the neighbourhood where they had planted themselves. This summit, however, as always elsewhere, was near the sea. When the army of Xerxes passed through the Troad, the Aeolic city seems to have not yet extended into the plain below. The long-deserted lower town of the prehistoric Ilion was not again covered with buildings until the Macedonian age.

Dr. Schliemann has been vaguely accused of obscuring his facts by his theories, and the public has been warned that a strict distinction should be made between the theories he has put forward and the facts he has discovered. In reality, however, it is his critics themselves, rather than Dr. Schliemann, who have been guilty of propounding theories which have no facts to support them. As compared with most explorers, he has been singularly free from the fault of hasty generalization, or the far worse fault of bending the facts to suit pre-conceived views. Admiration of the Homeric Poems, and the growing conviction that if the Troy of Homer ever had any existence at all it could only have been at Hissarlik, can hardly be called theories. His works are for the most part a record of facts, brought into relation with one another by means of those inductive inferences, which the scientific method of modern archaeology obliges us to draw from them. And, with the true scientific spirit, he has never hesitated to modify these inferences whenever the discovery of new facts seems to require it, while the facts themselves have invariably been presented by him fully and fairly, so that his readers have always been able to test for themselves the validity of the inferences he has based on them. To forbid him to make any suggestion which is supported only by probable or possible evidence, is to deprive him of a privilege enjoyed both by the critics themselves and by every scientific enquirer. But such suggestions will be found to be rare, and the fact that so much has been said about them makes me suspect that the critics do not possess that archaeological knowledge, which would enable them to distinguish between a merely possible or probable theory and an inference which is necessitated by the facts. The very peculiar pottery found immediately below the Greek stratum proves to the archaeologist, more convincingly than any architectural remains could do, that a separate and independent settlement once existed between the fifth and the Greek cities, just as the objects found on the plain below prove that the Greek city must once have extended thus far, even though the walls by which it was surrounded have now wholly disappeared. On the other hand, the theory that this settlement was of Lydian foundation is a theory only, about which Dr. Schliemann expresses himself with the needful hesitation.

One of the most disheartening signs of the little knowledge of prehistoric and Levantine archaeology there is in this country, is to be found in the criticisms passed upon *Ilios* in respectable English publications. Nowhere but in England would it have been possible for writers who enjoy a certain reputation to pass off-hand judgments and propound new theories of their own on archaeological questions, without having first taken the trouble to learn the elementary principles of the subject about which they treat. What can be said of a critic who does not know the difference between prehistoric and Hellenic pottery on the one hand, or archaic and classical Greek pottery on the other, and covers his ignorance by misquoting the words of an eminent French archaeologist who has made the early pottery of the Levant his special study? The English public is apt to think that a man who is reputed to be a great scholar is qualified to pronounce an opinion upon every subject under the sun. As a matter of fact, he knows as little as the public itself about those subjects in which he has not undergone the necessary preliminary training, and his writing about them is but a new form of charlatanry. The power of translating from Greek and Latin, or of composing Greek and Latin verses, will not enable a scholar to determine archaeological problems, any more than it will enable him to translate the hymns of the Rig-Veda, or to decipher a cuneiform inscription. Theories in regard to Dr. Schliemann's discoveries at Hissarlik have been gravely put forward of late, which have derived an importance only from the influential character of the organs in which they have appeared. It has been maintained in sober earnest, that the fifth stratum of ruins represents the Macedonian Ilion, which was embellished by Lysimakhos about 300 B.C., and sacked by Fimbria in 85 B.C., while the fourth city was that visited by Xerxes, and the third city the old Aeolic settlement. It is only necessary for the reader who does not pretend to a knowledge of archaeology to examine the woodcuts so lavishly distributed throughout the pages of *Ilios*, in order that he may judge of the value of such a hypothesis, or of the archaeological attainments that lie behind it. The pottery, the terra-cotta "whorls," the idols, the implements and weapons of stone and bone, found in the prehistoric strata of Hissarlik, are all such as have never been found—nor are likely to be found—on any Greek site even of the prehistoric age. We shall look for them in vain at Mykênae, at Orkhomenos, at Tiryns, or in the early tombs of

Spata and Menidi, of Rhodes and Cyprus. On the other hand, the distinctive features of Greek daily life are equally absent; there are neither coins nor lamps, nor alphabetic inscriptions, nor patterns of the classical epoch; there is no Hellenic pottery, whether archaic or recent. We now know pretty exactly what were the objects left behind them by the Greeks and their neighbours in the Levant during the six centuries that preceded the Christian era; and, thanks more especially to Dr. Schliemann's labours, we can even trace the art and culture of that period back to the art and culture of the still older period, which was first revealed to us by his exploration of Mykênae. It is too late now, when archaeology has become a science and its fundamental facts have been firmly established, to revert to the dilettante antiquarianism of fifty years ago. Then, indeed, it was possible to put forward theories that were the product of the literary, and not of the scientific, imagination, and to build houses of straw upon a foundation of shifting sand. But the time for such pleasant recreation is now gone; the study of the far distant past has been transferred from the domain of literature to that of science, and he who would pursue it must imbue himself with the scientific method and spirit, must submit to the hard drudgery of preliminary training, and must know how to combine the labours of men like Evans and Lubbock, or Virchow and Rolleston, with the results that are being poured in upon us year by year from the Oriental world. To look for a Macedonian city in the fifth prehistoric village of Hissarlik is like looking for an Elizabethan cemetery in the tumuli of Salisbury plain.: the archaeologist can only pass by the paradox with a smile.

A. H. Sayce.

OXFORD,
October, 1883.

CONTENTS.

	PAGE
PREFACE. By PROFESSOR SAYCE	v
COMPARATIVE TABLE of French and English Measures	xxxiv
LIST OF ILLUSTRATIONS	xxxv

CHAPTER I.

NARRATIVE OF THE EXPLORATIONS AT TROY AND IN THE TROAD IN 1882 1

CHAPTER II.

THE FIRST PREHISTORIC SETTLEMENT ON THE HILL OF HISSARLIK 29

CHAPTER III.

THE SECOND CITY; TROY PROPER; THE 'ILIOS' OF THE HOMERIC LEGEND 52

CHAPTER IV.

THE THIRD, FOURTH, FIFTH, AND SIXTH SETTLEMENTS ON THE SITE OF TROY 175
§ I.—THE THIRD PREHISTORIC SETTLEMENT . 175
§ II.—THE FOURTH PREHISTORIC SETTLEMENT ON THE SITE OF TROY . . . 184
§ III.—THE FIFTH PREHISTORIC SETTLEMENT ON THE SITE OF TROY 188
§ IV.—THE SIXTH OR LYDIAN SETTLEMENT ON THE SITE OF TROY 193

COMPARATIVE TABLE OF FRENCH AND ENGLISH MEASURES, EXACT AND APPROXIMATE.

Metric.	Inches.	Ft.	Inch.	Approximate.
Millimètre	0·0393708		0·03937	·04 or $\frac{1}{25}$ of inch.
Centimètre	0·393708	,,	0·39371	·4 ,, $\frac{2}{5}$,,
Décimètre	3·93708	,,	3·9371	4 inches.
Mètre	39·3708	3	3·3708	$3\frac{1}{4}$ feet.
2	78·7416	6	6·7416	$6\frac{1}{2}$,,
3	118·1124	9	10·1124	10 ,,
4	157·4832	13	1·4832	13 ,,
5	196·8540	16	4·8540	$16\frac{1}{3}$,,
6	236·2248	19	8·2248	$19\frac{2}{3}$,,
7	275·5956	22	11·5956	23 ,,
8	314·9664	26	2·9664	$26\frac{1}{4}$,,
9	354·3372	29	6·3372	$29\frac{1}{2}$,,
10	393·7089	32	9·7080	33 ,,
11	433·0788	36	1·0788	36 (12 yds.)
12	472·4496	39	4·4496	$39\frac{1}{3}$ feet.
13	511·8204	42	7·9204	$42\frac{2}{3}$,,
14	551·1912	45	11·1912	46 ,,
15	590·5620	49	2·5620	$49\frac{1}{4}$,,
16	620·9328	52	5·9328	$52\frac{1}{2}$,,
17	669·3036	55	9·3036	$55\frac{3}{4}$,,
18	708·6744	59	0·6744	59 ,,
19	748·0452	62	4·0452	$62\frac{1}{3}$,,
20	787·416	65	7·4160	$65\frac{2}{3}$,,
30	1181·124	98	5·124	$98\frac{1}{3}$,,
40	1574·832	131	2·832	$131\frac{1}{4}$,,
50	1968·54	164	0·54	164 ,,
100	3937·08	328	1·08	328 (109 yds.)

N.B.—The following is a convenient approximate rule:—" To turn *Mètres* into *Yards*, add 1-11th to the number of Mètres."

LIST OF ILLUSTRATIONS.

(The *figures*, as 15 M. &c., denote the *depths* at which the Objects were found.)

                                                                                               PAGE

No. 140. MAP OF THE TROAD .. .. *Frontispiece*

No. 1. Fragment of a lustrous black Bowl, with an incised decoration filled with white chalk (15 M.) 31

No. 2. Fragment of a lustrous black Vase, with an incised ornamentation filled with white chalk (15 M.) 31

No. 3. The reverse side of No. 2, with two vertical holes for suspension (15 M.) 32

No. 4. Small lustrous black Cup (14–15 M.) .. 34

No. 5. Lustrous black wheel-made Jug (14–15 M.) 34

Nos. 6, 7. Two lustrous black Cups, with hollow foot and upright handle (14 M.) 35

No. 8. Lustrous black Cup, with horizontal flutings, hollow foot, and vertical perforated handle (14 M.) 36

No. 9. Lustrous black Vessel, with convex foot, and vertically perforated excrescences on the sides (14 M.) 36

No. 10. Axe of Green Jade (14 M.) 41

No. 11. Battle-axe of Grey Diorite (14 M.) 43

No. 12. Brooch of Copper or Bronze, with a globular head (14 M.) 47

No. 13. Brooch of Copper or Bronze, with a spiral head (14 M.) 47

No. 14. Huckle-bone (*Astragalus*) (14 M.) 51

No. 15. View of the great Substruction Wall of the Acropolis of the second city on the west side, close to the south-west gate 55

No. 16. Section of the Tower G M on the east side of the Acropolis; showing the arrangement of the channels for the artificial baking of the brick wall 60

No. 17. Ground Plan of the South-western Gate 68

No. 18. Ground Plan of the Southern Gate. NF on Plan VII. 71

No. 19. View of the remains of the South-east Gate 74

No. 20. External Side of a Wall of Temple A, showing the arrangement of the horizontal channels and of those which go right through the wall 77

LIST OF ILLUSTRATIONS.

	PAGE
No. 21. Section of a Wall of Temple A, showing the arrangement of the horizontal channels	77
No. 22. Section of a Wall of Temple B, showing the arrangement of the horizontal channels	77
No. 23. Plan of a Wall of Temple B, showing the arrangement of the cross channels	77
No. 24. Plan of a Wall of Temple A, showing the arrangement of the cross channels	77
No. 25. Ground plan of the Temple A	79
No. 26. Ground plan of the Temple B	79
No. 27. Parastades on the front ends of the lateral walls of Temple A, consisting of six vertical wooden jambs	80
No. 27A. Temple of Themis at Rhamnus	83
No. 28. Copper Nail of a quadrangular shape with a disk-like head, which has been cast independently of the nail and merely fixed on it (8·50 M.)	91
No. 29. Quadrangular copper Nail without the disk-like head (8·50 M.)	92
No. 30. Quadrangular copper Nail without the disk-like head (8·50 M.)	92
No. 31. Copper Nail with round head (8·50 M.)	93
No. 32. Bronze Battle-axe (8·50 M.)	93
No. 33. Bronze Lance-head; with the end broken off (8·50 M.)	97
No. 34. Bronze Dagger; with the handle and the upper end curled up in the great fire (8·50 M.)	97
No. 34A. Gimlet of bronze (8·50 M.)	99
No. 35. Bronze Knife (8·50 M.)	99
No. 36. Surgical instrument (8·50 M.)	106
No. 37. Whorl of Terra-cotta, in which is stuck a copper or bronze nail with a round head (8·50 M.)	106
No. 38. Staff or sceptre-knob of gold, with a geometrical ornamentation (8·50 M.)	107
No. 39. Bundle of bronze Brooches, intermingled with Earrings of silver and electrum, and fastened together by the cementing action of the carbonate of copper: on the outside is attached a gold earring (8·50 M.)	107
No. 40. Knife-handle of Ivory (8·50 M.)	115
No. 41. Object of Ivory with 5 globular projections (8·50 M.)	116
No. 42. Knife-handle of Ivory in the form of a Ram (8·50 M.)	117
No. 43. Small Spoon of Ivory (8·50 M.)	117
No. 44. Arrow-head of Ivory (8·50 M.)	117

LIST OF ILLUSTRATIONS.

xxxvii

	PAGE
No. 45. Knife-handle of Bone (8·50 M.) ..	117
No. 46. Egg of Aragonite (8·50 M.)	118
No. 47. Sling-Bullet of Haematite (8·50 M.)	118
No. 48. Axe of Diorite (8·50 M.) ..	119
Nos. 49–52. Four Whorls of Terra-cotta, with incised signs which may be written characters (8·50 M.) ..	120
No. 53. Vase-head (8·50 M.)	130
No. 54. Vase with two handles, and two ear-like excrescences perforated vertically (8·50 M.)	130
No. 55. Tripod-vase in the form of a hedgehog (8·50 M.)	131
No. 56. Oenochoë of oval form with a long neck (8·50 M.)	131
No. 57. Oenochoë of oval form, with a long straight neck and trefoil mouth (8·50 M.)	132
No. 58. Oenochoë with a long straight neck and a trefoil orifice (8·50 M.)	133
No. 59. Vase with vertically perforated excrescences and an incised ornamentation of leaf patterns (8·50 M.)	134
No. 60. Vase in the form of a hunting-bottle with a flat bottom, and an ear-like excrescence on each side (8·50 M.) ..	137
No. 61. Vase in the form of a hunting-bottle, with a convex bottom and an incised linear ornamentation (8·50 M.)	138
Nos. 62, 63. Brooches of bronze or copper with spiral heads (8·50 M.)	139
Nos. 64, 65. Brooches of bronze or copper with a semiglobular head and a quadrangular perforation (8·50 M.)	139
No. 66. Punch of bronze or copper (8·50 M.)	139
No. 67. Head of a Vase in the form of a hog, ornamented with incised fish-spine patterns; the eyes are of stone (9 M.)	139
Nos. 68, 69. Side view and front view of a Vase with four feet, in the form of a cat (8·50 M.) ..	140
No. 70. Headless female Idol of terra-cotta, with an incised ornamentation (9 M.) ..	141
No. 71. Very rude figure of Terra-cotta (8 M.) ..	142
No. 72. Fragment of an Idol of terra-cotta, with two large owl's eyes (8·50 M.) ..	142
No. 73. Oenochoë, with a straight neck and convex bottom (9 M.)	143
No. 74. Tripod-vase with four excrescences, two of which are perforated vertically (9 M.)	144
No. 75. Tripod Oenochoë with a straight neck (9 M.) ..	144
No. 76. Vase-cover with two vertically perforated horn-like excrescences (9 M.) ..	145

LIST OF ILLUSTRATIONS.

	PAGE
No. 77. Lentiform terra-cotta Bottle with a convex bottom and four wart-like excrescences (9 M.)	145
No. 78. Lustrous brown Goblet with two handles (δέπας ἀμφικύπελλον) (9 M.)	164
No. 79. Lustrous dark-brown Goblet with two handles (δέπας ἀμφικύπελλον) (9 M.)	165
No. 80. Battle-axe of copper with a perforation in the upper end (9 M.)	166
No. 81. Battle-axe of copper (9 M.)	166
No. 82. Knife of bronze (9 M.)	166
No. 83. Ring of bronze or copper (9 M.)	167
No. 84. Female Idol of bronze or copper (9 M.)	168
No. 85. Mould of Mica Slate (9 M.)	170
No. 86. Stone Hammer with a groove on two sides (8·50 M.)	173
No. 87. Object of white marble, a *phallus* (8·50 M.)	173
No. 88. Object of granite with two furrows (9 M.)	173
No. 89. Accumulation of *débris* before the Gate. The form of the strata of *débris* indicates that after the great conflagration the third settlers continued to go in and out on the same spot as before, although the paved road was buried deep under the brick-*débris* and ashes	177
No. 90. Ground Plan of the South-eastern Gate, marked OX on Plan VII.	179
No. 91. Jug with two spouts (8 M.)	183
No. 92. Vase with a hollow foot and vertically perforated excrescences for suspension (8 M.)	183
No. 93. Cup with an ear-like ornament in relief on either side (8 M.)	183
No. 94. Clay-ring (8 M.)	183
Nos. 95, 96. Two Astragals (ἀστράγαλοι) (8 M.)	184
No. 97. Vase with an owl-face, the characteristics of a woman, and two wing-like upright projections (5 M.)	186
No. 98. Vase with the characteristics of a woman and two wing-like upright projections. The cover has an owl-face (5 M.)	187
No. 99. Entrance to the great north-eastern Trench SS on Plan VII. To the left, a huge Roman wall of large well-wrought blocks. To the right, the great wall of the fifth city, consisting of irregular stones	189
No. 100. Vase with an owl-head, the characteristics of a woman, and two wing-like upright projections (3 M.)	191
No. 101. Vase with an owl-head and the characteristics of a woman (3 M.)	191

LIST OF ILLUSTRATIONS.

	PAGE
No. 102. Object of ivory (3 M.)	192
No. 103. Object of ivory (3 M.)	192
Quarry-marks on Blocks of the Roman Wall	196
No. 104. Entablature and capital of the small Doric Temple	197
No. 105. Marble Metope of the Macedonian period, representing a warrior holding a kneeling man by the hair (1 M.)	198
No. 106. Fragment of a marble Metope of the Macedonian period, representing a man holding up a sinking woman	199
No. 107. Fragment of a Metope of marble of the Macedonian period, representing a helmeted warrior, and a shield held by a second figure, of which only the left hand remains	200
No. 108. Fragment of a Metope of marble of the Temple of Athené of the Macedonian period, representing a goddess, probably Athené, with a large shield; holding by her left a warrior with a shield, who vainly strives to liberate himself from her grasp	201
No. 109. Capital, triglyphon, and corona of the great Doric Temple	202
No. 110. Cymatium of the Temple of Athené, of the Macedonian time	203
No. 111. Cymatium of the Temple of Athené, Roman restoration	204
No. 112. Fragment of a Pediment-relief	205
No. 113. Portion of a Frieze representing a procession of chariots preceded by a winged Niké on a swift chariot. Probably of the Macedonian time	205
No. 114. Fragment of a Frieze with a Gorgon's head, on each side of which is a Niké	206
No. 115. Small Relief representing two gallopping horses. Certainly of the Macedonian period	206
No. 116. Pediment-relief representing a man holding his right arm over his head	207
No. 117. Ground plan of the Roman Propylaeum in its present state	208
No. 118. Restored ground plan of the Roman Propylaeum	208
No. 119. Entablature and capital of the Roman Propylaeum	209
No. 120. Restored view of the Roman Propylaeum	210
No. 121. Ground plan of the great Theatre of Ilium	211
No. 122. Medallion in relief; representing the she-wolf suckling Romulus and Remus	212
No. 123. Corinthian Capital of the theatre	213
No. 124. Restored Acanthus-leaf of the capital of the theatre	213

LIST OF ILLUSTRATIONS.

	PAGE
No. 125. Portrait-statue in the shape of a Hermheracles (1 M.)	214
No. 126. River-god, probably the Scamander, with a cornucopiae and an urn (1 M.)	215
No. 127. Female head of marble (2 M.)	215
No. 128. Horse's head of marble belonging to a Metope (1 M.)	216
No. 129. Male Mask of terra-cotta (1 M.)	216
No. 130. Archaic Greek Vessel (1·50 M.)	216
No. 131. Archaic Greek painted terra-cotta Bottle, in the form of a huge hunting bottle, with two handles and three feet (1·50 M.)	217
No. 132. Arrow-head of bronze or copper without barbs (γλωχῖνες). Found in the tumulus of Achilles (6 M.)	247
No. 133. Tumulus of Protesilaus on the Thracian Chersonesus, opposite the Plain of Troy	255
No. 134. Hammer and Axe of Diorite, with perforation; found on the surface of the tumulus of Protesilaus	258
No. 135. Perforated Ball of serpentine, found in the tumulus of Protesilaus	259
No. 136. Bronze Knife found in the tumulus of Protesilaus	259
No. 136a. Vase-handle found in the tumulus of Protesilaus	259
No. 137. Wall of the first and oldest epoch: on the Bali Dagh	264
No. 138. Wall of the first and oldest epoch: on the Bali Dagh	265
No. 139. Wall of the second and later epoch: on the Bali Dagh	265
No. 139, a. Egyptian Women weaving and using spindles	294
No. 139, b. Men spinning and making a sort of net-work	295
No. 139, c. Egyptian Spindles found at Thebes	295
No. 139, d. A Woman spinning: from a Roman bas-relief	298
No. 139, e. A Slave bringing the work-basket to her mistress, in whose hand is something that looks like the lower end of the distaff	299
No. 139, f. An Egyptian weighing rings (of silver) with Weights in the form of Ox-heads	301

MAPS AND PLANS AT THE END OF THE BOOK.

MAP OF THE PLAIN OF TROY.

Plan VII.* The Acropolis of the Second City.
Plan VIII. The Homeric Troy and the Later Ilium.

* NOTE.—The *numbers* are in continuation of the Plans at the end of the Author's 'Ilios.'

TROJA.

CHAPTER I.

NARRATIVE OF THE EXPLORATIONS AT TROY AND IN THE TROAD IN 1882.

BY my excavations on the hill of Hissarlik in 1879, in company with Professor Rudolf Virchow of Berlin and M. Emile Burnouf of Paris, I supposed that I had settled the Trojan question for ever. I thought I had proved that the small town, the third in succession from the virgin soil, whose house-substructions I had brought to light at an average depth of from 7 to 8 mètres beneath the ruins of four later cities, which in the course of ages had succeeded each other above them on the same site, must necessarily be the Ilium of the legend immortalized by Homer; and I maintained this theory in my work *Ilios*, which I published at the end of 1880. But after its publication I became sceptical, not indeed regarding the position of Troy, for there could be no question but that Hissarlik marked its site, but respecting the extent of the city; and my doubts increased as time wore on. I soon found it no longer possible to believe that the divine poet—who, with the fidelity of an eye-witness and with so much truth to nature, has drawn the picture, not only of the plain of Troy with its promontories, its rivers, and its heroic tombs, but of the whole Troad, with its numerous different nations and cities, with the Hellespont, Cape Lectum, Ida, Samothrace, Imbros, Lesbos, and Tenedos, as well as all the mighty phenomena of nature displayed in the country—that this same poet could have represented Ilium as a great,* elegant,† flourishing, and well-inhabited,‡ well-built§ city, with large streets,‖ if it had been in reality only a very little town; so small indeed, that, even supposing its houses, which appear to have been built like the present Trojan village-houses, and, like them, but one story high, to have been six stories high, it could hardly have contained 3000 inhabitants. Nay, had Troy been merely a small fortified borough, such as the ruins of the third city denote, a few hundred men might have easily taken it in a few days, and the whole Trojan war, with its ten years' siege, would either have been a total fiction, or it would have had but a slender foundation. I could accept neither hypothesis, for I found it impossible to think that, whilst there were so many large cities on the coast of Asia, the catastrophe of a little borough could at once have been taken up by the bards; that the legend of the event could have survived for centuries, and have come down to Homer to be magnified by him to gigantic proportions, and to become the subject of his divine poems.

Besides, the tradition of all antiquity regarding the war of Troy was quite unanimous, and this unanimity was too characteristic not to rest on a basis of positive facts, which so high an authority as Thucydides¶ accepts as real history. Tradition was even unanimous in stating that the capture of Troy had taken place eighty years before the Dorian invasion of the Peloponnesus. Furthermore, as mentioned in my *Ilios*,** the Egyptian documents give us historic evidence that Ilium and the kingdom of Troy had a real existence; for in the poem of Pentaur,

---

* *Il.* II. 332, 803 : ἄστυ μέγα Πριάμοιο
† *Il.* V. 210 : ὅτε Ἴλιον εἰς ἐρατεινήν
‡ *Il.* XIII. 380 : Ἰλίου ἐκπέρσῃς εὐναιόμενον πτολίεθρον.
§ *Il.* XXI. 433 : Ἰλίου ἐκπέρσαντες ἐϋκτίμενον πτολίεθρον.
‖ *Il.* II. 141 : οὐ γὰρ ἔτι Τροίην αἱρήσομεν εὐρυάγυιαν.
¶ I. 10, 11.   ** *Ilios*, p. 123.

in the "Sallier" hieratic papyrus, preserved in the British Museum, the Dardani or Dandani (Dardanians) and the people of Iluna (Ilion) * are mentioned, together with the Liku (Lycians) and the people of Pidasa (Pedasus), the Kerkesh or Gergesh (the Gergithians), the Masu (Mysians), and the Akerit † (Carians), among the confederates who came to the help of the Hittites (or Khita) under the walls of Kadesh on the Orontes, in the fifth year of Ramses II. (cir. 1333–1300 B.C.). What struck me still more was, that these are precisely the same peoples who are enumerated in the second book of the Iliad as auxiliaries of the Trojans in the defence of their city. It is therefore an established fact, that there was in the Troad, probably about the 14th century B.C., a kingdom of the Dardanians, one of whose principal towns was named Ilium; a kingdom which ranked among the most powerful of Asia Minor, and sent its warriors into Syria to do battle with the Egyptian troops for the defence of Asia; and this agrees admirably with what Homer, and in fact all Greek tradition, says of the power of Troy. Besides, Professor Henry Brugsch-Pasha mentions,‡ that in the mural paintings and inscriptions on a pylon of the temple of Medinet Abou at Thebes may be seen in two groups thirty-nine nations, countries, and cities, which joined in a confederacy against Ramses III. (cir. 1200 B.C.), invaded Egypt, and were defeated by that king. In the first group appear the peoples called Purosata or

---

* Professor Henry Brugsch-Pasha, in his appendix to my *Ilios*, pp. 746, 747, recognizes the identity of the Dardani with the Dardanians or Trojans, of the Liku with the Lycians, of Pidasa with the Trojan city Pedasus, of the Kerkesh or Gergesh with the Gergithians of the Troad, of the Masu with the Mysians; but he is sceptical regarding the identification of Ilion with Iluna (Iliuna, Iri-una), for he thinks that this latter name ought to be rectified into Ma-una, Mauon, the Mæonians or Meonians (the ancient Lydians).

† François Lenormant, in the *Academy* of the 21st and 28th of March, 1874, holds the Akerit to be probably identical with the Carians.

‡ In his Appendix to *Ilios*, pp. 748, 749.

Pulosata (Pelasgians—Philistines!), Tekri, Tekkari (Teucrians),* and Danau (Danai?). In the second group he finds names which are of particular interest for us: Asi, which suggests the name of Assos, a Mysian city in the Troad, or of Issa, the ancient name of Lesbos, which equally belongs to the Troad, or of Issus in Cilicia; Kerena or Kelena, which seems to be Colonae in the Troad; U-lu, which brings Ilium to mind and seems to be identical with it; Kanu, which may be Caunus in Caria; L(a)res, Larissa, which may or may not be the Trojan city Larissa or Larisa, there being many cities of that name; Maulnus or Mulnus, which recals to mind the Cilician Mallus: Atena, which may be Adana; and Karkamash, which Prof. Brugsch identifies with Coracesium, both likewise in Cilicia.† Now it is a remarkable fact, to which M. François Lenormant ‡ has already called attention, that the Dardanians, who stand prominent among the confederates against Ramses II., do not appear in these two groups of invaders, who fought, a little more than a century later, against Ramses III., and that the Teucrians appear in their stead. May not this change of name of the Trojans have been caused by the war and capture of Troy and the destruction or dispersion of the people? It is, however, to be remarked that Herodotus always calls the ancient Trojans of epic poetry Teucrians, whereas the Roman poets use the names Teucrians and Trojans as equivalent.§

To this overwhelming testimony for the power and greatness of Troy, a further proof has been added by the ten

---

* Professor Brugsch-Pasha has no doubt regarding the identity of the Tekri or Tekkari with the Teucrians.

† Professor Sayce remarks to me that other Egyptologists identify Karkamash with Carchemish, the Hittite capital on the Euphrates.

‡ In the *Academy* of the 21st and 28th of March, 1874.

§ Virgil, *Aeneid*. I. 38, 172; II. 248, 252, 571; V. 265; XII. 137; Horace, *Od*. IV. 6, 15; Ovid, *Met*. XII. 67. Stephanus Byzantinus, s.v. Τεῦκροι, says: Τεῦκροι, ὀξυτόνως οἱ Τρῶες, ἀπὸ Τεύκρου τοῦ Σκαμάνδρου, καὶ Ἰδαίας νύμφης. Λέγεται καὶ Τευκρὶς θηλυκῶς ἡ Τροία, καὶ Τεύκριον.

treasures of gold ornaments which I found in my excavations on Hissarlik, confirming the epithet "πολύχρυσος" which Homer gives to Troy. I therefore resolved upon continuing the excavations at Hissarlik, for five months more, to clear up the mystery, and to settle finally the important Trojan question. The *firman* obtained for me in the summer of 1878 by the good offices of my honoured friend Sir A. H. Layard, then English Ambassador at Constantinople, having expired, I had in the summer of 1881 applied to H. H. Prince Bismarck, through whose kind intervention I received, at the end of October in the same year, a new *firman* for continuing the excavations at Hissarlik, and on the site of the lower town of Ilium. As a supplement to the firman, he obtained for me some months later the permission to make, simultaneously with the exploration of Troy, excavations on any other site in the Troad I might desire, provided these latter were limited to one site at a time, and were made in the presence of a Turkish delegate. In order to be able to secure for science any light which might be obtained from ancient architectural remains, I engaged the services of two eminent architects—Dr. William Dörpfeld of Berlin, who had for four years managed the technical part of the excavations of the German Empire at Olympia, and Mr. Joseph Höfler of Vienna; both of whom had taken the first prizes in their respective Academies, so as to obtain State stipends for scientific travels in Italy. The monthly salary of the former was £35, that of the latter £15 and travelling expenses. I also engaged three able overseers; two of them were Peloponnesians, who had already served and distinguished themselves in the same capacity in the excavations at Olympia; one of them, Gregorios Basilopoulos, a native of Magouliana, near Gortynia, received for this Trojan campaign the name of Ilos; the other, Georgios Paraskevopoulos, a native of Pyrgos, was now baptized Laomedon. The latter was of great use to me by his gigantic frame and herculean strength, which inspired awe in my labourers and made them blindly obey him; each of them received 150 francs monthly. As third overseer I engaged Mr. Gustav Battus, son of the late French Consul Battus at the Dardanelles, with 300 fr. monthly wages. Fortunately, in June, 1879, I had left a Turkish watchman at Hissarlik, to guard my wooden barracks and the magazine, in which were stored all my machinery and implements for excavating. Thus I now found everything in the best order, and had only to cover my houses with new waterproof felt. As all of them were built in one continuous line, the danger of fire was great. I therefore separated them and put them up in different places, so that, in case one of the barracks caught fire, none of the others could be reached by the flames, even with the heaviest storm blowing. The barrack in which I and my servants lived had five rooms, two of which I occupied; another had two, a third had three, and a fourth had four bedrooms. We had, therefore, ample room, and could also conveniently lodge seven visitors. One barrack, of only one room, served as a dining-hall, and was called by that proud name, though it consisted of rude planks, through whose crevices the wind blew incessantly, so that frequently it was impossible to burn a lamp or light a candle. Another large barrack served as a store for the antiquities, which were to be divided between the Imperial Museum at Constantinople and myself. My honoured friends, Messrs. J. Henry Schröder & Co., of London, had kindly sent me a large supply of tins of Chicago corned beef, peaches, the best English cheese, and ox-tongues, as well as 240 bottles of the best English pale ale.* We could always get fresh

---

* I was the sole consumer of these 240 bottles of pale ale, which lasted me for five months, and which I used as a medicine to cure constipation, from which I had been suffering for more than thirty years, and which had been aggravated by all other medicines, and particularly by the mineral waters of Carlsbad. This pale-ale-cure proved perfectly effectual.

mutton, and as the Trojan wine of the villages of Yeni-Shehr, Yeni Kioi, and Ren Kioi, is magnificent, and excels even the very best Bordeaux wine, we had an abundance of good food; but of vegetables we could only get potatoes and spinach; the former are not grown at all in the plain of Troy, and had to be fetched from the town of the Dardanelles, whither they are imported probably from Italy. It appears very extraordinary that the villagers of the Troad, Greeks as well as Turks, do not use potatoes for food, though the soil is well adapted for the cultivation of this vegetable, and that they should use bread in its stead. In June and July we were supplied by the villagers with an abundance of hog-beans, kidney-beans, and artichokes, which appear to be, besides spinach, almost the sole kinds of vegetable they cultivate. It seems that garden peas are not cultivated in the Troad, for I could only buy them in June and July in the town of the Dardanelles, whither they were imported by sea.

I heard that the country was infested by marauders and highway robbers; besides that, the continual acts of brigandage in Macedonia, where a number of opulent men had been carried off by the robbers to the mountains and ransomed for heavy amounts, made me afraid of a like fate at Hissarlik. I therefore required at least eleven gendarmes for my safeguard. During my excavations at Hissarlik in 1878 and 1879 I had always kept ten gendarmes; but these were refugees from Bulgaria and Albania, and to such men I would not now entrust myself. I therefore applied to Hamid Pasha, the civil governor at the Dardanelles, to give me as a guard the eleven surest men he could find. By his permission they were picked out for me by his first dragoman and political agent, M. Nicolaos Didymos, from among the strongest and most trustworthy Turks of the Dardanelles. Their wages were £30 10*s.* monthly. So I had now eleven brave gendarmes of a powerful frame; all of them were well armed with rifles, pistols, and daggers; their firearms were not precisely of the latest invention, for they had for the most part only flint-locks; but some of them had Minié rifles, which they boasted of having used in the Crimean war. These shortcomings, however, were made up by the courage of the men, and I trusted them entirely, for I was sure they would have defended us bravely even if our camp had been attacked by a whole band of brigands. They were headed by a corporal (called *shaush* in Turkish), who superintended the other ten gendarmes and regulated the night and day watches. Three of these gendarmes always accompanied me every morning before sunrise to my sea-bath in the Hellespont, at Karanlik, a distance of four miles; as I always rode at a trot, they had to run as fast as they could to keep up with me. These daily runs being, therefore, very fatiguing to the men, I paid them 7*d.* every morning as extra wages. I further used the gendarmes to keep close watch on my workmen in the trenches, and never allowed excavations to be made at any point without at least one gendarme being on the look-out. In this way I forced my workmen to be honest, for they knew that if they were taken in the act of stealing they would be thrown into prison. I housed my eleven gendarmes in a large wooden barrack covered with waterproof felt, which I had built for them close to the stone house containing the kitchen and the chamber of my purser, for in this way they were about in the centre of my camp; but as there were constant disputes among them, some of them preferred to sleep in the open air even in the coldest weather, rather than endure the company of their comrades.

As majordomo and purser I had again Nicolaos Zaphyros Giannakes, from the village of Ren Kioi, who had served me in the same capacity in all my archæological campaigns in the Troad since March, 1870. Seeing that he was indispensable to me, he refused to serve me now for less than £15 monthly and his food; but I gladly granted him these terms, and also made him, when I left, a present of all my barracks at Hissarlik, for he is perfectly honest, and as purser and majordomo in a large camp in the wilderness, or in exploring expeditions, he can never be excelled. But his wages were the least advantage he had with me, for he derived enormous profits from the shop which was kept on his account by his brother, and in which he sold bread, tobacco, and brandy, on credit to my workmen, whose debts to him he always deducted in paying them on Saturday evening.

I had brought with me from Athens an excellent servant named Oedipus Pyromalles, a native of Xanthe, whose monthly wages were £2 16s., and a female cook, named Jocasté, who got £1 12s. monthly. I kept also a wheelwright, whose wages were £9 monthly, and a carpenter who received £4 a month. I had brought a good riding-horse with me from Athens, which stood well the great fatigue of the five months' campaign, but in the last week he broke down, so that I had to leave him behind. The stables stood on the south side against the store-barrack and the stone kitchen.

My instruments for working consisted of forty iron crowbars, some of them 2·25 m. long and 0·05 m. in diameter;* two jacks; a hundred large iron shovels, and as many pickaxes; fifty large hoes (called here by the Turkish name *tchapa*), such as are used in the vineyards, and which were exceedingly useful to me in filling the *débris* into the baskets; a windlass; 100 wheelbarrows, most of which had iron wheels; twenty man-carts, which were drawn by one man and pushed by two from behind, and a number of horse-carts. As I had to provide my workmen with good drinking water, I kept a labourer and a boy exclusively

---

* I here call attention to the rule, that I give *all measurements* according to the *metric system*. Their English values can be found from the *Tables* prefixed to the work.

for the service of fetching water from the nearest spring,* distant 365 mètres from Hissarlik. The boy's work was to fill the barrels; that of the man to load two of them at a time on a donkey, and to convey them to the trenches or to the barracks; and so great was the consumption of water, that in hot weather he could hardly fetch water enough, though ten barrels were in constant use.

Thus equipped and installed, I recommenced the excavations on the 1st of March with 150 workmen, which remained the average number of my labourers during the five months of the Trojan campaign of 1882. I employed, besides, a large number of ox-teams and horse-carts. The daily wages of my labourers, which were at first 9 piastres, or 1s. 7d., gradually increased with the season, and were in the hot summer months 11 and 12 piastres, equal to from 2s. to 2s. 1¾d. The horse and ox-carts were paid 1 piastre, equal to $2\tfrac{1}{10}d.$, for each load. Work was commenced regularly at sunrise and continued till sunset. Until the 12th of April no rest was allowed, except one hour for dinner; but as the days became longer, I allowed, after the Easter holidays, another half-hour at 8.30 A.M. for breakfast; this latter break was, from the 1st of June, increased to one hour.

As the work with the pickaxe is the heaviest, I always selected for it the strongest workmen; the rest were employed for the wheelbarrows, for filling the *débris* into the baskets, for loading the carts, and for drawing or pushing the man-carts and shooting the *débris*.

The workmen were for the most part Greeks from the neighbouring villages of Kalifatli, Yeni Shehr, and Ren Kioi; a few of them were from the islands of Imbros or Tenedos, or from the Thracian Chersonese. Of Turkish workmen I had on an average only twenty-five; I would gladly have increased their number had it been possible, for

---

* See *Ilios*, p. 110.

they work much better than the Asiatic Greeks, are more honest, and I had in them the great advantage that they worked on Sundays and on the numerous saints' days, when no Greek would have worked at any price. Besides, as I could always be sure that they would work on with unremitting zeal, and never need to be urged, I could let them sink all the shafts and assign to them other work, in which no superintendence on my part was possible. For all these reasons I always allotted to the Turkish workmen proportionally higher wages than to the Greeks. I had also now and then some Jewish labourers, who likewise worked much better than the Greeks.

I may take this occasion to mention that all the Jews of the Levant are descendants of the Spanish Jews who, to the ruin of Spain, were expelled from that country in March, 1492, under Ferdinand and Isabella. Strange to say, in spite of their long wanderings and the vicissitudes of their fortunes, they have not forgotten the Spanish language, in which they still converse among themselves, and which even the Jewish labourer speaks more fluently than Turkish. If one of these Jews now returned to Spain, his vocabulary would of course excite much amusement, for it abounds with antiquated Spanish words, such as we find in *Don Quixote*, and it also contains many Turkish words. But still it is a wonder that the Spanish language could have been so well preserved here in the East for four centuries, in the mouths of a people who do not write it with Latin, but solely with Hebrew characters, whenever they have to correspond among themselves. Thus, to all the Spanish letters I addressed to the Jew S. B. Gormezano at the Dardanelles, who happened to be for a time my agent, I got the answers always in Italian, and was assured that the writer did not know how to write Spanish with Latin characters, as from his childhood he had been accustomed to use the Hebrew alphabet in writing Spanish.

I had two Turkish delegates, one of whom, called Moharrem Effendi, was supplied to me by the local authorities; I had to provide him with lodgings and to pay him £7 10s. monthly. The other delegate, Beder Eddin Effendi, was sent to me by the Minister of Public Instruction at Constantinople, by whom he was paid; I had merely to provide him with a bedchamber. I have carried on archæological excavations in Turkey for a number of years, but it had never yet been my ill-fortune to have such a monster of a delegate as Beder Eddin, whose arrogance and self-conceit were only equalled by his complete ignorance, and who considered it his sole office to throw all possible obstacles in my way. As he was in the employ of government, he had the telegraph to the Dardanelles at his disposal, and he used it in the most shameless way to denounce me and my architects to the local authorities. At first the civil governor listened to him, and sent trustworthy men to investigate the charges; but having repeatedly convinced himself that the man had basely calumniated us, he took no further notice of him.

A Turk will always hate a Christian, however well he may be paid by him, and thus it was not difficult for Beder Eddin Effendi to bring all my eleven gendarmes over to his side, and to make so many spies of them. The man became particularly obnoxious and insupportable to us when my architect, Dr. Dörpfeld, having in April imported a surveying instrument for taking measurements and making the plans of Ilium, the circumstance was reported to the military governor of the Dardanelles, Djemal Pasha, who at once communicated it to Said Pasha, the Grand Master of the Artillery at Constantinople, hinting to him his suspicions that we were merely using the excavations at Troy as a pretext for taking plans of the fortress of Koum Kaleh. Said Pasha, who took the same view of the case, at once telegraphed to him to prohibit, not only our use of the surveying instrument, but even our making any plans at all.

Beder Eddin Effendi no sooner heard of this, than he began to denounce us repeatedly to the military governor, alleging that, in spite of the prohibition, we measured and took plans clandestinely; and he succeeded in irritating that officer against us so much, that he prohibited us from taking any measurements at all within the excavations. Having obtained this, Beder Eddin Effendi declared that he and the watchmen, whom he had placed over us, could not distinguish whether we were measuring, or merely taking notes, or making drawings; he therefore interdicted us from taking notes or making drawings within the excavations, and continually threatened to arrest my architects and send them in chains to Constantinople in case of their disobedience.

I applied for redress to the German Embassy, explaining that the miserable fortress of Koum Kaleh was at a distance of five miles from Hissarlik, and altogether invisible from here; that I merely intended to make new plans of the Acropolis and of the lower city, instead of the old plans (I. and II. in *Ilios*), which, in consequence of my excavations of this year, were no longer quite correct. The chargé d'affaires of the German Empire at Constantinople, Baron von Hirschfeld, took the matter at once in hand, but neither he nor his excellent first dragoman, Baron von Testa, could effect anything against the obstinacy of the Grand Master of the Artillery, who did not even attend to the orders of the Grand Vizier.

It is true that, in spite of Beder Eddin Effendi's vigilance, we succeeded in taking all the notes we wanted, but to take measurements came to be out of the question. In this manner the five months' Trojan campaign went on, and finished at the end of July, with continual vain efforts on the part of the German Embassy at Constantinople to obtain for us permission to make the plans, and amidst the daily and hourly vexations caused us by our insufferable delegate, Beder Eddin Effendi; in short, a wretch like him is an unmitigated plague in archæological pursuits.

In August I made a direct application to the Chancellor of the German Empire, Prince Otto von Bismarck, who kindly took the matter in hand, at once gave new instructions to his Embassy at Constantinople, and obtained for me, in September, permission to take new plans, provided these were limited to my works below the level of the ground and no measurements were made above ground. The permission thus limited was of course useless. Further long delays and disappointments would probably have been in store for me, had it not been for the lucky circumstance that, in the beginning of November, my honoured friend Herr von Radowitz was appointed ambassador of the German Empire at Constantinople, who is one of the most excellent diplomatists Germany has ever had; he is besides animated by the holy fire of science, and has unbounded energy. Having addressed himself on my behalf direct to H. M. the Sultan, he at once obtained an *iradé* which permitted me to make the plans. I now fulfil a most agreeable duty in thanking His Excellency publicly and most cordially for the immense service he has rendered me, without which I could probably never have brought my work to a close.

I therefore again dispatched Dr. Dörpfeld to Troy on the 18th of November; but, being pressed for time, he only made the Plan VII. of the Acropolis of the Second City. It was not till April 18:3 that I was able to send to Troy the surveyor, Mr. J. Ritter Wolff, who made the Plan VIII. of the whole city of Ilium.

To return to the order of our proceedings. We had a south wind for only the first three days in March; afterwards until the end of April, and therefore for fifty-eight days uninterruptedly, we had a strong north wind,* in-

---

* The ἐτησίαι (sc. ἄνεμοι) of the ancients, also called ἐτησίαι βορέαι, Aristot. *Probl.* 26, 2.

creasing at least four times a-week to a severe storm, which blew the blinding dust into our eyes, and interfered seriously with the excavations. Only a few of my labourers had dust-spectacles; those who had none were obliged to cover up their faces with shawls, and thus the host of my veiled workmen looked very like the muffled attendants at Italian funerals. At the same time the weather was very cold, the thermometer often falling at night below freezing-point ($0°$ Celsius $= 32°$ F.)[*], and sometimes, even in April, the water froze to solid ice in our barracks; nay, the thermometer often did not mark above $3°$ C. $= 37°·4$ F. at noon. Mount Saoce, on Samothrace, remained covered with snow till about the end of March. The chain of Ida was entirely covered with snow till about the 20th of March. Afterwards only the higher peaks remained snow-clad; but the snow gradually diminished, and by the end of May snow could only be seen on and near their summits. For particulars regarding the weather from the 22nd of April to the 21st of July, I refer the reader to the meteorological tables at the end of the volume. Unfortunately these observations were not made for the first fifty-three days; and I was prevented by my malaria-fever from continuing to write them up after the 21st of July.

The winter of 1881–1882 had been extraordinarily dry, and later on rain was still extremely rare. We had in all March and April only five or six very slight showers of rain, and all the time, up to the end of July, there was no rain except during two thunderstorms. From this cause, the

---

[*] It may be convenient here to give the simple rule for converting degrees of the centigrade thermometer (Celsius) into those of Fahrenheit. Multiply by $1·8$, *i.e.* double the number and multiply by $0·9$, and add $32°$; or, if the degrees are *minus* (below zero of Celsius), subtract from $32°$. Thus, $3°·2$ C. $= 6°·4 \times ·9 + 32° = 37°·76$ F. For, as the interval between the freezing and boiling points, $100°$ C. $= 212° - 32° = 180°$ F., every $5°$ C. $= 9°$ F. and each degree of C. $= 1·80$, or $9:5$ F.

water of the Simois, which was only a few inches deep in the beginning of March, was entirely exhausted by the end of April, and the river bed became perfectly dry in the beginning of May. The same occurred in the Thymbrius by the middle of May, and (a thing unheard of) even the course of the Scamander in the plain of Troy had no running water in the beginning of July, and thenceforward consisted only of a series of pools of stagnant water, the number of which diminished in proportion as the season advanced.* As stated in *Ilios*,† it happens on an average once every three years, in August or September, that the Scamander has no running water; it also happens, perhaps as often, that the Simois and the Thymbrius dry up completely in August or September; but the oldest inhabitants of the Troad do not remember that this phenomenon ever occurred in any one of the three rivers so early as it did this year.

While speaking of the Scamander, I may here add that, on the 14th of March, I investigated the junction of the Bounarbashi Su with the Scamander, which does not occur in two places, as P. W. Forchhammer ‡ states, but only in one place, about a mile to the south of the bridge of Koum Kaleh.§ The rivulet of the Bounarbashi Su was, at the junction, 2 mètres broad and 0·30 m. deep. In examining the soil in the neighbourhood, I was struck by the conical shape of the hillock on which one of the two windmills stands, which are immediately to the east and south-east of Yeni Shehr,|| and, having investigated it most

---

* The inhabitants of the village of Yeni Shehr, who have to fetch their whole supply of water from the Scamander, are badly off when the river dries up, for they have then to sink wells in the river bed, and to dig the shafts deeper and deeper in proportion as the river bed becomes drier and drier. † Page 94.

‡ *Topographische und Physiographische Beschreibung der Ebene von Troia*, p. 14.

§ See the large Map of the Troad. || Ibid.

carefully, I found it to be an artificial tumulus, a so-called heroic tomb; indeed, the fragments of ancient pottery, which peep out from it here and there, can leave no doubt on the point. This tumulus had never yet come under the notice of any modern traveller, but it was evidently known to Strabo,* who mentions here three tombs, namely, those of Achilles, Patroclus, and Antilochus; whilst until now we knew only of the two tombs attributed to the two former heroes. I shall revert to the newly discovered tumulus in the subsequent pages.

The Plain of Troy used to be covered in April and May with red and yellow flowers, as well as with deep grass; but this year, for want of moisture, there were no flowers and barely any grass at all, so that the poor people had hardly anything for their flocks to feed upon. We had not, therefore, to complain this year of being annoyed, as in former years, by the monotonous croaking of millions of frogs, for the swamps being dried up in the lower Simois valley, there were no frogs at all, except a few in the bed of the Kalifatli Asmak. The locusts appeared this year later than usual, namely, towards the end of June, when nearly all the grain had been harvested; they therefore did not do much damage.

The first flocks of cranes passed over the Plain of Troy on the 14th of March; the first storks arrived on the 17th of March. The cranes do not make their nests here; they merely stop a few hours for food, and fly on to more northerly regions.

A slight shock of earthquake occurred on the 1st of April, at 5 h. 15½ minutes P.M.

One of my first works was to bring to light all the foundations of the Hellenic or Roman edifices in the part of Hissarlik still unexcavated, and to collect the sculptured

---

* XIII. p. 596, Casaubon. Compare Chap. VI. p. 242.

blocks belonging to them, as well as to other buildings, of which the foundations could no longer be traced. I also continued on the north side, at the place marked V— N O,* at a depth of 12 mètres below the surface, the excavation commenced there in the summer of 1872. But finding that the soil consisted solely of prehistoric *débris*, which had been thrown down there to enlarge and level the hill, I soon gave it up again.

As I expected to find more metopes on the northern slope, at the place (see the upper V on Plan I. in *Ilios*) where in 1872 I had found the beautiful metope of Apollo and the quadriga of the sun, I stationed twenty-five labourers there, who worked for nearly two months, first in removing the enormous mass of *débris* which I had thrown out on the slope in 1872 and 1873, and afterwards digging away from the latter a slice 3 mètres deep from front to back. The layer of *débris* to be removed being on an average 6 mètres deep, 28 mètres high, and 20 mètres broad, the excavation had to be made in terraces, for in this way the work became much easier and the distance the *débris* had to be carried was reduced to a minimum. We worked here with pickaxes, shovels, and wheelbarrows, which are always more advantageous than carts, so long as the distance is less than 30 mètres. But no second metope was found there, nor any other sculpture of great interest, and only a marble female head of the Macedonian period, which I represent in the chapter on Ilium. I struck in this excavation a very remarkable wall-corner of the Macedonian time, which I describe in the following pages. I also explored the gigantic theatre, immediately to the east of the Acropolis,† of which I give a detailed account in the chapter on Ilium. In this, as well as in the excavations on Hissarlik, we found a vast number of venomous

---

* See Plan I. in *Ilios*.
† See Plan II. in *Ilios*, and Plan VIII. in the present work.

serpents, but my labourers were not afraid of their bite, for they declared they had drunk, before coming to work with me, an antidote which they called "*sorbet*," and which made the bite even of the most poisonous snakes harmless. But I was never able to obtain this antidote from them, though I promised a large reward for it.

I proceeded to empty the Hellenic well in the Acropolis,* the mouth of which I had brought to light in the autumn of 1871, about 2 mètres below the surface. At the depth of 18 mètres I found in it many rude prehistoric stone hammers of diorite and a polishing-stone of jasper, and below these implements large masses of Greek and Roman tiles of various forms, which seem to prove that the stone implements had been thrown into the well at a later time, together with other *débris*. On reaching the depth of 22 mètres I had to stop this work on account of the water, which rose faster than I could draw it up. The last objects taken out of the well were six sheeps'-skulls.

I also sunk in the eastern part of the Acropolis a shaft 3 mètres square, in which I struck the rock at the depth of 14 mètres.†

One of my greater works was a trench (marked S S on Plan VII.), 80 mètres long and 7 mètres broad, which I dug in March and April, from the point K to the point L,‡ across the eastern part of the Acropolis, which was then still unexcavated, in order to ascertain how far the citadel of the earliest prehistoric cities extended in this direction. This work was exceedingly difficult, on account of the immense masses of small stones and huge boulders which we had to remove, as well as on account of the depth (no less than 12 mètres) to which we had to dig to reach the rock. The trench was excavated simultaneously

---

* See a z on Plan I. in *Ilios*, and t z on Plan VII. in the present work. † This shaft is marked R on Plan VII.
‡ See Plan I. in *Ilios*.

throughout its whole length, the *débris* being carried off by wheelbarrows as well as by man-carts and horse-carts; but the deeper we penetrated the more difficult and fatiguing did the labour become, for we were obliged to carry up the *débris* in baskets on narrow zigzag paths, which became steeper and steeper with the increasing depth. When we had reached a depth of from 10 to 12 mètres, the side paths had to be cut away, and all the *débris* had to be removed by man-carts, and shot out on the slope at the point K. But this fatiguing work has been rewarded by interesting results for the topography of the ancient Acropolis; since it has enabled us to ascertain that this whole eastern part of the citadel-hill originated after the destruction of the fourth city, and that it was heaped up to extend the original Pergamos; because we brought to light in the trench the exterior or eastern side of the brick wall of the citadel of the second city (marked N N on Plan VII.), whence the layers of *débris* fell off abruptly. Further investigation has proved to us with certainty, that from the foot of the citadel-wall the ground fell off originally with a steep inclination to the east, and that, during the time of the first four cities, a deep valley here separated the Pergamos on the east side from the mountainous ridge, of which it formed the spur. The citadel-hill must consequently have increased on the east side full 70 mètres since the catastrophe of the second city.

In excavating the trench we struck gigantic foundations, composed of well-wrought blocks of limestone: some of these foundations certainly belong to the Roman time; their construction, as well as the stonecutters' marks which they bore, can leave no doubt of this. After having taken note of their exact position, we had to break through these foundations in order to dig the trench deeper; but, not being able to move the stones on account of their ponderous weight, we had to crush them with enormous hammers, a work which only two or three of all my labourers were able to do, and which was always rewarded by additional pay in the evening. We reserved only those blocks which had a peculiar interest in an architectural point of view. It was impossible for us to ascertain to what edifices these foundations had belonged, for they had been already partly demolished in the Middle Ages, and had been in modern times a welcome quarry for building-stones. Among these foundations, those on the north-east side are particularly distinguished by their gigantic proportions and their good construction.

Having broken through them, we struck at the north-east end of the trench a large fortress-wall of rudely-wrought stones, which my architects ascribe with the very greatest probability to the fifth prehistoric city, and of which the woodcut No. 99, p. 189, gives a good view. We brought it to light to a depth of 6 mètres, and were obliged to cut it through in order to make a road for the man-carts which worked in the trench. It is distinguished by its masonry from the substruction-walls of the more ancient prehistoric cities, for it consists of long plate-like slabs of stone, joined in the most solid way without cement or lime, which have enormous dimensions, particularly in the lower part, whilst the lower part of the walls of the second prehistoric city consists of smaller stones of rather a cubical shape. This peculiar construction gave us the clue to find on the opposite side of the Acropolis the continuation of this wall of plate-like slabs, and it thus enabled us to indicate the course of the wall of the fifth prehistoric settlement, at least in general.

The exterior side of this wall is slightly curved; its upper breadth is 2·50 m., its lower breadth being 5 m., owing to an enlargement in the middle of its height. On a level with this prehistoric citadel-wall many house-walls were brought to light, consisting partly of quarry-stones, partly of unbaked clay-bricks. It is very remarkable that below the Hellenic layer of ruins we found, from the point K to about half the distance to the point L, only Lydian terra-cottas, such as are described in Chapter X. of *Ilios*, and pottery of the fifth and fourth settlements, but none at all of the three lowest cities. In the other half of the trench we found, beneath the *débris* of the fourth settlement, deep layers of *débris* of bricks falling off from the brick wall of the second citadel (N N on Plan VII.) to the east, which must have originated at a time when the second and the fourth cities had been destroyed. Of this brick wall, which here forms a tower (G M on Plan VII.), I give a detailed account in the description of the second city. Below the slanting layers of *débris* of bricks I found a layer of natural soil, 0·50 m. deep, which had evidently been dug away from another place and had been shot here. We found this layer of natural soil on the whole south and east sides of the Acropolis: it was most likely dug up and shot here by the second settlers when they levelled the ground for the foundations of this brick wall, which, as we shall see in the following pages, belongs to the second period in the history of their town. This is the more probable, as below this natural soil we found a layer of *débris* of baked bricks, which seems to have been derived from the destruction of the citadel-wall of the first period, which was more to the west. Still deeper, down to the rock, we found pottery of the first and second cities.

Another of my larger works was to excavate, as far down as the house-ruins of the second city, the whole part of the earthblock D (on Plan I. in *Ilios*), which extends between the south-western extremity of the trench W and L (see Plan I. in *Ilios*). Here, too, the enormous foundations of the Hellenic or Roman edifices gave us most trouble; below them we brought to light, in regular succession, the foundations, with part of the house-walls, of the fifth, fourth, and third settlements, all of which we had unfortunately to remove. The masonry of these three cities did not differ much from each other, consisting of crude bricks or of small calcareous stones joined with clay. In a house-wall of the fifth city were some courses of crude bricks between the courses of stone-masonry. As a strange phenomenon I may mention that, in this excavation, we picked up in several places corn-bruisers and rude hammers of stone immediately below the stratum of the Aeolic Ilium. As in the case of their presence in the Hellenic well, they were, no doubt, thrown here together with other *débris*.

The Greek and Latin inscriptions, of which many were found here and elsewhere, are given in the subsequent pages.

Another of our great labours was to cut away nearly the whole of the great block of *débris* marked B on Plan I. in *Ilios*, and to remove in the excavated parts all the walls and the remaining *débris* of the third settlement, so as to bring to light all the foundations of the second city, and what else remained of its house-walls. I only left *in situ* the largest house of the third city (marked H S on Plan I. in *Ilios* and on Plan VII. in this work), which I formerly attributed to the town chief. I also excavated the trench (Z'—O on Plan I. in *Ilios* and N Z on Plan VII.) much deeper, carefully cleared the great western wall, and excavated the whole space A—O (Plan I. in *Ilios*), so as to bring to light the south-western gate (R C and F M on Plan VII.) with the adjacent part of the great wall down to below their foundations. I further removed the *débris* which rested on the south-western gate-road,* cleared out the *débris* from between the two great walls of the second city,† *c* and *b* on Plan VII., and brought to light their prolongation in an easterly direction. In doing so, I was led by certain indications to suspect the existence of a second gateway, leading up from the south side to the Acropolis of the second city, at the points marked G, G' (on Plan I. in *Ilios*). I therefore excavated there, and

---

* See in *Ilios* the engraving No. 144, and T U on Plan VII. in this volume. † *Idem*, and Plan VII.

in fact discovered a second large gate (marked N F on Plan VII.), which I shall discuss in the subsequent pages. As I had to cut away a large part of the blocks of *débris* G, G' and a considerable part of the earthblock J E (Plan I. in *Ilios*), and had to dig down to an enormous depth, this excavation was one of the most troublesome and fatiguing, the more so as we had no other outlet than the great northern trench (X—Z on Plan VII.) into which the *débris* were shot, and had to be removed thence by horse or ox-carts, to be thrown out on the northern slope.

I also excavated to the north-west of L (see Plan I. in *Ilios*) at the place where, in 1873, I had discovered the altar represented in *Ilios*, p. 31, No. 6; and brought to light there a second gate of the third city, and, at 1·50 m. beneath it, a third large gate of the second city (marked O X on Plan VII.): both these gates will be discussed in the subsequent pages. I further cleared the southern part of the building L and L' (see Plan I. in *Ilios*), in which we now recognized a large gate of the Roman age of Ilium. In order to bring to light more of the first city, I enlarged and excavated down to the rock the great northern trench (X on Plan I. in *Ilios*, and X—Z on Plan VII. in this volume), as far as was possible without demolishing any of the foundations of the second city. In doing so I discovered many interesting walls of the first city (marked *f* and *fa*, *fb*, *fc*, on Plan VII.), which I shall discuss in the following pages.

My researches in the spring of 1873, on the plateau to the east, south, and west of the Acropolis, had been but very superficial. As may be seen from Plan II. in *Ilios*, they had been limited to twenty shafts sunk at random over the vast extent of the lower city of Ilium, and in five instances in places where the rock was only covered with a layer of *débris* a few feet deep. Besides, in three of the deeper shafts (see D, O, R, and the vignette on Plan II. in *Ilios*), I struck tombs cut into or built upon the rock. In three other shafts (see E, F, I, and in the vignette on Plan II.) I struck large walls; in four more I struck house-walls, in building all of which walls the rock must necessarily have been cleared of the ancient *débris* with which it had been covered. Therefore, fifteen out of twenty shafts had given no result at all.

I now therefore wished to explore the plateau systematically and thoroughly, and I began this work by digging on the south-western slope of Hissarlik, close to the shafts marked K, I, G on Plan II. in *Ilios*, at right angles to the axis of the south-western gate (FM—TU on Plan VII.) a trench 60 mètres long by 3 mètres broad (see Plan VIII. in this volume). Besides investigating the soil, I hoped to bring to light the prolongation of the south-western gateway, and to find tombs on both sides of it. As the slope rises here at an angle of 15°, I thought that the accumulation of *débris* would be rather insignificant, and I hoped, therefore, to obtain great results from this excavation. But I was greatly disappointed, for I only struck the rock at 12 mètres below the surface, and whoever has seen excavations will know that to search for tombs at such a depth is altogether out of the question, the difficulties of removing the *débris* from narrow trenches being too enormous. As I found there no trace of the south-western gate-road, we must suppose that this road—just as I found to be the case with the southern gate-road (N F on Plan VII.)—lay upon the bare rock. I found in this trench very large quantities of fragments of Hellenic pottery, and in the lowest layers masses of fragments of those kinds of very ancient pottery which are peculiar to the two most ancient cities of Hissarlik; namely the thick lustrous black pottery peculiar to the first city, with an incised ornamentation filled with chalk, having long horizontal tubes in the rim, or two vertical tubular holes for suspension in the body; and the dark-red, brown, or yellow tripod vases, and fragments of thick, perfectly flat, lustrous red terra-cotta trays or plates, which are peculiar to the second city.

I further dug a trench 40 metres long close to the Acropolis on the north-west side (see Plan VIII. in this volume), where I hoped to find the prolongation of the great wall of the second city. In fact, I found there, at the exact place where it must be supposed to have existed, the rock artificially levelled, so that there can be no doubt that the wall once stood here; but not a stone of it remained *in situ*.

I also dug a trench, 110 metres long, 3 metres broad, on the plateau of the lower city of Ilium, on the south side of Hissarlik (see Plan VIII.). Here the excavation was much easier, the depth of the *débris* being 6 metres close to the citadel-hill, and only 2 metres at the end of my trench. I struck here a portico of syenite columns with Corinthian capitals of white marble. It is paved with large well-wrought blocks of calcareous stone, and has evidently been destroyed at a late period, for the columns had only fallen when the pavement was already covered up with *débris* 0·30 m. deep; and, as all the columns which are visible lie in a north-westerly direction, it is probable that the edifice was destroyed by an earthquake.* In this trench we also struck many Hellenic house-walls, and found masses of Hellenic pottery, but in the lowest layers of *débris* again a very large quantity of prehistoric terra-cottas of the first two cities of Hissarlik. Visitors can easily convince themselves of the existence of this pottery, if they will only take the trouble to pick with a knife in the sides of the trench from the rock to 0·30 m. or 0·40 m. above it. I also sunk a large number of shafts on the plateau, south and east of the citadel-hill, as well as on the

---

* Mr. Calvert calls my attention to the statement of Pliny, *H. N.* II. 86: "Maximus terrae memoria mortalium exstitit motus, Tiberii Caesaris principatu; XII. urbibus Asiae una nocte prostratis," which proves that earthquakes occurred here in earlier times.

slope west of it, all of which are indicated on Plan VIII.; in all of them I obtained the same results.

I also excavated the tumuli at the foot of Cape Sigeum attributed to Achilles and Patroclus, the tomb of Protesilaus * on the opposite shore of the Thracian Chersonesus, as well as the three tumuli on the high headland above In Tepeh. I excavated on the site of the small city, which I believe to be Gergis, on Mount Bali Dagh above Bounarbashi; in the ancient city called Eski Hissarlik opposite those heights, on the eastern bank of the Scamander, and further north-east in the ancient ruins on the Fulu Dagh or Mount Dedeh. I further excavated in the ancient cities on Mount Kurshunlu Tepeh † near Beiramich, at the foot of the range of Ida. I went thither on the 1st of July, accompanied by four mounted gendarmes, the Turkish delegate Moharrem Effendi, two workmen, who carried the baggage and the implements for excavating on pack-horses, and two servants, one of whom was Nicolaos.

We went by way of Chiblak, through the plain of Troy, to Bounarbashi. About a mile south of Chiblak, we passed four solitary columns of grey granite, which by their position form a regular quadrangle, about 100 m. long by 40 m. broad. These columns have often been mistaken by travellers for the remains of a large ancient temple, whilst in reality they mark the site of a comparatively recent Turkish sheep-fold or stable for sheep, to which they served as corners; they must have been brought hither from the lower city of Ilium, where similar granite columns abound. On a small hill close to Bounarbashi, and on the north-east side of it, we saw a number of similar granite columns, of which four also form a regular quadrangle; these columns have often been mistaken by

---

* See the large Map of the Troad, and Chapter VI.
† See the small Map of the Troad, No. 140, p. 303.

modern travellers for remnants of ancient Troy, whereas in reality they have likewise been brought hither from Ilium, and have been used to ornament the "konak" (mansion) of a Turkish Aga, which still existed here a century ago, and of which we find a fine engraving in Count Choiseul-Gouffier's *Voyage pittoresque de la Grèce*. The road leads from Bounarbashi over the heights of which the Bali Dagh is the north-eastern spur, and close to a still unexplored "heroic tomb" (see the large Map of the Troad). It turns gradually to the east, and descends to the winding bed of the Scamander, which we had to pass not less than six times in one hour; leading afterwards, across long tracts of uncultivated land thickly overgrown with dwarf oaks, juniper, etc., to Iné, where I was kindly received by the Caïmacam (mayor) Chevket Abdoullah, who has some education and speaks French fluently. He gave me two additional gendarmes, the country being very unsafe. It was in the height of summer; my thermometer marked $34°$ C. = $93°\cdot 4$ F. in the coolest room of the mayor's house. I arrived in the evening at Beiramich, and the next morning early on Mount Kurshunlu Tepeh (see the small Map of the Troad, No. 140, p. 303). The temperature was already at 8 A.M. $36°$ C.=$96°\cdot 8$ F.: it increased by 10 A.M. to $38°$ C.= $100°\cdot 4$ F.

I had taken ten workmen with me from Beiramich, each of whom had to receive 10 gros = 1*s*. 9½*d*. a day. Pickaxes, shovels, and baskets, I had brought with me from Hissarlik. I shall give in the subsequent pages the result of my researches on Kurshunlu Tepeh, as well as of those I made immediately afterwards on Mount Chali Dagh, the site of the ancient city of Cebrené.

I terminated the excavations at Hissarlik by the end of July, but a week before I had caught the malaria fever. I got rid of it by means of quinine and black coffee, but it soon returned, and continued to torment me for nearly four months afterwards.

CHAPTER II.

THE FIRST PREHISTORIC SETTLEMENT ON THE HILL OF HISSARLIK.

MY excellent architects have proved to me, beyond any doubt, that the first settlers built on the hill of Hissarlik only one or two large edifices. The length of this first settlement does not exceed 46 mètres, and its breadth can hardly have been greater. Of the walls which we have brought to light, the northern (fc on Plan VII.) and the two southern ones (fa and fb) are particularly remarkable, because they are fortification walls (see Plan VII.). Of the two southern walls, the inner one (fb) belongs, no doubt, to an older epoch of the first settlement, the outer wall to a later extension of it. These fortification-walls are made of unwrought calcareous stones, and in such a way that their outside is somewhat slanting, and consists of larger stones. It is difficult to ascertain their thickness accurately, their upper part having fallen on the inner side, but it is approximately 2·50 m. The extension of the settlement on the south side was a little more than 8 m. Between these fortification-walls there are, at intervals of 2½, 4, 5, 5½, and 6 mètres, five thinner walls, nearly parallel, 0·60 m. to 0·90 m. thick; besides two smaller walls and two cross walls (see Plan VII.). We have only been able to excavate them for the breadth of my great northern trench (X—Z on Plan VII.), say for a distance of 15 mètres; unfortunately we could not extend this excavation of the first city without destroying the ruins of the following city, which, as we shall see in the following pages, are of capital interest to science. The masonry of the walls consists of small stones joined with earth; the clay coating has been preserved in several places. Neither baked nor unbaked bricks were found here. The settlement stood on the slope, which fell off from south to north, the ground being 2 m. higher on the south side than on the north. We found here many small shells, but not in such masses as in the following prehistoric cities; besides, they seem to have been contained in the clay of the house-walls or terraces, and consequently cannot be considered as kitchen refuse, like a large part of those of the later settlers.

As before mentioned, the ruins denote only one or two large edifices on Hissarlik: we may therefore presume, with the greatest probability, that this first settlement had a lower city, which extended on the plateau to the west, south, and south-east; and indeed the large masses of pottery I found there in the lowest stratum in my trenches and shafts, the form and fabric of which is perfectly identical with that of the first settlement on the Acropolis hill, can leave no doubt in this respect. This first settlement appears to have existed here for a great number of centuries, for the *débris* had time to accumulate and to form a stratum having an average depth of 2·50 m.

As even mere fragments of pottery from this first and most ancient settlement are remarkable, and welcome to every museum, I gathered all we found, and was able to fill with them no less than eight large boxes. I also carefully collected all the bones I could find, and sent a whole box-full of them to Professor Rudolf Virchow at Berlin for investigation. (See Appendix II.) Nearly all the pottery is lustrous black; but lustrous red, brown, or yellow terracottas are not rare. I collected separately all the more characteristic fragments, particularly all the vase-rims with long horizontal tubular holes, of which I gathered hundreds, and put carefully aside those with an incised ornamentation, which is always filled with chalk in order to strike the eye. This ornamentation is always more or less like that which we see on the fragments represented in *Ilios*, p. 216, Nos.

28–35. But an ornamentation of wave-lines, like those at p. 225, Nos. 53, 54 in *Ilios*, also occurs now and then.

I represent here only the two most interesting vase-fragments.

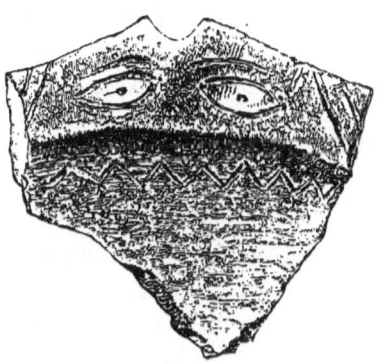

No. 1.—Fragment of a lustrous black Bowl, with an incised decoration filled with white chalk. (Size 1 : 2, about. Depth, 15 m.)

No. 1 is a rim-fragment of a large bowl, on which are distinctly incised two lentiform eyes with brows, probably meant for human eyes; to the right and left are two parallel strokes; below, a zigzag line; just above the eyes the rim forms a semicircle.

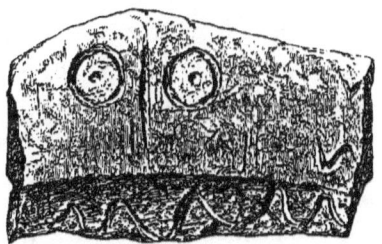

No. 2.—Fragment of a lustrous black Vase, with an incised ornamentation filled with white chalk. (The reverse side, No. 3, p. 32.)

No. 2 is a similar fragment of a bowl-rim, on which we see a very curious incised ornamentation resembling an owl's face in monogram; the eyes are particularly large; the stroke between them may be intended to indicate the beak; below the rim we see a line of curves; all these incisions are filled with chalk. To the right of the owl's-face are two or more incised signs. Professor Sayce thinks that the eyes may have been intended to ward off the effects of the *evil eye*, like the eyes painted on the boats of China, Malta, and Sicily. In Marocco small pieces are broken out of earthenware vessels for the same purpose.

It deserves particular attention that these incised ornamentations, Nos. 1 and 2, are on the inner side of the bowl rims, and that there is no ornamentation at all on the outside. The bowls to which Nos. 1 and 2 belong had on the outside two excrescences, each with two vertical tubular holes for suspension: one of these excrescences (belonging

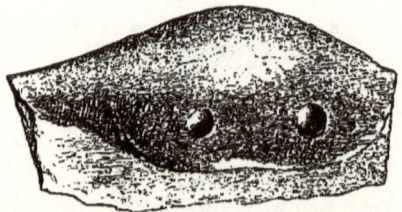

No. 3.—The reverse side of No. 2, with two vertical holes for suspension. (Size 1 : 2, about. Depth, 15 m.)

to No. 2) is represented by the engraving No. 3; in order to photograph it, the reverse side of the fragment had to be put almost horizontally. We have illustrated this system of vases and bowls with two vertical tubular holes for suspension on each side by the engravings, pp. 214, 215, Nos. 23, 24, and 25 in *Ilios*. To the few places enumerated on p. 215 in *Ilios*, in which vases with a like contrivance may be found, I have to add the Museum of Parma, of which Mr. Giovanni Mariotti is the learned keeper. This museum contains a vase found in the terramare of the Emilia, which has on each side two vertical tubular holes for suspension.

The pottery of the first city in general, particularly these large bowls, is but very slightly baked; the clay contains a great many small coarse pieces of granite, the mica of which shows its presence by numerous small flakes, glittering like gold and silver; but it must be observed that this granite was contained in the clay, and that, consequently, there was no need for the potter to add it.

The celebrated manufacturer of earthenware, Mr. Henry Doulton, of Lambeth, who, at my request, has made experiments with some of these lustrous black bowl-fragments of the first city, has obtained the following results. The fragments which he submitted merely to a red heat turned a light yellow, whilst those which he subjected to a high degree of heat, in fact to quite a white heat, such as vitreous stoneware is submitted to, got a red brick colour. The material of the pottery has proved to be very refractory, standing a high degree of heat. Mr. Doulton's experiments perfectly confirm, therefore, the theory of Dr. Lisch,* as to the manufacture of the clay vessels in prehistoric times.

Though I thought that in *Ilios* (pp. 218–220) I had exhausted the discussion of the manufacture of the Trojan pottery in general, and of that of the first city in particular, yet I cannot refrain from giving here an extract of a letter on the same subject from Dr. Chr. Hostmann, of Celle, because his theory differs from those I have advanced. " I have found in my excavations in the ancient necropolis of Darzau, vases with the same lustrous black colour which is conspicuous on those of the first settlement at Troy. Now, in the most varied experiments I have made, and for which my manufacture of printing-ink gave me an excellent opportunity, I have found that that colour can never have been produced in a slow fire with much smoke, but that it has been obtained merely by dipping the vases in oil, covering them with a thin layer of

---

* See *Ilios*, p. 219.

melted pine-resin, to which may have been added a little oil, and, when this had become cold, exposing them to the action of the fire, so that the layer of resin became carbonized."

No. 4 is a very small lustrous black cup, with a handle and a convex foot. No. 5 is a lustrous black jug: the body is globular, the foot flat, the neck straight and cylindrical; the handle long and slender. The clay of this jug is only three millimètres thick, of which hardly one millimètre is baked; it is one of the lightest vases I ever found in any of the prehistoric settlements at Hissarlik,

No. 4.—Small lustrous black Cup. (Size 1 : 4. Depth, 14-15 m.)

No. 5.—Lustrous black wheel-made Jug. (Size 1 : 4. Depth, 14-15 m.)

and is of capital interest to science, because it is wheel-made and, except the vase, p. 214, No. 23 in *Ilios*, which is manufactured in like manner, it is the only entire wheel-made vase of the first city that I can boast of: fragments of wheel-made pottery sometimes occur in the first city, but they are rare.

Although the ruins of this first and most ancient Trojan settlement may be more than a thousand years older than Homer, I cannot refrain from mentioning in this place, that the art of making pottery by means of the wheel existed already as a handicraft and a profession at the time of the poet; as we see it in the admirable simile, in which, in order to depict the light and rapid movements of the dancing youths and virgins represented by Hephaestus on the shield of Achilles, he compares these movements to the rapid rotation of the wheel, which the potter, in commencing his work, sets turning rapidly round its axis, in order to try whether it can aid the skill of his hands.* I may add that as early as the time of the first dynasties of the old Egyptian empire the potter's wheel was in general use, and all pottery was thoroughly baked in ovens.†

Nos. 6 and 7 are two lustrous black cups with a high hollow foot and a large handle, standing upright on the rim; the clay is thick, but slightly baked, and heavy. These are the first entire cups of this shape I ever found,

Nos. 6, 7.—Two lustrous black Cups, with hollow foot and upright handle.
(Size 1 : 4. Depth, about 14 m.)

but, as similar handles and hollow feet are of frequent occurrence in the *débris* of the first settlement, there can be no doubt that this form of cup was in general use here. A very singular vessel is No. 8, which is also of a lustrous black colour, and of thick clay only slightly baked. The body, which resembles that of our present drinking-glasses,

---

* *Il.* XVIII. 599-601 :

οἱ δ' ὁτὲ μὲν θρέξασκον ἐπισταμένοισι πόδεσσιν
ῥεῖα μάλ', ὡς ὅτε τις τροχὸν ἄρμενον ἐν παλάμῃσιν
ἑζόμενος κεραμεὺς πειρήσεται, αἴ κε θέῃσιν·

† See George Perrot et Charles Chipiez, *Histoire de l'Art*, Paris, 1882, vol. i. pp. 818, 819. See also S. Birch, *Ancient Pottery*, p. 14.

is encircled by five concave furrows deeply impressed; the rim is slightly bent over; the long handle, but slightly curved, is very curious; the large perforation we see in it probably indicates the use of the vessel, for it seems to have been let down with a string into the well to draw up water; the hole must also have served to suspend it on a nail. I never found here a similar vessel, nor am I aware that this form has ever occurred elsewhere.

No. 9 is a very pretty lustrous black vase, with a convex foot and an excrescence on either side perpendicularly perforated for suspension. To the list of the few places given on pp. 222, 223 in *Ilios*, where vases with a similar con-

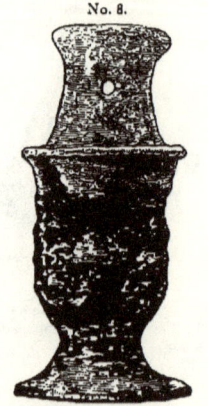

No. 8.—Lustrous black Cup, with horizontal flutings, hollow foot, and vertical perforated handle. (Size 1 : 4. Depth, about 14 m.)

No. 9.—Lustrous black Vessel with convex foot, and vertically perforated excrescences on the sides. (Size 1 : 4. Depth, 14 m.)

trivance may be seen, I must add the Prehistoric Museum of Madrid, which contains five fragments of hand-made vases found in caverns of the stone age in Andalusia, having on each side a tubular hole for suspension. Another vase-fragment with vertical perforations for suspension, likewise found in a cavern in Andalusia, is in the Museum at Cassel. The same system may be seen on several fragments of hand-made vases found by me in my excavations at

Orchomenos in Boeotia;* also on three hand-made vases found in the terramare of the Emilia, one of which is preserved in the Museum of Parma, the other two in the Museum of Reggio, of which Professor Gaetano Chierici is the learned keeper. Two more hand-made vases, with vertical tubular holes for suspension, may be seen in the prehistoric collection of the Museo Nazionale in the Collegio Romano at Rome; one of them was found in the terramare of Castello, near Bovolone (province of Verona), the other in the lake-dwellings of the Lago di Garda; another, which was found in an ancient tomb near Corneto (Tarquinii), is preserved in the museum of this latter city. A hand-made vase with a vertical hole for suspension on four sides was found in a terramare of the Stone age near Campeggine, in the province of Reggio in the Emilia.† I may also mention some hand-made funereal urns, having the very same contrivance, which were found in ancient tombs near Bovolone (province of Verona), held to be of the same age as the terramare of the Emilia.‡ A vase with a similar system for suspension, found in Umbria, is in the prehistoric collection of the Museum of Bologna; another, found in the cavern of Trou du Frontal-Furfooz, in Belgium, is in the Museum of Brussels. A box of terra-cotta, with a vertical hole for suspension in the cover and in the rim, was found in the district of Guben in Prussia.§ The prehistoric collection of the Museum of Geneva contains some fragments of vases found in France,|| which have the same kind of vertical holes for suspension. Finally, I may mention a vase with four excrescences,

---

* See my *Orchomenos*, Leipzig, 1881, p. 40, fig. 2, and p. 41, fig. 3.

† *Bulletino di Paletnologia Italiana*, 1877, pp. 8, 9, Plate I. No. 3.

‡ *Bullctino di Paletnologia Italiana*, 1880, pp. 182-192, and Table XII. Nos. 1, 2, 4, 5.

§ *Zeitschrift für Ethnologie*, Organ der Berliner Gesellschaft für Anthropologie, Ethnologie und Urgeschichte, 1882, pp. 392-396.

|| The place where this interesting discovery was made is not indicated.

each of which has two vertical perforations; it was found, last year, in a tomb of the stone age near Tangermünde in the Altmark, and is preserved in the *Nordische Abtheilung* of the Royal Museum at Berlin; my attention was called to it by Mr. Ed. Krause of the Royal Ethnological Museum.

I call the reader's particular attention to the great resemblance of these Trojan vases to the *kipes* (Latin, *cupa;* French, *hotte*) which workmen use in the fields, and which have the very same kind of vertical tubular holes for suspension as the vases. But I must also mention the discovery, lately made by Dr. Philios on account of the Hellenic Archæological Society, of a certain number of most ancient terra-cotta vases and idols, at the base of the temple of Demeter at Eleusis, among which is a small vessel having on each side an excrescence perpendicularly perforated for suspension; whereas nearly all the other vases have on each side merely a hole for suspension in the foot and rim. All these vases have a painting of circular red bands, and they are so primitive that I do not hesitate to claim for them an age antecedent even to that of the royal tombs of Mycenae. The idols found with them are even still more primitive than the rudest ever found at Troy.

Fragments of hand-made bowls of terra-cotta, with two long horizontal tubular holes for suspension, such as are represented by Nos. 37-42, pp. 217, 218 in *Ilios*, were again found in large masses in the ruins of the first settlement; so that I have been able to recompose twenty-five of them. The Museum of Bologna contains fragments of bowls with a similar contrivance, found in the Grotta del Diavolo,* near Bologna, the antiquities of which are considered to belong to the first epoch of the reindeer.† The same museum contains also a large number of fragments

---

* Avv. Ulderigo Botti, *La Grotta del Diavolo*, Bologna, 1871, Pl. V., figs. 1 and 4. † Idem, p. 36.

of bowls with the same system of horizontal tubular holes, from 0·03 m. to 0·07 m. long in the brim, found in the grottoes of Farneto, Pragatto, and Rastellino, in the province of Bologna, all of which are of the Stone Age. Fragments of bowls, with precisely the same system, found in the terramare of the Emilia, may also be seen in the Museum of Bologna, as well as in the Museo Nazionale in the Collegio Romano at Rome. I also found similar bowl fragments in my excavations at Orchomenos,* as well as in those I made with Mr. Frank Calvert at Hanaï Tepeh.†

On this occasion I may mention, concerning the curious goblet of the first city represented in *Ilios*, p. 224, No. 51, that the Prehistoric Museum at Madrid contains four cups of the same form, but without handles, which were found in caverns in Andalusia; inhabited in the Stone Period; further, that three goblets of the same form, one with one handle, the others with two, found in Rhodes, are in the Museum of the Louvre. A goblet of a similar form, recently found in the lowest layers of *débris* in the Acropolis of Athens, is in the Acropolis Museum.

Of terra-cotta whorls, both plain and with an incised ornamentation, a very large number, not less than 4000, were again found in the five prehistoric settlements in this year's excavations. My opinion, that all the many thousands of whorls which I gathered here in the course of years, have served as votive offerings, is strenuously supported by Mr. H. Rivett-Carnac,‡ who found a great many similar ones at Sankisa, in Behar, and other Buddhist ruins in the North-west Provinces of India. On many of these Indian whorls the incised ornamentation, in which he

---

* See *Orchomenos*, Leipzig, 1881, p. 41, fig. 4.
† See *Ilios*, p. 710, fig. 1543-1545.
‡ Memorandum on Clay Discs called *Spindle Whorls*, and Votive Seals, found at Sankisa, in the *Journal of the Asiatic Society of Bengal*, Vol. XLIX. part i. 1880.

recognises religious symbols, and generally a representation of the sun, is perfectly identical with that of the Trojan whorls.

Dr. W. Dörpfeld calls my attention to Richard Andree's *Ethnographische Parallelen und Vergleiche*,* pp. 230-232, fig. 8A and 8C; where it is stated that perforated whorls of terra-cotta or glass, which according to the engravings are of a form identical with that of the Trojan whorls, and with a similar ornamentation, are used as money on the Palau or Pelew Islands in the Pacific Ocean: "They are called there Audou, are regarded as a gift of the spirits, and are held to have been imported, no native being able to make them for want of the material. The quantity of them in circulation is never augmented. Some of those whorls are estimated at £750 sterling each."

The most ancient terra-cotta whorls found in Italy appear to be those of the Grotta del Diavolo, the antiquities of which, as I have stated above, are attributed to the first epoch of the reindeer:† they are unornamented, and are preserved in the Museum of Bologna. But they are of no rare occurrence in the Italian terramare, particularly in those of the Emilia, and, besides the places enumerated at pp. 229-231 of *Ilios*, I may mention the museums of Reggio and Corneto as containing a few ornamented with incisions: the museum of Parma also contains six ornamented ones, instead of only two, as stated in *Ilios* (p. 230).

Many terra-cotta whorls with an ornamentation similar to that of the Trojan whorls were gathered by the indefatigable Dr. Victor Gross in his excavations in the Swiss Lake habitations.‡

Unornamented terra-cotta whorls occur also on the Esquiline at Rome, and in the Necropolis of Albano. Pro-

---

* Stuttgart, 1878.
† Avv. Ulderigo Botti, *La Grotta del Diavolo*, Bologna, 1871, p. 36, and Pl. IV. figs. 7 and 8.
‡ Victor Gross, *Les Protohelvètes*, Paris, 1883, Pl. XXVI.

fessor W. Helbig* holds them to have been used partly as spindle-whorls and partly as beads for necklaces; but this latter use is out of the question for the large whorls. Dr. Victor Gross is of opinion that the terra-cotta whorls must have been used partly as buttons of garments, partly as pearls of necklaces, and last, not least, as whorls for the spindle. He says this latter hypothesis is corroborated by the discovery of several of these whorls in which the spindle-stick still remains fixed, and by the striking resemblance of the terra-cotta whorls to those which are still used by spinsters in some countries.†

Of stone axes, like those represented at p. 445, Nos. 668-670 in *Ilios*, eight were found this year in the ruins of the first settlement at Troy; five of them being of diorite, and three of jade.‡ Of these latter I represent one, No. 10, in the actual size. It is of transparent green jade.§ Professor H. Bücking has had the kindness

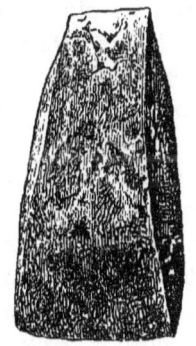

No. 10.—Axe of Green Jade.
(Actual size. Depth, 14 m.)

* Wolfgang Helbig, *Die Italiker in der Po-Ebene*, Leipzig, 1879, pp. 21, 22, 83.

† Dr. Victor Gross, *Les Protohelvètes*, Paris, 1883, pp. 100, 101. See Note XVI. on *Spindle Whorls and Spinning*, p. 293.

‡ I have discussed jade (nephrite) at length in *Ilios*, pp. 238-243, 445-451; but to those who wish to read more on this important subject, I recommend Professor Heinrich Fischer's excellent work *Nephrit und Jadeit nach ihren mineralogischen Eigenschaften, sowie nach ihrer urgeschichtlichen und ethnographischen Bedeutung*, Stuttgart, 1875; as well as his learned dissertation, "Vergleichende Betrachtungen über die Form der Steinbeile auf der ganzen Erde," in the journal *Kosmos*, V^{er}. Jahrgang, 1881.

§ A constantly severe critic of mine, E. Brentano, *Troia und Neu Ilion*, Heilbronn, 1882, p. 70, footnote, endeavours to throw ridicule on me for having always called similar instruments "Axes" in *Ilios*. But if he had had the most superficial knowledge of archæology, he would have known that this is the proper and only name for them; they are called "axes" in all archæological works in the world, and I have no right to change the name to please ignorant critics.

to send me the following interesting note on Jade: "Jade and Jadeite, the appearance of which is perfectly similar, may, according to the latest investigations by A. Arzruni * and by Berwerth, † be easily distinguished, because Jade belongs to the group of the Amphibols, Jadeite to the group of Pyroxen-minerals, and consequently they differ considerably in the size of the angles of cleavage in which the finer fibres may be recognised."

There were also found two of those curious instruments of diorite (like that represented in *Ilios*, p. 243, No. 90), which have the same shape as the axes, with the sole difference that at the lower end, where the edge ought to be, they are blunt, perfectly smooth, and from a quarter to half an inch thick. Two precisely similar implements, found in caverns of the stone period in Andalusia, are in the Prehistoric Museum at Madrid; another, discovered in the cavern called " Caverna delle Arene," near Genoa, is in the Prehistoric collection of the Museo Nazionale in the Collegio Romano at Rome.

There were also found four whetstones of indurated slate, with a perforation at the smaller end, like that represented in *Ilios*, p. 248, No. 101. Besides the places enumerated in *Ilios* (p. 248), at which similar whetstones were found, I may mention that one, discovered in a tomb at Camirus in the island of Rhodes, is in the Louvre, and three, found in Swiss lake dwellings, are in the Museum of Geneva; another whetstone, of an identical form, was found in the prehistoric cemetery of Koban in the Caucasus.‡

No. 11 represents a battle-axe of grey diorite; it is of rude manufacture, and but little polished. It has only one

---

* See *Verhandlungen der Berliner Anthropol. Gesellschaft*, Session of July 16th, 1881, pp. 281–283, and Session of December 16th, 1882, pp. 564–567.

† *Sitzungsberichte der k. k. Akademie der Wissenschaften*, Wien, 1880, I. 102-105.

‡ Rudolf Virchow, *Das Gräberfeld von Koban im Lande der Osseten*, Berlin, 1883, p. 21, Pl. IV. fig. 18.

sharp edge; the opposite end is blunt, and must have been used as a hammer; in the middle of each side may be seen a shallow groove, which proves that the operation of drilling a hole through it had been commenced, but was abandoned. A very similar stone battle-axe, in which the boring was commenced but abandoned, was found in the terramare of the Stone age near Mantua, and is preserved in the Museo Nazionale in the Collegio Romano at Rome. Another stone battle-axe of a similar shape, but in which the perforation is completed, was found in Denmark.*

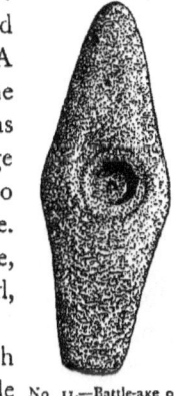

No. 11.—Battle-axe of Grey Diorite. (Size 1 : 4. Depth, about 14 m.)

As stone hammers and axes, in which the operation of drilling a hole on each side has been begun, are of very frequent occurrence, Dr. Dörpfeld suggests to me that it may not have been intended to perforate the instruments, as a wooden handle may easily have been fastened to them by some sort of crotchet.

There were also found in the *débris* of the first settlement numerous very rude stone-hammers, like that represented in *Ilios*, p. 237, No. 83. Some similar rude stone hammers, found in Chaldæa, are preserved in the museum of the Louvre; others, found in the terramare of the Emilia, are in the Museums of Reggio and Parma. I may also mention the rudely-cut, nearly globular, stone instruments, like Nos. 80 and 81, p. 236, in *Ilios*, which occur by hundreds in all the four lower prehistoric cities of Troy. Besides the localities mentioned on pp. 236, 237, 442, in *Ilios*, these rude implements, which are usually called corn-bruisers, are also very frequent in the Italian terramare, and many of them may be seen in the Museums

---

* J. J. A. Worsaae, *Nordiske Oldsager i det Kongelige Museum i Kjöbenhavn*, Copenhagen, 1859, Plate XIII., fig. 38.

of Reggio and Parma; others, found among the ancient ruins in Chaldæa, are in the small Chaldæan Collection in the Louvre.

I also collected a large number of saddle-querns of trachyte, like those represented in *Ilios*, p. 234, Nos. 74, 75, and p. 447, No. 678, which abound in all the four lower prehistoric cities of Troy. Besides the places mentioned at p. 234 in *Ilios*, they are also frequent in the terramare of the Emilia, and a large number of them may be seen in the Museums of Reggio and Parma; others, found in the "Caverna delle Arene Candide," near Genoa, are in the Museo Nazionale in the Collegio Romano at Rome. Six similar saddle-querns of ferruginous sandstone are in the Museum of Saint Germain-en-Laye; the Prehistoric Museum of Geneva contains four, which were found in the Swiss lake dwellings. Many similar saddle-querns of trachyte have recently been found in the lowest layers of *débris* in the Acropolis of Athens.

In *Ilios* (pp. 234, 235) I have already explained the fact that the grain was bruised between the flat sides of two of these querns, but that only a kind of groats, not flour, could have been produced in this way, and that the bruised grain could not have been used for making regular bread. I have further pointed out that in Homer we find it used as porridge,* and also for sprinkling on roasted meat.† I may add that, according to another passage in Homer, it was used as an ingredient of a peculiar mixed beverage, which Hecamede prepares in the tent of Nestor, of Pramnian wine, rasped goat's-cheese, and barley-meal (ἄλφιτα).‡ Although no regular bread, such as we have, can be made of bruised grain, yet something must have been prepared

---

* *Il.* XVIII., 558–560.   † *Od.* XIV., 76, 77.
‡ *Il.* XI., 638–640:

ἐν τῷ ῥά σφι κύκησε γυνὴ εἰκυῖα θεῇσιν,
οἴνῳ Πραμνείῳ, ἐπὶ δ' αἴγειον κνῆ τυρόν
κνήστι χαλκείῃ, ἐπὶ δ' ἄλφιτα λευκὰ πάλυνεν·

from it which passed by the name of bread (σῖτος), and which in the Homeric poems we always find on the table as an indispensable accessory of all meals. The poet nowhere tells us how it was made or what was its form, nor does he ever mention ovens, which are certainly not found also in the ruins of Troy. I would suggest that the Homeric bread was probably made in the same way as we see the Bedouins of the desert make theirs, who, after having kneaded the dough, turn it into the form of pancakes, which they throw on the embers of a fire kindled in the open air, where it gets baked in a few moments. A similar mode of baking bread seems also implied by the fact that leathern bags filled with such meal (ἄλφιτα) were taken for use on the road in a journey; thus, for example, we see that, when Telemachus prepares for his journey to Pylos, he orders Euryclea to put him up twenty measures of this meal in leathern bags.* Professor W. Helbig † calls attention to the fact that, as I have stated with regard to the Trojans, there is among the inhabitants of the terramare villages no trace of any arrangement for baking bread, and he holds that we must conclude from this that, like the Germans, they prepared a sort of porridge from pounded grains. Helbig adds: "In the public Roman rite, which here, as nearly everywhere else, kept up the ancient custom, not bread was offered, but always parched spelt-grains, the *far tostum*, flour spiced with salt, the *mola salsa*, or porridge, *puls*. Varro ‡ and Pliny § are therefore perfectly right in stating that for a long time the Romans

---

* *Od.* II., 354, 355:
  ἐν δέ μοι ἄλφιτα χεῦον ἐϋρραφέεσσι δοροῖσιν·
  εἴκοσι δ' ἔστω μέτρα μυληφάτου ἀλφίτου ἀκτῆς.

† Wolfgang Helbig, *Die Italiker in der Po-Ebene*, Leipzig, 1879, pp. 17, 41, 71.

‡ Varro, *R. R.* V. p. 105 : "de victu antiquissima puls."

§ Pliny *H. N.* XVIII. 83 : "pulte autem, non pane vixisse longo tempore Romanos manifestum, quoniam et pulmentaria hodieque dicuntur." See Juvenal, *Sat.* XIV. 171.

knew no other form of food from grain than *puls*. It was only at a time comparatively late that leaven, the addition of which is so essential to make flour into wholesome savoury bread, came into general use. It was still considered as an unusual innovation at the time when the Romans regulated the discipline of the Flamen Dialis; for the priest was forbidden to touch *farinam fermento imbutam*.* Tradition has even preserved a trace of the fact that there existed no proper apparatus for grinding at the time of the oldest Italic development; because the *mola versatilis*, the more perfected apparatus, whose upper part was turned by a handle above the lower one, was, according to Varro, † an invention of the Volsinians. This tradition, therefore, presupposed an older epoch, during which people put up with other more imperfect means, possibly with two stones such as were used by the ancient inhabitants of the terramare villages for pounding the grains. I may here remind the reader that the identical Greek and Latin words, $\mu\acute{\upsilon}\lambda\eta = mola$, $\pi\tau\acute{\iota}\sigma\sigma\omega = pinso$, $\pi\acute{o}\lambda\tau o\varsigma = puls$, prove that the Graeco-Italians used the cereals in the same manner as the inhabitants of the terramare villages—a fact which is not without significance for our investigation, as among all Italic settlements these villages stand in time and space nearest to the Graeco-Italic stage of civilization (*stadium*)."

Of well-polished perforated axes like No. 91, p. 244 in *Ilios*, only two halves were found in the first city; of single and double-edged saws of white or brown flint or chalcedony, like Nos. 93–98, p. 246 in *Ilios*, a very large number were again gathered in all the four lower prehistoric settlements of Troy. Besides the localities enumerated on pp. 245 and 246 of *Ilios*, I must mention seventeen similar saws, which were found in the recess of a rock at

---

* Gell. X., 15, 19. Festus, p. 87, 13, Müller.
† Ap. Plinium *H. N.* XXXVI. 135, see Serv. *ad Vergil. Aen.* 1, 179.

CHAP. II.] BRONZE OR COPPER INSTRUMENTS. 47

Beït-Sahour, near Bethlehem in Palestine, and which are preserved in the Museum of Saint Germain-en-Laye. Some similar flint saws were also found in the very ancient grotto already mentioned, called "Grotta del Diavolo," near Bologna.* Several saws of silex, as well as knives of silex and obsidian, found at Warka and Mugheir in Assyria, are in the British Museum.

Of polishers of serpentine, jasper, diorite, or porphyry, a large number were again found in all the four lower prehistoric settlements of Troy.

Of bronze or copper, there were found in the *débris* of the first settlement only a knife, like that represented under No. 118, p. 250 in *Ilios*, some punches similar to those under Nos. 109 and 110, p. 249 in *Ilios*, and from twelve to fifteen brooches, some of which have a globular

No. 12.—Brooch of Copper or Bronze, with a globular head. (Size 1 : 3. Depth, 14 m.)

No. 13.—Brooch of Copper or Bronze, with a spiral head. (Size 1 : 3. Depth, 14 m.)

head, others a head in the form of a spiral. I here give one of the former under No. 12, of the latter one under No. 13: both of them are bent at right angles. Both these forms of brooch served the ancient Trojan settlers instead of the fibula, which never occurs here in any one of the five prehistoric cities, nor in the Lydian city of Hissarlik, and which must have been invented at a much later period.† It deserves very particular attention, that

---

* Avv. Ulderigo Botti, *La Grotta del Diavolo*, Bologna, 1871, p. 36, and Plate III.

† A. Dumont and J. Chaplain (*Les Céramiques de la Grèce Propre*, Paris, 1881, p. 4) erroneously state that fibulae have been found in the first city of Troy; they must have mistaken for a fibula the small flat

brooches of bronze or copper with globular heads are also very frequent in the terramare of the Emilia, in which the fibula has never yet been found.* On the other hand, these brooches are never found in the funeral hut-urns discovered at Marino near Albano and in the environs of Corneto, in which the fibulae are very abundant. It appears, therefore, certain that these hut-urns, for which a very high antiquity is generally claimed, belong to a later time than the latest prehistoric city, and even to a later time than the Lydian settlement of Troy. In most of the Swiss lake dwellings both the brooches with globular heads and those with spiral heads are found together with fibulae, from which we must naturally conclude that these lake dwellings belong to a comparatively late time; for, as Professor Rudolf Virchow † justly remarks, the fibula has been "engendered" by the straight brooch. This scholar also found fibulae, together with brooches with spiral or globular heads, in his excavations in the prehistoric Necropolis of Upper Koban in the Caucasus,‡ which belongs to the 9th or 10th century, B.C.§ I must say the same of the ancient necropolis of Samthawro near Mtskheth, the ancient capital of Georgia, which has been excavated by the "Société des Amateurs d'Archéologie du Caucase," ‖ where fibulae also occur together with globular-headed or spiral-headed

---

crescent-like earring of very thin silver leaf, represented in *Ilios*, p. 250, No. 122. Like the nine earrings of an identical form, made of very thin gold leaf, which are represented by No. 917, p. 501, in *Ilios*, the small silver object can be nothing else than an earring.

    * Dr. Ingvald Undset assures me, however, that in carefully examining the *débris* in the terramare of the Emilia he discovered fibulae in them, of which he gathered in all thirteen.

    † Rudolf Virchow, *Das Gräberfeld von Koban im Lande der Osseten*, Berlin, 1883, p. 24.

    ‡ Idem, p. 32, Plate I. No. 20, Plate II. No. 7.

    § Idem, p. 124.

    ‖ *Objets d'Antiquité du Musée de la Société des Amateurs d'Archéologie au Caucase*, Tiflis, 1877, p. 19, Pl. VI. No. 9.

brooches. I may still further mention that a bronze brooch with a spiral head was found in the ancient cemetery on the Kattenborn road in the district of Guben.*

I think it not out of place to observe here that we do not find in Homer any special word to designate metals; but we find in the poems the verb μεταλλάω,† with which is connected the later substantive μέταλλον, which the ancients acknowledged to be derived from μετ' ἄλλα. Consequently μεταλλᾶν signified " *to search for other things*," and μέταλλον the *research*, the *spot where researches were made, and the object of research itself.*‡ From this was developed the more special signification of *mines*, shafts in which metals, minerals, &c., were searched for; and thence the expression μέταλλα was transferred to the minerals, and especially metals, obtained from the mines.§

Having discussed at great length in *Ilios* (pp. 253–260) the interesting question, whence the Trojans obtained their gold, I may here add that Mr. Calvert has called my attention to a passage in Strabo not noticed by me, according to which Demetrius of Scepsis received from Callisthenes and some other authors the legend, "that the wealth of Tantalus and the Pelopids was derived from the mines in Phrygia and the Sipylus; that of Cadmus, from those in Thrace and the mountain of Pangaeus; that of Priam, from the gold-mines of Astyra near Abydos, of which a little has remained until now, and of which the numerous heaps of earth thrown out, as well as the underground

---

* *Zeitschrift für Ethnologie, Organ der Berliner Gesellschaft für Anthrop. Ethn. und Urgeschichte,* 14ter Jahrgang, 1882, pp. 392–396.

† *Il.* I., 550, 553; III., 177; V., 516; X., 125; XIII., 780; *Od.* I., 231; III., 69, 243; VII., 243, 401; XIV., 128, 378; XV., 23, 361; XVI., 287, 465; XVII., 554; XIX., 115, 190; XXIII., 99; XXIV., 320, 477.

‡ Buttmann, *Lexil.* I., p. 140; Köpke, *Ueber das Kriegswesen der Griechen im heroischen Zeitalter*, p. 40.

§ E. Buchholz, *Die Homerischen Realien*, Leipzig, 1873, p. 299.

passages, prove the ancient mining industry: that the riches of Midas were derived from the mines of the mountain of Bermion; the wealth of Gyges, Alyattes, and Croesus, from those of Lydia and one near a small desert town between Atarneus and Pergamum, which has exhausted mines."* Mr. Calvert further calls my attention to the passage in Pliny:† "Gemmae nascuntur et repente novae, ac sine nominibus: sicut olim Lampsaci in metallis aurariis una inventa, quae propter pulchritudinem Alexandro regi missa fuit, ut auctor est Theophrastus."‡ Lampsacus is not more than 30 kilomètres to the north of Abydos, and 55 from Ilium. Mr. Calvert also cites to me the passage of the famous Dr. Chandler: "The principal countries whence the Greeks procured their gold were India, Arabia, Armenia, Colchis, and the Troade." It affords me pleasure to add that Mr. Calvert is now exploring the mines of Astyra, of which he has obtained from the Sublime Porte the concession for ninety-nine years.

There was found a large number of awls and needles of bone; also some small objects of ivory, like those represented in *Ilios*, p. 261, Nos. 123–140.

Besides the places enumerated on p. 262 in *Ilios*, bone-needles of a similar form were found in the Grotta del Diavolo, near Bologna,§ the antiquities of which, as mentioned above, are attributed to the first epoch of the reindeer. They also occur in the terramare of the Emilia.

Huckle-bones (*astragali*) occur in all the prehistoric

---

* Strabo, XIII. p. 680 : ὡς ὁ μὲν Ταντάλου πλοῦτος καὶ τῶν Πελοπιδῶν ἀπὸ τῶν περὶ Φρυγίαν καὶ Σίπυλον μετάλλων ἐγένετο· ὁ δὲ Κάδμου [ἐκ τῶν] περὶ Θρᾴκην καὶ τὸ Παγγαῖον ὄρος· ὁ δὲ Πριάμου ἐκ τῶν ἐν Ἀστύροις περὶ Ἄβυδον χρυσείων, ὧν καὶ νῦν ἔτι μικρὰ λείπεται· πολλὴ δ' ἡ ἐκβολὴ καὶ τὰ ὀρύγματα σημεῖα τῆς πάλαι μεταλλείας· ὁ δὲ Μίδου ἐκ τῶν περὶ τὸ Βέρμιον ὄρος· ὁ δὲ Γύγου καὶ Ἀλυάττου καὶ Κροίσου ἀπὸ τῶν ἐν Λυδίᾳ ... τῆς μεταξὺ Ἀταρνέως τε καὶ Περγάμου πολίχνη ἐρήμη ἐκμεμεταλλευμένα ἔχουσα τὰ χωρία.   † *H. N.* XXXVII., 74.   ‡ *De Lapidibus.*

§ Avv. Ulderigo Botti, *La Grotta del Diavolo*, Bologna, 1871, p. 36, and Pl. IV. fig. 15.

cities of Troy, and Professor R. Virchow found a number of them, but all perforated, in his excavations in the prehistoric necropolis of Upper Koban in the Caucasus.*

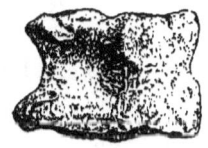

The huckle-bone given in *Ilios*, p. 262, No. 143, having been badly photographed, I represent here, under No. 14, another which was found in the *débris* of the first city.

No. 14.—Huckle-bone *(Astragalus).* Half-size. Depth about 14 m.

It is impossible to ascertain from the ruins of this first settlement, whether it was peacefully abandoned by its inhabitants, or whether it was destroyed by the hand of an enemy, for there are no signs of either a partial or a general catastrophe.

* Rudolf Virchow, *Das Gräberfeld von Koban im Lande der Osseten*, Berlin, 1883, p. 21, Pl. XI. fig. 16.

CHAPTER III.

THE SECOND CITY; TROY PROPER; THE 'ILIOS' OF THE HOMERIC LEGEND.

My architects have proved to me that, together with M. Burnouf, my collaborator in 1879, I had not rightly distinguished and separated the ruins of the two following settlements, namely, the Second and Third; that we had rightly considered as foundations belonging to the second city the walls of large blocks, 2·50 m. deep (marked *q*, R, on Plan III. in *Ilios*); but that we had been mistaken in not connecting with it the layer of calcined ruins which lies immediately upon these walls, and belongs to the second city, and in attributing this burnt stratum to the third settlement, with which it has nothing to do. We had been led into this error by the colossal masses of *débris* of baked, or, more rightly, of burnt bricks of the second city, which in a very great many places had not been removed by the third settlers, and were lying on a level with their house-foundations, and often even much higher. These *débris* of burnt bricks are partly derived from houses destroyed in a terrible fire, partly they are the remains of brick walls, which, after having been completely built up of crude bricks, have for solidity's sake been artificially baked by large masses of wood piled up on both sides of them and set on fire simultaneously. The Burnt City proper is, therefore, not the Third, but the Second city, all of whose buildings have been completely destroyed; but, the third city having been built immediately upon it, the layer of *débris* of the second city is often but insignificant, and in some places even only 0·20 m. deep. The house-foundations of the third settlers having been sunk into the calcined *débris* of the second city, we erroneously attributed these latter to the third settlement, with which they have nothing to do.

The slanting strata of *débris* of the first city, 2·50 m. deep (see N—N on Plan III. in *Ilios*), are succeeded in the Acropolis by a layer of earth 0·50 m. deep, which contains no traces of walls, and extends uninterruptedly above it; proving that the site had been left deserted, and had not been built upon for a long time. Above this earth we see a layer of *débris* of baked bricks, 0·25 m. deep, which may be followed in the great northern trench (Plan III. in *Ilios*) almost for its entire length, and which had its origin from the very foundation of the second city. This settlement developed itself gradually to what it was at the time of its great catastrophe, for in several of its buildings we recognize great changes, which I shall describe in detail in the following pages. The first and most remarkable change introduced by the second settlers, a change which testifies to their wonderful building activity, was that they completely levelled the site, which before slanted to the north. To this end they heightened the ground on the south side by 0·50 m., on the north side by 3 mètres; at the same time they extended the site of the Acropolis considerably in a southerly direction. The large edifices could not be erected immediately on this "planum;" they were therefore provided with foundations sunk 2·50 m. deep, of larger and smaller stones (see *q*, R, on Plan III. in *Ilios*), which were laid on the older and more solid soil. These foundations, in which we formerly thought we recognized the fillings-up of funnel-like holes made by the rain-water, are particularly conspicuous on the north-east side in the great northern trench (see *q*, R, on Plan III. in *Ilios*). Just below these foundations we found a house-floor of large white pebbles, which extended to the very wall on the north side, and of which a large part may still be seen in the north-east corner of my great northern trench (see V on Plan III. in *Ilios*). This singular house-floor must naturally have belonged to one of the first buildings of the second inhabitants here.

These people surrounded their settlement on the hill of Hissarlik with a large fortress-wall, which is preserved on the south and south-west sides, and served as the substruction of a large brick wall. It consists of quarry-stones, on an average 0·45 m. long by 0·25 m. broad, which are somewhat irregularly joined in easily recognisable horizontal courses, without any binding material. It is represented with dark colour on Plan VII. in this work. Very remarkable is the excellently preserved southern part of this great fortress-wall, which is marked *c* on Plan VII. in this volume, as well as on Plan I., and on the engraving, No. 144, p. 264, in *Ilios*, and which we have now brought to light for a considerable distance further in a north-easterly direction; because, as is proved by the later erected wall *b*, it evidently belongs to the first period in the history of the second city, and has a tower (marked O on Plan VII.), which corresponds with the tower *o w* at the north-west corner of the great southern gate N F, as well as with the two towers, *p* and *p w*, to the north-west of the gate F M and R C (see Plan VII.). It is impossible to say how the upper part of this wall may have been constructed, for we have not found the slightest vestige of it. The upper part was probably demolished by the second settlers themselves, who filled up the inward projecting angle of their Acropolis by erecting the new great wall *b* (see Plan VII. in this volume, and Plan I. and engraving No. 144 in *Ilios*). The demolition of the upper part of the wall *c* cannot have taken place in the great catastrophe, for the great hollow between the walls *c* and *b* does not contain any *débris* of bricks, but only the black earth and gravel with which it had been filled up. The front of the wall *c* slants at an angle of 45°; the other side is vertical.

No. 15.—View of the great Substruction Wall of the Acropolis of the second city on the west side, close to the south-west gate.

a, is the paved road, which leads from the south-west gate down to the plain, and which is marked T U on Plan VII., and on the sketch No. 17, p. 68.
b, is the continuation of the great Acropolis-wall of the second city on the west side of the south-west gate.
c, the foundation of the paved road and the quadrangular pier to strengthen it, marked V on Plan VII., and on the sketch No. 17, p. 68.
d, masonry added by the third settlers.

In spite of the most eager researches, we have not been able to find out the course of the wall *c* on the north-east side. But, from the direction of the layers of *débris* in the trench S S, my architects ascertained with certainty, that the older Acropolis-wall of the second city lay more to the west than the prolongation of the later wall *b*, and consequently the new citadel wall was intended for extending the Acropolis on the east side. We have further brought to light in a southerly and easterly direction the wall *b*, which, as above mentioned, belongs to the second period of the second city. All the walls of the first period of the second city are marked on Plan VII. by a black tint, those of the second period have a red colouring. I give under No. 15 (p. 55), a view of the continuation of the wall (see Plan VII., O Z), on the west side of the south-west gate. Here it is built at an ascending angle of 60°; it has a slanting height of 9 mètres, and a perpendicular height of 7·50 m. On the north side, this substruction of the great Acropolis-wall consisted of much larger blocks, some of which were as much as 1 mètre in ength and breadth. But I had to destroy it on this side in 1872, in excavating my great northern trench. The course of the whole Acropolis-wall formed a regular rectilinear polygon, the projecting corners of which were fortified with towers. These towers stood, approximately, at equal distances of a little more than 50 mètres; in which measure we must certainly recognize the number of 100 ancient Trojan cubits, though the precise length of the Trojan cubit is unknown to us. From the analogy of the oriental and the Egyptian cubit it may, however, be fixed at a little more than 0·50 m. I call particular attention to the fact, that on this computation the gate R C and F M is exactly 10 cubits broad; the vestibulum of the edifice A, precisely 20 cubits both in length and breadth. The form of the projecting towers cannot now be exactly determined, there being only left on the east, south, south-west, and west sides, some remains of the tower-like spurs (G M, *o w*, O, *p*, and *p w* on Plan VII.), on which the towers proper stood, but probably most of them were quadrangular.

I may mention here that the wall of the Homeric Troy was likewise provided with numerous towers.* With the exception of the wall *c*, we found all these substruction walls still crowned with brick walls, more or less preserved, and we may assume with certainty that all of these belonged to the second city, and that they had merely been repaired by the third settlers. This appears the more certain, as on the east side the brick wall of the second city is for the most part in an admirable state of preservation, and still about 2·50 m. high. The third settlers, consequently, needed only to repair the upper part of the destroyed Acropolis-wall in some places, in order to be able to use the wall again. For this reason we may consider it also certain, that the great treasure found by me at the place Δ,† at the end of May 1873, was contained in the brick-*débris* of the second city; the more so as, by excavating the substruction wall to its foundations, we have brought to light, precisely in this place, a tower of the second city (*p* on Plan VII.). It is even possible that the brick-*débris*, in which the great treasure was found, was the real brick wall. I call particular attention to the fact, that for a layman it is next to impossible to distinguish what is Trojan brick-*débris* and what Trojan brick-masonry, and thus it may be that what I called "red and calcined ruins" was really a brick wall. Nay, it is even in the highest degree probable that the whole space between the western city wall (O Z on Plan VII.) and the large house of the third settlement, marked H S, (which, on account of the wealth found near

---

* *Il.* VIII. 517–519:
κήρυκες δ' ἀνὰ ἄστυ Διῒ φίλοι ἀγγελλόντων
παῖδας πρωθήβας πολιοκροτάφους τε γέροντας
λέξασθαι περὶ ἄστυ θεοδμήτων ἐπὶ πύργων·

† See Plan I. in *Ilios*.

it, I used to ascribe to the town-chief or king), had remained filled with brick-*débris* of the second city wall, which had not been removed by the third settlers, and that the many treasures discovered by me there in 1878 and 1879 were contained in this stratum. That the deep mass of brick-*débris* here belonged to the second city, seems to be proved with certainty by two facts: first, by the non-existence of a door on this side of the edifice H S, and secondly, by the absence of a wall-coating on this side of the house-wall which faces the fortress-wall O Z; for such a coating exists on both sides of all the other walls of the house, nor is it missing on the internal side of its western wall. But a still more weighty proof that all the treasures belong, not to the third, but to the second, the burnt city, is found in the condition of the more than 10,000 objects of which they are composed, for every one of them, even to the smallest gold drop, bears the most evident marks of the fearful incandescence to which it has been exposed. But these marks of heat are still more striking on the bronze weapons than on the gold ornaments. Thus, for example, of the weapons found in the largest gold-treasure, one bronze dagger (see p. 482, No. 813 in *Ilios*) has been completely curled up in the conflagration; a mass of lance-heads, daggers, and battle-axes (p. 482, No. 815 in *Ilios*) have been fused together by the intense heat; there are, further, lance-heads fused to battle-axes (p. 476, Nos. 805, 807, in *Ilios*); and a lance and battle-axe firmly fused to a copper caldron (p. 474, No. 800 in *Ilios*).

The preserved brick wall (N N) on the east side of the Acropolis is from 3·50 m. to 4 mètres thick, and is still 2·50 m. high; but my architects infer from its thickness that it must have been originally at least 4 mètres high, and they think there cannot be a doubt that the upper wall of the citadel had an equal thickness and height throughout.

The construction of this brick wall may best be recognized on the east side, where an excellent view of it may be obtained in the great north-eastern trench (S S). It consists of a substruction, more or less deep, of unwrought calcareous stones, on which was erected the wall proper of bricks. The manner in which the latter was made is especially remarkable. Visitors may best realize the following description by comparing it with the above-mentioned tower G M. The sketch No. 16, on p. 60, gives a section of this tower, which is about 3·50 m. broad, and projects about 2 mètres from the wall.

The foundations of the wall and the tower are only from 1 m. to 1·50 m. deep, and consist of calcareous stones, which are on an average 0·25 m. long and broad, and are bonded with clay. On this substruction was erected the wall proper of sun-dried clay bricks, with which material straw was mixed abundantly. The bricks are on an average 0·09 m. high by 0·23 m. broad; their length could not well be ascertained, as it is exceedingly difficult to recognize the joints, but it is probably 0·45 m. A very fine light-coloured clay, mixed with straw or hay, has been used as cement, and has been put on from 0,010 mm. to 0,015 mm.* deep in the horizontal joints as well as in the vertical ones. We find in the bricks numerous small fragments of pottery and masses of small shells, which prove that the clay has not been cleaned, but that it was used for brickmaking just as it was found.

In order to render this wall of sun-dried bricks more solid, it was artificially baked, when *in situ*, by a great fire kindled on its west side. The same could not be done on its east side, on account of the abrupt slope. On account of its considerable thickness, the wall could not have been baked through by the fire, for the heat could not have

---

* I explain this notation one for all. The decimal numbers to which *m*. is affixed are *mètres* with their decimal parts. Those to which *mm*. is affixed are *millimètres*: thus 0,010 mm. and 0,015 mm. mean 10 and 15 millimètres respectively.

penetrated into the interior. In order to effect this, channels 0·30 m. high and broad were made in the interior of the wall at various heights, the arrangement of which may be seen in the engraving No. 16. But the wall could of course not be baked equally throughout in this way, for, whilst the bricks around the channels are thoroughly baked, those on the east side are perfectly crude and unbaked. Even the different stages of baking may be distinctly observed on a number of the bricks; for, whilst that part of them which faced towards the channel is completely baked, the part which faced the other way has but slight traces, or none, of the incandescence. It is highly instructive to follow up the effect of the fire round the channels. Dr. Dörpfeld observed round the channel, first,

No. 16.—Section of the tower G M on the east side of the Acropolis; showing the arrangement of the channels for the artificial baking of the brick wall.

a circle which had been completely raised to a glowing heat throughout, and has now a light colour: this is followed by a black ring, which has received its colour from the black vapour of the fire. Still farther from the channel the bricks are completely baked, and have a dark red colouring; the joints, which consist of another material, being light red. The farther the bricks are distant from the channel, the less red is their colour, and the less thorough their baking. In the less baked or badly baked portion of the wall, the shells contained in the bricks have preserved their white colour, whereas in the thoroughly baked portion they have been blackened by the fire. The wall is covered on both sides with a clay-coating, 0,001 mm. thick. It is highly probable that the brick wall of the second city was built throughout in a similar manner; but this is certainly the first example ever found of a citadel-wall having been erected of crude bricks and having been baked *in situ*.

The reason why the great brick-wall on the east side has a substruction of stones, only 1 m. or 1·50 m. high, is because no high substruction-wall was needed here, on account of the abrupt slope which served in its stead; besides, the foot of the brick-wall here was exactly on a level with the upper part of the stone substruction-walls on the other sides of the Acropolis.

When the whole wall of the Acropolis was still entire, and when the gigantic substruction-wall was still surmounted by the brick-wall crowned with numerous towers, it must have had a very imposing aspect, particularly on the high north side which faces the Hellespont; and this may have induced the Trojans to ascribe its construction to Poseidon,* or to Poseidon and Apollo.†

But the legend that the walls of Troy were built by Poseidon may have a much deeper meaning, for, as Mr. Gladstone has ingeniously proved,‡ a connection with Poseidon frequently denotes Phoenician associations; and further, as Karl Victor Müllenhoff has proved in his *Deutsche Altertumskunde*,§ Herakles is the representative of the Phoenicians, and the tradition of his expedition to Ilium‖ may point to an early conquest and destruction of the city by the Phoenicians, just as the building of Troy's

---

* *Il.* XXI. 435-446. † *Il.* VII. 452, 453.
‡ See his Preface to my *Mycenæ*, pp. viii. and xxiv., and his *Homeric Synchronism*, pp. 42, 43, 177.
§ W. Christ, *Die Topographie der Troianischen Ebene*, p. 225.
‖ *Il.* V. 640-642:

ὅς ('Ηρακλῆς) ποτε δεῦρ' ἐλθὼν ἕνεχ' ἵππων Λαομέδοντος
ἒξ οἴης σὺν νηυσὶ καὶ ἀνδράσι παυροτέροισιν
'Ιλίου ἐξαλάπαξε πόλιν, χήρωσε δ' ἀγυιάς.

walls by Poseidon may denote that they were built by the Phoenicians.

But this second settlement on the hill of Hissarlik constituted only the Acropolis, to which a Lower City was attached on the east, south, and south-west sides. The existence of this lower city is proved, in the first place, by the wall which runs off in an easterly direction (see B, in the engraving No. 2, p. 24 in *Ilios*), and which is not slanting, like the fortress-wall of the Acropolis, but is built vertically, and is composed of large unwrought blocks joined with small ones. This fortress-wall runs from the Acropolis in an easterly direction, and consequently cannot belong to the citadel itself. A second proof of the existence of this lower city is the large mass of prehistoric pottery, which, as before mentioned, occurs in the lowest layers of *débris* on the plateau beneath the hill; for in form, fabric, and material, this pottery is identical with that of the first and second settlements on Hissarlik. As a third reason for the existence of a lower city, I may mention that the Acropolis of the second city had three gates (R C and F M, N F, and O X, on Plan VII.). I lay stress on the fact, that two of these gates must at all events have been in use simultaneously, for if there had been no lower city, considering the proportionately small extent of the citadel, it could have been much more easily defended if there had been only one gate. But a far more important reason still for the existence of a lower city is found in the number and the ground-plan of the edifices situated on the Acropolis, of which there can have been only six, and which are laid out on a grand scale.

As, however, not one of the succeeding cities, until the foundation of the Aeolic Ilium, had a lower city, and as all of them were limited to the former Pergamos, with the exception of the fifth settlement which extended somewhat beyond it (see Chapter IV., § 3), the site of the lower city of the second settlement was left deserted for ages. Its ruins remained solitary; the brick-walls crumbled away; the stones of their substructions and the house-foundations were employed for the new constructions on the Acropolis; and I now see no reason which clashes with the tradition preserved by Strabo,* according to which Archaeanax, the Mitylenaean, built the walls of Sigeum with the stones of Troy; for by this could of course only be meant the stones of the lower city of the second settlement, and probably those of the city walls. It is, therefore, but natural that, in spite of the numerous and extensive excavations I made on the site of the lower city of Ilium—except the city-wall represented under No. 2 B in *Ilios*—I found no fragments of the wall belonging to the lower city of the second settlement; but I found in several places the platform of rock on which it must have stood, and which had been purposely levelled for it.

We cannot determine now with certainty how far the lower city extended. In indicating its walls, which we have marked in Plan VIII. with dotted lines, we were guided by their two junctions with the Acropolis-wall. On the north-east side it is the above-mentioned wall of large calcareous blocks in the trench W †; on the west side it is at the point where also in the Macedonian and Roman time the wall of the lower city joined the Acropolis-wall. For the rest we were guided by the formation of the ground, and by the pottery belonging to the second city.

I have given in *Ilios* (p. 625, No. 1480) an engraving of a mysterious cavern situated just outside the lower city, about 300 yards to the west of the hill of Hissarlik, at a place where the site of Ilium slopes from the city wall gently down to the plain (see Plan VIII.); it is beneath a protruding rock crowned with three fig-trees, which have grown up from the same root. Having excavated it in 1879, I found a vaulted passage, 3 m. broad by 1·68 m.

---

* XIII. p. 599. † See Plan I. in *Ilios*.

high, cut out in the limestone-rock. At about 10 mètres from the entrance is a vertical hole, 1 m. in diameter, artificially cut in the superincumbent rock; it served, no doubt, to admit both air and light. At a distance of 18 mètres from the entrance, the large passage divides into two very narrow passages and a broad one, the former being only wide enough for one man to enter; the third passage, which turns to the north, is nearly as broad as the principal passage; of the two others, one turns to the east, the other to the south-east.

My architects having in 1882 thoroughly excavated the space before the cavern, as well as the cavern itself and the three narrow passages, we found that the passages which turn to the east and south-east are about as long as the large passage, namely, 18 m., but that the passage which turns to the north is somewhat shorter; and that at the end of each of them there is a spring, from which the water flowed out into the large gallery, and ran off by an earthen pipe of the Roman time; but this pipe being broken in many places, my collaborators and I in 1879 had not even observed it, and we thought the water flowed off, by an open channel in the floor, into an earthen pipe which we found outside. But now, on clearing the large passage most carefully of all the earth and dirt still contained in it, we discovered beneath the earthen pipe on the natural soil a water-conduit of a very primitive sort, composed of unwrought calcareous stones laid without any binding material, and covered with similar plates, which extends all along the large passage and its northern arm. It has the very closest resemblance to the Cyclopean water-conduits found by me at Tiryns and Mycenae (see my *Mycenae*, pp. 9, 80, 141). The channel was filled up with clay and dirt, and this may probably have been the case from a remote antiquity.

This conduit, which certainly belongs to a remote antiquity, appears not to have been noticed at all by the people of the Aeolic Ilium, for they laid the earthen pipe high above it, on the earth in which the Cyclopean water-conduit lay hidden, and in this way the water of the three springs must for ages have flowed out into the large wash-basins built of bricks and lime, and therefore of the Roman time, which we brought to light just in front of the entrance, and which prove that the inhabitants of Ilium continued to fetch water and to wash their clothes here. As soon as the springs and the conduit had been cleared, they gave again good potable water.

Supposing now these springs did not exist, and we were asked to indicate the place best suited for the situation of the two Trojan springs flowing into the Scamander, with the stone wash-basins, in which the women of Troy used to wash their clothes, and where the single combat between Hector and Achilles took place,* we should certainly indicate this precise spot, because it answers in all its details to the Homeric description. In fact, the cavern with the three springs is in the great plain, on the west side of the lower city of Troy, immediately outside the city-wall, and a little to the south of the depression of the ground between the Acropolis and the lower city, in which the road now leads up to Chiblak, and in which the road to the city and the Acropolis, and consequently also the Scaean Gate, must always have been situated. It is further, as above mentioned, very close to the Acropolis (about 300 yards), so that a person on the wall could see what was going on at the springs, and even call to a man standing by them. Besides, these springs fulfil the indispensable condition of being close to the road (ἁμαξιτός) † which led from the Scaean Gate, for the ancient road must necessarily have been about in the same situation as the present road, the position of which is deter-

---

* *Il.* XXII. 147-364.   † *Il.* XXII. 146.

mined on the east side by the slope, on the west side by the swamp and the ancient bed of the Scamander. But we find a still more weighty reason for the identity of these springs with the Homeric sources, in the fact that they flowed directly and at a distance of a few hundred yards into the Scamander, and the springs might, for this reason, be called by the poet the sources of this river,* whilst the three springs which still exist on the north side of Ilium flow into the Simois, and may perhaps for that reason have been called by the Trojans " Springs of the Simois," to distinguish them from the springs of the Scamander. Being for all these reasons perfectly convinced that Homer could not possibly have had in mind any other springs than these, we endeavoured to find here the lukewarm spring he refers to,† and with this object we carefully excavated the soil around, but all our researches were in vain. The water of the three springs had a uniform temperature of $15°·6$ C. ($60°·8$ F.) But the absence of the warm spring must not astonish us, for it no longer existed in the time of Demetrius of Scepsis‡ (210–180 B.C.), and it may have been already destroyed by an earthquake at a remote antiquity, or changed by the same cause into a cold-water spring.

To the many proofs I have given in *Ilios*, pp. 83–96, of the identity of the ancient bed of the Scamander with the immense bed of the small rivulet Kalifatli Asmak, which flows at the foot of the hill of Hissarlik, and immediately on the west side of the lower city of Ilium, I may

---

* *Il.* XXII. 147, 148.

κρουνὼ δ' ἵκανον καλλιρρόω, ἔνθα δὲ πηγαί
δοιαὶ ἀναΐσσουσι Σκαμάνδρου δινήεντος.

† *Il.* XXII. 149, 150:

ἡ μὲν γάρ θ' ὕδατι λιαρῷ ῥέει, ἀμφὶ δὲ καπνός
γίγνεται ἐξ αὐτῆς, ὡσεὶ πυρὸς αἰθομένοιο·

‡ Strabo, XIII. p. 602.

add the passage of Aeschylus,* where Cassandra, the daughter of Priam, pathetically invokes the banks of the Scamander, on which she had been accustomed to play in her childhood. This passage seems to prove that, in the opinion of Aeschylus, the Scamander flowed at the foot of Troy, and consequently that it was held to be identical with the immense bed of the small rivulet (Kalifatli Asmak), which really flows at the foot of Hissarlik.

The south-western gate of the Acropolis of the second city (R C on Plan VII.), the ground plan of which is represented in the engraving No. 17 (p. 68), served for the inhabitants of the western part of the Acropolis, and more particularly perhaps for the inmates of the large edifice immediately to the north-west of it. The road to this gate ascended from the lower city at an angle of 20° by a ramp (T U on Plan VII. and the ground plan No. 17), about 8 m. broad, built of large rudely wrought blocks, and paved with large slabs of calcareous stone. The gate was strengthened by two quadrangular piers (see ground plan No. 17, and Plan VII. Y, Y), on both sides of the road. The interior width of the gate itself was 5·15 m. The lateral walls of the gate (marked $v\ b$ on No. 17 and Plan VII.) consisted of baked bricks, and rested on substructions of calcareous stones, which are still preserved. The architecture of this gate proves with certainty that it had at first only one portal (indicated by R C on No. 17 and by a dark colouring on Plan VII.), formed by two projecting quadrangular pillars (xx on Plan VII. and ground plan No. 17) to which the folding gates were fixed, and the foundations of which still exist, being formed of unwrought stones cemented with clay. One of these piers stands out to a

---

Agamemnon, 1156-1159 (ed. Tauchnitz):

ἰὼ γάμοι, γάμοι Πάριδος ὀλέθριοι
φίλων· ἰὼ Σκαμάνδρου πάτριον ποτίν·
τότε μὲν ἀμφὶ σὰς ἀϊόνας τάλαιν'
ἠνυτόμαν τροφαῖς·

distance of 0·83 m., the other to a distance of 0·92 m.; both are 1·08 m. high, and 1·25 m. thick. The pillars which rested on these foundations, like the lateral walls from which they projected, consisted of bricks, and served with them no doubt to support the roof, which seems to have been crowned with an upper building of brick.

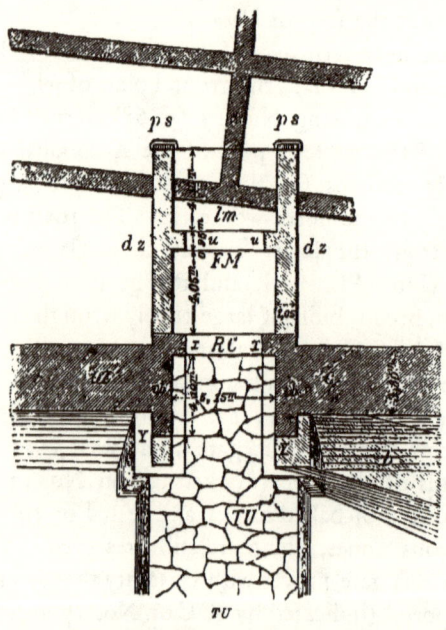

No. 17.—Ground Plan of the South-western Gate. (Scale, 1 : 333.)

Just in front of this ancient gateway, and separated from it by an open space, perhaps a street, about 6 m. wide, there stood in the interior of the Acropolis a large edifice, which was demolished by the second settlers when they added to this gate a second portal (marked F M on No. 17, and with red colouring on Plan VII.) with far-extending lateral walls (*d z* on Plan VII. and on No. 17), whose end-faces (*p s, p s* on Plan VII. and No. 17) were strengthened with wooden *parastades;* the well-wrought base-stones of the latter being still *in situ*. Instead of the demolished edifice, of which the long foundation wall (*l m* on Plan VII. and engraving No. 17) still exists, they erected to the right and left of the gate new edifices, of which the still extant foundations are marked on Plan VII. by *r b* and *r x* and with red colour.

The second portal consisted likewise of two projecting quadrangular brick-pillars (*u* on No. 17 and Plan VII.), to which the gates were attached, and of which the foundations, of unwrought stones cemented with clay, still exist; they are 0·60 m. high, more than 0·90 m. broad, and project about 0·75 m. The tower-like upper building was, no doubt, also continued over the second portal. Visitors will recognize at a glance that this gate has been constructed at two different periods, the walls of the older part being built of larger stones, those of the second epoch of much smaller ones. The later addition to the southern part of the gate is visible on the engraving No. 144, p. 264 in *Ilios*, to the right of the Greek with the spade; being separated from the more ancient part by a vertical joint, which extends from the top of the wall to the bottom. All the masonry of the first period of the second city is marked on Plan VII. with a black colouring, that of the second period with red. Some remains of the bricks of the lateral walls may still be seen on the foundations. I call the particular attention of visitors to the ancient road-surface of this gateway, of beaten clay, remains of which are still visible between the stones of the foundations of the lateral walls. This surface is higher than the square foundations of the gate-pillars, which were consequently not visible at the time when the gate was in use. The above-mentioned ramp (T U on Plan VII. and No. 17), paved with large slabs and plates, rose gradually to this clay roadway.

Much grander is the southern gate (N F on Plan VII.), which we brought to light at a vertical depth of 14 m.

below the surface of the hill. Whilst the south-western gate is on the level of the Acropolis, and its ramp-like road (T U) paved with large slabs ascends from the lower city, the southern gate has been erected at the foot of the Acropolis hill, and the road, which leads through it, and the surface of which consists of beaten clay, commences only in the interior of the Pergamos to ascend gently to the level, which is 4 m. higher. The surface can be easily recognized by the charcoal with which it is invariably covered. As may be seen from the accompanying sketch, No. 18, the ground plan of this gate forms a rectangle 40 m. long by 18 m. broad, which projects for about 18 m. from the Acropolis wall. From the massive walls ($x g$ on Plan VII. and engraving No. 18), which consist of calcareous quarry-stones, and are on each side about 7·50 m. thick by 4 m. high, as well as from the broken bricks and burnt wooden beams with which the whole gate-road was filled, we may conclude with certainty that these walls were mere substructions, and were surmounted by an enormous upper building of bricks and wood, of whose shape and construction, of course, we have no knowledge. But the substructions, with the far-extending gateway, are almost perfectly preserved. The bricks, with which the gateway was filled, had the same height as the bricks of the edifice B, namely, 0,085 mm.; their breadth is 0,305 mm. Without supposing the existence of such an upper edifice we could not explain the heat which has prevailed here, and which has been so intense that many stones have been burnt to lime, while the pottery has either crumbled away or melted into shapeless masses.

Having passed the gate proper ($f y$ on Plan VII. and the engraving No. 18), which had probably a double portal, one enters into the long gallery N F, which is 3·50 m. broad, and leads up to the higher plateau crowned by the principal edifices of the Acropolis. The southern portions of its lateral walls ($x g$ on No. 18 and Plan VII.) are built of small calcareous stones of somewhat polygonal form, united with a coarse brick cement of clay and straw, which has been completely baked and is perfectly similar to the cement used in the edifice A. The northern part of the lateral walls (*i* on No. 18 and Plan VII.) consists of smaller stones, more rectangular in form, united with a light-

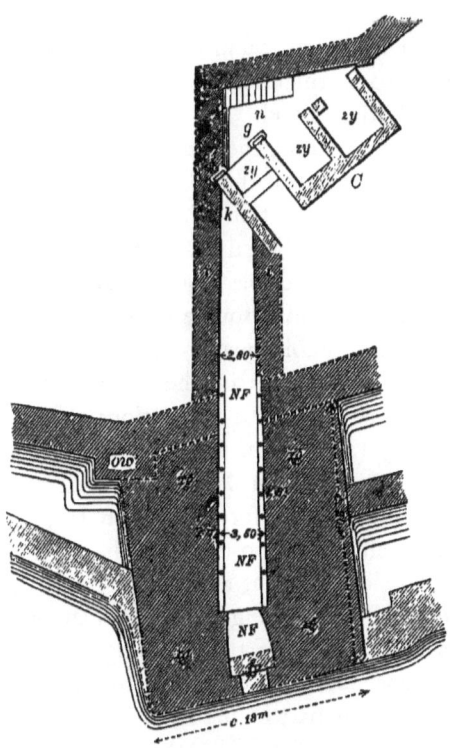

No. 18.—Ground Plan of the Southern Gate. NF on Plan VII. Scale 1 : 500.

coloured clay cement, which is perfectly similar to the clay cement in the edifice B. (Of both these edifices, A and B, I shall speak in the following pages.) The exterior sides of the lateral walls are covered with a clay coating which is still partly preserved. Being built in this way, the walls could not have supported an upper edifice, the less so as their interior sides are vertical, if they had not been strengthened with wooden posts ($z\,m$ on No. 18), which were placed vertically against the walls, at intervals of from 2 m. to 2·50 m. and of which considerable remains are still visible, of course in a carbonized state. We recognize them also by the impressions they have left on the walls. In order to make them firmer, they were set 0·50 m. deep into the ground of the gateway: they must have been 0·20 m. thick, this being the diameter of the holes in which they stood. At several places where these wooden posts have stood, the heat produced by their combustion has been so great that the stones have been burnt to lime, which, by the action of rain, has been fused with the wall-coating into so hard and compact a mass, that we had the very greatest trouble to cut it away with pickaxes. These wooden posts had a double purpose; first, to prop up and sustain the unstable quarry-stone walls, and secondly, to support the crossbeams of the ceiling and the upper edifice. But in spite of these precautions, the northern part of this gateway ($i\,i$ on No. 18 and Plan VII.) appears to have at some time broken down, or at least to have been very near breaking down, for it has been faced on the east side with a panelling, the posts of which, consisting of two beams side by side, stand at average intervals of 0·60 m.; the intermediate space being filled up with quarry-stones. The whole exterior side of the panelling is covered with a clay coating and daubed over with a thin layer of clay.

In the southern part of the gate, where the entrance is ($f\,y$ on No. 18 and Plan VII.), the masonry is composed of larger stones joined with clay-cement, no doubt in order to make it more solid. It even appears that, for the same reason, this wall has been artificially baked, as an additional precaution, for the clay cement between the stones is baked much more than the exterior coating of the wall. So far as the gate-road was covered by the upper edifice, its walls were vertical; but at its northern end (k on the engraving

No. 18 and Plan VII.), where the upper edifice ceased and where the road lay in the open air, its lateral walls were slanting. It led up on the left to the large edifices by a ramp (*n* on No. 18 and Plan VII.) paved with large stone slabs; the gate-road itself turned to the right, but we could not ascertain how it ended there, for a later edifice (C on No. 18 and Plan VII.) of the second city, which had been built over the northern part of the gateway, prevented us from making further researches in that direction.

I have cleared this gateway in front for a length of 45 m., and have found that at the end of that distance (*g* on Plan VII.), its clay surface ceases, and the road proceeds on the bare rock into the lower city. It was easy for us to bring the clay surface to light up to that point, it being, as already mentioned, everywhere covered with charcoal. This gateway (N F on No. 18 and Plan VII.) was at all events destroyed by fire before the great catastrophe, and it remained ever after unused and buried; the edifice (C on No. 18 and Plan VII.) of the second city, which has been built over and above it, can leave no doubt of this fact.

As a substitute for the southern gate, a new large gate (O X on the sketch No. 90, p. 179, and on Plan VII.), of which the accompanying engraving No. 19 gives a good view, was erected immediately to the east, which we shall call the south-east gate. Its ground plan is given under No. 90, in the description of the third city. We have only been able to bring this gate partially to light, the third settlers having erected, 1·50 m. above it, a new and narrower gate, which we should have had to destroy in order to excavate that of the second city. We can therefore describe the latter but incompletely. Its interior breadth is 7·50 m., and it is about three times as long. It has two portals, which are both marked with the letter *a* on No. 19, on No. 90, and on Plan VII.

The south-western lateral wall is visible in the foreground, and is marked with the letter *b* in the engraving

No. 19 also in the ground plan No. 90, and *w* on Plan VII. The same letters mark also the second lateral wall, which has been brought to light only for a short distance, and which is visible further back. The masonry of both these walls consists of unwrought calcareous stones, and is about 2·50 m. thick. The upper projecting quadrangular crosswalls of the gate (*v* on the ground plan No. 90 and on Plan VII.) are also more than 2·50 m. in thickness. This gate is directed towards the entrance of the two great edifices on the north side, A and B.

The great brick wall described above (see Plan VII. NN) is joined to this gate, from which it extends to the north-east. Thus, instead of only one gate, we have now found three. But I must remind the reader that all these three gates are the Acropolis gates of Troy, which Homer never had occasion to mention. His Scaean gate was, as I have mentioned above, not in the Pergamos, but on the west side of the lower city, and by it people went out to the great plain.*
I have shown in *Ilios*† that this Scaean gate is the only gate of the lower city mentioned in the poems, that there is no allusion to other gates, and that, whenever Homer mentions gates (πύλαι), he means by the plural the two wings of the gate, and, consequently, but one gate. With respect to this, Dr. Dörpfeld calls my attention to the inscription of the Parthenon (*Corpus Inscriptionum Atticarum*, II. 708, and Michaelis, *Parthenon*, p. 316), in which the plural θύραι is used for the single doublewinged door of the *cella* of the Parthenon, for here we have a perfect analogy with the foregoing interpretation of the πύλαι of Troy.

As will be seen from Plan VII., there are only a few large buildings on the Acropolis, the most remarkable of which

---

* *Il.* VI. 392, 393 :
εὖτε πύλας ἵκανε διερχόμενος μέγα ἄστυ
Σκαιάς—τῇ γὰρ ἔμελλε διεξίμεναι πεδίονδε.

† Pages 143, 144.

are two edifices on the north side, of which we shall call the larger one A, the smaller one B. The layer of calcined ruins and *débris*, which, as I have stated, is in general but insignificant in the second city and frequently only 0·20 m. deep, is in these two edifices considerably deeper, but only for the reason that the brick walls of A are 1·45 m. thick, those of B 1·25 m., and consequently these walls could not be so easily destroyed, and necessarily produced a much larger quantity of *débris*. The part of the walls of these edifices still standing is 1·50 m. high.

To the edifice A belong the three blocks of bricks marked H on Plan III. in *Ilios*, in which my former collaborator, M. Burnouf, had erroneously seen the remains of the great city wall. These two large edifices of the second, the burnt city, are most probably temples: we infer this in the first place from their ground plan, because they have only one hall in the breadth; secondly, from the proportionately considerable thickness of the walls; thirdly, from the circumstance, that they stand parallel and near each other, being only separated by a corridor 0·50 m. broad; for if they had been dwelling-houses they would probably have had one common wall—a thing never found yet in ancient temples. Both are built of bricks, which—like the above-mentioned fortification-wall of the second city—have only been baked after the walls had been completely built up. The ground being level here, the walls could be baked both on the exterior and interior sides, but the effect of the fire of the wood-piles simultaneously kindled on both sides of the walls was further considerably increased by the holes which had been provided in them in all directions. Some of these holes go right through the wall; others, which may rather be called grooves, are arranged lengthwise in the external sides of the walls, as represented by the woodcut No. 20. In the temple A they may be seen on the external sides of the wall in each fourth course of bricks, in such a manner that the lowest groove was immediately

CHAP. III.] BRICK WALLS BURNT AFTER BUILDING. 77

above the stone foundation (see the woodcuts Nos. 20, 21). These longitudinal grooves penetrate into the wall from 0·25 m. to 0·35 m. deep, and are from 0·15 m. to 0·25 m. high. The cross holes or channels are arranged in the walls at distances of about 4 mètres, in such a way that one of them is invariably in the corner of the halls. In this manner the cross walls are enclosed on both sides by such cross channels in the places where they join the lateral walls (see the ground plan No. 24). In the temple B

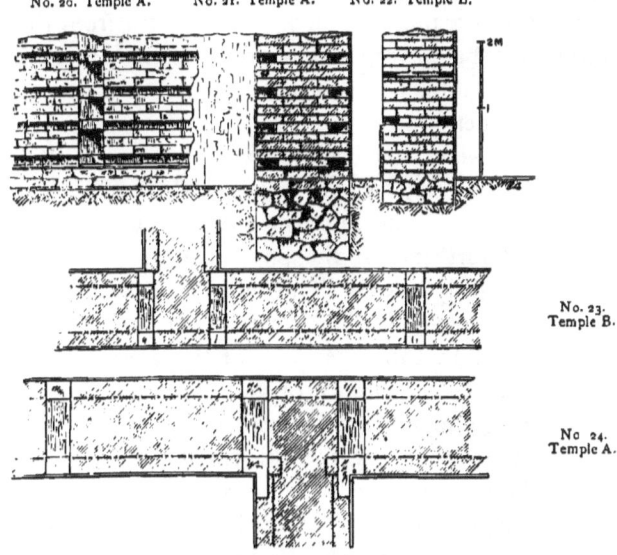

No. 20. Temple A.   No. 21. Temple A.   No. 22. Temple B.

No. 23. Temple B.

No 24. Temple A.

No. 20.—External Side of a Wall of Temple A, showing the arrangement of the horizontal channels and of those which go right through the wall.
No. 21.—Section of a Wall of Temple A, showing the arrangement of the horizontal channels.
No. 22.—Section of a Wall of Temple B, showing the arrangement of the horizontal channels.
No. 23.—Plan of a Wall of Temple B, showing the arrangement of the cross channels.
No. 24.—Plan of a Wall of Temple A, showing the arrangement of the cross channels.

the channels are arranged in a similar manner (see Nos. 20, 22, 23); the only difference is that here the longitudinal grooves are in each sixth course of bricks (see No. 22), and the cross-channels at shorter distances, according to the length of the rooms.

All these longitudinal grooves, as well as all the cross holes, had been originally filled with wooden beams; as is proved with the greatest certainty by their form and by the impressions the branches have left in the clay cement. But it is a curious fact, that in none of the grooves or holes have we been able to discover the slightest vestige of charred wood. In some rare cases these grooves and holes had, after the artificial baking of the brick walls, been left open, either intentionally or by inadvertence; but in general they were filled with baked brick matter mixed with vitrified pieces of brick, probably such as had fallen from the walls during the baking operation, for we find occasionally a fragment of pottery in this brick *débris*.

As further proofs that the walls were built of crude bricks and were baked after having been erected, I may state that the clay cement between the bricks has been baked exactly in the same manner as the bricks themselves, and further that the upper parts of the walls were but very slightly baked. This again is proved by a fragment of a cross-wall, which contains clay-bricks still quite unbaked, and by the upper parts of the lateral walls, which have fallen into the interior of the edifice, portions of their bricks being altogether unbaked.

The foundations of the brick walls of this temple A consist throughout of walls of unwrought calcareous stones, 2·50 m. high, which are covered with large limestone or sandstone slabs, on which the brick walls rested. These foundations protrude in the south-eastern part of the edifice 0·30 m. above the floor; but, as the latter rises gradually towards the north-west, the foundations are there on a level with the floor. The bricks are on an average 0·45 m. broad, 0·67 m. long, and about 0·12 m. thick. With this proportion of 2 : 3 in the breadth and length of the bricks, the walls could be regularly bonded in such a way that, together with the joints, three and two bricks alternately formed the thickness of the wall, viz. 1·45 m.

CHAP. III.]   FIRST TEMPLE OF THE ACROPOLIS.   79

The width of the joints varies from 0·02 m. to 0·04 m. The material used for the bricks is a greenish-yellow clay, mixed with straw. The walls were covered, both on the inside and outside, with a coating about 0·02 m. thick, which consisted of clay and was pargetted with a very thin layer of clay. The floor consisted of a layer of beaten clay, from 0,005 mm. to 0,015 mm. thick, which has been laid on simultaneously with the wall-coating after the wall had been baked. For this reason the remains of the

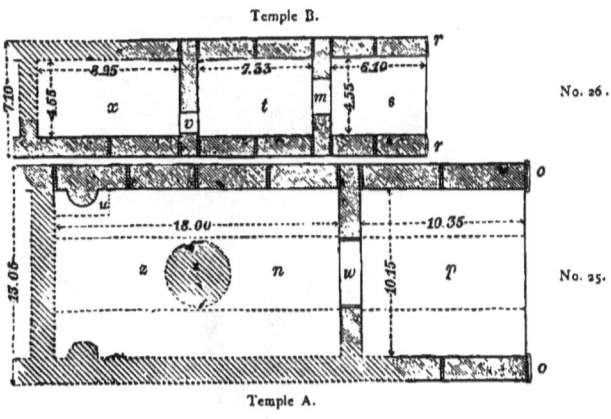

No. 25.—Ground plan of the Temple A.
No. 26.—Ground plan of the Temple B.

charcoal derived from the baking of the walls are found *below* the floor.

As will be seen from the adjoining ground-plan, No. 25, the temple A consists of a pronaos or vestibulum, marked *p*, which is open to the south-east, and of the naos proper (*n*). The latter is indicated in the sketch (No. 25), as 18 mètres long, for close to the semicircle *u* there appeared to be the remains of a cross-wall belonging to the edifice. But having again most carefully examined the premises, my architects conclude with the highest probability, from the arrangement of the holes in the lateral wall, that the length of the naos (*n*) must have extended to somewhat more than 20 m., and that, consequently, the proportion of its breadth to its length is exactly as 1 : 2. It cannot be determined now whether there was still a third room on the north-west side (in correspondence with the division of the temple B), because the western portion of the edifice has been cut away by the great northern trench.

The pronaos, *p*, is 10·15 m. broad by 10·35 m. deep, and therefore just a square. The front ends of the lateral walls (marked *o*) were cased with vertical wooden jambs,

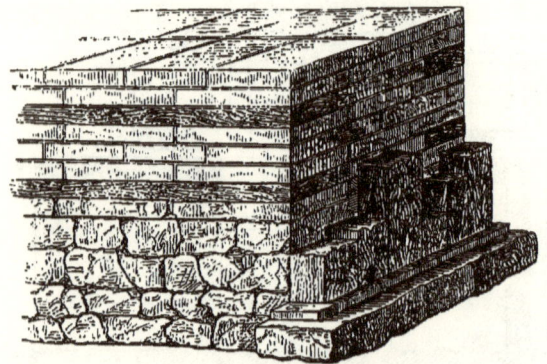

No. 27.—Parastades on the front ends of the lateral walls of temple A, consisting of six vertical wooden jambs.*

for, as the wall-corners consisted of bricks, they might have been easily destroyed without this consolidation (see woodcut, No. 27). These jambs, of which there were six at each extremity, stood on well-wrought foundation-stones; their lower parts are preserved, standing on the stones, but, of course, in a calcined state. Each of these wooden jambs was about 0·25 m. square, so that the six jambs made up fully the wall thickness of 1·45 m. We thus see in this temple, that the *parastades* or *antae*, which are customary in the Greek temples, and merely fulfilled in them an

---

* The dark horizontal bands between the courses of bricks in this engraving No. 27 indicate the grooves which had once been filled with wood, and were now found empty. The shading of these empty grooves is not well done; it ought to be much darker.

artistic purpose, have been used here principally for constructive reasons; first, because they served to secure the corners of the walls against direct injury, and, secondly, because they served to render the walls strong enough to support the great beams of the roof. This discovery of *parastades* in their original form, and with the primitive use for which they were employed, is of capital interest to archæology, the more so as the discovery has been made in Troy divine.*

---

* Karl Boetticher, *Die Tektonik der Hellenen*, Berlin, 1874, I. pp. 194, 195, 198, writes on the *parastades* as follows: " *Antae* v. *Anta*.— In the ancient (original) cella with parastas-spaces, where the side-walls are extended to the edge of the stylobate, so as to range with the pillars, both the walls are ended or finished by a *parastas* or *anta* at the point of junction. The *anta* corresponds here with the entablature of the pillars, and, together with them, encloses the space requisite to form the portico.

" The *antae* have neither a static nor a constructive function. It is not a pillar to sustain a weight ; it is essentially an artistic form to accentuate the end of the wall and the beginning of an epistylion. Its employment is necessitated only from its relation to the epistylion, and consequently it requires only a very slight degree of relief from the face of the wall, and a marked difference in the form of the capital from that of the pillars. As it ends the mass of the wall, its front face must be the whole thickness of the wall, but as the inner side receives only the mass of the epistylion or entablature, its breadth must be governed by that of the epistylion ; while its outer face is only marked by sufficient projection to distinguish it from the face of the wall itself..

" When the *anta* is in such a situation that a space is enclosed on both sides of it, so that two epistylia rest on it, the breadth of the *anta* is governed by the breadth of the epistylia, and the *anta* then assumes the function of a pillar. When the epistylion rests neither on the end nor the middle of the wall, the *anta* is marked only by two small facets.

" The capital (of the *anta*) consists of a necking with a slight projection adorned with an anthemion (or honeysuckle ornament) ; above this is a slight Doric cymatium with a necking of several annulets, like the echinus of the pillars, thus connecting the two parts together in design. A narrow abacus marks its junction with the pillars of the pteron, and is ornamented with a meander (fret) on its face, like the abacus of the pillars. Originally this abacus had no cymation to separate it from the pteron, as was universally the case in later monuments.

" The reason why originally the *antae* were not constructed with a

7

I am indebted to my friend, Mr. James Fergusson, for the accompanying sketch (No. 27A) of the temple of

separate base, as was usually the case, is evident enough. It was for artistic reasons—the same that prevented the pillars and the walls from being furnished with bases. Such a separation from the stylobate would have prevented it from having a common significance with the other two forms. When however a base to the wall was introduced, with or without mouldings, it was also added to the *anta;* but in that case it is a sure sign of the introduction of an Attic-Ionic element; as is found, for instance, in the Theseum, and in the Temple of Artemis-Propylaea at Eleusis, where a reversed cymatium appears as a base.

"In a technical sense, an *anta* or *parastas* signifies any part of a building that stands in juxtaposition with another; thence it applies to a wall at the side of an entrance, and also to the artistic form which terminates any projecting wall. For this artistic form, as well as for every such projecting wall, the Latin term *anta* is used. The term *parastas* came eventually to be applied to the space between the side walls, a use shown, as already said, by the term being applied to designate both the pronaos and posticum, when they are called 'in parastades.' The so-called parastas-space, or space between the *antae,* is a term used not only to designate this particular portion, but also to describe a form of temple, and to distinguish a particular form of temple, whether prostyle, amphiprostyle, or peripteral. The existence of the *antae* alone would not be sufficient for the purpose, as these exist in all known forms of temples."

Boetticher gives the following citations from ancient authors regarding *parastades.* The scholiast to Euripides, *Androm.* 1089 (where Neoptolemus takes down the arms from a *parastades* wall in the temple of Delphi) explains : παραστάδας λέγει τὰς κατὰ τὴν εἴσοδον ἑκατέρωθεν παρισταμένας τύχας. The *parastas* becomes the vestibulum, as distinct from the cella, in Eurip. *Iphig. Taur.* 1159 : Ἄναξ, ἐχ᾿αὐτοῦ πόδα σὸν ἐν παραστάσι; Eurip. *Phoen.* 418 : Ἀδράστου δ᾿ ἦλθον ἐς παραστάδας. Vitruvius, 6, 7, 1, uses παραστάς for the space—(*antae* for the two projecting walls)—forming the vestibulum, prothyron, or prostomiaion, with a roof, as also is the case in the Puteolanian inscription given by Gruter : "ex eo pariete antas duas ad more morsum proiicito longas P. II, crassas P. I." Hesychius explains παραστάδες · οἱ πρὸς τοῖς τοίχοις τετραμμένοι κίονες. The *antae* of the door-opening are likewise *parastades,* being rendered by *phliai, stathmoi.* Hesychius: φλιᾶς · τῆς θύρας παραστάδος, though φλιά is often confounded with threshold, as in the Schol. Hom. *Iliad,* I. 591. Hesychius also explains παραστραθμίδες τῆς θύρας τὰ πρὸς τῷ στρόφιγγι. *Poll.* 1, 76 : σταθμοὶ δὲ τὰ ἑκατέρωθεν ξύλα κατὰ πλευρὰν τῶν θυρῶν, ἃ παραστάδες φασίν. Herodotus speaks of them as being of

PRIMITIVE PARASTADES.

Themis at Rhamnus, which gives an excellent example of an ancient Greek temple of polygonal masonry, to which parastades (p) in hewn stone have been added, probably at some later date, certainly in a later style. It is to be found in the volume of the unedited antiquities of Attica published by the Dilettanti Society in 1817, Chapter VII., plate 1, where the difference of masonry is carefully distinguished, and certainly appears to be a subsequent addition.

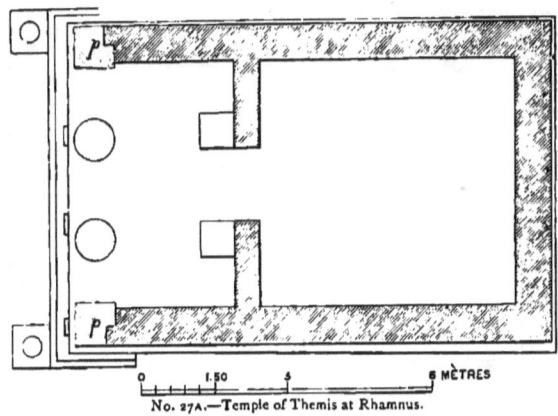

No. 27A.—Temple of Themis at Rhamnus.

It could not be ascertained whether there have been, between the *parastades* of the temple A, wooden columns such as we are led to expect, with a span exceeding 10 mètres, for we could not find the particular foundation stones on which they ought to have stood. I may say the same of any columns which may have stood in the interior to diminish the great span of the roof.

copper in the gates of Babylon: καὶ σταθμοὶ δὲ καὶ ὑπέρθυρα. The doorposts are likewise called σταθμοί in Homer, *Odyssey*, VII. 89; Scholiast, αἱ παραστάδες. *Anecd. Bachm.* I. 369, 21, σταθμῶν· τῶν παραστάδων τῆς θύρας. Hesychius, σταθμόνες and σταθμῶν, also ἁρμοστῆρες in ἁρμοστής. *Etym. M.* 609, 34, σταθμὸς τῆς θύρας ἡ φλία. Zonaras, *Lex.* p. 1814, φλία δέ ἐστιν τὸ πλάγιον τῆς θύρας ἡ παραστάς, ὅπου τὶς ἵσταται καὶ ἐπερείδεται. Apion, *Gloss. Homer.* σταθμός . . . τῆς θύρας ἡ φλία, and Schol. Lycophr. *Alexandra*, v. 290, καὶ ἡ παραστὰς δὲ σταθμὸς λέγεται. Phot. σταθμῶν τῶν τῆς θύρας παραστάδων.

PRIMITIVE PARASTADES.

Themis at Rhamnus, which gives an excellent example of an ancient Greek temple of polygonal masonry, to which parastades (*p*) in hewn stone have been added, probably at some later date, certainly in a later style. It is to be found in the volume of the unedited antiquities of Attica published by the Dilettanti Society in 1817, Chapter VII., plate 1, where the difference of masonry is carefully distinguished, and certainly appears to be a subsequent addition.

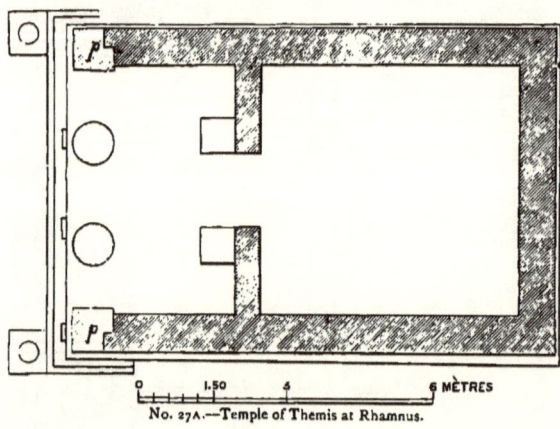

No. 27A.—Temple of Themis at Rhamnus.

It could not be ascertained whether there have been, between the *parastades* of the temple A, wooden columns such as we are led to expect, with a span exceeding 10 mètres, for we could not find the particular foundation stones on which they ought to have stood. I may say the same of any columns which may have stood in the interior to diminish the great span of the roof.

---

copper in the gates of Babylon: καὶ σταθμοὶ δὲ καὶ ὑπέρθυρα. The doorposts are likewise called σταθμοί in Homer, *Odyssey*, VII. 89; Scholiast, αἱ παραστάδες. *Anecd. Bachm.* I. 369, 21, σταθμῶν· τῶν παραστάδων τῆς θύρας. Hesychius, σταθμόνες and σταθμῶν, also ἁρμοστῆρες in ἁρμοστής. *Etym. M.* 609, 34, σταθμὸς τῆς θύρας ἡ φλία. Zonaras, *Lex.* p. 1814, φλία δέ ἐστιν τὸ πλάγιον τῆς θύρας ἢ παραστάς, ὅπου τις ἵσταται καὶ ἐπερείδεται. Apion, *Gloss. Homer.* σταθμός . . . τῆς θύρας ἡ φλία, and Schol. Lycophr. *Alexandra*, v. 290, καὶ ἡ παραστὰς δὲ σταθμὸς λέγεται. Phot. σταθμῶν τῶν τῆς θύρας παραστάδων.

deep, and are not covered with large stone slabs like those of the temple A. The construction of these brick walls is similar to that of the walls of the temple A, and only differs from it in details. The *antae* (*r*) are formed in like manner. This temple (B) has been built later than A, because its south-western lateral wall has no coating on the exterior side, as it could not be seen on account of the close proximity of the temple A. On the other hand, the whole exterior side of the north-eastern lateral wall of the temple A is covered with a coating, which must necessarily belong to the time when this large sanctuary still stood alone, and when the temple B had not yet been built. It deserves particular attention, that the north-eastern wall of the temple B is much less baked than the south-western wall; the reason seems to be that in the baking of the latter the heat must have been more intense on account of the close proximity of the edifice A. The narrow passage between the two temples was filled with *débris* of baked bricks, among which we found a very large number of thoroughly vitrified bricks, called in Germany Ziegelschlacken (brick scoriae). The material of the bricks is identical with that of the temple A, whereas the cement consists of a much lighter-coloured clay, which is mixed with fine hay, and also shows after the baking a much lighter colour than the bricks.

The ground plan (see No. 26) consists of three rooms : first, the pronaos (*s*), which is open on the south-east side, and is 6·10 m. in length and 4·55 m. in breadth ; secondly, the cella or *naos* proper (*t*), which is 7·33 m. long by 4·55 m. broad, and is connected with the *pronaos* by a doorway (*m*) 2 m. wide. In the western corner a narrower doorway (*v*) leads into the third room (*x*), which is 8·95 m. long by 4·55 m. broad. The floor, which consists of beaten clay, has been made later than the wall-coating, for this latter can be followed as far as 0·10 m. deep below the floor. As the wall-coating terminates at the doorways, and as remains of charcoal still exist there, it is evident that the lateral faces of the doors were dressed with some other material, most probably with wood.

It deserves particular attention that to a height of 0·50 m. above the floor the clay walls of neither temple are vitrified; which we explain by the evident fact that the material of the terraced roof, the clay and the charred wood, fell in the conflagration and covered up the floors to this height. In many places even the upper part of the walls is not vitrified, but only much burnt: this must be attributed to the larger or smaller mass of burning wood which fell at different places. Very remarkable is the mass of small shells found in the bricks, and which must have been contained in the clay of which they were made. These shells are invariably black in the baked bricks, and have retained their natural colour in those which have not been exposed to the great heat. It is uncertain whether there was still a fourth room on the north-west side, for it cannot be proved by the existing fragments of foundations.

Although the division of the temple B into three rooms answers in a striking manner to the division of the house of Paris, according to Homer's description,

οἵ οἱ ἐποίησαν θάλαμον καὶ δῶμα καὶ αὐλήν *

"they [the architects of Troy] built him a chamber (thalamos), a dwelling-room (dòma) and a vestibule (aulé)," nevertheless the reasons given above seem to prove, with the greatest probability, that both the edifices, B as well as A, were temples. Both these temples have been destroyed in a fearful catastrophe, together with all the other buildings of the second settlement.

At the north-west end of the temple B, large remains of more ancient house-walls stand out from beneath its floor,

---

* *Il.* VI. 316. I may here observe that by later authors αὐλή is often used for a dwelling-house: see *e.g.* Aeschyl. *Prometh.* 122 (ed. Tauchn.), ἡ Διὸς αὐλή; also Monk in Euripid. *Hippolyt.* v. 68 (ed. Tauchn.).

evidently belonging to an edifice of the first epoch of the second city. These ancient house-walls may also be followed up beneath the floor of the temple A, and are marked with black colour and the letters *v a* on Plan VII. They must naturally belong to an edifice which stood here before the temples A and B were built. It would, of course, have been impossible to ascertain the ground plan of these ancient house-walls, without destroying both temples.

Between the two temples A and B and the south-eastern gate (O X on Plan VII.) we discovered, as I have mentioned, the remains of an edifice, which had been erected precisely over the entrance to the southern gate, and which is marked on Plan VII. with the letter C. It came to light in a very ruined state, the houses of the third city having been built in this place only about 0·20 m. above the level of the second city : for this reason we can say but little of the ground plan of this edifice. The part best preserved is a vestibule (*w v*), which is 3·13 m. broad. The north-western ends of its lateral walls (*g*) are faced with wooden *parastades*, similar to those of the temple A (see the engraving No. 27). Each lateral wall-end, 1 mètre broad, had probably four vertical wooden posts, which stood on an enormous hard calcareous block, well wrought and well polished, on which may be seen a rebate. As in the temples A and B, these wooden posts served to protect the front ends of the walls, which were built of bricks and had not a sufficient solidity ; the wooden posts served at the same time to support the terraced roof. At a distance of 2·50 m. from the *parastades* (*g*) may be seen a well-wrought and well-polished block of hard limestone, 2·65 m. long, 1·20 m. broad, which lies across the vestibule of the edifice C and fills up the whole breadth between its lateral walls. On its south-east side we see a rebate. Most probably this remarkable block formed the threshold of a large doorway which existed here ; but we could not ascertain this with certainty, the lateral walls having been entirely destroyed in the places where the doorway ought to have been. We at first supposed this edifice to have formed a separate gate for the precinct of the two temples. But we have again become sceptical about this, through the discovery on the north side of several chambers (*z y*), which are joined to it, the extent of which, however, we could not ascertain. In all the rooms of this edifice the floor consists of beaten clay, which has apparently been artificially baked, and which extended also over the large threshold and the base-stones of the *parastades*, so far as these had not been occupied by the wooden posts.

As may be seen from Plan VII. the north-eastern part of the Acropolis is occupied by a number of house-walls (marked W on Plan VII.), some of which run parallel with the temples, others at right angles to them; of all of them, however, there remain only the foundations of calcareous stones cemented with clay. Here also the third settlers had erected their houses immediately over the edifices of the second city, and in doing so they had so completely destroyed the upper part of them, that it is now hardly possible to determine their ground plan. But we can at least recognize from the remains that there existed here a very large edifice, containing many large halls.

We are somewhat better informed regarding the great edifice which occupied the whole western part of the Acropolis, though here too all the upper walls have been destroyed, either in the great catastrophe of the second city or by the third settlers when they built their town. Among the house-walls of the second city, which we brought to light in the western part of the citadel, beneath those of the third settlers, we must distinguish two different kinds of walls, which, as before mentioned, we have indicated on Plan VII. with black and red colour. The walls with black colour are the most ancient; they belong to the period of the second city when the south-western gate had only one portal (R C). The red walls have been erected later, and are at all events contemporaneous with the extension of the south-western gate. Though we cannot completely reconstruct the ground plan of the more ancient edifice from the walls which are preserved, yet we recognize with certainty that it consisted of several halls (marked D on Plan VII.), from 5 to 7 mètres long and broad, which were grouped around an interior rectangular central hall or court (marked E), 11 m. long by 7·50 m. broad. At the northern corner of this great hall (E) may be seen the Hellenic well (*t z*), built of calcareous stones joined with lime. As before mentioned, when the south-western gate (R C) was to be provided with a second portal F M, that large edifice had to be altered, for the lateral walls (*d z*) of the new gateway (F M) passed over some of its foundation walls (*l m*). The reconstruction of the edifice (the red walls on Plan VII.) was effected with a somewhat altered direction, in such a way that a building was erected to the north-west (*r x*), and another to the south-east (*r b*), so that between them there remained a free space for access to the gate. Like the more ancient edifice, these houses seem also to have consisted of several successive rooms. That this reconstruction took place simultaneously with the extension of the Acropolis to the south and east may be recognized particularly from the fact, that a wall of the south-eastern edifice passed across the substruction of the more ancient fortification-wall (*c* on Plan VII. in this volume, as well as on Plan I. and No. 144, p. 264, in *Ilios*).

I call particular attention to the fact that, like the front ends of the lateral walls of the edifices in the eastern part of the Acropolis and those of the gate-extension, the front ends of the lateral walls of this edifice also had wooden *parastades*, resting on well-wrought and well-polished blocks of hard limestone (marked *d d*), one of which (*a*) may still be seen *in situ* on the ancient fortification-wall *c*. Consequently all the edifices of the Acropolis of the second city had the same kind of architecture; but for the most part they had also the same mode of construction, the foundations consisting of calcareous stones cemented with clay, the upper walls of bricks, with terraced roofs of wooden beams, rushes, and clay. In many halls of these edifices we see well-formed floors, consisting either of small pebbles, or of clay intermixed with very small pebbles, or merely of beaten clay: in the last case the floors have nearly always been vitrified in the great fire. We found only one floor of clay covered with plates of green slate. How total and complete was the catastrophe in which the second city perished, is seen from the fact that most of its edifices have been destroyed to their very foundations, as well as from the tremendous masses of vitrified brick-*débris* and calcined wooden beams, which we found especially in the larger edifices and in the gates. In places where the great quantity of wood gave an abundant aliment to the fire, as for instance the *parastades* and the doors, large parts of the brick walls have been completely melted and transformed into a kind of spongy glass-metal. As I have mentioned in *Ilios* (p. 313), for a long distance on the north side the floors resembled a sort of vitrified sheet, which was only interrupted by the house-walls.

I found in the *débris* of the second city very large masses of green slates, which must once have served for paving the house floors, and perhaps also the streets between the houses; but strange to say, the above-mentioned floor, in the great edifice *r x* in the western part of the citadel, is the only one which is still covered with them, and it was only in a chamber of the edifice C that I found a few of them still *in situ*. The plates of slate were found almost exclusively in small pieces, owing to the intense incandescence which must have prevailed in the catastrophe of the second

CHAP. III.]   OBJECTS FOUND IN FIRST TEMPLE.   91

city. By this heat the thin plates have nearly all been burst to pieces, and have partly assumed a red colouring.

In passing now to the description of the objects of

No. 28.—Copper Nail of a quadrangular shape with a disk-like head, which has been cast independently of the nail and merely fixed on it.   Size 2 : 3 ; depth 8·50 m.

human industry discovered in the second city, I begin with those found in the temple A.

With the carbonized beams was found a large number

of huge copper nails, some of which have the enormous weight of 1190 grammes (above 2½ lbs. avoirdupois). They were doubtless used in the wooden structures of the terrace and the *parastades*. As may be seen from the engraving No. 28, they are quadrangular, run out at one end into a point, and have at the other end a disk-like head, which has been cast independently of the nail and has merely been fixed on it. Some of these largest nails were

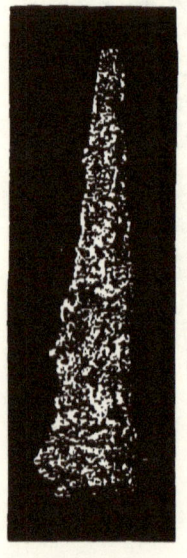
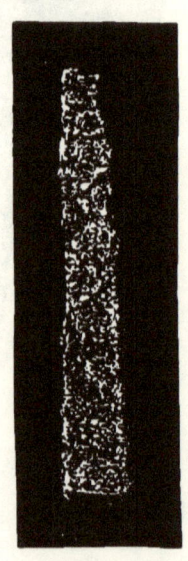

No. 29.—Quadrangular copper Nail without the disk-like head. Size 1:3; depth 8·50 m.

No. 30.—Quadrangular copper Nail without the disk-like head. Size 1:3; depth 8·50 m.

stuck vertically in the carbonized wood and clay, and it was not easy to extract them with the hands. I represent here under Nos. 29 and 30, in only one-third of their actual size, two more such nails, which have lost their disk-like heads. There were also found some very large quadrangular copper nails with a hammerlike head, which has been cast together with the nail. Of these I represent one under No. 31, likewise one-third of the size. As in

CHAP. III.]   OBJECTS OF BRONZE OR COPPER.   93

the Italian terramare, all the bronze and copper at Troy was worked solely by casting, and not yet by forging.

Of other objects found in the temple A, I may mention a copper cup with an omphalos, like the one represented in *Ilios*, p. 469, No. 786; and a number of bronze battle-axes of the usual Trojan form, of which I represent one under No. 32. To the list of places given in *Ilios*, p. 479, where similar battle-axes may be seen, I may add that a battle-axe

No. 31.—Copper Nail with round head. Size 1 : 3 ; depth 8·50 m.

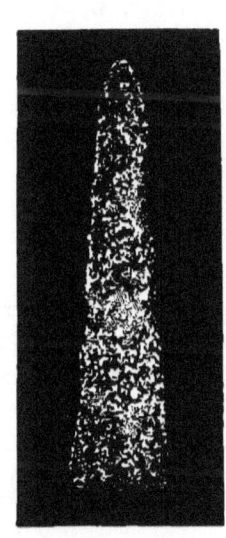

No. 32.—Bronze Battle-axe. Size 1 : 3 ; depth 8·50 m.

of identical form is in the Musée de Cluny at Paris, but the place where it was found is not indicated. A second battle-axe of the same shape, found in Cyprus, is in the collection of M. Eugène Piot in Paris, a third in the Egyptian collection in the Museum of Turin, and a fourth in the British Museum. I have already pointed out in *Ilios*, p. 479, that this form of battle-axe must probably have been copied from the stone battle-axes, many of which have exactly the same type: see *e.g.* J. J. A. Worsaae,

Nordiske Oldsager i det Kongelige Museum i Kjöbenhavn, Copenhagen, 1859, Pl. 9, figs. 5, 6, 8; Pl. 10, figs. 11, 12; Pl. 37, fig. 178. See also A. P. Madsen, *Antiquités Préhistoriques du Danemark*, Copenhagen, 1872, Pl. xv., 14, 15; Pl. xxvi., Nos. 1, 2; Pl. xxvii., Nos. 5, 6; Pl. xxviii., Nos. 16–23; Pl. xxix., Nos. 1, 2, 13; Pl. xxx., No. 2.

I also found here some bronze lance-heads of the common Trojan form, of which I give one under No. 33, p. 97. It is a remarkable fact, of which every one can convince himself with his own eyes in the Schliemann Museum at Berlin, that *nearly all the lance-heads contained in the great treasure, or found elsewhere in my excavations at Troy, are indented on both sides like saws, though of course they could not have been intended for anything else but lance-heads.* Similar serrated lance-heads of bronze or copper have never yet been found elsewhere. On the other hand, none of the lance-heads found in my excavations at Troy in 1882, of which No. 33 is a fair specimen, are serrated. But serrated lance-heads of flint are frequently found in Denmark, and many specimens of them may be seen in the museum in Copenhagen. See J. J. A. Worsaae, *op. cit.* Pl. 15, No. 56, Pl. 16, Nos. 67–72; A. P. Madsen, *op. cit.*, Pl. xxxvi., Nos. 2, 12; Pl. xxxvii., Nos. 27, 28, 30–32. Four of these serrated stone lance-heads were found in a tumulus at Borreby in Zealand (Denmark), together with four unserrated ones. These indented Danish lance-heads resemble the Trojan type of lance-heads as exactly as if they had been their prototype.

Another fine specimen of a serrated lance-head of silex, found on the bank of the Labionka in the north-western Caucasus, is represented under No. 28, p. 78 in Professor Rudolf Virchow's great work *Das Gräberfeld von Koban im Lande der Osseten, Kaukasus*, Berlin, 1883. The learned author justly remarks, with reference to this lance-head, that the original form of the bronze dagger was perfectly developed in the stone age, and that it served as a type for lance and arrow heads as well as daggers of bronze. Many of the double-edged bronze daggers (which Virchow discusses on pp. 76-82, and represents on Pl. ii., No. 1, Pl. iii., Nos. 8, 9, Pl. iv., No. 9), have the very closest resemblance to the Trojan weapons (like No. 33), which I take to be lance-heads and call them so. He points (p. 79) to their resemblance to the ancient Chinese * and ancient Egyptian † daggers, as well as to those of Nineveh, and remarks (p. 80), that the double-edged dagger of the lancet-form has obviously first of all been prolonged to the double-edged sword of the sedge-leaf or sword-lily (xiphion) form, such as we see in a specimen from Samthawro (Caucasus) and in the swords of the Lake dwellings.‡

Like the Trojan lance-heads,§ those of the prehistoric cemetery of Koban run out at the hinder end into a tongue for a handle, or they have a broad end, and were fastened with rivets to the shaft, which was probably of wood.∥

Just as at Troy, swords have never yet been found in the prehistoric cemetery of Koban, but neither do they occur in the Italian terramare,¶ nor in the necropolis of Alba Longa,** although in this latter as well as at Koban

---

* J. J. A. Worsaae, *Mémoires de la Société Royale des Antiquités du Nord*, 1880, p. 194, figs. 8, 9, 11.

† *Idem*, 1872-1877, p. 128, fig. 2 ; Montélius, *Congrès International d'Anthropologie et d'Archéologie Préhistorique*, Stockholm, II., p. 917, figs. 65-67.

‡ The same view is taken in an interesting paper on "The Forms and History of the Sword," by Frederick Pollock, in *Macmillan's Magazine*, July, 1883.

§ See No. 33 in the present work and *Ilios*, p. 476, Nos. 801-803, 805 ; p. 482, No. 815.

∥ Rudolf Virchow, *Das Gräberfeld von Koban im Lande der Osseten*, Berlin, 1883, Pl. iii., figs. 8, 9 ; Pl. x., fig. 8.

¶ Wolfgang Helbig, *Die Italiker in der Po-Ebene*, Leipzig, 1879, p. 5.   ** *Idem*, p. 78.

the fibula is very frequent. Professor W. Helbig * remarks regarding swords, that, when a longer bronze blade was to be made, the primitive metallurgist had to contend with great difficulties. Bronze itself being a rare and precious material, the manufacture of stone weapons continued for a long time. Herodotus † says of the Sagartians, that they possessed no metal weapon except daggers. Helbig ‡ points to the passage in Homer,§ where it is stated that the only weapon of the Locrians was the sling, and that they had neither swords, nor helmets, nor spears, and he adds that, the Locrians having remained behind in their development and having maintained many ancient usages, this passage of the *Iliad* seems to give an important hint regarding the most ancient equipment and manner of fighting among the Greeks. Swords appear even to have been unknown to the Anglo-Saxons, who still fought at the battle of Hastings, in 1066 A.D., with spears, axes, and clubs, all of which weapons consisted of stone and were attached to wooden shafts. Even as late as towards the end of the 13th century, stone axes were still wielded by the Scots whom William Wallace led into the field against the English.‖ At all events it is certain, says Helbig,¶ that although some Indo-European peoples worked bronze from ancient times, they nevertheless continued to adhere, along with it, to the manufacture of stone weapons. The words *hamar* "hammer," and *sahs* "knife," "dagger," which originally meant *a hard stone*,** prove this in the case of the Germans.

One of the most interesting objects found in the temple A is the dagger of bronze, No. 34, which, like that

---

* *Idem*, p. 20.
† Herodotus, vii. 85 ; ὅπλα δὲ οὐ νομίζουσι ἔχειν οὔτε χάλκεα οὔτε σιδήρεα ἔξω ἐγχειριδίων.   ‡ W. Helbig, *op. cit.*, p. 5.
§ *Il.* xiii. 712–718.   ‖ W. Helbig, *op. cit.*, pp. 42, 43.
¶ *Idem*, p. 115.
** Grimm, *Deutsche Mythologie*, 4th ed. I., p. 151.

CHAP. III.] LANCE AND DAGGER OF BRONZE. 97

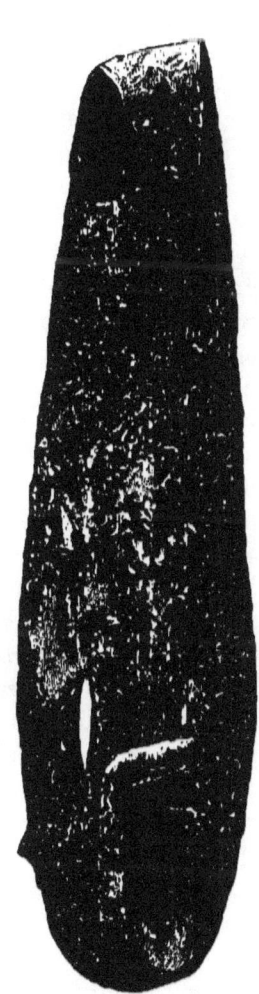

No. 33.—Bronze Lance-head; with the end broken off. Size 2:3; depth 8·50 m.

No. 34.—Bronze Dagger; with the handle and the upper end curled up in the great fire. Size 2:3; depth 8·50 m.

represented on p. 482, No. 813, in *Ilios*, has been partly rolled up in the heat of the great conflagration. It had originally precisely the form of the silver dagger represented in *Ilios* under No. 901, on p. 499; only that the handle, instead of being round, is quadrangular. Its end is bent round almost at a right angle, which proves that it had been cased in wood; it can hardly have been cased in bone or ivory, as all the bone and ivory I found was well preserved. This handle has been bent over so completely, in the incandescence of the great conflagration, that it now lies flat on the blade. Near the lower end of the blade there are two openings, each 0,015 mm. long, and 0,002 mm. broad in the broadest place. The upper end of the dagger is curved for a distance of 0·03 m., so that the point touches the blade. There was found besides in the temple A a bronze dagger of the same form and also with two holes; but it is not curled up and its handle is broken. Seven similar bronze daggers were contained in the great Trojan treasure (see *Ilios*, p. 453 and p. 482, Nos. 811–815). I also found a few in other places in my excavations at Hissarlik; but they have never been found elsewhere.

Of other copper weapons found here I can only mention the curious quadrangular bolts, which run out at one end to a sharp edge, and of which Nos. 816 and 817, p. 482, in *Ilios*, give fair specimens. A similar weapon, but of iron, is in the Egyptian collection in the Museum of Turin. One of the most interesting objects found in my excavations of 1882, was a bronze gimlet which I represent here under No. 34*a*; for, as far as I know, no instrument of this kind has ever been found in prehistoric remains, and the one before us is the more remarkable as it was found in the principal temple of Troy divine.

Regarding other tools of bronze or copper, my architect, Dr. Dörpfeld, rightly observes to me, that the construction and grandeur of the temples A and B, and of all the other edifices of the Acropolis, denote already a high civilization,

CHAP. III.] GIMLET AND KNIFE OF BRONZE. 99

and it seems altogether impossible that a people who could erect such sumptuous buildings, and who possessed such masses of gold treasure of elaborate workmanship as I have represented and described in *Ilios*, pp. 455–504, should

No. 34A.—Gimlet of bronze.
Size 2 : 3 ; depth about 8·50 m.

No. 35.—Bronze Knife.
Size 1 : 3 ; depth 8·50 m

not have had regular tools of bronze or copper. But if we found none of these, the reason must be, that the carpenters and the other handicraftsmen probably did not live in the Acropolis, which we must suppose to have been reserved merely for the king with his family, and for the temples of the gods. We must hold it to be impossible that the immense masses of wooden beams, or the large number of well-wrought and polished base-stones of the *parastades*, could have been cut and wrought without good instruments. It certainly seems absurd to suppose that this would have been done with stone axes by a people who used copper and bronze abundantly for making battle-axes, lances, knives, arrow-heads, brooches, &c. But then, again, I must confess that I never found at Troy a trace of moulds for casting such working implements, whereas the number of moulds found for casting battle-axes, lance-heads, and small instruments, is very large.

There were also some bronze knives found in the temple A, of which I represent one under No. 35. Of the round heads of the pins by which the handle of the knife was fixed in the wooden casing, two may be seen in the handle, and one in the lower part of the blade. All these curious huge nails, battle-axes, lance-heads, daggers, knives, &c., have been cast in moulds of mica-slate, like those represented in *Ilios*, pp. 433, 435, under Nos. 599–601. That the art of casting gold, and metals in general, was in common use at the time of Homer, is proved by the designation, "melter of gold" (χρυσοχόος), which the poet gives to Laërces,* who is sent for to gild the horns of an ox.

Prof. J. Maehly † observes, that there are in Homer several passages which seem to corroborate the assertion of Lucretius, ‡ that copper was in remote antiquity valued

---

* *Od.* III. 425, 426 :

εἰς δ' αὖ χρυσοχόον Λαέρκεα δεῦρο κελέσθω
ἐλθεῖν, ὄφρα βοὸς χρυσὸν κέρασιν περιχεύῃ.

† *Blätter für Literarische Unterhaltung,* 1881, Nos. 15, 16.

‡ V. 1268–1273 :

"Nec minus argento facere haec auroque parabant,
Quam validi primum violentis viribus aeris :
Nequidquam ; quoniam cedebat victa potestas,
Nec poterant pariter durum subferre laborem.
Nam fuit in pretio magis aes, aurumque jacebat
Propter inutilitatem, hebeti mucrone retusum."

even more highly than gold or silver. But the contrary seems to be proved most decidedly by a famous passage of the *Iliad*,* where the proportionate value between a suit of armour of gold and one of copper or bronze is given as 100 to 9. This latter proportion, as Dr. Dörpfeld observes to me, agrees pretty accurately with the proportion between gold and silver, which, according to Herodotus, was customary in the coins of Babylon, and in fact in the whole Eastern world.

I have in *Ilios* † called attention to the general belief that, besides alloying copper with tin, the ancients had still another way of hardening their copper, namely, by plunging it in water, for we read this apparently in Homer, ‡ Virgil,§ and Pausanias; ‖ and Pollux seems to confirm it by a remarkable example, when, noticing the use of βάψις instead of βαφή, he observes that Antiphon speaks of the hardening (βάψις) of copper and iron.¶ Regarding the meaning of the word tempering, Professor W. Chandler Roberts, of the Royal Mint, has kindly sent me the following interesting note.** "It must be remembered that tempering is *softening*, not hardening: a piece of steel when it has been *hardened* by rapid cooling, is heated to a certain definite temperature, which makes it *softer;* this is

---

* VI. 234-236:
> ἔνθ' αὖτε Γλαύκῳ Κρονίδης φρένας ἐξέλετο Ζεύς,
> ὃς πρὸς Τυδείδην Διομήδεα τεύχε' ἄμειβεν,
> χρύσεα χαλκείων, ἑκατόμβοι' ἐννεαβοίων.

† Pages 481, 482.

‡ *Od.* IX. 391-393:
> ὡς δ' ὅτ' ἀνὴρ χαλκεὺς πέλεκυν μέγαν ἠὲ σκέπαρνον
> εἰν ὕδατι ψυχρῷ βάπτῃ μεγάλα ἰάχοντα,
> φαρμάσσων· τὸ γὰρ αὖτε σιδήρου γε κράτος ἐστίν·

§ *Aen.* VIII. 450 ; *Georg.* IV. 172:
> "Accipiunt redduntque, alii stridentia tinguunt
> Aera lacu : gemit impositis incudibus Aetna."

‖ II. 3, 3 : καὶ τὸν Κορίνθιον χαλκὸν διάπυρον καὶ θερμὸν ὄντα ὑπὸ ὕδατος τούτου βάπτεσθαι λέγουσιν, ἐπεὶ χαλκός γε οὐκ ἔστι Κορινθίοις.

¶ Pollux, *Onomast.* VII. 409, ed. Simon. Grynaeus, Basil. 1536 : 'Αντιφῶν δὲ εἴρηκε βάψιν χαλκοῦ καὶ σιδήρου.

** Some further remarks from Professor Roberts are given on p. 104.

called 'tempering.' The confusion possibly arises from the French word *trempe* being the word used for hardening, while in English tempering is softening."

According to Dr. Chr. Hostmann, of Celle, all the above passages of the classics must be understood in a different way, for he writes to me: "Any coppersmith can assure you of the fact, that it is altogether impossible to harden copper by immersion in cold water; and for this reason the βαφὴ χαλκοῦ mentioned by some ancient authors cannot be understood and explained as a method of hardening. The fact is this: every malleable metal, and therefore gold, silver, copper, bronze, and wrought-iron, loses its dilatability, after having been for some time wrought or stretched. But then the workman puts the metal into the fire until it becomes incandescent and cools it in cold water. By this means the original flexibility of the metal is restored, and the work can begin anew. This would, therefore, be the softening effect of the immersion in cold water, the βαφὴ χαλκοῦ καὶ σιδήρου. As a proof that the ancients knew this effect perfectly well, I remind you of the important passage in Plutarch, *de Def. Oracul.* c. 47, where he speaks of the celebrated tripod of Glaucus, which was made of wrought-iron and richly ornamented with sculptures, and he adds very rightly, that such a work would have been impossible without the μάλαξις διὰ πυρὸς καὶ ὕδατος βαφήν. Quite in the same sense Sophocles makes Ajax say (verse 651, ed. Tauchnitz): βαφῇ σίδηρος ὡς ἐθηλύνθην στόμα. However, the same Plutarch speaks a little before (cap. 41 and elsewhere), in apparent contradiction with this, of the hardening of iron by immersion. But he was perfectly justified in saying so, for it must be considered that *in this case* the question is not about malleable wrought-iron, but specifically about *steel*, for *this metal alone* and *no other* has the property of being hardened by immersion in cold water. The same is the case in Homer, who, in the celebrated passage, had in view *steel*, not wrought-iron, and far less, of course, copper.

From what precedes it must, therefore, appear certain, that by βαφὴ χαλκοῦ nothing else can be meant than the softening of copper which had been wrought with the hammer. I must also very strongly doubt whether any one of the ancient classical authors *really* speaks of the *hardening* of copper. For the rest you have rightly observed that the ancient kitchen-utensils are harder than the copper of trade. But for this hardness they are indebted solely to the circumstance that, after having been cast, they have been wrought and fashioned with the hammer; for the same reason their surface is less subject to become oxidized and to form the well-known patina."

But as regards iron and steel at all events, the opinion of Professor G. Richard Lepsius, of Darmstadt, and Professor Hugo Bücking, of Kiel, is altogether different; for they write to me on the subject as follows: " It is a well-known fact that iron, like steel, if made red-hot, and then cooled by being suddenly plunged into cold water, acquires a greater amount of hardness than when it is allowed to cool slowly. On this quality of iron depends its applicability to numerous uses; but since it never becomes as hard as steel, it can never take the place of the latter. Steel however, that is, the result of a chemical union of iron with a certain quantity of carbon, was certainly not known to the ancients; at least no fact with which we are acquainted speaks in favour of the supposition. On the other hand, it is true that iron is softened by the action of fire (iron wire, for instance, is annealed to make it more flexible and malleable); and it is well known that pieces of iron, if exposed to a white heat, can be united and welded together by hammering. Hardened iron becomes malleable again, if made red-hot and then allowed to cool *slowly*; whereas, if suddenly plunged into cold water, it once more becomes as hard as before." This is confirmed by Professor W. Chandler Roberts, of the Royal Mint, who writes the following interesting note:

" Steel is hardened, and not tempered, by cooling from a

red heat in cold water; but it must also be remembered that while steel is *hardened* by rapid cooling, certain alloys of copper and tin can be *softened* by rapid cooling. Thus M. Alfred Riche, of the Paris Mint, has shewn that alloys of copper containing much tin can be so hardened by rapid cooling, but this rapid cooling (*la trempe*) produces an almost insensible degree of softening in alloys of copper and tin which contain less than from 6 to 12 per cent. of tin, and it is to this class that the alloys of which analyses are given in the following pages belong."*

There were also found in the temple A some very primitive arrow-heads of bronze or copper, like those represented in *Ilios*, p. 505, under Nos. 931, 933, 942, 944, 946. The Museum of Parma contains several copper arrow-heads of the same shape, which were found in the terramare of the Emilia. I also found one arrow-head with two barbs, like that represented under No. 955, p. 505, in *Ilios*. All these arrow-heads were made to be attached with a string to the shaft, as we find described in Homer.†

I sent to Professor Rudolf Virchow at Berlin the borings of three Trojan battle-axes, a lance-head, a quadrangular weapon like that represented in *Ilios*, p. 482, No. 816, and a brooch. He submitted these borings to the eminent chemist, Prof. Rammelsberg of Berlin, whose analysis gave the following results:

	Tin.	Copper.	Lead.	Iron.
1. Battle-axe:	2·90	97·10	traces	
2. ,,	2·89	97·11	,,	
3. ,,	4·11	95·38	,,	
4. Brooch.	6·27	93·73	,,	
5. Quadrangular weapon	0·84	99·16	,,	
6. Lance-head	5·43	94·57	,,	

---

* "Professor Roberts considers that, unfortunately, the view that copper may be rendered exceptionally hard by the presence of small quantities of rhodium is wholly unsupported by experimental evidence."

† *Il.* IV. 151:

ὡς δὲ ἴδεν νευρόν τε καὶ ὄγκους ἐκτὸς ἰόντας,

Prof. Virchow adds: "Nos. 1 and 2 contain so little tin that they do not answer at all to the common mixture of bronze, such as the analysis of the Orchomenian metals reveals." Of these latter I had sent the borings of a quadrangular weapon like the above, as well as the fragment of a nail, and a whole nail, found by me in my excavation in the Treasury of Orchomenos, and used to attach the bronze plates to the walls; the analysis of which gave—

	Tin.	Copper.	Lead.	Iron.
1. Quadrangular weapon	8·42	90·76	0·32	0·50
2. Fragment of a nail	8·26	91·74	—	traces
3. Entire nail	—	99·53	0·27	0·20

I also sent the borings of a lance-head, a large battle-axe, and two large quadrangular nails, all of which objects had been found in the temple A, for analysis to the celebrated chemist and metallurgist, Dr. Theodor Schuchardt at Görlitz, who obtained the following results:

	Tin.	Copper.	Lead.	Iron.
1. Lance-head	9·04	90·96	—	—
2. Large battle-axe	5·80	93·50	—	0·70
3. Large quadrangular nail	0·45	98·65	—	0·85
4. Largest quadrangular nail	traces	99·55	—	traces

Dr. Schuchardt desires me to add, that the analytical investigation has been principally conducted by his able assistant, Mr. Hugo Schröter. I may add that the bronze found by Professor Rudolf Virchow in his excavations in the prehistoric cemetery of Koban contained from 10 to 12 per cent of tin.*

There was also found in the temple A the very curious object of bronze, No. 36 (p. 106), which seems to be a surgical instrument; further, numerous brooches of copper with spiral or globular heads. No. 37 is an unornamented terra-cotta whorl: it appears to have been nailed to a wall with a copper pin, which is preserved, and its round head

* Rudolf Virchow, *Das Gräberfeld von Koban im Lande der Osseten, Kaukasus*, Berlin, 1883, p. 23.

may be distinctly seen in the engraving. The presence of this pin in the whorl seems rather to corroborate my opinion, that all the whorls served as votive offerings to Athené Ergané, the tutelary deity of Troy.

Of gold there was found in the temple A only a very small and simple unornamented frontlet, and a staff or sceptre knob with a geometrical ornamentation in *repoussé*.

No. 36.—Surgical instrument.
Half size; depth, 8·50 m.

No. 37.—Whorl of terra-cotta in which is stuck a copper or bronze nail with a round head.
Size 1 : 3 ; depth, 8·50 m.

work, which I represent here under No. 38. The reverse side of this object can leave no doubt of its use as a staff button. Just in front of the temple A, and only about a yard to the south of its *antae*, was picked up a bundle of a dozen copper brooches with globular heads, intermingled with earrings of silver and electrum, and fastened together by the cementing action of the carbonate of copper: to the outside of the bundle was cemented by the same agency a gold earring, which is conspicuous in the accompanying engraving, No. 39. It will be seen that the gold earring is of the shape represented by Nos. 754–764, p. 462, in *Ilios*. Of the same form are also the other earrings, but they cannot be seen well in the engraving, as only part of them shows itself.

Regarding this gold earring, which is made of wire

soldered together, I may remark that the art of manufacturing gold wire, and of forming with it objects of art, is mentioned by Homer, and attributed by him to Hephaestus,

No. 38.—Staff or sceptre knob of gold, with a geometrical ornamentation. Size 2 : 3 ; depth, 8·50 m.

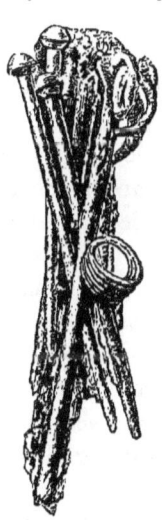

No. 39.—Bundle of bronze Brooches, intermingled with Earrings of silver and electrum, and fastened together by the cementing action of the carbonate of copper : on the outside is attached a gold earring. (Size 2 : 3 ; depth, 8·50 m.)

who made of gold wire the crest of Achilles' helmet,* and the tassels of Athené's aegis ;† he also made a net of wire

---

* *Il.* XVIII. 611, 612 :

τεῦξε δέ οἱ κόρυθα βριαρὴν κροτάφοις ἀραρυῖαν,
καλήν, δαιδαλέην· ἐπὶ δὲ χρύσεον λόφον ἧκεν·

Il. XIX. 380-383 :

. . . .˙. . . περὶ δὲ τρυφάλειαν ἄειρας
κρατὶ θέτο βριαρήν· ἣ δ', ἀστὴρ ὥς, ἀπέλαμπε
ἵππουρις τρυφάλεια· περισσείοντο δ' ἔθειραι
χρύσεαι, ἃς Ἥφαιστος ἵει λόφον ἀμφὶ θαμειάς.

† *Il.* II. 446-448 :

. . . . . . μετὰ δὲ γλαυκῶπις Ἀθήνη
αἰγίδ' ἔχουσ' ἐρίτιμον, ἀγήραον, ἀθανάτην τε·
τῆς ἑκατὸν θύσανοι παγχρύσεοι ἠερέθονται,

to catch Ares and Aphrodité (but it is not stated of what metal it was), which was as fine as the threads of a spider's web.*

It is very remarkable that the art of soldering, which was universally known at Troy, and of which we found there hundreds of examples (as for instance the gold goblet, No. 772, p. 465, and all the gold earrings, such as Nos. 694, 695, 698-708, 752-764, pp. 460, 462 in *Ilios*), was entirely unknown at Mycenae,† where no trace of it was found in the immense gold treasures discovered by me in the royal sepulchres, though these certainly denote a higher civilization than the Trojan antiquities. I have stated in *Ilios*, p. 465, that, according to Mr. Carlo Giuliano, the celebrated London goldsmith and jeweller of antiques, who kindly devoted six hours of his precious time to examining the Trojan jewels with me, "this soldering could only be done by mixing silver with gold, by beating the mixture very fine, and by cutting it into very small pieces, which would melt, whilst the pure gold would not melt; thus the soldering could easily be made by means of the mixture and a little borax: instead of borax, glass might have been used." But Mr. Achilles Postolaccas, keeper of the National Collection of Coins at Athens, calls my attention to the fact that, though this is the method of soldering used by Mr. Giuliano and all goldsmiths and jewellers of the present day, it was certainly not the way in which the ancients soldered; for they knew the art of soldering gold to gold without using any mixture of silver, and without borax. The best proof is, that all the gold soldering done

---

* *Od.* VIII. 279-281 :

πολλὰ δὲ καὶ καθύπερθε μελαθρόφιν ἐξεκέχυντο,
ἧῦτ' ἀράχνια λεπτά, τά γ' οὔ κέ τις οὐδὲ ἴδοιτο,
οὐδὲ θεῶν μακάρων· πέρι γὰρ δολόεντα τέτυκτο.

† I thought I had found some soldering on the Mycenean golden greaves, and stated this at p. 466 in *Ilios*. But it has since been proved that I was mistaken, there being no trace of soldering either on the greaves or on anything else at Mycenae.

now-a-days has (in consequence of the silver and the borax) a dark tint, whereas we never see an ancient gold-soldering which is not perfectly pure. This art of soldering gold to gold, without employing silver or borax, was perfectly well known to the Trojan goldsmith, for all the solderings of the Trojan jewels are perfectly pure, and no dark tint can be seen on them with the strongest lens. Indeed, we cannot look without admiration on the Trojan filigree work (such as the examples on p. 487, Nos. 830, 831; p. 488, No. 834, 835; p. 489, Nos. 841–844, in *Ilios*), when we see that, in the remote antiquity to which this work belongs, the goldsmiths, without a lens, could solder on such almost microscopic pearls, with an art which now baffles the comprehension of the most skilful of the skilful. This art is lost, and it is doubtful whether it will ever be reinvented.

The art of soldering was certainly known at the time of Homer, for he mentions a silver basket belonging to Helen, which had an orifice of gold.* The silver mixing-vessel, also, which Telemachus received from Menelaus, was ornamented with rims of gold.†

With reference to the golden bottle, No. 775, p. 466, in *Ilios*, I may here observe that golden bottles containing oil are mentioned by Homer.‡ I even believe the Homeric word for bottle, "λήκυθος," to be probably nothing else than an abbreviation of ἐλάκυθος, that is to say, ἐλαιόκυθος, a vessel containing oil. The derivation of λήκυθος from ληκέω, 'to crock,' 'to sound,' is altogether impossible.

I may here mention regarding the curious gold ornament represented in *Ilios*, p. 489, Nos. 836, 838, and p. 490,

---

* *Od.* IV. 131, 132:
χρυσέην τ' ἠλακάτην, τάλαρόν θ' ὑπόκυκλον ὕπασσεν,
ἀργύρεον, χρυσῷ δ' ἐπὶ χείλεα κεκράαντο.

† *Od.* IV. 615, 616:
δώσω τοι κρητῆρα τετυγμένον· ἀργύρεος δέ
ἔστιν ἅπας, χρυσῷ δ' ἐπὶ χείλεα κεκράανται.

‡ *Od.* VI. 79:
δῶκεν δὲ χρυσέῃ ἐν ληκύθῳ ὑγρὸν ἔλαιον.

110   THE SECOND CITY: TROY.   [CHAP. III.

No. 853, of which I found so many fine specimens at Troy, and a large number at Mycenae,* that a perfectly similar ornament, but of copper, was found in an ancient sepulchre in the environs of Bologna, and is preserved in the museum of that city. It is an exceedingly curious fact that six ornaments, of exactly the same form, have been found by Bastian among the ancient petroglyphs at Saboya, on the Rio Suarez or Saravita, in Columbia.†

A spectacle-like pattern, similar to Nos. 834, 835, p. 488, Nos. 848, 849, p. 489, which occurs also seventy-two times on the two bracelets, Nos. 873, 874, p. 495, and is frequent on the Mycenae jewels (see *Mycenae*, Nos. 266, 292, 295, 296, 305, 458, 500), has been found by the "Société des Amateurs d'Archéologie du Caucase" in their excavations in the necropolis of Samthawro near Mtskheth, the ancient capital of Georgia.‡ The same pattern appears on a bronze ornament found near Lopöhnen in Prussia,§ on another in the museum at Mitau,‖ on another in the Royal Museum at Berlin,¶ and on another in the Museum at Hanover.** The spectacle-like spiral ornament may also be seen in the form of a mould for casting jewels, which was found by Sir A. H. Layard in his excavations at Koyunjik.†† Professor Rudolf Virchow found the same spectacle-like spiral ornament of bronze in his excavations in the prehistoric cemetery of Koban.‡‡ He reminds us at

---

* See my *Mycenae*, p. 196, Nos. 297, 299.
† Bastian, *Zeitschrift der Berliner Gesellschaft für Erdkunde*, XIII. 1, Pl. 1 and 2.
‡ *Objets d'Antiquité du Musée des Amateurs d'Archéologie au Caucase*, Tiflis, 1877, p. 12, Pl. I. No. 14.
§ Ingvald Undset, *Das erste Auftreten des Eisens in Nord-Europa*, German edition by Miss J. Mestorf, Hamburg, 1882, p. 154, Pl. XVI. 4.
‖ *Ibid.* pp. 168, 170, Pl. XVII. 8.
¶ *Ibid.* p. 205, Pl. XXIII. 4.
** *Ibid.* p. 284, Pl. XXVII. 1.
†† See George Perrot et Charles Chipiez, *Histoire de l'Art*, Paris, 1883, No. 437, p. 766.
‡‡ Rudolf Virchow, *Das Gräberfeld von Koban im Lande der Osseten*, Berlin, 1883, p. 45, Pl. I. fig. 7, and p. 47, Pl. VI. fig. 8; Pl. XI. fig. 10.

the same time * that Mr. Désor found in the lake-dwellings of Auvernier a (bronze?) earring on which a similar ornament was suspended; that Dr. Victor Gross found one of gold in the lake-dwellings of Moeringen,† and that Mr. Angelucci possesses some of the same kind from Naples and Ordona. This spectacle-like ornament is also found in the tombs of Spata.‡

Regarding the six silver wedges found in the great Trojan treasure (see *Ilios*, pp. 470, 471, Nos. 787–792), I have already cited the passage of the *Iliad*, XXIII. 262–270, to prove that the Homeric talent was but very small. I can still cite other passages of the poet to the same effect; such as that, where each of the twelve ἡγήτορες or μέδοντες, and the king himself, presents to Ulysses a talent of gold, which is the last mentioned in the list of the presents.§ In another passage ten gold talents are also mentioned last in the list of presents offered to Menelaus by King Polybus of Egypt.‖ But the most striking proof of the smallness

---

* Virchow, *Ibid.* p. 45.

† This spectacle-like gold spiral ornament is discussed in Dr. Victor Gross's new work, *Les Protohelvètes*, Paris, 1883, p. 78, and represented Pl. XVIII. fig. 19. The author shows in the same work, Pl. XXIII. figs. 12, 21, two perfectly similar spectacle-like spiral ornaments of bronze, of which the former was found at the station of Corcelettes, the latter at the station of Moeringen (see also the same work, p. 78); he further represents in Pl. XI. fig. 3; Pl. XII. fig. 3, and pp. 32, 33, a sword of bronze (found at the station of Corcelettes), having a precisely similar spectacle-like spiral ornament at the lower part of the handle.

‡ A. Dumont et Jules Chaplain, *Les Céramiques de la Grèce Propre*, Paris, 1881, p. 61, No. 36.

§ *Od.* VIII. 390–393:

δώδεκα γὰρ κατὰ δῆμον ἀριπρεπέες βασιλῆες
ἀρχοὶ κραίνουσι, τρισκαιδέκατος δ᾽ ἐγὼ αὐτός·
τῶν οἱ φᾶρος ἕκαστος ἐϋπλυνὲς ἠδὲ χιτῶνα
καὶ χρυσοῖο τάλαντον ἐνείκατε τιμήεντος·

‖ *Od.* IV. 128, 129:

ὃς Μενελάῳ δῶκε δύ᾽ ἀργυρέας ἀσαμίνθους,
δοιοὺς δὲ τρίποδας, δέκα δὲ χρυσοῖο τάλαντα.

of the Homeric talent is given in the passage, where two gold talents are deposited in the midst of the judges, to be presented to him who should pronounce the most equitable judgment.* A *tongue* of gold of 50 shekels is mentioned among the spoil of Jericho, in Josh. vii. 21, 24, which not only reminds us of the shape of the Trojan silver wedges, but also implies an object of small size.

To Prof. Sayce's interesting dissertation † on the same six silver wedges, I have to add that the most ancient coins do not appear to be anterior to the 7th century B.C. Among the ancient Egyptians gold and silver were, as the engineer Winer remarks,‡ estimated by weight. The weights used for these metals had commonly the form of animals, and principally of bulls or oxen; hence the Roman name "pecunia," from "pecus." In like manner, a large number of the Assyrian weights are in the form of ducks. But that Mr. Winer's theory is altogether unsound is proved by the explanation of Friedrich Hultsch,§ to which Dr. Dörpfeld calls my attention: "Much more distinctly than in the case of the Greeks, we can follow up among the Romans the traces of development which, from the most ancient simple exchange by barter, gradually led to the use of coined money. Precisely as among the Greeks at the time of Homer, the ox, and with it the sheep, served until a late period among the Romans as the medium of barter. It really was their oldest money, and consequently they were unable to express this conception better in their language

---

* *Il.* XVIII. 507, 508:

κεῖτο δ' ἄρ' ἐν μέσσοισι δύω χρυσοῖο τάλαντα,
τῷ δόμεν, ὃς μετὰ τοῖσι δίκην ἰθύντατα εἴποι.

† See *Ilios*, pp. 471, 472.

‡ The engineer Winer, in the journal, *Berg- und Hüttenmännische Zeitung*, 1881, No. 46, p. 439. My attention was called to this article by Professor Xavier Landerer at Athens.

§ *Griechische und Römische Metrologie*, Berlin, 1882, p. 254.

than by a derivation from *pecus*.* It is attested with certainty that the most ancient legal penalties were in oxen and sheep, and only much later were they expressed in coined money." †

Dr. Dörpfeld has also called my attention to the highly interesting dissertation on the Homeric talent by Friedrich Hultsch : ‡ " The customary denomination of the principal weight of the Greek system, τάλαντον, is derived from the same root as τλῆναι, and signifies first of all the balance, and then also that which is put on the balance to be weighed, the amount of its weight.§ In Homer it is still the expression for a small gold-weight, the amount of which, as was observed in antiquity by Aristotle and others, cannot be accurately determined. But from the results of modern investigations, it is very probable that the Homeric τάλαντον is identical with that Babylonian-Phoenician weight, which in the Semitic languages is called *shekel*; indeed, the comparison of the various prizes, which the poet mentions in several passages, leads us to suppose, that it was the *heavy shekel* of gold, the double of which was in one case

---

* Varro *de L. L.* 5, 19, "pecus—a quo pecunia universa, quod in pecore pecunia tum consistebat pastoribus ;" Colum. *de R. R.* 6, praef. ; Festus, p. 213 ; Paulus, p. 23, *s. v.* abgregare. See also Marquardt, *Röm. Staatsverw.* II. p. 4 ; Lenormant, I. p. 74, sqq.

† The principal passage is in Festus, p. 202 ; and the fact is further proved by Cic. *de Rep.* 2, 9, 16 ; Varro *de R. R.* 2, 1 ; Pliny *H. N.* 33, 1, 7. Further details are given by Marquardt, p. 4, note 1. In the Lex Aternia Tarpeia of the year 454 B.C., the penalties were still fixed in sheep and oxen, and, instead of these, only 24 years later, penalties in money were introduced. See Lange, *Röm. Altert.* I. p. 620, sqq. ; Marquardt, II. p. 6, sq.

‡ *Griechische und Römische Metrologie,* Berlin, 1882, pp. 128–131.

§ The former interpretation is given by the *Etym. M.*, the latter is based especially on a comparison with the Latin *libra.* According to A. Fick, *Vergleichendes Wörterbuch der Indogermanischen Sprachen,* I. p. 601, τάλαντον is derived from the original root in the European family of languages *tal*, lift, weigh, compare ; this root has then, in the Graeco-Italic family of languages (II. p. 105), the forms *tal* (τάλαντον) and *tol* (Latin tuli, tollo, etc.). For further details see G. Curtius, *Grundzüge der Griechischen Etymologie,* p. 220, sqq.

9

fixed as the fourth prize among five, and the half of which was at another time set out as the last prize of three.* The Homeric talent weighed, therefore, 16·8 grammes (a little above half an ounce Troy); it was brought out in the customary longish-round bar-form, the prototype of the oldest gold stater, which was coined at the beginning of the 7th century B.C., at Phocaea, and in other cities of Asia Minor. As we have just seen, its half was also in circulation in Homer's time; it was a small bar weighing 8·4 grammes, and with this weight it was afterwards issued by Croesus and Darius as a royal coin. Another small talent, the origin of which reaches back to the earliest time of the civilization of Western Asia, is the weight of three staters or six Attic drachms of gold (= 26·2 grammes, or above 4-5ths of an ounce Troy).

"By Greek authors the talent is first mentioned on the occasion of the victory which the Sicilian Greeks won over the Carthaginians at Himera in 480 B.C., and then frequently until the second century B.C., to determine the weight of golden presents of honour or offerings, particularly of wreaths.† It is mentioned by the comic

---

* *Il.* XXIII. 262-270; 740-751. By comparing these passages with the others, where prizes are mentioned, or where talents of gold are spoken of with other references, B. Bortolotti, "Del Talento Omerico" in the *Commentationes Mommsenianae*, Berlin, 1877, pp. 282-290, concludes that the Homeric talent was one shekel of gold, and probably the double of the later Daricus. Under the Persian dominion, such a talent was afterwards fixed, in the Syrian provincial coinage (Brandis, p. 235, below 51, 6), as the principal unit for the small silver coins and for the copper coinage. The Homeric talent is put on a par with the Daricus by the anonymous Alexandrian (*Metrol. Script.* I. p. 301, 6-8; De Lagarde, *Symmict.* I. p. 167, where the text has erroneously δωρικῷ instead of Δαρεικῷ).

† Diod. XI. 26, 3, informs us that Damareta, wife of Gelon king of Syracuse, received from the Carthaginians, after the conclusion of peace, a golden wreath of 100 talents = 2·62 kilogr., nearly $5\frac{3}{4}$ lbs. avoirdupois. He further tells us that Gelon consecrated to the Delphian Apollo, from gratitude for the victory, a golden tripod of 16 talents = 419·1 gr. (about 9-10ths of a lb.).

poet Philemon,* towards the end of the fourth, or at the beginning of the third century B.C., probably to express the value of an Egyptian copper-talent. Besides Nicander of Thyatira, Pollux and Eustathius give the value and weight of the small gold talent as three staters. † The last writer also calls it Macedonian, but the reason of this denomination is uncertain."

There were further found in the temple A some curious objects of ivory, of which I represent five under Nos. 40–44. The object No. 40, of which two examples were found,

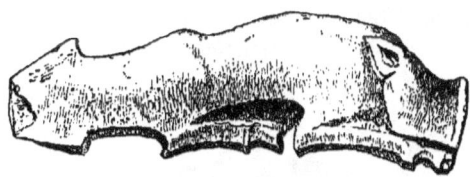

No. 40.—Knife-handle of Ivory. Size 2 : 3 ; depth about 8·50 m.

represents a crouching hog, rudely carved; it is very similar to a like object of ivory given in *Ilios*, p. 423, No. 517, which I supposed at the time to have been used in some way or other in weaving. But I now rather think that all these three crouching hogs have been used as knife handles, because that is certainly the purpose of two very similar objects, in the form of lions, which are in the Assyrian collection in the Louvre. I think this the rather, as the back part of our ivory hog, which is broken off here, but is complete in figure 517 in *Ilios*, runs out into something like a fish-tail, has a vertical opening, and is perforated horizontally.

Much more difficult is it to determine the use of the

---

* *Etymol. M.* under τάλαντον : τὸ τάλαντον κατὰ τοὺς παλαιοὺς χρυσοῦς εἶχε τρεῖς· διὸ καὶ Φιλήμων ὁ κωμικός φησι· Δύ' εἰ λάβοι τάλαντα, χρυσοῦς ἓξ ἔχων ἀποίσεται.

† Nicander in the *Lexic. Seguer.* p. 306, 1 (see Boeckh, p. 40); Pollux, 4, 173, 9, 53; Eustath. *ad Il.* IX. p. 740, 19 (*Metrol. Script.* I. p. 299, 21).

very singular object of ivory, No. 41, which is solid and has five semi-globular projections like loaves of bread, each of which stands on two circular bands; the base is not unlike a small flat boat. The only other object, to which we might fairly compare it, is represented in *Ilios*, p. 514, No. 983; it consists of a substance which is lighter than Egyptian porcelain, and has traces of blue colour on the external side; it has nine semiglobular projections, each of which is surrounded by two impressed circles : it has at one end one perforation, at the other two, by which it was pinned to some other object. But the object before us, No. 41, has no perforation. Nevertheless it may have served as an ornament of a wooden box, as it would be easy to let it

No. 41.—Object of Ivory with 5 globular projections. Size 2 : 3 ; depth about 8·50 m.

into the wood. Regarding the object made of the white substance (*Ilios*, 514, No. 983), I have already expressed the opinion that it must have been imported; and we have, of course, the certainty that the material, at least, for the object No. 41 (viz. ivory) was imported, probably from Egypt. As no other similar ornaments ever occur at Troy, the supposition is natural, that it was imported ready carved. At all events this object, as well as Nos. 40, 42, 43, 44, vividly call to our memory the passage in Homer : " Thither came the Phoenicians, mariners renowned, covetous merchant-men, bringing countless gauds in a black ship." * No. 42 is a lamb of ivory, which was probably also represented as crouching; but its feet, as well as its

---

* *Od.* XV. 415, 416:
      Ἔνθα δὲ Φοίνικες ναυσίκλυτοι ἤλυθον ἄνδρες,
      τρῶκται, μυρί' ἄγοντες ἀθύρματα νηΐ μελαίνῃ.

back part, are broken off. I have no doubt that, like the object represented under No. 40, as well as that represented at p. 423, No. 517, in *Ilios*, it has served as a knife handle.

No. 42.—Knife-handle of Ivory in the form of a Ram. Size 2 : 3 ; depth about 8·50 m.

No. 43.—Small Spoon of Ivory. Size 2 : 3 ; depth about 8·50 m.

Under No. 43 I represent a small spoon of ivory, with the handle broken off. No. 44 is an arrow-head of ivory,

No. 44.—Arrow-head of Ivory. Size 3 : 4 ; depth about 8·50 m.

having two long barbs and a stem, 0,085 mm. long, which must have been fastened in the shaft. There was further found in the temple A a curious object of bone, represented under No. 45 ; it has a hole in the upper end, which can leave no doubt that it has served as the handle of a knife or some other instrument: this seems also to be proved by the two parallel furrows all round the upper end, which have probably been made with flint saws, and must have served to strengthen the upper end with twine. In the handle may be seen hundreds of cuts, apparently made with knives. A similar knife-handle of bone is represented

No. 45.—Knife-handle of Bone. Size 1 : 3 ; depth about 8·50 m.

in *Ilios*, under No. 542, p. 427. To the list of places where such knife-handles can be seen, I may add that there is one in the Egyptian collection in the Louvre.

There were also found two very pretty eggs of aragonite, of which I represent one under No. 46; they probably served as offerings or ex-votos, for we do not know for what else they could have been used: also many sling bullets of haematite or magnetic iron, of which I represent one under No. 47 in the actual size. Some of these sling bullets were much larger, though always of the same shape: the largest found weighed 1130 grammes (nearly 1½ lb. avoirdupois); the second largest, which weighs 520 grammes (nearly 11 ounces), was found in the temple B.

No. 46.—Egg of Aragonite.
Size 2 : 3, depth about 8·50 m.

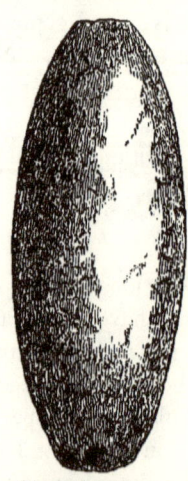

No. 47.—Sling-Bullet of Haematite. Actual size; depth about 8·50 m.

To my argument on sling bullets in *Ilios*, p. 437, I may add that the sling, which is mentioned but twice in Homer, appears to have been, besides the bow, the only weapon of the Locrians.* " He bound up his hand with a sling of

---

* *Il.* XIII. 599, 600:

αὐτὴν δὲ ξυνέδησεν ἐϋστρόφῳ οἰὸς ἀώτῳ,
σφενδόνῃ, ἥν ἄρα οἱ θεράπων ἔχε ποιμένι λαῶν.

Il. XIII. 712–718:

οὐδ' ἄρ' Ὀϊλιάδῃ μεγαλήτορι Λοκροὶ ἕποντο·
οὐ γάρ σφι σταδίῃ ὑσμίνῃ μίμνε φίλον κ.ρ.   [οὐ γὰρ

twisted sheep's wool, which an attendant carried for the shepherd of the people;" and again, "The magnanimous Locrians did not follow the son of Oïleus; for their heart was not firm in the ranged battle; they had no copper helmets with crests of horsehair; they had neither round shields nor ashen lances; but they came to Ilium trusting to their bows and to their slings of twisted sheep's wool; with these arms they did not cease to harass the Trojans and to break their phalanxes." The sling was consequently made of sheep's wool, instead of which leather was used in later times. As the sling is never mentioned in the poems except in these two passages, it appears to have been a weapon which was not much esteemed.*

There were also found in the temple A some axes of diorite, among which I represent the most remarkable under No. 48. It has only one edge; the other end, which is convex, must have been used as a hammer, for it bears the marks of such usage. A groove on each side, half a centimètre deep, proves that the boring had been commenced but abandoned. It is well polished and expanding towards the edge; on all its four sides there are two slightly concave bands, 0·01 m. wide, which give the axe a very pretty appearance.

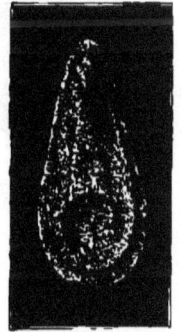

No. 48.—Axe of Diorite. Size 1 : 3; depth about 8·50 m.

Of particular interest is an object of Egyptian porce-

οὐ γὰρ ἔχον κόρυθας χαλκήρεας ἱπποδασείας,
οὐδ' ἔχον ἀσπίδας εὐκύκλους καὶ μείλινα δοῦρα·
ἀλλ' ἄρα τόξοισιν καὶ ἐυστρόφῳ οἶος ἀώτῳ
Ἴλιον εἰς ἅμ' ἕποντο πεποιθότες· οἷσιν ἔπειτα
ταρφέα βάλλοντες, Τρώων ῥήγνυντο φάλαγγας.

* Whoever wishes to learn more about sling-bullets should read Gottfried Semper's excellent work *Ueber die Schleudergeschosse der Alten und über zweckmässige Gestaltung der Wurfkörper im Allgemeinen*, Frankfurt-on-the-Maine, 1859.

lain in the shape of a thick needle with two pointed ends, each of which is perforated; its use is quite unintelligible to us.*

There were further found in the temple A very numerous whorls of terra-cotta with an incised ornamentation: twenty-six of them were found in one heap immediately in front of the pronaos. I give four of them under Nos. 49–52, ornamented with very curious scratchings, which may perhaps turn out to be written characters. The only thing we can recognize is a branch on the left side of the whorl

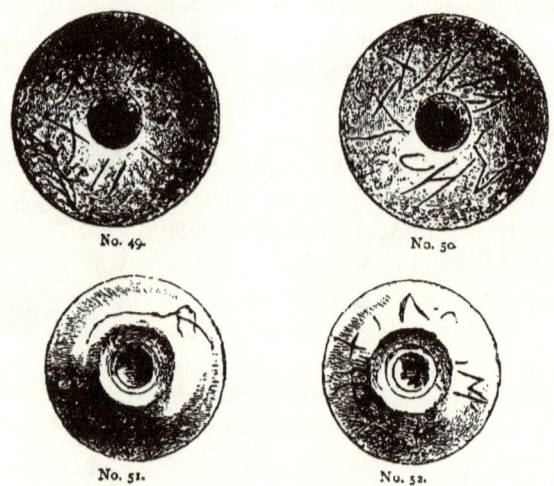

Nos. 49–52.—Four Whorls of Terra-cotta, with incised signs which may be written characters. Size 2:3; depth about 8·50 m.

No. 49. The scratching on the upper part of No. 51 may represent a bird, for two legs and a beak seem to be indicated.

---

* George Perrot et Charles Chipiez, *Histoire de l'Art dans l'Antiquité*, Paris, 1882, I. p. 820, say of Egyptian porcelain : " Ce terme est inexact ; on devrait bien plutôt l'appeler *faïence égyptienne*. Elle (la porcelaine égyptienne) est composée d'un sable blanc, légèrement fondu, que recouvre une glaçure d'émail coloré, faite de silice et de soude, avec addition d'une matière colorante. Elle a été cuite avec assez de soin pour supporter, sans être endommagée, la haute température du four à porcelaine."

Among the different incised patterns on the whorls, the sun ornament, like Nos. 1821, 1823, 1824, 1828, 1829, 1833, 1841, 1845, 1848, in *Ilios*, is the most frequent. I may add that the pattern of No. 1824, representing the sun with his rays, often finds its parallel in the petroglyphs, as for example in those in the grotto of Dowth in Ireland.*

The same may be said of the whorls frequently found with a rude linear representation of three quadrupeds with horns, probably meant for stags, like No. 1881 in *Ilios*. In fact these stags find their most curious parallels among the petroglyphs in the Wadi Mokatteb (written valley), in the Sinaitic peninsula; † on the Rio Uâpes; ‡ in the province of Ceará, in Brazil; § in the ravine called Quebrada de las Inscripciones in Nicaragua.|| The same may be further said of the monstrous Trojan manikins which we see now and then scratched on the whorls or balls, as Nos. 1826, 1883, 1954, 1994 in *Ilios*.¶ Rude linear representations of horned quadrupeds also occur sometimes in the so-called "Gesichtsurnen," or urns with rude human faces in relief, found in the province of Pommerellen, in Prussia; for example, on an urn found in Hoch-Kelpin, in the district of Danzig,** as well as on an urn from the said province preserved in the Royal Museum at Berlin. An urn with impressed drawings of three animals, probably intended for

---

* See Richard Andrée, *Ethnographie. Parallelen und Vergleiche*, p. 270, Pl. II. 9.
† *Idem*, p. 260, Pl. II. fig. 1.
‡ *Idem*, p. 278, Pl. III. fig. 14.
§ *Idem*, p. 278, Pl. III. fig. 16.
|| *Idem*, p. 284, Pl. IV. fig. 31, *a*, *b*, *c*.
¶ See A. von Humboldt, *Ansichten der Natur*, I. 238, 241, 244; and A. von Humboldt und Bonpland, *Reise in den Aequinoctial-Gegenden*, III. 408; Richard Andrée, *Ethnographie, Parallelen und Vergleiche*, p. 278, Pl. III. 15, 16, 19; Pl. IV. 27; Pl. V. 43-52.
** Ingvald Undset, *Das erste Auftreten des Eisens in Nord-Europa*. German edition by Miss J. Mestorf, Hamburg, 1882, p. 129, Pl. XIV. No. 13.

horses, was found in the ancient graveyard of Kluczewo, in the district of Posen; another urn, found in a field of the village of Darzlubie, near Putzig in Prussia, has an incised linear representation of a four-wheeled waggon drawn by two horses, before which stands a man; in front is a man on horseback holding in his right hand a spear, in his left hand the bridle.*

Among the whorls there were five ornamented with four incised 卍, another with five 卐, and a third with only two 卍 and the sign ℼ. As I have represented in *Ilios* a vast number of whorls with these signs (as in Nos. 1849, 1850, 1851, 1852, 1855, 1859, 1905, 1912, &c.), I abstain from giving more of them here. To the long list of places cited at pp. 350, 351 in *Ilios*, I may add that we see the 卐 five times repeated on one of the ancient hut-urns in the Etruscan collection in the Museum of the Vatican at Rome, which are said to have been found below the ancient lava at Marino, near Albano. The 卐 is also very frequent on the small vases found together with similar hut-urns near Corneto (Tarquinii) and preserved in the Museum of this latter city, of which Antonio Frangioni is the obliging keeper. One of these small vases has no less than eight, another four, a third three, and three have two 卐 each. I have already mentioned (*Ilios*, p. 351), a bowl from Yucatan, ornamented with a 卐, in the Berlin Ethnological Museum; and during the last excavations in Yucatan this sign was found several times on ancient pottery.† It seems to have been preserved by the aborigines in various parts of America, for we find it scratched on a pumpkin bottle of the tribe of the Lenguas in Paraguay, which has recently been sent to the Royal Museum at Berlin by a traveller of the Berlin Ethnological

---

* *Verhandlungen der Berliner Gesellschaft für Anthropologie, Ethnologie und Urgeschichte*, Vierzehnter Jahrgang 1882, pp. 392–396 and 532, 533. † See Plongeon, *Fouilles au Yucatan*.

Museum; we also see a 卍 scratched on two terra-cotta bowls of the Pueblos Indians of New Mexico, preserved in the Ethnological section of the Royal Museum at Berlin, to which Mr. Ed. Krause kindly called my attention. A 卍 and a 卐 may further be seen in the Royal Museum at Berlin incised on a balustrade relief of the hall which surrounded the temple of Athené at Pergamum; also a 卍 impressed in the bottom of a terra-cotta vase which was discovered in the district (Feldmark) of Loitz.* It is frequent at Pompeii, and may be seen there sixty times in the mosaic floor of a house. The 卍 and the 卐 may also be seen on one or on both extremities of many cylinders of terra-cotta found in the terramare at Coazze, in the province of Verona, preserved in the Museo Nazionale in the Collegio Romano at Rome; also on the exterior side of a vase-bottom found by Dr. Chr. Hostmann in the ancient cemetery of Darzau, in Hanover;† and again on the bottom of an urn found by Professor Rudolf Virchow in a pre-Slavic tomb near Wachlin in the Prussian province of Pommern.‡ The 卐, in the spiral form, which is of the greatest frequency on the Trojan terra-cotta whorls and the Mycenean gold ornaments, is also represented innumerable times in the sculptured ceiling of the thalamos in the Treasury at Orchomenos.§ Dr. Arthur Milchhoefer‖ calls attention to the occurrence of the 卍 in the spiral form, as well as of the triquetrum and its variations, in the

---

* *Verhandlungen der Berliner Gesellschaft für Anthropologie, Ethnologie und Urgeschichte*, edited by Rudolf Virchow, extraordinary Session of February 10th, 1883.

† Chr. Hostmann, *Der Urnenfriedhof bei Darzau*, Braunschweig, 1874, Pl. VI. No. 53.

‡ See *Verhandlungen der Berliner Gesellschaft für Anthropologie, Ethnologie und Urgeschichte*, Jahrgang 1882, Session of 17th June, pp. 398–402, figs. 4, 5.

§ See my *Orchomenos*, Leipzig, 1881, Pl. 1.

‖ Dr. A. Milchhoefer, *Die Anfänge der Kunst in Griechenland*, Leipzig, 1883, pp. 25, 26.

types of the Lycian coins, which must have taken these signs from a very ancient indigenous ornament. Both the 卐 and the 卍 are very frequent on the most ancient Attic vases with geometrical patterns.

I may here remind the reader of M. E. Burnouf's theory,* that the 卍 and the 卐 represent the two pieces of wood, which were laid crosswise upon one another before the sacrificial altars, in order to produce the sacred fire (*Agni*), and the ends of which were bent round at right angles, and fastened by means of four nails 卐, so that this wooden framework might not be moved; further that the Greek word for cross, σταυρός, is either derived from the root *stri*, which signifies lying upon the earth, and is identical with the Latin *sternere*, or from the Sanskrit word "stâvara," with the meaning "firm, solid, immovable." I might add that in Homer,† the word σταυρός means the same as πάσσαλος or σκόλοψ, a peg or stake. Eustathius remarks that in his time crosses were called στάβαρα, which seems to corroborate M. Burnouf's opinion as to the derivation of the word σταυρός from the Sanskrit " stâvara."

Mr. R. P. Greg, who has been for six years endeavouring to discover the real meaning of the 卐 and the 卍, and who thinks he has now got to the bottom of the question, read an elaborate paper on the subject, on the 23rd of March, 1882, before the Society of Antiquaries in London. He argued: That the two symbols were identical, and, in the first instance, exclusively of early Aryan use and origin; and, whatever their subsequent adaptation may have been, that down to about 600 B.C. it was the emblem or symbol of the supreme Aryan god, Dyaus or Zeus; and later of Indra, the rain-god in India; of Thor or Donnar, among the early Scandinavians and Teutons; and of Perrun or Perkun among the Slavs. Dyaus, originally

---

* *Ilios*, pp. 351, 352. † *Il.* XXIV. 453; *Od.* XIV. 11.

the 'Bright Sky' god, came more especially to mean the god of both sky and air, and the controller of the rain, wind, and lightning; as in Jupiter Tonans and Jupiter Pluvius. Not improbably the emblem itself, resembling two Z's or Zetas placed crosswise, may have been a holy or mysterious cross, intended also to represent the forked lightning by the addition of feet or spurs; and possibly the letter Z itself of the early Attic Greek alphabet may have arisen in the first instance, as being a letter required by the Greeks to give better expression to the earlier sound of *ds* or *ts*, equivalent to the English *j*, as the initial sound of Z in Zeus, and borrowed partly from the emblem itself. Subsequently, in certain cases, the 卍 may have been occasionally employed as a symbol either of the sun or of water; and in the latter case it may have been not improbably the origin of the Greek fret or meander pattern. Later still it was even adopted by the Christians as a suitable variety of their own cross, and became variously modified geometrically, or used as a charm. In India and China, the swastika was adopted and propagated, doubtless by the Buddhists, either as an auspicious sign or a holy emblem. Mr. Greg, in contending for the 卍 being the early emblem of the supreme Aryan god of the sky and air, drew attention further to several suggestive examples from early coins and pottery, as, for example, from Bactria, Greece, and Ilium, where the symbol was appropriately placed, as it were, midway between the solar disk (often at the top) and the earth, water, or animals; and as being sometimes in obvious connection with the bull, as an emblem of Indra or Jove, and with the soma-plant or sacred tree, fire-altars, and other religious emblems.

 Mr. Greg has since informed me that he has found a 卍 on a Hittite cylinder, which, in his belief, shows probably that the Hittites had an Aryan origin or cult. Prof. A. H. Sayce kindly informs me that he saw in the Museum at Carthage four pieces of mosaic with the 卍 upon them;

also in the Museum of Castelvetrano a vase with the same sign. He further informs me that Mr. W. M. Ramsay has copied the dress of the Hittite king sculptured on the rocks of Ibreez in Lycaonia, and that the border of the dress is ornamented with Trojan swastikas. He adds: "I thought we should discover that the Trojan swastika was derived from the Hittites."

I have still to add a few words with regard to the sign ⊓⊓, which, as before mentioned, occurs on one of the terra-cotta whorls, and the sign ⊓⊓⊓. These signs, which are very frequent on the Trojan antiquities, occur also in *relief* over the door and on the back part of nearly every one of the ancient hut-urns found below the lava at Marino, near Albano, or in ancient tombs near Corneto. Only on the hut-urns these signs are a little more ornamented, ⋒ and ⋒. We find it impossible to accept the theory of L. Pigorini and Sir John Lubbock,* that these signs were meant to indicate the windows of the hut-urns, the less so as on both sides of the latter, and immediately above the signs, there are openings of a triangular, a circular, or a semicircular shape, with a projecting frame. Two such hut-urns from Marino, in the Etruscan Collection of the Vatican Museum, have on each side the former sign, while two others have the latter sign, in *relief*. The sign ⋒ is also seen twice in *relief* on a similar hut-urn from Marino, in the Royal Museum at Berlin. Of the five similar hut-urns, of the very same form and fabric, which have been found near Corneto, two have the ⋒, twice in *relief*, two others the ⋒. One of these hut-urns is in the Museo Nazionale in the Collegio Romano at Rome; the others in the Museum of Corneto. I cannot accept Professor Rudolf Virchow's † theory that these signs merely indicated

---

* L. Pigorini and Sir John Lubbock, *Notes on Hut Urns and other objects from Marino near Albano*, London, 1869, p. 12, Plate IX. Nos. 7–9.

† Rudolf Virchow, *Die Hüttenurnen von Marino bei Albano und von Corneto* (Tarquinii). Berlin, 1883.

the beams on the front and back sides of the huts, and that they had no deeper signification. I may add that, in my opinion, the Italian archaeologists are right in claiming for all these hut-urns the time of the 11th or 12th century B.C., and in attributing them to the people who preceded the Etruscans. But, as I have before mentioned, these hut-urns, or at least those of Corneto, abound with bronze fibulae, which never occur in the prehistoric settlements of Troy. The ᝰ also occurs *incised* on two terra-cotta whorls in the Museum of Bologna, and *in relief* on a funeral urn found by Dr. Chr. Hostmann in the ancient necropolis of Darzau in Hanover.*

Prof. A. H. Sayce informs me that the sign ᝰ is found among the Hittite hieroglyphs, and that, in the opinion of some scholars, it signifies a chair. The same friend informs me that Mr. W. M. Ramsay purchased at Kaisariyeh a terra-cotta whorl, identical in material, form, and ornamentation, with the Trojan whorl represented in *Ilios* under No. 1940, at the same time that he bought the clay contract tablets in the Cappadocian cuneiform character. Clay whorls with incised patterns, some of which are similar to those of the Trojan whorls, occur also in Cyprus.

There were further found in the temple A two balls of lustrous black clay, 0,0425 mm. in diameter. The surface of the one is divided by two cross-lines into four equal fields, which are filled up with concave hollows, from 0,004 mm. to 0,005 mm. in diameter, in the centre of each of which is a point. The other ball is very similar to that represented in *Ilios* under No. 1991, for it is likewise ornamented with a sun, a ᝰ, and a zigzag line, which may be intended to represent lightning, and with very numerous concave hollows with a point in the centre. It appears

---

* Chr. Hostmann, *Der Urnenfriedhof bei Darzau*, Braunschweig, 1874, Pl. III. p. 22.

very probable that the primitive artist intended to represent on these, as well as on numerous similar terra-cotta balls found by me at Hissarlik, as Nos. 1986, 1991, 1993, 1999 in *Ilios*, the starry heavens. But I have also found terra-cotta balls, the surface of which is divided by numerous parallel lines into as many zones. As a fair specimen of this kind of balls, I have represented in *Ilios*, p. 349, under Nos. 245, 246, a ball divided by fourteen incised parallel circular lines into fifteen zones, of which two are ornamented with points, and the middle, which is the largest of all, with thirteen 卐 and 卍. A constantly severe critic of mine, Dr. E. Brentano,* of Frankfurt-on-the-Maine, lately made a tremendous attack on me with respect to this ball, which he considered as a weighty argument against the antiquity of the prehistoric ruins at Hissarlik. He wrote: " Nobody who sees this ball will doubt that the zones of the earth are here indicated, not apparently, but in reality. In the middle zone is an *inscription*† which, strange to say, is not mentioned at all in the Appendix III. (the inscriptions of Hissarlik). It is well known that for the globular form of the earth, which was first taught by Pythagoras, Eudoxus of Cnidus (370–360 B.C.) gave the mathematical proofs, and to him is due the division into zones. Crates of Mallus (160–150 B.C.) made at Pergamum a colossal globe, to which the miniature ball in question is in some way a pendant." Dr. Brentano further considered it a fact, established by this ball, that in the city where it was found the globular form of the earth was well known, and was already utilized by the hieratic ceramic art as a pattern in the manufacture of small objects. He therefore took the ball for another proof that the Trojan antiquities are comparatively modern, and proclaimed in the most sarcastic manner

---

* *Troia und Neu-Ilion*, Heilbronn, 1882, p. 73.
† My bitter critic, therefore, recognized in the 卐 and 卍 written characters ! Surely this is a sufficient *reductio ad absurdum !*

that the foundations of my theories are brittle and rotten. Using, as I needs must, all requisite freedom in refuting the arguments of Dr. Brentano, the tone of just severity is restrained by his sad end. While these pages are in the press, he has died by his own hand in a fit of insanity, on the 25th of March, 1883. But strange to say, his most ridiculous criticism is strenuously supported by another constantly severe critic of mine, Professor R. C. Jebb, of Glasgow, who, after having triumphantly repeated Brentano's most absurd of all absurd criticisms, enthusiastically exclaims: "Here again, then, in the stratum of Troy, is an object referable to circa 350–150 B.C." *

Having submitted the Trojan balls to the judgment of the celebrated astronomer, Dr. Julius Schmidt, Director of the Observatory at Athens, I received from him the following letter on the subject: "If an astronomer had to judge of these balls merely by the engravings, and without knowing the place where they had been found, then the circles on some of these figures might indeed deserve his attention. But the circumstance, that the numerous similar balls appear principally to represent mere decorations, warns us to be cautious in our conclusions. If we admit that certain circles on the heavens may be represented here, then I would only attempt to work out the meaning of the balls represented in *Ilios* under Nos. 1986 and 1999, but *not* of Nos. 245, 246, p. 349. Here (on the ball No. 1986) we recognize the equator by two parallel circles, which are close to each other, the two arctic circles, and, in the arch which stands obliquely to the equator, the ecliptic. The black spot in the middle would then indicate the place of the sun at the time of the equinox. But this spot, to which a second one corresponds on the other side of the ball, is in reality a hole, and regarding the ecliptic

---

* "The Ruins of Hissarlik; their relation to the Iliad," in the *Journal of Hellenic Studies*, vol. iii. No. 2, October 1882, p. 192.

Dr. Dörpfeld rightly observes that, if this line were really intended to represent it, the arch would not be one-sided, but it would be indicated on both sides of the equator. If the balls were of the year 1500 B.C., it might be said, that at that time there may have lived in Japan, China, Babylon, and Egypt, some students who knew how to infer from the phenomena of the heavens the most important circles; but that such knowledge could at that time scarcely have passed over to the Greeks, or even to Troy."

In both the temples, A and B, much burnt grain was found. There was also found in the temple A some pottery, of which I represent the most remarkable pieces.

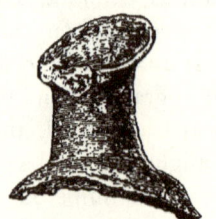

No. 53.—Vase-head. Size 1:3; depth 8·50 m.

No. 54.—Vase with two handles, and two ear-like excrescences perforated vertically. Size 1:3; depth 8·50 m.

No. 53 exhibits a very curious vase-head, of a kind never found before; it is of an unusually fine clay, and of a lustrous black colour; the rim, which expands considerably, gives to the vase-head a peculiarly interesting appearance. Of the same clay and colour is also the vase, No. 54, which has on two of its sides small handles, on the other two sides ear-like excrescences with vertical perforations, to which the holes in the rim correspond; it has a small flat bottom. No. 55 is a curious tripod vase in the form of a hedgehog, of a thick clay and a lustrous dark-brown colour. Unlike all the other Trojan animal-vases, the hedgehog before us has a tail distinctly indicated. As usual, the mouth-piece is here on the hinder part, and joined to the back by a handle;

CHAP. III.] VASE IN THE FORM OF A HEDGEHOG. 131

contiguous to the latter is a second very small handle, which may have served to hang up the vase by a string. There are two incised lines round the lower part of the mouth-piece, and as many round the neck of the animal; the eyes are in relief, the snout or muzzle is turned up.

No. 55.—Tripod-vase in the form of a hedgehog.
Size 1:3; depth about 8·50 m.

No. 56.—Oenochoë of oval form with a long neck
Size 1 : 4; depth about 8·50 m.

To the list of places given in *Ilios*, p. 294, where vases in the form of animals may be seen, I have to add the Museum of Posen, which contains a vase in the form of an ox, having the orifice on the back; it was found in the ancient cemetery of Kazmierz-Komorowo.* I may further mention a tripod-vase with a horse's head, found in a

---

* Professor Dr. F. L. W. Schwartz, *Zweiter Nachtrag zu den Materialen zur praehistorischen Kartographie der Provinz Posen*, Posen, 1880, p. 6, Pl. II. fig. 6.

sepulchre near Corneto and now preserved under No. 244 in the Royal Museum at Berlin, to which Dr. Furtwaengler kindly called my attention; it appears to be approximately of the 8th century B.C.

No. 56 is a lustrous dark-brown *oenochoë* of oval form,

No. 57.—Oenochoë of oval form, with a long straight neck and trefoil mouth. Size 1:4; depth about 8·50 m.

with a convex foot and a very long straight neck, which is joined by a long handle to the body; the rim is bent over all round. Of a somewhat similar shape and a like colour is the oenochoë, No. 57; but its mouth is trefoil and straighter. A vase with a long straight neck, similar to this, but of a lustrous black colour and with a flat bottom, was found below the ancient lava at Marino near Albano, and is preserved in the British Museum; another somewhat similar one is in the collection of Consul A. Bourguignon, partner of Messrs. Meuricoffre & Co. at Naples.

No. 58.—Oenochoë with a long straight neck and a trefoil orifice. Size 1 : 4; depth about 8·50 m.

Still more interesting is the oenochoë No. 58, which is remarkable for its long tall handle and neck, and beautiful straight trefoil mouth. Another highly interesting vase is represented by No. 59: it is of a dark-brown colour, has a flat bottom, and on each side a long vertically perforated excrescence for suspension with a string: each side of the vase is adorned with incised leaf-patterns, hanging down vertically. All these terra-cottas are thoroughly baked, and have evidently been exposed to an intense heat. Another remarkable object found in the temple A is a vase which has been almost altogether melted into a shapeless mass, and thus testifies again to the white heat to which it has been exposed in the catastrophe.

No. 59.—Vase with vertically perforated excrescences and an incised ornamentation of leaf patterns. Size 1:3; depth about 8·50m.

Among the objects found in the temple A I may lastly mention more than a hundred perforated clay cylinders, of the shape of those represented in *Ilios* under Nos. 1200 and 1201, p. 559. To the list of places given on pp. 559 and 560 in *Ilios*, where similar clay cylinders have been found, I may add the terramare of the Emilia, from which several are preserved in the Museo Nazionale in the Collegio Romano at Rome. The British Museum contains also some such clay-cylinders which were found in

Cyprus. Her Majesty Queen Olga, of Greece, who has repeatedly done me the honour to visit my Trojan collection, is of opinion that these clay-cylinders must probably have served as weights for the looms of weavers. I think Her Majesty is perfectly right, for they can hardly have been used for any other purpose.

In the temple B also there was found some pottery, among which were some fragments of a vase perforated like a sieve, such as that represented in *Ilios* under No. 1193, p. 557. Similar vases perforated all over were in general use at Mycenae, for I found numerous fragments of them in my excavations in the Acropolis, as well as in the great treasury excavated by Mrs. Schliemann.* Mr. Ed. Krause, of the Royal Ethnological Museum at Berlin, kindly called my attention to a very curious tripod-vessel of terra-cotta in the form of a one-handled pitcher, which stands on its side, supported by three feet, and is pierced all over with holes like a sieve. It came from Puno in Peru, and is preserved in the Ethnological Collection in the Royal Museum at Berlin. Except the handle, which is placed somewhat differently, it is precisely similar to the sieve-like perforated tripod-vessels, of which No. 327, p. 373, in *Ilios*, is a fair specimen.

Fragments of a large sieve-like perforated vase have also been found in the "Urnenfeld" of Fresdorf in Prussia.† These perforated vases occur also in the terramare of the Emilia, and several fragments of them may be seen in the Museums of Parma and the Collegio Romano at Rome. The prehistoric collection in the Museum of Bologna contains several such fragments of vases perforated all over, found among antiquities of the stone age in the grottoes of Pragatto, Rastellino, and Farneto, in the

---

* See *Mycenae*, fig. 156.
† *Zeitschrift für Ethnologie, Organ der Berliner Gesellschaft für Anthropologie, Ethnologie und Urgeschichte*, 1881, vol. iv. pp. 102, 103.

province of Bologna. The director of this collection, M. Brizio, thinks they may have served for cheese-making. Professor Rudolf Virchow is of the same opinion, the more so as he has seen in a peasant's house in Suggenthal, near Freiburg in Baden, a terra-cotta bowl,* perforated all over like a sieve, still in use for the same purpose. But this use of the sieve-like bowl by no means explains the use of the large sieve-like perforated Trojan vases, with a narrow orifice, like Nos. 1193, 1194, p. 557 in *Ilios*, for unless it be admitted that the vase was knocked to pieces when the cheese was ready, we do not well see how it could be got out. Fragments of similar vases were also found in the lowest layers of *débris* in the Acropolis of Athens, and may be seen in the Acropolis Museum. His Majesty King George of Greece, who has also repeatedly done me the honour to visit my Trojan collection, has expressed the opinion that these sieve-like vases may have served as a sort of flower-pots, for plants sown in them which would creep out by the holes and thus cover the whole outside of the vase. I think His Majesty's opinion is the soundest of all the explanations which have hitherto been given respecting the use of these mysterious vases.

Similar vessels also occur at Hanaï Tepch, as well as in the caverns of Gibraltar, and in the Rinnekaln in Livonia. †

I may further mention a small flat tripod dish of terra-cotta, and twelve wheel-made plates similar to those represented in *Ilios* under Nos. 461-468, on p. 408.

Among the other terra-cotta vases found in the temple B, I find none which has not yet been represented in

---

* *Verhandlungen der Berliner Gesellschaft für Anthropologie, Ethnologie und Urgeschichte*, Jahrgang 1882, Session o: 21st October, p. 485; and Rudolf Virchow, *Alttroianische Gräber und Schädel*, Berlin, 1882, p. 90.

† Rudolf Virchow, *Alttroianische Gräber und Schädel*, Berlin, 1882, p. 90.

Chapters VI. and VII. of *Ilios*, except Nos. 60 and 61, both of which are of a lustrous brown colour, and have the shape of hunting-bottles with one handle. No. 60 has a flat bottom, and on each side of the body a semicircular ornament in relief: on the lower part of the neck we see a protruding circle ornamented with straight incisions, above which is a circular concave depression. The bottle, No. 61 (p. 138), has a convex bottom, and is decorated all over with

No. 60.—Vase in the form of a hunting-bottle with a flat bottom, and an ear-like excrescence on each side. Size 1 : 3 ; depth about 8·50 m.

incised vertical and horizontal lines. To the list of places given on p. 402 in *Ilios*, where terra-cotta bottles of a somewhat similar shape may be seen, I have to add the Egyptian Museums in Florence and Turin.

One thing, which the Trojan terra-cottas have in common with those found in the Italian terramare, is that they have solely the natural colour of the clay, and no artificial painting; if they have any decoration at all, it is either incised or impressed in the clay, or worked out of it in relief.

Of copper or bronze there were found in the temple B a number of brooches with globular or spiral heads, of which latter form I represent two under Nos. 62 and 63; those given in *Ilios* under No. 104, p. 249, and No. 114, p. 250, not being distinct. I further represent here, under Nos. 64 and 65, two of the very curious needles having a protruding semi-globular head; from 0,010 mm. to

No. 61.—Vase in form of a hunting-bottle, with a convex bottom and an incised linear ornamentation. Size 1:3; depth about 8·50 m.

0,013 mm., below this head the needles are slightly beaten out, and they have here a very symmetrical quadrangular perforation, 0,008 mm. long by 0,002 mm. broad in the broadest part; so that, if these brooches were cut off immediately above this hole or eye, they would resemble our present sail-needles. It is a puzzle to us how these needles may have been used; they could certainly not have been employed for sewing, as the large head would have prevented the needle being drawn through the linen. I would there-

CHAP. III.] BRONZE NEEDLES, BROOCHES, &c. 139

fore suggest that they were used as brooches, and that the quadrangular perforation served for suspending some ornament. A perfectly similar brooch of bronze or copper,

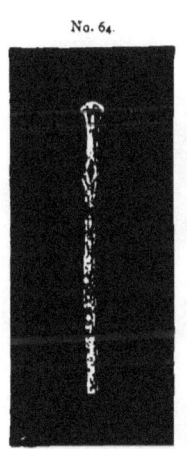
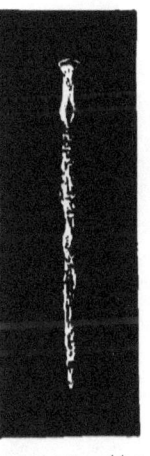

No. 62.   No. 63.   No. 64.   No. 65.   No. 65.

Nos. 62, 63.—Brooches of bronze or copper with spiral heads. Half-size; depth about 8·50 m.

Nos. 64, 65.—Brooches of bronze or copper with a semiglobular head and a quadrangular perforation. Half-size; depth about 8·50 m.

No. 66.—Punch of bronze or copper. Half-size; dept about 8·50 m.

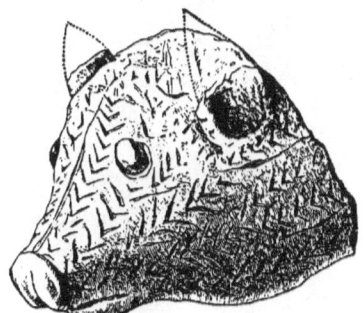

No. 67.—Head of a Vase in the form of a hog, ornamented with incised fish-spine patterns; the eyes are of stone. Half-size; depth about 9 m.

which was found in Cyprus, is in the British Museum. No. 66 is a punch of bronze or copper.

An enormous mass of pottery was found elsewhere in the *débris* of the second settlement. I represent here only

140   THE SECOND CITY: TROY.   [CHAP. III.

such forms as have not occurred before. No. 67 is the very well made head-fragment of a dark-brown vase in the shape of a hog; it is ornamented all over with incised fish-spine

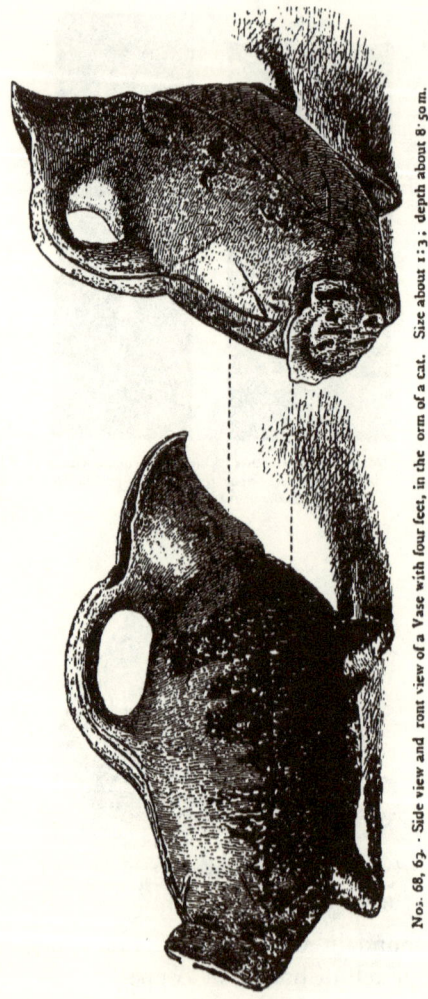

Nos. 68, 69. Side view and front view of a Vase with four feet, in the orm of a cat. Size about 1:3; depth about 8·50m.

patterns; the eyes, which are of stone, are very characteristic. No. 68 presents a side view, and No. 69 a front view, of a very curious animal-vase with four feet. It is difficult to say what animal the primitive artist intended to represent here; the head resembles that of a cat more than anything else. But if a cat was really intended to be represented here, then we must suppose that the vase was imported from Egypt, where the domestic cat appears to have been already introduced from Nubia under the eleventh dynasty. A Trojan artist can hardly have known the domestic cat, which, except in Magna Graecia, was unknown in Greece until a comparatively late period: it is therefore difficult to admit that it could have existed in Asia Minor in the remote antiquity to which the ruins of Troy belong. As usual, the mouthpiece, which is here uncommonly large, is on the hinder part, and is joined to the back by a handle; there is an incised arrow-like ornament on the neck and on both sides.

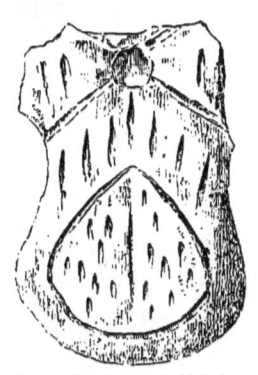

No. 70.—Headless female Idol of terracotta, with an incised ornamentation. Nearly actual size; depth about 9 m.

The taste for animal vases has survived in the Troad, and the Turkish potters' shops in the town of the Dardanelles abound with vases in the form of lions, horses, donkeys, &c.

No. 70 is, no doubt, a headless female idol, of which the arms are also broken off: in its present state it resembles very much the common Trojan stone idols.* The breast is ornamented by two incised lines which cross each other; at the place of their juncture is a concave circle, which is perhaps meant to represent an ornament: to the right and left of it are two short incised strokes, and seven more such below the cross band; beneath them is an incised ornamentation resembling a pear, but no doubt intended to

---

* See *Ilios*, pp. 334–336, Nos. 204–220.

represent the delta or vulva of the goddess; it has a long vertical stroke in the midst; the space in the vulva is filled up with seventeen small strokes.

An idol (?) much ruder still is represented by the figure No. 71; the projections to the right and left are doubtless meant to indicate arms. No. 72 is the head of a very curious terra-cotta idol, the lower part of which was unfortunately not found. Very characteristic are the immense owl-eyes, between which a vertical stroke is no doubt meant to denote the beak: the horizontal stroke above it doubt-

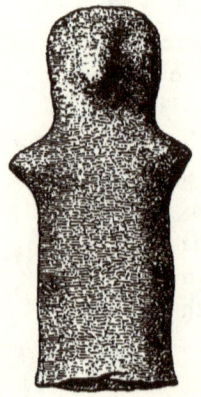

No. 71.—Very rude figure of terra-cotta. Size 3:4; depth about 8 m.

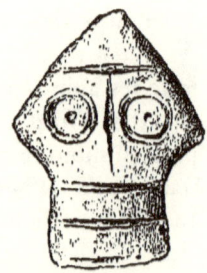

No. 72.—Fragment of an Idol of terra-cotta, with two large owl's eyes. Size 3:4; depth about 8·50 m.

less indicates the eyebrows; three incised lines on the neck may perhaps be meant to represent necklaces.

No. 73 is a terra-cotta *oenochoë*, with a straight neck bent back, a pretty handle, and a convex bottom. The taste for vases with long straight necks has also survived in the Troad, and enormous masses of them may be seen in the Turkish potters' shops in the Dardanelles. In spite of their gildings and their other ornamentation, they cannot be compared to the Trojan vases, either for fabric or for elegance of form. But nevertheless they give us another remarkable proof that, in spite of all political revolutions, certain types of terra-cottas may be preserved in a country for more than three thousand years.

A terra-cotta vase similar to No. 73 is in the Etruscan collection in the Museum of the Vatican, and two are in the Museum at Turin. Another, found at Ovieto, is in the Cypriote collection in the Egyptian Museum at Florence. The Etruscan collection at Corneto (Tarquinii) contains two somewhat similar vases, which are, however, of a much

No. 73.—Oenochoë, with a straight neck and convex bottom. Size 1:4; depth about 9 m.

later period. I may also mention vases with a straight neck, though with a painted linear ornamentation, one of which is in the Cabinet des Médailles, the other in the Musée du Louvre, at Paris. I also found in my excavations at Mycenae ten * similar jugs, but with the spout turned slightly backwards; two similar ones, with necks bent

---

* Instead of only three, as I stated erroneously in *Ilios*, p. 387.

back, are in the Louvre, and two in the private collection of M. Eugène Piot at Paris. All other places where *oenochoae* like No. 73 may be seen are indicated in *Ilios*, p. 387.

Of terra-cottas of the second settlement I further represent under No. 74 a lustrous black tripod vase with four excrescences on the sides, two of which have vertical perforations for suspension. No. 75 is a curious tripod *oenochoë* of a lustrous red colour, with a handle and a straight neck: by a deep compression all round the middle of the body, this *oenochoë* is made to resemble two vases

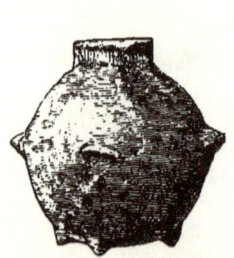

No. 74.—Tripod-vase with four excrescences, two of which are perforated vertically. Size 1:3; depth about 9 in.

No 75.—Tripod Oenochoë with a straight neck. Size 1:3; depth about 9 m.

placed one on the other. No. 76 is a curious vase-cover with two vertically perforated horn-like excrescences: it evidently belonged to a vase having the usual vertically perforated excrescences on the sides, by means of which the cover could be fastened hermetically to the vase. No. 77 represents a lentiform terra-cotta bottle, with a convex bottom and four wart-like excrescences on the body, each of which has a small hollow, and is surrounded by three incised concentric circles, the two larger of which are connected by numerous incised strokes.

There was further found a large mixing-vessel of terra-cotta, like No. 438, p. 403 in *Ilios*, besides fragments of many others. All these κρατῆρες testify to the praiseworthy habit of the ancient Trojans in always drinking their wine mixed with water. That this wise custom was also universally prevalent in the time of Homer, we find confirmed by very numerous passages in the poems; in fact, pure wine was only used for libations to the gods.* But there can be no doubt that in later times the Romans occasionally drank *merum*, and the Greeks ἄκρατον, for it appears by many passages in Athenaeus † that all great drinkers drank

No. 76.—Vase-cover with two vertically perforated horn-like excrescences. Size 1:4; depth about 9 m.

No. 77.—Lentiform terra-cotta Bottle with a convex bottom and four wart-like excrescences. Size 1:4; depth about 9 m.

pure wine. The same author cites the wise but severe law of the Locrian legislator Zaleucus, which interdicted to the Locrians of Magna Graecia (Λοκροὶ 'Επιζεφύριοι), upon pain of death, the drinking of ἄκρατον, except when ordered by a physician.‡

Of lamps, as before, no vestige was discovered; in fact, I have never found a lamp even in the latest prehistoric settlement at Hissarlik, nor in the Lydian settlement, nor at Mycenae, nor at Orchomenos; and it may be taken as certain that in all antiquity, previous to the fifth century B.C.,

---

* *Il.* II. 341, and IV. 159. † *Deipnosophistae*, X.

‡ X. 429 : παρὰ δὲ Λοκροῖς τοῖς 'Επιζεφυρίοις εἴ τις ἄκρατον ἔπιε, μὴ προστάξαντος ἰατροῦ θεραπείας ἕνεκα, θάνατος ἦν ἡ ζημία, Ζαλεύκου τὸν νόμον θέντος.

11

people used torches for giving light. It is true that once in Homer* Pallas Athené lights Ulysses and Telemachus by holding in her hand a λύχνος, which word is generally translated "lamp." But I must absolutely protest against such an interpretation, for Homer knew no kind of lamp proper, and this is confirmed by the Scholiast and by Eustathius. Consequently the λύχνος which Athené carried could not be anything else than a δαΐς, a piece of resinous wood, or a λαμπτήρ (a pan in which dry wood was burned).† We certainly find the oil-lamp mentioned in the *Batrachomyomachia*,‡ but this proves nothing else than that the latter poem is *not* by Homer and belongs to a time centuries later.

Of vases with spouts in the body, and which may have served as babies' feeding-bottles, such as are represented in *Ilios*, pp. 406, 407, under Nos. 443-447, several more were found. Besides the places enumerated in *Ilios*, p. 406, similar bottles with spouts are not rare in the Swiss Lake-dwellings. Two such bottles have been found by the sagacious Dr. Victor Gross in his excavations at the station of Corcelettes in the Lake of Neufchâtel,§ and two at the station of Estavayer.‖ Another, which was found under the ancient tufa at Marino near Albano, is in the Museo Nazionale in the Collegio Romano at Rome.

There were also found half-a-dozen vases having on each side a spiral decoration in relief, like the Cypriote character *ko*, such as is conspicuous on the vases Nos. 306, 354, and

---

* *Od.* XIX. 33, 34:
πάροιθε δὲ Παλλὰς Ἀθήνη,
χρύσεον λύχνον ἔχουσα, φάος περικαλλὲς ἐποίει.

† See *Ilios*, p. 405.

‡ 178-180:
. . . . . ἐπεὶ κακὰ πολλά μ' ἔοργαν,
στέμματα βλάπτοντες καὶ λύχνους εἵνεκ' ἐλαίου.

§ Victor Gross, *Station de Corcelettes*, Neuveville, 1882, Pl. V. fig. 3 et 7.

‖ *Résultat des Recherches exécutées dans les lacs de la Suisse occidentale* par Victor Gross, Zurich, 1876, Pl. XVIII. fig. 7 and 7*a*.

355, pp. 369, 383, 384, in *Ilios*. Two vases with an identical sign on two sides were found, one in a tomb at Monte Conato near Cavriana, the other in the terramare at the station of Coazze in the province of Verona; both are in the Museo Nazionale in the Collegio Romano at Rome. Strange to say, two funeral urns with an identical sign in relief have been found by Chr. Hostmann in the ancient necropolis near Darzau in Hanover.*

There were also found in the ruins of the second settlement, as well as in those of the subsequent prehistoric cities, a large number of those very pretty vase-covers, like Nos. 328-331, p. 374, in *Ilios*, having either a tripod-like handle, or a handle consisting as it were of two arches; in both cases with a large knob; giving to all these vase-covers a crown-like appearance. Dr. Furtwaengler, of the Royal Museum in Berlin, has called my attention to four large Etruscan vases, found at Caere and preserved in the Louvre, which have exactly similar vase-covers. One of them has on its large knob four feet, so that it could be stood upside down and used as a cup. I have noticed in the Etruscan collection in the Louvre a fifth vase-cover of the same form, which stands apart from the other vases of a similar shape. Dr. Furtwaengler has also called my attention to a vase-cover with a similar crown-like handle, but with four vertical perforations by means of which it was fastened on the orifice of a vase having the same number of vertical holes. This vase-cover, which appears to be of the 6th century B.C., is in the Antiquarium of the Royal Museum of Berlin, but the place where it was discovered is not indicated. But, so far as I know, similar vase-covers have not been found elsewhere. Of vase-covers with only one plain handle, like No. 332, p. 375 in *Ilios*, three were found in a sepulchre at Pozzo near Chiusi, and

---

* Chr. Hostmann, *Der Urnenfriedhof bei Darzau in der Provinz Hannover*, Braunschweig, 1874, Pl. I. fig. 9; Pl. V. fig. 46.

are preserved in the Museo Nazionale in the Collegio Romano at Rome.

I may further mention vases or cups consisting of two or three conjoint vessels, similar to No. 356, p. 384, and Nos. 1110, 1111, p. 540, in *Ilios*. To the list of museums given in *Ilios*, p. 384, where similar vessels may be seen, I may add the following examples. A vessel with four cups, but without feet, found in a tomb at Camirus in Rhodes, is preserved in the Musée du Louvre. A vase consisting of three cups joined by hollow arms, found near Petschkendorf in Silesia, is in the Museum at Breslau;[*] a vessel with two conjoined cups is in the Museum at Posen,[†] and a similar one, found in the Neumark, in the Royal Museum in Berlin.[‡] The Museum of Corneto (Tarquinii) contains a large number of vessels with joined cups; but these vases are late Etruscan, and probably more than a thousand years later than their Trojan brethren. The same museum contains a cup exactly similar to that represented in *Ilios*, p. 554, No. 1181. I have to add that a vessel consisting of two conjoined cups, and another of three cups, were found by Dr. Victor Gross in his excavations in the Swiss Lake habitations at the station of Hauterive.[§]

Of lilliputian vases, like those represented at p. 534, Nos. 1054–1078, in *Ilios*, a great many were again found in the *débris* of all the prehistoric settlements of Troy.

I also found two more very rude one-handled long pitchers, like No. 347, p. 381, in *Ilios*, which are exceedingly heavy in the lower part, and appear, therefore, to have been used as buckets to draw water from a well. I noticed two very similar vessels, but with two handles, in the Egyptian collection in the Museum of Turin.

---

[*] Ingvald Undset, *Das erste Auftreten des Eisens in Nord-Europa*, German edition by Miss J. Mestorf, Hamburg, 1882, p. 67, Pl. IX. No. 15.
[†] *Ibid.* p. 85, Pl. XI. 8.   [‡] *Ibid.* p. 187, Pl. XX. 2.
[§] Victor Gross, *Les Protohelvètes*, Paris, 1883, Pl. XXXII. figs. 3, 17.

The gigantic jars (πίθοι) are very numerous in all the four upper prehistoric settlements, and particularly so in the second and third. They served as cellars or as reservoirs for wine or water; their positions in the houses are different: in many cases they are dug into the ground, so that the mouth was on a level with the floor of the house; but most frequently they stand, two, three, four, or five together, on the floor, into which they have been sunk to one-fourth or one-third of their height. Of the jars of the second settlement, with mouths on a level with the floor, a great number may be seen *in situ;* they do not, however, occur in the temples. But it is not worth while to attempt taking them out, for they have been injured so much by the heat of the catastrophe, that they fall to pieces on being exposed to the open air. Of the jars which stood upright in the houses of the second settlement, only the lower part has remained; for, as the third settlers built their houses immediately upon the ruins of the second city, they naturally cut away whatever objects stood out above the ground. It is curious to see how these third settlers planted their jars, now right into the halves of those of the second city which had been left in the *débris*, now into the fragments of brick walls which had remained, now again into their house floors. In general the jars are plain and unornamented, but in many instances they are decorated with an incised ornamentation, representing bands of fish-spines, of concentric circles, of crosses, &c.

As I have stated in *Ilios*, p. 281, two such jars are mentioned in Homer as standing on the ground floor in the hall of the Palace of Zeus. But the poet also mentions them as being used for wine, and placed along the walls of the store-room in the Palace of Ulysses,* in the same

---

* *Od.* II. 340-342:

ἐν δὲ πίθοι οἴνοιο παλαιοῦ ἡδυπότοιο
ἕστασαν, ἄκρητον θεῖον ποτὸν ἐντὸς ἔχοντες,
ἑξείης ποτὶ τοῖχον ἀρηρότες,

way as we often see them placed on the ground floor of the Trojan houses.* In another passage they serve for the same use.† In a fourth passage these πίθοι are called κέραμοι,‡ and are also used as reservoirs for wine: according to Eustathius,§ κέραμοι are πίθοι.

I have mentioned in *Ilios*, p. 281, fragments of terra-cotta plates, from 0,0125 mm. to 0,0167 mm. thick, thoroughly baked and of a dark lustrous red colour, which are peculiar to the second city, and occur in enormous masses in its *débris*, but are never found in any one of the subsequent prehistoric settlements. As they are almost completely flat, having only an insignificant curvature, they have been a great puzzle to me ever since 1871; for I could not believe them to be fragments of vessels, and rather thought them to have been used as a decoration to case the house-walls. But having brought together a number of the largest rim-fragments of them we could find, my architects have proved to me that the rim of all is curved, though almost imperceptibly, and that, therefore, they are the fragments of gigantic dishes, almost flat, *whose diameter must have exceeded* 1 *mètre*. These dishes may have been employed as tables on a frame of wood, and if so, they testify to the cleanliness and good taste of the people. Owing to their enormous size and disproportionate thinness, it is but natural that every one of them should have been broken into a thousand fragments in the great catastrophe. But what strikes me is, that I never found the fragments of one dish together in one spot, so as to be able to recompose it. Except the πίθοι, these gigantic dishes are evidently the only articles of pottery which have been

---

* See the engraving No. 8, p. 33, in *Ilios*.
† *Od.* XXIII. 305 :
   . . . . πολλὸς δὲ πίθων ἠφύσσετο οἶνος.
‡ *Il.* IX. 469 :
   πολλὸν δ' ἐκ κεράμων μέθυ πίνετο τοῖο γέροντος.
§ *Ad Iliadem*, IX. 469.

thoroughly baked at the time of making them. It is therefore evident that the baking was intended to increase the solidity of the dishes: the baking operation must have been easy, as the fire could strike the dishes on both sides at once. All the other pottery had been but slightly baked, but it was thoroughly burnt or baked in the great catastrophe.

Of terra-cotta vases with owl-faces, two wings, and the characteristics of a woman, a very large number was found in all the four upper prehistoric cities, but as they are all more or less like those represented in *Ilios*, Nos. 157–159, pp. 290, 291, Nos. 227–235, pp. 340–343, Nos. 988–991, pp. 521–523, Nos. 1291–1299, pp. 574–576, and for the most part like No. 988, I abstain from representing here any of those last found, and shall only give in the paragraphs on the fourth and fifth settlements the four owl-vases which slightly differ in shape (see pp. 186, 187, 191).

I would call particular attention to the fact, that the Trojan owl-vases have not only the shape of the Trojan idols of marble or trachyte (see *Ilios*, pp. 332–336, Nos. 197–220) but that with their two long wings they have the greatest resemblance to the hundreds of horned or winged idols found by me at Mycenae and Tiryns.*

Of idols of marble a very great number were found. Many of them have an owl-face rudely incised, like figs. 204, 205, 212–218, pp. 334, 336, in *Ilios;* on many others it is merely indicated by a black colour, which I take for black clay, like Nos. 206–210, pp. 334, 335, in *Ilios*. These Trojan idols are so rude, that even the rudest idols found in the Cyclades, and of which I gave a list at p. 338 of *Ilios*, appear masterpieces of workmanship if compared to them. I may add to that list three idols from Paros, and three from Babylon, in the Musée du Louvre, on all of which the vulva is indicated by a triangle.

---

* See *Mycenae*, p. 12, Nos. 8 and 10; Pl. XVII. Nos. 94, 96; p. 72, No. 111.

Of large urns or vases, like those represented in *Ilios*, pp. 398–401, Nos. 419–432, or pp. 541, 542, Nos. 1112, 1119, a vast number were found. Strange as it may appear, urns or vases of like shapes have never yet been found elsewhere. Though I have most carefully examined all the prehistoric collections of Europe, I have not found a single analogue, with the exception of the type of the urn, No. 424, p. 399, in *Ilios*, which is somewhat approached by one in the Museo Nazionale of the Collegio Romano at Rome, found in the necropolis of Carpineto near Cupra Marittima in the province of Ascoli Piceno; and excepting also the shape of the vases, No. 419, p. 398, Nos. 422, 423, p. 399, which is somewhat approached by three vases of the Egyptian Collection in the Museum of Turin.

I found another barrel-vase in fragments, like No. 439, p. 404, in *Ilios*. Dr. Chr. Hostmann calls my attention to a vase of identical form, found in a very ancient tomb near Halberstadt;[*] but that is probably the only one of the same shape ever found outside of Troy or Cyprus.

Of polished black one-handled hand-made plates (or rather bowls) of the shape of No. 455, p. 408, in *Ilios*, two were found. Similar but much ruder one-handled handmade bowls are frequent in the pre-Etruscan tombs of Corneto (Tarquinii), where, strange to say, they always served as covers for the large one-handled funeral urns.

Of very rude wheel-made plates without handles, like those represented under Nos. 456–468, p. 408, in *Ilios*, a vast number was found in the ruins of both the second and third settlements. Those of the second city are always of a dark yellow colour, which I take to be the effect of the heat in the great catastrophe. Similar rude wheel-made plates may be seen, besides the places indicated on p. 408 of *Ilios*, in the Egyptian Collection of the Louvre, which contains two of them.

---

[*] Chr. Hostmann, *Zeitschrift für Ethnologie*, IV. p. 211.

I cannot leave unnoticed the unglazed red wheel-made pottery, which occurs sometimes in the second city; but it is very rare.

I also found in the second, third, and fourth cities, more of those small boat-like cups of but slightly baked clay, like those shewn under Nos. 471–473, p. 409, in *Ilios*, which, in the opinion of Dr. John Percy and Prof. W. Chandler Roberts, have been used in primitive metallurgy. Three similar vessels, found in the ancient tombs near Corneto (Tarquinii), are in the Museum of that city; of four others, found in the terramare of the Emilia, three are in the Museum of Reggio, the fourth in the Museum of Parma; this latter one has rather the form of a small ship, like No. 471, p. 409, in *Ilios*. Now, I am ready to believe that the people of the terramare, like the Trojans, may have used these small vessels in metallurgy, but I am sceptical as to the same use having been made of a similar vessel, which was found in the famous Grotta del Diavolo near Bologna, for the antiquities of which the remote age of the first epoch of the reindeer is claimed,* because the inhabitants of that grotto seem to have been totally unacquainted with metals.

Among my discoveries of this year I may further mention such small rude terra-cotta spoons as those represented under Nos. 474, 475, p. 410, in *Ilios*. Of similar spoons, found in the terramare of the Emilia, one is in the Museum of Reggio, the other in that of Parma. Another spoon of the same sort was found by Dr. Victor Gross in his excavations in the Lake habitations at the station of Hauterive.† I also found some more funnels of terra-cotta, in the second and third settlements, of the same form as No. 476, p. 410. Four very similar funnels of

---

* Avv. Ulderigo Botti, *Grotta del Diavolo*, Bologna, 1871, Pl. IV. fig. 10, p. 36.
† Victor Gross, *Les Protohelvètes*, Paris, 1883, Plate XXXII. fig. 1.

terra-cotta are in the Museum of Parma, with the indication that they were found in the terramare of the Emilia; but the exact station of their discovery is not given. Another very similar terra-cotta funnel, found in the terramare of the Emilia at Imola, Monte Castellaccio, is in the Museo Nazionale in the Collegio Romano at Rome.

Two more rattle-boxes of terra-cotta were found. One of them has the form of a woman, but it is of such rude fabric and so much defaced, that, without having in mind the rattle-box represented in *Ilios*, p. 413, fig. 487, it would hardly be possible to recognize in it the human shape; it has on its lower end some perforations, by means of which it may be seen that it contains small pebbles which produce the rattling noise; but others, such as Nos. 486 and 487, p. 413, in *Ilios*, seem to contain small lumps of bronze or copper, for they produce a metallic sound when shaken. Rattle-boxes of terra-cotta occur also in Swiss lake-dwellings, as well as in Egyptian tombs; one, of oval shape, was found by Dr. Victor Gross in his excavations at the station of Corcelettes in the Lake of Neufchâtel; two similar ones were discovered by M. de Fellenberg in his diggings in the lake dwellings at the station of Moeringen.*

I also found one more of those large well-polished funnels of terra-cotta, lustrous dark-yellow or rather brown, of semi-globular form, with sieve-like holes, of which the only two specimens previously found are represented under Nos. 477 and 478, pp. 410, 411, in *Ilios*. Tripod-vases of terra-cotta with two vertically perforated excrescences on the sides, like those represented in *Ilios*, pp. 357–363, Nos. 252–263, 268–281, were just as abundant as before, so that I was able to collect some hundreds of them.

But still far more plentifully than in any one of my

---

* Dr. Victor Gross, *Station de Corcelettes*, Neuveville, 1882, p. 10, Pl. I. 6.

former excavations at Troy have I now found the long straight goblets, in shape like a trumpet, with two enormous handles, such as Nos. 319, 320, p. 371, and Nos. 321-323, p. 372, in *Ilios*. I have tried to prove by my full dissertation on the subject (pp. 299-302, in *Ilios*) that under the denomination δέπας ἀμφικύπελλον Homer cannot possibly have had in view anything else than a cup with two large handles. This certainly appears to be also proved by the word ἀμφίθετος in Eustathius, which means "with two handles" or ἀμφιφορεύς.* As this form of goblet was in general use in all the four upper prehistoric settlements of Troy, and even occurs among the Lydian pottery of the sixth settlement, I suggested it as highly probable that cups of an identical shape still existed at the time of Homer, and that it is to this very same sort of double-handled goblet that he gives the name of δέπας ἀμφικύπελλον.†

It appears that my arguments have convinced most philologists; and no less an authority than Professor J. Maehly, of Basle, ‡ has accepted it as an undoubted fact, that to the Homeric δέπας ἀμφικύπελλον no other interpretation can be given than that of double-handled simple cup. An authority equally high, Professor Wolfgang Helbig, of Rome,§ now also accepts my theory; he brings forward a long series of new and highly interesting arguments, from which I give the following extracts:

"(p. 221.) The chopin (French *chope*; German *Schoppen*) and the champagne-glass are the images of the extremes of social life." (p. 222.) " In the Homeric poems,

---

* Eustath. apud *Il.* XXIII. 270: Ἀμφίθετος δὲ φιάλη ἡ ἀμφοτέρωθεν αἰρομένη τῶν ὤτων κατὰ τοὺς ἀμφιφορεῖς κ.τ.λ.
† See *Ilios*, pp. 596, 597.
‡ *Blätter für Literarische Unterhaltung*, 1881, Nos. 15, 16.
§ *Annali dell' Instituto di Corrispondenza Archeologica*, vol. liii. pp. 221-238. "*Sopra il Depas Amphikypellon*, Discorso letto da W. Helbig nell' adunanza solenne del 9 decembre 1881."

δέπας ἀμφικύπελλον is the usual name of a drinking-cup, synonymous with which are the oft-recurring abbreviations, δέπας and κύπελλον. The ancient grammarians have limited themselves to explaining the form of the drinking-cups by more or less doubtful etymologies (p. 223) of their names. So it happens that some of them make κύπελλον come from κύπτειν, *bend, curve,* or from κυφός, *curved.* Others explain ἀμφικύπελλον by τὸ ἀμφοτέρωθεν κυπτόμενον, that is to say, a goblet curved all round.* Others again explain κύπελλον as a ποτήριον ἔσω κεκυφός, and therefore ἀμφικύπελλον as a drinking-cup, the whole rim of which is curved equally inwards."† (p. 224.) "Aristarchus and other grammarians supposed the ἀμφικύπελλον to be a cup with curved handles.‡ This hypothesis is the most probable. Winckelmann, § from the analogy of ἀμφιθέατρον, considered ἀμφικύπελλον to mean the goblet with its cover; but this type seems not to have been in use earlier than the time of Alexander the Great."

(p. 225.) "Dr. Henry Schliemann explains δέπας

---

* Schol. *Od.* III. 62 : δέπας ἀμφικύπελλον) τὸ ἀμφοτέρωθεν κυπτόμενον. Schol. *Od.* XIII. 57 : τὸ περιφερές, τὸ πανταχόθεν κεκυφός. Schol. *Od.* XX. 153; Athen. XI. p. 482 E : ἀπὸ γὰρ κυφότητος τὸ κύπελλον, ὥσπερ καὶ τὸ ἀμφικύπελλον (cf. Eustath. ad *Od.* XV. 120, p. 1775, 24, p. 1776, 38), *Etym. Mag.* p. 90, 42 : τὸ ἐκ περιφερείας κύφον. Hesych.: ἀμφικύπελ(λ)ον περιφερὲς ποτήριον. Apoll. *Lex.* p. 25 : ἀμφικύπελλον ἀμφίκυρτον· οἷον περικεκυφωμένον, ὅπερ ἴσον τῷ κεκυρτωμένον. Further, several grammarians maintained that the Homeric goblet had no handles, in order that the continuity of the curve might be in no way interrupted. Athen. XI. 482 F : Σειληνὸς δέ φησι · κύπελλα ἐκπώματα σκύφοις ὅμοια, ὡς καὶ Νίκανδρος ὁ Κολοφώνιος. Hesych. κύπελλον · εἶδος ποτηρίου ἄωτον.

† Eustath. ad *Il.* I.596, p. 158, 41 sqq.; ad *Od.* 1, 142, p. 1402, 26 sqq.

‡ *Etym. Magn.* s. v. ἀμφικύπελλον (pp. 90, 44) : Ἀρίσταρχός φησι σημαίνειν τὴν λέξιν τὴν διὰ τῶν ὤτων ἑκατέρωθεν περιφέρειαν. Athen. XI. c. 24, p. 783 B: Παρθένιος δὲ διὰ τὸ περικεκυρτῶσθαι τὰ ὠτάρια · κυφὸν γὰρ εἶναι τὸ κυρτόν (repeated from Eustath. *Od.* XV. 120, p. 1776, 36) ; XI. c. 65, p. 482 F : ἀμφίκυρτα ἀπὸ τῶν ὤτων. Anicetus apud Eustath. *Od.* XV. 120, p. 1776, 38 : ἀπὸ γὰρ κυφότητος κύπελλον καὶ ἀμφικύπελλον, ὡς οἷον κυρτὸν καὶ ἀμφίκυρτον, ἀπὸ τῶν ὤτων.

§ *Geschichte der Kunst des Alterthums*, XI. 1 paragr. 15.

ἀμφικύπελλον as a goblet with two handles, such as that of which he has found many specimens in his excavations at Troy, as well as in the Acropolis of Mycenae. This opinion seems to be the right one, and we shall here endeavour to prove it. Buttmann* and Frati† suppose that, since Aristotle compares the cells of bees to ἀμφικύπελλα, this must decide the form of the Homeric goblet. Frati mentions handleless vases, found in the necropolis of Villanova, near Bologna, which have indeed the shape indicated by Aristotle,‡ for they are of a cylindrical form contracted somewhat towards the central part. The bottom is nearly in the middle of the cylinder, which forms, consequently, two cups (p. 227).§ But the goblet of Homer cannot have had this type, for in his time it was not customary to drink two different sorts of wine at table. Such a habit would have been in contradiction to the primitive simplicity of the Homeric bill of fare, and the poems have no trace of it. Besides, according to the poems, the δέπας ἀμφικύπελλον served also for dipping out wine from the mixing vessels (κρητῆρες).|| But for this purpose the cylindrical vases from Villanova are altogether unfit. In fact, it would have been necessary to hold the rim of the upper cup in the hand, and to press the vessel down with much force, so as to overcome the

---

* *Lexilogus*, I. pp. 160–162.

† Apud Gozzadini, *Di un sepolcreto etrusco scoperto presso Bologna*, p. 18 (Pl. III. 19, 18) ; cf. Gozzadini, *Intorno ad altre 71 tombe del sepolcreto scoperto presso Bologna*, p. 5.

‡ *Hist. Anim.* IX. 40 (I. p. 624a, 7th ed. Bekker) : αἱ δὲ θυρίδες καὶ αἱ τοῦ μέλιτος καὶ τῶν σχαδόνων ἀμφίστομοι· περὶ γὰρ μίαν βάσιν δύο θυρίδες εἰσίν, ὥσπερ ἡ τῶν ἀμφικυπέλλων, ἡ μὲν ἐντὸς ἡ δ' ἐκτός—a passage quoted by Eustath. *ad Il.* I. 596, p. 158, 45 sqq.

§ Such vases with double cups have been figured by Gozzadini, *Di un sepolcreto etr. scop. presso Bologna*, Pl. III. 19, 18, and *Intorno agli Scavi fatti dal sig. Arnoaldi Veli*, Pl. III. 2 ; see also G. de Mortillet, *Le signe de la croix*, p. 64, fig. 31 ; p. 166, fig. 91. See also Issel, *L'uomo preistorico in Italia*, p. 833, fig. 65, and Crespellani, *Del Sepolcreto scoperto presso Bazzano*, Pl. III. 1.

|| *Il.* III. 295 ; XXIII. 219 sqq.

resistance of the air in the other cup. Such a shape of vase is in contradiction with, and not at all adapted to, the form of goblet which could have been used in libations, or for the welcoming of guests on their arrival. In this case one and the same δέπας ἀμφικύπελλον was handed round among the guests,* and if a new guest arrived, the banquetters welcomed him, presenting to him δέπα ἀμφικύπελλα full of wine; the guest took one of them, drank it up, and gave back the goblet to the person from whom he had received it.† Now it would be very difficult to make such handleless vases full of wine circulate, without spilling the liquid. In fact it would have required the firm hand of the conjuror, not those of banquetters who have already made large libations to Bacchus (p. 228). Besides it is much easier to hold such a handleless cylindrical vase with two hands than with one,‡ whereas the poems expressly state that the δέπας ἀμφικύπελλον was taken with one hand.§ The Villanova vases with a double cup may have received this form because it was the most easy to make. The diaphragm, which separated the two cups, consolidated the sides of the plastic cylinder and prevented them from bending before they were baked."

(p. 229.) "But the fact, that Aristotle describes an ἀμφικύπελλον as a goblet forming a double vessel, does not prove that the δέπας ἀμφικύπελλον of the poems had the same form. Aristotle himself has not said so, and even if we supposed that he recognized in the ἀμφικύπελλον of his time a direct descendant from the Homeric goblet, his

---

* *Od.* III. 35 sqq.
† *Il.* XV. 86; XXIV. 101, 102.
‡ According to the measures which Count Gozzadini has communicated to me, the larger internal diameter of these vases varies between 0,124 and 0,150 mm.; the smaller one, between 0,075 and 0,121 mm.
§ *e.g. Od.* XIII. 57:

'Αρήτῃ δ' ἐν χειρὶ τίθει δέπας ἀμφικύπελλον,

XXII. 17:

δέπας δέ οἱ ἔκπεσε χειρός.

opinion would have been a mere conjecture. We know besides that the word κύπελλον, which in the poems is synonymous with δέπας ἀμφικύπελλον, signified in other Greek dialects a different type from that indicated by Aristotle; the Cypriots called by this name a goblet with two handles, the Cretans (p. 230) a goblet with two or with four."* Now a name which was in general use among Cypriots has in our enquiry the same and even greater weight than a designation employed by Aristotle, for it is well known that the Greek population of that island preserved many peculiarities of the Homeric language.† Professor Helbig goes on to repeat the Homeric testimonies, which were first pointed out by me (see *Ilios*, pp. 299-301), that δέπας ἀμφικύπελλον, δέπας, κύπελλον, ἄλεισον, and ἄλεισον ἄμφωτον, are synonymous, and he thinks that from the same Homeric evidence Aristarchus must have taken the idea of the two handles of the δέπας ἀμφικύπελλον. (p. 231.) "Drinking-cups with a double vessel and two handles cannot have existed, because such a goblet has never yet been found, and it has left no trace of its existence among the monumental evidence. The Homeric δέπας ἀμφικύπελλον can have been nothing else than a simple goblet with two handles, and this theory corresponds with the monumental examples, because, as Dr. Schliemann's excavations at Troy and Mycenae have proved, this kind of drinking-cup was in common and general use long before the Homeric poems originated

---

* Professor W. Helbig seems not to have been aware that I had cited these instances in *Ilios*, p. 302.

† This peculiarity of the Cypriot dialect has been noticed by Deecke and Siegesmund, apud G. Curtius, *Studien zur griechischen und lateinischen Grammatik*, VII. (1875) p. 262; also by M. Bréal, *Sur le déchiffrement des inscriptions cypriotes*, pp. 16, 17 (*Journal des savants*, Août et Sept. 1877); further by Ahrens in the *Philologus*, XXXV. pp. 36, 49. We may also remind the reader that the Cypriots preserved the use of the Homeric war-chariots till the beginning of the fifth century B.C. Herodot. V. 113.

(p. 232). The same may be said of the examples which follow in date the Homeric age, in the cemeteries of Camirus and Etruria.* To this evidence may be added, that in later times also this type of goblet occupied a place of great importance in the rites of worship; on sepulchral monuments, priests hold it in their hands as a distinctive mark of their dignity.† It is nearly always the attribute of Bacchus, the god of wine,‡ and it is never missing in the hands of the Chthonian god in Spartan relief sculptures.§ The later Greeks call such a goblet κάνθαρος, whilst an Ionian contemporary of the Homeric poems would have called it δέπας ἀμφικύπελλον or ἄλεισον. Such a type of goblet suits all the uses of it mentioned in the Homeric poems (p. 233). A simple goblet with two handles was suitable for dipping out wine from the mixing vessel (κρητήρ); held by one handle, it could be lifted to the mouth; it was well adapted to be handed round among the guests at the libations, and to be offered by the banquetters to the arriving guest. The handles are either horizontal ‖ or vertical ; ¶ but the indications in the poems do not give us to understand which of the two types was preferred in the Homeric age."

(p. 234.) *Etymologies.*—" G. Curtius ** compares κύπελ-

---

* Salzmann, *Nécropole de Camiros*, Pl. 2, 33, 38.

† *E.g.* on the stélé of Lyseas, *Mittheilungen des Archaeologischen Instituts in Athen*, 1879, Pl. I. p. 41.

‡ It is also held in hand by the archaic idol of Bacchus on the vase figured in the *Mon. dell' Inst.* VI. Pl. XXXVII.

§ *Mittheilungen des Archaeologischen Instituts in Athen*, 1877, Pl. XX., XXIII., XXIV.

‖ Such are two goblets from Camirus (Salzmann, *Nécropole de Camiros*, Pl. 33, 38), published by Urlichs, *Zwei Vasen ältesten Stils*, Würzburg, 1874.

¶ So are all the goblets found by Schliemann at Troy and at Mycenae.

** *Grundzüge der griechischen Etymologie*, 4th ed. p. 158. For the rest, the same scholar, to whom I wrote, submitting my etymology to his authoritative judgment, kindly answered me that he thinks it admissible, and furnished me some materials to substantiate it still further.

λον with κύπη, 'cavern,' and cup-a, 'barrel.' If this were right, then ἀμφικύπελλον would be a goblet with a double vessel, which we have found to be inadmissible. If the δέπας ἀμφικύπελλον means a goblet with two handles, then it seems obvious that the root is καπ-, as in *capere*. As the Latins formed from this root *cap-ulus*, a handle, *cap-i-s*, a cup or goblet with a handle, the Umbrians *cap-i-s*, which has the same signification as the last-mentioned Latin word, so it appears highly probable that in remote antiquity the Greeks made of it a substantive κυπ-έλη (cf. νεφ-έλη), handle. The υ being an Aeolic peculiarity, κυπ-έλη would be connected with κώπ-η, a common word to designate a 'handle,' as πρύτανις is connected with πρό, ἀμύμων with μῶμος, πίσυρες with τέσσαρες, κύπη with κάπη (p. 235).* From κυπέλη was afterwards formed an adjective κυπέλ-ιο-ς, κύπελλος (cf. φύλλον = *folium*, ἄλλος = *alius*) to express 'handled,' and hence ἀμφικύπελλος, 'furnished with handles on both sides.' At the time of Aristotle the word ἀμφικύπελλον may have had a different meaning from that which it had in Homer, and it may have designated a vase with two cups. Even in Homer κύπελλον is employed as a substantive without δέπας; in the course of time, it may well have designated simply a cup, with or without handles. It was then but natural that Aristotle should have called a vase with two cups ἀμφικύπελλον. The δέπας ἀμφικύπελλον from which Ulysses drank when he took leave of Arete, as well as the δέπα ἀμφικύπελλα which we see in the hands of the suitors of Penelope, must therefore be supposed to have been similar to the κάνθαρος of Bacchus.

"This fact is not without importance for judging of the state of society at the time of Homer. The civilization of the Greeks at the time of the poems presents a singular mixture of incongruous elements. On one hand we see rem-

---

* I do not include here the word *cupa*, by which Cato, *De Re Rustica*, 21, indicates the handle of an oil-mill, for the quantity of the *u* is unknown, and it may be that the word is derived from κώπη.

nants of the primitive Indo-Germanic stage of barbarism. Achilles still honours the shade of Patroclus with human sacrifices (p. 236).* Cleanliness, which is one of the most characteristic qualities of the classical time, leaves much to be desired.† The use of the bath is still rare; the food is of a primitive simplicity.‡ On the other hand, with these barbarous elements are mingled the refinements of Oriental civilization; elegance and luxury in dress, particularly that of the women. The wives of the *basileis*, in their costumes of the Asiatic style, resemble rather the Odalisces (women of the harem) of King Solomon than the Athenian women of the Periclean epoch, and exhale the scent of Asiatic perfumes,§ which contrasts strangely with that rising from the dung in the courtyard.‖ But the people whose external life generally presents such a mixture of barbarism and Asiatic luxury, are in the development of their inward feelings, already quite Hellenic or classical. This quality finds a splendid expression in the plastic precision of the epic descriptions. The enthusiasm for physical beauty is truly classical. In no popular poetry does any figure exist, which represents, so fully as Helen, the daemonic power of beauty. When Hector is slain and stripped of his armour, the Achaeans admire the perfect form of his naked body.¶ They have already the same aesthetic sentiment which, many centuries later, the Athenian warriors manifested near Plataea before the corpse of the Persian general Masistius ** (p. 237). The types of the divinities

---

* *Il.* XVIII. 336; XXI. 27–32; XXIII. 175.
† Helbig, *die Italiker in der Po-Ebene*, p. 4.
‡ Idem, pp. 74–76.
§ *Il.* XIV. 171–174; XXIII. 185–187; *Od.* II. 339; VIII. 364; XVIII. 192–194; *Hymn. hom.* IV. (in Venerem), 61; XXIV. 3; *Il.* VI. 483: κηώδεϊ κόλπῳ (of Andromache). Cf. Hehn, *Kulturpflanzen und Hausthiere*, 3rd ed. pp. 90–93.
‖ *Il.* XXIV. 640; *Od.* XVII. 290–300.
¶ *Il.* XXII. 370, cf. also XXII. 71–76.
** Herodotus, IX. 25.

presented themselves before their mind as very like those expressed by the art of the 5th century b.c., and the celebrated verses of the *Iliad*, which describe how Zeus nods assent to the prayer of Thetis, already contain the essential conception which Phidias represented in his Olympian Jove.* There was only wanted the capacity to give to the poetical ideas an adequate form in clay or stone." Prof. Helbig goes on to say that his lecture aimed at establishing a new fact which unites the social life of the contemporaries of Homer with that of the classical period : " the goblet with two handles, which the Ionians used when the Homeric songs first resounded at their banquets, was the direct ancestor of the high κάνθαρος, as well as of the flat and finely profiled κύλιξ, which glittered in the hands of Pericles and Sophocles."

In a postscript, Professor Helbig states that he had consulted Mr. Bezzenberger on the etymology of κύπελλον, and that the latter answered, "If you put κύπελλον in relation with *capere*, I see only a slight difficulty in the fact that, in the words which are certainly allied to *capere*, the *a* remains unchanged (Gothic *haban*, Lithuanian *kampt*, &c.), and that the words ἀμύμων, πίσυρες, πρύτανις, &c., which you cited as analogies, belong to a category which is slightly different from a word κύπελλον derived from καπ-. Notwithstanding this, your etymology can be sustained; but I would support it further by pointing to κυπασσίς, which is founded on κυπασσο, corresponding to the Latin *capitiu-m*. I would also not lose sight of the analogy of

---

* *Il.* i. 528-530:

Ἦ, καὶ κυανέῃσιν ἐπ' ὀφρύσι νεῦσε Κρονίων·
ἀμβρόσιαι δ' ἄρα χαῖται ἐπερρώσαντο ἄνακτος
κρατὸς ἀπ' ἀθανάτοιο· μέγαν δ' ἐλέλιξεν Ὄλυμπον.

Besides the Olympian Jove of Phidias, these lines gave Milton the pattern for those sublime verses in the *Paradise Lost* (III. 135-137):

" Thus while God spake, ambrosial fragrance fill'd
All heaven, and in the blessed spirits elect
Sense of new joy ineffable diffused."

the German words, Gefäss, Fass, fassen. But I would ask whether the root of κύπελλον must not be sought for in the Lithuanian *kuprs*, the ancient German *hovar*, 'a boss,' the Lithuanian *kùmpis*, 'curved,' the ancient German *hubil*, 'hill,' &c. Then the comparison could be maintained as to κύπη, *cupa*, &c.; and ἀμφικύπελλον would in like

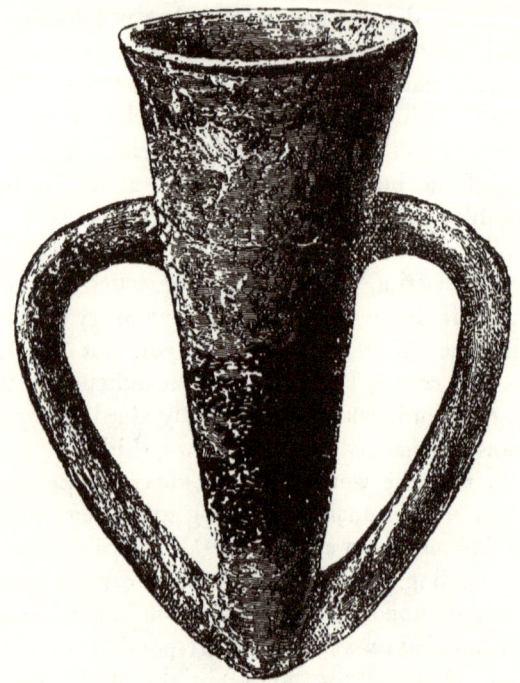

No. 78.—Lustrous brown Goblet with two handles (δέπας ἀμφικύπελλον). Size 1:3; depth about 9 m.

manner signify 'provided with two bosses, or with two handles.'"

Among the double-handled goblets found in my Trojan campaign of 1882 there are some of very large size. The largest of them, which has the shape of the cup No. 321, p. 372, in *Ilios*, contains not less than ten bottles of Bordeaux wine; filled with wine it would therefore be sufficient for a company of forty persons, if each of them were supposed to drink as much as a quarter of a bottle. I represent here under No. 78 and No. 79, two of these goblets which were found in the second city, and which have a somewhat different form from those represented in *Ilios*.

With but few exceptions, these double-handled cups are always wheel-made. All the unpolished plates, like those represented at p. 408, Nos. 461-468, in *Ilios*, are also

No. 79.—Lustrous dark-brown Goblet with two handles (δέπας ἀμφικύπελλον). Size 1·3; depth about 9 in.

wheel-made. But otherwise wheel-made terra-cottas are exceedingly rare, nearly all the pottery being hand-made.

One of my most interesting discoveries in 1882 was a small treasure of objects of copper and bronze, which was found in the layer of *débris* of the second settlement, at the place marked *r* on Plan I. in *Ilios*, where I had found a gold treasure on the 21st of October, 1878.* It consisted

---

* See *Ilios*, p. 490.

of two quadrangular nails, 0·09 m. and 0·18 m. long respectively, like those found in the temple A, but without disks; of six well-preserved but very plain bracelets, two of which are treble; of three small battle-axes, from 0,105 mm. to

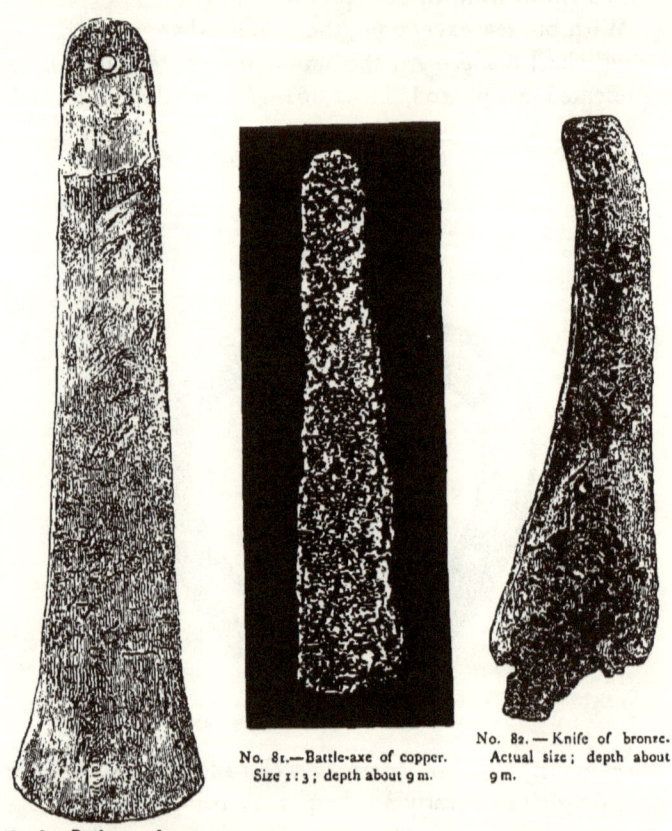

No. 81.—Battle-axe of copper. Size 1:3; depth about 9 m.

No. 82.— Knife of bronze. Actual size; depth about 9 m.

No. 80.—Battle-axe of copper with a perforation in the upper end. Actual size; depth about 9 m.

0,120 mm. long, of which two have the upper end perforated. I represent one of these in the actual size under No. 80. The use of the perforation is not clear to me: may these perforated battle-axes perhaps have been used as chisels, and may the artist have used the perforation to suspend them on his belt? I may here mention that the British Museum contains six battle-axes of copper or bronze of a similar shape, which were found in the island of Thermia in the Greek Archipelago, and of which three are perforated in like manner.

There were also a large battle-axe, 0·23 m. long, which I give here under No. 81, and the lower part of another. Also a curious object of copper in the form of a seal, on which however no engraved sign is visible. Further, three small but well-preserved knives of bronze, of which I represent one under No. 82; a bronze dagger, precisely similar to that found in the temple A, and represented before under No. 34, but rolled up in the conflagration,

No. 83.—Ring of bronze or copper. Size 2 : 3 ; depth 9 m.

so that it forms nearly a circle, like the dagger No. 813, p. 482, in *Ilios*. The treasure further contained a bronze lance of the usual Trojan form, such as I have represented under No. 33, and a most curious ring of bronze or copper, which I represent under No. 83. It is of the size of our napkin rings, but rather thick and therefore very heavy; it is 0,045 mm. broad and 0,068 mm. in diameter; it has five compartments, each ornamented with a cross. The use of this ring is altogether a riddle to us.

168   THE SECOND CITY: TROY.   [CHAP. III.

But by far the most interesting object of the little treasure was a copper or bronze idol of the most primitive form, which I represent here, under No. 84, in about 7-8ths of the size. It has an owl's head, and round protruding eyes, between which the beak is conspicuous. There is a hole in each ear, which, however, does not go through, and therefore cannot have served for suspension. The neck is disproportionately long, indeed, fully twice as long as a human figure of this size would have; no breasts are indicated; the right arm is represented by a shapeless projection, which is bent round so as to make the end, where the hand ought to be, rest on the place where the right breast ought to be; and this circumstance can hardly leave a doubt that a female figure was intended. The left arm is broken off; but the stump which remains of it extends too far horizontally to admit the supposition that this arm could have had an attitude similar to that of the right arm; we rather think it stood out in a straight line, and this is also probably the reason that it was broken when the idol fell. No delta or vulva is indicated. The legs are separated: probably merely to consolidate them, a shapeless piece of copper has been soldered to them from behind, which protrudes 0,012 mm. below

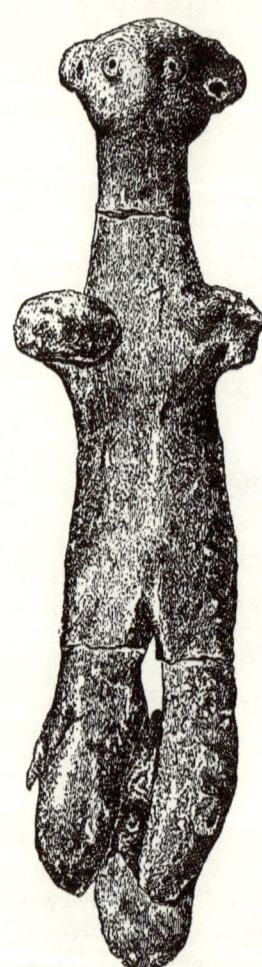

No. 84.—Female Idol of bronze or copper.
Size about 7:8; depth about 9 m.

the feet, and ought not to be mistaken for a stay or prop, because it can never have served as such, for the simple reason that it is longer than the feet, and is fastened almost parallel with them. But it is difficult to say how the Trojans may have managed to place the idol upright; its back has no marks of any fastenings, and we cannot think they could have suspended it with a wire round the neck, for in later times at least that would have been considered as a sacrilegious act, and have revolted the religious feelings of the people. We presume, therefore, that the shapeless piece of copper, which we see projecting below the feet, may have been sunk into a wooden stand; we see no other way to explain how the idol could have been placed upright.

The figure is 0,155 mm. long, and weighs 440 grammes (nearly 1 lb. avoird.). I think it probable that it is a copy or imitation of the famous Palladium, which was fabled to have fallen from heaven,* the original of which was probably much larger, and of wood. Fortunately, as may be seen in the engraving, it had broken into three fragments; I am indebted to this lucky circumstance for having obtained it in the division with the Turkish Government; for the three pieces were covered with carbonate of copper and dirt, and altogether undiscernible to an inexperienced eye.

Among the objects found I may further mention many fragments of stone moulds, as well as three entire ones, all of mica slate; one of them has a bed in the form of a ㅜ, such as we see in the mould, p. 435, No. 602, in *Ilios;* the two others have the shape of the moulds, Nos. 599, 600, p. 433, in *Ilios*, with beds for similar weapons or instruments on six sides. Conspicuous among the forms is the disk-like one which we see in Nos. 599, 600, and which can in our opinion only have served to cast copper

---

* Apollodorus, III. 2, 3 : τῷ δὲ Διὰ σημεῖον εὐξάμενος αὐτῷ τι φανῆναι, μεθ' ἡμέραν τὸ διϊπετὲς Παλλάδιον πρὸ τῆς σκηνῆς κείμενον ἐθεάσατο.

disks to serve as nail-heads, such as we see on the nail No. 28. It deserves particular attention that in these Trojan moulds the beds have exactly the size of the whole weapon or implement which was to be cast. The fused copper was therefore poured into the forms, and these were simply covered with a flat stone. A mould likewise of mica slate, and of exactly the same shape and size as these Trojan moulds, and having, like them, deep beds for the entire weapon or implement, was found in the terramare of Gozzano, in the province of Modena, and is preserved in

No. 85.—Mould of Mica Slate. Size 1 : 3 ; depth about 9 m.

the Museo Nazionale in the Collegio Romano at Rome; but it has the beds only on four sides, and not on six as in the Trojan moulds. This kind of mould is the most common at Troy. The other Trojan moulds contain beds having exactly the size of the arms or implements, but *only half their depth*. Moulds of this kind, of which I represent one under No. 85, have always the bed only on one side, and never on more. As the bed in each of these stones represents only one-half of the thickness of the object to be cast, there were necessarily always two stones, whose beds contained conjointly the entire form. These two stones having been fitted exactly on each other, the whole mould was complete. As we see in No. 85, in each of these moulds there is a little furrow leading from the border to the bed, and when both stones were joined, and consequently the two furrows fitted exactly on each other, they constituted together a small funnel-like tubular hole, through which the liquid metal was poured into the mould. In general each mould of this kind has two perforations, by means of which the two halves were fastened together (see No. 603, p. 435, in *Ilios*); but the stone before us, No. 85, has no such perforation. Numerous moulds of this kind, of sandstone, terra-cotta, or bronze, have been found, principally by the enterprising Dr. Victor Gross, in his excavations in the Swiss Lake-habitations at the stations of Estavayer, Corcelettes, Moeringen, Auvernier, Cortaillod, etc.* Most of these moulds have four perforations, one in each corner; in some of these holes Dr. Victor Gross still found the pegs of wood by means of which the two halves of the moulds were attached to each other.†

Of stone disks with a hole in the centre many were found in the second city, as well as in the three upper pre-historic settlements. Similar disks found in the terramare of the Emilia are in the Museum of Parma, where may also be seen clay disks of the same size, found in the terramare. Such perforated clay disks occur also at Hissarlik, but they are here always much smaller.

There were further found, one more egg of aragonite, beautifully polished, and four fine axes of jade (nephrite), similar to those represented in *Ilios* under Nos. 86, 87, 89, on p. 238; three of them are of green, the fourth of white jade. This latter kind of jade is exceedingly rare and has never yet been found worked into an axe, except in one specimen found by me some years ago at Troy (see

---

* Victor Gross, *Les Protohelvètes*, Paris, 1883, pp. 53–63, Pl. XXVII. Nos. 10–14; Pl. XXVIII. Nos. 1–6; Pl. XXIX. Nos. 1–12; Pl. XXX. Nos. 1–7. † *Op. cit.* pp. 56, 57.

Ilios, p. 573, No. 1288). This is therefore only the second white jade axe which has been found up to this time. I may here add that five more green jade axes were found in this last Trojan campaign, in the *débris* of the fourth and fifth prehistoric settlements. According to Mr. N. J. Witkowsky,* "jade belongs to the neolithic period. The valley of Yarkand gives white, the environs of the Lake of Baikal green jade. The largest piece of green jade in the Mausoleum of Tamerlane at Samarkand is 2·25 m. long, 0·45 m. high, and weighs 50 poods = 1805·6 pounds Troy."

There were also found a large number of axes of diorite, like Nos. 667-670, p. 445, in *Ilios*, as well as an entire well-polished double-edged axe of green-gabbro rock, like No. 620, p. 438, and some halves of the same kind of axes, like No. 91, p. 244, in *Ilios*. Whetstones of green or black slate, with a perforation at one end, like No. 101, p. 248, in *Ilios*, are very frequent here, as well as in all the other prehistoric cities of Troy. I also found a large number of polishing-stones of porphyry or jasper, which were used to smooth the still unbaked pottery, like those represented in *Ilios*, p. 443, under Nos. 645, 647, 649; and badly polished perforated hammers of granite, as well as a large number of very rude ones unperforated. No. 86 is a stone hammer with grooves on either side, which prove that the operation of perforating the instrument had been commenced, but abandoned. There was also found a curious object of white marble, which I represent here under No. 87. From its shape it can hardly be anything else than a *phallus* or *priapus*, regarding the mythology and worship of which in antiquity I refer the reader to what I have said in *Ilios*, pp. 276-278. No. 88 is an object of granite with two furrows, which run round it in

---

* *Zeitschrift für Ethnologie*, Organ der Berliner Gesellschaft für Anthropologie, Ethnologie und Urgeschichte, p. 82, Session of 21st Sept. 1882.

different directions; it may have served as a weight for the weaver's loom or for fishing nets. I may also mention a number of the kind of stone-implements having a groove all round them, like No. 1286, p. 570, in *Ilios*. Two similar ones, found in the terramare of the Emilia, are in the Museum of Parma.

Single and double-edged saws, as well as knives, of flint, chalcedony, or obsidian, similar to those represented in *Ilios*, p. 246, Nos. 93–98; p. 445, Nos. 656–665, were again collected in large quantities in all the five prehistoric

No. 86.—Stone Hammer with a groove on two sides. Size 1 : 4; depth about 8·50 m.

No. 88.—Object of granite with two furrows. Size 1 : 4; depth about 9 m.

No. 87.—Object of white marble, a *phallus*. Size about 1 : 3; depth about 8·50 m.

settlements, and particularly in the four lower ones. On the important question of how the flint saws were made, the eminent American architect, Dr. Joseph Thacher Clarke, who has been for two years at the head of the expedition sent out by the Archaeological Institute of America for the exploration of Assos, kindly sent me the following most interesting contribution:—

"The method of making flint-saws practised to-day by savages in several parts of the world, notably by the more debased Indian tribes of the south-west of the United States, is without doubt that employed in prehistoric antiquity. A sharpened stick of hard wood is set on fire. When its tip becomes a bright coal, this is pressed firmly against the side edge of the flint to be serrated, and the coal blown quickly to intense heat. A scale-like chip is thereby split from the stone, indenting its outline, and leaving sharp and quite regular edges. The process being repeated at given intervals makes from a thin flake of flint a saw capable of more service than one not familiar with the tools of savages might suppose. A proof that this simple method was customary in the earliest ages of mankind is found in the quantities of such peculiar scale-like and easily recognizable chips, met with in those prehistoric deposits which evidently contain the *débris* of primitive workshops of flint instruments."

In further illustration I may cite what a writer in the *Quarterly Review* says from his own observation of the Indians in California:—"We found the first traces of their presence on the side of a river twenty miles from the Yosemite valley. The sandy banks had been their camping ground, and *the place was strewn with chips and cores of obsidian*—the refuse of a manufactory of those beautiful little arrow-points with which they still bring down small game."—(*Q. R.*, Jan. 1881, vol. 151, p. 65.)

Prof. Rudolf Virchow observes to me that I have unfortunately confounded in *Ilios* his descriptions of two of the Trojan skulls, and that the explanation and measures given for the skull, p. 508, Nos. 969–972, really belong to the skull represented on the following page under Nos. 973–976; whilst the description and measures attributed by me to the latter belong to the skull, Nos. 969–972.

CHAPTER IV.

THE THIRD, FOURTH, FIFTH, AND SIXTH SETTLEMENTS ON THE SITE OF TROY.

§ I.—THE THIRD PREHISTORIC SETTLEMENT.

AFTER the great catastrophe of the second city, the Acropolis formed an immense heap of ruins, from which there stood forth only the great brick wall and the thick walls of the temples. It is impossible to say, even approximately, how long the Acropolis lay deserted; but, judging from the very insignificant stratum of black earth, which we find between the *débris* of the second settlement and the house floors of the third, we presume, with great probability, that the place was soon rebuilt. The number of the third settlers was but small, and they consequently settled on the old Pergamos. They did not rebuild the lower city, and probably used its site as fields and pasture-ground for their herds. Such of the building materials of the lower city, as could be used, were no doubt employed by the new settlers for the construction of their houses. On the old Acropolis the ruins and *débris* were left lying just as the new-comers found them; they did not go to the trouble of making a level platform. Some of them erected their houses on the hillock formed by the ruins and *débris* of the temples, whilst others built on the space before these edifices, on which there lay only a very insignificant stratum of *débris*. The house-walls of this third settlement consist, in general, of small unwrought stones joined with clay, but brick walls also occur now and then. They are covered on both sides with a clay coating, which has been pargetted with a thin layer of clay to give it a smoother appearance. The thickness of the walls varies generally between 0·45 m. and 0·65 m. The foundations of these house-walls are only 0·50 m. deep, and have simply been sunk into the *débris* of the second city, without having any solid foundation. For this reason the houses, with but few exceptions, cannot have been more than one story high; they have no particular characteristic ground plan, but consist of several small chambers irregularly grouped, the walls of which are often not even parallel. The largest and most regular house is the habitation repeatedly mentioned, to the north-west of the south-western gate (see p. 325, No. 188 in *Ilios*), which I used to consider as the royal house of the burnt city. But as we have now recognized as the Ilios of the Homeric legend the second city, which had a lower town, and which perished in a tremendous catastrophe, this largest house of the third settlement can have nothing whatever to do with that original Troy. I found the substructions of this house, as well as those of the buildings to the north of it, buried about three mètres deep in bricks, which were baked, much like those of the temple A. Hence I conclude that this house, as well as the adjacent buildings, must have had at least one high story of bricks above their substructions of small stones; and that, in the same manner as the walls of the temples and the fortification walls of the second city, these house-walls must have been baked *in situ* after they had been erected, by large quantities of wood being piled up on both sides of each wall and kindled simultaneously. The condition of the bricks can leave no doubt on this point, for all of them had evidently been exposed to a great fire, and besides they were very fragile; had they been baked separately, they would have been much more solid. Among the houses of the third settlement on the east side of the great northern trench X–Z (Plan VII.), there also occurred walls consisting partly of unbaked and partly of baked bricks, which latter appear to have been extracted from the heaps of ruins of the second city. Remains of such a mode of building were found, for instance, on the space before the temple A of the second city, and we are inclined to recognize in them the scanty remains of the temple of the third settlement. We infer this, first, from the considerable thickness of these walls, and secondly from the fact that the edifice stands on about the same place as that where the second settlers had their sanctuaries, for we know with what a wonderful tenacity people clung in antiquity to sacred sites.

As above mentioned, the third settlers found still, particularly on the west, south, and east sides, large remains of the Acropolis-wall of the second city, which they merely

No. 89.—Accumulation of *débris* before the Gate. The form of the strata of *débris* indicates that after the great conflagration the third settlers continued to go in and out on the same spot as before, although the paved road was buried deep under the brick-*débris* and ashes.

repaired. But on the north-west side, where the citadel-hill falls off directly to the plain, and has thus a higher slope, the ancient wall had been almost totally destroyed, and here, therefore, a new fortification-wall had to be erected, which is of far inferior masonry to that of the wall of the second city, and has been indicated on Plan VII. by the letters *x m* and with blue colour.

The third settlement had in the fortification-wall two gates; the one just above the south-western, the other just above the south-eastern gate of the second city (see Plan VII.). The same positions had been maintained, probably because they gave easiest access to the Acropolis, and because the country-roads commenced and ended at these points. As may be seen from the accompanying engraving,

No. 89, which represents a profile of the road leading up to the south-west gate, when the third settlers went in and out by it, the stone slabs paving the gateway of the second city were no longer visible; they were hidden beneath a layer of *débris*, which was about 0·50 m. deep at the gate-portals *u u* and *x x* (see Plan VII.), and about 1·50 m. outside the fortification-wall at the place TU (see Plan VII.). Even now these different heights of the pavements may be easily recognized outside the gate, in the high block of *débris* marked F on the Plan VII., which is still unexcavated. The gate-portals were probably arranged by the third settlers in the same way as they had been in the second city. When I excavated this gateway in the spring of 1873, I found it covered from 2 to 3 m. deep with burnt bricks, *débris* of bricks, and wood ashes, which prove with certainty that at the time of the third settlers also the gateway had high lateral brick walls, on which most probably some sort of an upper building was raised; but it is of course impossible to say now how much of these lateral walls had escaped the great catastrophe of the second city, and what part of them was the work of the third settlers.

In the second, the south-eastern gate (OX on Plan VII.) also, great alterations were made, but we have not been able to find out how far these belong to the second settlers, and how far to the third. The ground plan of this gate, with all the alterations, is given in the sketch No. 90. Its surface lay, at the time of the third settlement, about 1·50 mètre higher than it had been at the time of the catastrophe of the second city. Within the gate stood the sacrificial altar represented in *Ilios* under No. 6, p. 31. Through the gate runs a large channel or gutter of a very primitive masonry, much like the water conduit, mentioned above (p. 64) in the mysterious cavern, and the cyclopean water-conduits discovered by me at Tiryns and Mycenae.* It

---

* See *Mycenae*, pp. 9, 80, 144.

§ I.]   THE SOUTH-EASTERN GATE.   179

is formed of rude unwrought slabs of limestone joined without cement, and covered with similar stones. This channel cannot have served for carrying off the blood of the sacrificed animals, as I at first supposed (*Ilios*, p. 30); it is too deep for that; besides, it extends in a north-westerly direction into the city, and therefore probably served for carrying off the rain-water.

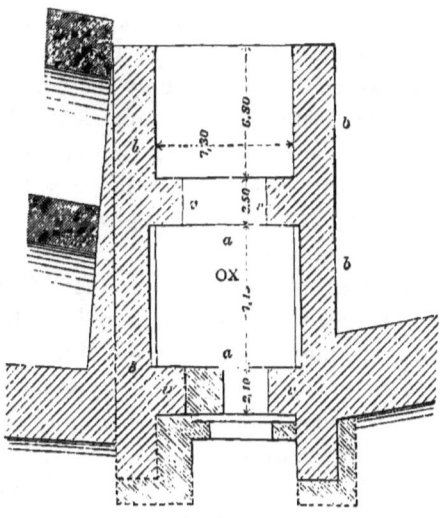

No. 90.—Ground Plan of the South-eastern Gate, marked OX on Plan VII. Scale 1 : 333. This gate had likewise two portals (*a, a*).

Like the south-western gate, this south-eastern gate also must have had on the substructions (*b, b* in the engraving No. 90 and *w* in Plan VII.) long and high lateral walls of bricks, and must have been crowned with a tower of the same material, for otherwise we should be at a loss to account for the masses of fallen baked or burnt bricks and *débris* of bricks, 3 mètres deep, in which we found the sacrificial altar and its surroundings imbedded. But I may say of these lateral walls the same that I said of those of the south-western gate, namely, that it is impossible to say now what part, if any, of these walls belongs to the second city. But the great difference in the level of the surface of the two gates rather induces us to believe that the old lateral walls had been at least in great part destroyed, and that most of the bricks and brick *débris* which encumbered the upper gateway belong to the lateral walls and upper construction built by the third settlers, and that the latter employed in both gateways the system repeatedly described as used by their predecessors, of baking the brick walls entire. The altar may already have stood in the gate when the walls were fired, for not only the outward appearance of the square plate of slate granite with which it was covered, and the great block of the same stone cut out in the form of a crescent which stood above it, but also the fractures of these slabs, all denote that they have been exposed to a great incandescence.

Professor Sayce observes to me that "brick walls, similarly baked after their construction, have been found elsewhere. For example, the sixth stage of the great temple of 'the Seven Lights of Heaven,' built by Nebuchadnezzar at Borsippa, and now known as the Birs-i-Nimrûd, was composed of bricks vitrified by intense heat into a mass of blue slag after the stage was erected. In Scotland, also, vitrified forts have been discovered, of which the best known is Craig Phadric, near Inverness, where the walls have been fused into a compact mass after they have been built. Here, however, the walls are made of stone and not of brick."

Mr. James D. Butler, President of the State Historical Society of Wisconsin, writes me on this interesting subject as follows:—

"*Madison, Feb.* 14, 1883.
" HENRY SCHLIEMANN, ESQ.

"In the London *Times* of January 26, I am pleased with your Trojan letter, especially with your discovery of an *inversion* of our mode of making brick.

"It seems odd to lay them up crude and then bake them. But I came to the same conclusion regarding a ruin near here which I explored last summer.

"The place, 50 miles east of here, on the way to Milwaukee, is called *Aztalan*. At that point about 18 acres were inclosed by a breast-work forming three sides of a parallelogram, the fourth side lying along a stream too deep to ford. There were 33 projections, considered flanking towers. The wall, when discovered in 1836, was about 4 feet high. It seems to have been once higher. The ground was first heaped up— and then coated with clay; the clods matted and massed together with the coarse prairie grass and bushes. Over all similar grass and bushes were piled and set on fire. The clay, of course, became brick, or an incrustation of brick. The soil still abounds in brick fragments, though the ploughshare has already for forty years been destroying this grand unique relic of some prehistoric race.

"This 'ancient city,' as it is locally styled, was first described in the *Milwaukee Advertiser* in 1837, in the *American Journal of Science*, New Haven, 1842, vol. xliv. p. 21, and more fully in 1855 by Lapham, in the *Smithsonian Contributions to Knowledge*, vol. vii. pp. 41–51.

"No explorer before myself, last May, appears to have felt that the brick or *terra-cotta* crust was baked *in situ*, as you describe the walls of Troy. An article of mine was published in the *State Journal* of this city, May, 22, 1882. I stated that one fragment I brought away had a stick an inch thick in the middle of it burned to charcoal, and that every bit of the terra-cotta showed holes where the sedge from the river bank had been mixed with the clay to help in burning it to brick."

The destruction of the third settlement was not total, for its city-wall and its house-walls have remained standing to a considerable height down to the present time.

Though we see traces of fire in several houses of the third settlement, yet nothing here testifies to a catastrophe such as took place in the second city, where all the edifices were destroyed to the very foundations, and only the thick walls of the temples, the citadel-wall, and perhaps the lateral walls of the gateways, have partly escaped destruction.

As explained in the preceding pages, my collaborators at Troy in 1879 agreed with me in attributing erroneously to the second city only the strata of *débris*, from 3 to 4 mètres thick, which succeed to the layer of ruins of the first city, and which we now find to have been artificially heaped up by the inhabitants of the second city to make a great "planum" for their Pergamos. Consequently the objects of human industry found in this layer and represented in *Ilios*, pp. 271–304, Nos. 147–181, as belonging to the second city, certainly belong to it. About this there is no mistake; but we have now ascertained with certainty that they belong to the oldest epoch in the history of the second city, and that to the second city belong also the thousands of objects which I found in the calcined ruins, and which I had formerly attributed erroneously to the third settlement. Now as some places in the house-floors of the third settlers are only separated by a layer of *débris* 0·20 m. thick from those of the burnt city, the objects of human industry which belong to them have naturally become mixed up with those of the second city. As we have had in this last Trojan campaign thousands of opportunities to convince ourselves by gradually excavating layer by layer from above, the third settlers could only have been very poor, for we found but very little in their houses. There can consequently be no doubt that nearly all the objects discussed and represented in *Ilios* in the chapter on the third city, pp. 330 to 514, Nos. 190–983, really belong to the second, the burnt city. It might even be very easy now to make the separation, for all the objects found in the burnt city bear the most evident marks of the intense heat to which they have been exposed in the great catastrophe, and all the pottery has become thoroughly baked by it, whilst, like all other Trojan pottery, the pottery of the third settlement proper is but very superficially baked. But it would lead us too far to undertake the separation now; we prefer to leave it for a new edition of *Ilios*, and here merely to put the facts on record.

I give under Nos. 91–96 a few objects which I picked up in the houses of the third settlement, and which differ slightly from those represented before. No. 91 is a one-handled hand-made jug with two separate spouts, one behind the other, though there is no separation in the body of the vessel. The front is ornamented with three breast-like excrescences. No. 92 is a vase with a hollow foot and a long perpendicularly perforated excrescence on each side of the body, and corresponding holes in the rim. No. 93 is a cup with a handle, a flat bottom, and an ear-

No. 91.—Jug with two spouts. Size 1:3; depth 8 m.

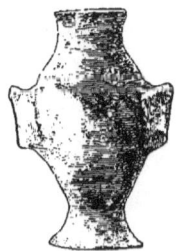

No. 92.—Vase with a hollow foot and vertically perforated excrescences for suspension. Size 1:3; depth 8 m.

like ornament in relief on each side of the body. All this pottery is but very slightly baked. More thoroughly baked is the clay ring No. 94, probably because it was to be used as a stand for vases with a convex bottom. Nos.

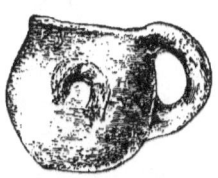

No. 93.—Cup with an ear-like ornament in relief on either side. Size 1:3; depth 8 m.

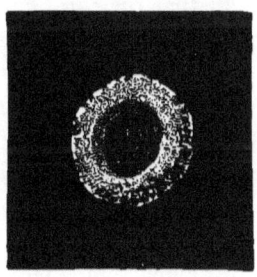

No 94.—Clay-ring. Size 1:3; depth about 8 m.

95, 96 are two astragals (huckle-bones). I represent them here instead of the two astragals Nos. 530, 531, p. 426, in *Ilios*, which were badly photographed. To avoid repetitions I represent here no more pottery. The whorls, both ornamented and unornamented, occurred by hundreds. Of brooches of bronze with a globular or a spiral head perhaps a dozen were gathered; also many awls and needles of bone, like those shown in *Ilios*, p. 261, Nos. 123–140, and p. 430, Nos. 560–574; hundreds of saddle-querns of trachyte,

Nos. 95, 96.—Two Huckle-bones (ἀστράγαλοι). Size 1 : 2; depth about 8 m.

like those at p. 234, No. 75, and p. 447, No. 678; rude stone hammers, like those at p. 237, No. 83, and p. 441, Nos. 632–634; corn-bruisers, like those at p. 236, Nos. 80, 81; saws and knives of flint or chalcedony, like those at p. 246, Nos. 93–98, p. 445, Nos. 656–664, etc.

§ II.—The Fourth Prehistoric Settlement on the Site of Troy.

As above mentioned, my architects ascertained beyond all doubt that the third settlement never perished in a catastrophe, for the remains of its house-walls still stood from 2 to 3 mètres high, and its walls of fortification were more or less well preserved. The fourth settlers built their houses on the gradually accumulated ground of the hill, and on the ruined house-walls of their predecessors. My architects further found that the fourth settlers used the brick walls of the third settlement, after having repaired them, and perhaps having built them somewhat higher, in proportion to the increased height of the ground. The fourth settlement, therefore, did not extend any further than the third, and consequently, like the latter, it only occupied the Pergamos of the second city. It had its gates, which were probably of wood, exactly at the same places as the third settlers had had theirs, but, as visitors may observe in the still standing vertical block of *débris*, F on Plan VII., the surface within the gates had again become 1·50 m. higher. The whole ground within the fortification-walls was covered with the houses of the fourth city, their ground-plans having no regular form, but consisting, like the houses of the third settlement, of small chambers irregularly grouped together. The house-walls were built of a masonry of small quarry-stones joined with clay; but their dimensions were in general still smaller than those of the house-walls of the third city; we even see some house-walls only 0·30 m. thick. Besides, some of the house-walls were built of bricks, partly baked, partly unbaked. I call the attention of visitors to a wall of unbaked bricks, which may still be seen in the great block of *débris*, marked G on Plan VII., which has remained standing to the south of the temple A. The bricks are made of clay mixed with straw, and are 0·45 m. square and 0·07 m. high; they are joined with a cement of a whitish clay. The thickness of the walls, only one brick in breadth, measures, inclusive of the coating on both sides, 0·47 m. Considering the thinness of most of the house-walls of this fourth settlement, it is not probable that there could have been an upper story above the ground floors, which are still partially preserved: in fact, as in the third settlement so also in the fourth, most houses appear to have had only a ground floor. Both these settlements, as brought to light by the excavations, certainly give the impression of mere villages. No tiles were found in the fourth settlement, for, as in the preceding cities, all the houses were roofed with horizontal terraces, which, as we still see in the villages of the Troad, were made of wooden beams, reeds, and a layer of clay about 0·25 m. thick. It is especially the existence of these horizontal terraces, the clay of which is constantly being washed away by the rain and must always be renewed, that explains that rapid accumulation of the ground, which we find in the prehistoric settlements on the hill of Hissarlik, and which has never yet been observed elsewhere in anything like such proportions. This also explains the tremendous masses of mussel and other small shells, some of which are still closed. The house-walls of clay-bricks must also have contributed to the rapid accumulation of *débris*, for by the alternate influence of rain, sunshine, and wind, these bricks get completely dissolved.

We cannot say with certainty how the fourth settlement

No. 97.—Vase with an owl-face, the characteristics of a woman, and two wing-like upright projections. Size 1:4; depth about 5 m.

came to an end; but, as we found the upper part of its fortification-walls destroyed, it is natural to suppose that the settlement may have perished by the hand of enemies. We see in several houses traces of fire, but these are not more considerable than those in the third settlement, and certainly there has not been a general destruction.

We found again in the *débris* of the fourth settlement a very large quantity of pottery, like that represented and discussed in *Ilios*, pp. 521-562, Nos. 986-1219, but no

OWL-FACED VASES.

new types, except two vases with owl-faces and the characteristics of a woman, which I represent here under Nos. 97, 98, because they differ from any of those I have shown in *Ilios*.

On the vase No. 97, the owl-face is very rude; the beak is long and pointed, the eyes are indicated by semi-globular dots; the eyebrows by a horizontal line in relief; the female breasts and vulva are well marked; the rim of the orifice

No. 98.—Vase with the characteristics of a woman and two wing-like upright projections. The cover has an owl-face. Size 1 : 4; depth about 5 m.

is bent over; the bottom is flat; the wings are indicated by vertical projections. No. 98 is one of those vases which have two wing-like vertical projections, two female breasts and the vulva, but a smooth cylindrical neck, on which is put a separate cover with an owl-face. This vase-cover is particularly remarkable for its large semi-globular eyes and high protruding eyebrows.

The forms of these sacred Trojan vases have changed

somewhat in the course of ages; but, although they have lost their owl-heads and wings, yet their types may easily be recognized in the vases with two female breasts with which the potters' shops in the Dardanelles abound.

There also occurred in this stratum hundreds of ornamented and unornamented terra-cotta whorls, and many brooches of bronze, some knives of the same metal, many needles and awls of bone, innumerable rude stone hammers as well as saddle-querns, and a large number of well-polished axes of diorite, like those represented in *Ilios* under Nos. 1279–1281, p. 569.

§ III.—THE FIFTH PREHISTORIC SETTLEMENT ON THE SITE OF TROY.

The fifth settlers extended their city further to the south and east than the two preceding settlements; for, owing to the great accumulation of *débris*, and the insignificant difference of height between the hill of Hissarlik and the adjoining ridge, the level top had increased very considerably in those directions. For this reason we see how the houses of the new settlers extend over the old fortification-walls and far beyond them. The house-walls are built partly of quarry-stones joined with clay, partly of clay-bricks: of such clay-brick walls of the fifth settlement, many may be seen in the great north-eastern trench below the Roman propylæum (see L on Plan VII.) above the southern gate (see NF on Plan VII.), and in the great block of *débris* (G on Plan VII.) to the south of the temple A. They consist of bricks 0·30 m.–0·33 m. broad and long, by 0,065 mm.–0,075 mm. in height, their thickness not exceeding the length of a brick. The material of the bricks is, as in the preceding cities, a dark clay; the cement is a light-coloured clay, almost white. These brick walls are for the most part unbaked; only in rare cases are baked bricks seen. All the brick walls have foundations

No. 99.—Entrance to the great north-eastern Trench SS on Plan VII. To the left, a huge Roman wall of large well-wrought blocks. To the right, the great wall of the fifth city, consisting of irregular stones.

of quarry-stones, which probably projected partly above the floors, to prevent the disintegration to which the lower parts of the walls were most exposed. As no traces of tiles have been found, all the houses in this settlement also must have had horizontal roofs of wood, reeds, and clay.

The fifth settlers cannot have used the old fortification walls, for the accumulation of *débris* had been so great that those walls were completely buried. Although my architects have not succeeded in finding a fortification-wall which could with certainty be attributed to the fifth settlement, yet we have brought to light in two places a citadel-wall of large rudely-wrought calcareous blocks, which we can, at least with the highest probability, indicate as the wall of the fifth city. This wall is now visible, first, in the great north-west trench ($n\ z$ on Plan VII. in this work and Z'-O on Plan I. in *Ilios*); and, again, at the north-eastern end of the great north-eastern trench (SS on Plan VII.). We struck it immediately below the Roman and Greek foundations, at a depth of about 2 m. below the surface of the ground, and excavated it to a depth of 6 m. As before mentioned, it is distinguished by its masonry from the fortification-walls of the more ancient prehistoric cities, for it consists of long plate-like slabs, joined in the most solid way without cement or lime, which have very large dimensions, particularly in the lower part, whilst the lowest part of the walls of the second city consists of smaller stones of rather a cubical shape. The accompanying woodcut, No. 99, gives a good view of this wall of the fifth city, as it was brought to light in the great north-eastern trench (SS on Plan VII.). It deserves attention that this wall is outside and to the north-east of the Acropolis of the second city, in fact near the north-east end of the Greek and Roman Acropolis of Ilium.

The objects of human industry found were of the same kind as those described and represented on pp. 573–586 in *Ilios*; I have no new types to record, except two vases with owl-heads, and two small objects of ivory, which I represent here under Nos. 100–103.

The vase, No. 100, is peculiar for the long pointed owl's beak and the well-indicated closed eyelids; only two female breasts are indicated, and no vulva. The neck of the vase, which is very long and cylindrical, is ornamented with three incised circular lines, meant possibly to represent necklaces. The rim of the orifice is turned over; the bottom is flat; two long upright projections indicate the wings.

No. 100.—Vase with an owl-head, the characteristics of a woman, and two wing-like upright projections. Size 1 : 4 ; depth about 3 m.

No. 101.—Vase with an owl-head and the characteristics of a woman. Size 1 : 4 ; depth about 3 m.

On the vase No. 101 the eyes are large and protruding; the ears are not indicated; the beak is but small and on a level with the eyes; just below it is a small round groove, in the centre of which is a minute perforation ; probably this is meant to represent the mouth; the two female breasts and the vulva are very large and conspicuous; the latter is peculiarly interesting on account of the incised ⊕ with which it is ornamented, and which seems to corroborate M. Emile Burnouf's* opinion, that the 卐 represents the two pieces of wood laid across, in the junction of which the holy fire was produced by friction, and that the mother of the holy fire is Mâjâ, who represents the productive force in the form of a woman. This appears to us the more probable as we also see a 卐 on the vulva, of the idol No. 226, p. 337, in *Ilios*; and very often crosses, as for example, a cross with the marks of four nails on the vulva of the owl-faced vase No. 986, p. 521 ; a simple cross on that of the vase No. 991, p. 523, &c. Instead of the usual wings, we see on the vase No. 101 mere stumps, which do not appear to have been longer ; three incised lines round the back seem to indicate necklaces ; two other lines run across the body ; there is a groove at their juncture.

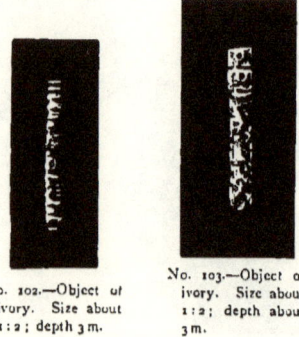

No. 102.—Object of ivory. Size about 1 : 2 ; depth 3 m.

No. 103.—Object of ivory. Size about 1 : 2 ; depth about 3 m.

No. 102 is a curious object of ivory with sixteen rude circular furrows, which seem to have been made by a flint-saw ; the use of this object is a riddle to us, for it can hardly have been used in ladies' needle-work. Another curious object is No. 103, which is hollow and has three perforations and two circular incisions, apparently made by a flint-saw. The object may have served as a handle to some small bronze instrument.

* *La Science des Religions*, p. 256.

§ IV.—THE SIXTH OR LYDIAN SETTLEMENT ON THE
SITE OF TROY.

Above the layer of ruins and *débris* of the fifth prehistoric settlement, and just below the ruins of the Aeolic Ilium, we found again a large quantity of the pottery described and represented in *Ilios*, pp. 590–597, Nos. 1363–1405, which, as explained in *Ilios*, p. 587, from the great resemblance this pottery has to the hand-made vases found in the ancient cemeteries of Rovio, Volterra, Bismantova, Villanova, and other places in Italy, and held to be either archaic-Etruscan or prae-Etruscan pottery, as well as in consideration of the colonization of Etruria by the Lydians, asserted by Herodotus (I. 94), I attribute to a Lydian settlement that must have existed here for a long time. There were again found the same vase-handles as before, in the form of snakes' heads, or with cow-heads (see *Ilios*, pp. 598, 599, Nos. 1399–1405). Regarding the latter I may mention that I found at Mycenae a large painted vase, the handles of which are modelled with cow-heads (see *Mycenae*, p. 133, No. 213, and p. 139, No. 214). An Etruscan vase ornamented with a cow's head is in the Museum at Corneto (Tarquinii). Dr. Chr. Hostmann, of Celle, kindly informs me that vases with handles terminating in cow-heads have been discovered at Sarka near Prague, and that they are preserved in the Museum of the latter city. A similar vase, found in an excavation at Civita Vecchia, is in the Museum of Bologna.

There were again found six of the pretty, dull-blackish, one-handled cups, with a convex bottom and three hornlike excrescences on the body, similar to those represented in *Ilios*, p. 592, Nos. 1370–1375. The Etruscan Museum in the Vatican contains two similar cups, the Museo Nazionale in the Collegio Romano three. These latter were found in the necropolis of Carpineto near Cupra Maritrima. I may further notice the discovery of two more double-handled

14

cups like No. 1376, p. 593, in *Ilios*: two similar ones, found at Corneto (Tarquinii), are preserved in the museum of that city. Also two more of those remarkable one-handled vessels, like No. 1392, p. 596 in *Ilios*, which are in the shape of a bugle with *three feet*. Similar vessels, but without feet, may be seen elsewhere: the Etruscan Collection in the Musée du Louvre contains a number of them; one may also be seen in the Etruscan Collection in the Museum of Naples; another, found in Cyprus, is in the collection of Eugène Piot at Paris.

I repeat here from *Ilios*, pp. 588, 589, that with rare exceptions all this pottery, which I hold to be Lydian, is hand-made, and abundantly mixed with crushed silicious stones and syenite containing much mica. The vessels are in general very bulky; and as they have been dipped in a wash of the same clay and polished before being put to the fire, besides being but very slightly baked, they have a dull black, in a few cases a dull yellow or brown colour, which much resembles the colour of the famous hut-urns found under the ancient layer of peperino near Albano.* This dull black colour is, however, perhaps as much due to the peculiar mode of baking as to the peculiar sort of clay of which the pottery is made, for, except the πίθοι, nearly all the innumerable terra-cotta vases found in the first, third, fourth, and fifth prehistoric settlements of Hissarlik are but very superficially baked, and yet none of them have the dull colour of these Lydian terra-cottas. Besides, the shape and fabric are totally different from those of any pottery found in the prehistoric settlements or in the upper Aeolic Greek city. The reader of *Ilios* and the visitor to the Schliemann Museum at Berlin, will recognize this great difference in shape and fabric in the case of every object of pottery represented in *Ilios* (pp. 589–599) or exhibited in that Trojan collection at Berlin.

---

* L. Pigorini and Sir John Lubbock, *Notes on Hut-urns and other Objects from Marino near Albano*, London, 1869, pp. 2, 13.

CHAPTER V.

THE SEVENTH CITY—THE GREEK AND ROMAN ILIUM.[*]

§ I.—BUILDINGS, AND OBJECTS FOUND IN THEM.

As I am describing our works at Troy in 1882 in the order of the antiquity of the settlements, I come now in the last place to the ruins of Ilium, though, in commencing our labours from the top of the hill of Hissarlik, these were naturally the first we had to excavate and to study. As before mentioned (see p. 18), I brought to light in the excavation on the northern slope (in the place marked by the most northern letter V on Plan I. in *Ilios*) a very remarkable wall-corner. It is about six mètres above the plain, and consists of large well-wrought blocks of shelly limestone, joined without any binding material. It belongs apparently to the Macedonian time, and probably formed part of the grand wall of defence which Lysimachus built for Ilium. It has courses of masonry, alternately higher and lower, which are wrought on the outside with rusticated surfaces. It appears that all the more ancient buildings here, with the exception of the great temple of Athené, built by Lysimachus, consist of a shelly conglomerate,

---

[*] I here remark that I use for the historic Ilium of the Greek and Roman age the *simple and only name* by which it occurs in the classical writers; for Strabo's ἡ νῦν πόλις, τὸ σημερινὸν Ἴλιον, are merely distinguishing phrases, not names; and even these are used by no other writer. It is the more important to mention this, as the *modern* phrase, *Ilium Novum*, or *Novum Ilium*, which I reluctantly adopted in *Ilios*, has been mistaken even by some scholars for a genuine classical appellation; and this has helped to perpetuate the delusion of the two different sites, which have been marked on maps, since Lechevalier *invented* the distinction, as *Ilium Novum* (at Hissarlik, which he never visited), and *Troja Vetus* (at Bounarbashi).

whereas those of the Roman time consist for the most part of marble, with foundations of a soft calcareous stone.

The Roman wall is better preserved, and we have been able to trace it nearly everywhere, at least in its general outlines, in the Acropolis as well as in the lower city (see the Plan VIII. in this work).

In the woodcut No. 99 (p. 189), is represented the entrance of the great north-eastern trench, with the great corner of the Roman wall in the foreground, and the great fortress-wall of the fifth city in the back-ground. Each visible stone of the former bears a quarry mark, consisting of a single letter. But on the large foundation stones of the edifices these quarry marks are more complicated. I give here a few examples of them.

In the part of the Acropolis previously unexcavated my architects bestowed great care on the uncovering of all the immense foundations of Greek and Roman edifices, which consist of huge boulders, and on bringing together the sculptured blocks belonging to those edifices, as well as to other buildings, of which the foundations could no longer be ascertained.

Among the latter, a small Doric temple deserves particular attention, as it might seem to be identical with that "small and insignificant" sanctuary of Pallas Athené which Alexander the Great saw here.* But, in the opinion of my architects, the sculptured blocks of it which remain are not archaic enough to belong to that temple of the goddess, to which, according to Herodotus,† Xerxes ascended.

The entablature and a capital of this little Doric sanctuary are shown in the adjoining drawing, No. 104.

---

* Strabo, XIII. p. 593 : τὸ ἱερὸν τῆς Ἀθηνᾶς μικρὸν καὶ εὐτελές.
† VII. 43.

THE SMALL DORIC TEMPLE.

The material of the sculptured blocks is a rude shelly limestone, the exterior side of which has been covered with a thin coating of lime. This is the same rude building material which we find in many Greek temples of Southern Italy, Sicily, and Greece. Of the capitals we found two specimens, both of which are much damaged. The *echinus* is almost a straight line; it is united by three rings to the shaft of the column, which has twenty flutings, and is 0·45 m. in diameter at the upper end. Its lower diameter

No. 104.—Entablature and capital of the small Doric Temple. Scale 1 : 15.

cannot be determined with precision; but it appears to have been 0·59 m., this being the diameter of the thickest of the drums of columns which we found. The architrave is particularly remarkable for the fact that its *taenia* or ledgment (Tropfenleiste) has only five *guttae* (Tropfen), instead of six as usually. This peculiarity has as yet been noticed but very rarely. The height of the architrave could not be determined; it has been restored according to the height of the triglyphs, which are 0,355 mm. high and

0,276 mm. broad; they are arranged in such a way that three of them come in an intercolumniation of about 2 mètres. The *corona*,* together with the *cymatium*, has been worked out of one block. In contrast with the arrangement of the architrave, the mutules (*viae*, Hängeplatten) have six *guttae* (Tropfen). All the sculptured blocks of this temple are well made, and were bound together with simple iron bolts and iron cramps, having this form ‖▭‖. From

No. 105.—Marble Metope of the Macedonian period, representing a warrior holding a kneeling man by the hair. Size about 1 : 12; depth about 1 m.

all these characteristics, my architects conclude with certainty that the temple was not built earlier than the fourth century B.C.; and consequently that it cannot be identical with the sanctuary which Xerxes saw here. We have not been able to ascertain the exact site of this temple in the Acropolis, for among all the foundations we brought to light there are none which are adapted for it. The sculp-

---

* I adopt here the terms used by English architects, which differ in some respects from those used in Germany. For example, the Latin terms *corona* and *cymatium* answer to the Greek *geison* and *sima*, which I adopt in my German edition.

§ I.]　　THE LARGE DORIC TEMPLE.　　199

tured blocks which belong to it had been used in various walls, as well as in the foundations of a later portico.

The oldest of the other later edifices is a very large Doric temple of white marble, to which belongs the beautiful metope representing Phoebus Apollo with the quadriga of the Sun,* which I discovered here eleven years ago, and which now ornaments the Schliemann Museum at Berlin, as well as the mutilated metope which I represent here under No. 105. This latter is of the Macedonian time,

No. 106.—Fragment of a marble Metope of the Macedonian period, representing a man holding up a sinking woman. Size about 1 : 9.

and seems to have been exposed for centuries to the inclemency of the seasons, for it is much worn and mutilated; but it is not difficult to recognize on it a warrior holding a kneeling man by the hair, and apparently about to strike him with his uplifted arm. I attribute to this temple also with much probability the fragment of another metope, which has served for centuries as a tombstone in the old Turkish cemetery of Koum Kioi, whence we removed it to enrich the Schliemann Museum at Berlin. As will be seen by the engraving No. 106, it seems to represent a man holding up a sinking person, apparently a woman. The sculpture is excellent, and belongs with certainty to the Macedonian

---

* See *Ilios*, pp. 622–625.

period. I give further, under No. 107, the engraving of another fragment of a metope which has also stood for ages as a tombstone in the old cemetery of Koum Kioi, and which likewise I attribute with high probability to the great Doric temple, the more so as it is also of the Macedonian period. It represents a helmeted warrior with a shield held by some other warrior, whose hand alone remains. I attribute to it also, with great likelihood, a much better preserved metope from the Ilium of the Macedonian period, which has stood for twenty-five years before Mr. Calvert's farmhouse at Thymbra, and which I bought of him to present it to the Schliemann Museum at Berlin.

No. 107.—Fragment of a Metope of marble of the Macedonian period, representing a helmeted warrior, and a shield held by a second figure, of which only the left hand remains. Size about 1 : 10.

For the accompanying drawing of this metope, No. 108, I am indebted to the skilful hand of my friend Mr. Schöne, Director General of the Royal Museums at Berlin, who kindly gives me the following description of it:

"A goddess, evidently Athené, is in-lively movement towards the left. She has lifted her right arm, of which only the shoulder is preserved, probably in order to deal a stab with the lance upon the warrior to her right, who has sunk down at her feet. With her left hand she has caught hold of his head, but it is not clear whether she is grasping him by the hair or by the helmet, as the head is for the most part broken away. She wears an overhanging *chiton*, which is girdled below the breast, and has on her left arm a large round shield. It cannot be recognized with certainty whether she wears an aegis on her breast. Her head is broken off. The warrior, who with his right is trying to liberate himself from the left hand of the goddess, appears to have been quite naked, only having a large round shield on his left arm."

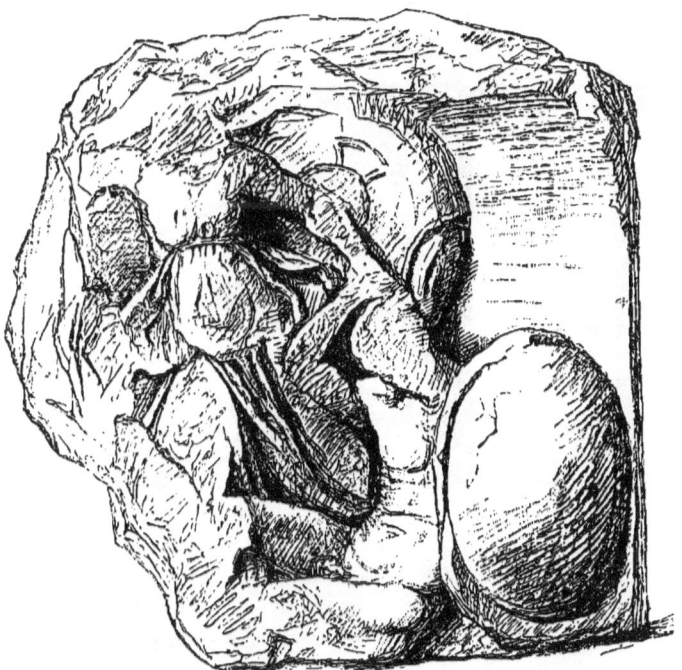

No. 108 —Fragment of a Metope of marble of the temple of Athené, of the Macedonian period, representing a goddess, probably Athené, with a large shield; holding by her left a warrior with a shield, who vainly strives to liberate himself from her grasp. Size about 1 : 9.

This sanctuary is, no doubt, identical with the temple which was built here by Lysimachus.* In my excavations I found its sculptured marble blocks scattered about over the whole north-eastern part of the hill of Hissarlik. On the

* Strabo, XIII. p. 593: Λυσίμαχος μάλιστα τῆς πόλεως ἐπεμελήθη καὶ νεὼν κατεσκεύασε.

same side were brought to light several large foundations consisting of well-wrought blocks of calcareous stone, but they were too much destroyed for my architects to determine which of them had belonged to the great temple. Besides the sculptured blocks of the temple found in the

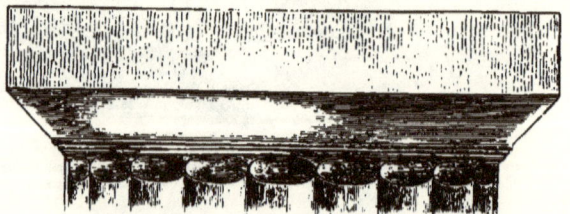

No. 109.—Capital, triglyphon, and corona of the great Doric Temple.

Acropolis, we have found in several ancient Turkish cemeteries in the neighbourhood so many fragments of columns and entablatures, that my architects have been enabled to make the accompanying restoration of the upper part of the temple (see the engraving, No. 109).

The temple was of the Doric order, and all its visible parts were of white marble. The columns have twenty flutings; their upper diameter is 1·01 m.; their lower diameter, as well as their height, are both unknown. The profile of the *echinus* approaches a straight line; the *echinus* has three rings. Of the architrave no fragment has been found, because it furnished the destroyers with the very best building blocks. The frieze (*triglyphon*) had been arranged in such a way that two triglyphs always came on an axis-distance of about 2·90 m. Each triglyph is 0·58 m. broad and 0·84 m. high, and has been wrought together with an

No. 110.—Cymatium of the Temple of Athené, of the Macedonian time. Size about 1 : 12.

adjoining metope, from one block. To one of these slabs a second triglyph is joined. All the metopes had been decorated with reliefs, and thus they formed the peculiar ornamentation of the temple. The *corona* of this temple presents the common Doric forms: it supported a *cymatium* of marble, which was ornamented with leaves in relief, and with lions' heads for water-spouts. The roofs, as well as the panelled ceiling of the interior, were of marble. The destruction of this temple by Fimbria, and its restoration by Sulla,* may be easily recognized from several sculptured blocks. This is particularly manifest from the *cymatium*, of which most of the fragments found have been made in the Roman time. as is evident from the style of the sculptures.

---

* Strabo, XIII. p. 594. See also *Ilios*, pp. 176, 177.

Indeed, the *cymatium* was just that part of the temple which would suffer most damage in a conflagration. I represent here, under No. 110, a *cymatium* of the Macedonian, and under No. 111 one of the Roman period. We cannot indicate with precision the date of the last and total destruction of the temple; but many of the sculptured blocks throw light on the object of this destruction, for they show us a great number of holes bored close to each other, evidently intended to facilitate the breaking of the large blocks into splinters, in order to burn the marble to lime. The same intention is also indicated by the innumerable marble splinters, which covered the whole north-eastern part of the hill of Hissarlik. But we often find large marble blocks, particularly blocks of *strotera*-ceilings, which have escaped

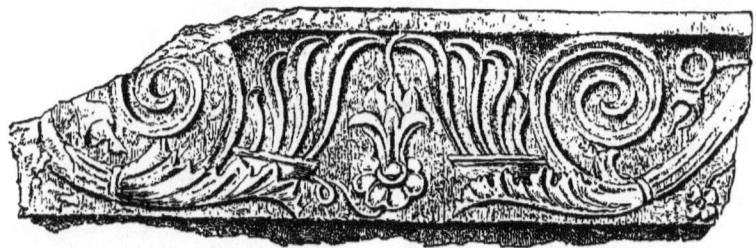

No. 1.1.—Cymatium of the Temple of Athené, Roman restoration. Size about 1 : 12.

destruction, probably because they were too heavy and unwieldy to be moved and to be cut into splinters.

We thought ourselves authorized to call this large sanctuary the temple of Pallas Athené, because, just as she was the tutelary and patron deity of Troy, so this temple was by far the largest and most magnificent sanctuary of Ilium. Besides, the architectural forms, as well as the reliefs of the metopes, point to the fourth century B.C. as the time when this temple was built, and this agrees perfectly with the statement of Strabo,* that Lysimachus built here a temple of Athené. I show here, under No. 112, the fragment of a

---

* XIII. p. 593.

§ 1.] SCULPTURES FROM THE GREAT DORIC TEMPLE. 205

relief, on which was represented a prostrate man. We recognize an arm leaning on a leather bag. The hand holds a drinking-horn.

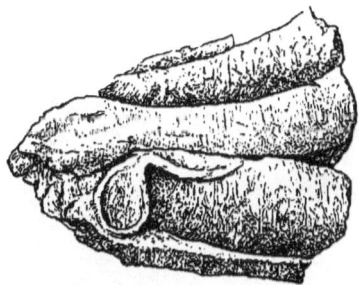

No. 112.—Fragment of a Pediment-relief. Size about 1 : 12.

No. 113 is a portion of a frieze, probably of the Macedonian time, which appears to represent a train of chariots in procession, preceded by a Niké on a swift chariot; only a part of one of her horses is visible. Of the chariot which follows her we see only a horse gallopping, and on his back the foot of another.

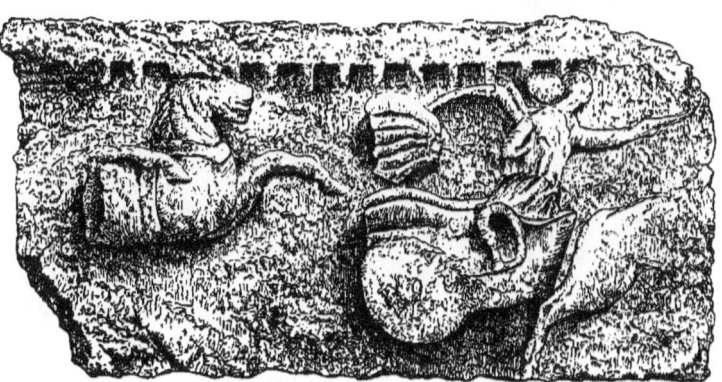

No. 113.—Portion of a Frieze representing a procession of chariots preceded by a winged Niké on a swift chariot. Probably of the Macedonian time. Size about 1 : 12.

No. 114 undoubtedly belongs to the same frieze; it likewise represents a winged Niké and the fragment of another. Between these two Nikés is seen a Gorgon's head with two small wings. Of the same frieze we found more fragments in the Turkish cemeteries, but they are for the most part much damaged.

No. 114.—Fragment of a Frieze with a Gorgon's head, on each side of which is a Niké. Size about 1 : 12.

No. 115 shows a small relief, representing two horses gallopping, which is certainly of the Macedonian age.

No. 116 is the fragment of a relief which probably

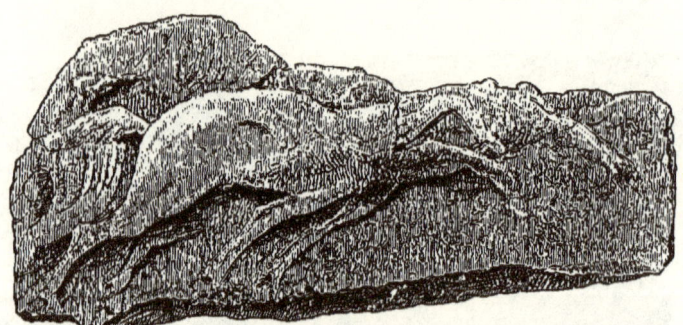

No. 115.—Small Relief representing two gallopping horses. Certainly of the Macedonian period. Size about 1 : 5.

ornamented a pediment, representing the figure of a man holding his right arm over his head.

It is probable that all, or nearly all, of these sculptures belong to the great Doric temple of Athené, but it is impossible to assert this with certainty.

I take this occasion to assure the reader, on the testimony

of my architects, that I was mistaken in believing that I had, in 1873, destroyed the temple of Pallas Athené, in the south-eastern part of Hissarlik, and that it was merely the substruction of a Roman portico which I had to destroy for the most part, in order to be able to excavate the prehistoric cities underneath.

The many other edifices, of which we found isolated fragments, seem to belong to the Roman time. Nearly all these edifices were built of marble; most of them are in the Doric style; some few show the Ionic or Corinthian style Of the Doric edifices, there are only two which could

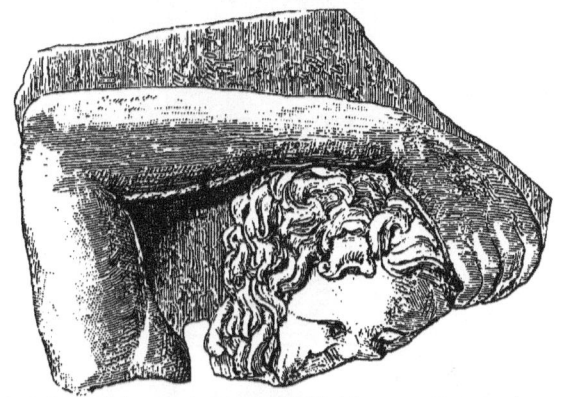

No. 116.—Pediment-relief representing a man holding his right arm over his head. Size about 1 : 5.

be partially restored, and the foundations of which are still preserved ; namely a Roman gate which led up to the Acropolis, and a portico erected in the Acropolis. The foundations of this gate, which consist of large square blocks, have been brought to light in the great south-eastern trench,* to the south-east of the south-eastern gate, and are marked L on Plan VII. in the present work, and on Plan I. in *Ilios*. They form a rectangle, 12·50 m. long, 8·50 m. broad, which is divided by an interior traverse into two parts. (See the engraving No. 117.) The numerous sculptured

---

* See Plan IV. in *Ilios*.

blocks of the upper edifice, which are lying about in close vicinity to the foundations, such as Doric columns, architraves, triglyphs, *coronae*, and Corinthian semi-columns,

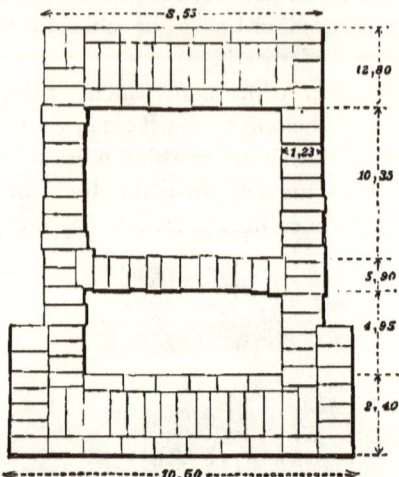

No. 117.—Ground plan of the Roman Propylaeum in its present state. Scale 1:200.

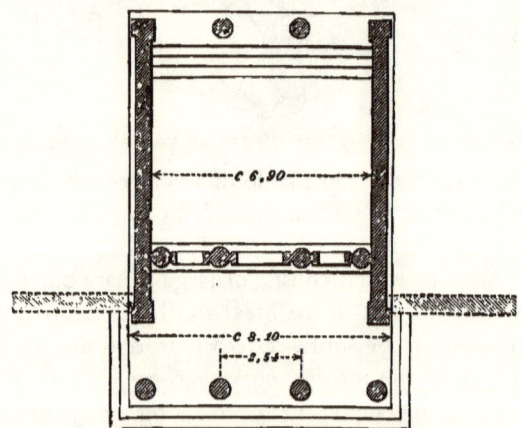

No. 118.—Restored ground plan of the Roman Propylaeum.

furnished the grounds on which it was possible to make the accompanying sketches (Nos. 118–120) of the gate as restored. On the southern outer side of the gate stood four

Doric columns; on the interior side there were probably two similar columns between two *parastades*. The portal proper was formed by three doors in the interior traverse, which were encompassed with Corinthian semi-columns. The lateral walls of the gate joined, on the east and west, the walls of the sacred precincts of the temples

No. 119.—Entablature and capital of the Roman Propylaeum. Scale 1:15.

The above-mentioned Roman portico, which was visible on the block of *débris* G' on Plan I., and of which a far projecting slab is marked f on the engraving, p. 264, No. 144, in *Ilios*, appears to have formed the western
15

boundary of this *temenos*. The length of this portico cannot now be determined. The width between the axes of the columns, which stood on two marble steps on the east side of the portico, was 2·30 m. and contained three marble triglyphs in the entablature.

Of the other Doric edifices there exist only a few capitals and entablatures; we cannot, therefore, make up the plan of them. Of Corinthian edifices I discovered no other than the before-mentioned portico in the lower city (p. 26). Its columns, being of syenite, are of course not fluted; the

No. 120.—Restored view of the Roman Propylaeum. Scale 1 : 100.

capitals and the entablature are of white marble. Many of the small foundations in the Greek and Roman stratum of Ilium seem to have served for erecting statues.

Much larger still than any one of all the edifices hitherto mentioned is the gigantic theatre, which is immediately to the east of the Acropolis (see Plan VIII.), and of which I brought to light the lower part of the stage-buildings, the walls of which are nearly all preserved to the height of a mètre. The accompanying sketch, No. 121, represents its ground plan.

§ I.] THE GREAT THEATRE OF ILIUM. 211

The theatre was most magnificently ornamented with marble columns, of the Doric, Ionic, and Corinthian orders, of which, as well as of the entablature, I found thousands of fragments; and it was moreover completely cased with marble, as is proved by some remains of the casing which are still *in situ*. We found a large number of the seat-steps, which are of a hard calcareous stone and have the usual form of the benches in ancient theatres;

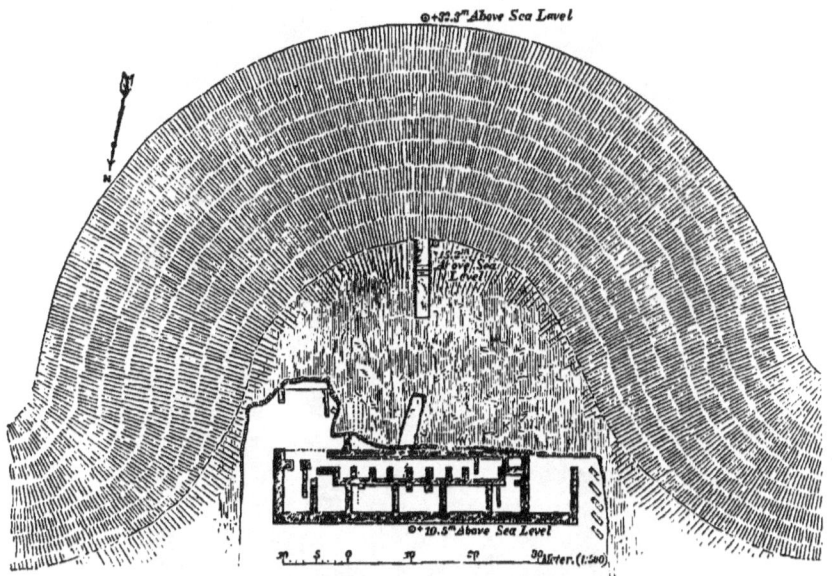

No. 121.—Ground plan of the great Theatre of Ilium.

but none of them were *in situ*. The κοιλόν, or space for the spectators, is formed by a semi-circle cut out in the limestone rock of the northern slope of the ridge, and affords room for more than 6000 persons. From the higher seats, which overlooked the stage and its buildings, the spectators enjoyed a splendid view over the lower plain, the Hellespont, and the Aegean Sea with its islands. Apparently the whole theatre was built only in the Roman time; for, although the inscriptions, which I shall give in the subsequent pages, prove that sacred games were celebrated here much earlier, yet it seems that only temporary buildings were used for them. We found in the theatre enormous masses of splinters of marble statues, as well as a kiln, in which all the statues and other sculptures, which could easily be cut to pieces, seem to have been burnt to lime. One of the few sculptures which have escaped destruc-

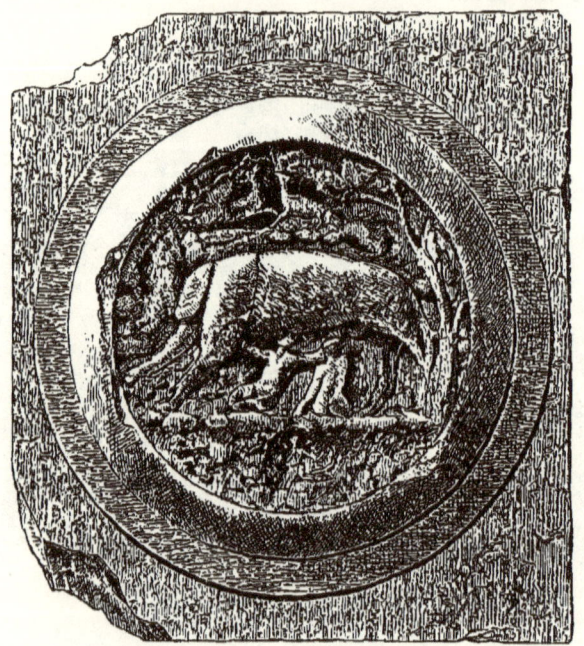

No. 122.—Medallion in relief, representing the she-wolf suckling Romulus and Remus. Size 1 : 13.

tion is a large medallion in relief, measuring 1·20 m. in diameter, representing the she-wolf suckling Romulus and Remus, of which I give an engraving under No. 122, though it is of no great artistic value. It is divided into three compartments: in the middle one the she-wolf is represented on a rocky ground covered with a forest; in the upper compartment, above the animal, are two stags, probably intended to characterize the locality; in the lower compartment, beneath the twins, we see a grotto in which is represented the god Pan with his goat's feet. The head of the she-wolf was probably in high relief and turned

No. 123.—Corinthian Capital of the theatre.

towards the twins, in consequence of which it was broken off when the block fell.

I show under No. 123 a Corinthian capital of the theatre, and under No. 124 a restored acanthus-leaf of the same.

I may further mention a marble fountain ornamented with a human head, from which the water poured into a large marble basin; also a head and many feet of colossal statues. There were found in the theatre several Greek inscriptions, which will be given in the subsequent pages, together with a good many others found in the Acropolis and in the cemeteries. One of them, which, as the letters testify, is of a late Roman time, is engraved on a small marble column 0·25 m. high, the upper diameter being 0,125 mm., the lower 0,145 mm. It has on its top a hollow, which may have served for a sacred offering.

No. 124.—Restored Acanthus-leaf of the capital of the theatre.

At the west end of the theatre we found at a small depth two tombs, each composed of four limestone slabs, which appear to belong to a late Byzantine period.

In one of the shafts before-mentioned, sunk by me in the lower city, close to the Acropolis, on its south side, I found two marble statues of the Roman time; one of them, which I represent here under No. 125, is a Hercules holding a lion's skin; it evidently represents the portrait of an eminent personage. The other statue, which I represent under No. 126, is in a reclining posture; it is a river god; probably the Scamander, holding in his right hand a cornucopiae; close to the arm, on the ground, is an urn. The figure is obese; the vesture has been intentionally drawn down in order to show the very full form of the body. The head is missing. The feet are naked. Neither of these statues is of any great artistic value.

No. 125.—Portrait-statue in the shape of a Hermheracles. Size 1:18; depth 1 m.

In five other shafts I found mosaic floors, among which were some with good patterns, but all of them were more or less damaged.

Of other objects found in the ruins of Ilium I may mention a small female head, which I give here under No. 127. It was found in the excavation on the northern slope (the more northern V on Plan I. in *Ilios*), close to the remarkable ancient wall-corner, and is certainly of the Macedonian age. Together with it was found a helmeted male head belonging to a metope, which, however, is too much mutilated to be represented here. Dr. H. G. Lolling, member of the German Archaeological Institute at Athens, kindly calls my attention to the peculiar manner in which

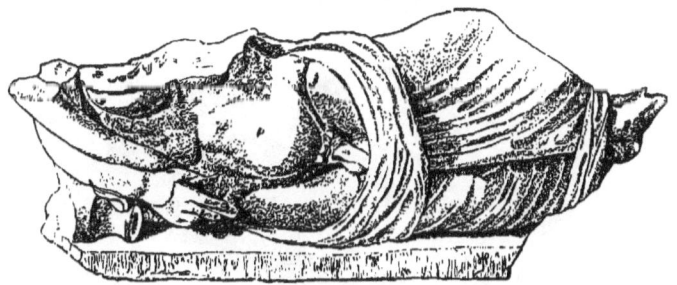

No. 126.—River-god, probably the Scamander, with a cornucopiae and an urn. Size 1 : 18 ; depth 1 m.

the upper part of the skull of the figure, No. 127, has been worked, in order that a helmet might be fixed upon it; for a like treatment of the skull is seen in the head of Athené on the monument of Eubulides, published in the Annals of the Institute, VII., Plate V. The bronze helmet, with which this head of Athené was covered, was probably Corinthian, as Dr. Julius thinks.

I have further to mention a horse's head, which has apparently also belonged to a metope, or to the sculptures of a pediment, and of which I give an engraving under No. 128 (p. 216).

Among other objects found, I may mention thirty heads of terra-cotta figures, of which I give here the most remarkable under No. 129. It represents a male mask with abundant hair; the brows are contracted in a frown; the eyes shut; the

No. 127.—Female head of marble. Size about 1 : 2; depth about 2 m.

cheeks are puffed out; the nose very thick; the mouth wide open; the beard long and pointed. There were again found a very large number of watch-shaped objects of terra-cotta with two perforations, many of which have a

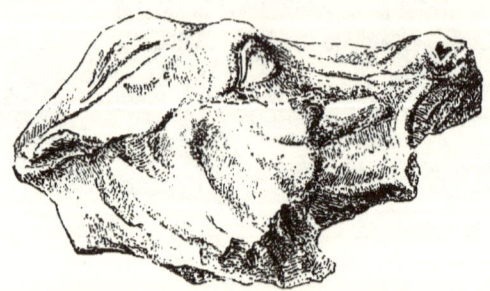

No. 128.—Horse's head of marble belonging to a metope. Size about 1:4; depth about 1 m.

stamp with different figures, like those represented in *Ilios*, p. 619, Nos. 1466–1472; also a number of terra-cotta tablets, with the winged thunderbolt of Zeus in relief, like

No. 130.—Archaic Greek Vessel. Size 1:4; depth about 1·50 m.

No. 129.—Male Mask of terra-cotta. Size about 2:3; depth 1 m.

Nos. 1459–1461, p. 618; further, a large mass of archaic painted pottery, precisely like Nos. 1439–1446, p. 615, as well as other pieces with a spiral ornamentation similar to that on the Mycenean pottery. I represent under No.

130 a very remarkable archaic Greek vessel, which resembles a turtle, but has no feet; the mouth-piece is on the left side, on which the rim projects horizontally: the vase is rudely ornamented with red cross-lines, which, owing to the dirt with which it is covered, have not come out in the photograph. A terra-cotta vase of perfectly the same shape as

No. 131.—Archaic Greek painted terra-cotta Bottle, in the form of a huge hunting bottle, with two handles and three feet. Size about 1:4; depth about 1·50 m.

No. 130, but of uniform black colour, was found, with hut-urns, under a stratum of peperino at Marino near Albano, and is preserved in the British Museum. A similar ornamentation of red cross-lines, forming lozenges, like No. 130, is seen on the remarkable archaic Greek flat two-handled tripod-bottle, No. 131, which has the form of a huge hunting-bottle. A perfectly similar archaic Etruscan bottle, but without either feet or painted ornamentation, is in the British Museum.

There occur here besides, in the lowest layers of the Hellenic *débris*, two kinds of wheel-made pottery, which we cannot ascribe either to the Aeolic city or to a prehistoric settlement; of both types we found only fragments, all of which are derived from large vases. The one kind is thoroughly baked, has the red colour of the clay, and is either polished but superficially or not polished at all. The other kind is but very slightly baked, very coarse and heavy, but well polished and glazed, of grey or blackish-grey colour, and somewhat resembles the Lydian pottery described in the tenth chapter of *Ilios*; but it cannot be confounded with that, the less so as the fragments denote larger and more bulky examples, of shapes entirely different; besides they are without exception wheel-made, a thing which is of very rare occurrence in the Lydian pottery. For all these reasons I think that these two kinds of pottery are later than the Lydian pottery, and we shall see in the following pages that they most probably belong to the age from the ninth to the fifth century B.C.

The extreme rarity of glass in the *débris* of Ilium is very remarkable; and even the few fragments of it occasionally found seem to belong to a late Roman period. There was found, however, a round perforated object made of a green glass paste with regular white strokes, much like No. 551, p. 429, in *Ilios*. I may mention that very similar objects of green glass paste with white lines, found by M. Ernest Renan in his excavations in Phoenicia, are preserved in the Museé du Louvre.

§ II.—GEMS AND COINS FOUND AT ILIUM.

Of incised gems I picked up five in my trenches, but none of them is of any great artistic value. Mr. Achilles Postolaccas attributes the three most remarkable of them with certainty to the Roman time, and explains them as follows:—One is of cornelian, and represents the Dioscuri, holding each a spear and a short sword; each of them has a star above his head. The other stone represents a caduceus between two cornucopiae, this being the symbol of the Senate of Rome. The third is a glass-paste imitation of amethyst, on which a Muse is incised. The fourth, which is also of a glass-paste, shows in pretty intaglio Jupiter sitting on his throne, holding in his right hand a lance, on his flat left hand a small Niké; at his feet is an eagle.

The same friend kindly calls my attention to the passage of Pliny (*H. N.* XXXVII. 5): "Gemmas plures, quod peregrino appellant nomine dactyliothecam, primus omnium habuit Romae privignus Sullae Scaurus. Diuque nulla alia fuit, donec Pompeius Magnus eam quae Mithridatis regis fuerat inter dona in Capitolio dicaret, ut M. Varro aliique ejusdem aetatis auctores confirmant, multum praelatam Scauri. Hoc exemplo Caesar dictator sex dactyliothecas in aede Veneris Genetricis consecravit: Marcellus Octavia genitus in aede Palatini Apollinis unam."

Mr. Postolaccas also reminds me of the incised gem which ornamented the ring of Pompey the Great, and which according to Plutarch * represented a lion carrying a sword, but according to Dion Cassius † three trophies; the latter historian adds that Sulla had an identically similar seal-ring.

I again found a great many coins; and I bought many others of the shepherds who had found them on the site of Ilium; most of them are Macedonian and imperial Roman coins. Of well-preserved coins of Ilium there were found forty-two, but all of them are of bronze; for the most part they are of the types represented in *Ilios*, pp. 641–647;

---

* *In Pompeio*, LXXX. 18 : ἦν δὲ γλυφὴ λέων ξιφήρης.

† XLII. 18 : ἐνεγέγλυπτο δὲ ἐν αὐτῷ τρόπαια τρία, ὥσπερ καὶ ἐν τῷ τοῦ Σύλλου.

the new types are described by Mr. Postolaccas as follows:—

"*Autonomous Coins of Ilium.*

"There are fifteen, five of which bear on one side the head of Pallas, in left and right profile, with a three-crested helmet; on the other side a Pallas standing, holding on her right shoulder a spear, in her left hand a spindle, with the legend IΑI. One of these four coins has a counter-mark with a star. Of the other ten coins eight are perfectly identical with these, the sole difference being that the head of Pallas on them is in three-quarter profile. These fifteen coins are of the Macedonian period. Of the time of the first Roman entrance into Asia Minor appear to be two other autonomous coins, representing on one side Hector 'festinans' and fully armed, holding in his left hand a lance and shield, in his right a firebrand to set fire to the Greek ships, with the legend ΕΚΤΩΡ; on the other side a she-wolf suckling Romulus and Remus, with the legend IΑI.

"*Of Roman Imperial Coins.*

1 coin, representing on one side Augustus, standing, with the legend ΣΕΒΑΣΤΟΥ; on the other side the bust of Pallas, with the legend IΑI . . . .
1 coin of the same with a standing Pallas, holding spear and spindle.
1 coin, having on one side the head of Augustus, without a legend; on the other a Pallas Nicephora gradiens, with the legend IΑI and a small monogram.
1 coin, on one side a head of Augustus, with the legend IΑI; on the other, an owl standing between two monograms.
1 coin, with the bust and legend of Marcus Aurelius; on the other side a Palladium, with the legend IΑIΕ–ΩΝ.
1 coin, with the bust and legend of Commodus Cæsar; on the other side a Palladium, with the legend IΑIΕ–ΩΝ.

1 medallion, with bust and legend of Commodus, and a counter-mark with a bust of Pallas; on the other side a bust of the helmeted Pallas with the aegis; the legend is obliterated.

1 medallion, precisely the same but smaller, with the legend ΙΛΙ-ΕΩΝ; no counter-mark.

1 medallion, large, with bust and legend of Commodus, and a counter-mark with a bust of Pallas; on the other side we see the she-wolf suckling Romulus and Remus, with the legend ΙΛΙ-ΕΩΝ; behind the wolf is a rock on which sits a bird.

1 coin, with bust and legend of Commodus; on the other side Pallas Nicephora, standing, with legend ΙΛΙΕΩΝ.

1 coin, with bust and legend of Crispina; on the other side the she-wolf suckling Romulus and Remus; behind the animal is a tree with a bird.

1 coin, with bust and legend of Julia Domna; on the other side a Pallas Nicephora, standing, with the legend ΙΛΙ-ΕΩΝ.

1 coin, with bust and legend of Julia Domna; on the other side a Palladium, with the legend ΙΛΙ-ΕΩΝ.

1 coin, with bust and legend of Caracalla; on the other side the same, standing, in full armour as Imperator Nicephorus, with the legend ΙΛΙ-ΕΩΝ.

1 coin, with bust and legend of Caracalla; on the other side a bust of the helmeted Pallas, with the legend ΙΛΙ-ΕΩΝ.

Coins of Alexandria Troas.

Of these there are twenty of bronze, well preserved.

1 coin, having a full-faced bust of Apollo with a laurel crown; on the other side, within a laurel crown, a lyre, with the legend—

Α—ΛΕ
ΞΑ—Ν

This is the only coin of the Macedonian time.

"Of *numi coloniae autonomi* there are:

1 coin, with the turretted bust of the personified city, with the legend [COL]–ALE–AVG, and a vexillum with the legend— CO. AV

On the other side Apollo, standing on a pedestal and sacrificing on a tripod before him, and holding in his left hand a bow.

1 coin, with an identical bust of the city and the legend COL–TROAD, and a vexillum with AV; on the other side is an eagle sitting on a bull's head with neck, and the legend CO–LAVGTRO.

1 coin, with an identical bust and the legend AL–EX–TRO, and a vexillum with CO. AV;

the other side has the same type as the foregoing, with the legend CO–L–AV–TR.

4 coins, with an identical bust and the legend CO–ALEXTRO; on the other side the she-wolf suckling Romulus and Remus, with the legend COLAVG–TRO.

"Of *numi coloniae imperatorii* there are:

1 coin, with bust and legend of Septimius Severus; on the other side the she-wolf suckling Romulus and Remus, with the legend COL–AVG–TROAD.

1 coin, with bust and legend of Caracalla, who is represented as very young; on the other side is a tripod, with the legend COL–AVG–TRO.

1 coin, with bust and legend of Caracalla; on the other side a horse grazing, with the legend, COLALEX–AVG.

1 coin, with bust and legend of Severus Alexander; on the other side Apollo standing on a pedestal, holding in the right hand a patera, in the left a bow, with the legend COLAVG–TROA.

1 coin, with bust and legend of Volusianus; on the other side an eagle on a bull's head with neck, and the legend COL–AVGTRO.

2 coins, with bust and legend of Valerianus the Elder; on the other side the same type as on the foregoing, with the legend COLAVGO (*sic*)–TROA.

2 coins, with bust and legend of Valerianus the Elder; on the other side a horse grazing, with the legend COLAVG–TRO.

1 coin, with head and legend of Gallienus; on the other side the she-wolf suckling Romulus and Remus, with the legend COLAVG–TRO.

1 coin, with bust and legend of Gallienus; on the other side a horse grazing, with legend COLAV–TRO; behind the horse is a tree.

"Of well-preserved coins of *Sigeum* there are four:

1 coin, with a head of Pallas, in nearly full face, with a three-crested helmet; on the other side two owls joined in one head, this being the type of the di-obol of Attica, with the legend ΣΙΓΕ.

1 coin, with an identical head of Pallas; on the other side an owl standing, behind which in the field is a crescent; legend ΣΙΓΕ

1 coin, with an identical head of Pallas; on the other side an owl standing, without the crescent, legend Σ–Ι
Γ–Ε.

1 coin, the same head of Pallas; on the other side an owl standing, with an upright crescent and legend Σ–Ι
Γ–Ε.

"Of well-preserved coins of *Tenedos* there was only 1 coin of bronze, with a double head, male and female; on the other side a double axe, an owl, and a cluster of grapes, with the legend ΤΕΝΕΔΙΩΝ. The double head on the Tenedian coins has generally been considered to represent Zeus and Hera; but Professor Percy Gardner (*The Types of Greek Coins*, Cambridge, 1883, p. 175), interprets it differently. He says: "Aristotle (apud Steph. Byzant. *s. v.* Tenedos) entertained a fancy that the type arose from a decree of a king of Tenedos, punishing adultery with death. But he, Professor Gardner, thinks François Lenormant's opinion far more probable, that the double head is that of the dimorphous or androgynous Dionysus.

"There were found besides, 1 coin of Thyatira in Lydia, 1 of Parion, 1 of Pergamus; 1 of Teos, 1 of Panticapaeum, and several of Greece proper, among which latter is one of Ithaca, representing on one side a head of Ulysses with a Phrygian cap, on the other a cock, with the legend ΙΘΑΚΩΝ. Of non-Asiatic Roman coins more than a hundred were found."

There were gathered at least a dozen coins of monasteries; and, as similar coins are frequently picked up by shepherds on the site of Ilium, I now firmly believe that a monastery flourished here in the Middle Ages, and that even the statement of Constantinus Porphyrogennetus,* who cites Ilium as a bishopric, may be referred to part of the Acropolis of Ilium. What strengthens me in this belief is the fact, that my architects found in the Acropolis foundations of buildings, in which capitals of the great Doric temple of Athené had been used instead of common stones. We can hardly admit that such an act of vandalism could have been committed as early as the end of the fourth century; it must have happened later. The existence of some sort of settlement here, at least in the earlier part of the Middle Ages, seems certainly indicated also by a moat, 6 mètres deep by 2·50 wide, which we found in the north-east corner of the Acropolis, and which seems to have surrounded a fort that stood there in the Middle Ages; but this fort must have been exceptionally small, because my architects find that the space enclosed by the moat

---

* *De Caerem.* II. 54, pp. 792, 794. See *Ilios*, p. 183.

hardly occupies one-eighth part of the Acropolis. The moat is entirely filled with river sand, which proves with certainty that, at the time the fort existed, the great Roman aqueduct, by which the water was brought to Ilium from the upper Thymbrius, was still in use. A large arch of this aqueduct may still be seen spanning the Thymbrius, about three miles above its confluence with the Scamander. We found on the surface or at a small depth in the sand many marble fragments of the edifices of the Acropolis, and we conclude from this, with much probability, that the moat was already filled up as far back as the time when the temples were destroyed.

But though the sanctuaries and other large edifices still existed in the 5th century A.D., and there may have been a monastery, perhaps even a bishopric, with a small fort on the Acropolis, up to a later time, the city of Ilium seems to have been deserted and lying in ruins when it was visited by the Empress Eudoxia (421-444 A.D.), the consort of Theodosius II., for in her *Ionia* she breaks out into the lamentation : " Ilios between the Ida and the sea, the city once so magnificent, merits that we shed tears over it, for it is so completely ruined that not even its foundations remain. *She who saw it bears witness to this,* to speak according to the gospel." But again it may be that, especially as Eudoxia does not call the city *Ilion,* but *Ilios,* she speaks here solely of the disappearance of the Homeric city,* for she was so excellent a Homeric scholar that she was able to write a *Life of Jesus Christ* in Homeric verses.

---

* If this interpretation be admitted, it may furnish another example of that constant habit of speaking of the destruction and desolation of *heroic Troy*, without regard to the existence of the historic Ilium, which appears to be the key to the true meaning of such passages as that cited, as if it were conclusive, from the orator Lycurgus. Such utterances indicate a sentiment rather than a site, a religious and poetical tradition, not a topographical opinion.

§ III.—The Greek and Latin Inscriptions of Ilium.

I. On a stélé of white marble, 0·79 m. long, having an upper breadth of 0,445 mm., a lower one of 0.48 m. and a thickness of 0,085 mm., found in the Acropolis of Ilium, about 0·60 m. below the surface:

```
ΤΕΙΣΑΝΔΡΩΙΑΙΣΧΙΝΗΙΧΑΡΟΓΓΗΙ
ΝΙΚΑΣΙΔΙΚΩΙΑΡΙΣΤΟΞΕΝΟΥΓΑΙΣΙΤΕ
ΝΕΔΙΟΙΣΓΡΟΞΕΝΟΙΣΚΑΙΕΥΕΡΓΕΤΑΙΣ
ΑΥΤΟΙΣΚΑΙΕΓΓΟΝΟΙΣΙΛΙΕΙΣΕΔΟΣΑΝ
ΑΤΕΛΕΙΑΝΓΑΝΤΩΝΚΑΙΟΣΑΝΩΝΗΤΑΙ
ΓΑΡΑΤΟΥΤΩΝΗΓΩΛΗΙΓΡΟΣΤΟΥΤΟΥΣΑ
ΤΕΛΗΣΕΣΤΩΤΟΥΤΕΛΟΥΣΕΑΝΔΕΤΙΣ
ΓΡΑΞΗΤΑΙΔΕΚΑΓΛΟΥΝΑΓΟΔΟΤΩΤΟΤΕΛ
ΟΣΤΟΙΣΓΡΟΞΕΝΟΙΣΕΙΝΑΙΔΕΚΑΙΑΣΥΛΙΑ
ΝΑΥΤΟΙΣΚΑΙΕΝΓΟΛΕΜΩΙΚΑΙΕΙΡΗΝΗΙ
ΚΑΙΕΝΚΤΗΣΙΝΚΑΙΓΗΣΚΑΙΟΙΚΙΩΝΚΑΙΑΛ
ΛΟΥΟΤΟΥΑΝΘΕΛΩΣΙΝΕΓΑΤΕΛΕΙΑΙΚ
ΑΙΙΛΙΕΙΑΣΕΙΝΑΙΚΑΙΕΙΣΦΥΛΗΝΕΙΣΙΟΝΤΑ
ΣΗΝΑΝΘΕΛΩΣΙΝΚΑΙΑΝΥΓΟΤΟΥΑΔΙΚΩΝ
ΤΑΙΞΕΝΩΝΕΞΕΙΝΑΙΣΥΛΑΝΕΚΤΗΣΙΛΙ
ΑΔΟΣΣΥΝΛΑΝΒΑΝΕΙΝΔΕΚΑΙΤΟΚΟΙΝΟ
ΝΤΟΙΛΙΕΩΝΓΑΡΑΚΑΛΕΙΝΔΕΚΑΙΕΝΤΟΙ
ΣΓΑΝΑΘΗΝΑΙΟΙΣΕΙΣΓΡΟΕΔΡΙΑΝΟΝΟΜΑΣ
ΤΕΙΓΑΤΡΟΘΕΝΚΑΙΑΥΤΟΥΣΚΑΙΕΓΓΟΝΟΥΣ
ΕΙΝΑΙΔΕΑΥΤΟΙΣΚΑΙΕΝΓΡΥΤΑΝΕΙΩΙΣΙΤΗ
ΣΙΝΕΑΝΔΕΤΙΣΤΟΥΤΩΝΤΙΛΥΗΙΚΑΤΑΡΑ
ΤΟΣΕΣΤΩ
```

Two of the brothers mentioned in this inscription, ΧΑΡΟΓΓΗΣ and ΝΙΚΑΣΙΔΙΚΟΣ, have names which occur here for the first time. Attention may also be drawn to the spelling of the word ΣΥΝΛΑΝΒΑΝΕΙΝ. Judging from the forms of the characters, we may assign this inscription to the 3rd century B.C.

II. On a plaque of white marble found in the Acropolis of Ilium, about 0·50 m. below the surface, 0·31 m. long, from 0·22 to 0·24 m. broad, and 0·10 m. thick, we read the following inscription, of which the beginning is lost; the beginnings of the lines are also wanting.

```
. . . . . . . ΝΕΥΕΡΓΕΤΗΙΤΙΜΗΘ(ΕΝΤΙ
. . . . . ΨΗ)ΦΙΣΜΑΕΙΣΣΤΗΛΗΝΤΟΥ
. . . . . . . ΤΟΙΕΡΟΝΤΗΣΑΘΗΝΑΣ
. . . . . ΣΑΝΟΙΙΕΡΟΝΟΜΟΙΜΕΤΑΤΟΥ
. . . . . ΗΣΑΝΜΕΝΑΝΔΡΟΣ
. . . . . ΥΘΟΥΤΙΜΟΘΕΟΣΔΩΚΟΥ
. . . . . ΥΣΓΟΛΥΧΑΡΜΟΣΜΕΛΑΝΙΓΓΙΔΟΥ
```

This inscription is interesting from the mention in it of

the ιεροnομοι, or managers of the sanctuary of the Ilian Athené. The name ΔΩΚΟΣ occurs here for the first time The inscription may be assigned to the 3rd century B.C.

III. Fragment of a white marble stélé found in the Acropolis of Ilium, about 1 m. below the surface·

```
 . . . . . ΝΗΣΑΓΟΚΑ . . . . . .
 . . ΗΜΕ)ΡΑΙΣ ΤΡΙΣΙΝΕΙΣ : . . . . .
```

This inscription seems to belong to the 3rd century B.C.

IV. Pedestal of a statue, of white marble, found at a depth of less than 1 m. below the surface, in the Acropolis of Ilium, with the following inscription:

```
ΚΙΣΣΟΦΑΝΗΣ
ΑΠΟΛΛΩΝΙΔΟΥ
```

Cissophanes is a new name. The forms of the characters show that the inscription belongs probably to the 2nd century B.C.

V. Pedestal of a statue, of white marble, found in the Acropolis of Ilium, near the surface, bearing the following inscription:

```
ΙΛΙΕΙΣΚΑΙΑΙΠΟΛΕΙΣΑΙΚΟΙΝΩΝΟΥΣΑΙ
ΤΗΣΘΥΣΙΑΣΚΑΙΤΟΥΑΓΩΝΟΣΚΑΙΤΗΣ
ΠΑΝΗΓΥΡΕΩΣΜΕΛΙΤΕΙΑΝΘΥΓΑΤΕΡΑ
ΑΠΕΛΛΕΙΟΥΣΤΟΥΛΥΣΑΝΙΟΥΙΛΙΕΩΣ
ΚΑΛΩΣΚΑΙΦΙΛΟΔΟΞΩΣΚΑΝΗΦΟΡΗΣΑΣΑΝ
ΕΥΣΕΒΕΙΑΣΕΝΕΚΕΝΤΗΣΠΡΟΣΤΗΝΘΕΑΝ
```

It follows from this inscription, which by its characters appears to be of the 1st century B.C., that on the pedestal on which it was engraved stood the statue of Meliteia, daughter of Apelleies (a name which occurs here for the first time), an Ilian, and granddaughter of Lysanias, who had distinguished herself by her zeal in the service of the goddess. This inscription furnishes another confirmation of the fact, made known by the inscription which I published in *Ilios*, pp. 633–635, that there existed a κοινόν, or union of cities, situated between the Propontis and the

Gulf of Adramyttium, and, as Droysen * remarks regarding the latter inscription, it thus explains several inscriptions already known : " According to Strabo (XIII. p. 593) the so-called Ilion was, until Alexander's arrival, a village with a small and insignificant temple of the Ilian Athené; Alexander celebrated there a sort of preliminary consecration of his campaign against Persia, and ordered that the temple should be adorned with offerings, that the place should be raised to the dignity of a town and enlarged, ἐλευθέραν τε κρῖναι καὶ ἄφορον. Later on, after the destruction of the Persian empire, he made [promised to make], as Strabo says, further additions : ἐπιστολὴν καταπέμψαι φιλάνθρωπον, ὑπισχνούμενον πόλιν τε ποιῆσαι μεγάλην καὶ ἱερὸν ἐπισημότατον, καὶ ἀγῶνα ἀποδείξειν ἱερόν. Then follows what Lysimachus and Antigonus had done for the town.

" Since Ilion was first made a city by Alexander, the union of the cities, of which it was the centre, cannot be traced back to an earlier period, but must have been established by him, because from the inscription, line 9 (pp. 633–635 in *Ilios*), where Antigonus is not indicated as βασιλεύς, as is done in line 24, we may conclude that this union existed already before 306 B.C. If Alexander united the liberated Hellenic cities of this district in a κοινόν, and did not induce them to enter into the κοινόν of the Hellenes, which had its synedrion at Corinth, we have gained an important fact bearing upon the political condition of Alexander's empire.

" From the statement of the Lampsacenian at the end of the inscription, we must conclude that Lampsacus belonged to the union, like Gargara on the Gulf of Adramyttium; and we are authorized to suppose that the cities situated between these two points, and especially Alexandria Troas, belonged to this κοινόν.

---

* Joh. Gust. Droysen, *Geschichte des Hellenismus*, Gotha, 1878, pp. 386, 387.

§ III.]   GREEK INSCRIPTIONS OF ILIUM.   229

"That these cities were free cities, or were intended to be such, may be seen from the mission mentioned in line 24: εἰς τὸν βασιλέα (Antigonus) ὑπὲρ τῆς ἐλευθερίας τῶν πόλεων τῶν κοινωνουσῶν τοῦ ἱεροῦ καὶ τῆς πανηγύρεως. The συνέδριον of these cities is therefore connected, not only with the festival in Ilion and the games which were celebrated there, but also with the political position of the united cities."

VI. On a fragment of marble, 0·35 m. in height and 0·65 m. in breadth, found at Bounarbashi, but doubtless brought thither from Ilium.

```
(ΗΒΟΥΛΗ ΚΑΙ) ΟΔΗΜΟΣΕΤΙΜΗΣΑΝ
. . . . . . . ΔΙΑΒΙΟΥΑΥΤΟΚΡΑΤΟΡΟΣ
. . . . . . . ΟΥΥΙΟΥΣΕΒΑΣΤΟΥ
. . . . . . . ΕΥΘΥΔΙΟΥΥΙΟΝ
. . . . . . . ΙΔΙΑΤ...ΙΝΠΡΟΣΤΟΝ
. . . . . . . ΕΥΣΕΒΕΙΑΝΚΑΙΔΙΑ
. . . . . . . ΡΙΛΑΕΥΕΡΓΕΣΙΑΣ
```

The inscription, if we may judge from the forms of the characters, belongs perhaps to the 2nd century A.D. The name of Euthydius occurs here for the first time.

VII. On the upper part of the pedestal of a statue discovered at Hissarlik.

```
ΗΒΟΥΛΗΚΑΙΟΔΗΜΟΣ
ΓΟΓΛΙΟΝΟΥΗΔΙΟΝ ΓΩΛ
ΛΙΩΝΑ
```

Publius Vedius Pollio is mentioned in an inscription found in the Acropolis of Athens, and published in Boeckh, C. I. G. 366. He was a friend of Augustus and famous for his luxury (Tacit. *Ann.* i. 10).

VIII. On a fragment of basalt discovered in the Acropolis of Ilium.

```
ΚΟΝΑ
ΩΝ
ΔΕΓΛ
ΑΜΦΙ
```

In the first line we should probably read ΕΙΚΟΝΑ.

IX. A small white marble column of rude workmanship, found in the theatre of Ilium, at a depth of about 1 m.,

0·25 m. high, upper diameter 0·125 m., lower diameter
0·145 m., with the following inscription :

ΛΟΥΚΙΟC
CATPEIOC
ΝΕΜΕCΙΕΥ
ΧΗΝΕΥΗΚ
Ω

I may add that the Satrii were a Roman family, and that a Lucius Satrius Abascantus is mentioned by Pliny the Younger (*Ep.* x. 6), as having been recommended by him to the Emperor Trajan. The form of the characters of this inscription would seem to show, however, that it belongs to a later date.

X. Fragment of a plaque of white marble, found on the northern slope of the Acropolis-hill of Ilium :

. . . . . HEN . . .
. . . . TΩNΔH . . .
. . . . ITATE . . .
. . . . . ΣΘΟ . . .

The forms of the characters lead us to assign the inscription to the 1st or 2nd century A.D.

XI. A fragment of white marble, found on the northern slope of the Acropolis-hill of Ilium, contains the word

ΠΑΡΗ
ΝΟΙ

surrounded by a laurel-wreath.

XII. Plaque of white marble, found in the theatre of Ilium, at a depth of about 1 m.; it is 0·40 m. long by 0·26 m. broad and 0·04 m. thick; it is broken on the left side :

. . . . TIΒΕΡΙΩΚΛΑΥΔΙΩΙΟΥΛΙΑΝΩ
. . . . . ΗΤΗΡΙΟΝΥΠΟΤΟΝ
. . . . . ΗΔΟΓΜΑΤΙ

The forms of the characters lead us to assign this inscription to the 2nd or 3rd century A.D.

XIII. Votive tablet of white marble, with two ears in

relief, found in the theatre of Ilium, at a depth of about
1 m. It bears the unfinished inscription:

ΕΥΤΕΡ

It is evidently later than the Christian era.

XIV. Pedestal of white marble, 0·90 m. high, 0·53 m.
broad, found in the Turkish cemetery of Halil Kioi, with
the following inscription:

ΓΑΠΑΤΡΙΗΓΑΘΟΝΤΑ
ΚΑΤΕΣΧΕΜΕΙΛΙΑΣΑΙ
Α
ΑΛΚΑΝΕΛΛΑΔΙΚΑ(Ν
ΚΕΥΘΟΜΕΝΑΛΑΓΟ
ΣΙΝ

This inscription has been wrongly copied and explained
by Boeckh, *C. I. G.*, No. 3632. He has not seen the first
letter, which is a very plain Γ, and has read ΑΠΑΤΡΙΗ, a
word which has no existence in the Greek language, and
which, strange to say, he translates by "peregrina habita-
tione." ΓΑΘΩΝ is a proper name, whereas Boeckh assumes
that ΓΑΘΟΝΤΑ is the participle of γήθω, which is found
only in very late writers instead of the classical γηθέω.
Boeckh has not seen the I and second A at the end of the
first line, and merely conjectures them. His fourth error
is that in his copy he reads ΛΑΓΩΣΙΝ, which he is forced
to correct into ΛΑΓΟΣΙΝ, whilst in reality the original has
an Ο. The translation is: "My fatherland, the soil of
Ilium, holds me, Gathon, hiding in its flanks one of the
strong men of Greece" (literally "Grecian strength").
ΓΑΘΩΝ is a perfectly new name, which has never occurred
before. The reader will notice that the forms of the words
used in this inscription are not Ionic: thus we have ΓΑ
instead of ΓΗ; ΑΛΚΑΝ instead of ΑΛΚΗΝ; ΚΕΥΘΟΜΕΝΑ instead
of ΚΕΥΘΟΜΕΝΗ. On the other hand, the hiatus ΜΕΙΛΙΑΣΑΙΑ
shows that the phrase has been taken from the old epic
poetry of Greece, in which the word ΙΛΙΑΣ still preserved
its original digamma.

XV. Round a base of white calcareous stone, 1·41 m. high, 0·60 m. in diameter, found in the Turkish cemetery of Halil Kioi, is the following inscription of nineteen lines:

ΑΝΤΩΝΙΑΝΤΗΝ
ΑΔΕΛΦΙΔΗΝΤΗΝΘΕΟΥ
. . . ΣΕΒΑΣΤΟΥΓΥΝΑΙΚΑΔΕΓΕ
ΝΟΜΕΝΗΝΔΡΟΥΣΟΥΚΛΑΥ
ΔΙΟΥΑΔΕΛΦΟΥΤΟΥΑΥ
ΤΟΚΡΑΤΟΡΟΣΤΙΒΕΡΙΟΥΣΕΒΑΣ
ΤΟΥΚΑΙΣΕΒΑΣΤΟΥΜΗΤΕΡΑ
ΓΕΡΜΑΝΙΚΟΥΚΑΙΣΑΡΟΣ
ΚΑΙ)ΤΙΒΕΡΙΟΥΚΛΑΥ
ΔΙΟΥΓΕΡΜΑΝΙΚΟΥ
ΚΑΙΛΕΙΒΙΑΣΘΕΑΣΑΦΡΟ
ΔΕΙΤΗCΑΝΧΕΙCΙΑΔΟC
ΠΛΕΙCΤΑCΚΑΙΜΕΓΙC
ΤΑCΑΡΧΑCΤΟΥΘΕΙΟΤΑ
ΤΟΥΓΕΝΟΥCΠΑΡΑCΧΟΥ
CΑΝΦΙΛѠΝΑΠΟΛ
ΛѠΝΙΟΥΤΗΝΕΑΥΤΟΥ
ΘΕΑΝΚΑΙΕΥΕΡΓΕΤΙΝ
ΕΚΤѠΝΙΔΙѠΝ

There is no inscription in the *C. I. G.* which gives such full details of the relationship of Antonia, who is here stated to be, as in fact she was, a niece of Augustus, wife of Drusus Claudius, the brother of the Emperor Tiberius, and mother of Germanicus Caesar and Tiberius Claudius Germanicus, as well as of Livia (the younger, here written ΛΕΙΒΙΑ), and called the goddess Aphrodite belonging to the race of Anchises. As the younger Livia was born in 9 B.C. and died in 31 A.D., we may be certain that this inscription belongs to the beginning of the 1st century A.D. As regards the characters, it will be observed that a remarkable change takes place in the middle of the inscription in the shape of the Σ, Ε and Ω.

XVI. On the cornice of a white marble base in the Turkish cemetery of Halil Kioi, which is 0·89 m. high, 0·31 m. broad in the upper part, and 0·36 m. in the lower, and 0·32 m. thick:

ΦΔ'ΘΕΟΔѠΡΟC
ΑΠιϕΡ'ΖΑΤΕѠC
· · Τ · · · · · ΤΗ · · ·

Below the cornice are traces of three lines of characters, probably forming part of an older inscription, which has been effaced and replaced by the three lines on the cornice. The forms of the characters prove that the inscription is later than the Christian era.

XVII. Fragment of a Doric architrave of white marble in the Turkish cemetery of Halil Kioi, with the following inscription :
EPM . . . . .

The characters are of immense size, being 1·20 m. high.

XVIII. Plaque of white marble in the same cemetery, 0·52 m. long, 0·30 m. broad, and 0·11 m. thick; on the right and lower side it is broken; on the left side are the marks of another plaque, to which it has been attached. It has the following inscription :

. . . . . ENA(Ξ) . . . . .
. . . . . . ΟΥ . . . . . .

XIX. On the base of a statue of white marble in the old Turkish cemetery of Koum Kioi. The upper part of the base is destroyed, but traces of the feet of the statue which stood upon it are still visible :

HBOYΛHKAIOΔH
MOΣETEI*MHΣAN   * Sic.
ΛIKINNIONΠPOKΛ(ON
Θ)EMIΣΩNATONΦIΛ
ONKAIΠPOΣTATHNK(AI
K)OΣMONTOYΣYNEΔPI
ϹY)TΩNENNEAΔHMΩN
KAI)EYEPΓETHNTOYΔHMOY
APET)HΣENEKENKAIE(Y
NOIAΣ TH)ΣEIΣTHNΠO(ΛIN

This inscription is of capital importance, since it states that the ΣΥΝΕΔΡΙΟΝ, referred to in the inscription No. V., as well as in the inscription given on pp. 633-635 in *Ilios*, consisted of nine cities. A Licinnius Proclus is mentioned in a Greek inscription found at Smyrna and given in the *C. I. G.* No. 3173, and he may be the same person as the Licinnius Proclus of our inscription. The Smyrna inscription is dated in the year 80 A.D., and the forms of the characters in our inscription would show that it belongs to the same period.

XX. Plaque of white marble, found in the old Turkish

cemetery of Koum Kioi, 1,240 mm. long, 0,685 mm. thick, and 0,460 mm. broad. It seems to have belonged to a large base, on which stood two statues; the left side is broken:

ΓΟΝΘΕΟΝ

ΑΥΤΟΚΡΑ(ΤΟΡΑΤΙ
ΤΟΝΚΑΙΣΑΡΑΘ(ΕΟΝ
ΘΕΟΥΟΥΕΣΠΑ(ΣΙΑ
ΝΟΥΥΙΟΝΣΕΒΑΣ(ΤΟΝ

This inscription belongs to the reign of Titus.

XXI. On a plaque of white marble, found in the house of the peasant Masitsi in the village of Koum Kioi. The beginning is lost, as well as the ends of all the lines, while the beginnings only of the last three lines are preserved. The plaque is 1 m. long, 0·34 m. broad, 0·13 m. thick:

. . . . E)OPTAI . . . .
. . . . ΝΑΠΗΤΟ . . . .
. . . . ΩΝΙΕΡΟΝ . . . .
. . . . ΨΗΦΙ)ΣΜΑΤΗΣΒΟΥ(ΛΗΣ . . .
. . . . ΧΑΡΙΣΤΙΑΝΤΗΝΠΡ . . . . . .
ΝΑΙΔΕΚΑΙΤΩΘΕΙΟΤΑ(ΤΩ . . . .
ΝΩΣΕΒΑΣΤΩΩΣΕΚΤ . . . .
ΤΗΣΙΕΡΕΙΑΣΑΥΤΟΥ

The lost name of the emperor seems to be that of Hadrian or one of the Antonines.

XXII. Block of white marble, with three crowns of olive, each containing the inscription ΟΔΗΜΟΣ. It was found built into the house of the peasant Gianakis Psochlous in Koum Kioi. The inscription which followed has been lost.

XXIII. Fragment of white marble, found in the Turkish cemetery of Koum Kioi, with the inscription:

ΟΣ
Τ)ΟΥΣΚΑΜΑ

The name is evidently either Scamander or Scamandrius.

XXIV. I owe to the kindness of Mr. Frank Calvert a squeeze of the following interesting inscription, engraved on a small marble slab found at Kurshunlu Tepeh. It was probably headed by the words ΣΥΝΕΔΡΙΟΝ ΤΕΧΝΙΤΩΝ, or something similar. The name ΛΕΥΚΙΟΣ (Lucius), which occurs in it, makes it probable that it is later than the first Roman invasion of Asia (190 B.C.). The inscription is difficult to decipher, the letters being much worn. The letter Σ in ΒΑΣΜΟΥΣ, in place of Θ, can leave no doubt that Θ was pronounced at the time this inscription was written in the same way as that in which it is pronounced in modern Greek. The name of the town referred to in the inscription is unknown to us. It is probably the city which stood on Mount Kurshunlu Tepeh and occupied the site once occupied, in my opinion, by Palaescepsis, and at an earlier epoch by Dardanié. But the name of the city which succeeded to Palaescepsis we do not know.

```
 1. ΙΕΡΑΔΙΟΝΥΣΟΥ . . . . . . . . . . . . . .
    ΒΑΤΡΙΟΥΤΡΙΑΚΑΔΙΕΠΡΥΤΑΝΕΥΟΝΣΚΑ
    ΜΑΝΔΡΙΟΣΗΡΑΚΛΕΙΔΟΥΔΙΟΝΥΣΙΟΣΒΑΚΟ
    ΥΜΙΛΗΣΙΟΣΑΝΔΡΗΡΑΤΟΥΗΡΑΚΛΕΙΔΗΣΑΕ
 5. ΛΛΙΚΩΝΤΟΣΕΠΕΣΤΑΤΕΙΛΕΥΚΙΟΣΜΙΛΗΣΙ(ΟΣ)
    (Ε)ΓΡΑΜΜΑΤΕΥΕΣΙΜΙΑΣΣΙΜΙΟΥΕΒΑΣΙΛΕΥΕΜΗ(Τ)
    ΡΟΔΩΡΟΣΜΙΜΑΝΤΟΣΗΡΑΚΛΕΙΔΗΣΑΒΑΝΤΟΣ(ΕΛΕ)
    ΞΕΝΑΓΑΘΗΙΤΥΧΗΙΣΥΝΤΕΤΑΧΘΑΙΠΕΡΙΤΩΝΧΟΡ(ΩΝ)
    ΟΠΩΣΚΑΘΕΚΑΣΤΟΝΕΤΟΣΗΠΟΛΙΣΠΟΗΙΤΩΙΔΙΟΝ
10. (Υ)ΣΩΙΘΕ(Α)ΝΤΟΔΕΑΡΓΥΡΙΟΝΕΙΝΑΙΤΟΕΙΣΤΗΝΘΕΛΝ
    ΤΟΠΕΡΙΓΙΝΟΜΕΝΟΝΑΠΟΤΩΝΙΕΡΕΙΩΝΕΚΑΣΤΟΥΕΤΟ(Υ)
    ΣΣΤΑΤΗΡΑΣΔΙΑΚΟΣΙΟΥΣΚΑΤΑΣΚΕΥΑΣΑΙΔΕΚΑΙ(Τ)
    (Ο)ΘΕΑΤΡΟΝΚΑΙΑΝΕΛΕΙΝΤΟΥΣΑΡΧΑΙΟΥΣΒΑΣΜΟΥΣ
    ΚΑΙΑΝΑΧΩΣΑΙΩΣΚΑΛΛΙΣΤΑΚΑΙΟΣΟΣΜΕΝΑΝΤΟ(Υ)
15. ΥΠΑΡΧΟΝΤΟΣΛΙΘΟΥΧΡΗΣΙΜΟΣΗΙΕΙΣΤΟΥΣΒΑΣΜΟ(ΥΣ)
    ΚΑΙΤΑΛΛΑΤΟΥΤΩΙΧΡΗΣΑΣΘΑΙΤΟΔΕΛΟΙΠΟΝΕΠΙΤ(Ε)
    (Λ)ΕΙΝΚΑΘΕΚΑΣΤΟΝΕΤΟΣΑΠΟΤΟΥΑΡΓΥΡΙΟΥΤΟΥΠΕΡΙ
    ΓΙΝΟΜΕΝΟΥΑΠΟΤΗΣΘΕΑΣΚΑΤΑΣΚΕΥΑΣΑΙΔΕΚΑΙΤ(Ο)
    (ΠΡΟ)ΣΚΗΝ˙ΟΝΩΣΑΝΔΟΚΗΙΤΟΙΣΑΠΟΔΕΙΧΘΕΙΣΙΟΙΚΟ
20. (ΔΟΜ)ΗΣΑΙΔΕΚΑΙΤΟΤΕΙΧΙΟΝΤΟΕΠΑΝΩΤΟΥΘΕΑΤΡΟΥ [Κ]*ΑΙ
    (Τ)ΟΥΓΥΡΓΟΥΕΩΣΤΩΝΣΚΑΜΑΝΔΡΙΟΥΟΙΚΙΩΝΚΑΙΝ
    ΗΣΑΙΤΕΤΡΑΠΗΧΥΚΑΙΓΕΙΣΟΝΕΙΝΑΙΤΟΔΕΠΕΡ(Υ)
    ΣΙΚΑΙΤΟΤΡΙΤΟΝΕΤΟΣΠΕΡΙΓΙΝΟΜΕΝΟΝΑΡΓΥΡΙΟΝ
    ΤΟΤΩΝΙΕΡΕΙΩΝΑΝΑΛΙΣΚΕΙΝΕΙΣΤΕΤΗΝΑΝΑΧΡ(ΕΙΑΝ)
25. ΤΟΥΘΕΑΤΡΟΥΚΑΙΕΙΣΑΛΛΗΝΕΠΙΣΚΕΥΗΝΑΝ  . . . .
    ΕΛΛΕΙΠΗΙΔΙΔΟΝΑΙΤΟΝΤΑΜΙΑΝΜΗΕ . . . . . . . .
    ΟΥΑΡΓΥΡΙΟΝΕΙΣΜΗΘΕΝΑΛΛΟΚΑ . . . . . . (ΩΣ)
    ΠΕΡΣΥΝΤΕΤΑΚΤΑΙΤΑ . . . . . . . . . . . . .
    . . . ΤΕΤΡΑΜΜΕΝΑ . . . . . . . . . . . . .
30. . . . . . ΗΚΟΝΤΑ . . . . . . . . . . . . .
```

The latter part of the first line is obliterated, and ΒΑΤΡΙΟΥ is the end of a name, so that the meaning is "The sacred rites of Dionysos . . . the son of . . . ΒΑΤΡΙΟΣ," etc. The only names found in Pape are ΣΙΜΙΑΣ (ΣΙΜΜΙΑΣ), ΜΙΜΑΣ and ΑΒΑΣ, all of which seem to be Thracian. The names ΒΑΚΗΣ or ΒΑΚΟΣ may belong to Asia Minor. ΑΕΛΛΙΚΩΝ is a patronymic from ΑΕΛΛΙΚΟΣ, which is derived from ΑΕΛΛΑ.

---

* Omitted in the text.

XXV. The two following inscriptions are in Latin. Both were found in the cemetery of Koum Kioi. The first is engraved on the quadrangular white marble pedestal of a statue, 1·18 m. high, by 0·49 m. broad, on which may be seen the traces of feet belonging to more than one figure. The stone on which the inscription is engraved originally served for another inscription, which has been erased to make way for the later one.

```
         DN
    L. CLAUDIULIANU
    DImPERAUF
```

This inscription is in late Roman characters, and contains the dedication of a statue by a certain Aufidius to Lucius Claudius Julianus.

XXVI. The second Latin inscription is on a plaque of white marble, broken on all its sides. It reads·

```
. . . . . . ROU . . . .
. . . . . UICTOR . . .
. . (A)UREL-IOU . . . .
. . . LICIAUG . . . . .
. . A)UR'HERMOGE . .
. . . OCONSUL' X . . .
```

§ *IV. My Critics.*— I cannot conclude the discussion of the seven settlements on the citadel-hill of Hissarlik without adding a few words in reply to my persistently bitter critic, Professor R. C. Jebb, who in his long dissertation on "The Ruins at Hissarlik; their Relation to the *Iliad*," in the *Journal of Hellenic Studies*, October 3, 1882, has propounded the following theory :—That the uppermost stratum, about 2 m. deep, marks the Greek Ilium of the Roman age subsequently to its destruction by Fimbria in 85 B.C.;—that a Lydian settlement had no real existence, and must altogether disappear;—that the next stratum below, 2 m. deep, the fifth prehistoric settlement, described and illustrated in the ninth chapter of *Ilios*, is the Greek Ilium of the Macedonian age, which was embellished by Lysimachus about 300 B.C., and was sacked by Fimbria in 85 B.C.;—that the next stratum of ruins, about 3 mètres deep, the fourth prehistoric settlement, extensively described and illustrated in the eighth chapter of *Ilios*, is in reality the Greek Ilium as it existed before the Macedonian age;—that the stratum of *débris* immediately beneath, about 3 mètres deep, the third prehistoric city, described and illustrated in the seventh chapter of *Ilios*, is in reality the Greek Ilium in its earliest form, that is, the first settlement of Aeolian colonists on the hill of Hissarlik, about 560 or perhaps 700 B.C.*;—that the next stratum of ruins, about 4 mètres deep, the second prehistoric city, described and illustrated in the sixth chapter of *Ilios*, may be the city, the capture and siege of which gave rise to the legend of Troy;—and finally, that the last stratum of *débris*, 2·50 m. deep, which lies on the virgin soil, and is described and illustrated in the fifth chapter of *Ilios*, is still earlier.

If in Professor Jebb's whole tone, in this and his other discussions of my discoveries, I trace an *animus* of which I might with good right complain, I will certainly be no party to bringing down this great scientific question to the level of a personal dispute. But no courtesy on my part can save Professor Jebb from the fate on which an eminent classical scholar rushes when he mingles in an archaeological debate in ignorance of the first principles of archaeology :

οἴῳ πεπνῦσθαι· τοὶ δὲ σκιαὶ ἀΐσσουσιν.

As his authorship of the anonymous article on my *Ilios* in the *Edinburgh Review* of April, 1881, has been since acknowledged, I must assume that he has read the book, in the whole substance of which (apart from my opinions), as well as in the thousands of objects in my Trojan collection, which he might have seen for three years and a half in

---

* *Journal of Hellenic Studies*, III. 2, p. 213. I may remark on this, that the age of the elder Cyrus, "when the Persian power was becoming predominant," was *not* in "the *earlier* half of the sixth century, B.C." I may also observe that Professor Jebb adopts without question Kramer's reading of κατὰ Κροῖσον in Strabo (XIII. p. 593), for the old reading κατὰ χρησμόν, which has at least as good MS. authority, and is more likely to have been altered into the former, than *vice versâ*.

the South Kensington Museum, there is an overwhelming mass of evidence, which I should have thought it impossible for the veriest tyro to reconcile with this crude hypothesis.

The Lydian settlement, which Professor Jebb so jauntily disposes of, cannot be got rid of by a stroke of the pen; for just below the stratum, 2 m. deep, of the Roman and Greek Ilium, there occur by hundreds very curious hand-made, and sometimes also wheel-made, terra-cotta vases, which, as is shown by the forty-four illustrations given in *Ilios*, pp. 589–599, Nos. 1362–1405, are entirely different in shape from all the pottery found in the five prehistoric settlements at Hissarlik, as well as from all Greek and Roman pottery ever met with; the same may be said of its material, fabric, and colour, which bear a great resemblance to the material, fabric, and colour, of the Albano hut-urns published by Sir John Lubbock.* As I have explained in *Ilios*, p. 587, it is merely from the great resemblance this pottery bears to the hand-made vases found in the ancient cemeteries of Rovio, Volterra, Bismantova, Villanova, and other places in Italy, which are held to be either archaic Etruscan or pre-Etruscan, that I think it likely that there may have been a Lydian settlement on Hissarlik, contemporary with the colonization of Etruria by the Lydians, which is asserted by Herodotus. But if any one can prove that this pottery is not Lydian, but belongs to another people, who had their settlement on Hissarlik, I shall gladly acknowledge my error. Mr. Albert Dumont, indeed, whom Professor Jebb repeatedly misquotes in his attacks on me, seems to claim for this very Lydian pottery an enormous antiquity, since he includes the vase No. 1392, p. 596, in *Ilios*, reproduced on p. 10 under No. 27 in his work *Les Céramiques de la Grèce Propre*, Paris, 1881, among the pottery which he considers *more ancient* than that of Thera, which latter he holds to belong to the people

---

* L. Pigorini and Sir John Lubbock, *Notes on Hut-urns, and other Objects from Marino near Albano*, London, 1869.

who inhabited the island before the great volcanic catastrophe and cataclysm, supposed by him to have taken place between the sixteenth and the thirteenth centuries B.C. (See his work mentioned above, p. 30). But I repeat here what I have stated in *Ilios*, p. 587, that all I am able to show of this Lydian settlement is an enormous mass of curious pottery: there is no wall of defence nor any house-wall left, which I can with any degree of probability attribute to it.

Professor Jebb asserts, that the last or fifth prehistoric city of Hissarlik is the Greek Ilium destroyed in 85 B.C.; that the fourth is the Greek Ilium as it existed before the Macedonian age, which was destroyed in 359 B.C., and that the third is the Aeolic Ilium of 560 or 700 B.C. This assertion must sound to any one who has but the most superficial knowledge of archaeology, just as absurd as if he heard it asserted that horses have five legs; since the character of Greek pottery ought to be known to the least instructed student of archaeology, all museums and private collections being full of it, so that we are perfectly well acquainted with it in all its various forms, from the remote age of the royal tombs at Mycenae down to the Roman period. Even the most archaic Greek pottery, of which thousands of fragments have been found at Hissarlik at a depth of from 1·30 to 2 m. (see *Ilios*, pp. 613–615, Nos. 1435–1446), is *painted;* whereas colours and the artistic use of them were perfectly unknown at Troy, not only to all the prehistoric colonists, from the first settlement up to the last, but also to the Lydian settlers, or whatever be the people to which the pottery described and illustrated in the tenth chapter of *Ilios* may belong. Everybody who has visited my Trojan collection during the three years and a half that it was exhibited at the South Kensington Museum, or during the three years that it has now been exhibited in the Schliemann Museum at Berlin, and has not intentionally shut his eyes, must have seen this to be the case, and must at the same time have convinced himself that the shape, manufacture, and clay, of all the Trojan pottery, are totally different from those of any Greek pottery whatsoever. I can assure my readers that among the many thousands of prehistoric objects of terra-cotta contained in the Schliemann Museum at Berlin, and in the museum in my own house at Athens, and of which about 1400 are illustrated in *Ilios*, in the chapters on the five different settlements to which each of them belongs, there is hardly one which has any resemblance to Greek terra-cottas. And what shall we say of the stone battle-axes, rude stone hammers, and other stone utensils, which occur even in the uppermost prehistoric city (Chapter IX. in *Ilios*), and which are found by thousands in all the four lower settlements, and particularly in immense masses in the fourth from below, which Professor Jebb imagines to be the original Greek Ilium, destroyed in 359 B.C.? I would ask him where he has learned that the Greeks of the historic period used such weapons and implements of stone? If Professor Jebb could remove by witchcraft the Trojan collections, and all that has been written about them by scholars, from the surface of the earth, he might possibly carry his point, and convince the world that all the three upper prehistoric settlements were Greek, and that the Lydian pottery was a dream of mine.

In support of his wild theories, Professor Jebb refers to Mr. Albert Dumont, who, in his work mentioned above, notices among the Trojan pottery a piece of earthenware, from the character of which he infers that it is not older than the second century B.C., *i.e.* contemporary with the Macedonian Ilium; but at the same time he prudently leaves unnoticed Mr. Dumont's footnote on page 4, in which that scholar acknowledges his error, and says that the object is figured in *Ilios* (No. 1468, p. 619), in the chapter upon the Greek Ilium, with the indication that it had been found at a depth of from 2 to 6 feet (0·60 to 1·80 m.). Mr. Dumont honourably makes the same acknowledgment in a footnote on page 10, regarding two pieces of archaic painted pottery (Nos. 20, 21, on p. 9), but to these notes

Professor Jebb has suppressed all allusion. Certainly Mr. Dumont sometimes makes mistakes, which he does not retract. Thus, for instance, he sees (page 4) in fig. 103 as given in *Ilios*, a mould for ornaments, though in reality it is a mould with beds for very primitive arrow-heads, one of which has two long barbs. He further sees in the small flat, very thin, crescent-like object of silver, given in *Ilios* under No. 122, a fibula, whereas in reality it is an earring of precisely the same form as the nine gold earrings represented by No. 917, p. 501, in *Ilios*. I repeat that there is no trace of a fibula at Hissarlik, either in any of the prehistoric settlements or in the Lydian settlement. For the rest, Mr. Dumont acknowledges in his work (p. 3) that the vases, arms and ornaments found by me at Hissarlik belong to one of the most ancient civilizations of which traces have as yet been discovered in Greek countries. Besides, Mr. Dumont expresses (page 72) the firm conviction, that the pottery of Thera is earlier than the sixteenth century B.C., but that it is *later* than the pottery of Hissarlik, in which, as is evident from what he states (pp. 2–18), he includes not only the pottery of all the five prehistoric cities, but also the pottery of the Lydian settlement. All this Professor Jebb wisely leaves unnoticed, for it would at once upset his scheme of turning the prehistoric pottery into Roman and Greek pottery; he only quotes Dumont's erroneous statements as tangible proofs against me, and chooses to pass over his corrections of those very statements in silence.

On pages 128–130 I have answered in full Professor Jebb's and Dr. Brentano's fancies about the terra-cotta ball divided into zones, which was found in the Trojan stratum, and I have shown the complete absurdity of their assertion, that it is referable to circa 350–150 B.C. I shall say no more on the subject; and be content to add, that it is no part of the duty of a discoverer to waste his time in giving his critics elementary lessons in archaeological science.

CHAPTER VI.

THE CONICAL MOUNDS, CALLED HEROIC TUMULI.

§ *I. The Tumulus of Achilles.*—Another object of special interest was my exploration of eight more of the conical mounds, the so-called Trojan Heroic Tumuli. I began with the excavation of the two tumuli situated at the foot of Cape Sigeum, the larger of which the tradition of all antiquity attributed to Achilles, the smaller one perhaps to his friend Patroclus. But this is by no means quite certain, for, according to Strabo,* there were at the foot of Cape Sigeum the tombs of Achilles, Patroclus, and Antilochus, and, as before mentioned, I discovered that one of the large massive windmills to the south-east of Sigeum is actually built on the top of an ancient conical tumulus, which makes up the number three, as stated by Strabo. With regard to the large conical hill on the projecting headland, there can be no question that it is the very tumulus to which tradition unanimously pointed as the sepulchre of Achilles; but we have nothing to guide us as to which of the two remaining tumuli was attributed by the ancients to Antilochus, and which to Patroclus, for the name "tomb of Patroclus," which the smaller unencumbered tumulus now bears, seems to have been given to it less than a century ago by Lechevalier or Choiseul-Gouffier,† and the other tumulus, which is crowned by the windmill, has not come under the notice of any modern traveller, and is therefore marked on no map. But for brevity's sake I

---

* XIII. p. 596.
† Carl Gotthold Lenz, *Die Ebene von Troia nach dem Grafen Choiseul-Gouffier*, Neu-Strelitz, 1798, p. 64.

shall still call the small unencumbered conical hill the tumulus of Patroclus.

That the large tumulus on the jutting headland was considered in the historical times of antiquity as the sepulchre of Achilles, is evident from Strabo,[*] Arrian,[†] Pliny,[‡] Lucian,[§] Quintus Smyrnaeus,[||] Dion Cassius,[¶] and others. It was situated within the fortified town of Achilleum,[**] which seems to have extended to and enclosed the site of the present little Turkish town of Koum Kaleh; for fragments of marble columns and other architectural blocks, which are found near the surface, denote the existence of an ancient city on that site. The existence of an ancient settlement to the south and east of the tumulus is attested by the masses of ancient pottery with which the ground is covered.

The tumulus of Patroclus is about 350 yards to the south-east of the sepulchre of Achilles, and the third tumulus, on which the windmill stands, is about a thousand yards still farther to the south.[††]

The tomb of Achilles was, according to Choiseul-Gouffier,[‡‡] a century ago vulgarly called "Thiol," whilst now this tumulus, as well as that of Patroclus, are indifferently called "Cuvin" by the villagers. The former tumulus is situated immediately to the north-east of Cape Sigeum, at a lesser height, on the very border of the high table-land which falls off abruptly, and is about 250 yards from the Hellespont.[§§] On account of its high situation it can be seen from a great distance out at sea, and it answers

---

[*] XIII. p. 595.
[†] Anab. I, 11, 12; compare Cicero, pro Arch. 10.
[‡] H. N. V. 33.   [§] Charon, 521.
[||] VII. 402.   [¶] LXXVII. 16.
[**] See the authors just cited.
[††] See the large Map of the Troad at the end of this volume.
[‡‡] See C. G. Lenz, Die Ebene von Troia, etc., p. 64.
[§§] See the large Map of the Troad.

therefore very well to the indications of Homer.* "Then we the holy host of Argive warriors piled over them (thy bones) a great and goodly tomb on a jutting headland upon the wide Hellespont, that it might be visible far off from the sea, to men who now are, and to those that shall hereafter be born."

In the spring of 1879 the proprietors of these tumuli asked me £100 for permission to explore the tomb of Achilles, and as much for that of Patroclus, but now they had considerably modified their pretensions and asked only £20 for each, whilst I offered only £1. Happily the civil governor of the Dardanelles, Hamid Pasha, came out in April to see my works, and I profited by this opportunity to explain the matter to him, and to convince him that the demand of the proprietors was exorbitant and ridiculous. He thereupon decided that I should at once commence the exploration of the two tumuli, with or without the consent of the proprietors; and that, in case they were not satisfied with £2, or at the utmost £3, he would, after the exploration had been finished, send out an expert to get the damage estimated and ascertain the indemnity the two proprietors were entitled to. Being afraid to come off second best by waiting, the two men now eagerly accepted £3 in full settlement of their claim. But as by the Turkish law they were entitled to one-third of any treasure-trove that might be discovered, they watched the progress of the excavation most vigilantly, and never left it for a moment. But they were greatly disappointed, not I; for, having found no gold or silver in the six tumuli which I had explored before, I had not the slightest hope of discovering any now. All I expected to find was pottery,

---

* *Od.* XXIV. 80–84:

ἀμφ' αὐτοῖσι δ' ἔπειτα μέγαν καὶ ἀμύμονα τύμβον
χεύαμεν Ἀργείων ἱερὸς στρατὸς αἰχμητάων,
ἀκτῇ ἐπὶ προὐχούσῃ, ἐπὶ πλατεῖ Ἑλλησπόντῳ,
ὥς κεν τηλεφανὴς ἐκ ποντόφιν ἀνδράσιν εἴη,
τοῖς οἳ νῦν γεγάασιν καὶ οἳ μετόπισθεν ἔσονται.

§ I.] EXPLORATION OF THE TUMULUS OF ACHILLES. 245

and this I found in abundance. I assigned to each tumulus a gendarme and four of my very best Turkish workmen, of whom I was sure that they would work just as assiduously without an overseer as with one. The duty of the gendarme was to look sharp that all, even to the smallest potsherds, were carefully collected, and nothing thrown away. On the western slope of the tumulus of Achilles, fragments of the foundation-walls of the farmhouse, which Choiseul-Gouffier saw here, may still be seen peeping out from the ground.

Into both these tumuli I sank shafts from the top, three mètres long and broad. We worked at first only with pickaxes and shovels, with which the *débris* were thrown out as long as the shafts were less than two mètres deep; afterwards the *débris* were carried out in baskets. The diameter of the tumulus of Achilles is thirty mètres at its foot, its upper diameter being fifteen mètres; its lowest height is four mètres, its greatest height twelve. It had been explored in 1786 by a Jew, by order and on account of Count Choiseul-Gouffier, who was at that time the French ambassador at Constantinople. The Jew pretended that he had sunk a shaft from the top,* and had found the upper part of the tumulus to consist of well-beaten clay to a depth of two mètres; that he had then struck a compact layer of stones and clay, resembling masonry, 0·60 m. deep, that he had found a third stratum consisting of earth mixed with sand, and a fourth of very fine sand, and had reached at a depth of 9·70 m. a quadrangular cavity, 1·33 m. in length and breadth, formed of masonry, and covered with a flat stone, which had broken under the ponderous weight pressing upon it. It is not quite clear whether the Jew meant that the cavity was in the rock or above it; at all events he described the rock as consisting of *granite*. He pretended to have found in the cavity a large quantity of charcoal, ashes impregnated with fat,

---

* See C. G. Lenz, *Die Ebene von Troia nach dem Grafen Choiseul-Gouffier*, Neu-Strelitz, 1798, p. 65.

several bones, among which were the upper part of a tibia and the fragment of a skull; also the fragments of an iron sword, and a bronze figure seated in a chariot with horses, as well as a large quantity of fragments of pottery, exactly similar to the Etruscan, some of which was much burnt and vitrified, whereas all the painted terra-cotta vessels were unhurt. But as no man of experience or worthy of confidence was present at the exploration, scholars appear to have distrusted the account from the first, and to have thought that the Jew, in order to obtain a large reward, had procured and prepared beforehand all the objects he pretended to have found at the bottom of the tumulus.

In the first place I can assure the reader, that the rock here, as well as everywhere else in the plain of Troy north of Bounarbashi, is calcareous, and that no granite exists here; in the second place, that the Jew made only a small excavation in the southern slope of the tumulus, and that he remained far away from its centre; in fact, so far away from it, that in the shaft, three mètres in length and breadth, which I sunk from the top of the tomb, and precisely in its centre, I found all the different strata of earth, of which the tumulus is composed, perfectly undisturbed. As my shaft remains open, and as I cut steps in it, visitors can easily convince themselves that ·

The upper layer,	0·70 m.	deep,	consists of black earth.
„ second „	0·30 m.	„	„	sand, clay, and small stones.
„ third „	0·10 m.	„	„	white and yellow clay.
„ fourth „	0·30 m.	„	„	light-coloured clay, with small stones.
„ fifth „	0·10 m.	„	„	blue clay.
„ sixth „	1·70 m.	„	„	sand and light-coloured clay.
„ seventh „	0·10 m.	„	„	black earth.
„ eighth „	0·20 m.	„	„	light-coloured clay.
„ ninth „	3·00 m.	„	„	light-coloured lumps of clay mixed with pieces of sandstone.
	6·50 m.			

§ I.] EXPLORATION OF THE TUMULUS OF ACHILLES. 247

Thus we get a total depth of 6·50 m. from the top to the bottom of the tumulus, which differs by not less than 3·20 m. from the depth of 9·70 m. which the Jew pretended to have reached,* though in reality he appears to have excavated to a depth of only one mètre. All the Jew's other statements are likewise mere fictions: his description of the different layers of earth of which the tumulus consists is false; and equally false are his assertions that he found a large quantity of charcoal, human bones, and a mass of fragments of pottery similar to the Etruscan, a bronze figure seated in a chariot with horses, or even a quadrangular cavity consisting of masonry; for the tumulus contains nothing of all that, nor ever did contain it. As in all the tumuli of the Troad explored by me in 1873 and 1879, I found in the tumulus of Achilles no trace of bones, ashes, or charcoal—in fact no trace of a burial. Of bronze or copper I found, at a depth of about six mètres, a curious arrowhead without barbs (γλωχῖνες), in which are still preserved the heads of the little pins by which it was fastened to the shaft; I represent it here under No. 132. According to Dr. L. Stern† this form of arrow-head is the most ancient, and occurs already in Egypt in the time of the XIIth dynasty. A perfectly similar arrow-head was found by Professor Virchow in his excavations in the prehistoric cemetery of Upper Koban.‡ Similar ones were also found at Olympia, as well as on the battlefield of Plataeae and in tombs in Bohemia, as *e.g.* at

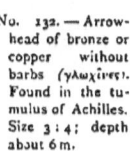

No. 132.—Arrowhead of bronze or copper without barbs (γλωχῖνες). Found in the tumulus of Achilles. Size 3 : 4; depth about 6 m.

---

* See C. G. Lenz, *Die Ebene von Troia nach dem Grafen Choiseul-Gouffier*, Neu-Strelitz, 1798, p. 65.

† Rudolf Virchow, *Das Gräberfeld von Koban im Lande der Osseten*, Berlin, 1883, p. 90.

‡ *Ibid.* p. 90, Table I. No. 21.

Blovica and Korunka, and in Denmark.* I also found a fragment of an iron nail.

Of fragments of pottery large quantities were turned up, among which there are two or three pieces of the lustrous black hand-made pottery which is peculiar to the first and most ancient city of Hissarlik. But these potsherds must have lain on the ground when the tumulus was erected. There were also a number of fragments of but slightly baked lustrous grey or blackish wheel-made pottery, which, as before mentioned, occur also in the lowest layer of *débris* of the Greek Ilium, and which somewhat resemble the Lydian pottery described in the tenth chapter of *Ilios*. But by far the greater proportion is thoroughly baked wheel-made Hellenic pottery, of very different types and fabric. For example, many pieces of it are 0,008 mm. thick, and have on both sides or only on one side a glazed faint lustrous black colour; or this colour is only on the outer side and extends to about half the height of the vase, the other half having a light-yellow, the inner side a glazed dark-red colour; or the outside is dark lustrous black and the inside dark-brown; or the outside is covered all over with alternate glazed black and dark-red stripes, the inside being unpainted and having the natural light-yellow colour of the clay; or with the latter colour on the inside we see on the outside a glazed brown. For all these terra-cottas no archaeologist will hesitate to claim the ninth century B.C., or even a remoter age, for the appearance of this pottery is so archaic that, even if it had been found among the oldest Mycenean pottery, outside the royal tombs, it would not have appeared out of place there. But there is a quantity of much finer wheel-made Hellenic pottery, from 0,003 mm. to 0,006 mm. thick, which baffles the ingenuity of the most experienced

---

* J. J. A. Worsaae, *Nordiske Oldsager*, Table 38, No. 192.

archaeologist, and makes him think at first sight that it is of the Roman time. It is not till after looking at it for a while that he sees the mistake, and begins to refer it piece after piece to the Macedonian period; but afterwards, when he has examined it for a long time most carefully, and compared it with the Mycenean pottery, he at last fully realizes the antiquity of these terra-cottas, and becomes convinced that they belong probably to a time five centuries before the birth of Alexander the Great. What perplexes the archaeologist most are the fragments of a primitive monochrome glazed lustrous black pottery; for, until recently, we were accustomed to consider such as of the Roman or, at the utmost, of the Macedonian age. But I found at Mycenae a fragment of most excellent varnished lustrous black Hellenic pottery, with an inscription scratched on it, the characters of which prove with certainty that it belongs to the sixth century B.C.* The fragment itself is in the Mycenean Museum at Athens, and it will be seen that it is as good as any pottery of that kind made in later times. But such excellent varnished lustrous black terra-cotta ware cannot possibly have been invented at once; it naturally leads us to suppose a school of potters, which had worked for centuries to reach such a perfection in the art, and, if all the other pottery of the tumulus of Achilles can claim the ninth century B.C. as its date, we must necessarily attribute to the same period the fragments of glazed lustrous black ware, which were found there. It should besides be considered, that such perfect pottery as the Mycenean fragment can never lose its beautiful lustrous black colour; whilst on the primitive pottery of the Achilles-tomb the glazed lustrous black colour has in a great many instances been more or less effaced. The other terra-cottas either have on the outside alternate lustrous black and red bands, with a uniform black on the inside, or they are light-yellow

---

* See this inscription in my *Mycenae*, p. 115.

on the outside and black on the inside; or they are black on both sides; or they are black on the outside and yellow on the inside; or they have on the outside a light-red colour with a black rim, and are black on the inside; or they have on the outside black bands on a light-yellow or red ground, and inside the natural clay colour; or they have on the outside dark-red bands on a light-red ground, and are inside of a uniform dark-red; or they have on the outside a very rude meaningless lustrous black ornamentation on a light-yellow or red ground, and are monochrome black on the inside. There was further found a whorl of that very slightly baked greyish pottery, already mentioned, which somewhat resembles the Lydian pottery described in the tenth chapter of *Ilios;* it is ornamented with four incised wedges, which form a cross round the perforation. All this pottery was found scattered about in the *débris* in sinking the shaft. There is also a fragment of a varnished monochrome red vase, which certainly cannot claim a higher antiquity than the Macedonian period; but, as this was found only a few inches below the surface, it probably comes from sacrifices made here in later times, and cannot be taken into account.

The tumulus described in the *Odyssey,* XXIV. 80–84,* as the tomb of Achilles, situated on the jutting headland on the shore of the Hellespont, can be no other than this mound; and there can be no doubt that the poet had this one also in view, when he makes Achilles order the tumulus of Patroclus to be erected: "I do not, however, advise you to make the tomb too high, but as is becoming; at a future time you may pile it up broad and high, you Achaeans who survive me and remain in the ships with many oars."†

---

* Cited above, p. 244.
† *Il.* XXIII. 245–248:

τύμβον δ'οὐ μάλα πολλὸν ἐγὼ πονέεσθαι ἄνωγα,
ἀλλ' ἐπιεικέα τοῖον· ἔπειτα δὲ καὶ τὸν 'Αχαιοί
εὐρύν θ' ὑψηλόν τε τιθήμεναι, οἵ κεν ἐμεῖο
δεύτεροι ἐν νήεσσι πολυκληῖσι λίπησθε.

§ *II. Tumulus of Patroclus.*—The passage just cited seems to prove that in Homer's mind there was only one tumulus raised for Patroclus and Achilles. But it is highly probable that the two neighbouring tumuli also existed in the Homeric age, or at least the one which is now attributed to Patroclus. This latter had been excavated in 1855 by Mr. Frank Calvert, of the Dardanelles, in company with some officers of the British fleet. They sank an open shaft in it and dug down to the rock, without finding anything worth their notice. But at that time archaeologists had not yet given any attention to the fragments of ancient pottery. Even when in 1876 I made the large excavations at Mycenae, the delegate of the Greek Government, the Inspector of Antiquities, Mr. P. Stamatakes, pronounced the immense masses of fragments of highly important archaic pottery which were brought to light, and which far exceeded in interest anything of that kind ever found in Greece, to be useless *débris*, and urgently insisted that they should be shot from the hill with the real rubbish; in fact I could not prevent this being done with quantities of such fragments. It was in vain that I telegraphed to Athens, begging the Minister of Public Instruction, as well as the President of the Archaeological Society, Mr. Philippos Ioannes, to stop this vandalism. Finally I invoked the aid of the Director-General of Antiquities, Mr. P. Eustratiades, and of Professor E. Castorches, and I owe it solely to the energy of these worthy scholars, that the Archaeological Society was at last induced to put a stop to that outrage, and to command Stamatakes to preserve all the fragments of pottery. Since that time people have begun to regard pottery as the cornucopiae of archaeological knowledge, and to employ it as a key to determine approximately the age of the sites where it is found. Science will, therefore, be grateful to me for having saved the really enormous masses of fragments of most ancient Mycenean pottery from certain destruction.

For similar reasons I was very anxious to excavate the tumulus of Patroclus again, in order to gather the potsherds, which I felt sure of finding. The diameter of this tumulus at the base is 27 mètres, whilst according to the measurement of Choiseul-Gouffier * it was only 16 feet, or 5·33 m.: he must therefore have had a strange mode of measuring; but his whole work † is of the same character, and abounds with errors not less absurd and ridiculous. The diameter at the top is 8 mètres; the perpendicular height, 6 mètres. I sank in it from the top a shaft 3 mètres long and broad, and dug it down to the rock. I found this tumulus, from the top down to a depth of 3·45 m., to consist of light-coloured clay mixed with stones; then followed a layer, 0·40 m. deep, of red and light-coloured clay mixed with sand, and afterwards a layer, 0·40 m. deep, of very light-coloured clay; the lowest stratum, 1·25 m. deep, consists of dark brown clay. As we reached the rock at a depth of 5·50 m., it is evident that there was an elevation of the ground 0·50 m. high at the spot.

I found in this tumulus exactly the same archaic pottery as in the tumulus of Achilles, though in a much less considerable quantity; further, a long fragment of a flute of potstone, the *lapis ollaris* of Pliny, of which also the flutes are made which I found in my excavation in Ithaca and Mycenae.‡ I found here likewise neither human bones, nor ashes, nor charcoal, nor any other traces of a burial. We have, therefore, to add the conical mounds of Achilles and Patroclus to the six other tumuli, which my previous exploration had proved to be mere *cenotaphia* or memorials. That such *cenotaphia* or memorials were in general use at a remote antiquity, is proved by various passages in Homer. Thus, Pallas Athené directs Telemachus to erect a cenotaph

---

* C. G. Lenz, *Die Ebene von Troia*, etc., p. 64.
† *Voyage Pittoresque de la Grèce*, Paris, 1820.
‡ See *Mycenae*, p. 78.

§ III.] EXPLORATION OF TUMULUS OF ANTILOCHUS. 253

to his father if he learns his death.* Menelaus erects in Egypt a cenotaph to Agamemnon.† So Virgil tells us that Andromache, who had married Helenus and become queen of Chaonia, had erected in the shade of a sacred grove, on the bank of another Simois, a cenotaph in honour of Hector.‡

§ *III. Tumulus of Antilochus.*—In spite of all my endeavours, I have not been able to persuade the proprietor of the third tumulus, which is crowned by the large massive windmill, to permit me, for an indemnity of £3, to sink a shaft within the building or to run in a tunnel at the foot of the hillock; for he apprehends that, by this operation, the heavy walls of the mill might fall in. I could only obtain from him permission to dig with the pickaxe small holes in the slope of the tumulus. In these holes I gathered many fragments of the very same archaic pottery which I had found in the tumuli of Achilles and Patroclus. All that remains, therefore, to be done, is to put on record the re-discovery of this tumulus which was so well known in antiquity,§ and to insert it on the map of the Troad as the Tumulus of Antilochus, in

---

* *Od.* I. 289-291:

εἰ δέ κε τεθνηῶτος ἀκούσῃς, μηδ' ἔτ' ἐόντος,
νοστήσας δὴ ἔπειτα φίλην ἐς πατρίδα γαῖαν,
σῆμά τέ οἱ χεῦαι, καὶ ἐπὶ κτέρεα κτερεΐξαι.

Od. II. 222, 223 :

σῆμά τέ οἱ χεύω, καὶ ἐπὶ κτέρεα κτερεΐξω
πολλὰ μάλ', ὅσσα ἔοικε, καὶ ἀνέρι μητέρα δώσω.

† *Od.* IV. 583, 584:

αὐτὰρ ἐπεὶ κατέπαυσα θεῶν χόλον αἰὲν ἐόντων,
χεῦ' Ἀγαμέμνονι τύμβον, ἵν' ἄσβεστον κλέος εἴη.

‡ *Æneid.* III. 302-305 :

ante urbem in luco, falsi Simoentis ad undam,
libabat cineri Andromache, Manesque vocabat.
Hectoreum ad tumulum, viridi quem cespite inanem
et geminas, causam lacrymis, sacraverat aras.

§ Strabo, XIII. p. 596.

order to distinguish it from the so-called Tumulus of Patroclus. But as Strabo,* in describing the shore of the plain of Troy, first mentions Cape Rhoeteum, and then, in succession, Cape Sigeum, the tomb of Achilles, the sepulchre of Patroclus, and in the last place the Tumulus of Antilochus, it is highly probable that this latter was the one farthest from the shore, and, consequently, that the tumulus which is crowned by the windmill was in antiquity really attributed to Antilochus.

§ *IV. Tumulus of Protesilaus.*—Far more interesting than any of the tumuli explored by me in the Troad, is the mound attributed by the tradition of all antiquity to the hero Protesilaus, who led the warriors of Phylacé in Thessaly against Troy, and not only, on the arrival of the fleet, was the first Greek who jumped on shore,† but also the first who was killed, either by Hector,‡ or Achates,§ or Aeneas,|| or Euphorbus.¶ His tomb was shown on the Thracian Chersonesus, near the city of Elaeus,** where he had a *heroum* and a celebrated oracle.†† Of this city very extensive ruins may be seen in the background of the old Turkish fort of Eski Hissarlik,‡‡ which was abandoned thirteen years ago. It is about two

---

* Strabo, XIII. p. 596.
† *Il.* II. 695-699:

Οἳ δ' εἶχον Φυλάκην καὶ Πύρασον ἀνθεμόεντα,
Δήμητρος τέμενος, Ἴτωνά τε, μητέρα μήλων,
ἀγχίαλόν τ' Ἀντρῶν' ἠδὲ Πτελεὸν λεχεποίην·
τῶν αὖ Πρωτεσίλαος Ἀρήϊος ἡγεμόνευεν,
ζωὸς ἐών· τότε δ' ἤδη ἔχεν κάτα γαῖα μέλαινα.

XIII. 681 ; XV. 705 ; Philostr. *Heroica*, II. 15.
‡ Lucian, *D. M.* XXIII. 1 ; Tzetzes, *Lycophr.* 245, 528, 530 ;
Ovid. *Met.* XII. 67 ; Hyg. *Fab.* 103.   § Eustath. p. 326, 5.
|| Dictys Cret. II. 11.   ¶ Eustath. p. 325, 38.
** Strabo, XIII. p. 595 ; Pausanias, I. 34, 2 ; Tzetzes, *Lycophron*, 532.
†† Philostr. I. 1 ; Herodot. VII. 33 ; IX. 116, 120 ; Pausan. III. 4, 5.
‡‡ See the large Map of the Troad.

No. 133.—Tumulus of Protesilaus on the Thracian Chersonesus opposite the Plain of Troy.

and a half miles to the north of the large Turkish fortress of Seddul Bahr, which is situated close to the extreme point of the peninsula, and was built in the year 1070 of the Hegira, or 1658 A.D. The tumulus of Protesilaus lies near the further end of the small but beautiful valley of exuberant fertility, which extends between Seddul Bahr and Elaeus. This sepulchre, of which I give an engraving under No. 133, is not less than 126 mètres in diameter. It is now only 10 m. high, but as it is under cultivation, and has probably been tilled for thousands of years, it must originally have been much higher. In order to facilitate its cultivation, its west, south, and east sides have been transformed into three terraces, sustained by masonry, and planted with vines, almond-trees, and pomegranate-trees. The top and the northern slope are sown with barley, and also planted with vines, olive-trees, pomegranate-trees, and some beautiful elms, which last vividly called to my recollection the dialogue in Philostratus* between an ἀμπελουργός (vine-dresser) and a Phoenician captain, in which the former speaks of the elm-trees planted round the tomb of Protesilaus by the Nymphs, of which he says that the branches turned towards Troy blossomed earlier, but that they also shed their leaves quickly and withered before the time.† It was also said that if the elms grew so high that they could see Troy, they withered away, but put forth fresh shoots from below.‡ Pliny certainly believed in this story, for he says,§ "Sunt hodie ex adverso Iliensium urbis, juxta Hellespontum, in Protesilai sepulcro arbores, quae omnibus aevis, quum in tantum accrevere ut Ilium adspiciant, inarescunt, rursusque

---

* In *Heroicis*.
† Philostr. *Heroica*, II. 1. Περὶ τῶν τοιούτων ἄκουε, ξένε· κεῖται μὲν οὐκ ἐν Τροίᾳ ὁ Πρωτεσίλεως, ἀλλ' ἐν Χεῤῥονήσῳ ταύτῃ, κολωνὸς δὲ αὐτὸν ἐπέχει μέγας οὑτοσὶ δήπου ὁ ἐν ἀριστερᾷ, πτελέας δὲ ταύτας αἱ νύμφαι περὶ τῷ κολωνῷ ἐφύτευσαν καὶ τοιόνδε ἐπὶ τοῖς δένδρεσι τούτοις ἔγραψάν που αὗται νόμον · τοὺς πρὸς τὸ Ἴλιον τετραμμένους τῶν ὄζων ἀνθεῖν μὲν πρωί, φυλλοῤῥοεῖν δὲ αὐτίκα καὶ προαπόλλυσθαι τῆς ὥρας—
‡ *Anthol. Pal.* VII. 141, 385. § Plin. *H. N.* XVI. 88.

§ IV.] EXPLORATION OF TUMULUS OF PROTESILAUS. 257

adolescunt." This tumulus is now called "Kara Agatch Tepeh," which means, "hill planted with black trees." On my visit to the place, I went in company with my Turkish delegate Moharrem Effendi, a servant, two gendarmes, and four strong workmen, on horseback down to Koum Kaleh, whence we crossed the Hellespont in a boat to Seddul Bahr, and proceeded thence on foot. I was amazed to find not only the tumulus, but also the gardens around it, strewn with fragments of thick lustrous black pottery; of bowls with long horizontal tubes for suspension on two sides of the rim, like Nos. 37-42, pp. 217, 218, in *Ilios*; or of vases with double vertical tubular holes for suspension on the sides, like Nos. 23-25, pp. 214, 215, in *Ilios*; also with fragments of shining black bowls, with an incised ornamentation filled with chalk to strike the eye, like Nos. 28-35, p. 216, in *Ilios*. This pottery only occurs at Troy in the first city, and it is by far the most ancient I have ever seen. It is therefore quite inconceivable how, after having been exposed here for perhaps four thousand years to frost and heat, rain and sunshine, it could still look quite fresh; but it bewilders the mind still more to think how the chalk, with which the ornamentation was filled in, could have withstood for long ages the inclemencies of the seasons. I also picked up there many feet of terra-cotta tripods; saddle-querns of trachyte (like Nos. 74, 75, p. 234, and No. 678, p. 447, in *Ilios*); small knives or saws of chalcedony or flint (like Nos. 93-98, p. 246, in *Ilios*); some rude hammers of black diorite (like No. 83, p. 237, in *Ilios*), together with a very fine specimen of a perforated hammer and axe of diorite, which I represent here under No. 134, and a fine axe and hammer of grey diorite (like No. 621, p. 438, in *Ilios*), with grooves on both sides, showing that the perforation had been commenced but abandoned. I also picked up there a certain number of corn-bruisers of silicious stone (like Nos. 80, 81. p. 236, in *Ilios*).

258   THE HEROIC TUMULI IN THE TROAD.   [CHAP. VI.

Having heard that the proprietor of the tumulus, a Turk in Seddul Bahr, was in prison for the theft of a horse, and feeling sure that I could easily settle the indemnity later on by the intervention of the kind civil governor of the Dardanelles, Hamid Pasha; being moreover afraid that the ever suspicious and envious military governor of the Dardanelles, Djemal Pasha, might throw obstacles in my way;—I did not lose a moment of my precious time, and, having brought with me pickaxes, shovels, baskets, etc., I at once ordered the four workmen to sink, just in the middle of the summit, a shaft three mètres in length and breadth. I had done exceedingly well to hurry on the work, for the commandant of the fortress of Seddul Bahr reported my doings to the military governor of the Dardanelles, who, not being able to conceive how a man could waste his time in excavating a lonely hillock, suspected that I was merely using the excavation of the Protesilaus-tomb as a pretext for making plans of the fortress of Seddul Bahr, and investigating the lines of torpedoes recently sunk in the Hellespont; and so he issued an order to suspend the excavation. But happily this order arrived only on the evening of the second day. I at once telegraphed and wrote to the German Embassy in Constantinople to seek redress, but all the endeavours of the excellent first dragoman, Baron von Testa, were of no avail. I then proposed that the excavation of the tumulus should be continued at my expense by the commandant of Seddul Bahr, with his own men and one of my Turkish gendarmes; I promised neither to visit the tumulus myself nor to send thither either of my architects; but even this proposal was rejected with disdain. But, happily, in those two days my four workmen had dug down to a depth of

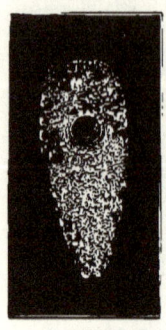

No. 134.—Hammer and Axe of Diorite, with perforation. Size about 1 : 3; found on the surface of the tumulus of Protesilaus.

2·50 m., and had found large quantities of most ancient pottery, similar to that of the first and second cities of Hissarlik; some perforated balls of serpentine, of which I represent one under No. 135; a number of excellent axes of

No. 135.—Perforated Ball of serpentine, found in the tumulus of Protesilaus. Size about 3:4.

No. 136.—Bronze Knife found in the tumulus of Protesilaus. Size about 1:4.

diorite; large masses of rude stone hammers, corn-bruisers, saddle-querns, and other interesting things, among which was the pretty bronze knife which I represent here under No. 136; at its lower end are preserved the heads of the nails with which the wooden handle was fastened on.

I further represent here, under No. 136*a*, the fragment of a lustrous black vase with a handle of a very curious form.

At a depth of 1·50 m. we struck a layer of slightly baked bricks, mixed with straw, very similar to the bricks found in the second and third cities of Hissarlik.

No. 136*a*.—Vase-handle found in the tumulus of Protesilaus. Size about 1:4.

The pottery with which the tumulus and the gardens around it are strewn, and which also predominates among the terra-cottas in the hill, is most decidedly identical with that of the first city of Troy, and proves with certainty that here, on the Thracian Chersonese, there lived in a remote prehistoric age a people of the same race, habits, and culture, as the first settlers on the hill of Hissarlik. With the *débris* of this ancient settlement, and probably long after it had ceased to exist, was erected the tumulus of Protesilaus, to the probable date of which we have a key in the latest pottery contained in the tomb. Now as I find among the pottery a great quantity of a similar type and of a like fabric to the pottery of the second, the burnt city of Troy, and nothing later, we may attribute the tumulus with the very greatest probability to the time of the catastrophe, which gave rise to the legend of the Trojan war. But I must remind the reader, that this is the only tumulus yet found having in it Trojan pottery. The tumulus of Besika Tepeh, explored by me in 1879,* contains a large quantity of prehistoric pottery, which appears to be contemporaneous with that of the second city of Troy, or may even be still more ancient, but its material, fabric, and forms, are totally different from anything found at Troy, and it most decidedly denotes a race of people altogether different. The same may be said of the tumulus of Hanaï Tepeh, which I explored together with Mr. Calvert,† for here too the pottery is totally different from the Trojan pottery. But Hanaï Tepeh has only the form of a vast tumulus; in reality the *débris* of which it is composed denote a succession of human settlements.

As the latest pottery contained in Kara Agatch Tepeh is identical with that of the second settlement of Troy, there is nothing to contradict the tradition, that this tumulus belongs to the actual time of the Trojan war; and who then shall gainsay the legend, that it marked the tomb of the first Greek who leaped down on the Trojan shore on the arrival of the fleet? We may find it more difficult to

---

* See *Ilios*, pp. 665–669. † See the note in *Ilios*, p. 720.

imagine that the name of this hero should have been Πρωτεσίλαος, which means "the first of the army or the people," for, unless we believe in predestination, we must think that he received this name from the glorious feat in which he perished.

With respect to this name, Professor Sayce remarks to me :—

(1) With Πρωτεσί-λαος, we must compare ναυσί-κλυτος, Ναυσι-κάα, &c., -λαος being "people."

(2) Πρώτεσι- ought to be a dative plural like ναῦσι, but from a nominative singular πρώτυς (like γλυκύς).

(3) Πρώτεσι- *may* stand for πρώτεσσι, which *may* be formed from πρωτεύς, "the chief;" BUT "People among the first," has no sense.

(4) Perhaps Πρωτεσί-λαος has been formed after the analogy of ἑλκεσί-πεπλος, not grammatically but analogically. As ἑλκεσί-πεπλος means "trailing the robe," so πρωτεσί-λαος may, ungrammatically, have been supposed to mean "first among the people."

Besides the tumulus of Protesilaus, there certainly existed at the time of the Trojan war the oft-mentioned tumulus of Besika Tepeh, and that called Hagios Demetrios Tepeh, which is a natural rock of a conical shape, exactly resembling the so-called heroic tumuli, and probably considered at all times to be one of them.*

Professor Sayce observes to me: "It is very remarkable that, whereas the pottery found in the first two prehistoric cities of Hissarlik does not occur elsewhere in the Troad, it should nevertheless be met with on the European side of the Hellespont on the site of the tumulus of Protesilaus. We may infer from this fact that the first settlers in Troy came from Europe rather than from Asia. Now this inference is curiously borne out by a fragment of the

---

* See *Ilios*, p. 650.

Lydian historian, Xanthus, preserved in Strabo.* He there states that the Mysians ' for a time lived about (the Trojan) Olympus; but when the Phrygians crossed over from Thrace, they captured both the ruler of Troy and the neighbouring country, and while they settled here the Mysians settled about the sources of the Caïcus, near the Lydians.' This must have been before the Trojan war, since after it, according to Strabo,† the Troad was occupied by Greek colonists, Tréres, Cimmerians, and Lydians, then by Persians and Macedonians, and finally by Gauls."

§ *V. The Three Nameless Tumuli on Cape Rhoeteum.*—I also commenced with twelve workmen sinking shafts, three mètres long and broad, in the three tumuli on Cape Rhoeteum to the north-east of the tumulus of Ajax,‡ having obtained the permission of the proprietor of the field, a Turk in Koum Kaleh, for £3. But, alas! I had been digging only one day, when this work too was prohibited by the military governor of the Dardanelles. Strange to say, though my workmen had reached in each tumulus a depth of about 1·50 m., not a single fragment of pottery turned up, and thus this excavation remained wholly without result.

§ *VI. The so-called Tomb of Priam.*—I also sank a shaft, three mètres long and broad, in the tumulus which is situated on Mount Bali Dagh behind Bounarbashi,§ and is 25 m. in diameter by 2·50 m. in height: it used to be ascribed, by the adherents of the Troy-Bounarbashi theory, to King Priam himself. But I found there nothing

---

* XII. p. 572. Τέως μὲν γὰρ οἰκεῖν αὐτοὺς περὶ τὸν Ὄλυμπον· τῶν δὲ Φρυγῶν ἐκ τῆς Θρᾴκης περαιωθέντων, εἵλοντο τόν τε τῆς Τροίας ἄρχοντα καὶ τῆς πλησίον γῆς· ἐκείνους μὲν ἐνταῦθα οἰκῆσαι· τοὺς δὲ Μυσοὺς περὶ τὰς τοῦ Καΐκου πηγὰς πλησίον Λυδῶν.   † XII. p. 573.
‡ See the large Map of the Plain of Troy.
§ See the large Map of the Plain of Troy.

else than fragments of that sort of pottery, very slightly baked, wheel-made, exceedingly heavy, glazed, of a gray or blackish colour, which, as before mentioned, is frequent in the lowest layers of *débris* of the seventh city at Hissarlik, the Aeolic Ilium, and of which also many fragments were gathered in the tumulus of Achilles. The resemblance it bears to the Lydian pottery, described in Chapter X. of *Ilios*, is but very slight; the only points that both kinds of pottery have in common are, their very slight baking, their colour, and the large mass of mica they contain. For the rest, they are altogether different in form and in fabric; the Lydian pottery being, with rare exceptions, hand-made, whilst all the pottery of Priam's tumulus is wheel-made, and for this reason it is certainly of a later time than the former. As in the nine other "heroic tombs" explored by me, I found here no vestige of either bones or charcoal, and no trace of a burial. Like all the others, therefore, this is a mere cenotaph or memorial.

CHAPTER VII.

OTHER EXPLORATIONS IN THE TROAD.

§ *I. The Ancient Town on the Bali Dagh.*—I also most carefully explored with my architects the site of the small town situated on the mount just named, immediately to the south and south-east of the "tumulus of Priam," which I hold with Mr. Calvert to be the ancient city of Gergis, and which for nearly a century has had the undeserved honour of being considered as the real site of Troy. Nothing is visible above ground of the wall of

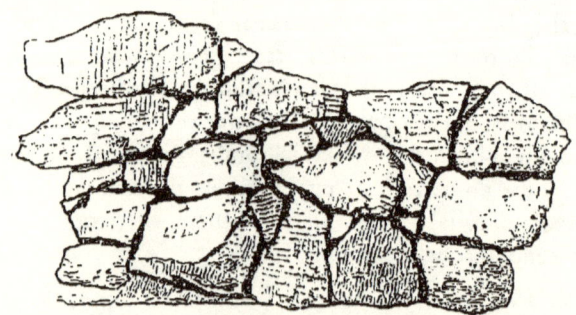

No. 137.—Wall of the first and oldest epoch.

the lower city; but its northern part seems to be buried in a far extending low elevation of the ground. The site of the lower city is indicated by a number of house-foundations, which peep out from the ground, and by very numerous fragments of Hellenic pottery. The site is crowned at its south and south-eastern extremity by a small Acropolis, which is about 200 mètres long by 100 mètres broad, and these also are approximately the dimensions of the lower town. In this citadel the late Austrian

Consul, J. G. von Hahn, of Syra, made some excavations in the spring of 1864, in company with the famous astronomer Dr. Julius Schmidt, and the architect Ernest Ziller of Athens. The altitude of the Acropolis is, according to Dr. Julius Schmidt's measurement, 142 m. They brought

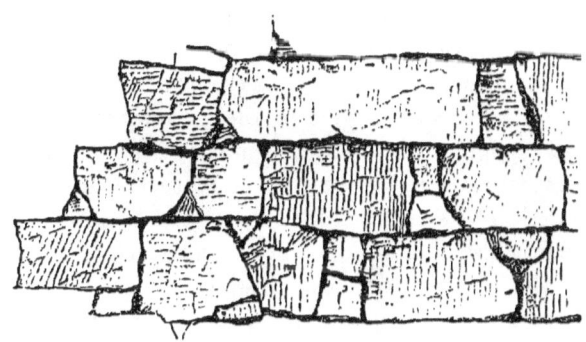

No. 138.—Wall of the first and oldest epoch.

to light in a number of places the walls, which clearly show two different epochs. Those of the first epoch are nearly vertical, and are built of large blocks, more or less unwrought, filled in with smaller ones (see the engravings Nos. 137,

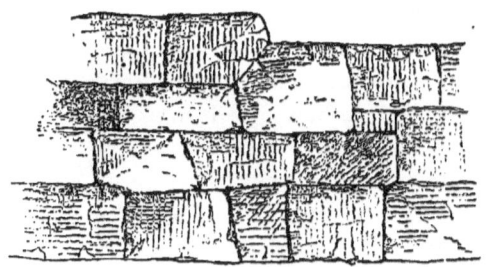

No. 139.—Wall of the second and later epoch.

138); those of the second epoch are built of regularly wrought stones, laid in regular courses, with the joints fitting exactly (see the engraving, No. 139). To the first and oldest epoch we may also attribute a wall of almost unwrought polygons, each about 0·60 m. long, filled in with small stones; to the second epoch a wall of well-joined stones, almost rectangular, which lie in horizontal courses like steps, each course projecting 0·10 m., from the lowest to the highest; also a wall, the lower part of which consists of well-wrought blocks, about 1 mètre long, the upper courses consisting of well-joined rustic quoins, that is to say, of square stones with an unwrought projecting square panel in the middle of the exterior side of each, which were intended to give to the masonry the character of great weight and solidity. Similar rustic quoins have been especially used in the palaces of the renaissance age in Italy. There are besides some walls of small stones, apparently also belonging to the second epoch.

I also found these two distinct epochs in all the trenches I dug and in all the shafts I sank, both in the Acropolis and in the lower city. In a trench, 25 m. long by 2·50 m. deep, which I dug in the middle of the little citadel, I found in the layer of the second epoch, which reached to a depth of 1·80 m. below the surface, several house-walls of small stones, and very numerous fragments of Hellenic pottery, for the most part of a very common monochrome red, green, or black; a great deal of it is not varnished at all; some cups or vases are only varnished black or red on the outside, the inside retaining the natural colour of the clay; others are left unpainted on the outside, the inside being ornamented with black bands; again, others have a black varnish with red bands on the outside, the inside being left unpainted. There also occur common plates, which are unpainted on the outside, but varnished red on the inside, with a very rude ornamentation of black bands. But there occur also a good number of fragments of well-made pottery, carefully varnished black both on the outside and the inside, and red on the bottom with two small concentric circles in the centre. There also occurs common fluted black pottery, which archaeologists cannot ascribe to a remoter time than about 200 B.C. The other

Hellenic pottery is evidently of the 2nd, 3rd, 4th, and 5th centuries B.C. Every doubt that one may have felt regarding the great antiquity of the Hellenic pottery of the tumuli of Achilles and Patroclus will disappear on comparing it with this Bounarbashi pottery, which looks quite modern alongside of the other. Below this layer of Hellenic pottery was the stratum of the first epoch, 0·70 m. deep, with the remains of a house-wall built of small stones, and masses of that very coarse, heavy, glazed, grey or blackish wheel-made pottery, described above, which is so slightly baked that its whole fracture has a light grey colour.

In this trench I struck the natural rock at a depth of 2·50 m. In a second trench, dug on the east side of the Acropolis, I found the accumulation of *débris* to be only 1·50 m. deep, of which 0·60 m. belongs to the second epoch, and 0·90 m. to the first. I brought to light here the substructions of an edifice of neatly-wrought quadrangular blocks of conglomerate rock, and the same gray, black, red, or brown, glazed Hellenic pottery in the upper layer, the same very coarse, heavy, glazed gray or black wheel-made pottery in the lower. I obtained the same result in the trench I dug at the west end of the Acropolis, where the rock was reached at a depth of 2·50 m., as well as in the trench dug at the eastern extremity, where, besides the same kinds of pottery, two iron nails and a copper one were found in the upper layer; also in a shaft which I sank 3·50 m. deep in an ancient building in the Acropolis, and in other shafts which I sank in the lower city. Among the architectural curiosities of the latter I may mention a large and a small stone circle, which are contiguous. In a shaft sunk in the larger circle I found numerous fragments of Hellenic pottery, and below them the repeatedly-mentioned coarse gray wheel-made terra-cottas.

It deserves particular notice that, in all the trenches I dug and in all the shafts I sank, I found the layer of *débris* of the first epoch, with the coarse slightly baked gray wheel-made pottery, succeeded abruptly by the second layer, which contains the Hellenic pottery. Nowhere is there any trace of black earth between them, such as we should expect if, after the first settlement, the site had lain deserted for a number of years. We may conclude from this that the place, on being abandoned by the first settlers, was at once, or at least very soon, reoccupied by a Greek colony. Now, as we certainly found no vestige of Hellenic pottery which could claim an earlier date than the fifth century B.C., while the bulk is of the Macedonian time and later, we may with the greatest probability infer, that the coarse heavy gray or black wheel-made pottery was still in use among the first settlers when they abandoned the site in the fifth century B.C. This we may, therefore, with the greatest probability, regard as its latest or minimum date. Regarding its earliest date I repeat that all the pottery, without exception, is wheel-made, whereas the Lydian pottery of Hissarlik, to which it has some resemblance, is nearly all hand-made; and if, therefore, we take as the latest date of the Lydian settlement the tenth century B.C., we are probably near the mark if we attribute the ancient pottery on the Bali Dagh to the period between the 5th and 9th centuries B.C.; and we must ascribe to the same time the so-called "tumulus of Priam," which I excavated, and in which none but this ancient pottery was found. This chronology is the more likely to be correct, as in the oldest layer of *débris* on the Bali Dagh there is no trace of the whorls, with or without an incised ornamentation, of which I collected at least twenty-two thousand in the five prehistoric settlements of Troy, and which are not wanting in the Lydian settlement. There were only found three unornamented whorls in the Hellenic layer of *débris*.

As (to my no small annoyance) I have for a long number of years been exhorted, verbally and by letter, by the adherents of the Troy-Bounarbashi theory, to excavate the *marble wash-basins* at the springs of Bounarbashi, I must assure the reader that nothing of the kind exists, and that my architects and I could discover at those springs only one block which had been worked by the hand of man. It is a Doric *corona*-block of white marble, on which the women now do their washing; the *campanas* (or *guttae*) are still visible on it; it must certainly have been brought thither from Ilium.

§ *II. Eski Hissarlik.*—I also explored the ruins of the ancient town called Eski Hissarlik (old fortress), which is situated on the rock on the eastern bank of the Scamander, opposite the Bali Dagh, and only separated from it by a few hundred yards.* The Acropolis, the walls of which are preserved almost in their entire circuit to a height of several mètres, and are only covered by the fallen upper parts of the wall, was situated on the top of the rock, at an altitude of 153 m.; whilst the lower town, which is marked by numerous house-foundations, extended on its northern and eastern slope. Immediately in front of the lower town is a tumulus of very small stones, which has lost its conical shape, and seems to have been explored by some traveller. As the Acropolis as well as the lower city are built in slopes, the earth and the remains of human industry have naturally been washed away by the rains, and it so happens that the accumulation of *débris* is here even much more insignificant than on the Bali Dagh; the bare rock peeps out in many places, and, wherever we excavated, the depth of the *débris* did not exceed from 0·50 m. to 0·70 m. We found there nothing else but the coarse heavy slightly-baked wheel-made pottery of the first epoch of the Bali Dagh. BOTH FORTRESSES, ESKI HISSARLIK AND BALI DAGH, WHICH ARE ONLY SEPARATED FROM EACH OTHER BY A FEW HUNDRED YARDS, MUST—AS THEIR IDENTICAL POTTERY PROVES—HAVE EXISTED SIMULTANEOUSLY, PROBABLY FROM THE 9TH TO THE 5TH CENTURIES B.C.; THEY SEEM TO

---

* See the large Map of the Troad.

HAVE FORMED ONE WHOLE, FOR THEY ARE BUILT OPPOSITE EACH OTHER ON LOFTY HEIGHTS RISING ALMOST PERPENDICULARLY FROM THE RIVER, AND IN THIS SITUATION THEY COMPLETELY DOMINATED THE ROAD WHICH LEADS FROM THE VALLEY OF THE SCAMANDER INTO THE INTERIOR OF ASIA MINOR.

§ *III. Excavations on the Fulu Dagh, or Mount Dedeh.*—I also explored the ancient settlement on a hill called Fulu Dagh or Mount Dedeh,* about 1½ mile to the northeast of Eski Hissarlik, where I found, at a distance of about fifty mètres from each other, two concentric circles of fortification walls, of which the inner is sixty mètres in diameter; but all the walls have fallen and are shapeless heaps of ruins. I found there only some very rude unglazed and unpainted wheel-made pottery, which is thoroughly baked and has a dull-red brick colour. As before mentioned, a very similar rude red pottery occurs also in the *débris* of Ilium below the Macedonian stratum; we may, therefore, probably be right in attributing to it the same age which we found for the coarse, almost unbaked, wheel-made pottery of the Bali Dagh. This is the more likely, as I found among the Fulu Dagh terra-cottas a certain number of fragments of the latter kind. The altitude of the Fulu Dagh is 68 m.

§ *IV. Ruins on the Kurshunlu Tepeh.*—As before mentioned, I also explored the Kurshunlu Tepeh, which means "leaden hill," and is situated on the right bank of the Scamander, at a short distance from Mount Ida. At the foot of the Kurshunlu Tepeh lies the miserable Turkish village of Oba Kioi (altitude 244 mètres). In the walls of the village houses may be seen well-wrought marble slabs and fragments of Doric entablatures. The summit of Kurshunlu Tepeh has an altitude of 345 mètres,

---

* See the small Map of the Troad, No. 140, and the large Map of the Troad.

§ IV.]   THE RUINS ON KURSHUNLU TEPEH.   271

and is, therefore, 101 mètres higher than the village. The temperature of the air on the 2nd of July, both in the village and on the summit of the hill was 36° C. (96·8 F.) When in the beginning of the present century Dr. Clarke visited this hill, it was still covered with ruins of ancient edifices, though these building materials had then already for a long time past been the great quarry for Beiramich, where a mosque, the tomb of a Dervish, a bridge with three arches, and many large houses, had been built with them.* All the ruins which could be used for building purposes had disappeared when P. Barker Webb visited the hill in 1819.† Nevertheless, ancient remains may still be seen in many places. The first object which strikes the eye of the archaeologist is the ruin of the great wall, which is 2·80 m. thick, and of the same kind of masonry as the walls of Assos, fo it has on both sides wedge-like blocks, between which, as well as in the interior, the space is filled up with small stones. On the summit are the foundations of a chamber, 3 m. long by 1·80 m. broad, the walls being 0·60 m. thick; but outside of it are large rudely-wrought blocks, between which and the foundations of the chamber the space is filled up with small stones. The position of the large blocks seems to indicate that the building had an oval form, and it may probably, therefore, have been a tower. In excavating this chamber, I found it to have an accumulation of *débris* only 0·30 m. deep. To the north-west of it is a spacious hollow in the rock, which perhaps marks the site of a large edifice, but here I struck the rock at a depth only from 0·15 m. to 0·20 m. To the north of this hollow are the foundation walls, 0·50 m. thick, of another edifice, which is 18 m. long by 11 broad. To the north-west of it are some remains of a smaller building; and again to the north of the latter, on a terrace about 12 m. below the summit, some ruins of larger

---

* P. Barker Webb, *Topographie de la Troade*, p. 80.   † *Ibid.*

edifices. Traces of several large buildings may also be seen on a terrace on the south side. I dug in these four latter places, as well as in twenty others where the formation of the soil held out any hope of finding a deeper accumulation of *débris*. But everywhere I struck the rock at a depth of from 0·15 m. to 0·30 m. Nevertheless, I found a good deal of pottery, the bulk of which consisted of well-baked, very common wheel-made, unpainted and unvarnished terra-cottas, very similar to those found on the Fulu Dagh. They were intermixed with rude, very slightly baked, wheel-made pottery of white clay, such as I had found in abundance in my excavations in Ithaca; also with slightly baked, coarse, light-yellow, gray, dark-blue, or black pottery, very similar to that of the first epoch at Gergis on the Bali Dagh and at Eski Hissarlik, for which, as well as for the coarse red pottery of Fulu Dagh, we had found the date of from the 9th to the 5th centuries B.C. The Hellenic pottery found on Kurshunlu Tepeh consisted of monochrome glazed red or black terra-cottas, of the Macedonian and Roman times. Of prehistoric or archaic Hellenic pottery no trace was found.

As Mount Kurshunlu Tepeh runs out to an obtuse point, it appears probable that the *débris* were washed down the slopes by the winter rains, and that this is the cause of the scanty vestiges of human industry on the declivity of the hill. But it is altogether inexplicable to me that the accumulation of *débris* should be as insignificant in the large hollow on the north-west side, and on the flat terraces, as it is everywhere else. Several travellers mention, on the east and west side of the hill, two circles of stones resembling cromlechs, for which they claim the remotest antiquity. I also saw these stone circles, but at once recognized in them the substructions of shepherds' huts, laid by modern Turkish herdsmen. The surface of the hill is strewn with fragments of very rude pottery, apparently of large jars.

The panorama the traveller enjoys from the summit of Kurshunlu Tepeh is beautiful beyond description. He sees at his feet the large valley of Beiramich, through which the Scamander meanders in innumerable curves; the valley being enclosed on all sides by the ridges of Ida, whose highest peaks, Garguissa (Gargarus) and Sarikis, tower majestically above it.

I also sank a shaft 2 mètres square into the artificial conical hill called Kutchek Tepeh (small hill) situated on the bank of the Scamander, about a mile to the south of Kurshunlu Tepeh; but I could not make much progress there on account of the enormous stones I encountered, for moving which I had no crowbars with me. Probably, like the tower in Ujek Tepeh, these blocks were intended to consolidate the mound. I found there nothing else but bones of animals, and very uninteresting fragments of tiles and of large jars.

§ *V. Kurshunlu Tepeh was the ancient Dardanié and Palaescepsis.*—I had always thought that the Homeric Dardanié, as well as the ancient Scepsis (Palaescepsis), had both been on high plateaux near the summit of Mount Ida. But for weighty reasons, to be explained in my "Journey in the Troad," (Appendix I. to this work) it is certain that no human settlement is, or ever was, possible there. In fact Homer nowhere tells us that Dardanié was situated high up in the mountains; he tells us that it was situated on the ὑπορείαι Ἴδης, that is to say, at the foot of Mount Ida;* and I am perfectly convinced that no place could have been meant here higher up than Kurshunlu Tepeh, for the city could only have been built on a spot whose environs were fertile enough to feed its inhabitants;

Il. XX. 216–218:

κτίσσε δὲ Δαρδανίην· ἐπεὶ οὔπω Ἴλιος ἱρή
ἐν πεδίῳ πεπόλιστο, πόλις μερόπων ἀνθρώπων,
ἀλλ' ἔθ' ὑπωρείας ᾤκεον πολυπίδακος Ἴδης.

but this is not the case with the highest villages on the mountain, namely, Oba Kioi * and Evjilar, the land of which hardly produces enough to feed their scanty population. Further, we must consider that Dardanié was situated in Dardania, the dominion of Aeneas, which, according to Strabo,† was limited to the small mountain slope, and extended in a southerly direction to the environs of Scepsis, and on the other side, to the north, as far as the Lycians about Zeleia. I therefore presume that Kurshunlu Tepeh was the original site of Dardanié, whose position Strabo ‡ could not determine, and of which he only says that it was probably situated in Dardania. As moreover, according to the tradition preserved by Homer,§ the inhabitants of Dardanié emigrated and built Ilios, I presume that the abandoned city on Kurshunlu Tepeh received other colonists, and was called Scepsis, because, as Strabo ǁ thinks, it had a high position and was visible at a great distance. Just as, according to Homer, Dardanié was the residence of the ancient kings, so, according to Demetrius, as cited by Strabo,¶ the ancient Scepsis remained the residence of Aeneas. It was situated above Cebrené, namely, nearer to Ida, and was separated from it by the Scamander.** Strabo †† proceeds to tell us that the inhabitants of Scepsis built, at a distance of 60 stadia from the ancient city, the new Scepsis, which still existed in his time, and was the birthplace of Demetrius. Now as the distance from Kurshunlu Tepeh to Beiramich is just two hours, and therefore about 60 stadia, and also as Beiramich is evidently the site of an ancient city, and as many coins of the later Scepsis are found there, I hold the two to be identical.

---

* This Oba Kioi is not to be confounded with the village of the same name at the foot of Kurshunlu Tepeh. See the small Map of the Troad, No. 140.
† XIII. pp. 592, 593, 596.
‡ XIII. p. 592.
§ *Il.* XX. 215-218.
ǁ XIII. p. 607.
¶ XIII. p. 607.
** XIII. pp. 597, 607.
†† XIII. 607.

§ VI. *The City of Cebrené.*—I went from Kurshunlu Tepeh to explore the site of the ancient city of Cebrené on Mount Chalidagh (bush-mountain), so called, no doubt, on account of the underwood with which it is overgrown. A good road leads up by zigzags to the site of the lower city, the altitude of which, at the foot of the little Acropolis, is 515 mètres. This Acropolis is on a steep rock, its highest point having an altitude of 544 mètres. Some foundations of houses, and a cistern cut out in the rock, 6 m. long, 5·50 m. broad, and 4 m. deep, are all that can be seen in the Acropolis; there is no accumulation of *débris*, and no trace of walls; but in fact walls were not needed, as the rock falls off vertically on all sides but one. Even on the site of the lower city the accumulation of *débris* is but very insignificant; but here, at least, may be seen a great many foundations of ancient houses of large well-wrought stones. The walls, which are more than two miles in circumference, may be traced in their entire circuit on the uneven ground: they are built in exactly the same way as the walls of Assos, and five gates may be recognized in them. In the upper part of the lower city are the foundations of a vast edifice of large wrought quadrangular blocks, also many walls of large unwrought stones; but as these latter consist only of one course of stones, and merely serve to support the terraces, they cannot be called cyclopean walls.

Having engaged in the village of Chalidagh Kioi ten workmen for 7 piastres (= 1½ francs) each, I selected on the plateau of the lower town fourteen places where the accumulation of *débris* appeared to be deepest, and began at once to excavate. But everywhere I struck the rock at the very insignificant depth of about 0·20 m., and only in a few places did I find an accumulation of *débris* 0·50 m. deep. The pottery I found is but very slightly baked, wheelmade, of a heavy gray or black, precisely identical with the pottery of the first epoch of Gergis on the Bali Dagh, but sparingly intermixed with rude thoroughly-baked red ware, such as was found on Fulu Dagh, and with monochrome glazed red or black Hellenic pottery of the Macedonian time. As all the excavations I made were on the perfectly flat plateau of the city, I am altogether at a loss to explain the insignificant accumulation of *débris*, for Cebrené is mentioned by Xenophon,* Scylax,† Stephanus Byzantinus;‡ and others, and, as the site is so well fortified by nature, there can hardly be a doubt that it was inhabited from a remote prehistoric period. But all we know of its history is, that Antigonus forced the inhabitants of Cebrené to settle in Alexandria Troas. Strabo§ mentions the Thracian Cebrenes, by whom the city of Cebrené may have been founded. In two of the holes I dug I struck rock-hewn tombs, containing human skeletons, which had suffered so much from moisture that they crumbled away when brought in contact with the air. In one of the tombs there was nothing else; the other contained a pair of silver earrings, an iron tripod, a bronze or copper bowl, and some utensils of the same metal, which were too much broken for their form or use to be recognized. The date of these sepulchres I do not venture to fix even approximately.

I found in my excavations a number of bronze coins and a silver coin of Cebrené, having on one side a ram's head with the legend K E, on the other a head of Apollo. I bought of the villagers on the hill many other Cebrenian bronze coins, as well as two bronze coins of Scepsis. The latter have on one side a palm-tree with the legend ΣΚ, or a Dionysus standing on a panther and holding a bunch of grapes in his hand; on the other side a hippocampus or a Roman emperor's head. The usual size of the bronze coins of Cebrené is 0,009 mm., but there are a vast number which are only 0,005 mm. in diameter, less than a sixth part of the diameter of a penny. If we are to judge of the

---

* *Hellenica*, 3, 1, 17.　　　　　† *Periplus*, 96.
‡ *S. v.* Κεβρήια.　　　　　　　§ XIII. p. 590.

wealth of a people by the size and value of their coins,* the Cebrenians must have been a very poor people, and this seems also to be confirmed by the rudeness of their pottery. But, in spite of their extreme poverty, they were far more advanced in the art of coining than even the most civilized nations of our time; nay, the fineness of the representation of the Apollo-heads, even on their smallest bronze coins, has hardly ever yet been equalled even by the best American or English gold coins.

From the Acropolis of Cebrené the traveller sees, beyond the heights which encompass the valley of Beiramich on the north side, the islands of Imbros and Samothrace, and to the left the vast Aegean Sea, from which the pyramidal Mount Athos rises majestically in the distance.

§ *VII. Results of the Explorations in* 1882.—Now to recapitulate the results of my five months' Trojan campaign of 1882 : I HAVE PROVED THAT IN A REMOTE ANTIQUITY THERE WAS IN THE PLAIN OF TROY A LARGE CITY, DESTROYED OF OLD BY A FEARFUL CATASTROPHE, WHICH HAD ON THE HILL OF HISSARLIK ONLY ITS ACROPOLIS, WITH ITS TEMPLES AND A FEW OTHER LARGE EDIFICES, WHILST ITS LOWER CITY EXTENDED IN AN EASTERLY, SOUTHERLY, AND WESTERLY DIRECTION, ON THE SITE OF THE LATER ILIUM ; AND THAT, CONSEQUENTLY, THIS CITY ANSWERS PERFECTLY TO THE HOMERIC DESCRIPTION OF THE SITE OF *SACRED ILIOS.* I HAVE FURTHER ONCE MORE BROUGHT TO NAUGHT THE PRETENSIONS OF THE SMALL CITY ON THE BALI DAGH BEHIND BOUNARBASHI TO BE THE SITE OF TROY, INASMUCH AS I HAVE SHOWN THAT IT BELONGS TO A MUCH LATER TIME, AND THAT IT CANNOT BE SEPARATED FROM THE STRONGLY FORTIFIED CITY ON ESKI HISSARLIK, WHICH, AT A DISTANCE OF ONLY A FEW HUNDRED YARDS FROM IT, CROWNS A LOFTY HILL ON THE

---

* I may remind the reader here that 1000 Chinese or 4000 Japanese zinc-coins have the value of one dollar.

OPPOSITE BANK OF THE SCAMANDER, HAVING BEEN BUILT SIMULTANEOUSLY WITH IT, AND HAVING BEEN TOGETHER WITH IT THE KEY TO THE ROAD WHICH LEADS THROUGH THE VALLEY OF THE SCAMANDER INTO ASIA MINOR. I have further proved that the accumulation of ancient ruins and *débris*, which exceeds sixteen mètres in depth on the hill of Hissarlik, is quite insignificant on the Bali Dagh, as well as at Eski Hissarlik and on Mount Fulu Dagh, and amounts to nothing in the only two places in the Troad where the most ancient human settlements ought to have existed, and where the archaeologist might confidently expect to find a rich abundance of most ancient prehistoric ruins, namely, Kurshunlu Tepeh (Dardanié and Palaescepsis), and the Chalidagh (Cebrené). I have proved that the most ancient remains on all these sites, scanty as they are, belong most probably to the period between the ninth and the fifth centuries B.C., and that there is no trace among them of prehistoric pottery

By my exploration of the "heroic tombs," I have further proved, that the tumulus which by Homer and the tradition of all antiquity had been attributed to Achilles, as well as one of the two tumuli ascribed to Antilochus and Patroclus, cannot claim a higher antiquity than the ninth century B.C., that is to say, the Homeric age; whereas the tumulus, to which tradition pointed as the tomb of Protesilaus, may with the very greatest probability be attributed to the age of the second city of Hissarlik, which perished in a direful calamity. My excavations in this tumulus have also confirmed the ancient tradition which brought the earlier inhabitants of Ilium from Europe and not from Asia. I have further discovered at the foot of Cape Sigeum a large tumulus, which was known in antiquity and was probably attributed by tradition to the hero Antilochus, but which has not come under the notice of any modern explorer and is indicated on no map of the Troad. My exploration in 1882 has also been of capital importance from an architectural point of view, for I have proved for the first time that, in the remote antiquity to which the ruins of Troy belong, not only the walls of the city, but even the walls of the large edifices were made of raw bricks, and were artificially baked *in situ* after having been completely built; and that the *antae* or *parastades*, which in later ages fulfilled only a technical purpose, were nothing else than a reminiscence or "survival" of the ancient wooden *parastades*, which had two important constructive purposes; for they served both to consolidate and secure the front faces of the lateral walls, and to render them capable of supporting the ponderous weight of the superincumbent cross-beams and the terraced roof.

My work at Troy is now ended for ever, after extending over more than the period of *ten years*, which has a fated connection with the legend of the city. How many tens of years a new controversy may rage around it, I leave to the critics: *that* is their work; *mine* is done. I content myself with recalling to the memory of my readers the words which I wrote from Hissarlik in the first year of my excavations * (Nov. 3, 1871):

"*My expectations are extremely modest;* I have no hope of finding plastic works of art. The *single object* of my excavations from the beginning was only TO FIND TROY, whose site has been discussed by a hundred scholars in a hundred books, but which as yet *no one has ever sought to bring to light by excavations.* If I should not succeed in this, still I shall be perfectly contented, if by my labours I succeed only in penetrating to the deepest darkness of prehistoric times, and enriching archaeology by the discovery of a few interesting features from the most ancient history of the great Hellenic race."

Such was my simple purpose in beginning the great work: how it has been performed I now leave finally to the judgment of candid readers and honest students: to those of another spirit—how provoked I leave to their own conscience—I hope, as I can well afford, henceforth to be indifferent.

* *Troy and its Remains*, p. 80.

NOTES

Note I.—THE CAUCASUS.

As some of the oldest Greek myths are located in the Caucasus, I had always thought that antiquities might possibly be found there, of an age even more remote than those of Troy. But it seems that I have been mistaken, for Professor Rudolf Virchow, of Berlin—who attended the Archaeological Congress at Tiflis in September and October, 1881, and who himself made excavations in the most ancient cemetery of the country, the prehistoric necropolis of Upper-Koban, which has been explored since 1869—ascertained that even this necropolis belongs to the very beginning of the *iron-age*, though bronze is still preponderant in it, and that neither there nor elsewhere in the Caucasus have any prehistoric antiquities, in the proper sense of the word, as yet been found, nor have any stone-implements ever yet occurred. Nevertheless the celebrated explorer thinks that the necropolis of Upper-Koban may probably belong to the tenth century before our era.*

---

* Rudolf Virchow, *Das Gräberfeld von Koban im Lande der Osseten, Kaukasus, eine vergleichende archaeologische Studie*, Berlin, 1883. This work is not only quantitatively a gigantic performance, but it is also qualitatively a real masterpiece of comparative investigation. It contains 20 printed sheets of large size with 50 excellent woodcuts, and is accompanied by an Atlas containing 11 tables and about 200 magnificent representations in autotype (Lichtdruck) of the most remarkable objects found in the 500 tombs, and more, hitherto unearthed in the Necropolis of Upper-Koban. The celebrated investigator remarks that, by the copiousness and the variety of its bronzes, the necropolis of Koban stands among all ancient European cemeteries nearest to the famous necropolis of Hallstadt in Austria. With all the richness of his deep and extensive learning, with the vast abundance of his long experience, and with the mature judgment of the practical archaeologist, he has proceeded to investigate the connection in which each of the numerous bronze and other objects found in the necropolis of Koban stands to every other discovery made by himself or by any other explorer on any other prehistoric site. The rich abundance of the contents may be conceived when it is considered that, besides numerous quotations in the text, the work contains more than a thousand notes and quotations below the text. I enthusiastically recommend this new and splendid masterpiece of the most conscientious and deeply-learned investigator and explorer to all who take an interest in archaeology.

Note II.—Callicoloné.

I mentioned in *Ilios*, p. 59, that, as Homer* makes Ares leap alternately from Ilium to Callicoloné on the Simois, and from Callicoloné to Ilium, Prof. R. Virchow considered it to be implied that Callicoloné must be visible from Ilium, and he therefore identified Mount Oulou Dagh with it, this being the only great height in the neighbourhood of the Simois from which Ilium is visible, as well as nearly every point of the plain of Troy. But the Oulou Dagh is ten miles distant from Ilium, a leap too great even for the war god ; besides it is fully three miles on the further side of the Simois to the east. I therefore adhere still to the old belief that, in mentioning Callicoloné, Homer had in view Mount Kara Your,† and not Mount Oulou Dagh. The former, which is 206 mètres high, and only four and a half miles from Ilium, was evidently held by Demetrius of Scepsis to be identical with the Homeric Callicoloné, for Strabo‡ says that it is five stadia from the Simois: ἡ Καλλικολώνη λόφος τις, παρ' ὃν ὁ Σιμόεις ῥεῖ πεντοστάδιον διέχων, and such is the actual distance of the Kara Your from the river. The only difficulty is, that this mountain is not visible from Ilium. But Dr. Dörpfeld reminds me that Homer mentions Callicoloné, in describing the battle raging between the Greek camp on the shore of the Hellespont and Ilium. The gods participate in it, and Ares stands opposite to Pallas Athené.§ As the latter shouted, standing now beside the deep trench, without the wall, now on the resounding shore,‖ Dörpfeld thinks it would be unreasonable to suppose that the war god, in fighting against Pallas Athené and animating the Trojans to battle, could have done this, now from Ilium's Acropolis, now from a hill situated in a side valley, seven kilomètres from the battlefield and at least ten kilomètres from the Greek camp, for it is said of him " Ares on the other side, like a black storm, shouted to the Trojans, now from the citadel and now, running along the Simois, on Callicoloné."¶ Dr. Dörpfeld therefore thinks that Καλλικολώνη must absolutely be looked for on the high ridge which runs out

---

* *Il.* XX. 52, 53. † See the large Map of the Troad.
‡ XIII. p. 597.
§ *Il.* XX. 69 :
    ἄντα δ' Ἐνυαλίοιο θεὰ γλαυκῶπις Ἀθήνη·

‖ *Il.* XX. 48–50 :
    . . . . αὖε δ' Ἀθήνη,
    στᾶσ' ὁτὲ μὲν παρὰ τάφρον ὀρυκτὴν τείχεος ἐκτός,
    ἄλλοτ' ἐπ' ἀκτάων ἐριδούπων μακρὸν ἀύτει.

¶ *Il.* XX. 51–53 :
    αὖε δ' Ἄρης ἑτέρωθεν, ἐρεμνῇ λαίλαπι ἶσος,
    ὀξὺ κατ' ἀκροτάτης πόλιος Τρώεσσι κελεύων,
    ἄλλοτε πὰρ Σιμόεντι θέων ἐπὶ Καλλικολώνῃ,

in Cape Rhoeteum, and which extends on the south side parallel with the Simois, on the west side parallel with the In Tepeh Asmak, the ancient bed of the Scamander. I would not hesitate a moment to accept this ingenious theory, if there were on that ridge a solitary hillock which could in any way be called Καλλικολώνη. The word κολώνη occurs three times in Homer; in the first passage it means a conical tumulus, a so-called "heroic tomb." "In front of Ilium there is a lofty hillock, standing apart in the plain, which can be passed round. It is called Batieia by men, whilst the gods call it the tomb of the swift Myrina." * In the second passage it is a steep hill; "there is a city Thryoessa on a lofty hill." † In the third passage it is either a hill near Aleisium, or a conical tumulus of Aleisius.‡ If, therefore, κολώνη means sometimes a conical tumulus, sometimes a steep hill, we must infer that Καλλικολώνη can only signify a beautiful, high, steep hill, the form of which strikes the eye. Such a hill is Mount Kara Your, whose roof-like top will remain for a long time in the memory of visitors to the plain of Troy. Besides, there are on the top of this hill the foundations of a larger edifice, which may have been a temple of Ares, and which would explain why he shouts now from Ilium's Acropolis, now from Καλλικολώνη. Again, the poet describes in more than one place the immense proportions and enormous strength of the war-god, who shouts as loud as ten thousand warriors,§ and who, when struck down by Athené, covers a space of seven plethra = 216 mètres, on the ground.‖ Of still much larger proportions is his sister Eris, who, whilst walking on earth, touches with her head even the heavens.¶ I may add that Athené's helmet

---

* *Il.* II. 811–814:

"Ἔστι δέ τις προπάροιθε πόλιος αἰπεῖα κολώνη,
ἐν πεδίῳ ἀπάνευθε, περίδρομος ἔνθα καὶ ἔνθα·
τὴν ἤτοι ἄνδρες Βατίειαν κικλήσκουσιν,
ἀθάνατοι δέ τε σῆμα πολυσκάρθμοιο Μυρίνης·

† *Il.* XI. 711:

ἔστι δέ τις Θρυόεσσα πόλις, αἰπεῖα κολώνη,

‡ *Il.* XI. 757, 758:

πέτρης τ' Ὠλενίης, καὶ Ἀλεισίου ἔνθα κολώνη
κέκληται . . . . . .

§ *Il.* V. 859, 860:

. . . . . . ὁ δ' ἔβραχε χάλκεος Ἄρης,
ὅσσον τ' ἐννεάχιλοι ἐπίαχον ἢ δεκάχιλοι

‖ *Il.* XXI. 406, 407:

τῷ βάλε θοῦρον Ἄρηα κατ' αὐχένα, λῦσε δὲ γυῖα.
ἑπτὰ δ' ἐπέσχε πέλεθρα πεσών, ἐκόνισε δὲ χαίτας·

¶ *Il.* IV. 443:

(Ἔρις) οὐρανῷ ἐστήριξε κάρη, καὶ ἐπὶ χθονὶ βαίνει.

was large enough to cover the troops of a hundred cities.* The distance of seven kilomètres can, therefore, be no obstacle to our supposing that Mount Kara Your is the Homeric Καλλικολώνη. I think it not out of place to mention here, that Eustathius,† who accepts without criticism Strabo's theory regarding the identity of Troy with the Ἰλιέων Κώμη, has misunderstood the phrase cited above, ἡ Καλλικολώνη, λόφος τις, παρ' ὃν ὁ Σιμόεις ῥεῖ πεντασταδίων διέχων, and has understood it to mean that Καλλικολώνη is a hill five stadia long, close to which the Simois flows, for he says: Καλλικολώνη, λόφος τις πενταστάδιος, παρ' ὃν ῥεῖ ὁ Σιμόεις. I have still to remark that only the north-western corner of the above-mentioned ridge is called Cape Rhoeteum, which does not, however, denote a height projecting above the rest.

Note III.—THE ADVANCE OF THE SEA UPON THE SHORES OF THE HELLESPONT.

Having cited in *Ilios*, p. 91, Mr. Frank Calvert's learned dissertation on *the Asiatic Coast of the Hellespont*, in which he proves beyond any doubt the cessation of the growth of the land on the coast, and the gradual inroad of the sea on the land, I may here state that Mr. Calvert writes to me, that he has found still further proofs of the advance of the sea in the Gulf of Artaki, on the northern coast of the Hellespont, where the foundations of houses may be seen extending into the sea for a long distance from the shore.

Note IV.—THE POSITION OF THE TUMULUS OF ILUS, ACCORDING TO THE ILIAD.

As I have mentioned in *Ilios*, p. 147, at a certain distance in front of Ilium was the confluence of the Scamander and the Simois, as well as the ford of the Scamander; and near this was the Tumulus of Ilus, surmounted by a pillar, against which Paris leant when he shot an arrow at Diomedes and wounded him. ‡ This position of the monument is also proved by the Agora which Hector held far from the ships, on the banks of the Scamander,§ and close by the Tumulus of Ilus, far from the tumult.‖ In another passage ¶ it is described as situated in the midst of the plain, but not at all meaning—as the passage is generally interpreted—that it was close to the Erineos, which, as is evident from other passages,** was close to the city-wall; nay, it is distinctly stated that the Trojans, in flying through the plain to the city, passed the tumulus of

---

* *Il.* V. 743, 744:
κρατὶ δ' ἐπ' ἀμφίφαλον κυνέην θέτο τετραφάληρον,
χρυσείην, ἑκατὸν πολίων πρυλέεσσ' ἀραρυῖαν.

† *Ad Iliadem*, XX. 53.   ‡ *Il.* XI. 369-372.
§ *Il.* VIII. 489, 490.   ‖ *Il.* X. 414, 415.
¶ *Il.* XI. 166-168.   ** *Il.* VI. 433, 434, and XXII. 145.

Ilus and the Erineos, and there is not a word which alludes to the proximity of the two:

οἱ δὲ παρ' Ἴλου σῆμα παλαιοῦ Δαρδανίδαο,
μέσσον κὰπ πεδίον παρ' ἐρινεὸν ἐσσεύοντο
ἱέμενοι πόλιος·

But from none of these passages can we infer whether the tumulus of Ilus was situated on the right or on the left bank of the Scamander. In this respect we neither find an indication in the passage from which it follows that the thousand watch-fires of the Trojan camp were seen between the ships and the river;* nor in that in which it is stated that Hector, who (from the Greek point of view) fought on the left side of the battle, on the shore of the Scamander, knew nothing of the carnage † made by Ajax, for we are left perfectly ignorant as to the distance between the scene of that slaughter and the tumulus of Ilus. Thus there is nothing to contradict the sole passage in the *Iliad* which fixes the position of the Tumulus of Ilus, and indicates it as on the right bank of the Scamander, for on his way to the tent of Achilles Priam first passes the Tumulus of Ilus and then reaches the ford of the Scamander:

οἳ δ' ἐπεὶ οὖν μέγα σῆμα παρὲξ Ἴλοιο ἔλασσαν,
στῆσαν ἄρ' ἡμιόνους τε καὶ ἵππους, ὄφρα πίοιεν,
ἐν ποταμῷ·‡

Note V.—DEMETRIUS OF SCEPSIS.

I have explained in *Ilios*,§ that, from the indications given by Strabo, the Ἰλιέων Κώμη of Demetrius must have occupied the site of a low hill on Mr. Calvert's farm to the north-east of Thymbra, and just in front of the swamp, now dried up, which used to be called the Duden-swamp. Among many other proofs adduced by Prof. August Steitz,‖ to show how little reliance can be placed on the statements of Demetrius (in Strabo), he points to the contradiction regarding the position of the Erineos, which, according to one passage,¶ lies close to Ἰλιέων Κώμη (τῷ μὲν ἀρχαίῳ κτίσματι ὑποπέπτωκεν), whilst in the preceding paragraph it is expressly stated that the Erineos lies in the plain of the Scamander.** Respecting Ἰλιέων Κώμη, as Steitz remarks, Demetrius evidently sought only for the name of a second Ilium, just as people disputed which of several places named Pylos was the city of Nestor; and since there was no other city of Ilium, he was satisfied with a village, the appellation of which probably indicates only that it had belonged to the Ilians of Ilium. In proclaiming the identity of Ἰλιέων Κώμη with Troy, he was content with putting forward the scruples which he professed to have

---

* *Il.* VIII. 560-563.   † *Il.* XI. 497-499.
‡ *Il.* XXIV. 349-351.   § Pages 79, 176.
‖ "Die Lage des Homerischen Troia," in the *Jahrbücher für Classische Philologie*, ed. Alfred Fleckeisen, Jahrgang XXI. Band III., Leipzig, 1875, p. 246, seq.
¶ Strabo, XIII. p. 598.   ** Strabo, XIII. p. 597.

against the site of Ilium, and he thought it unnecessary to give positive proofs.

Note VI.—MENTION OF OYSTERS IN HOMER.

Homer * compares the mortally wounded Hebriones, precipitated from his chariot, to a diver who searches for τήθεα, which is generally explained as oysters; † but as this word does not occur again in Homer, whereas the very similar τήθυον means, in Aristotle and others, merely ascidia (ἀσκίδια, acephalous molluscs), which are still used on the Mediterranean coast as food, the former interpretation is considered by Herr von Martens, the eminent physiologist of Berlin, ‡ as at least doubtful. But on this I have to observe that the translation of the Homeric word τῆθος (plural τήθεα) by 'oyster' is confirmed by Athenaeus,§ and there can consequently be no doubt of its correctness. I may add that oysters appear to have been a favourite dish with all the early settlers on Hissarlik, for oyster shells occur in large numbers in the ruins of all the five prehistoric settlements; their abundance in the first and oldest city is confirmed by Prof. R. Virchow (See Appendix II.).

Note VII.—AUTHORS ON TROY.

To the list given in *Ilios*, pp. 186–188, of scholars who adhered to the theory of Lechevalier and Choiseul-Gouffier, that ancient Troy had been situated on the heights of Bounarbashi, I have to add the following:—

Friedr. Gottlieb Welcker: "Ueber die Lage des Homerischen Ilion," in the *Augsburger Allgemeine Zeitung*, 1843, Nos. 38, 39, 40 (Supplement).

W. Forchhammer: "Der Skamandros," in the *Augsburger Allgemeine Zeitung*, 1881, No. 298 (Supplement).

G. Nicolaïdes: Ἰλιάδος Στρατηγικὴ Διασκευή, Athens, 1883.

To the list given in *Ilios*, pp. 189–190, of scholars who have recognized the identity of Ilium with the site of the Homeric Troy, I have to add :—

Gustav von Eckenbrecher: "Ueber die Lage des Homerischen Ilion," in the *Augsburger Allgemeine Zeitung*, 1843, Nos. 225, 227, 228 (Supplement). (Answer to F. G. Welcker's above-mentioned article in the same journal, Nos. 38, 39, 40.)

F. C. Schlosser: Weltgeschichte für das Deutsche Volk, 1844. The author says, I. p. 200: "The city was completely razed. Later on, a

---

Il. XVI. 746, 747 :
εἰ δή που καὶ πόντῳ ἐν ἰχθυόεντι γένοιτο,
πολλοὺς ἂν κορέσειεν ἀνὴρ ὅδε, τήθεα δηφῶν.

† So e.g. by Suidas.   ‡ See *Ilios*, pp. 114–116.

§ *Deipnosophistae*, 1. 22 : οὐ μόνον δὲ (οἱ ἥρωες) ἰχθύσιν ἀλλὰ καὶ ὀστρείοις ἐχρῶντο, καίτοι τῆς τούτων ἐδωδῆς οὐ πολὺ ἐχούσης τὸ ὠφέλιμον καὶ ἡδύ, ἀλλὰ κἂν τῷ βυθῷ κατὰ βάθος κειμένων · καὶ οὐκ ἔστιν εἰς ταῦτα ἄλλῃ τινὶ τέχνῃ χρήσασθαι ἢ δύντα κατὰ βυθοῦ
ἢ μάλ' ἐλαφρὸς ἀνὴρ ὃς ῥεῖα κυβιστᾷ
ὃν καὶ λέγει πολλοὺς ἂν κορέσαι τήθεα διφῶντα.

new Troy or Ilion was built on the site of the old one." This remark of Schlosser is of importance, considering the great conscientiousness which characterizes that historian.

J. de Witte: *Discours prononcé à la Séance publique de l'Académie d'Archéologie de Belgique*, June 28, 1874.

P. M. Keller van Hoorn: *Heinrich Schliemann en zijne archeologische Onderzoekningen*, Dordrecht, September 25, 1874.

Ernest Chantre: *L'Age de la Pierre et l'Age du Bronze en Troade et en Grèce*, Lyon, 1874.

W. Rossmann: "Ueber Schliemann's Troja," in the journal *Deutsche Rundschau*, 1875.

August Steitz: " Die Lage des Homerischen Troia," in the *Jahrbücher für Classische Philologie*, ed. Alfred Fleckeisen, Jahrgang XXI., Band III.; Leipzig, 1875.

S. A. Naber: *Gladstone over Homerus*, Amsterdam, 1876 (reprinted from the periodical *De Gids*).

Ludolf Stephani, in the *Compte Rendu de la Commission Impériale Archéologique pour l'année* 1877, p. 52, recognizes the identity of Hissarlik with the site of ancient Troy; but nevertheless he maintains that the antiquities which I gathered there in my excavations, as well as the immense gold treasures discovered by me in the royal sepulchres of Mycenae, belong to the time of the migration of the nations, and consequently to the end of the fourth and the beginning of the fifth century, A.D. He says, "As, in order to prove that the objects found in the Mycenean tombs belong to the twelfth century B.C., stress has often been laid on their resemblance to the objects discovered during the last ten years on the site of ancient Troy, it will not be superfluous to remind the reader that these latter also belong to the time of the migration of the nations, namely, that the Trojan gold ornaments and utensils have been brought from the south of Russia by other bands of the same Goths and Scythians, to whom also the treasures of Mycenae belong." I may add that this most fantastic of all fantastic theories has been received with ridicule and sarcasm by all archaeologists throughout the world.

W. J. Manssen: *Heinrich Schliemann*, Haarlem, 1880.

A. H. Sayce: "Notes from Journeys in the Troad and Lydia," in the *Journal of Hellenic Studies*, vol. i.; London, 1880.

Karl Blind: "Schliemann's Discoveries" in the *Examiner* of 11th December, 1880; further, "Germanische Wassergottheiten," in the *Vossische Zeitung* of July, 1880, to March, 1881 (Sunday Supplement), see the number of 13th March, 1881; further, "Der Troja Forscher und die Ur-Germanen des Ostens," in the *Neue Freie Presse* of Vienna, of 2nd August, 1881; further, "Schliemann's Ehrenbürgerrecht und seine Troja Funde," in the *Westliche Post* of St. Louis, Missouri, August, 1881; further, "Scottish, Shetlandic, and Germanic Water Tales," in the *Contemporary Review* of August, September, and October,

1881 (see the August number); further, "Schliemann's Entdeckungen und Forschungen," in the Berlin periodical *Gegenwart* of 29th April, 1882; further, "Virchow's Old Trojan Tombs and Skulls," in the *Academy* of 17th March, 1883. (See Appendix III. to the present work.)

J. Maehly: "Schliemann's Troja," *Blätter für Literarische Unterhaltung,* Nos. 15, 16, 1881.

G. Perrot: "Les Découvertes archéologiques du Docteur H Schliemann, à Troie et à Mycènes," in the *Revue politique et littéraire* of 9th April, 1881.

Arthur Milchhoefer: "Heinrich Schliemann," in the *Deutsche Rundschau,* VII., September, 1881, Heft 12, p. 392, *seqq.*; further, " Heinrich Schliemann und seine Werke," in the periodical *Nord und Süd,* XXI., April, 1882; Heft 61, p. 65, *seqq.*

Edmund Jörg and Franz Binder: "Schliemann und Ilios," in the journal *Historisch-politische Blätter für das katolische Deutschland,* 5th and 6th Heft, Nos. 87⁵, 87⁶; Munich, 1881.

Anonymous: "Schliemann's Trojanische Sammlung," in the periodical *Die Grenzboten,* No. 9; Leipzig, 24th February, 1881.

Signature A. K.: "Schliemann's Ilios," in the periodical *Die Grenzboten,* No. 12; Leipzig, 17th March, 1881.

Anonymous: "The True Site of Troy," in the New York *Nation* of 5th May, 1881.

R. C. Jebb: "Schliemann's Ilios," in the *Edinburgh Review* of April 1881; and "Homeric and Hellenic Ilium," in the *Journal of Hellenic Studies,* vol. ii.; London, 1881.

F. A. Paley: "Schliemann's Ilios," in the *British Quarterly Review,* of April, 1881.

Philip Smith: " The Site of Homer's Troy," in the *Quarterly Review* of July, 1881.

Rudolf Virchow: " Die Petersburger Angriffe gegen die Schliemannschen Funde," in the periodical *Ausland,* No. 12, 1881; further, " Die Lage von Troja," in the *Verhandlungen der Berliner Anthropologischen Gesellschaft,* Session 21st May, 1881; further, *Alttrojanische Gräber und Schädel,* Berlin, 1882.

J. P. Mahaffy: "The Site and Antiquity of the Hellenic Ilion," in the *Journal of Hellenic Studies,* vol. iii. No. 1, April, 1882. (See Appendix V. to the present work.)

A. E. Holweda: "Schliemann's Troie," in the periodical *De Gids,* February, 1882.

K. Hertz: "Генрихъ Шлиманъ, его жизнь, раскопки и литературные труды," въ Русскомъ Вѣстникѣ, 1882.

Christian Belger: "Generalfeldmarschall Graf Moltke's Verdienste um die Kenntniss des Alterthums," in the 51st volume of the *Preussische Jahrbücher,* 1882.

Edmund Hardy: " Schliemann und seine Entdeckungen auf der

Baustelle des alten Troja," *Frankfurter zeitgemässe Broschüren*, vol. iii. Heft 10, 1882.

William W. Goodwin: "The Ruins at Hissarlik," in the *Academy* of 9th December, 1882.

Wm. Dörpfeld: "Troia und Neu Ilion," in the *Allgemeine Zeitung*, No. 272 of 1882 (Supplement); further, "Ilian Theories," in the *Times* of 22nd March, 1883; further, "Noch einmal Troia und Neu Ilion," in the *Allgemeine Zeitung*, No. 89 of 1883 (Supplement).

Dr. Fligier: In the *Correspondenzblatt* of the German Society for Anthropology, Ethnology, and Prehistoric History, of August, 1882. Also in the *Literarische Beilage der Montag's Revue*, Vienna, 15th January, 1883.

Prince Karl von Schwarzenberg: Vijlet ua Hissarlik, Prag, 1882

A theory differing from those of the sites of Bounarbashi and Ilium (Hissarlik) is only adopted by:

E. Brentano: Ilion im Dumbrekthale, Stuttgart, 1881, further "Zur Lösung der Trojanischen Frage," in the *Deutsche Literatur-Zeitung*, 1881, No. 40, and *Troia und Neu-Ilion*, Heilbronn, 1882, who believes Troy to have been situated in the valley of the Simois.

R. C. Jebb, who in his above-mentioned two publications acknowledged the identity of Hissarlik with the Troy of the legend, has changed his theory in his latest dissertation, "The Ruins at Hissarlik, their relation to the Iliad," in the *Journal of Hellenic Studies*, III. No. 2, October, 1882, and now expresses the opinion that the topography of the Iliad is probably eclectic.

Note VIII.—THE PROPHECY OF JUNO IN THE ODE OF HORACE, "JUSTUM ET TENACEM." (*Carm.* III. 3.)

As I have mentioned in *Ilios*, pp. 204–206, this prophecy has been repeatedly cited by the adherents of the Troy-Bounarbashi theory, as a decisive proof against the identity of the site of Ilium with the Homeric Troy. Prof. J. Maehly* is of opinion: "that Horace really had here Ilium in view; but to leave this provincial city in its comparative insignificance, or to elevate it to the importance of a second Rome, were two altogether different things. Juno, or whoever may have urged his remonstrance in her person, was opposing a design to raise Ilium to the grandeur of a new capital; and the goddess is made to express herself somewhat hyperbolically, 'ne tecta velint reparare Troiae.'"

Note IX.—LETTER OF THE EMPEROR JULIAN.

In the translation of this letter given in *Ilios*, pp. 181, 182, there is a mistake; the phrase "ἡ μὲν οὖν εἰκὼν οὐχ ὑγιής," having been erro-

---

* *Blätter für Literarische Unterhaltung*, Nos. 15, 16, 1881.

neously rendered by "it is true the statue is not uninjured," whereas it ought to be "it is true the comparison is not sound."

To explain the phrase : "he (Pegasius) did none of the things those impious men are wont to do, who make on the forehead the memorial of the impious (one), nor did he hiss to himself (*i.e.* 'aside') like those (men), for their high theology consists in these two things, hissing against the daemons and making the sign of the cross," I have called attention to the fact that at that time the term δαίμονες was applied to the ancient gods who were identified with the devils, and that the Christians hissed to themselves in order to avert their energy, just as now in the Greek church, when the priest baptizes a child, he blows thrice into the baptismal water and spits thrice on the child, in order to avert the power of the devils from it. I may add that the custom of spitting thrice in order to avert the "evil eye," seems to belong to a remote antiquity, for we find, *e.g.* in Theocritus : " To avert being bewitched I spat thrice in my bosom." * And in Lucian : "After the magic sentence, he spat thrice in my face and returned without looking at any one of those he met." †

The number three was also customary in reciting formulae, as we see in Pliny : ‡ "Caesarem dictatorem post unum ancipitem vehiculi casum, ferunt semper, ut primum concedisset, id quod plerosque nunc facere scimus, carmine ter repetito securitatem itinerum aucupari solitum."

This letter of the Emperor Julian proves that in the fourth century A.D. Ilium was a favourite resort of tourists, because Julian speaks of the Periegetae as professional guides for strangers. That the same was the case in the first or second century A.D., appears to be proved by the tenth of the spurious letters which bear the name of the orator Aeschines. §

I do not stay to discuss the doubts which have been raised as to the genuineness of this letter ; for, if it were the spurious work of a rhetorician (like so many epistles ascribed to famous Greeks), this would merely extend the duration of Ilium to a still later time.

Note X.—POLEMON.

I stated in *Ilios*, p. 168, by mistake, that Polemon, who lived at the end of the third and at the beginning of the second century B.C., who was therefore older than Demetrius of Scepsis, and who wrote a descrip-

---

Idyll. VI. verse 39 :

ὡς μὴ βασκανθῶ δέ, τρὶς εἰς ἐμὸν ἔπτυσα κόλπον.

† Μένιππος ἢ Νεκυομαντεία, p. 465 : μετὰ δ' οὖν τὴν ἐπῳδὴν τρὶς ἔν μου πρὸς τὸ πρόσωπον ἀποπτύσας, ἐπανῄειν πάλιν οὐδένα τῶν ἀπαντώντων προσβλέπων·

‡ *H. N.* XXVIII. 4. § See also Philostratus, *Apoll.* 4, 11.

tion (περιήγησις) of Ilium, was a native of Ilium ; whereas, in fact, he was a native of the Ilian village of Glykeia.* I further stated by mistake that Polemon speaks (in the fragments preserved) of the altar of Zeus Herkeios, on which Priam had been slain ; for this altar is, so far as I know, only mentioned by Arrian, † who says that Alexander the Great offered sacrifices on it to Priam, praying him to relinquish his wrath against the race of Neoptolemus, to which he (Alexander) belonged. But Arrian does not say whether the Ilians held this to be the identical altar of Zeus Herkeios on which Priam was slain.

Note XI.—TESTIMONY OF PLATO FOR THE SITE OF TROY.

The testimony of Plato for the site of Troy is of capital interest. In the discussion on the origin of government between Cleinias and the Athenian stranger, the latter proposes to pass in review the successive forms of civilization since the deluge. The waters having receded, there was an immense desert, and the organization of human society had to recommence from its first elements. The arts had perished in the general catastrophe, and many generations had to pass before they could revive. Wars and discords had ceased for a time ; legislation had not yet reappeared. But there must already have existed that form of government, in which every one is the master in his own house. Such a δυναστεία is attributed by Homer to the Cyclopes : " They have neither an *agora* for national assemblies, nor oracles of law ; they inhabit caverns on the tops of high mountains ; every one makes the law for his children and his wives, and they have no care one for another." ‡ In the second stage, the primitive men descended from the heights, and built larger cities at the foot of the mountains ; they surrounded them with fences to protect themselves against the wild beasts, and engaged in agriculture. In the third stage, men had become so courageous that they began building cities in the plains. These two last stages (the second and the third) are indicated by Homer § in the passage where he puts into the

---

* See Polemon in Suidas.
† *Anab.* I. 11 : Θῦσαι δὲ αὐτὸν καὶ Πριάμῳ ἐπὶ τοῦ βωμοῦ τοῦ Διὸς τοῦ Ἑρκείου λόγος κατέχει, μῆνιν Πριάμου παραιτούμενον τῷ Νεοπτολέμου γένει, ὃ δὴ ἐς αὐτὸν καθῆκεν.
‡ *Od.* IX. 112-115 :
    τοῖσιν δ'οὔτ' ἀγοραὶ βουληφόροι, οὔτε θέμιστες
    ἀλλ' οἴγ' ὑψηλῶν ὀρέων ναίουσι κάρηνα
    ἐν σπέσσι γλαφυροῖσι · θεμιστεύει δὲ ἕκαστος
    παίδων ἠδ' ἀλόχων, οὐδ' ἀλλήλων ἀλέγουσιν.

§ *Il.* XX. 215-218 :
    Δάρδανον αὖ πρῶτον τέκετο νεφεληγερέτα Ζεύς,
    κτίσσε δὲ Δαρδανίην · ἐπεὶ οὔπω Ἴλιος ἱρὴ
    ἐν πεδίῳ πεπόλιστο, πόλις μερόπων ἀνθρώπων,
    ἀλλ' ἔθ' ὑπωρείας ᾤκεον πολυπίδακος Ἴδης ·

mouth of Aeneas the tradition : "Dardanus founded the city of Dardanié, for the sacred town of Ilios had not yet been built in the plain, and my ancestors still dwelt at the foot of Mount Ida rich in fountains." Plato's Athenian adds: "*We say that the inhabitants descended from the heights and founded Ilium in a large and fair plain, on a hill of moderate height, watered by several rivers which descend from the heights of Ida.*" *

It appears to me impossible that Plato could have better indicated the situation of Ilios on Hissarlik, to distinguish its site from 'Ιλιέων Κώμη, Bounarbashi, or any other place.

Note XII.—TESTIMONY OF THE ORATOR LYCURGUS.

The very greatest stress is laid by the defenders of the Troy-Bounarbashi theory, and other antagonists of Troy on Hissarlik, on the testimony of the orator Lycurgus, † who says in his speech against Leocrates, accused of treason after the battle of Chaeronea : "Who has not heard that Troy, the greatest city of its time, and the sovereign of all Asia, after having been destroyed by the Greeks, has remained uninhabited ever since?" This mere brief rhetorical allusion has been cited, with a strange air of triumph, to prove that in classical times Ilium was not acknowledged to mark the site of the Homeric city.

Prof. August Steitz, of Frankfurt-on-the-Main, ‡ gives the following striking answer to this argument: "That the people of Attica had at least a right idea of Ilium, and thus of the situation of Troy on Hissarlik, is proved by the passage in Plato, κατῳκίσθη Ἴλιον ἐπὶ λόφον τινὰ οὐχ ὑψηλόν κ.τ.λ.§, which would not be adapted to the situation of Bounarbashi, but well to that of Hissarlik. It is true that, side by side with the local tradition preserved by the *Iliad*, there was also the poetical tradition to which Strabo (XIII., p. 601) refers. Proceeding from the Homeric passages on the destruction of Troy, the later poets know nothing of the continuation or the re-construction of the city, and this is particularly the firm belief established in tragedy (Welcker, *loc. cit.* XXXVI.). We must therefore not be astonished if an enthusiast for tragic poetry, like the orator Lycurgus (in his speech against Leocrates), asserts it as a well-known fact that Troy, after its destruction by the

---

* *De Legibus*, III. p. 682, *b, c, d, e.* κατῳκίσθη δή, φαμέν, ἐκ τῶν ὑψηλῶν εἰς μέγα τε καὶ καλὸν πεδίον Ἴλιον, ἐπὶ λόφον τινὰ οὐχ ὑψηλὸν καὶ ἔχοντα ποταμοὺς πολλοὺς ἄνωθεν ἐκ τῆς Ἴδης ὡρμημένους.

† Lycurgus *In Leocratem*, p. 62, ed. Carol. Scheibe : τὴν Τροίαν τίς οὐκ ἀκήκοεν, ὅτι μεγίστη γεγενημένη τῶν τότε πόλεων καὶ πάσης ἐπάρξασα τῆς Ἀσίας ὡς ἅπαξ ὑπὸ τῶν Ἑλλήνων κατεσκάφη, τὸν αἰῶνα ἀοίκητός ἐστι.

‡ "Die Lage des Homerischen Troia," in the *Jahrbücher für Classische Philologie*, ed. Alfred Fleckeisen, Jahrgang XXI. Band III., Leipzig, 1875.

§ *De Legibus*, III. 682 *b.* This passage has just been cited.

Greeks, had remained desert and had never been rebuilt. The tone and the conception of the whole passage prove with certainty that the orator does not give here the result of historical research, but that he brings forward as an example a case universally known through the poets. But perhaps Lycurgus knew no more about it. How little poetical tradition cares about historical truth, we see from the brilliant passage in Lucan (*Pharsalia*, pp. 9, 961, *seqq.*), who represents Troy as still lying in ruins at Cæsar's time, and attributes to him the intention of founding a new Roman Troy, just as if he had had no knowledge of Ilium or of its pretensions, or of the faith of the Romans in its identity with Troy. He certainly had no knowledge of the little city on the Bali Dagh. But I cite all this only to refute the opinion that the ancients had doubts, based on real facts, regarding the identity of the site of Ilium with the Homeric Troy."

Note XIII.—THE CULTUS OF APIS.

As I have cited in *Ilios*, p. 285, the tradition according to which Apis, king of the Peloponnesus, ceded his dominion to his brother, and became king of Egypt, where, as Serapis, he was worshipped in the shape of a bull *—I think it not out of place to remark here, that I asked the celebrated Egyptologist, Prof. Henry Brugsch Pasha, whether the cultus of Apis could possibly have been introduced from Greece into Egypt. He has answered me in the negative, and adds: "The cultus of Apis is as old as the most ancient monuments of Egypt. His name and cultus are already mentioned at the period of the fourth dynasty (towards the middle of the fifth millennium, B.C.); in fact, his cultus extends like a red thread through the whole course of Egyptian history down to the Roman time. The same is the case with Isis and Osiris, whose names and worship are likewise as ancient as the most ancient Egyptian monuments. The cradle of the worship of Apis, Isis, and Osiris, must be looked for at Memphis, whence it migrated to the Libyan city of Apis, on the south of the Lake of Mareotis (Mariût), on the south-west of Alexandria. From this second station the worship became known to the Greeks who settled on the western part of the coast of Egypt, and who understood under the name of Apis itself a Libyan (*i.e.* an occidental) king."

Note XIV.—DOMESTIC FOWLS UNKNOWN AT TROY.

Domestic fowls were introduced comparatively late into Asia Minor and Greece, and certainly not before the Persian invasion. †

---

* Euseb. *Chron.* part I. pp. 96, 127, 130, ed. Aucher ; Augustin. *de Civit. Dei*, XVIII. 5.

† See V. Hehn, *Culturpflanzen und Hausthiere*, p. 280, et seq. of the 3rd edition.

NOTES.] SITE OF THE SLAUGHTER BY PATROCLUS. 293

Note XV.—THE SLAUGHTER OF THE TROJANS BY PATROCLUS BETWEEN THE SHIPS, THE RIVER, AND THE HIGH WALL OF THE NAVAL CAMP.

Among the many reasons given in *Ilios*, pp. 92, 93, in order to prove that in Homer's imagination the Greek camp was on the left or western side of the Scamander, and not on the right or eastern side, as would have been the case if the Scamander had then had its present course, I have quoted the passage of the Iliad—where, after Patroclus had cut off the foremost Trojan troops, he drove them back again to the ships, baffled their attempts to gain the town, and attacked and slew them between the ships, the river, and the high wall.* But Dr. Dörpfeld calls my attention to the fact, that I erroneously referred τείχεος ὑψηλοῖο to the high wall of Troy, whilst nothing else can be meant than the high wall of the naval camp. This is perfectly right. But as the passage proves that the Scamander flowed on the right or eastern side of the camp, and therefore fell into the sea at Cape Rhoeteum, it gives us also a further proof that this river must have flowed between Troy and the naval camp.

Note XVI.—SPINDLE WHORLS AND SPINNING AMONG THE ANCIENTS.

After all that has been said, in this and my former works, about the objects which occur in enormous masses in the ruins of Troy, and which I have called *whorls*, from their resemblance to the *whorls* (or *whirls*), used with the spindle in hand-spinning (whether such was their sole use, or not), it has occurred to me that a few words on that almost forgotten art may not be out of place. For it would be a curious enquiry, how many of my readers have any precise knowledge of an industry, which has long since been superseded, at least in all civilized countries, first by the spinning-wheel, which in its turn has given place to machinery. Some account of the process seems the more in place here, as it carries us back to the remote period in which the earliest settlers on the site of Troy lived and worked.

Like other origins of civilization, the industry of *spinning* is set before our eyes in full practice on the primeval monuments of Egypt; and that not only in pictures so vivid that description is hardly needed, but with the interpretation added by hieroglyphs, among which we constantly find the word *saht*, which in Coptic signifies "to twist." † Women for the most part practised the industry, from which a maiden

---

* *Il.* XVI. 394-398:

Πάτροκλος δ' ἐπεὶ οὖν πρώτας ἐπέκερσε φάλαγγα
ἂψ ἐπὶ νῆας ἔεργε παλίμπετες, οὐδὲ πόληος
εἴα ἱεμένους ἐπιβαινέμεν, ἀλλὰ μεσηγύ
νηῶν καὶ ποταμοῦ καὶ τείχεος ὑψηλοῖο
κτεῖνε μεταΐσσων, πολέων δ' ἀπετίνυτο ποινήν.

† Sir Gardner Wilkinson's *Ancient Egyptians*, vol. ii. p. 171; new edition by Dr. S. Birch, 1878.

still derives her legal designation of *spinster;* * and the wonderful mural pictures in the sepulchral grottoes of Beni-hassan, of the time of the XIIth Dynasty, have preserved for nearly forty centuries the graphic exhibition of spinning and weaving, here set before the reader in outline. (No. 139, *a.*)

No. 139, *a.*—Egyptian Women weaving and using spindles. *Beni-hassan.*†

Figs. 1 and 3, weaving. Fig. 2, the loom. Fig. 4, male overseer. Fig. 5, hackling. Fig. 6, twisting the double threads for the woof. Figs. 7, 8, 9, twisting single threads with the spindle. The hieroglyphs are: *a (sxet)* 'weaving'; *b (mer sxet)* 'chief of loom'; *c (m sua)* 'facing'; *d (sta)* 'pulling out'; *e (siiga)* 'weaving'; *f (xes)* 'spinning.'

That men also were employed in such work (as is incidentally observed both by Herodotus and Sophocles),‡ is proved by another of the paintings at Beni-hassan. (No. 139, *b.*)

The *Egyptian spindles* "were generally small, being about one foot three inches in length, and several have been found at Thebes, and are now preserved in the museums of Europe. They were generally of wood, and in order to increase their impetus in turning, the circular head [answering the purpose of the *whorl*], was occasionally of gypsum or composition; some, however, were of a light plaited work, made of

---

* Genealogists too distinguish the sexes as the *spear-side* and the *spindle-side*.

† From Birch's Wilkinson, vol. i. p. 317; only the upper row of figures are spinning; but, as the picture is complete, the explanation of the lower row is also given here.

‡ Herod. ii. 35; Sophocles, *Oedip. Col.* 352; but, as we now see, they were wrong in the point of their contrast, which supposed such work to be that of the Egyptian *men* only.

rushes or palm leaves, stained of various colours, and furnished with a loop of the same materials, for securing the twine after it was wound."* (See No. 139, c.)

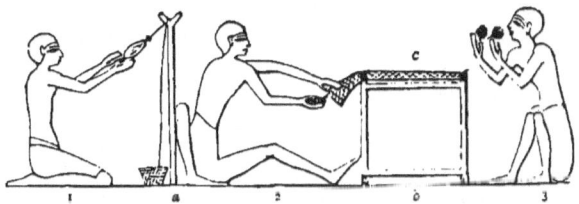

No. 139, b.—Men spinning and making a sort of net-work. *Beni-hassan.**
Fig. 1, man spinning; a, pole and vase. Figs. 2, 3, men netting; b, stand; c, net.

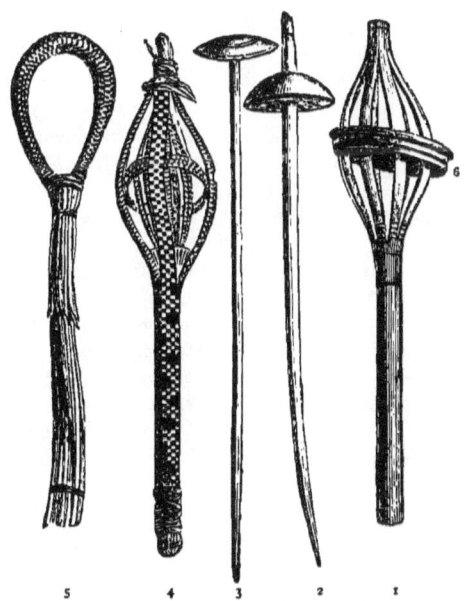

No. 139, c.—Egyptian Spindles found at Thebes.—*British and Berlin Museums.*
Fig. 1 is of a sort of cane, split at the top to give it a globular shape. 2 has the head or whorl of gypsum. 3 is entirely of wood, with a flange for a whorl. 4, of plaited or basket work. 5, the loop to put over the twine. 6, a ring of wood for securing the twine.

Here the spindle No. 2 deserves special notice for the parallel it furnishes to several spindle-sticks, found by Dr. Victor Gross in the Swiss Lake dwellings, *still sticking in the terra-cotta whorl* (see p. 41);

---

* From Birch's Wilkinson, vol. ii. p. 171. The cut No. 139, c is from the same, p. 172.

as well as from the fact that this Theban spindle, which may be seen in the British Museum, *has still some of the linen thread attached to it.*

It is remarkable that no *distaff* is seen in any of these Egyptian pictures; but it is also to be observed that, in some cases (figs. 8 and 9, No. 139, *a*), the spindle and thread are depicted without the mass (of wool or flax) from which the thread was drawn, so that this *may* have been on a distaff, not shown. But it would rather seem to have been in a vase (or basket), as in No. 139, *a* (fig. 7), and in No. 139, *b* (fig. 1), where the thread is drawn out from such a vase over a sort of crook. Observe also the two vases at the feet of fig. 9, in No. 139, *a*.

The next most ancient mention of spinning is in two passages (and two only) of the Old Testament, as a female industry, Exod. xxxv. 25: "All the *women* that were wise did *spin with their hands*," &c.; and in King Lemuel's famous character of the virtuous woman, Prov. xxxi. 19: "She layeth her hands to the *spindle* and her hands hold the *distaff.*" So we read in the English A. V.; but Hebrew scholars tell us that "here the *distaff* appears to have been dispensed with, and the term so rendered (פֶּלֶךְ) means the *spindle* itself, while that rendered *spindle* (כִּישׁוֹר) represents the *whirl* (or *whorl*) of the spindle (*verticillus*, Plin. *H. N.* xxxvii. 11), a button or circular rim which was affixed to it, and gave steadiness to its circular motion. The *whirl* of the Syrian women was made of amber in the time of Pliny." *

If this interpretation of the Hebrew words is correct, we have a remarkable example of the very ancient use of spindle whorls.

Coming now to Homer, we find, among other passages about spinning, one which is of particular interest from its relation to Egypt. Among the presents bestowed on Helen by "Alcandra, the wife of Polybus, who dwelt in Egyptian Thebes," was a *silver basket*, with a golden or gilt rim, filled with *wrought yarn*, on which was laid an ἠλακάτη charged with purple-dyed wool. † This word ἠλακάτη commonly signifies the *distaff*, the *spindle* being ἄτρακτος, but ἠλακάτη is also used for *both*, and it is applied to various spindle-shaped objects, as a

---

* Dr. Wm. Smith's *Dict. of the Bible*, art. SPINNING, vol. iii. p. 1371. Professor Sayce observes that פֶּלֶךְ is literally a *round stick* (which would apply either to the distaff or the spindle), and that the phrase "she layeth her hands to the כִּישׁוֹר" seems to imply a *whorl*.

† Hom. *Od.* iv. 125-7, 130-5:

Φυλὼ δ' ἀργύρεον τάλαρον φέρε, τόν οἱ ἔδωκεν
'Αλκάνδρη, Πολύβοιο δάμαρ, ὃς ἔναι' ἐνὶ Θήβῃς
Αἰγυπτίῃς, ὅθι πλεῖστα δόμοις ἐν κτήματα κεῖται·

. . . .

χρυσίην τ' ἠλακάτην τάλαρον θ' ὑπόκυκλον ὔπασσεν
ἀργύρεον, χρυσῷ δ' ἐπὶ χείλεα κεκράαντο.
Τόν ῥά οἱ ἀμφίπολος Φυλὼ παρέθηκε φέρουσα
νήματος ἀσκητοῖο βεβυσμένον· αὐτὰρ ἐπ' αὐτῷ
ἠλακάτη τετάνυστο ἰοδνεφὲς εἶρος ἔχουσα.

reed, the joint of a reed, an arrow, a top-mast, &c. In the passage before us, Sir Gardner Wilkinson * takes it for the *distaff*, which agrees with its having the purple wool upon it. But *it may*, on the other hand, signify the *spindle*, especially as the basket is filled with *spun yarn*, and if the gift was a complete apparatus for spinning, and ἠλακάτη was the *distaff, where is the spindle*—the really essential implement for the work? One is therefore disposed to recognize here the *basket and spindle*, as seen in the Beni-hassan paintings. (Of the *basket*, however, we have to say more presently.)

Be this as it may, in historic times the combination of the *distaff and spindle* was—and has remained to modern times—essential to the operation, which cannot be better described than in the words of the late accomplished archaeologist, Mr. James Yates.† "The *spindle* (ἄτρακτος, *fusus*) was always, when in use, accompanied by the *distaff* (ἠλάκατος, *colus*), as an indispensable part of the same apparatus.‡ The wool, flax, or other material, having been prepared for spinning, and having sometimes been dyed,§ was rolled into a ball (ταλύπη, *glomus*),‖ which was however sufficiently loose to allow the fibres to be easily drawn out by the hand of the spinner. The upper part of the distaff was then inserted into this mass of flax or wool (*colus comta*),¶ and the lower part was held in the left hand, in such a position as was most convenient for conducting the operation. The fibres were drawn out, and at the same time spirally twisted, chiefly by the use of the forefinger and thumb of the right hand; ** and the thread so produced (νῆμα, fr. νέω 'spin'; *filum, stamen*), was wound upon the spindle, until the quantity was as great as it would carry.

"The *spindle* was a stick, ten or twelve inches long, having at the top a slit or catch (ἄγκιστρον, *dens*),†† in which the thread was fixed, so that the weight of the spindle might continually carry down the thread as it was formed. Its lower extremity was inserted into *a small wheel*,

---

* Vol. ii. p. 172, note. This is also the ordinary view of commentators and lexicographers with regard to the Homeric use of ἠλακάτη. But it is remarkable that it is used in combination with ἱστός, *Il.* vi. 491, *Od.* i. 357 : ἱστόν τ' ἠλακάτην τε—"the loom and—" *one* instrument for spinning—the *spindle* being the essential one. Homer's use of ἠλάκατα (pl. only), in such phrases as ἠλάκατα στρωφᾶν and στροφαλίζειν ("to twist the yarns") may denote either the spun wool (yarn) on the spindle, or the wool drawn off the distaff in spinning.

† In Dr. Wm. Smith's *Dictionary of Greek and Roman Antiquities*, art. FUSUS, p. 565, 2nd ed. I cannot mention the name of Mr. Yates, without a record of the lasting gratitude due to him as the founder of the Chair of Archaeology in University College, London, which is so worthily filled by my distinguished friend Mr. Charles T. Newton, C.B.

‡ Ovid. *Metam.* iv. 220–9. § Hom. *Od.* iv. 135 (as cited above).
‖ Horat. *Epist.* i. 13, 14; Ovid. *Metam.* vi. 19. ¶ Plin. *H. N.* viii. 74.
** Eurip. *Orest.* 1414, δακτύλοις ἕλισσε. Claudian. *de Prob. Cons.* 177.
†† Compare the *loops*, &c., in the Egyptian spindles shown above; and observe how exactly the Beni-hassan pictures illustrate Mr. Yates's description of the process.

called the WHORL (*verticillum* or *verticillus*), made of *wood, stone,* or *metal*,* the use of which was *to keep the spindle more steady and to promote its rotation* (see No. 139, *d*). For the spinner, who was commonly a

No. 139, *d.*—A Woman spinning. Drawn by Mr. G. Scharf from a Roman bas-relief.

female, every now and then twirled round the spindle with her right hand,† so as to twist the thread still more completely; and whenever, by its continued prolongation, it let down the spindle to the ground, she took it out of the slit, wound it upon the spindle, and, having replaced it in the slit, drew out and twisted another length. All these circumstances are mentioned in detail by Catullus. ‡

"The accompanying woodcut is taken from a series of bas-reliefs, representing the arts of Minerva, upon a frieze of the Forum Palladium at Rome. It shows the operation of spinning, at the moment when the woman has drawn out a sufficient length of yarn to twist it by twirling the spindle with her right thumb and fore-finger, and previously to the act of taking it out of the slit, to wind it upon the bobbin (πήνιον) already formed.

"The *distaff* was about three times the length of the spindle, strong and thick in proportion, commonly either a stick or a reed, with an expansion near the top for holding the ball. It was sometimes of richer materials and ornamented. Theocritus has left a poem,§ written on sending an ivory distaff to the wife of a friend. Golden [distaffs and] spindles were sent as presents to ladies of high rank;‖ and a golden distaff is attributed by Homer and Pindar to goddesses, and other females of remarkable dignity, who are called χρυσηλάκατοι.¶

"It was usual to have a *basket* (κάλαθος, καλαθίσκος, *calathus, calathiscus*, also τάλαρος), in Latin *qualus* and *quasillus*, to hold the distaff and spindle, with the balls of wool prepared for spinning, and the

---

* This was published in 1848, when the Trojan terra-cotta whorls lay *perdus* in the hill of Hissarlik, besides the numbers of others elsewhere. We use type to call special attention to the part of the description most apposite for our purpose.

† Herod. v. 12; Ovid. *Metam.* vi. 22.

‡ *Carm.* lxiv. 305-319. § *Idyll.* xxviii.

‖ Homer, *Od.* iv. 131; Herod. iv. 162. The correction of the text is required by the latter passage, where queen Pheretima, the exiled widow of Battus, of Cyrene, is received at Salamis in Cyprus by Evelthon, who presents her, besides other gifts, with a *golden spindle and distaff* and plenty of wool, like the gifts of Alcandra to Helen: τελευταῖόν οἱ ἐξέπεμψε δῶρον ὁ Εὐέλθων, ἄτρακτον χρύσεον καὶ ἠλακάτην—a striking contrast to the Scotch nobleman, who drove out an abbess from her convent with the taunt—"Go spin, jade, go spin."

¶ It is needless to observe that this epithet would be equally appropriate, whether ἠλάκατος is the distaff or the spindle.

NOTES.] THE SPINDLE &c. AS OFFERINGS. 299

bobbins already spun." * As Mr. Yates observes in another article,†
"Pollux (x. 125) speaks of both τάλαρος and κάλαθος as τῆς γυναικωνίτιδος
σκεύη, and in another passage (vii. 29), he names them in connection
with spinning, and says that the τάλαρος and καλαθίσκος were the same.
These baskets were made of osiers or reeds,‡ whence we read in Pollux
(vii. 173), πλέκειν ταλάρους καὶ καλαθίσκους, and in Catullus (lxiv. 319) :—

"Ante pedes autem candentis mollia lanae
Vellera *virgati* custodiebant *calathisci*,"

No. 139, *e.*—A Slave bringing the work-basket to her mistress, in whose hand is something that looks like the lower end of the distaff.

"They frequently occur in paintings on vases, and often indicate, as Böttiger § remarks, that the scene represented takes place in the *gynaeconitis*, or women's apartments. In the following woodcut, taken from a painting on a vase,‖ a slave, belonging to the class called *quasillariae*, is presenting her mistress with the calathus."

It is a striking social fact, that the industry, which was deemed by the Greeks worthy of goddesses and princesses (though also practised by servants), became in the times of Roman luxury the type of degradation; for the *quasillariae* (bearers of the work-basket, or spinsters) were the lowest class of slaves. It was a reversion to the society of Egypt, where we have seen the omnipresent taskmaster standing over the women as they spin and weave; the *rod* not being spared in either case.

I quote with particular interest Mr. Yates's observations (in the article *Fusus*) on the *sacred associations* of the implements used for spinning :—"The distaff and spindle, with the wool and thread upon them, were carried in bridal processions; and, without the wool and thread, they were often suspended by females as offerings of religious gratitude, especially in old age, or on relinquishing the constant use of them. ¶ *They were most frequently dedicated to Pallas, the patroness of*

---

* Ovid. *Metam.* iv. 10; Brunck, *Anal.* ii. 12.
† *Dictionary of Greek and Roman Antiquities*, art. CALATHUS, p. 220.
‡ Hence we may infer, with all probability, that Helen's silver work-basket in Homer was made in imitation of wicker-work, with its rim of twisted golden or gilt rods. I have mentioned this basket at p. 109.
§ *l'asengem.* iii. 44.
‖ Millin, *Peintures de Vases Antiques*, vol. i. pl. 4. We might fancy that this was Alcandra's maid-servant, Phylo, bringing the basket to Helen (as in *Od.* IV. 125, cited above).
¶ Plin. *H. N.* viii. 74, s. 48. This was, in fact, an example of a general principle in making votive offerings; "Individuals who gave up the profession or occupation by which they had gained their livelihood, frequently dedicated in a temple the instruments which they had used, as a grateful acknowledgment of the favour of the gods." (*Dictionary of Greek and Roman Antiquities*, art. DONARIA, p. 433.)

spinning and of the arts connected with it. This goddess was herself rudely sculptured with a distaff and spindle in the Trojan Palladium."* This dedication of the distaff and spindle is perfectly analogous to the offering of the whorls to Athené Ergané, which I have constantly suggested. Nor is it at all inconsistent with their use in spinning; for their *ultimate destination* as offerings would be a sufficient reason for engraving them with religious emblems. The *particular examples* of several whorls which were found by Dr. Victor Gross in the Swiss Lake dwellings, with the *stick of a spindle* sticking in them (p. 41), and one found by me, with a *nail* by which it may have been fastened to the temple wall (p. 107, No. 37), will thus serve as *types* of the *common* and *sacred uses* of these objects, which have now become familiar to archaeological science.

In conclusion, I cannot deny myself the pleasure of adding to this matter-of-fact exposition, the imaginative passage in which the prince of novelists describes the process as dying out in Britain. It is more than "Sixty years since" Sir Walter Scott drew in the *Antiquary* that vivid picture of a fisherman's cottage with its portraiture of the aged Elspeth, which fancy may be tempted to transfer to the old days of primitive Troy. "*With her distaff in her bosom and her spindle in her hand,* she plied lazily and mechanically the old-fashioned Scottish thrift, according to the old-fashioned Scottish manner. The younger children, sprawling among the feet of the elder, *watched the progress of granny's spindle as it twisted,* and now and then ventured to interrupt its progress, as *it danced upon the floor in those vagaries* which the more regulated spinning-wheel has now so universally superseded, that even the fated princess of the fairy tale might roam through all Scotland without the risk of piercing her hand with a spindle, and dying of the wound." Well! since then the Fates have still drawn out their thread; the wheel has followed the spindle, except in remote cottages, or as a lady's toy, or in the chorus of an opera,—silenced by the more powerful whirr of the factory; and, if we may parody Aristophanes—

Δῖνος βασιλεύει, ἠλάκατον ἐξεληλακώς.

I may add that the ancient mode of hand-spinning is even now still in general use among the shepherds' women on Mount Parnassus and on the mountains of the Peloponnesus.

---

* Apollodorus, iii. 12, 3. I have already referred to this passage in *Ilios*, p. 641, note 5, as well as to the statement of Pausanias (vii. 5, § 4), describing the statue of Athené Polias, at Erythrae, as having ἠλακάτην ἐν ἑκατέρᾳ τῶν χειρῶν, where common sense requires us to understand ἠλακάτην in the *twofold* sense—a *distaff* in one hand, a *spindle* in the other (or she would not be drawn holding *two distaffs* or *two spindles*). On the coin of Ilium engraved on the same page of *Ilios* (No. 1481) the Palladium is shown holding in the left hand what seems clearly to be *a spindle with its whorl*, rather than a distaff.

NOTES.]   PRIMITIVE MONEY BY WEIGHT.   301

Note XVII.—THE PRIMITIVE USE OF THE PRECIOUS METALS BY
WEIGHT AS MONEY.

For some further illustrations of what has been said in the discussion of the Old Trojan and Homeric Talents (pp. 111, f.), I am chiefly indebted to the excellent article 'Money' by my friend, Dr. Reginald Stuart Poole, in Dr. William Smith's *Dictionary of the Bible* (vol. ii. pp. 405, f.).

The frequent pictorial representations on the Egyptian monuments, of which the appended woodcut (No. 139, f.) is an example, shew three points of interest for our subject.

Besides the process itself of weighing, we see that the weights are in the forms of ox-heads, and of some other animal (see the dish), as well as simple cones, like sugar-loaves. The use of similar weights by the Assyrians is attested by Sir A. Layard's discovery, in the palace of Sennacherib at Nineveh, of a series of sixteen copper or bronze *lions couchants*, so graduated in size as to be multiples or submultiples of some standard unit, doubtless the Babylonian talent.* There are some of stone in the form of ducks.

No. 139, f.—An Egyptian weighing rings (of silver with Weights in the form of Ox-heads. From Lepsius, *Denkmäler*, Abth. iii. Bl. 39, No. 3.

The other point of interest is, that the metal weighed (which we know to have been generally *silver*, gold being reserved for ornament),' is not in mere rude masses, but in rings, a *definite form*, shewing a first approach to true *money*.

The question is too wide to discuss here, whether the system of *weighed money* (as we may now venture to call it) had its origin in Egypt, or in Babylon, the well-known source of the metrical systems of Greece and Rome. But, long before the age of the Theban monuments, which furnish the above illustrations, we find it in full use *out of Egypt*, among the people whom every new discovery is revealing as the great connecting link between the old Chaldaean civilization and that of Western Europe and Asia; I mean the *Hittites*. The very earliest mention of some sort of money in written history, in the transaction between Abraham and Abimelech, king of Gerar (on the south frontier of Palestine), shews us *silver* as a currency, but leaves the mode of estimation

---

* For a full account of these weights, which bear the name of Sennacherib, see Layard, *Assyria and Babylon*, pp. 600, f.; and *Nineveh and its Remains*, abridged ed. pp. 89, 90.

obscure.* But there is no such obscurity in *the earliest commercial transaction on record* between the same Abraham and the *children of Heth*, the Hittites of Palestine (Gen. xxiii.). Here we have, first, *money* named as a standard of value (vv. 9, 13); next, the *price* fixed in *silver;* and finally, the *payment* described as follows (ver. 16): "And Abraham *weighed* to Ephron the silver, which he had named in the audience of the sons of Heth, 400 *shekels* of"—not *mere silver*, but "silver *current with the merchant*." It is natural to infer that its currency implies *form*, as well as weight, like the Egyptian *rings* and the Trojan *blades* of silver; but, be this as it may, the plain record of *a silver mercantile currency* among the *Hittites* of Western Asia, at the time of Abraham and the Middle Egyptian Monarchy, is a fact of capital interest for our whole enquiry.

Two generations later, we read of a similar transaction, in which Jacob buys from the Prince of Shalem, near Shechem, a field for a hundred *kesitahs*, a word of uncertain meaning; but, if rightly interpreted by the LXX. *lambs*, it again suggests weights in the form of animals.†

During the great Egyptian famine under Joseph, *money* was paid for corn, both by the natives and foreigners (Gen. xxxii. 56, 57), till the whole existing currency both of Egypt and Canaan, was absorbed into the royal treasury (xlvii. 14, f.); and not till then did the Egyptians fall back on barter, paying first with their cattle and then with their lands. The Canaanite silver money, which the sons of Jacob took to buy the corn (xlii.–xliv. *passim*), was reckoned by weight; for the money put back into their sacks was "*in full weight*" (xliii. 21). At the time of the Exodus, the Mosaic law makes frequent mention of money; and we now find the *shekel* as the standard, evidently of *weight*. This standard was sacred, and was doubtless kept by the priests; for it is defined as "the shekel of the *sanctuary* (of) twenty gerahs the shekel" (Ex. xxx. 13). Among the spoils of Jericho, as I have already mentioned (p. 112), we find, besides 200 shekels of silver, a *tongue of gold* of 50 shekels' weight (Josh. vii. 21, 24). May this be an indication that the Canaanites of that great city, enriched by commerce with Babylon (for "a goodly *Babylonish* garment" was among the spoil), had already a gold currency? Certainly the word *tongue* answers exactly to the blades or *laminae* of silver found in the great Trojan treasure. Of *coined* money we have no certain mention among the Jews till after the Captivity.

---

* Gen. xx. 16. As a munificently hospitable rebuke of his deception, Abimelech gives Abraham "a thousand of silver," to buy veils for Sarah and her maids. The LXX. supply the missing denomination by *didrachms*, meaning *shekels*, but unfortunately suggesting *coins*.

† Gen. xxxiii. 19. One of the weights in the dish (No. 139, f.) certainly looks very like a lamb. For the lost root of *kesitah* Dr. Stuart Poole suggests the Arabic بَحْث, meaning *equal division*, which might imply *definite parts* of a standard.

APPENDIX I.

JOURNEY IN THE TROAD, MAY, 1881.
BY DR. HENRY SCHLIEMANN.

THE following account of my journey in the Troad ought to have been added to *Ilios*, for it supplements many points of the Homeric geography which have until now remained obscure, and it tends to explode many theories, which have existed for thousands of years, and which have as yet never been contested or even doubted. It must further enhance the general interest attached to Hissarlik, for it shows that between the Hellespont, the mountains of Ida, Adramyttium, and Cape Lectum, there is nowhere any accumulation of prehistoric ruins, whilst the accumulation of such ruins at Hissarlik exceeds 14 mètres in depth. The measurement of the altitudes has been made with the greatest precision, and all the points which have been touched on the journey have been inserted with the greatest accuracy in the Map (No. 140: see *Frontispiece*), which I recommend to the reader's particular attention.

I had terminated the exploration of Hissarlik in June, 1879. The publication of my work, *Ilios*, which was brought out simultaneously in English by Messrs. Harper Brothers at New York, and Mr. John Murray at London, and in German by Mr. F. A. Brockhaus at Leipzig, kept me occupied during a year and a half. As soon as I had finished this, I proceeded to execute the plan I had formed for a long time past, of exploring the Minyan Orchomenos in Boeotia. I finished this exploration towards the middle of April 1881. There are only three cities to which Homer gives the epithet πολύχρυσος ("rich in gold"), namely, Troy, Mycenae, and the Minyan Orchomenos. The large treasures, which I brought to light in the two first cities, prove that they eminently deserved the Homeric epithet. I found no treasure of gold at Orchomenos; but the immense marble edifice called the "treasury," as well as the "thalamos," with its marvellously sculptured ceiling, which I discovered there, are the silent witnesses of a great accumulation of wealth, and of the justice of the Homeric epithet πολύχρυσος, as applied to Orchomenos. For fuller details of these excavations, I refer the reader to my work *Orchomenos*.*

Having done with that, I made a tour to the mountains of Ida, to see whether there are still any prehistoric ruins at other points of the Troad. Though I have so often visited the region, and for five years have spent many months excavating there, yet I always renew my visits with fresh delight, for the enchantment of the Trojan landscape is overpowering, and every hill and valley, the Sea, the Hellespont, and every river, all breathe of Homer and the *Iliad*. But on this occasion my journey was of especial interest, as it was made for the purpose of determining what other sites of ancient habitation, besides Hissarlik, demand archaeological investigation.

§ *I. From the Town of the Dardanelles to Hissarlik.*—I left the city of the Dardanelles (temperature 26°·5 C. = 79°·7 F.) on the 13th May, 1881, on horseback, in company with a servant, the owner of the horses, and an escort of two gendarmes, whom the civil governor of the Dardanelles had kindly put at my disposal, the country being unsafe. On leaving the town, we passed the shallow river of the Dardanelles, which has running water even in the hottest summer, and of whose identity with the Homeric Rhodius† there can be no doubt, for it had that name still at the time of Strabo,‡ who tells us that opposite its mouth, on the Thracian Chersonesus, there was the κυνὸς σῆμα (the tumulus of the bitch), held to be the tomb of Hecuba, who was said to have been changed, on her death, into a bitch.

In fact, a conical hillock is seen in the place indicated by Strabo; but Mr. Frank Calvert, who examined it, found it to consist of the natural rock, and to have only the form of a tumulus.

Riding along the shore of the Hellespont, I crossed, at half-an-hour's distance from the city of the Dardanelles, the site of an ancient town, which I am unable to identify, marked by millions of fragments of Greek and Roman pottery, with which

---

* Published by F. A. Brockhaus, Leipzig, 1881.
† *Il.* XII. 20.   ‡ XIII. p. 595.

the soil is strewn. Soon afterwards I passed a conical hillock to the right, and another to the left, both of which have been considered to be heroic tombs. But on examining them carefully I found the hillock to the right to consist of the natural rock, whereas that to the left is certainly artificial. The latter is 12 mètres high, and about 60 mètres in diameter at its base.

At a very short distance further on, upon the promontory of Gygas, I passed the site of the Aeolian city of Dardanus, which is often mentioned by Strabo,* and which must not be confounded with the Homeric city of Dardanié.† According to Strabo,‡ Cornelius Sulla and Mithridates VI., Eupator met here to treat of a peace. The excavations made, at my suggestion, by the military governor of the Dardanelles (Djemal Pasha) have proved that the accumulation of *débris* is here only from 0·60 m. to 0·90 m. deep, and that it consists almost entirely of black earth ; nothing is therefore to be done here by the archaeologist.

I passed afterwards, on a height to the left, the site of an ancient city, crowned by a conical hillock, always held to be an heroic tomb. But having carefully examined it, I found it to consist entirely of the natural rock. The fragments of Hellenic and Roman pottery, with which the slope of the height is strewn, seem to denote that the city once descended to the shore of the Hellespont. But the accumulation of *débris* is everywhere most insignificant. Mr. Calvert holds it to be the ancient city of Ophrynium, and as such it is also indicated on Admiral Spratt's most excellent map of the Troad. But I consider this identification to be erroneous, because, according to Strabo,§ close to Ophrynium is the swamp or pond called Pteleos, which certainly does not exist, nor can ever have existed, on this rocky height ; but such a swamp or pond exists at a distance of about two miles, near the site of an ancient city now called Palaeocastron, which has generally, and I think quite rightly, been identified with the ancient Ophrynium. Its position on a hill, which falls off abruptly and almost perpendicularly to the Hellespont, certainly also answers much better to the situation which seems to be indicated by the name Ophrynium, from Ὀφρύς. This site is abundantly strewn with Hellenic potsherds, and there are many fragments

---

* XIII. pp. 587, 590, 595, 600.
† *Il.* XX. 216. Mr. Grote, *Hist. of Greece*, I. p. 301, erroneously attributes to Dardanus the title to legendary reverence as the special sovereignty of Aeneas. He evidently confounds it with the Homeric Dardanié, which was situated far from Dardanus, at the foot of Ida, and of which no trace was left in the time of Demetrius. (See Strabo, XIII. p. 592.)   ‡ XIII. p. 595.   § *Ibid.*

of ancient walls; the accumulation of *débris* is here more considerable, and has an average depth of about 0·90 m. Between the two sites lies the pretty village of Ren Kioi (village of colours), which has an altitude of 188 mètres (temperature 23° C. = 73°·4 F.).

On the road thence to Hissarlik I passed the rivulet of Ren Kioi, which is fed by no spring, and has water only during the most heavy rains; otherwise it is always perfectly dry.*

I passed the night in my barracks at Hissarlik, and saw with pleasure that my trenches had sustained no injury since my departure in June 1879; the channels, which I had dug for the discharge of the rain water, having perfectly answered their purpose. I was astonished to see all the walls of my barracks, up to the roof, covered with a black mass which seemed to be moving. But as it was a dark night when I arrived, I could not recognize at once what this might be; only the following morning I saw that the masses consisted of locusts, which were more numerous in the Troad in 1881 than ever before, and made terrible havoc of the corn-fields and meadows. But I have never seen a field of corn entirely destroyed by them, for they never eat more than two-thirds or three-quarters of the green halms, and content themselves with eating, of those which they leave behind, only the leaves, and not the ears. They certainly appear to prefer grass to grain, for I often passed on my journey large tracts of land, on which they had literally not left a single blade of grass. (The temperature at Hissarlik at 8 A.M. was 17°·5 C. = 63°·5 F.)

§ *II. From Hissarlik to Kestambul.*—I proceeded by way of Kalifatli and Ujek Kioi, which latter place is at an altitude of 87 mètres (temperature 18° C. = 64°·4 F.).

When I crossed the Scamander, it had only a depth of 0·60 m. As in all other Turkish villages in the Troad, there are many storks' nests in Ujek Kioi, which are never to be seen in the villages inhabited by Greeks, as for instance in Kalifatli, Yeni Kioi, Yeni Shehr, &c. The reason is that the Turks have a sort of veneration for the stork, in consequence of which the Greeks

---

* To prove his impossible theory, that ancient Troy was situated in the Dumbrek valley, Dr. Brentano, *Ilion im Dumbrekthale*, Stuttgart, 1881, raises this watercourse to the honour of being the Homeric Simois, and gives to it on his map a thoroughly false position. The course of this rivulet is perfectly well indicated on the map of Admiral Spratt and that of Rudolf Virchow in his *Beiträge zur Landeskunde der Troas*, Berlin, 1880.

call it the sacred bird of the Turks, and do not allow it to build its nests on their houses.

Among the praiseworthy qualities of the Turks, I must further mention the great care they take to provide the thirsty wanderer and his horse with an abundance of good drinking water. In fact, no village is so small or poor as not to have at least one fountain, which is always encompassed by masonry of a monumental form, and flows into a quadrangular reservoir of trachyte, out of which the water runs to the right and left into several troughs of the same stone, which stand in a row and serve to water the cattle. All the roads are provided with fountains arranged in this or a similar way, and to each of them, for the convenience of the thirsty traveller, an earthen cup or a ladle of wood or zinc is fastened with a chain.* Above many of these fountains, and always above the fountains in the richer villages, we see long inscriptions, which, besides verses from the Koran, contain the name of the benefactor at whose cost the fountain has been established, as well as the date of its erection. Whenever such a fountain is on or near the site of an ancient city, we invariably see several sculptured blocks of marble in its masonry.

Another excellent quality of the Turks is their veneration for the dead; for our barbarous American and European custom of allowing the dead only one year's repose if the grave or tomb has not been paid for, does not exist here; on the contrary, the sepulchres are considered in Turkey as sacred ground and are never disturbed, not even for railway companies! Thus it happens that there are here an enormous number of graveyards, in which the tombs of the rich are always ornamented with two upright marble slabs, the smaller being placed at the foot, whilst the larger, whose upper end is sculptured in the form of a turban, marks the place of the deceased person's head. This headstone has commonly a painted margin, blue or green, and always a long inscription with pious verses and the name of the deceased, with the date of the burial; these inscriptions being often in gilt letters. The tombs of the poor are indicated by two such slabs, of common unpolished stone, without an inscription. Whenever a Turkish cemetery is in the

---

* I may cite the parallel of drinking fountains in England in the olden times. Bede tells us that Edwin, King of Northumbria and Supreme Lord of Britain (A.D. 624–633) caused bronze drinking-vessels to be hung on stakes beside the springs of clear water for the refreshment of travellers; and none dared either to touch these cups, except for their proper use, through the great fear of the King, nor wished to do so, through love of him.

neighbourhood of the site of an ancient city, we always see the sepulchres of the poor ornamented with drums of columns or sculptured blocks; and so it happens that, in the plain of Troy, for instance, all the Turkish graveyards are overloaded with fragments of marble columns and sculptures from Ilium. Near each Turkish cemetery we invariably see a table made of two uprights spanned with a large polished slab; with rare exceptions, this polished slab has been taken from some monument, and consists of well-wrought white marble; and the same is often the case also with the two uprights. On this stone table the coffin with the corpse is always placed, and prayers are recited over it before it is committed to the tomb.

From Ujek Kioi I proceeded, on a narrow path, in a southerly direction over the heights overgrown with juniper, oak-bushes, and pines. We reached, in about an hour, the village of Boskizi (altitude 47 mètres), which is close to a forest of oak-trees. In this poor little village may be seen many sculptured blocks of ancient edifices, some of which are so large that they can hardly have been brought here from a distance. Thus, for instance, we see in the stairs of the mosque very large blocks of granite, one of which is a threshold with the grooves for the door-hinges. In the vestibule of the same building are four columns: two of them are of granite, and have been taken from an ancient monument; the two others are of wood, one of them standing on an Ionic, the other on a Corinthian, capital of white marble. A second staircase contains also a threshold of white marble, and other blocks taken from ancient monuments. We also saw a column of white marble and another of granite in the circuit wall, and drums of granite columns lying on the terraces of two Turkish houses. All these monumental blocks seem to have been brought here from the site of an ancient town, which we see about 1000 yards from Boskizi, to the right of the road. But I cannot identify it with any one of the cities in the Troad mentioned by ancient writers. From the road only one single granite column can be seen standing on the site, which is strewn with fragments of ancient pottery; but the accumulation of *débris* here is very insignificant, being only a few inches deep. At an altitude of 32 mètres is the village of Gheukli Kioi, which we reached in fifty minutes from Boskizi. Here also may be seen several granite columns, and some sculptured marble slabs, which appear to have been brought from Alexandria Troas, for there is no site of an ancient town either at Gheukli Kioi or in its immediate neighbourhood. The road leads through a country partly cultivated, but for the most part covered with valonea oaks, until the hot springs of Ligia Hamam are reached, which are situated in a picturesque ravine at a distance of three miles to the south of Alexandria Troas. Here is a bath for women, and another for men. The former is dome-like and resembles a mosque; in its masonry may be seen many blocks taken from ancient buildings; in the middle is a walled basin, 3·90 m. square, into which a hot spring pours, having at the place where it spouts forth from the rock a temperature of $53°·5$ Celsius $= 128°·3$ F. The temperature of the water in the basin is only $34°$ C. $= 93°·2$ F. In the wall of this bath I saw a headless draped female statue of white marble. At a distance of about 39 mètres to the southwest of this spring there is another, which is so hot that I could not measure the temperature with my thermometer, for the mercury rose in a few seconds to above $60°$ C. $= 140°$ F. This spring flows into the bath for men, which is a miserable building with three exceedingly dirty and windowless rooms for lodging the sick, who have to lie down on the rugged paved floor, for there are not even stone benches.

There is a great number of smaller hot springs, which bubble forth from the crevices of the rock on the north side of the ravine; the water of all of them uniting at the bottom of the ravine, and forming a small rivulet. The water being hot and steaming, it is exceedingly difficult to make horses wade through it. All these springs, without exception, are saline and ferruginous, and very salutary and beneficial for rheumatic and cutaneous disorders; and if there were an able physician here, to prescribe to the sick how to use the waters, this watering-place might perhaps be one of the most celebrated in the world, whereas now it is entirely neglected, to such a degree indeed that, in spite of the advanced season, I found no living being there except a raven and a cuckoo, whose voices interrupted the death-like silence which reigned in the ravine.

But, at all events, this site bore an entirely different aspect in ancient times, for both slopes of the ravine, and particularly the northern side, are covered with the ruins of buildings, which still lie as silent witnesses to the important city which once stood here. Among the ruins, the gigantic remains of Roman baths attracted my particular attention. All round these baths I saw trenches but lately dug, which can have had no other purpose than to despoil the buildings of the marble plates with which they were formerly covered. The masonry of all these baths consists of small stones joined with lime or cement, amongst which are seen from time to time large wrought blocks of granite. But the interior hall, the bath proper, is always built of large wrought blocks, and its dome-like vaulting alone consists of masonry joined with lime or cement. In the walls are many niches, which may have served for offerings. Some of the baths, and probably all of them, had vestibules with colonnades; for there are a very large number of granite columns, as well as a fluted marble column, all more or less buried in the *débris*. There are also many ruins of baths and houses, which evidently belong to the Middle Ages. We may therefore take it for granted that the town has only been abandoned since late in the Middle Ages. The city having been built on the slopes, the accumulation of *débris* is insignificant, but still, here and there, it may be 2 mètres deep. The altitude of Ligia Hamam is 25 mètres (temperature $21°·5$ C. = $7c°·7$ F.).

I arrived in the evening at the village of Kestambul, which stands at an elevation of 185 mètres (temperature $18°$ C. = $64°·4$ F.). This village is inhabited exclusively by Turks, and so there are many storks' nests, and often two on the same roof. In the masonry of the house-walls there are many well-wrought marble blocks, as well as drums of columns. The great charm of Kestambul is a copious spring, overshadowed by noble plane-trees; the masonry with which it is encompassed has the form of a small quadrangular tower, on three sides of which are double water-cocks, as well as a ladle of zinc attached by a chain. On each side is a sculpture representing a flowery ornament, as well as a marble tablet, $0·43$ m. long by $0·70$ m. broad, with verses from the Koran, the name of the benefactor who built the fountain, and the date of its erection, 1193 after the Hegira. The fountain would therefore be now (in 1881) 104 years old.

In another fountain of this village may be seen a large ancient sarcophagus of basalt, on the upper margin of which is the inscription:

POSTVMIAVENERIA.

Below this is a rosette and a crown of flowers, as well as two figures of men, and a bird with a tree on its head. These sculptures, as well as the inscription, are evidently of the Middle Ages. To the right is another marble slab with geometrical patterns, which is probably more ancient. The high situation of this village, the many ancient ruins built into the masonry of the houses, the masses of fragments of ancient pottery with which the gardens and fields around are strewn, but especially the enormous mass of tremendous granite blocks, most of which have a monumental form,—all these various circumstances lead me to believe that Kestambul marks the site of the ancient city of Colonae. The situation certainly answers to the indications of Strabo,* that it was in the immediate neighbourhood of Achaeium, which lay close to Alexandria; but its distance from Ilium is fully 240 stadia instead of only 140 as he states. Colonae must have been indebted for its name to the innumerable gigantic blocks of granite just mentioned, with which all the fields in the environs are strewn, like enormous monuments. Kestambul has 110 Turkish houses.

§ *III. From Kestambul to Baba.*—I continued my journey by the village of Alampsa, which was in the year 1880 the theatre of a tragical event. In this village lives a Turkish merchant, named Hadji Uzin, who was known to possess £30,000 sterling: he had only one child, a son twenty-five years old. Twenty Greek brigands landed in a large boat on a Friday evening, in September, during the feast of the Ramazan, and went up to Alampsa, which is only half an hour's walk from the sea. At the hour of prayer, knowing Hadji Uzin to be in the mosque, they went up to his house, seized his son, and carried him off, in order to demand a heavy ransom for him. Unfortunately, the two guardians resisted, fired on the bandits, and wounded one of them. The musket shots having aroused all the inhabitants of the village, the brigands were afraid of being pursued by the Turks; they therefore fled, after murdering the two guardians, as well as the son of Hadji Uzin, who would gladly have sacrificed his whole fortune to have saved the life of his only child. A similar affray, in which two villagers and two brigands were killed, occurred in July 1879, in the village of Kalifatli, at a distance of only twenty minutes from Hissarlik.

Half an hour from Kestambul, on the road to Alampsa, may be seen nine granite columns lying on the ground; each of them is 1·35 m. in diameter and 11·40 m. in length. The country is wooded with beautiful valonea oaks. I passed, at an altitude of 239 mètres (temperature of the air 18° C. = 64°·4 F.), the village of Tawakli, and reached, in four hours from Kestambul, the large village of Kusch Deressi, a name which signifies "bird rivulet" It lies at an hour's distance from the sea, on the bank of a small river,

---

* XIII. pp. 589, 604.

at an altitude of 56 mètres, and consists of 200 houses, 190 of which are inhabited by Turks, and ten by Greeks. This village is on the site of an ancient city; as is evident from the ancient marbles built up in the masonry of the houses and of the garden walls, as well as from the layer of ancient *débris*, which, as I have ascertained in the trenches dug for laying the foundations of houses, is in some places from 2 to 3 mètres deep. Archaeological excavations could, however, give no result; for the site has always been inhabited, and the *débris* contain a mixture of fragments of pottery of all ages, and even Greek and Roman coins, as well as coins of the Middle Ages; but those of Larisa predominate, having on one side an amphora with the legend ΛΑ, on the other side a head of Apollo. I myself bought here a good bronze coin of Assos. I therefore feel sure of the identity of Kusch Deressi with Larisa, which, as Homer* tells us, was inhabited by Pelasgians, auxiliaries of the Trojans. Its situation answers perfectly to the indications of Strabo,† who says that Larisa was situated in the neighbourhood of Achaeium and the later Chrysa.

The Turkish graveyard of Kusch Deressi is one of the largest I ever saw; it is about half a mile long and 200 mètres broad, and, like most Turkish cemeteries, it is planted with cypresses. It is surrounded by a high wall, in which I saw many sculptured marble blocks, particularly in the front wall. The stairs consist almost exclusively of white marble blocks of ancient edifices, from one of which I copied the nearly effaced inscription :

ΦΕΡΜΟ
ΒΡΑΠΟΥ
ΟΜΗΡΟΥ.

Six miles further south, I reached the hot salt springs which are found at different places to the north and south of Toozla; there may be forty of them at this first place. The first spring which I tried had a temperature of 60° C. = 140° F.; another had 40° C. = 104° F. Two others I could not determine, on account of their great heat, the thermometer rising in a few seconds to above 62°·5 = 144½° F. The rock from which these salt springs bubble forth has a dirty red, yellow, or white colour, and in this respect it very much resembles the rocks around the Dead Sea. At this place there is only one spring of boiling salt water; I saw in it a porcupine which had been thoroughly boiled. The steep slope of the rock abounds with similar

---

* *Il.* II. 840, 841.   † XIII. p. 604.

springs, some of which may be seen at a height of 18 mètres ; but most of them are very insignificant, and come up only drop by drop. Some small salt springs bubble forth from the level ground at the foot of the rock. In front of all these springs are the salt-pans, at which, however, I saw nobody at work.

In half an hour from this place I reached the village of Toozla (altitude 65 mètres), which consists of only thirty houses, lying in a large mountain ravine, on both sides of which hot salt springs bubble forth, causing the high temperature of the air, which was 25° C.=77° F. At the extremity of the ravine is a very copious spring of boiling salt water, which dashes forth with vehemence and a great noise from the flat rock, to a height of 0·40 m.

The vast number of granite columns which we see at Toozla testify to the ancient importance and magnificence of the city of Tragasa, or Tragasae, which once stood here, and which is mentioned by Strabo,[*] together with its salt works (τὸ Τραγασαῖον ἁλοπήγιον). According to Athenæus[†] there was no duty on the salt produced here ; but when Lysimachus put a duty on it, the production of salt stopped altogether. Amazed at this he again abolished the tax, and then the production was continued. These salt works are also mentioned by Pliny,[‡] as well as by Pollux.[§] Strange to say, Stephanus Byzantinus[||] erroneously makes of Τράγασαι a district in Epirus, where he places the ἅλσιον πεδίον.

Large masses of wrought and polished marble slabs may be seen in the stairs and in the walls of the mosque, which was formerly a Byzantine church. On its dome is a stork's nest ; there is a second on the only minaret, and it is so near to the gallery that the Dervish, in calling to prayer, is obliged to stoop in order not to disturb the stork or to injure its nest ; there is a third nest on a cypress close by.

Toozla is at a distance of two hours from the sea. At a distance of a mile and a half to the south of this village I again

---

[*] XIII. p. 605.
[†] III. 73 : καὶ ἐν Τρῳάδι δὲ ἐξουσίαν εἶχον οἱ βουλόμενοι τὸν πρὸ τοῦ χρόνον τὸν τραγασαῖον ἅλα λαμβάνειν, Λυσιμάχου δέ τέλος ἐπιβαλόντος ἠφανίσθη · θαυμάσαντος δὲ καὶ ἀφέντος τὸν τόπον ἀτελῆ πάλιν ηὐξήθη.
[‡] *H. N.* XXXI. 41, 2 : "In igne nec crepitat nec exsilit Tragasæus (sal), neque Acanthius, ab oppido appellatus ; nec ullius spuma, aut ramentum, aut tenuis."
[§] *Onom.* VI. 10.
[||] S. v. Τράγασαι: Τράγασαι, χώρα ἐν Ἠπείρῳ, ἀπὸ Τραγάσου, οὗ εἰς χάριν ὁ Ποσειδῶν ἁλῶν πῆξιν ἐποίησεν. Ὅθεν Τράγασοι οἱ ἅλες, ὡς Ἑλλάνικος ἀγνοῶν ἐν πρώτῳ Λεσβιακῶν. Ἀφ' οὗ καὶ τὸ πεδίον Ἅλσιον καλεῖται.

saw a large number of hot salt-springs bubbling forth from the rock, which, like the rock in the upper ravine, has a dirty red, yellow, or white colour. In half an hour from Toozla we passed the river Satniois, on which, according to Homer,* was situated the city of Pedasus, inhabited by Leleges; but the ruins of this city, which was already deserted in Strabo's † time, must be covered up by the alluvia of the river. The water of the Satniois was only a foot deep.

Following the heights to the south of the Satniois valley, we reached in two hours the picturesquely situated village of Kulakli Kioi, which lies on the slope of a mountain, and seems to occupy exactly the site of the post-Homeric city of Chrysa. The highest point of the village is at an altitude of 148 mètres (temperature 20° C. =68° F.). At the foot of the mountain are beautiful gardens, in which may be seen the foundations of the temple of the Sminthean Apollo, excavated in 1866 by Mr. Pullan, at the cost of the Dilettanti Society of London; it was of white marble and of the Ionic order, octastyle and pseudodipteral. Some columns, capitals, and pieces of entablature, may be seen lying about in the gardens; as well as some curiously sculptured marbles, which seem to be fragments of large candelabra. Strabo ‡ mentions that the wooden statue of Apollo, a work of Scopas, had a mouse under its foot. The columns were 11·80 m. long, and 1·28 m. in diameter at the base. The foundations of this temple, which are 44·80 m. long, and 29·40 m. broad, are at an altitude of 27 mètres. A threshold of the door of this temple, which lies in the road, is 2·57 m. long, by 1·50 m. broad; a little higher up we see a second threshold of equal dimensions. Many large wrought blocks, as well as a column of basalt, which appear to belong to another edifice, may be seen in the walls of the gardens.

The narrow path from Kulakli Kioi to Baba (three hours) runs continually along rocks overgrown with juniper, oak-bushes, and pines. The village of Baba, which lies on the most westerly spur of Cape Lectum, now called Cape Baba, at an altitude of 38 m. (temperature 16° C.=60°·8 F.), is a modern place of 150 houses, inhabited exclusively by Turks. It was probably founded only 155 years ago, the year 1140 of the Hegira being inscribed above the gate of the fortress, as well as on the oldest fountain. There has never been an ancient city here. Baba has a splendid view to the south over Lesbos, to the north over Tenedos; the

---

* *Il.* XXI. 87.   † XIII. p. 605.   ‡ XIII. p. 604.

former island may be reached from here with a good wind in an hour and a half.

§ *IV. From Baba to Assos.*—Thence on the 16th of May, at half-past five in the morning, we rode along a narrow zigzag path, up the steep rocky height which overhangs the village, and which, like the whole ridge to a point far behind Assos, consists of ancient lava. It took me an hour and a half to reach the summit, which has an altitude of 274 mètres. But even this height cannot possibly be Cape Lectum proper, as there is a much higher point further east. It took me an hour and ten minutes to reach this summit, which has an altitude of 356 mètres, and overhangs the sea almost vertically. The temperature there was $19°$ C. $= 66°·2$ F. Assuredly Homer* can only have had in view this highest point, when he tells us that Hera and Hypnos, on their way to Ida, went up to this cape. I was also perfectly convinced that Strabo's† statement, that on Cape Lectum was the altar of the twelve gods, said to have been erected by Agamemnon, could only have referred to this highest summit; and in fact I found there a ruin of ancient massive masonry, $5·50$ m. long and $4·50$ m. broad, consisting of large and small stones joined without lime or cement. The present height of this monument above the ground is only $0·45$ m.; but its true height can only be determined by excavation; it seems, however, not to have been much higher. There can be no doubt that this is the real altar of the twelve gods, attributed to Agamemnon; but I am far from believing that this hero could really have erected it: the number 12 of itself contradicts such an idea. Nor do I believe that the monument can lay any claim to such high antiquity; for I found there no trace of prehistoric pottery, but I gathered among the stones many fragments of glazed red Hellenic vases, for which I cannot possibly claim a date higher than the Macedonian age. I must add that this is the only ancient masonry in the whole country between Chrysa (Kulakli Kioi), Baba, and Assos; and that in the whole region there is no trace of an ancient settlement. The altar of the twelve gods stands in the centre of a quadrangular enclosure, from $0·90$ m. to $1·50$ m. high, made of large stones put together

---

* *Il.* XIV. 284, 285:

  Λεκτόν, ὅθι πρῶτον λιπέτην ἅλα · τὼ δ' ἐπὶ χέρσου
  βήτην· ἀκροτάτη δὲ ποδῶν ὕπο σείετο ὕλη.

† XIII. p. 605: ἐπὶ δὲ τῷ Λεκτῷ βωμὸς τῶν δώδεκα θεῶν δείκνυται, καλοῦσι δὲ Ἀγαμέμνονος ἵδρυμα.

without cement. But I warn the traveller not to regard this, or any one of the four similar enclosures which are close by, and some of which have two or three small doorways, as ancient masonry, or to suppose them in any way connected with the altar of the twelve gods. In fact those enclosures are nothing but modern sheep-folds; many precisely similar sheep-folds may be seen only fifteen minutes to the north of these, and I saw sheep-folds like them all the way to Assos.

Near the altar of the twelve gods is a large well, built up with large and small stones without cement, and covered with a large polished plate of white marble; this well is doubtless ancient, for there is no marble in the whole region, and the herdsmen are too poor and unpretentious to fetch it from afar, the more so as they have an abundance of lava at hand.

I continued my journey by way of the villages of Paidenli Kioi (altitude 278 mètres), and Koiun Evi (altitude 286 mètres, temperature 22° C.=71°·6 F.). The volcanic ashes, with which the lava rocks are covered, are overgrown with thorny bushes and scattered pines. Even this sterile region is visited by the locusts, which leave the cattle hardly grass and weeds enough for their food. Billions of them may often be seen passing over a rich corn-field to a grass-field without damaging the former, and returning to it only after having destroyed the latter.

Let the traveller turn his eyes where he may, the landscape is everywhere beautiful and picturesque in the extreme. On all sides he sees tremendous masses of gigantic blocks of lava, lying either alone or in heaps, and often in three, five, or even ten rows, one upon another, like immense walls. Sometimes the upright blocks, rising one above another, resemble gigantic church organs; then again one sees them in the form of towers in long rows close to each other. The beauty of the landscape is enhanced by the continual sight of the sea; in fact I generally had the Aegean Sea and the Gulf of Adramyttium in view at the same time.

I passed Arablar Kioi (altitude 278 m.), and at four in the afternoon reached Assos, now called Behram, whose highest point is at an altitude of 233 mètres (temperature 19°C.=66°·2 F.). On this highest point there seems to have stood a great temple, the site of which may still be partly traced, and which is now being excavated by the Antiquarian Society of Boston; but it appears to me that the accumulation of *débris* can scarcely be more than 1 mètre deep, and I have therefore no hope that valuable sculptures can be found here. On the north side is a singular quadrangular edifice with a low cupola, which seems to have been a Byzantine church, afterwards changed into a mosque. Close by are two quadrangular towers, one of which is half destroyed; the other, which is pretty well preserved and provided with loop-holes, is about 20 mètres high by 12 m. broad. Both of these consist of wrought stones joined with lime, and belong evidently to the Middle Ages. ₀Close by are large arched vaults, probably cisterns, and large walls with bastions, all of which seem to belong to the Middle Ages. The principal buildings of the ancient city appear to have stood on the two large terraces on the south or sea side. Large walls lean against the perpendicularly cut rock of the upper terrace, on which the Agora may have stood; but here also the accumulation of ruins is very insignificant, Assos having for centuries furnished the stones for building the palaces and mosques in Constantinople. On the east side may be seen the ruins of a small building, believed to be a Nymphaeum; on the second terrace are the ruins of several large buildings, in which the work of the Boston Antiquarian Society may be rewarded with some fine sculptures. But of this there is still more hope in the great theatre, on which we look down from the second terrace, for although this monument is despoiled of nearly all its marble blocks, yet the accumulation of *débris* appears to be deeper there than anywhere else in Assos.

The walls of Assos, which consist of large wrought blocks of granite or trachyte, are better preserved than those of any other ancient Hellenic city, and they furnish the most perfect example extant of the ancient system of building fortresses. They were built so as to take advantage of the natural strength of the position, and divided the city into two parts, between which the Acropolis was situated. They are provided with numerous towers, which, with only one exception, are quadrangular. The walls are on an average 2·50 m. thick, and consist of wrought blocks, which are either wedge-shaped or quadrangular, and are put together in exactly the same way as the walls of Alexandria Troas and those of the large ancient fortress on Mount Chigri: that is to say, the interior of the walls, as well as the space between the wedge-shaped slabs, is filled up with small stones. Where the walls consist of quadrangular blocks, we see at regular distances between them wedge-shaped blocks, which serve to consolidate them in their position. It appears to me that the whole western wall is of the Roman time; the others are probably not older than the Macedonian period. But in two places we see later walls built above fragments of more ancient ones, which consist of well-joined polygons, and are generally described as Cyclopean, in consequence of which a high antiquity is claimed for them. But I can neither call these walls Cyclopean, nor can I attribute to them a very high age; since the blocks have the polygonal form only on the outside; for the rest they are wedge-shaped, and are built up exactly like the blocks of the later walls, namely, the space between the wedge-shaped blocks, as well as the whole interior of the walls, is filled with small stones. Consequently these walls have nothing in common with Cyclopean walls of polygonal blocks except their outward appearance. We have no example of a very ancient wall of such masonry, and therefore we cannot possibly attribute to these walls a higher age than the sixth or seventh century B.C. It deserves attention that these walls of polygonal stones stand obliquely, as if they had been bent.

Highly interesting are the many well-preserved streets, paved with large and small unwrought blocks. Such a street leads from the Acropolis eastward down the hill to a small height crowned by a tower, the exterior walls of which consist of wrought quadrangular blocks, 1·80 m. long by 0·39 m. broad, and 0·45 m. thick. From this point there is a splendid view over the valley of the Satnioïs and the hills of lava, covered with bushes and pines, which overhang it. The ancient pavement of the streets being here nearly everywhere visible, I presume that the accumulation of *débris* over the whole surface is very insignificant, and therefore excavations might easily be made. But precisely for that reason I have no hope that many interesting objects can be found here, except in the gardens on the west and east sides, to which I called the particular attention of the eminent American scholars who have been sent to Assos by the Boston Antiquarian Society, and whom I had the pleasure of meeting here.

Little or nothing is known of the history of Assos. Strabo * says that it was a colony of Methymna in Lesbos; but the imposing position of the town, as it overhangs the sea, leads us to think that a colony must have been established here at a very early period. I would suggest that Assos may be the ancient Chrysé, which had a celebrated temple of the Sminthean Apollo, and is mentioned five times in the *Iliad*.† The name of Apollonia, which it also bore, seems to be in favour of this supposition.‡ I

---

* XIII. p. 610.   † *I*. I. 37, 100, 390, 431, 451.   ‡ Plin. *H. N.* V. 32.

believe in this identity the more as, according to the *Iliad** the ancient Chrysé had a port, which is also attributed to it by Strabo,† whilst, on the whole northern coast of the gulf of Adramyttium, Assos is the only place which has a port. Strabo ‡ informs us that the cultus of the Sminthean Apollo was transferred from the ancient to the later Chrysé.

Assos, as well as Ilium and other Aeolic cities, enjoyed a peculiar system of self-government, forming together a kind of Hanseatic League. Their rulers, called Aesymnetae, were elected either for life or for a number of years. Under the Persian dominion, Assos was assigned to supply the Great King with wheat. According to Strabo§ Assos succeeded in obtaining its independence in the year 350 B.C. under the rulership of a eunuch named Hermias, who invited thither the philosophers Xenocrates and Aristotle, and gave the latter his niece in marriage. But the city soon fell again under the dominion of the Persians, who put Hermias to death; the philosophers escaping to Greece. After the death of Alexander, Assos formed part of the kingdom of Lysimachus, and passed afterwards under the rule of the kings of Pergamus; till finally, at the death of Attalus III., 130 B.C., it was incorporated in the Roman Empire. It was visited by the Apostle Paul in company with St. Luke, on their way from Alexandria Troas to Mitylene;‖ and was one of the earliest Greek colonies which received Christianity. The Bishop of Assos, Maximus, was present at the 3rd General Council at Ephesus (A.D. 431). We have no later information about the city of Assos. Strabo¶ says: "Assos is fortified by nature and well walled; it has a long and steep ascent from the sea and harbour, so that the musician Stratonicus seems aptly to have said of it, 'Hasten to *Assos*, so as the *quicker* to attain the summit of destruction'"**—(punning on the name, and the comparative adverb ἆσσον). The harbour was formed by a large mole. Here was born the stoic philosopher Cleanthes, who succeeded to the School of Zeno, and left it to Chrysippus

---

* *Il.* I. 431, 432:

ἐς Χρύσην ἵκανεν, ἄγων ἱερὴν ἑκατόμβην.
οἱ δ' ὅτε δὴ λιμένος πολυβενθέος ἐντὸς ἵκοντο,

† XIII. p. 612.   ‡ XIII. p. 612.   § XIII. p. 610.
‖ Acts XX. 13, 14.   ¶ XIII. p. 610.
** A quotation from Homer, *Il.* VI. 143:

ἆσσον ἴθ', ὥς κεν θᾶσσον ὀλέθρου πείραθ' ἵκηαι.

of Soli.* According to Pliny, the word sarcophagus is derived from a stone which was found in the neighbourhood of Assos.† This same sarcophagus stone is said by Pliny to be excellent for gout.‡

§ *V. From Assos to Papasli.*—The journey further eastward from Assos is very troublesome; lying at first along a narrow path covered with loose stones, through thorny bushes. In two hours this path leads gradually down from the heights to the seashore, where I rode all day in the deep sand. In four hours from Assos, close to a promontory, and only 18 mètres from the sea, I reached a well, the water of which had a temperature of 16° C. = 60°·8 F. (temperature of the air 23° C. = 73°·4 F.) and had a very strong sulphurous taste. About 300 yards further east stands a granite column, and on the height in the background to the north a conical tumulus, the only one I saw on this coast. There appears once to have been a city here, and I presume that it was Gargara, which, according to Strabo,§ stood at the foot of the cape, and 140 stadia from Assos: the distance certainly appears to agree, as well as the situation close to the promontory. Strabo ‖ says that, although the whole extent of sea from Lectum to Canae is called the Gulf of Adramyttium, this gulf, properly speaking, begins only from this promontory, called Pyrrha, under which stands the temple of Aphrodite. Gargara is also mentioned by Virgil,¶ Strabo,** Mela,†† and Pliny.‡‡

The landscape is everywhere highly interesting; for the mountain range sometimes approaches the seashore and overhangs it almost perpendicularly; again it withdraws from it to a distance of one or two miles, and forms splendid valleys planted with olives

---

* To those who wish to know more of Assos, I recommend Dr. Joseph Thacher Clarke's most excellent work, *Report on the Investigations at Assos*, 1881, in "The Papers of the Archaeological Institute of America," Classical Series I. The Report has an Appendix, containing inscriptions from Assos and Lesbos, and papers by Messrs. W. C. Lawton and J. S. Diller.

† Pliny, *H. N.* XXXVI. 27. "In Asso Troadis sarcophagus lapsis fissili vena scinditur. Corpora defunctorum condita in eo absumi constat intra XL diem, exceptis dentibus. Mucianus specula quoque, et strigiles, et vestes, et calciamenta illata mortuis lapidea fieri, auctor est. Ejus generis et in Lycia saxa sunt, et in Oriente, quae, viventibus quoque adalligata, erodunt corpora."

‡ *Idem, H. N.* XXXVI. 28. "Assius gustu salsus podagras lenit, pedibus in vas ex eo cavatum inditis. Praeterea omnia crurum vitia in i s lapicidinis sanantur, quum in metallis omnibus crura vitientur."

§ XIII. p. 606.   ‖ XIII. p. 606.   ¶ *Georgica*, I. 103.
** XIII. p. 610.   †† I. 18.   ‡‡ *H. N.* V. 32.

or sown with grain. For fear of pirates there is not a single village on the seashore from Alexandria Troas to Cape Lectum, and on both sides of the Gulf of Adramyttium all the villages lie on the heights, about an hour from the seashore; but each of them has on the shore a wooden barrack, serving as a timber-store, from which are shipped planks, beams, and rafters, as well as pine-bark. Near the timber store there is invariably a warehouse, in which bread, cheese, salt, and tobacco are sold, but no wine or rum, as these are not drunk by the Turks, and as there are no vineyards here. Such loading-places are always called by the Italian name of *Scala*

In seven hours from Assos we reached the scala of Arakli, a name which cannot be derived from any Turkish word, and seems to be a corruption of the Greek Ἡράκλειον; but no city of this name is placed here by the classics. Strabo,* it is true, mentions a Ἡράκλειον on the Gulf of Adramyttium, but next to Coryphantis, and therefore on the opposite shore. Half an hour further on I passed the scala of Mussaratli, near which the rivulet called Mussaratli Tsai flows into the sea. In an hour thence I reached the scala of Chepneh, which has several timber stores, and seems to ship a great deal of timber. As mentioned before, there is nowhere a port except at Assos, and the shipping of wood can therefore take place only in calm weather, though the *scalas* are somewhat protected by the islets of Moskonisi and Aivali, as well as by the island of Lesbos. In forty-five minutes from Chepneh I reached the scala of Ada, where I heard that, at a distance of two miles, near the village of Ada, there is a large cistern cut out in the summit of the rock, with steps leading down to it, but that there are no ancient ruins at all near it. I carefully obtained information at every halting-place, whether there were in the environs any traces of ancient walls, but there are none anywhere. The temperature of the air at Scala Ada was $20°·5$ C.$=68°·9$ F. During the whole journey we had rain daily for two hours on an average, and heard thunder at a distance.

A little beyond the scala of Ada, I passed the river Mochli Tsai, which is $0·90$ m. deep and 18 mètres broad. Thence, in thirty minutes, I reached the scala of Narli, and afterwards the rivulet Kutschuk Tsai (little river). I rode thence up to the village of Papasli, which has an altitude of 123 mètres; the temperature of the air was there $19°$ C.$=66°·2$ F. in the evening, and $17°$ C.$=62°·6$ F. in the morning. This village has a pictur-

---

* XIII. p. 607.

esque situation on the slope of a high mountain, planted with olives, which grow here very luxuriantly, and attain the size of enormous forest trees. The view over the valley and the sea is beautiful beyond description. Close to Papasli is the small river Tsatschenderessi. The village is inhabited by Turks and some Greeks; the latter do not distinguish themselves by an extraordinary cleanliness. In fact, however tired the traveller may be, he cannot lie down undisturbed for the night on his blankets spread on the floor, unless he has surrounded himself with a little wall of insect powder, and sprinkled the same over his whole body, because swarms of highly disagreeable insects pounce on him from all sides, and fall also from the ceiling. Unfortunately, it is not advisable to sleep in the open air, the nights being cold and moist. On asking whether there were ruins in the neighbourhood, I heard that there was an ancient fortress at a distance of an hour and a half.

§ *VI. From Papasli to Adramyttium.*—I visited this fortress on the following morning, accompanied by a guide. The way thither was exceedingly troublesome, for it led by a narrow path continually up and down, and I had to make a great deal of the journey on foot. I found the fortress in the background of a mountain ravine of white marble, overgrown with wild olives and pine-trees, and just above the source of the Tsatschenderessi. But I found my hopes very much disappointed, for it was merely a small fortress of the Middle Ages, built probably by the Genoese. The wall as well as the gate are well preserved. This fort is at an altitude of 103 mètres (temperature of the air 18° C. = 64°·4 F.).

On my way thence to the scala of Papasli, I was shown, at a distance of about three miles in an easterly direction, the site of an ancient town, which extends for about 1000 yards from E. to W. and the same from N. to S., and reaches down to the seashore. It is strewn with fragments of pottery of the Middle Ages, as well as of the Greek and Roman time. On its east side is a small hill with traces of ancient walls, which has, however, a height of hardly more than 10 mètres. Although this site is overgrown with large olive-trees, and though there is no human habitation here, it is nevertheless called Devrent, which cannot be derived from the Turkish language, and appears to be a corruption of Antandrus, the more so as the peasants in tilling the soil find here many silver coins of that city. Besides, in the external wall of the mosque in the neighbouring village of Avjilar, which I reached at 1 p.m. (altitude 144 mètres, temperature of the air 25° C. = 77° F.), may be seen a large marble slab with a Greek inscription upside down, in which the national assembly of Peltae congratulates itself on having sent an ambassador to the inhabitants of Antandrus to ask from them a judge and a secretary : it adds that the demand had been well received, that the excellent judge Satyrion, son of Satyrion, had been sent to them, who decided their lawsuit in conformity with the laws, with wisdom and justice ; that they had sent as secretary Demetrius, son of Athenaeus, who had also fulfilled his duty to their entire satisfaction ; that, consequently, the people of Peltae voted thanks to the people of Antandrus, as well as a gold crown and a bronze statue ; that they also conferred on the judge Satyrion, and on his secretary Demetrius, gold crowns and bronze statues, and that they named both of them πρόξενοι of the city of Peltae.* As this slab was no doubt set up in Antandrus, it corroborates our opinion regarding the identity of that city with Devrent. There are close to Avjilar, on the bank of the little river Monastir Tsai, the ruins of a small town, but this cannot be Peltae. According to Xenophon† this latter city was at a distance of ten parasangs from Celenae, and consequently to the S.E. of Sardes, and at a great distance from Antandrus. According to Pliny‡ and Stephanus Byzantinus,§ Antandrus was anciently called Edonis and Kimmeris. Alcaeus, quoted by Strabo,∥ calls it a city of the Leleges ; Herodotus¶ and Conon** call it a Pelasgian city. According to Thucydides†† the Antandrians were Aeolians, and this appears certainly to be most probable.

In the villages of Papasli and Avjilar I bought many Byzantine, Roman, and Greek coins, which have been found here ; amongst them a silver tetradrachm of Alexander the Great for 4 frs., and a didrachm of Philip the Second for 2 frs. Imperial Roman coins predominate here. There can be no doubt that the city was inhabited down to a late time in the Middle Ages. From what I could perceive in the banks of the rivulet, as well as in a ditch that had been dug, the accumulation of *débris* appears to be 2 mètres deep. But I think it hardly worth while to make systematic excavations here. In the village of Avjilar

---

* This inscription has been carefully copied by Dr. William C. Lawton, member of the American expedition for the exploration of Assos, who has kindly given me a copy of it.

† *Anabasis*, I. 2, 10.
‡ *II. N.* V. 32.   § S. v. Ἀντανδρος.   ∥ XIII. p. 606.
¶ VII. 42.   ** *Frag.* 41.   †† VIII. 108.

I copied the following inscription, which evidently belongs to the Middle Ages :—

ΜΗΤΡѠΕΡΜΑΙΟΥ
ΧΑΙΡΕ
ΦΙΛΙΣΤΑΕΠΙ
ΣΤΡΑΤΟΥ

In the masonry of a fountain here is a marble slab in bas-relief, with two persons sitting, one of whom holds aloft an animal, perhaps a bird ; to the right stands a man, who seems to hold a goblet in his hand. Although the Turkish population is predominant here, yet many Greeks live in Avjilar, amongst whom the oil merchant, Michael Cazazis, is the richest and most influential. All of them are from Lesbos. The Lesbian Greeks have the reputation of being the shrewdest merchants in the world ; as a proof it is alleged that in cities the commerce of which is in the hands of Lesbians not a Jew is to be found.

All the Greeks of Asia Minor, of whatever condition they may be, have a warm attachment for Greece, and it is indeed touching to hear them speak, with tears in their eyes, of their love for Greece, which they call their dear great mother country, though they have never visited it. All have the most sanguine hope, that by the rotation of the wheel of destiny the day will come, and cannot be far distant, when all the great provinces of Asia Minor will be annexed to Greece, towards which they gravitate daily and hourly more and more. They say : " We Greeks are hardworking people, whilst the Turks do not work at all, and are always in need of money, which we supply to them at high interest on their houses and land : as they do not pay, we foreclose the mortgages, and in this way their property is gradually passing into our hands. Besides the Turks are decreasing very fast. If, for instance, we look at Smyrna, it had but thirty-five years ago 80,000 Turkish and only 8000 Greek inhabitants, whereas now it numbers only 23,000 Turks and 76,000 Greeks. A like decrease of Turks may be found in all the cities ; they are also decreasing in the villages, but less quickly." The Greeks give expression to their sanguine hopes in the pictures with which they ornament their shops. In the middle of these we see the King and Queen of Greece represented, and around them, in twenty-four or more cartouches, the names of Turkish provinces or large cities, as for instance, Samos, Chios, Crete, Smyrna, Rhodes, &c.

As I am speaking of the village of Avjilar, I must add that in this region there are two villages of the name Evjilar, namely, the one near Beiramich, from which travellers ascend Mount

Ida, and a second in the mining district to the east of Adramyttium, of which I have spoken in *Ilios* (p. 57). From Avjilar to Beiramich is only eight hours, and seven hours to Evjilar at the foot of Ida. Evjilar means "hunter," and Avjilar is merely a corruption to distinguish the village from its two namesakes.

I rode from Avjilar to the famous hot mineral baths, which are called Lugia Hamam, to distinguish them from those of Ligia Hamam, which I have already described. Ligia is a Turkish word, signifying "mineral water." The bath-house consists of a quadrangular building with a roof in the form of a dome; in the middle is a large quadrangular basin, into which two springs run through iron pipes, one above the other. The upper spring is cool, and has a temperature of $14°$ C. = $57°·2$ F. The lower one is hot, and has a temperature of $52°·5$ C. = $126°·5$ F. The keeper of the bath assured me that the hot spring spouts from the ground at the very place where it flows into the basin through the little iron pipe; but I could not make him understand my enquiries about its healing virtue.

At a distance of about 30 mètres from this bath there is in the meadow a marsh-bath, consisting of a shallow pond of about 3 mètres in diameter, with a temperature of $37°·5$ C. = $99°·5$ F. This marsh-bath was described to me as having wonderful medicinal virtues, and in particular great sanative power for gout and rheumatism. This seems to be proved by the numerous ex-votos, or sacred offerings, consisting of rags of shirts and other garments, attached to the branches of the plane-tree which overshadows the marsh-bath; for the keeper of the bath assured me that all these singular gifts, of which I counted 150, had been suspended on the tree by the sick after they had obtained a complete cure.[*]

We sometimes see in the Egyptian Desert the trunk of an old tree, or a pole fastened in a heap of stones, ornamented with old rags; each pilgrim who passes adding a rag to it.[†] The origin of these tokens of thanksgiving for deliverance from the dangers of the journey is of the highest antiquity in Mussulman countries. The purpose of the expedition of the prophet

---

[*] This tree with its 150 ex-votos calls to my remembrance the beautiful verses of Horace (*Carm.* 1, 5):

..... Me tabulâ sacer
Votivâ paries indicat uvida
Suspendisse potenti
Vestimenta maris deo.

[†] Von Kremer, *Aegypten*, 1, 75.

Mahomet to Dat-er-Rika was probably such a tree ornamented with rags, which was the object of a superstitious veneration.* A very remarkable specimen of such a tree is the tamarisk, called Oumm-esh-sharamat (the mother of rags), between Dar-el-Beida and Suez.† Similar trees ornamented with rags are also found in other Mahometan countries in the north of Africa, where they are called *Marabout-Trees*; they are generally dwarf and stunted trees, to which a person transfers all his diseases and complaints, by fastening to them a rag of his garments. ‡ The custom of the Shilluks on the White Nile, who ornament with glass pearls and pieces of cloth the tree consecrated to the father of their race, Nickam, § is doubtless related to this Mahometan custom.

It appears certain that the baths of Lugia Hamam have had a high celebrity in every age; the great Genoese ruins which we see here are silent witnesses to their importance in the Middle Ages. The soil being swampy, it grows rapidly by the deposits of vegetable matter, so that nearly all the Genoese walls, which once stood on the level ground, are now almost entirely buried, and hardly any longer visible.

The baths of Lugia Hamam are situated in a meadow, at the foot of a conical hill called Lugia Tepessi, which is about 50 mètres high, and wooded with pines. May not this hill have been once called Plakos or Plax, and may not the Thebé of Eëtion, the native city of Andromache, have been situated in the meadow, and have received from the hill the epithet Hypoplakié (Θήβη ὑποπλακίη), which it has in Homer?‖ I suppose this for two reasons: in the first place, because a colony must have existed here from the remotest antiquity; in the second place, because in the whole plain of Adramyttium there is no other isolated hill or mount.

This entire absence of any other similar hill or mount appears also to be confirmed by Strabo, ¶ who rightly puts Thebé in the

---

* Richard Andrée, *Ethnographische Parallelen und Vergleiche*, p. 60.
† Von Kremer, *Aegypten*, I. 152.
‡ C. Devaux, *Les Kébailes de Djerdjera*, Paris, 1860.
§ Brun-Rollet, in the *Ergänzungsheft* of Petermann, No. 7, 23.
‖ *Il.* VI. 394-398:

ἔνθ' ἄλοχος πολύδωρος ἐναντίη ἦλθε θέουσα,
'Ανδρομάχη, θυγάτηρ μεγαλήτορος 'Ηετίωνος,
'Ηετίων, ὃς ἔναιεν ὑπὸ Πλάκῳ ὑληέσσῃ,
Θήβῃ 'Υποπλακίῃ Κιλίκεσσ' ἄνδρεσσιν ἀνάσσων·
τοῦ περ δὴ θυγάτηρ ἔχεθ' "Εκτορι χαλκοκορυστῇ.

¶ XIII. p. 614.

plain of Adramyttium, but evidently in another locality, for he says, "There is neither a Plakos nor a Plax in the country, and, in spite of the vicinity of Ida, there is no trace of an overhanging forest dominating the site in question." If, as appears probable to me, Lugia Tepessi is identical with the Πλάκος ὑλήεσσῃ of Homer, and if Thebé was situated at the foot of this hill, and received from it its epithet, then the ruins of this celebrated city must be buried in the swampy ground of the meadow. But the cost of an excavation here would be enormous, because in digging a hole water is found an inch or two deep below the surface, and therefore powerful steam-engines would be required to pump it out.

About 450 yards from Lugia Hamam I passed the river Gureliotissa, a name which is not Turkish, and has an Italian sound. About a mile further on to the east we passed the river Kisillkedjili, which is about 24 m. broad and 0·90 m. deep, the name of which cannot but be a corruption of Cillus (Κίλλος). On this river was situated the city of Cilla (Κίλλα) with a celebrated temple of the Cillaean Apollo.* The city and the temple still existed at the time of Strabo,† who says that close to the temple was a great tumulus of the hero Cillus.‡ If this tumulus still existed, we could easily find the site of the city of Cilla and of its temple; but it has been entirely carried away by the river Cillus, which continually changes its bed, and for a distance of several miles has covered the plain with a layer of pebbles so thick, that tillage is next to impossible there. The ruins of Cilla and its temple must therefore lie buried deep under the alluvia of the river.

About two miles further to the east I passed the river Zeitounli Tsai (so named from the Arabic word "Zeitoun," olive-tree, which has passed over into the Turkish language). It is about 40 m. broad, and 0·90 m. deep. This river, which is still larger than the Cillus, is also continually changing its bed: in fact, for a space of about ten square miles, one sees nothing but river-courses full of pebbles, which have been carried down by the waters from the mountains. The low plain is entirely ravaged by these river-beds, among which we see here and there little patches of land, which jut out like small oases, and are

---

* *Il.* I. 37, 38:
Κλῦθί μευ, 'Αργυρότοξ', ὃς Χρύσην ἀμφιβέβηκας
Κίλλαν τε ζαθέην, Τενέδοιό τε ἶφι ἀνάσσεις,

† XIII. p. 612.   ‡ XIII. p. 613.

covered with oleanders, alders, and planes. Cultivation is quite out of the question here. Lyrnesus,* Astyra,† Adramyttium,‡ and whatever other cities may have existed in antiquity in the plain, must be buried under the alluvia of this river, or of the rivers which flow further south, for on none of the neighbouring heights is there the slightest trace of human colonization.

I arrived at 6 P.M. at Adramyttium, which is at an altitude of 13 mètres, and at a distance of an hour and a half from the sea-coast (temperature $22°$ C.$=71°\cdot6$ F. in the evening, and $19°$ C.$=66°\cdot2$ F. in the morning). The city has a good export trade, particularly in olive oil. The Turkish population is predominant; there are about 4000 Turkish houses, and only 200 Greek; nearly all the Greeks are Lesbians. On the oldest fountains I found inscribed the year 1101 of the Hegira, or 1688 A.D., and this is approximately the date of the foundation of the town. Strange to say, there is no tradition whatever here regarding the position of ancient Adramyttium, though it was only abandoned two hundred years ago. Some think that it was situated on the seashore, and has been covered up by the alluvia of the rivers; and this seems to be the right opinion, as, according to Strabo,§ it had a port and roads. Others maintain that it was situated on one of the eastern heights. But, as already mentioned, on none of these heights is there a trace of walls or of potsherds.

Adramyttium is said by Strabo‖ to have been a colony of Athens, whereas, according to Stephanus Byzantinus, it was founded by the Lydians. It was a very flourishing and important port, particularly from the age of the Pergamenian dominion, and according to Pliny¶ it was a *conventus juridicus;* but it suffered much during the wars with Antiochus and Mithridates.** According to Pliny†† it exported the celebrated *unguentum oenanthinum;* its ancient name, according to the same author, was Pedasus.‡‡

The modern Adramyttium has an abundance of water, for there are a great many fountains; besides, the city is traversed by two rivers, each of which runs along one of the principal

---

* *Il.* II. 691; XIX. 60; Strabo, XIII. p. 612.
† Strabo, XIII. pp. 606, 613.   ‡ XIII. pp. 603, 611–614.
§ XIII. p. 606   ‖ *l. c.*
¶ *H. N.* V. 30, 32.   ** Strabo, XIII. p. 614; Livy, XXXVII. 19, 7.
†† *H. N.* XIII. 2, 2.   ‡‡ V. 32.

streets. They are embanked, so that on each side of them there is a pavement for foot passengers, from 3 m. to 3·30 m. broad. The larger of these two rivers, called Adramyt Tsai, is only 4·50 m. wide. But, to protect the city against inundation, its bed has been made twice as broad. Like the streets in Pompeii, the river-courses are crossed by five large flat blocks, which serve as a bridge. The streets not being lighted, people walk about in the evening with paper lanterns, and appear to the newly arrived stranger like wandering ghosts.

§ *VII. From Adramyttium over Mount Ida.*—As I wished to ascend Mount Ida and so to return to the Plain of Troy, I thought it in the interest of science to choose the route which, in Professor Virchow's opinion and my own, the army of Xerxes must have taken. Herodotus[*] describes it as follows: "The march of the army, after leaving Lydia, was directed upon the river Caïcus and the land of Mysia. Beyond the Caïcus the road, leaving Mount Cana on the left, passed through the Atarnean plain to the city of Carina. Quitting this, the troops advanced across the plain of Thebé, passing Adramyttium and the Pelasgic city of Antandrus; then, keeping Mount Ida upon the left hand, they entered the Trojan territory." Thus it is evident that the army went round the high peaks of Ida on the east side. But nobody in Adramyttium knew this road, there being no traffic with the poor and miserable villages of Oba Kioi and Evjilar, which lie on the other side of the pass; and the trade with Beiramich follows the road of Avjilar near Devrent (Antandrus). Finding it impossible to procure a guide, I went on, trusting to luck, in the direction where I expected to find the pass, because I had not the slightest doubt that it must exist. I reached the village of Kadi Kioi (altitude 32 mètres) at the foot of Ida, where I succeeded with great trouble in procuring a Turk of the name of Mehmet, who had a perfect knowledge of the topography of the Ida mountains, and was very useful to me. My first question was of course about ancient sites, but Mehmet swore to me that, from the foot of the mountains on this side to Oba Kioi on the other side, there was no trace of buildings, either ancient or modern, and that even on the other side there were only some Genoese walls on a hill near Oba Kioi. He added that there are no human habitations on the mountains, as they are inaccessible during six months of the

---

[*] VII. 42.

year, and because no horse, mule, ass, goat, or sheep can eat the grass which grows there before the middle of July, but that at that date herdsmen hasten thither from all parts and remain there till October. To my question, why the animals could not eat the grass which I saw growing on the mountains in rich abundance, he answered at first, because it is not ripe before July; but when I pressed him with questions, he declared that among the grass there is a poisonous herb called *Agil*, of which any animal dies in a few hours, but that it becomes ripe in July, and is then no longer noxious. All this was confirmed by my servant, by the owner of the horses, and by the two gendarmes, who had accompanied me from the Dardanelles. In fact, they were so afraid that the beasts might eat the grass of the mountains, that they muzzled them, and had taken with them a sufficient provision of barley for a day's fodder. Mehmet appeared to have some knowledge of plants, for he brought me the bulb of a species of Umbellifera, which had a ginger-like taste, and which he cut most dexterously out of the ground; but he was not able to bring me a specimen of the poisonous *Agil*. It is, however, certain that such a poisonous plant exists here in abundance, because I heard it confirmed the following day by the two guides whom I took with me from Evjilar, and who used the same precaution with their mules. The only thing which amazes me is that this highly important fact has never been observed by any traveller, and that even so distinguished a botanist as P. Barker Webb did not notice it; but it is true that he only came here in October, when the pasture is excellent and harmless to the animals; and besides, most travellers know neither Turkish nor Greek, and consequently cannot converse with the people.

As we are wont to paint in our imagination a picture of every unknown object which particularly interests us, so I had always represented in my mind the Homeric Dardanié, as well as the post-Homeric Palaescepsis, as situated on high plateaux near the summit of Ida, and probably others have formed the same idea. But, as I have explained in the preceding pages, these notions were false; nor can these cities have been situated even so high up as Evjilar.

After leaving Kadi Kioi, I came to the village of Zilenli Kioi, at which the river Zilenli pours down from the mountains, and flows into the Zeitounli Tsai.

The last village which I passed before ascending the heights was Zeitounli Kioi, at which the Zeitounli Tsai comes down from Ida. We rode up the steep slopes by a narrow zigzag path, and reached, in five hours from Adramyttium, a fountain called Turkoman-Tsesmesi (fountain of the Turkoman), at an altitude of 763 mètres. Thence we reached, in an hour and a quarter, on the summit of the lower height, the pass called Porta (Gate), which is about 20 mètres long and 5 mètres high, and which appears to have been artificially cut in the rock; it has an altitude of 1307 mètres. About 300 yards further on we came to the second pass, also called "Porta," which appears likewise to have been cut out artificially in the rock. It has approximately the same dimensions as the first pass, and an altitude of 1311 mètres. The rock consists of white marble, covered with pine-trees. From the second pass a footpath leads up to the Kazdagh (Geese-mountain), this being the Turkish name for the highest peaks of Ida. Its summit may be reached from hence in four hours; but as I should have been forced to camp out for the night on the summit, I preferred to go on to Evjilar, as was my intention from the first. Homer is right in describing Ida as πολυπίδαξ (rich in springs), for springs abound here; in fact, there is one at nearly every step. From the second "gate" the path descends gradually, and turns to the north-west, so that we enjoyed a splendid view over the lower ranges, the plains of Beiramich and Troy, the Hellespont, Imbros, Samothrace, and Mount Athos, which last we saw as a large pyramid, though it was scarcely 1 P.M., whereas from Hissarlik Mount Athos is only visible at sunset; its height is 1890 m.

In descending I passed three rivers, all of which flow into the Zeitounli Tsai: the first is the Altshulduren Tsai; the second, the Tshiisderessi; the third, the Bazarerek Tsai. Henceforward we saw no more marble. The rock consists of mica-slate, which has a somewhat greenish colour, and is covered with much black earth, in consequence of which the forest becomes gradually thicker and more varied: besides the pines, we saw at first only alders, to which were gradually added oak-trees, as well as planes, limes, and walnut-trees.

Finally, at 6.15 P.M., we reached the village of Oba Kioi (altitude 407 mètres), and at 8.15 the village of Evjilar (altitude 259 mètres, temperature of the air 16° C. = 68°·8 F.). Evjilar lies on the Scamander, into which here flows the river Atshikur, which we had passed shortly before.

Just as Homer mentions the absence of an agora (Council) among the Cyclops, in order to stigmatize their barbarous manner of living,* so my servants laughed at the poverty of the people of the two villages of Oba Kioi and Evjilar, exclaiming with indignation : " There is neither a coffee-house nor is there bread to be got." Indeed the condition of these villages was very critical, all the grass having been devoured by locusts, which had also nearly destroyed the corn-fields, so that the poor people had nothing for their herds to feed upon ; the grass-covered mountains of Ida were before their door, but their herds could not pasture there before the middle of July. Evjilar is a Turkish village with 100 houses.

§ *VIII. Ascent of Mount Gargarus.*—Though it rained on the morning of the 20th May, yet I was firmly resolved to ascend Mount Ida. The temperature of the air was $13°·5$ C. $= 56°·3$ F., that of the Scamander $11°$ C. $= 51°·8$ F. I left behind at Evjilar a gendarme and the owner of the horses, with the baggage and the horses, and ascended the mountain in company with the servant, the other gendarme, and two guides. We rode on mules, which are difficult to obtain here, even for $3s.\ 7d.$ a day. On the way to the mountains I saw the villagers ploughing with oxen ; some of the ploughs were entirely of wood, and had no iron at all ; others had a point of iron only about two inches long. Agriculture indeed is here still in the same primitive condition in which it was 3000 years ago, and the present Trojan plough is only a true copy of the plough which we find used by the plougher of the fallow ground on the shield of Achilles.† The first slope is so steep, that even mules cannot ascend it without the greatest trouble. In two hours from Evjilar we passed, at an altitude of 840 mètres, the source of the above-mentioned river Atshikur. At first we rode continually through a thick forest of pines, oaks, limes, alders, walnut-trees, chestnut-trees, planes, &c. ; but the higher we went, the fewer did the species of trees become, and for a long distance we saw none but pines. After a ride of four hours we reached the foot of the peak called Sarikis, where we halted in a beautiful valley overgrown with long grass. Here are two fountains, which

---

* *Od.* IX. 112 :

τοῖσιν δ' οὔτ' ἀγοραὶ βουληφόροι, οὔτε θέμιστες ·

† *Il.* XVIII. 541-543 :

'Εν δ' ἐτίθει νειὸν μαλακήν, πίειραν ἄρουραν,
εὐρεῖαν, τρίπολον · πολλοὶ δ' ἀροτῆρες ἐν αὐτῇ
ζεύγεα δινεύοντες ἐλάστρεον ἔνθα καὶ ἔνθα.

are conducted by long wooden channels into several large troughs, this being the great rendezvous of the shepherds with their herds from the middle of July till October. The altitude of this valley is 1491 m.; the temperature of the air at 11.36 A.M. was 14° C. = 57°·2 F. The temperature of the springs, where they bubbled forth from the rock, was 6° C. = 42°·8 F.

Here the mules were left, for they could climb no further; and henceforward we had to proceed on foot. Up to this plateau the pine-forest is thick, but further on, on account of the steep slope and the nature of the rock, which consists of mica slate and has no earth except in the crevices, only a few pines occur. Even these become gradually smaller, until, at an altitude of 1679 mètres, I found the last stunted pine, which was only 0·60 m. high. At a height of 1692 m., I reached the first snow, and at 1 P.M. the highest summit of Sarikis, which forms a plateau of about 100 mètres in diameter. Its altitude is 1767 mètres. The temperature of the air was 14° C. = 57°·2 F. It had taken me from the plateau forty-five minutes to reach the top. The weather had gradually cleared up, and we had on the summit of Sarikis a cloudless sky and beautiful sunshine.

The panorama, which here extended before my eyes, largely rewarded me for the pain and trouble of the ascent.

As on a plate, I saw before me the whole Troad with its hills and rivers, bordered on the north by the Sea of Marmora, on the north-west by the Hellespont, on the further side of which I saw the Thracian Chersonesus, and behind it the Sinus Melas, then the Thracian Sea with the island of Imbros, above which rose majestically Mount Saoce in Samothrace, the seat of Poseidon, whence he overlooked the battles before Troy: on the west by the Aegean Sea, with the island of Lemnos, above which proudly rose the gigantic pyramid of Mount Athos: on the south-west and south by the Gulf of Adramyttium and the Aegean Sea, with the island of Lesbos.

With special delight my eye rested on the plain of Troy, in which I could perceive Hissarlik, as well as the course of the Scamander, and even the so-called Heroic Tumuli; but the thought occurred to me that Jove must have had very keen eyes to distinguish from hence the movements of the troops and the battles before Troy, for Hissarlik appeared to me only of the size of a coat button. Several travellers, who have ascended Ida, affirm that they have seen hence even to Constantinople; but this appears to me a physical impossibility, which Jove himself could not have surmounted.

There are of course no ancient walls on the summit of Sarikis, but only several circles of stones laid one on another, which have been made by the herdsmen as substructions for their huts, and which are used by them when they come hither in the middle of July; but before that time no herdsman and no sheep are ever seen in these mountains. There is further on this summit a solitary Turkish tomb, probably that of a herdsman. The summit was free from snow; the vegetation had the appearance of having but just awoken from its winter's sleep; but there were already thousands of small spring flowers, which I shall presently describe.

According to Homer, Zeus had on the summit of Ida an altar and a sacred precinct (τέμενος), but I searched here in vain for traces of it.

As I saw to the north of Sarikis, and apparently close to it, another peak, which seemed to be much higher still, I asked its name, and heard to my extreme astonishment that its name is Garguissa, because this can be nothing else but a corruption of Gargarus. I hastened thither, running almost all the way, but as the path goes continually up and down, it took me fifty-five minutes to reach its summit. On looking back, it again appeared to me that Sarikis, which I had just left, towered above Gargarus. The latter had therefore appeared to me much higher merely by an optical illusion. My barometer showed at the summit of Gargarus an altitude of $1769\frac{1}{2}$ mètres, and consequently this latter is only 2·50 m. higher than Sarikis. Like the top of Sarikis, the summit of Gargarus was covered with spring flowers. Of all the plants I found there I have brought specimens to Athens, which have been determined as follows by Prof. Theodor von Heldreich, with the assistance of Dr. K. Müller of Halle, Prof. J. Müller of Geneva, and Prof. P. Ascherson of Berlin:—

Lichens: 1. Cladonia alcicornis, var. microphyllina, *Anzi.*
Fountain liver-worts: 2. Jungermania quinque-dentata, *Thed.*
Mosses: 3. Hypnum sericeum, *L.,* var. meridionale.
Gramineæ: 4. Poa bulbosa, *L.,* forma vivipara.
Festuca: 5. sp. ? (not in flower).
Liliaceæ: 6. Ornithogalum nanum, *Sibth. et Sm. ?*
Muscari racemosum: 7. (L.) *Medik.*
Thymelæaceæ: 8. Daphne oleides, *Schreb.* (not in flower).
Compositæ: 9. Taraxacum officinale, *Web.* (dandelion), var. alpinum, *Koch.*
Scrophulariaceæ: 10. Scrophularia olympica, *Boiss.*
Crassulaceæ: 11. Sedum, sp. (not in flower).
Ranunculaceæ: 12. Ranunculus, sp.
Cruciferæ: 13. Erophila vulgaris, *DC.*

Violaceæ: 14. Viola gracilis, *Sibth. et Sm.*
Caryophylleæ: 15. Scleranthus perennis, *L.*, var. confertiflorus, *Boiss.*
Cerastium: 16. Riaei, *Desm.*

Prof. P. Ascherson adds the following memorandum of the different sorts of crocus which occur on the Gargarus:

Crocus blossoming in Spring.
1. C. gargaricus, *Herb.* (yellow).
2. C. biflorus, *Mill.*, var. nubigenus (*Herb.*), *Baker* (blue).
3. C. candidus, *Clarke* (white).

Crocus blossoming in September and October.
4. C. autumnalis, *Webb* (probably blue).

Homer * mentions on the summit of Gargarus the λωτός (Lotus), the κρόκος (Crocus), and the ὑάκινθος (Hyacinthus), and Prof. Theodor von Heldreich thinks that the lotus is a kind of clover (*Lotus corniculatus*) or a Trifolium, which had perhaps not yet shot forth from the earth, and that the crocus, which is not rare on the high mountains in Greece and Asia Minor, grows also on Gargarus, and had probably already faded. The cluster-hyacinths, or grape-hyacinths (*Muscari racemosum*), which I gathered, are held by Prof. von Heldreich to be decidedly identical with the Homeric Hyacinthus.

On the plateau of the summit of Gargarus is an excrescence of mica slate, about 30 mètres long, and from 4 to 6 m. broad, which resembles a gigantic throne. It appears indeed that Homer had visited this summit, and that, precisely because of this throne-like excrescence, he assigned the top of Gargarus as the seat of Zeus. The crevices of this rocky throne are full of flowers, particularly of those blue hyacinths and violets, which reminded me vividly of the nuptial couch of Zeus and Hera. The beautiful passage of the *Iliad*, in which the nuptials of these two great deities are described, had always had a great interest for me, but here, on the very spot where the poet represents the event to have taken place, the interest was overpowering, and with delight I recited several times the divine verses describing the nuptials. †

The summit of Gargarus is not so spacious as that of Sarikis,

---

* *Il.* XIV. 347-349:
τοῖσι δ' ὑπὸ χθὼν δῖα φύεν νεοθηλέα ποίην,
λωτόν θ' ἑρσήεντα ἰδὲ κρόκον ἠδ' ὑάκινθον
πυκνὸν καὶ μαλακόν, ὃς ἀπὸ χθονὸς ὑψόσ' ἔεργεν.

† *Il.* XIV. 292-351.

and, as it is two hours distant from the above-mentioned high plateau with the two springs, the herdsmen do not put up their huts here, in consequence of which this hill-top has no stones upon it.

At a short distance to the south and north-west I still saw a great deal of snow on the mountain slopes, but the summit was free from it. The temperature of the air at 3 P.M. was 12° C. = 53°·6 F.

On the slope of this mountain (Gargarus), and about 1350 mètres below its summit, are the sources of the Scamander, which is called by Homer * διιπετής (flowing from Zeus), also a son of Zeus. † As, besides, the summit has that throne-like excrescence, as well as the sacred name of Gargarus, there can be no doubt that Homer assigns this summit as the throne of Zeus; but the altar cannot well have been here, because it was surrounded by a sacred precinct, and sacrifices were offered on it, "τέμενος βωμός τε θυήεις." ‡ But for all this there is no room on the summit, and it therefore appeared to me *a priori* probable, that the sacred precinct with the altar had been on the summit of the neighbouring Sarikis, which is of easier access, has more space for both, and may, as an appurtenance to Gargarus, have borne its name.

Returning, therefore, to Sarikis, which took me now one hour and thirty minutes, I searched carefully round its highest summit, and there in fact, at the foot of its northern vertical rock-wall, which is 33 mètres high, I found in a small chasm, formed by it and by the adjoining peak, a slab of white marble, 0·74 m. long, 0·60 m. broad, 0·35 m. thick. On what appears to have been the lower side, there are two round holes, 0·10 m. deep, and 0·12 m. in diameter, which no doubt served to place the slab on a base of wood or stone. It was rather difficult for my servant and me to turn this slab over, and I therefore presume that its weight cannot be less than 4 cwt. On the other side is a hollow, 0·68 m. long, 0·40 m. broad, and 0,075 mm. deep, with two holes, each 0·10 m. in diameter and 0·09 m. deep, which seem to indicate that the altar has had some sort of cornice or mounting. I also observed that on the two narrow sides there is a hollow, 0,075 mm. broad by 0,025 mm. deep. It at once occurred to my mind that very probably this was the marble slab of the altar of the Idæan Zeus, and that it had been

---

* *Il*. XXI. 268, 326. † *Il*. XIV. 434; XXI. 2; XXIV. 693.
‡ *Il*. VIII. 48.

cast down from the vertical rock-wall of Sarikis by the pious zeal of the first Christians.

This sanctuary of the greatest of the gods, situated as it was on so sacred a spot, which was visible for 100 miles around, and only accessible for six months in the year, must have had in all the ages of antiquity a great sanctity, and must have been a famous place of pilgrimage. The altar-slab must at all events have been hewn here on the summit of the mountain, because the smaller peak, which stands between Sarikis and Gargarus, consists of white marble, and besides, on account of the ponderous weight of the stone, it would have been difficult to carry it from the plain to the summit.

I recommend this singular altar-slab to the particular attention of all future travellers. It may easily be found, for it lies at the foot of the northern vertical rock-wall of the upper peak of Sarikis, at an altitude of 1734 m., and therefore 33 mètres below the summit of the peak. It would be exceedingly difficult and expensive to carry it down from the heights, for this could not be done otherwise than on rollers. But if the slab could be brought down to the foot of the mountains, it could easily be carried to the coast on a camel's back.

Homer calls Mount Ida $\mu\eta\tau\acute{\epsilon}\rho\alpha$ $\theta\eta\rho\hat{\omega}\nu$* (the mother of wild beasts), from which we might conclude that these mountains were once inhabited by wild animals. Bears certainly still live here, because they can feed on acorns ; but that wolves, bears, tigers, lions, or panthers, should ever have existed here seems to me impossible, because all these animals feed on grass-eating quadrupeds, which cannot live here for at least nine months in the year. I saw no living creature in the mountains, except the cuckoo, whose song is heard all over the Troad.

The descent is much more expeditious than the ascent. It had taken me almost five hours to reach the summit of Sarikis from Evjilar, whereas I returned thither in three hours.

The torches of resinous wood, which are used in the villages of the Troad, remind us vividly of the Homeric torches. †

§ *IX. From Evjilar to Bujuk Bounarbashi.*—I left Evjilar on the 21st of May at 5.15 A.M., and reached in three hours and a

---

* *Il.* XIV. 283; XV. 151.
† *Idem*, XVIII. 492, 493:
    νύμφας δ' ἐκ θαλάμων, δαΐδων ὕπο λαμπομενάων,
    ἠγίνεον ἀνὰ ἄστυ·

half Mount Kurshunlu Tepeh, which I have described in the preceding pages.* Thence I went to Beiramich (altitude 155 mètres), which, as before explained, I hold to mark the site of the later Scepsis, the birth-place of Demetrius. It is a badly built, dirty town, containing 620 houses of wood or unbaked bricks; 120 of them are inhabited by Greeks, the rest by Turks. There are also fifteen Jewish families. To the south-east of the city is a fine pine-forest.

Thence I visited the site of Cebrené on Mount Chalidagh, with its ruins, of which I say no more here, as I have given a full description of them in the text of this book. † I was quite touched in the village of Chalidagh Kioi, which occupies part of the site of Cebrené, by the patriarchal manners, the frankness, the urbanity, and the unbounded hospitality of the Turks, who, in spite of their poverty, treated me and my servants with sheep's milk curds (jaurt) and bread, and absolutely refused to accept any payment.

I descended thence to the village of Bounarbashi, where I arrived only at 7.40 in the evening. This village is usually called Bujuk Bounarbashi, to distinguish it from the village of Bounarbashi in the plain of Troy. The altitude of this village I found to be 147 mètres (temperature of the air 16° C.=60°·8 F. in the evening, 15° C.=59° F. in the morning). The village consists of only eighty Turkish houses, and derives its name from the three beautiful large fountains with which it is blessed, Bujuk Bounarbashi signifying "large fountain-head." The water of the springs is conducted hither from an unknown distance by means of three ancient underground conduits, built of large wrought stones put together without cement. They flow out from a pretty masonry of porous stone, which is ornamented with three pointed arches and four columns of the same stone. Close to each of these columns stands a granite column. These fountains form a large pond, embanked with masonry, from which the water flows out in a rivulet. At the extremity of the pond is a large washhouse. The pond is overshadowed by three gigantic plane-trees. The trunk of one of them has, at the height of one foot above the ground, a circumference of 13·10 mètres. Close to the fountains, to the south, are the ruins of a large ancient building, probably a temple, the threshold of which, still *in situ*, is 1·67 m. long by 0·84 m. broad. A large sculptured marble slab, probably from the pediment of a temple, lies on the wall of the pond,

---

See pp. 270-274. † See pp. 275-277.

which also contains other sculptured marble blocks. A polished marble slab, 2·60 m. long by 0·50 m. broad, which certainly also belonged to an ancient edifice, is now used by the women to stand on when they draw water. Many sculptured marble blocks serve as tombstones in the grave-yard; others may be seen built up in the bridges. All this seems to show that Bujuk Bounarbashi marks the site of a not insignificant ancient city, which, however, I cannot identify with any city of the Troad mentioned by the classics. But there is here no accumulation of *débris* whatever, and it would therefore be useless to attempt excavations.

§ *X. From Bujuk Bounarbashi to Alexandria Troas and Talian Kioi (Achaeium).*—We rode hence in the direction of Iné, or Eziné, and passed in three hours the rivulet Karkarideressi, which means "rivulet of the Lord." Two hours later we reached Iné (Eziné), which is situated on the Scamander, and after the city of the Dardanelles has the most extensive trade in the Troad. I had scarcely dismounted when I was assailed on all sides by sellers of ancient coins. The first coin offered me was a beautiful silver tetradrachm of Tenedos, having on one side the double head of Zeus and Hera, on the other the double axe, an owl, and a cluster of grapes, with the legend TENEΔIΩN, for which 20 frs. were demanded. I accepted it at once, but before I was able to pay the money the seller of the coin was pushed away by the crowd, and was kept for a time at a distance from me. Seeing my desire to possess the coin without bargaining, he thought it was worth more, and now demanded 40 frs., which I paid without hesitation, the value of the coin being at least 1000 frs. Besides many Roman imperial silver coins, such as of Gordian III., Philip the Elder, Severus Alexander, and others, which I bought at one franc apiece, I succeeded in obtaining many interesting bronze coins of the Troad, as, for instance, several of Neandria, having on one side either a horse grazing, or what appears to be a fish, with the legend NE, on the other a head of Apollo; others of Adramyttium, with a cornucopiae and the legend ADPAMYT; others of Larisa, having on one side an amphora, with the legend ΛA, on the other a head of Apollo; others of Scepsis, having on one side a palm-tree and ΣK, or a Dionysus standing on a panther, holding a cluster of grapes in his hand, on the other side a sea-horse or the head of a Roman emperor; these three types of coins were very abundant. Roman imperial coins of Alexandria Troas, having on one side a horse grazing or a she-wolf suckling Romulus and Remus, with the legend COLAVG and TROIA, constituted, perhaps, one-third of all the coins offered, and could be bought for a penny each. I also bought coins of Assos, Samos, Pergamus, Nicaea, etc.* Iné being the only place in the interior where the villagers can hope to dispose of their coins, they bring them here from all quarters, and even from Beiramich. Iné is a very small town of only 250 miserable houses, 150 of which are inhabited by Turks, the rest by Greeks or Jews; there are also some Armenians. In the excavations made here to lay the foundations for houses, I observed that there is a small accumulation of ancient *débris*, and innumerable fragments of ancient pottery are seen in the clay walls of the houses. It may therefore be taken for certain that there once stood here an ancient city, which I hold with Mr. Calvert to be Scamandria, because, as the name seems to imply, that city lay on the Scamander, on which I know of no other sites besides Kurshunlu Tepeh and Beiramich, the identity of which places with Dardanié, Palaescepsis, and the later Scepsis, I have tried to prove above; but we know Scamandria only from Pliny's mention of the town.† But probably the inscription (*Corpus Inscr. Gr.* No. 8804), which mentions Σκάμανδρος and No. 3597 *a b*, which mentions Σκάμανδροι, as well as No. 3597 *a*, Σκαμανδρεύς, and the bishopric Σκάμανδρος (in Hierocles, 662, 10), may be identical with Scamandria.

In two hours from Iné we reached the flourishing village of Kemanli Kioi, which certainly also marks the site of an ancient city, because we see the gardens strewn with ancient Greek potsherds, and now and then granite columns meet the eye. Built into the fountain are a large ancient sarcophagus of basalt, and a sculptured slab of granite 3 mètres long. There are also many sculptured marble slabs in the steps of the mosque, as well as marble columns supporting its vestibule. From a marble slab, 1 mètre long by 0·88 m. broad, I copied the following inscription:—

```
       LAVDIODRUS
     MANICIFILNERONI
         GERMANICO
      VRSODALIAVGVS7
       SODALTITIOCOS
        ORBANVS...EAN
       ADRATVSPE...PIL
      BMILITPRAEFCASTR
         AVGVR.II.VIR.
        TAMENTOPONI
            IVSSIT
```

---

* On my return to Athens, M. A. Postolaccas, Keeper of the National Collection of Coins, had the kindness to classify all these coins, for which I here express to him my warm gratitude. † *H. N.* V. 33, 2.

At the entrance of the mosque stands a marble arm-chair, similar to those in the theatre of Dionysus at Athens. In the mosque is a marble slab with two holes, spanning the window: it has a Latin inscription, which is, however, difficult to read. There is also a marble capital of a column. I hold this village, in all probability, to mark the site of the ancient city of Hamaxitus, the inhabitants of which were forced by Antigonus to settle in Alexandria Troas, for its situation agrees precisely with the indications of Strabo,* who states the distance of Hamaxitus from Ilium to be 200 stadia, and says that it lies below Neandria,† which, in agreement with Mr. Calvert, I recognize in the ancient city on Mount Chigri; this latter is in close proximity to Kemanli Kioi, and seems to tower above it. The altitude of Kemanli Kioi is 150 mètres (temperature of the air $24°$ C. = $75°\cdot 2$ F.). From thence I visited the ancient quarries near the village of Koch-Ali-Ovassi, which I have described in *Ilios*, p. 56.

Ruins of Alexandria Troas.—I went afterwards to Alexandria Troas, following the ancient road, which is 7 mètres broad, paved with large wrought blocks, and in many places well preserved; in fact I believe it to be well preserved in its entire length, and only covered up with earth in those places where it is not visible. On both sides of the road are many large tombs, some of which consist of large wrought granite slabs, others of small stones joined with lime. The site of Alexandria Troas is covered with a dense forest of valonea oaks. The walls are built in exactly the same way which I have described in speaking of the walls of Assos, of the ancient site on Mount Kurshunlu Tepeh, and of Cebrené. They are also precisely similar to those of Neandria on Mount Chigri. It therefore appears certain that walls consisting on both sides of large quadrangular or large wedge-shaped blocks, the space between the latter and in the interior being filled up with small stones, were in general use in the Troad during the whole historical period. The walls of Alexandria Troas have a circuit of not less than six English miles; they are provided with towers at regular distances, and are in many places well preserved. The enormous space enclosed by them is covered with the ruins of ancient edifices, a vast number of which the traveller still sees with the naked eye, towering above the oak forest, in passing along the coast on board the steamer.

---

* XIII. p. 605.   † Strabo, XIII. p. 606.

The largest ruin, about a mile distant from the shore, is called Bal Serai (Honey Palace), and seems to have been a bath, to which was joined a gymnasium. There was a large arch, which has now fallen, and behind it a large hall, nearly 100 mètres long by 30 mètres broad, extending through the entire length of the building. The vaulting rested probably on the pilasters which we see on the sides. In the middle were four quadrangular chambers ornamented with marble columns. At the north-east corner of the building we see the ruins of a water-conduit: there are in the neighbourhood ruins of other large edifices, probably temples. The port consists of two large embanked basins, which are nearly silted up with sand. The site, which was chosen by Alexander the Great for the city, was called, according to Strabo,* Sigia, and was therefore probably the site of a more ancient city. Antigonus appears to have built the city only after Alexander's death; he called it Antigonia, which name was afterwards changed by Lysimachus, in honour of Alexander, into Alexandria. Under the Roman dominion the city was very flourishing, and received a Roman colony under Augustus. As may be seen by the ruins of the walls and edifices, the accumulation of *débris* is here in general but very insignificant, and does not exceed 0·30 m. But I observed several places where it may be 3 mètres deep. Prehistoric ruins are here, of course, quite out of the question.

I passed the night in the village of Talian Kioi, on the seashore, close to Alexandria on the north. In the summer of 1868, I saw here only one single house. But since that time a considerable village has arisen, which may perhaps increase in the course of time to a large town. Talian Kioi doubtless marks the site of the ancient city of Achaeium, for it lies opposite to Tenedos and close to Alexandria, and it therefore answers precisely to Strabo's indications.† I observed in the wells that the accumulation of *débris* is here from 4 to 6 mètres deep, but it consists, of course, for the most part of sea-sand, and besides, as Achaeium cannot have been an important city, excavations are not advisable here.

§ *XI. From Talian Kioi back to the city of the Dardanelles.*— Riding thence some distance along the strand in a northerly direction, I saw masses of large granite cannon-balls, which have been cut by the Turks out of the columns of Alexandria.

---

* XIII. p. 604. † XIII. pp. 596, 603, 604.

I returned to Hissarlik by way of Ghcukli Kioi and the tumulus of Ujek Tepeh. The tunnel, 30 mètres long, as well as all the shafts I had sunk, and the galleries I had dug in this tumulus, in the spring of 1879, are well preserved ; but the villagers having taken out and stolen the wooden scaffolding with which I had consolidated the four sides of the great shaft to the depth of 14 mètres, part of the large quadrangular tower, which was originally built in the tumulus to render it more solid, had fallen in.

From this tumulus the traveller has a better view, than from any other point, over the sites of the ancient cities which once ornamented the plain of Troy. In a north-north-easterly direction he sees before him the now entirely uninhabited site of Ilium, which, judging by its extent and the size of its theatre, must have had at least 70,000 inhabitants, and to which the hill of Hissarlik, artificially heightened by the ruins of six preceding settlements, served as its Acropolis and the sacred precinct of its temples. Nearly in the same direction with Hissarlik, in the plain of the Simois, the site of Ophrynium rises on the high shore of the Hellespont. A little more to the north, in the middle of the great plain, the small village of Koum Kioi—consisting of a few miserable huts, only inhabited during harvest-time, and at all other times uninhabitable on account of its unhealthy position—marks the site of another ancient city, which I hold to be identical with the city of Polion, mentioned by Strabo * as called in his time Polisma. Some granite columns may be seen among the huts, and the whole site is covered with fragments of Hellenic pottery.

In the same direction, but farther north, the height of Cape Rhoeteum, covered with ancient *débris*, marks the site of the city of Rhoeteum, which often occurs in the ancient classics,†

---

* XIII. p. 601.

† Herodotus, VII. 43 ; Scylax, p. 35 ; Stephanus Byzantinus, p. 577 ; Mela, 18, 5 ; Pliny, *II. N.* V. 33 ; Thucydides, IV. 52 ; VIII. 101.

The city of Rhoeteum is marked in its right place on the map of Admiral T. A. B. Spratt, but Mr. Frank Calvert supposes it to have been about three miles further to the north-east, and to be identical with Palaeocastron, which I hold to be Ophrynium. But we read in Lucian, *Charon*, 521: ἐθέλω σοι δεῖξαι τὸν τοῦ Ἀχιλλέως τάφον. ὁρᾷς τὸν ἐπὶ τῇ θαλάττῃ ; Σίγειον μὲν ἐκεῖνό ἐστι τὸ Τρωϊκόν· ἀντικρὺ δὲ ὁ Αἴας τέθαπται ἐν τῷ Ῥοιτείῳ. (I will show you the tomb of Achilles. Do you see it on [the shore of] the sea? That is the Trojan Sigeum ; opposite to it on Rhoeteum Ajax is buried.) From this passage it is clear that the height at the north-eastern end of the plain of Troy, where the tomb of Ajax really exists, was called Cape Rhoeteum, and not the much higher mount of Palaeocastron (Ophrynium) ; and as the plateau of Cape Rhoeteum marks the site of an ancient settlement, this could be none other than the city of Rhoeteum.

and still existed at the time of Pliny. On a low spur of this cape is situated the later tumulus of Ajax, erected by the Emperor Hadrian;* the primitive tomb attributed to this hero was about 600 yards more to the north, on the shore of the Hellespont, where it is still marked by a low artificial hillock.† To the west, east, and south of this tomb, extends the site of the ancient city of Aeanteum, which is not spoken of by Strabo, but by Pliny,‡ who mentions it as no longer existing in his time.

In a northerly direction we see, on a neck of land in the Hellespont, the village of Koum Kaleh, with its miserable Turkish fortress, which latter is half covered up by sand. As before stated, it appears to lie on the site of the city of Achilleum, mentioned by Herodotus § and Strabo, ‖ which is also spoken of by Pliny ¶ as no longer existing in his time. A little further north stand the oft-mentioned tumuli of Achilles,** Patroclus, †† and Antilochus.‡‡ A little further still to the north may be seen, on the height of Cape Sigeum, the village of Yeni Shehr (new town), with its many windmills, which marks the site of the ancient city of Sigeum. This city is often mentioned by the ancient classics, but it no longer existed in Strabo's time. It was for years at war with the neighbouring city of Achilleum, §§ and was so rich as to erect in its temple of Pallas Athené an equestrian statue of gold in honour of King Antiochus. ‖‖

The eye of the traveller, wandering thence in a southerly direction along the shore of the Aegean Sea, observes on an artificially levelled plateau, a mile distant from Sigeum, the site of an ancient town, which is unknown to us, and of which only some fragments of walls are preserved. Another mile to the south, close to the natural conical rock called Hagios Demetrios Tepeh, are seen the ruins of a large temple of white marble, which was probably sacred to Demeter, and near it evident traces of an ancient settlement. Still further south, the village of Yeni Kioi, or Neo Chori (that is, new village), marks the site of another ancient city, probably the Oppidum Nee mentioned by Pliny. ¶¶

---

* See *Ilios*, pp. 652, 653.   † *Ibid.*
‡ *H. N.* V. 33.   § V. 94.   ‖ XIII. pp. 600, 604.
¶ *H. N.* V. 33.   ** See *Ilios*, pp. 654, 655.   †† *Ibid.* p. 656.
‡‡ See the chapter on the Heroic Tumuli and the large Map of the Troad in this volume.
§§ Mela, I. 18, 3 ; Pliny, *H. N.* V. 33 ; Serv. *ad Aen.* II. 312 ; Herodotus, V. 65, 94 ; Thucydides, VIII. 101 ; Strabo, XIII. pp. 595–602 ; Ptol. V. 23 ; Steph. Byz. p. 597 ; Hecataeus, p. 208 ; Scylax, p. 36.
‖‖ See *Ilios*, p. 631.   ¶¶ *H. N.* V. 33.

Still further south again, on the artificially smoothed rock to the east and north of the tumulus Besika Tepeh, which I explored, we see the site of a prehistoric city, of whose most remarkable pottery I brought very large quantities to light in my excavations of the tumulus.* At the southern extremity of the plain we see the village of Bounarbashi; behind which, on Mount Bali Dagh, are the ruins of the small town with its acropolis, which I explored, and where I found a settlement, dating from the 9th to the 5th century B.C., superposed by a later Greek one, which latter is probably Gergis.† Opposite to it, on the rock on the east side of the Scamander, are the ruins of the ancient fortified town of Eski Hissarlik, which I also investigated, and am bound to attribute likewise to a time from the 9th to the 5th century B.C.‡ Another prehistoric colony is marked by the hill of Hanaï Tepeh, which is situated on Mr. Calvert's farm of Thymbra, near the river Thymbrius;§ to the east of which extends the city of Thymbra, mentioned by Homer,‖ which had a temple of the Thymbrian Apollo, ¶ and must have existed till a late period of classical antiquity. About 1000 yards to the north of it, and on the same farm, is the site of the ancient settlement of Ἰλιέων κώμη (the Village of the Ilians), mentioned by Strabo,** who, as I have often had occasion to state, holds it, according to the theory of Demetrius of Scepsis, to be identical with the Homeric Troy.

Another ancient settlement is marked by the Fulu Dagh, about a mile to the east, which I explored, and to which also I assign a date from the 9th to the 5th century B.C. ††

Besides, therefore, the five prehistoric settlements and the Lydian city, whose ruins and *débris* we find below the remains of the Ilium of the classical period in Hissarlik—besides the other two prehistoric cities (the one close to the tumulus of Besika Tepeh, the other on Hanaï Tepeh), and besides the three towns, dating from the 9th to the 5th century B.C. (on the Bali Dagh, Eski Hissarlik and on Fulu Dagh);—we find that there were, in this plain of Troy, which is only eight miles long and less than half as broad in its widest part, eleven flourishing cities,

---

* See *Ilios*, pp. 665–669.
† See the exploration of the site in this work, pp. 264–269.
‡ See pp. 269–270 in the present work. § See *Ilios*, pp. 706–726.
‖ *Il.* X. 430. . ¶ Strabo, III. p. 598.
** XIII. p. 597. See *Ilios*, pp. 79, 175.
†† See p. 270 in the present work.

all of which were probably autonomous, and of which five—namely, Ilium, Ophrynium, Rhoeteum, Gergis, and Sigeum—coined their own money. If we further consider that the eleven cities, besides two villages, existed here simultaneously in classical antiquity, and that one of these—the city of Ilium itself—had at least 70,000 inhabitants, we are astounded and amazed how such large masses of people could have found the means of subsistence here, whilst the inhabitants of the present seven poor villages of the plain have the greatest difficulty in providing for their miserable existence. And not only had these ancient cities an abundance of food, but they were also so populous and rich, that they could carry on wars, and, as their ruins prove, they could erect temples and many other public buildings of white marble; Ilium especially must have been ornamented with a vast number of such sumptuous edifices.

This wealth of the ancient inhabitants of the plain of Troy can hardly be explained otherwise than by their great industry. They doubtless worked the gold, silver, and copper mines, mentioned by Homer,[*] Strabo,[†] and Pliny,[‡] as situated in their neighbourhood, and doubtless by their industry they had succeeded in entirely draining the plain of Troy, which has now become a swamp, and converting it into beautiful garden land. In the case of Ilium especially, the city was probably indebted for the greater part of its wealth to its temple of the Ilian Pallas Athené, which must have been a very celebrated place of pilgrimage, and have attracted innumerable worshippers, in all ages of classical antiquity.

Even a barbarian like Xerxes had heard of the great sanctity of this temple; for we have seen that,[§] according to Herodotus,[||] he ascended to it on his passage through the plain (480 B.C.), and sacrificed 1000 oxen to the goddess. That this sanctuary remained a highly celebrated place of pilgrimage at a time when the exercise of the Hellenic worship had long since been prohibited, and when the destruction of all heathen temples had long been decreed,[¶] we have seen from the letter of the Emperor Julian[**] (361–363 A.D.), who, when a prince, had visited Ilium in the year 354 or 355. Just as guides offer themselves in New York and London to the newly-arrived traveller, to show him

---

[*] *Il.* II. 856, 857.
[†] XIII. pp. 591, 603, 610, 680.
[‡] *H. N.* XXXVII. 74.
[§] See *Ilios*, p. 168.
[||] VII. 43.
[¶] Namely, through the edicts of the years 324, 326, and 341 A.D.
[**] See *Ilios*, pp. 180–182.

the curiosities of the city, so did guides offer themselves to Julian, to show him at Ilium the sacred relics of its glorious past.

I returned from the tumulus of Ujek Tepeh by way of Yeni Kioi and Yeni Shehr to Hissarlik, and thence by way of the city of the Dardanelles to Athens.

I was well content with the result of my laborious journey, for I now knew for certain that, whilst at Hissarlik the accumulation of prehistoric ruins, 14 mètres deep, is succeeded by a layer of Hellenic ruins and *débris* 2 mètres deep, there is in the whole Troad, between the Hellespont, the Gulf of Adramyttium, and the chain of Ida, no site containing prehistoric ruins, except at Hanaï Tepeh and Besika Tepeh. I now knew that, with the exception of Assos, which is being explored by distinguished American investigators, no excavations, with a view to find interesting antiquities of the classical times, are possible anywhere in the Troad, except perhaps on some spots in Alexandria Troas, but even there I certainly cannot advise any archaeologist to lose his time in digging.

All the altitudes given in this description of my journey have been calculated, according to my barometrical and thermometrical observations, by Dr. Julius Schmidt, the celebrated astronomer and director of the observatory, at Athens, who also rectified my thermometers, and to whom I here express my warmest gratitude.

The Map of the Troad, prefixed to this account of the journey, was drawn by Professor Ernest Ziller, of Athens, and Mr. Karl Heise, Cartographer at the Royal Prussian Landesaufnahme in Berlin, to whom I also tender my best thanks.*

The observations of the temperatures of springs, corrected by Dr. Julius Schmidt, are as follows:—

14 May.—Ligia Hamam, near Alexandria Troas, $53°·5$ C.$=128°·3$ F. The bath for men is too hot to be measured with the thermometer, which only goes as high as $62°$ C.$=143°·6$ F.
15 May.—Toozla salt spring, $60°·5$ C.$=140°·9$ F., another $39°·8$ C.$=103°·64$ F. The other springs are boiling.
17 May.—Near Assos on the shore, sulphurous well, $15°·8$ C.$=60°·44$ F.
18 May.—Lugia Hamam, $52°·51$ C.$=126°·52$ F.
18 May.—Lugia Hamam, marsh bath, $37°·3$ C.$=99°·14$ F.
20 May.—Spring on Mount Ida, $5°·8$ C.$=42°·44$ at an altitude of 1490 mètres.

HENRY SCHLIEMANN.

---

* The reader will observe that this Map (No. 140) takes in a larger space than the large Map of the Troad at the end of the volume.

APPENDIX II.

On the Bones Collected during the Excavations of 1882, in the First and most Ancient Prehistoric City at Hissarlik.

By PROFESSOR RUDOLF VIRCHOW.

THE bone-chest contained, unfortunately, so great a number of bones some quite freshly broken in pieces, and consequently no doubt broken in the carriage, that their determination was rendered extremely difficult, and in some cases quite impossible.

Among those that could be recognized were found a great number of small fragments, single teeth, etc., of a human being, and therefore in themselves very valuable objects. But with these also the attempts at restoration have led, for the present, to no satisfactory result. The skeleton to which they belonged was manifestly that of a person past middle life, probably a *man;* about which, however, I can venture to say no more than that the skull had a somewhat broad and flat-vaulted cranium. He might therefore possibly have been *brachycephalous*; at all events, not *dolichocephalous*. The skull found earlier in the second city * seems to have some resemblance to this one ; however, in the fragments of jawbones now furnished no trace of *prognathism* is shown, but, on the contrary, a short and quite vertical alveolar process, with the teeth likewise vertical, and very much worn down by use. .

Among the *animal bones*, those of *domestic animals* so greatly predominate, that it is difficult to discover the remains of *wild animals*. Of the latter I could only recognize with certainty the

---

* See *Ilios*, p. 270-1.

wild boar and *deer*. The antlers and other bones of deer belong undoubtedly, for the most part, to the *Cervus dama* (fallow deer).*

Among the *domestic animals*, I name first of all, on account of its rarity, the *horse*. I have already before mentioned the extreme rarity of the remains of the horse at Hissarlik;† a fact, which, of course, proves nothing against the possession of horses, since doubtless only the bones left from meals and sacrifices occur here. On this occasion also only two fragments of a jaw, and a tooth, have been recognized with certainty.

Bones of *cattle* are very numerous, the greater number being broken in pieces, and only the smaller, particularly bones of the hock (*astragali*) and of the foot, are preserved entire. Professor Müller, of the Berlin School of Veterinary Medicine, has had the goodness to institute a comparison with the bones of the present breed of Germany; and he is persuaded that the breed of cattle of the ancient Trojans must have been on the whole smaller, in some cases considerably so.

Both the *sheep* and *goat*, as well as *swine*, occur in such numbers that, besides cattle, they must have formed the regular stock of the flocks and herds. Single bones of the *dog*, a very few of *birds*, and a couple of large *vertebræ of fish*,‡ complete the osteological list.

On the whole, these results agree with those which I published in my "Contributions to the Natural History of the Troad,"§ founded on the earlier discoveries at Hissarlik, and in my essay on the "Ancient Trojan Graves and Skulls," ‖ founded on the discoveries at Hanaï Tepeh. The general conclusion is, that these most ancient inhabitants possessed all the necessary domestic animals, which still form the wealth of the Aryan peoples. The only one that appears to be wanting is the *cat*, which we also miss elsewhere among the discoveries of antiquity. The comparatively small number of bones of wild animals points distinctly to the inference, that *the chace* furnished only a supple-

---

* Compare Professor Virchow's account of the bones found in the Trojan houses, in *Ilios*, p. 319 :—" Horns of fallow deer and boar-tusks have been collected in large numbers."

† *Ilios*, pp. 319, 711 *b*.

‡ On the vertebrae of fish, previously found at Troy, see *Ilios*, pp. 323, 432.

§ *Beiträge zur Landeskunde der Troas;* see also *Ilios*, p. 319.

‖ *Alttrojanische Gräber und Schädel; Verlag der Kön. Akademie der Wissenschaften*, Berlin, 1882.

ment to the means of subsistence, but was not at all the principal condition of the people's existence. It occupied probably the same place as *fishing*, the products of which are represented, in the present contribution, by an abundance of *oyster-shells*.

For the rest, I may lay stress on the remark, that the circumstance of the larger bones being completely broken in pieces, must by no means be regarded as a proof of a low state of civilization. Many, indeed, infer from this that the bones were broken to get at the marrow, and that the marrow was eaten raw. But in cutting up the meat, in order to put it into the pot for boiling, the long bones are still broken in a way precisely like what we see here. The only conclusion therefore, from the broken state of the tubular bones appears to me to be, that the people of the most ancient Ilium already boiled their meat in the regular way.

It is, moreover, very interesting, that beef furnished at that time a much more considerable proportion of their food, than is now the case in the Troad and generally in the East; and that, besides the sheep and goat, the domesticated pig presents itself so conspicuously. Here we have another admirable coincidence with the descriptions of Homer.

APPENDIX III.

On Virchow's "Old Trojan Tombs and Skulls."

By KARL BLIND.

Alt-Trojanische Gräber und Schädel. Von Rudolf Virchow. (Berlin: Verlag der Kön. Akademie der Wissenschaften, 1882.)

THE reconstruction of Trojan ethnology is full of the greatest importance for a right estimate of Dr. Schliemann's wonderful excavations. From the remains at hand for the solution of this question, the great German physiologist, who has himself been for so many years active in unearthing mute testimonies of the past, both in Europe and Asia Minor, gives with due care and caution a highly interesting description in *Old Trojan Tombs and Skulls*. Considering the scantiness of the material, he does not strongly commit himself to any fixed theory as to the origin and kinship of the people who once dwelt on the hill of Hissarlik and its neighbourhood. But more than once he points to the possibility of a Thrakian connection; and here, I believe, the ultimate solution will be found.

For my own part, I have for some time past brought forward this hypothesis as a strong conviction, forced upon me by a comparison of all the passages in classic authors, which bear upon the Trojan, Thrakian, Getic, and Gothic tribes.

Professor Virchow's procedure is, it need not be said, based upon craniology. He tries to solve obscure race-questions from the outer structure of man, so far as this can be done with any degree of certainty. Frequent enquiries have, however, taught him, that points of extraordinary contact are often to be found among populations apparently the most widely divergent, so much so, that doubt now and then arises even as to the Aryan, Semitic—nay, Hamitic—character of a special skull whose origin is not known. In order to justify the extreme reserve with which he avoids too positive assertion, he refers to his examination of skulls from the Libyan oases, presented to him by Dr. Rohlfs, the African explorer. He found among them both long heads and heads of medium height, with more or less prominent jaws—in other words, dolichokephalic and mesokephalic, prognathous and less prognathous, specimens. In the same way he found, among the mummy skulls received from M. Mariette, a most ancient long-headed one, while others belong to the short-headed type. When we remember the successive waves of tribal conquests in Northern Africa, and the differences of race often embodied in caste-systems, these divergent results cannot create any surprise.

The skulls and bone-fragments which form the subject of Professor Virchow's present examination come from three places —Hanaï Tepeh, a hill of the Troad; Ren Kioi, near the site of the ancient Ophrynion; and Hissarlik, identified by Dr. Schliemann with Ilion. A solitary specimen of a skull was also furnished from Tchamlidcha by Mr. Frank Calvert, to whom Dr. Virchow owes most of his material. Unfortunately, the specimens from the probable site of Troy are so broken and defective, that they had to be taken to pieces and recomposed six or seven times, without any satisfactory result. Many bones had, during the long period of their being buried in the ruins, got entirely out of shape; large parts of the skulls are missing. A certain arbitrariness in the attempts at restoration cannot, therefore, be avoided. Experiments had, moreover, to be stopped at last from fear of entirely destroying the fragile material. This fact alone will show that hasty conclusions must be avoided, quite irrespective of the smallness of the number of specimens on which an opinion can in this case be founded.

Upon the whole, the oldest skulls from the three places mentioned have, according to Professor Virchow, more of a long-headed structure, with a single exception. The short heads and the heads of medium height prevail at Ren Kioi; the only two instances there of apparent dolichokephalic structure being due to an accident. "The idea"—Professor Virchow here says—"that Turanian admixture is the cause of relative short-headedness must for the nonce be relegated to the background, seeing that the other characteristics very little favour such an assumption. Since I have found that the Albanians as well as the Armenians are short-headed, the necessity of going back to Turanian sources for the explanation of brachykephalism among Aryan nations has become very small. On the other hand, the question, raised by me already in a previous lecture, as to whether Thrakian affinities should not be claimed for the Trojan population, has gained in probability by my new experience."

In a later part of his book, Professor Virchow remarks that, just as Bulgars and Albanians in our time are flocking over to Asia Minor from the opposite shores (the ancient Thrace), thus changing the ethnical character of the Anatolian population, so similar relations existed in farthest antiquity, as may be seen from classic authors and especially from the *Iliad*. "But the old, and more particularly the prehistoric, anthropology of Thrace has yet to be constructed; for the present, almost all material is wanting." Professor Virchow, of course, speaks here simply as an anthropologist. He does not refer to historical testimony bearing upon race-affinities. He then mentions the Armenian tribe of the Haig as a short-headed one, though of Aryan connection. Finally, he says the solution of the large prevalence of brachykephalism in Asia Minor may one day be found in the introduction of Thrakian race-elements; only he thinks this view has not yet been fully worked out.

It will be seen from the above that Professor Virchow does not believe Turanian admixture to be requisite any longer·for an explanation of the short-headed type. As to the Thrakian admixture in the population of Asia Minor, I think the material at hand is, in a historical sense, positively overwhelming. Physiologists naturally desire to solve ethnological questions as much as possible from the point of view of their own special science. Nor can it be denied that their labours excellently supplement, and partly check, the historical and linguistic evidence. Beyond a certain point, however, further enquiry and solution become well-nigh hopeless in matters of anthropology. Professor Virchow himself virtually states this difficulty by his remarks on the short-headedness of Albanians and Armenians; still more so by his observations on the strange points of contact even between many Aryan, Semitic, and Hamitic skulls. In one of his contributions to Schliemann's great work, *Ilios*, he had already said with good cause:—

"Our real knowledge of the craniology of ancient peoples is still on a very small scale. If it were correct that, as some authors suppose, the ancient Thracians, like the modern Albanians, were brachycephalic, we might perhaps connect with them the people represented by the brachycephalic head from Hissarlik. On the other hand, the dolichocephalism of Semites and Egyptians would permit us to go with our dolichocephalic

24

skulls from Hissarlik to so distant an origin. But if, besides the skull index, we take into consideration the entire formation of the head and the face of the dolichocephalic skulls, the idea that those men were members of the Aryan race is highly pleasing. Hence I believe the natural philosopher should stop in the face of these problems, and *should abandon further investigations to the archæologist.*"

Historically speaking, Asia Minor appears to have been inhabited, successively or simultaneously, by so many different nations—Aryan, Turanian, Semitic, and, may be, even partly Hamitic—that, in the absence of linguistic and other tests, many ethnical problems will perhaps for ever remain insoluble. Two great facts, however, I believe, stand out clearly before the eyes of those who will impartially read classic testimony; and, if we were to put out those lights (as an older English writer judiciously said), what other light would remain to us?

These facts are (1) that the great Thrakian stock—"the vastest," according to Herodotus, "next to the Indian"—was spread over both Eastern Europe and Asia Minor under many tribal names, such as Phrygians, Mysians, Lydians, Bithynians, and so forth; (2) that the Thrakians were of Getic, Gothic, Germanic, connection. It is not the place for me here to make out these statements in detail by ample quotations from Kallinos, Herodotos, Homer, Strabon, Stephanos, Capitolinus, Flavius Vopiscus, Claudian, Cassiodorus, Prokopios, and others—that is to say, from writers ranging over an epoch of from 1,400 to 1,500 years; not to mention the Goth Jornandes, among whose nation some ancient race-traditions must have been preserved. These points will be more fully considered on another occasion. Nor do they contain any new theory at all.

The third fact of importance is, that the Thrakian stock is at the bottom also of the Trojan or Teukrian population, as I will endeavour to show on the same occasion. Strabon was struck by the many Thrakian place-names in the Troad. A city called Ilion existed in European Thrace, as also in Asia Minor. Professor Virchow, as well as Dr. Schliemann, has found a great many analogies between Trojan and old Hungarian antiquities. Perhaps the mystery explains itself from the fact of Thrakian tribes having in ancient times been located on the Theiss as well as on the Skamandros. And taking "Thrakian" as a convertible term for "Teutonic," it is certainly remarkable that in classic times a Teutoburgion should have stood west of the river Theiss, at the confluence of the Danube and the Drau.

The very name of the Thrakians, as also that of the Phrygians, I hold to be of possible explanation from Teutonic philology. What we know of Phrygian speech, and of other Thrakian idioms, presents some remarkable affinities, partly with Old Norse, partly with German. The great influence which the musical, martial, and altogether highly gifted Thrakian race exercised on the Hellenic world, both in poetry and philosophy, stands recorded in Hellenic authors.

The skull-measurements taken by Professor Virchow among people at Ren Kioi in 1879, and the similar communications made by Mr. A. Weisbach ("On the Shape of the Greek Skull") to the Anthropological Society at Vienna, have brought out a remarkable coincidence between the mesokephalism or brachykephalism of the living population of the "purely Greek place" of Ren Kioi and the structure of the skulls found in the neighbouring Ophrynion. The words, "purely Greek," which Professor Virchow uses, are of course to be taken rather linguistically than in the strict sense of homogeneous descent. I think classic literature sufficiently proves that the early Hellenic conquerors not only became fused in Greece with indigenous "barbarous" tribes, but that Thrakian — that is, Germanic — as well as Semitic elements largely contributed, in course of time, to the formation of Greek nationality, both in Europe and in Asia Minor. Does not Herodotos (to give but one instance) say that, "from diligent enquiry," he found that even Aristogeiton and Harmodios were originally of Phoenikian descent—namely, "of the number of those Phoenikians who came over with Kadmos, and were admitted by the Athenians into the number of their citizens on certain conditions ; it being enacted that they should be excluded from several privileges"? When we remember such facts, it will be easily seen that "Greek" means, ethnologically, a great deal more than appears on the surface.

A definite decision from a purely anthropological point of view is, in the cases at issue, if not impossible, at least so extremely difficult, that the historian and the archaeologist must certainly come in with their own tests as to ethnical connection. In this respect, the fact of Dr. Schliemann's having found amid the prehistoric ruins of Hissarlik a well-preserved skull in a jar containing human ashes, appears to me a noteworthy fact. Professor Virchow gives it prominence by italics. A similar find, I may observe, was not long ago made in Germany ; and it seems to have puzzled archaeologists. I pointed out at the time that, as late as the seventh century of our era, some German tribes (for instance, the Thuringians) applied fire-burial only to the body, not to the head, of the dead : "Capite amputato, cadaver more gentilium ignibus traderetur." (See *Vita Arnulfi Metensis*). Perhaps the significance of the skull, in the way of judging a person's character and intellectual capacity, had already struck our forefathers; hence their funeral rites may have been adapted to that notion. The occurrence of the same extraordinary custom on German and Trojan ground looks at all events like an additional link in a very curious chain of connection, in which the eastern Teutons—that is, the Thrakians—form the large intermediate part.

Much interesting matter as to the remnants of Trojan civilization is contained in Professor Virchow's book. Thirteen plates, partly coloured, giving drawings of the skulls, of fragments of pottery, and other things discovered, are a useful adjunct. The author believes, both from the characteristics of the skeletons and from what was found in the graves and in the several layers of the ruins of Hissarlik, that the prehistoric populations in question had already made considerable progress in culture. This contribution to the solution of the Trojan question forms a valuable commentary on, at least, one aspect of that series of world-famed excavations which have recently brought forth a fresh surprise under Dr. Schliemann's ever active spade. The results of the last startling discovery are soon to be given to the public. So far as at present can be known, they will partly modify former conclusions, but in the main strengthen the view of those who look upon the once castled hill of Hissarlik as the site of the town which of old was sung in Greek ballads that were afterwards fused into the "Homeric" epic.

KARL BLIND.

(*The Academy* of March 17, 1883.)

APPENDIX IV.

The Teutonic Kinship of Trojans and Thrakians.
By KARL BLIND.

LONDON, *Dec.* 2, 1881.

TO DR. SCHLIEMANN.

DEAR FRIEND,

I believe it to be a thesis admitting of the clearest proof, that the Trojans, or Teukrians, were of Thrakian race ; that the Thrakians were of the Getic, Gothic, or Germanic stock ; hence, that the Trojans were originally a Teutonic tribe.

Like other Thrakians, the Trojans, in course of time, became partly Hellenized ; therefore, of mixed culture—probably also of mixed speech. But the direct as well as the circumstantial evidence of their Thrakian, and consequently Getic or Gothic, connection, seems to me overwhelming in presence of historical testimony ranging over more than a thousand years ; from Kallinos down to Jornandes.

Within the few pages of this letter, I can but make a rapid indication of some points. Kallinos and Herodotos mention the Trojans as Teukrians. At the time of Kallinos, these Teukrians were still the chief occupants of the Troad. The Paeonians (comp. Caesar's Germanic Pae-mani), a branch of the Thrakians, who lived on the Strymon (*Strom*), professed themselves to be a colony of Teukrians from Troy. The Teukrians—as Grote remarks— are mentioned together with the Mysians[*] by Herodotos in such a manner as to show that there was no great ethnical difference between them. Now the Mysians (whom, together with Thrakians, Phrygians, and kindred tribes, we find as allies of the Trojans in Homer) were, according to Strabon and Stephanos, Thrakians who had come from Europe into Asia ; and Strabon lays stress on the many Thrakian place-names in the Troad. No wonder a Thrakian city "Ilion" should have existed also in Europe.

The Phrygians, too, were a Thrakian people. Phrygians, Mysians, and the Bithynian branch of the Thrakians, according

---

[*] Compare the name of the sea-king Mysing in the Norse Skalda ("Menja and Fenja").

to Arrian, all likewise immigrated from Europe into Asia. The Thrakians, in fact, as Herodotos says, were "the largest of any nations, except at least the Indians." We can, therefore, scarcely be astonished that, although Trojans and Phrygians are represented as distinct in the Homeric Hymn to Aphroditê, the Attic tragedians and the Romans should nevertheless have called the old Trojans "Phrygians," whilst Herodotos calls them "Teukrians." The fact is, that various tribal names were alternately used, poetically or otherwise, for designating the widely scattered, only dialectically distinct, populations of the same vast Thrakian stock—just as Frank and Swabian, Bavarian and Saxon, nay, Dane, Swede, and Norwegian, belong in common to the Teutonic race.

Can, then, *primâ facie*, this "largest of any nations" be any other race than that which afterwards pushed forward in the Great Migrations?

The name of the Phrygians is explained as "freemen,"* aye, literally, as Franks. The Makedonians, who said "Aproditê" and "Bilippos"† for "Aphroditê" and "Philippos," called the Phrygians "Briges," "Bryges," or "Brykai;" but there is no doubt as to this name, Bryg, Bryk, or Fryk, having meant a freeman, a Frank. The omission of the nasal sound in that tribal name is found also in Old Norse "Frakkland" is, in the Edda, the Frankonian land on the Rhine, where Brynhild (Sigurdrifa) sleeps on the fire-encircled spell-bound rock.

I hold it possible that even "Thrax" (Thrakk-s), or Threïx (Threïk-s), as a Thrakian was called by the Greeks, may be connected with Frakk, Frank, Phryg, or Fryg, and "free," or *frei;* the phonetic interchange between the "th" and the "ph," or "f," being one easily proveable in other cases, both in the Greek tongue and in Germanic idioms.

So large was the Thrakian race, that some ancient writers divide the world into Asia, Libya (Africa), Europe, and Thrakê. Evidently the vast Teutonic race, which, under many tribal names, was spread over the region from Central Asia to the Baltic and the North Sea; which, as Teutons and Kimbrians, became the terror of Rome; and which, during the Migrations, broke like a torrent into southern and western Europe, and even

---

* Hesych. *Lexicon:* 'Ιόβας δὲ ὑπὸ Λυδῶν (ἀπο)φαίνεται Βρίγα λέγεσθαι τὸν ἐλεύθερον.

† A similar dialectic peculiarity still attaches to the speech of the Franconian Germans of the present day, even as to that of the Low Germans. Perhaps this circumstance may throw some light upon the mixed origin of the Makedonians themselves, who were held to be "barbarians" by the Greeks.

into Africa ;—was first known to the ancients under the Thrakian, Phrygian (Frankian), name.

Those Thrakians—blue-eyed, red-haired, according to an indication by Xenophanes, 500 years before our era—were a most martial and a highly musical people, much given to Bacchic habits, but also to philosophical speculation. Arês had his home in Thrakê. So had Orpheus. Pittakos, the son of the Thrakian Hyrrhadios, was the teacher of Pythagoras. Hermippos avers that Pythagoras had adopted the Thrakian philosophy. The Bithynian Thrakians produced a great many learned men.

Do not these martial, musical, Bacchic, and philosophical traits point strongly to the Teutonic stock?

The customs of the Thrakians, as portrayed in the famous scene of the banquet given by Seuthes (Seuth = Seyd, an abbreviation of Sigfrid) to Xenophon; the description of their dress and arms; the names of their chieftains, and all that we know of their language: all goes far to confirm this view. Among the Thrakian names there are many dagger- and spear-names, *Sig-* (Victory-), *As-* (God-), and *Teut-* (Folk-) names, such as were usual among Teutonic warriors. Again, most Thrakians, as well as the Germans of Tacitus, had scarcely any swords · the shield and spear were their chief weapons. Even the lance without a metal point, only hardened at the top by fire, occurs among the Thrakians of Herodotos, and, six hundred years later, among the Germans of Tacitus.*

You, my dear friend, have expressed an easily conceivable astonishment at not having found so much as the trace of a sword in the ruins of Hissarlik, nor even any moulds from which they might have been cast, whilst you found hundreds of bronze swords in the tombs of Mykenê.† But by the light of Herodotos' and Tacitus' account of the Thrakian and German armaments, and keeping in remembrance the Thrakian or Teutonic connection of the Trojans, the mystery seems to me cleared up.

In Strabon, the whole line of Germanic connection is traced out from the Getic neighbours of the Swabians to the Mysians, Lydians, Phrygians, and Trojans (VII. c. 3. 1-2). The Getes, in Herodotos, are "the noblest of the Thrakians;" and the Getes were Goths. The "Herkynian Forest," in which the Getes dwelt (and this Herkynian name is used for various thickly wooded parts of the Teutonic land in Aristoteles, Caesar, Strabon, Florus, Tacitus, Plinius, and Ptolemaios), is nothing but the Old German *Haruc*, the Norse *Hörgr;* meaning "forest.'

---

* Herod. VII. 74-77. Tac. *Germ.* VI.; *Annals*, II. 14. † *Ilios*, 483; Pref. xii.

According to Strabon and Menandros, Thrakians and Getes were of the same speech. Even Dakians (comp. *Degen*), living on the side towards Germany proper, were of the same speech with the Getes; hence, "the Getes hoped for German support against the Romans." Can we wonder, then, at Teutonic names —including even "Teutoburgion"—appearing in Roman times on what is now Hungarian soil?*

Nor should it be forgotten that Strabon mentions Thrakian Kebrenians in Europe, whose name is the same as that of those in Troy (XIII c. 1, § 21).

The Guttones of Pytheas, the Gythones of Ptolemaios, the Gothones of Tacitus, are but tribal varieties of Getes or Goths. The same race which Herodotos places as Getes near the outlet of the Danube and the Black Sea, turns up as Goths, in the fourth century, in the same quarter. When the Getic name begins to change into the Gothic, Spartianus bears clear testimony to their identity. Capitolinus, Flavius Vopiscus, Claudianus, Magnus Aurelius Cassiodorus (who served under Odoaker and Theodorich), and Prokopios, all bear witness to the same effect. Need the Goth Jornandes, then, be quoted at all?

The "Skaian" and "Sigaian" names, so widely distributed over Trojan, Phrygian, and Thrakian ground—and of which Prof. Haug said that most probably Sigo was a proper name, or a deity in Troy—I believe to be referable to a frequent Nikê- or Victory-name among the Teutons. (Comp. Sigi, Sigar, Sigebert, Sigebant, Sigfrid, Sigefugl, Sigegeat, Siggeir, Sigeher, Sighwat, Sigmund, Sigenot, Sigestap, Sigtyr, Sigtryg, Sigwart, Sigewein, Segest, Segimer; Sigyn, Sigrun, Sigrdrifa, Sigurlinn, Sigelind, Sigeminne, etc.) Strabon mentions certain Thrakians called Skaians, the river Skaios, a fort Skaion, and in Troy the Skaian Gate. Teutonic "As-" names are of equally wide distribution among the Thrakians and the kindred Lydians, Phrygians, and Mysians.

This Teutonic kinship of the Thrakians was already believed in by Fischart, and later by Voss, the author of the matchless translation of Homer. At the same time a careful comparison of classic authorities establishes the close kinship between Thrakians and Trojans. The Ilion of Asia Minor, and the Ilion of European Thrace, stand out therefore, in dim antiquity, like two watch-towers of the early Teutons of the East.

KARL BLIND.

---

* *Il. Ant.* p. 293. Ptol. *Geogr.* II. 16, 5.

APPENDIX V.

THE SITE AND ANTIQUITY OF THE HELLENIC ILION.

BY PROFESSOR MAHAFFY.

DR. SCHLIEMANN has asked me to reprint the following paper as an Appendix to his new book on Ilion. It is practically a reply to the attack volunteered by Professor Jebb upon the Appendix I contributed to the former *Ilios*—an attack which first appeared anonymously in the *Edinburgh Review*. Then it was republished with some modifications, for the readers of the *Hellenic Journal*, by the author, who is also one of the editors of that journal. The tacit reference to my original Appendix being so manifest that it required no proof, I sent this reply to the *Journal*. Since that time Brentano published a new pamphlet on the subject, and Mr. Jebb in a new article in the *Hellenic Journal* (vol. iii. No. 2, p. 203), has replied to my reply. He thinks I demanded this second reply. I was not aware that I had done so, though he calls the demand formal. I had intended to add nothing to this paper, but now append a few notes in reference to his last reply in the *Journal* (iii. 204), to show that he has not refuted my arguments.

There is an interesting historical question in relation to Dr. Schliemann's Trojan excavations; it is this: When was the historical Ilion really founded? And the answer to this question involves another of considerable interest: Was the historical Ilion on the site of the prehistoric Troy? If its foundation be recent, and in historical times, there is room to doubt the identity of the sites, and accordingly the ancient enquirers who denied this identity also denied the antiquity of Ilion. I propose, therefore, to review the evidence as briefly as possible by the light of recent discussions, and beg leave for this very brevity's sake to be allowed through the following argument to call the heroic city *Troy*, and the historical *Ilion*, without further specification.

Both Dr. Schliemann and I had come independently to the same conclusion on the second question just stated. He was led by his excavations, and I by a critical examination of the historical notices of the ancients, to assert the identity of the two sites; and we advanced from this to the further conclusion, that the alleged foundation of Ilion in historical times on a new site was not true, and that probably the earliest Ilion succeeded to the site and traditions of the latest Troy, without any considerable interruption. This was the general opinion throughout Greek history, till a very learned man, Demetrius of Scepsis, undertook to destroy the claims to a heroic ancestry of the Ilians, then rich and insolent through the favour of Lysimachus. Demetrius's conclusions were accepted and propagated by Strabo, and have thus passed into currency among older scholars. But most critics of our own day, and notably George Grote, our highest historical authority, have recognized that the theory of Demetrius was not only novel and paradoxical, but based on no real and solid evidence. This theory then, overthrown by Grote's critical acuteness, received a further deathblow from Dr. Schliemann's excavations. Any one who knows even the elements of archaeology now feels sure that the site of Ilion was a site occupied in heroic and prehistoric times, as the layers of many centuries' successive remains clearly testify. As there is no other site in the Troad for which the least evidence of this kind has been, or can be, produced, the argument that Troy and Ilion occupied the same site is as surely established as anything in ancient history.

It was accordingly interesting to consider why Demetrius was so zealous to overthrow this fixed belief; and both Dr. Schliemann and I think it may be ascribed to pedantic jealousy on the part of that author, who being himself a native of Scepsis, and anxious to claim Aeneas as a heroic ruler of that city, set himself to destroy the rival claim of Ilion to that honour. It would of course be a ridiculous hypothesis to assert that Demetrius deliberately chose a false site for Troy, 'through unwillingness to admit a claim which his critical conscience secretly ratified.' But such a clumsy piece of psychology (attributed to us by Mr. Jebb) was no part of our argument.* We only assumed (and have we no ample proofs before us?) that an envious pedant could persuade himself to argue a bad case, and could become so persuaded of it himself as to adopt it in the most serious earnest.

It was probably the rival claims of Ilion and Scepsis to be the seat of Aeneas's dynasty that stimulated this feeling in Demetrius. His only positive ground (so far as we know) for claiming this honour on behalf of Scepsis was the very weak argument, that Scepsis was half-way between the country assigned to Aeneas in the *Iliad* and Lyrnessus, to which he fled when pursued by Achilles (cf. Strabo, xiii. p. 607). So shadowy an argument could not stand for one moment till the claim of Ilion had been disposed of. For what did Homer prophesy?

Νῦν δὲ δὴ Αἰνείαο βίη Τρώεσσιν ἀνάξει
καὶ παίδων παῖδες, τοί κεν μετόπισθε γένωνται.†

Of course the obvious inference from this passage was that Aeneas reigned at Troy,‡ and so Strabo tells us it was generally understood (though Mr. Jebb thinks this an unnatural rendering, and thinks the avoidance of the name Troy implies a change of residence). It was asserted by divers legends preserved to us. Thus Dionysius of Halicarnassus (*Antiq. Rom.* i. 53) tells of legends asserting that Aeneas returned from Italy to Troy, and reigned there, leaving his kingdom to Ascanius—a legend based on the Homeric prophecy. There are other stories (hinted at by Homer) of Aeneas being disloyal to Priam, and thus saving his own party in the city. Against these legends, and the hero-worship of Aeneas at Ilion, Demetrius had to find arguments, if Scepsis could save its mythical renown. What were his argu-

---

* In his late reply (p. 215) Mr. Jebb adds: "This absurdity [viz. the absurdity he has invented and fathered upon us] becomes still more grotesque when it is observed that his own town, Scepsis, was not Ilium's rival. His own view was that the βασίλειον of Aeneas had been at Scepsis. Neither he nor anyone else ever dreamed of setting up Scepsis as Troy." What I said was this: That Aeneas was believed to have founded a dynasty in the Troad—the Ilians said at Ilion, Demetrius said at Scepsis. Ilion and Scepsis were therefore strictly rivals for this honour. The argument which showed that the Ilians had nothing to do with ancient Troy distinctly strengthened the case of Scepsis. I did not think any man of common sense could have mistaken this. † *Il.* xx. 307-8.

‡ The passage would never have been composed, had not what it prophesies been either actually existing, or at least generally believed. For it was undoubtedly a prediction "after the fact."

ments, and how did he persuade Strabo, and even some modern scholars, to adopt his theory?

I will state at the outset an important distinction, the neglect of which is sure to vitiate any argument on the subject; and yet the distinction is easy and obvious enough. When the destruction of Troy is to be considered, we have two points before us: (1) was it total? (2) was it final? Both cases are exceptional enough; for to destroy any city totally is an affair of no small labour and perseverance. But even when totally destroyed, a Greek city-site was sure to be re-occupied by fugitives as soon as the enemy had disappeared, and so there is hardly an instance in history where even a *total* destruction was *final*. It was effected in the case of Sybaris (a) by turning the course of a river over the levelled buildings, (β) by cursing solemnly the re-occupiers of the site, or (γ) by a διοίκισις, as in the case of Mantinea. These special precautions show that the ordinary pictures, poetical or otherwise, of the total ruin of a city, in no way imply its final disappearance from among the habitations of men. The party of Demetrius knew and felt this distinction very well. For they felt themselves obliged to assert an *abnormal* destruction of Troy. Thus Strabo, ἅτε γὰρ ἐκπεπορθημένων τῶν κύκλῳ πόλεων, οὐ τελέως δὲ κατεσπασμένων, some traces of them still remain; but Troy, he adds, was not only ἐκ βάθρων ἀνατετραμμένη, but all its atoms were carried away for building elsewhere—an amusing evidence of the way in which Demetrius (Strabo's authority) tried to meet the obvious objection, that the site he had discovered for Troy showed no traces of antiquity. Hence the first unproved conjecture. It was considered, even by its supporters, so weak, that they added another. According to Strabo: ὁμολογοῦσι δὲ οἱ νεώτεροι τὸν ἀφανισμὸν τῆς πόλεως, ὧν ἐστι καὶ Λυκοῦργος ὁ ῥήτωρ (whom he quotes), εἰκάζουσι δὲ (*they conjecture*) that the spot was avoided on account of its evil omen, or because Agamemnon cursed it. The νεώτεροι are of course not post-Homeric writers generally, as some have translated it, but the party of Demetrius, who have with them, among older authorities, the orator Lycurgus.*

---

* Mr. Jebb insists (*op. cit.* p. 210) that νεώτεροι means all post-Homeric writers, on the ground that *commentators on Homer* speak of post-Homeric writers in this way. It is natural enough that they should do so, when comparing the language of Homer with that of later literature. But in the case of *historians*, I am sure this is not the case, and could find plenty of evidence, were it worth while. I find two

It is perfectly clear that he was the only earlier authority asserting the *final* destruction of Troy by the Greeks.

Thus then we are warranted in declaring that there is no evidence to prove any settled belief on the part of the historical Greeks that Troy was *finally* destroyed. Some old authorities, such as Plato, Isocrates, and Xenophon, imply their belief that it was totally destroyed by the Greeks, but no one, except Lycurgus, ever asserted that it ceased to be inhabited. The weight of Lycurgus's evidence will be presently considered.

But this is not all. Can it even be said that there was a settled belief among the historical Greeks that the destruction of Troy was total, if not final? It is indeed true that Aeschylus, Euripides, and their Latin imitators, portray the destruction of Troy 'almost as Hebrew prophecy pictures the desolation of Tyre.' But are they indeed using no poetical liberty in so doing, and are they representing a tradition on this point inflexible? Far from it. What does Strabo say—Strabo, whom the followers of Demetrius quote as so important and trustworthy? "But the current stories (τὰ θρυλλούμενα) about Aeneas do not agree with the legends about the founding of Scepsis. For the former say that he came safe out of the war owing to his feud with Priam, 'for he had a lasting feud (says Homer) with noble Priam, because Priam would not honour him, brave though he was among men;' and so did the Antenoridae escape, and Antenor himself, through the guest-friendship of Menelaus. Sophocles indeed in his *Capture of Troy* * says that a leopard's skin was hung out before Antenor's door as a sign to leave his house unsacked." Strabo then speaks of these heroes' distant wanderings. "Homer, however, does not agree with these legends, or with what is told about the founders of Scepsis. For he indicates that Aeneas *remained in Troy*, and succeeded to the

---

cases in five minutes. Dionysius speaks of Hellanicus as τῶν παλαιῶν συγγραφέων in a passage which Mr. Jebb himself cites. But the latter never seems to foresee that a quotation, in an argument, can be turned against him in a new connection. Strabo, the very author now in question, speaks of Xanthus (xiii. p. 931) as ὁ παλαιὸς συγγραφεύς! Are these then the νεώτεροι? Such are the consequences of trying to refute everything an opponent has said.

* Mr. Jebb criticizes my translation, and says this means at the capture of Troy, and not in the play so called. If I am indeed wrong, I was misled by Eustathius, who quotes it as a play, omitting the article (τῇ); cf. Dindorf's *Poet. Scen.* Frag. Soph. Incert. 15. But I find the article used and not used in citations of plays, almost at random; e.g. ἐν Ἕκτορος λύτροις, and ἐν τοῖς Ἐ. λ., and so *passim* through the authorities.

sovereignty, and left the succession to his children's children." How can the legend of the total, far less the final, destruction of Troy, be called *inflexible* in the face of this famous and familiar authority? Homer was not inflexible on the point. Sophocles, the most Homeric of the tragedians, was not inflexible on the point. Polygnotus, in his famous pictures in the Lesché at Delphi, illustrated the Sophoclean view of the legend, and his pictures made it known to all visitors. They contemplate an incomplete destruction, followed (according to the *Iliad*) by a re-occupation of the place, and a restoration of the Trojan monarchy.*

Thus there was from the beginning an important addition— or I will admit it to be a variation—to the legend of the sack of Troy, which stated that the site had not remained desolate after the sack, but was occupied by the Aeneadae. Sophocles even implies that the destruction was not complete. And this, no doubt, was the reason why nobody through the earlier centuries of Greek history thought of denying the claim of the Ilians to represent the Troy of epic poetry. This too was the real reason why Strabo, with all his exact knowledge, mentions no other writer besides Hellanicus as having supported that claim. Everybody took it for granted.

Let us now lay aside the legend that the destruction was incomplete, and proceed to show the probability that the site was unchanged. This also was sustained by several important witnesses. Xerxes visited the place, and admired its famous relics, in a way which leaves no doubt whatever as to the then current opinion among his Greek subjects. Herodotus, by his language, indicates plainly his acquiescence in this belief. Mindarus proves the persistence of the same belief, and so does Alexander the Great. The historians, who cite these visits, never express any doubt or scepticism, and are thus additional and independent witnesses. What need have we of further evidence? what no one thought of questioning, no one thought

---

* As to the number of houses saved, I can say nothing but this : Had all Troy except one house been destroyed, the legends would doubtless have told us so, as they do in other cases. Nor did I contemplate a destruction so partial as to allow after-habitation without rebuilding. All I contend for is, that remnant enough was left to preserve the traditions of the site unbroken. The survival of one house would be enough to disprove the invention that the site was accursed, and would mark it, as the house of Rahab or of Pindar marked the site of their respective towns, which were presently rebuilt. Thus every fact adduced by Mr. Jebb tells against his own argument.

of asserting. The best modern judge of evidence in Greek history, George Grote, lays it down as self-evident, that this was the general belief of the Greek world. The best judge of Roman opinion, L. Friedländer, asserts it positively, and in the face of Strabo's theory, to have been the general belief of the Roman world.*

It is very characteristic of the attitude of Demetrius, that he seems to have passed over this strong historical proof from the acts and the acquiescence of leading *public men* in older days, and set himself to attack the statements of a *writer*, a compiler of local legends, who, being intimately acquainted with Ilion, had set down the legends there preserved in his *Troïca*, and thus given formal support to the identity of site. We do not know that he advocated a belief in a mere partial destruction; it is probable that he did. But it so happened that the very subject treated by this writer—Hellanicus—led him necessarily to contradict Demetrius's theory, and hence he must be refuted. He is alleged to have been over-partial to the Ilians. Surely when a man undertook to collect local legends he was not likely to succeed if he were not in sympathy with the inhabitants. He no doubt wrote down fully, without any sifting or sceptical criticism, what they had to say. Probably he was silent about Scepsis. There is no further evidence of any undue favouritism. It is clear that the main claim of the Ilians, beyond the venerable antiquity of their shrine of the Ilian Athené, rested on the annual pilgrimage of Locrian virgins, sent to expiate the crime of Ajax. Strabo and Demetrius object that this legend is not Homeric. It was certainly as old as the Cyclic poets. The annual sending of these virgins must have been in consequence of some misfortune which befel Locri, and owing to the behest of some ancient oracle. The statement of Strabo, that it did not begin till the Persian supremacy,† is devoid of probability and of evidence, and even if accepted, proves the recognition of the shrine at that date as that of Homer's Athené.

This refutation then of Hellanicus being very weak, and his

---

* This indeed Mr. Jebb concedes. Brentano, in the pamphlet praised by Mr. Jebb, tries to prove that even the Roman world rejected the claims of Ilion.

† I had said *the Persian wars*, meaning their wars in Ionia and Aeolis, but Mr. Jebb fairly misunderstood and corrected the expression. But in doing so he puts the date of the Persian supremacy (ἤδη κρατούντων) *in the earlier half of the 6th century* B.C.! If the sacrifice did go back beyond 600 B.C., it is amply sufficient for my argument.

authority as an ancient and respectable writer being capital in the question, the modern attacks on his credibility demand our attention. We may reject the evidence of Hellanicus, either on the general ground that he was an uncritical logographer, or on the special ground of his being untrustworthy in other cases where we can test his credibility. The former reason is by itself weak and insufficient, for, though it might not be in Hellanicus's power to criticize with acuteness the materials before him, he might nevertheless be an honest and careful collector of legends, and this is all we require in the present case. But so much we may safely allow him, for this strong and conclusive reason, that one of the severest critics of the logographers, Dionysius of Halicarnassus, though speaking with contempt of them as a class, alludes repeatedly to this particular man, Hellanicus, as an authority of importance on local legends. Thus, in the first book of his *Roman Antiquities*, he cites Hellanicus at least four times, once without remark, once (c. 35) to differ from him, though without disrespect. But the remaining cases are more important. He says (c. 38), "*The most credible of the legends about Aeneas's flight, which Hellanicus, of old historians, adopts, is as follows.*" In the other (c. 22) he sums up the legends of the passage of the Sicels into Sicily, as they are told ὑπὸ τῶν λόγου ἀξίων. Who are they? *Hellanicus*, Philistus, Antiochus, and *Thucydides!* This shows that Dionysius at all events respected Hellanicus's authority, and thus contradicted in this particular case his general depreciation of the logographers.* Nor need it surprise us, for Thucydides himself, who never cites other writers, selects Hellanicus alone for critical censure as to his chronology. This solitary citation clearly proves the importance of the man. Mr. Jebb, *as a controversialist*, is quite entitled to affect amazement at this argument. But to those who seek to find out the truth, I put it with some confidence. A very serious author, whose habit it is to quote no authorities, for once specifies a writer, and says that this man, who covered the same epoch, is inaccurate. From what I know of the habits of ancient historians, the proper inference is, that this stray mention is because of the writer's importance, often because the author has elsewhere copied him.

---

* I quoted this particular evidence from Dionysius as an *argumentum ad hominem*, because Mr. Jebb had unfortunately selected a general attack on the old logographers from this very writer, as against Hellanicus's credit.

But are there not distinct cases in which Hellanicus can be proved inaccurate and untrustworthy? This is the second line of argument. Of course there are. Strabo asserts that he had made mistakes in supposing old but obscure towns in Aetolia, Olenus and Pylene, to be still undisturbed, and indeed that his whole account was marked by great carelessness (εὐχέρεια). This may be true, but is his ignorance of Aetolian geography any proof of inaccuracy in Trojan affairs? The proper answer is to apply the same sort of argument to his critic Strabo. It is easy enough to hoist him on his own petard. In the account of Argolis, Strabo comes to speak of Mycenae, whose ruins were then, as they now are, among the most remarkable in Greece. What does the learned and accurate Strabo, whose authority is paramount with the modern followers of Demetrius, say about it, "In later times [and he was wrong about this too*] Mycenae was razed by the Argives, so that no trace of it is now to be found—ὥστε νῦν μηδ' ἴχνος εὑρίσκεσθαι τῆς Μυκηναίων πόλεως!"† Here we have almost the very words, applied by him to his imaginary site of Troy, applied to a great and famous ruin in Greece—no Olenus or Pylene, but royal Mycenae! Thus the argument, that a writer is generally untrustworthy because he has been wrong or negligent on one point, applies with equal force to Strabo himself. And yet those who attack Hellanicus on this very ground, extol the learning and accuracy of Strabo as beyond suspicion.

Let us now turn to the opposite side of the controversy, and having sufficiently defended Hellanicus, who asserted the transmission of Troy into Ilion without change of site, let us examine the only tangible witness from older days on the side of Demetrius—the orator Lycurgus. He says distinctly that Troy, after its total destruction, has remained uninhabited to his own day. Is this statement to outweigh all the consensus on the other side? Is it not notorious that the Attic orators were loose

---

* Mr. Jebb cites against me a couple of passages, which I had myself collected and discussed in my paper on the subject, as if they were a contribution of his own to the debate, and conclusive against my view!

† It is a curious evidence of how far prejudice can lead a man, to find Mr. Jebb arguing on this (*op. cit.* 214) that Strabo meant no more than to say that Mycenae *had no longer an inhabited house on it!* If Strabo had been searching for a strong phrase to express the total disappearance of a town, he could hardly have found a stronger. If such a statement could be found about the site of Troy, how Mr. Jebb would have paraded it as perfectly decisive!

in their historical allusions? Lycurgus is said indeed to have been steeped in legendary lore, and likely to represent the soundest opinion of his day on such a question. But so far as our positive evidence goes, he was rather steeped in the tragic literature, and so impressed by such plays as the *Hecuba* and *Troades*, that he would naturally speak in the strongest terms of the destruction of Troy. He may possibly have indulged in a mere rhetorical exaggeration, which would not have been seriously quoted, but for the dearth of evidence on that side of the question.* It seems to me on a par with Lucan's description of Caesar's visit to the deserted site of Troy, which is so clearly imaginary, that few have ventured to cite it as evidence.

But Lycurgus's statement has recently been supported by an argument of some ingenuity, which requires a moment's consideration. It has been argued that the speech in question was delivered shortly after the battle of the Granicus, and that then Ilion has just been "impressively aggrandised" [Mr. Jebb has found out since that this phrase of his implies no new building!] by Alexander, proclaimed a city, free of imposts, &c., so that the question of the site of Troy was at that moment prominent. This gives (it is urged) peculiar point to Lycurgus's expression, and makes it impossible that he could have used a random expression. In my Appendix to Schliemann's *Ilios* I had accepted this reading of the facts about Alexander and Ilion, but I now confess that I was here in error. It is clear enough in this case that Alexander only made promises, and gave orders; even after his complete success he is still only making promises, of which the fulfilment did not come till Lysimachus took the matter in hand. The point in Strabo's mind was the close imitation (as he thought) of Alexander by Augustus, and hence he gives prominence to a

---

* In arguing a very strong case against a very weak one, I am willing to concede that Lycurgus really intended by ἀνάστατος and ἀνοίκητος the total ruin and complete desertion of an inhabited site. But it is certain that ἀνάστατος is used rhetorically for mere political destruction, and I think it possible that, as οἰκίζειν constantly means not to people a deserted spot, but to make a new (Hellenic) polity on a spot inhabited by barbarians or villagers, so ἀνοίκητος may have been used by Lycurgus to signify, not the complete desertion of the site, but its disappearance from among the catalogue of Greek independent πόλεις. *As a matter of fact, even the site advocated by Demetrius, the 'Ιλιέων κώμη, was inhabited, and probably at Lycurgus's time, for had it been lately occupied, Demetrius would not have failed to mention it.* If this be so, the exaggeration of his language is manifest. I think, therefore, that had Lycurgus been attacked for gross inaccuracy, he could have defended himself in this way, and replied that he was only speaking politically, and not in the absolute sense of the words.

matter of no real importance in its day. It is however plain that we have been translating mere promises of Alexander into facts, for let us quote what follows (Strabo, xiii. p. 593). He had made his first promises as he was going up into Asia (ἀναβάντα). ὕστερον δὲ μετὰ τὴν κατάλυσιν τῶν Περσῶν ἐπιστολὴν καταπέμψαι φιλάνθρωπον, ὑπισχνούμενον πόλιν τε ποιῆσαι μεγάλην, καὶ ἱερὸν ἐπισημότατον, καὶ ἀγῶνα ἀποδείξειν ἱερόν. These words plainly convey the impression, that Alexander was apologizing to the Ilians for the non-performance of his early promises. Of course the mere promises of the young king were little talked of in the midst of the mighty events crowding upon the world. But the Ilians remembered them, and pressed them on Lysimachus. Afterwards, through the biographers of Alexander, the scene of the sacrifice became well known. The coincidence of time between Lycurgus's speech and Alexander's promises has no historical importance. For Alexander's solemn sacrifice to the Ilian Athené was a traditional thing, which had been so often repeated by Greek generals that it would excite no special remark. This acknowledgment of Ilion as the real site may have been "political and uncritical," but it proves, if anything can prove it, that the general tradition was not that of Lycurgus's speech, but that which Xerxes and Mindarus, and probably many others, had sanctioned by solemn acts, and which no one, so far as we know, had hitherto denied.

There is but one more point which requires comment, and one on which there has hitherto been little disagreement. "About 190 B.C. Demetrius of Scepsis," says Mr. Jebb (*Hellenic Journal*, vol. ii. p. 26), "then a boy, remembered Ilium to have been in a state of decay. It was a neglected place; the houses had not even tiled roofs. There is not the slightest reason to doubt this," &c. He thinks the neglect of the Seleucids after Lysimachus's death, and the Gallic invasions, are sufficient to account for the great foundation of Lysimachus falling into this condition. Mr. Grote thought differently, and is so perplexed by the personal statement of Demetrius (which he does not question), that he proposes to re-arrange the text of Strabo, and apply to Alexandria Troas the large dimensions and grandeur which Lysimachus is there said to have given Ilion. But I think the facts which Professor Jebb has himself clearly stated point to a different conclusion. No doubt Ilion was, during most of the historical period, very insignificant, but this point, on which he frequently insists, is only of moment to those who are playing Demetrius's part. However, two facts from the third century B.C., and from the latter part of it, show that, having once become a city, it maintained some position. About 228 B.C. some of Attalus's mercenary Gauls besieged Ilion, but were beaten off with the aid of 4,000 men from Alexandria. This shows that it was not only inhabited, but a garrison town with defences. An inscription found at Hissarlik, referred to the same time, possibly as late as the end of the third century, shows Ilion to have been *the head of a federal league of surrounding Greek towns* (Jebb, *op. cit.* p. 24). About 189 B.C. the Roman favours begin. I ask, is it likely that the head of a league of towns, which resisted a siege in 228 B.C., should have been dismantled and decayed between that date and 190 B.C.?* To me it seems very improbable indeed, and I cannot but suspect that Demetrius, when speaking of the great favours of the Romans, and the rapid rise of the town, drew somewhat on his imagination to describe the miserable place which they had chosen to honour.

My estimate of Demetrius therefore leads me to suspect strongly this personal statement of his recollections, and to doubt whether Ilion ever fell away into this condition at the close of the 3rd century B.C. The other escape from the difficulty, Mr. Grote's, does not seem to me so easy to adopt. But here I admit that the ground is uncertain, and that we are dealing with conjectures.

It remains for me to sum up briefly the conclusions which I maintain in accordance with Dr. Schliemann's text and the Appendix on the subject :—

1. The belief that Troy was completely destroyed, though very general, especially after the representations of the tragic poets, was not the whole of the Trojan legend. There were also

---

* Mr. Jebb (p. 216) now feels the effect of his former statement, which he did not expect to be quoted in this connection, and says " the league included only the petty towns of a portion of the Troad. Why should not a decayed town have still been the chief of such a district?" Because we have evidence that it resisted, about this time, an attack from a Gallic force large enough to draw 4000 men from Alexandria as a succour to Ilion. In the face of this statement he actually quotes as relevant the notice of Hegesianax, that in 278 B.C. Ilion was unfortified! What on earth has this to say to the question whether the Ilion of 228 B.C., which was certainly of some importance and fortified, could have decayed before 190 B.C.?

traditions of the partial survival of Troy, owing to the existence of a Greek party within the city.

2. The belief that the site had henceforth remained desolate was no part of the legend, and was not a necessary consequence even to those who held that the destruction had been complete.

3. The belief that Troy had survived under the Aeneadae was distinctly suggested by the Iliad, was therefore widely disseminated, and was stated as a generally received opinion even by Strabo.

4. The claim of the historical Ilion to occupy the site of the Homeric Troy, is not known to have been impugned by any writer before Demetrius (about 160 B.C.) except the orator Lycurgus, whose statement on this subject is outweighed by the rest of our evidence.

5. This claim is supported in ancient times by the solemn sacrifices offered to the Ilian Athené by Xerxes (480 B.C.), Mindarus, Alexander the Great, and other generals, *as well as from the statements and implications of Herodotus, Theophrastus, Dikaearchus,** &c.

6. More especially Hellanicus, an ancient and respectable authority, whom the critical Dionysius quotes as of peculiar weight, reported the local evidence of the Ilians, which depended not only on old shrines and relics, but on ancient customs founded upon the undoubted belief in the historical succession of Ilion from legendary Troy.

7. There is some evidence that Demetrius was personally hostile to the Ilian claim (1) on account of the sudden rise of Ilion and its offensive conduct towards the other towns of the Troad, backed up by royal favours from Lysimachus onward. He was certainly hostile (2) because the claim of Scepsis to Aeneas as its founder, which he advocated, would have been destroyed.

8. There is no evidence of the historical re-foundation of Ilion, the random guess of Demetrius that it occurred in Lydian days being merely the latest date to which he ventured to assign it. For it was old and recognised in the days of Xerxes.

---

* "What the soldier said," Mr. Jebb thinks no good evidence. Nor did I depend upon it. In this case it is not only what the soldiers said, but what those around them believed, and what the historians who report their acts sanction. Herodotus does not express one word of doubt about the correctness of Xerxes' belief as to the site of the temple of the Ilian Athené. Moreover there would have been no point in the sacrifice, or in Herodotus's mention of it, if the Greeks in Xerxes' army had not generally acquiesced in it.

9. The discoveries of Dr. Schliemann "may be said to clinch the proof of the point for which I am now contending," and render it certain that the Ilion of history was on the ancient site, and the inheritor of the traditions of many antecedent centuries.

When reviewing poor Brentano's tract in the *Academy*, I had said something, in a bantering way, about the idleness of criticizing either Hellanicus or Demetrius, because the works of both were lost, and that I conceived it the occupation of pedants to quarrel over such a topic. To this charge I am of course myself liable, and am guilty of having amused myself with these vanities. But there is a sort of logical interest in overthrowing an *a priori* argument, resting on merely speculative grounds, by setting up an opposing case of the same kind. I think I can show a better case for Hellanicus being trustworthy, and Demetrius untrustworthy, than Mr. Jebb can for the reverse, *and from the same texts*, but I cannot hope to have convinced him. And this is *because* we have not sufficient evidence to overcome stubborn opposition. Mr. Jebb says we have "abundant evidence" as to their general credibility, as reported by others, and that, he thinks, is quite sufficient. He adds that "the ancient citations of Hellanicus fill twenty-four large pages in Müller's work." Perhaps he hardly expected his readers would verify the statement, or question its meaning. Do *citations* mean quotations from the text of Hellanicus, or mere reports of his opinions? Do twenty-four *large pages* mean pages of large size, or pages containing much type? As to the former, I can tell the reader that *not ten lines in the whole twenty-four pages are verbatim quotations*. The rest is vague reference or report of facts mentioned by the author. I can also tell the reader that *nearly one-third of the twenty-four pages is Latin translation* of the Greek, and that *more than half the rest is either blank, or Latin explanation* of the authors quoted, and perhaps containing obscure references to Hellanicus. This is the "abundant evidence" on Hellanicus. The "abundant evidence" for Demetrius is still more grotesque. Not a word as to how many lines or words by him are extant. *But "a German has actually written a special treatise on Demetrius!"* Pending a closer account of this treatise, I ask whether it is not notorious, that many German philologists would rather write a treatise on an author irretrievably lost, than on an author now extant? But to state such a fact as evidence that we know a great deal about Demetrius—!

Yet in spite of all these difficulties, the Professor tells us [p. 203] that his views as to the ancient disbelief in the Ilian claim " have received the general assent of scholars whose attention has been directed to the point."

In the last number of the *Journal* (vol. iv. No. 1, p. 155) he also says: "Intelligent antiquity decisively rejected—as I have proved in this *Journal*—the Homeric pretensions of the historic Ilium."

I cannot conclude without a direct answer to such assertions. As to the former: among the host of scholars who have asserted, and do assert, that the Ilian claim was admitted by all antiquity up to Demetrius's date, I pick out two greater authorities than any Mr. Jebb could cite, Grote in the last generation, and Friedländer in this. Both of them decided the case before the tremendous corroboration of their decision by Dr. Schliemann's discoveries. They decided it against Mr. Jebb. Friedländer is still able to weigh any new evidence which has accrued. His last edition, containing a careful reconsideration of the debate, adheres strongly to his former view, that not even after the publication of the new theory by Demetrius and Strabo, did it receive any support from public opinion.

As to the second assertion, I have only to add that the "intelligent antiquity" of Mr. Jebb *includes:* Demetrius of Scepsis, Strabo, some learned men and women at Alexandria, the orator Lycurgus, the poet Lucan. It *excludes:* the Greeks who accompanied and advised Xerxes; the Greeks of the time when the Locrian sacrifice was established; Herodotus, Hellanicus, the Greeks about Mindarus, Xenophon, the Greeks about Alexander the Great, the Diadochi, the Romans both before and after Strabo's time, Tacitus, etc. etc.

But we can hardly hope that arguments, however strong, will close this long and bitter controversy.

J. P. MAHAFFY.

APPENDIX VI.

On the Earliest Greek Settlement at Hissarlik.

OBSTALDEN, CANTON GLARUS, *September* 15, 1883.

MY DEAR FRIEND SCHLIEMANN,

You wish to receive my testimony on the character of the objects found in those strata of the citadel-hill of Hissarlik, which correspond to the third, fourth, fifth, and sixth cities according to your division. Although here on the Lake of Wallenstadt I am away from all literary aids, and from my own notes, yet, in answer to your English critics, I will gladly report from my recollection what I observed as an eye-witness of your excavations in March and April, 1879. I can do this with so much the greater confidence, as it was precisely to the earthenware in its chronological order that I devoted very particular attention.

What appeared to me an eminently safe starting-point for these considerations was the wall of wrought blocks, which in its long course is preserved in its original situation, and which you held at that time to be the wall of Lysimachus. Whether this explanation was right or wrong, at all events in either case alike this wall supplied a *fixed datum line*, and at the same time a *totally new architectural element which does not occur in the deeper strata*. I therefore repeatedly examined, with my own hands, those layers of *débris* on which this wall had been erected. Nowhere did I find in them any fragments of terra-cottas whatever, or any other objects, which could be claimed as Roman. Here, too, were equally absent those remains (of pottery), which are so abundant throughout the uppermost strata—the strata of Ilium Novum—on which there is a painted ornamentation, geometrical or of figures, or which by their peculiar form, such as small plates or jugs with an elaborate foot, bear a marked Greek character.

On the contrary, there were found immediately below the wall, but in a layer of very insignificant depth, numerous fragments of light-coloured yellowish-grey terra-cottas, painted with brown colour of lustrous appearance. For the most part this colouring formed horizontal bands or stripes with diffused borders, never sharply-defined lines or zones, which would have shown the clear imprint of a more highly developed artistic skill. They were indeed fragments of archaic vases, whose technical style, to be sure, reminded one of archaic-Hellenic vases, but as to which, in my opinion, it could by no means be shown with certainty that they were necessarily of Greek origin. There did not, however, appear to me any reason to hesitate in terming them provisionally archaic-Hellenic.

I did not observe similar fragments of terra-cotta in any one of the deeper strata of *débris*. It is true that there are found in most of the deeper strata vases and fragments of vases, which in their manufacture have evidently been washed or rubbed with water or a wet object (such as a large or small brush or a cloth) and so smoothed over; also vases or fragments of vases, in the fabrication of which the water had probably been mixed with a colouring substance, particularly with a ferruginous matter, which was either red or received a red colour in the baking process. But this red colour is altogether different from the lustrous brown of the above-mentioned archaic fragments; it neither forms stripes nor bands, but a uniform tint.

Here, however, it is to be remarked, that in not a few cases there may be observed on these vases also lustrous stripes, which sometimes appear rather darker, and which at first sight might be brought into connection with the lustrous brown stripes on the fragments in the upper stratum. But I have already proved, in my lectures before the Berlin Anthropological Society, and in my treatise on the ancient Trojan tombs and skulls, that we have here to do with a very particular technical process, namely a subsequent *polishing* of the vessel already made, which had been performed with hard objects, probably with special *polishing-stones*. This kind of polishing, however, is met with even in the deepest stratum of Hissarlik, and on the very ancient pottery found in Besika Tepeh (see *Ilios*, p. 668). Besides the lustrous stripes are commonly not horizontal, but vertical, sometimes also slanting, and frequently irregular, crossing each other, and so forth.

The use, therefore, of a colour, properly so called, especially of a darkish brown, which *without any polishing at all* becomes lustrous in the baking, and which on a lighter back-ground shows itself as the *most primitive form of a real painting, though of a painting still altogether undefined and nowhere developed into sharp-edged figures*,—the use, I say, of such a colour proper is therefore comparatively modern in the strata of Hissarlik, and is the characteristic only of the layer of *débris* which follows next below the wall of wrought blocks. If then these vase-fragments were considered to be archaic-Hellenic, it would follow that *the earliest traces of Hellenic culture were met with not far below the surface*. To attribute this stratum to the *Macedonian* time would be, in fact, to presuppose a very strange conception of the ceramic art of that late period of Hellenic culture. Even in Italy, which can be proved to have adopted the ceramic patterns current in Greece, such pottery brings us to that rather more than less prehistoric period, which has lately again been frequently designated as Pelasgian.

Seeing, then, that this highly characteristic archaic pottery is totally absent in the deeper strata of Hissarlik, we are at a loss to discover what in all the world is to be called Greek in them. With equal truth might many kinds of vases from Mexico and Yucatan, nay even from the river Amazon, be called Greek! Not even do the terra-cotta vases from Santorin, which I thoroughly examined in the French school at Athens on returning from the Troad, permit a more general comparison, not to say an identification. They show much more relation to ancient Hellenic pottery than can be recognized at Hissarlik, at least in one of the strata disputed by an English critic. These strata, up to the sixth city inclusive, are Trojan proper, or if the term be preferred, Minor-Asiatic;* that is to say, they have a pronounced local character, and they resemble each other more than they resemble any known Hellenic local pottery.

For several of these strata comparative archaeology offers valuable analogies. Thus, for instance, as I have repeatedly proved, the black pottery of the first city repeats itself—technical style as well as patterns—in the Swiss lake habitations and in north-Italian and south-German tombs; and in the same way analogies to the terra-cotta vases of the sixth city can be found, as you have proved, in sepulchres of central Italy, and I think also in the terramare of the Emilia. Whether from these analogies we can infer direct connections between the ancient Trojans and the peoples of the West, must be left to the decision of further

---

* *Kleinasiatisch*, corresponding to Professor Sayce's convenient term *Asianic*.

and very extensive studies; at all events it appears to me inadmissible to assume at once direct ethnological relations, where numerous intermediate links may perhaps have to be inserted. For in such investigations we cannot limit ourselves to the pottery exclusively; but the totality of the objects discovered, particularly those of stone and metal, must be taken into consideration. In this respect, I believe I may venture to say that up to the present time *no place in Europe is known, which could be put in direct connection with any one of the six lower cities of Hissarlik.* Certainly if we assume the pottery with brown stripes to be Hellenic, and thus subject to European influence, this influence appears to have been altogether new and foreign, and to have come in suddenly at a comparatively late time.

But within the strata of *débris* of the six lower cities, which, according to my opinion, belong to an Asiatic local culture, and which for this reason I may designate as Trojan, there are striking differences, inasmuch as characteristic forms disappear and others come forward. Thus the black ware of the first city disappears, and thus also appear the vases of the sixth city, of a peculiar style, which you call Lydian. As I understand you, you yourself do not attach to this name any decisive value; you merely intend thereby a comprehensive expression of the fact, that a new and altered character of ceramic style presents itself in the sixth city; and I perfectly agree with you, that this revolution was not brought in by European influence. It appears to me beyond doubt, that the inhabitants of all the six lower cities were not only Asiatics, but also that they had not been subject to the influence of specific Greek culture. On the other hand, in my opinion, it is evident that the above-mentioned changes were not accomplished from within, nor were they the result of spontaneous progress in the taste or the technic skill of the Trojans, but that they were brought in by exterior influences. Several of these influences, such as the Egyptian, may have been introduced through the medium of navigators; others, and probably the larger number, seem to me referable to neighbours in Asia Minor. But, with regard to this, it can only be ascertained by a careful study of each particular layer, whether the change of style was produced by a completely new colonization of the citadel-hill, or only by the introduction of new patterns and by trade. Probably both had a share in the result; namely, the new colonization, when the second city was founded, the progressive variation of taste and technic skill in the subsequent cities.

With regard, however, to the censures of your critics, these considerations are of secondary interest. For the decision of the disputed question, the essential point is to determine the limit where the influence of Hellenic culture can first be recognized ; and that not an arbitrarily assumed Hellenic influence, answering perchance to what some now designate as "common Aryan," but an Hellenic influence of a distinct archaeological character, which can be connected with objects found at definite localities in Greece. As the result of what I have above stated, this limit lies very near the surface in the citadel-hill ; and, even if the vases with brown stripes be still allowed to be archaic Hellenic, the limit lies close under the foundation of the wall of wrought blocks. Immediately below this limit follow the strata, all of which I should most decidedly call *prehistoric*, but which, however, in my opinion, belong to different populations. The brachycephalic skulls, found hitherto only in the lowermost city, have their nearest analogues in those of the Armenians ; the dolichocephalous skulls of the burnt city cannot be brought into connection with them.

I trust these short remarks may answer to what you, my dear friend, expect from me. At all events they are the expression of a frank and perfectly independent and unprejudiced observation on the spot.

RUDOLF VIRCHOW.

APPENDIX VII.

METEOROLOGICAL OBSERVATIONS AT HISSARLIK FROM APRIL 22 TILL JULY 21, 1882.

(1.) For the *Barometer*, the scale is given in *millimètres*, which are converted into English inches approximately by multiplying by ·04 (more exactly ·03937). Thus 759 signifies about 31·36 inches.

(2.) For the *Thermometer*, the scale for converting + degrees of Celsius into those of Fahrenheit has been given on p. 15.

	Barometer.	Thermometer, Celsius.		Barometer.	Thermometer, Celsius.
April 22.			*April* 29.		
7¾ a.m. north storm	759	11	4.30 a.m. strong south wind	754	17
2¼ p.m. violent north storm	760	13	8 p.m. light south wind	755	15
7¼ p.m. violent north storm	759	15	*April* 30.		
April 23.			5.5 a.m. light south wind	754	11
5¾ a.m. violent north storm	758½	8½	12 noon, strong north wind	757	19
April 24.			*May* 1.		
			4.45 a.m. light east wind	760	11½
4 a.m. violent north storm	760½	20	12 noon, strong north wind	762	20
7¾ p.m. light north wind	760½	16	8.5 p.m. light north wind	765	15
April 25.			*May* 2.		
4.37 a.m. light north wind	758½	5	4.50 a.m. light north wind	764¼	10
1.5 p.m. strong west wind	761¼	22¼	12.35 noon, light north wind	766½	24
7.30 p.m. strong west wind	759	15	9.7 p.m. light east wind	764	15
April 26.			*May* 3.		
			4.25 a.m. light north wind	762	11
4.35 a.m. light south wind	756	15	4.12 p.m. strong north wind	763½	25
9.40 p.m. light south wind	757	14	9.25 p.m. light north wind	763	16
April 27.			*May* 4.		
4.45 a.m. light south wind	756½	13	4.5 a.m. light south wind	762	13
11.40 a.m. strong south wind	759	20	2 p.m. light south wind	763	27
8.30 p.m. light south wind	759	14	9 p.m. light north wind	761½	18
April 28.			*May* 5.		
4 a.m. light south wind	758	13	4.45 a.m. strong north wind	761	11
10 p.m. strong south wind with rain	756½	17	11.30 a.m. strong north wind	763	20
			8.45 p.m. light north wind	762½	15

	Barometer.	Thermometer, Celsius.		Barometer.	Thermometer, Celsius.
May 6.			*May* 16.		
4.23 a.m. calm	761	11	3.45 a.m. light south wind .	759	15
9.15 p.m. light north wind .	762	17	3.8 p.m. strong south wind .	762½	22
			10 p.m. south storm . . .	762	17
May 7.			*May* 17.		
4.50 a.m. light north wind .	762	12			
4 p.m. strong north wind . .	762½	21	4.15 a.m. light south wind .	760	16
9.40 p.m. light north wind .	762	15	9.30 p.m. light south wind .	758½	16
May 8.			*May* 18.		
4 a.m. calm.	761½	9	4.8 a.m. light north wind. .	756	11½
12 noon, strong north wind .	762½	23	2.50 p.m. strong west wind .	757	22½
9.25 p.m. light north wind .	765½	16½	8.30 p.m. light west wind .	756	17½
May 9.			*May* 19.		
4.15 a.m. light north wind .	759	11	3.50 a.m. light west wind .	755½	14
9.45 p.m. calm . .	759½	15	2.40 p.m. strong west wind .	758	20
			9.20 p.m. light west wind .	756	13½
May 10.			*May* 20.		
4.10 a.m. calm	758	13			
3 p.m. light south wind . .	760	26	5.25 a.m. light west wind .	757	14
8.50 p.m. light north wind .	758	16½	2.27 p.m. strong west wind .	759	21
			9.23 p.m. light east wind. .	758	16
May 11.			*May* 21.		
3.50 a.m. light north wind .	755½	15	4.15 a.m. light north wind .	756½	9
1.49 p.m. north storm . .	757	21	3.18 p.m. light west wind .	756	19
8.15 p.m. violent north storm	758	12	9.40 p.m. north storm . .	754	19
May 12.			*May* 22.		
5.45 a.m. violent north storm with rain	759½	7	3.52 a.m. north wind . .	752½	10
12 noon, violent north storm, clear sky	760¼	10	2.4 p.m. north storm . .	752½	15
			8.45 p.m. north storm . .	753½	12½
8.37 p.m. violent north storm, clear sky	763	10	*May* 23.		
			4.40 a.m. north storm. . .	753½	12
May 13.			12 noon, north storm . .	755½	20
3.59 a.m. light north wind .	762	9	9.45 p.m. north storm . .	753	15
12 noon, strong north wind .	763	16			
9.15 p.m. light north wind .	762	11	*May* 24.		
			4 a.m. north wind	758	11
May 14.			2.30 p.m. north wind . . .	761	21
4.55 a.m. calm	758	5	9.45 p.m. light north wind .	762	15
3.52 p.m. light south-west wind	760	21			
9 p.m. light south-west wind .	759	17	*May* 25.		
			3.25 a.m. calm	761	9
May 15.			11.10 a.m. light west wind .	764	24
4 a.m. light south wind . .	756½	9	10.30 p.m. calm.	762	16
9.23 p.m. light south wind .	760	16½			

	Barometer.	Thermometer. Celsius.		Barometer.	Thermometer. Celsius.
May 26.			*June* 6.		
3.40 a.m. calm	762	13	4.29 a.m. calm	763	14
1.23 p.m. strong north wind .	755	25	10.55 a.m. light west wind .	765	26
10.50 p.m. calm	755	19	9.20 p.m. light west wind .	762	20
May 27.			*June* 7.		
3.45 a.m. light north wind .	760	15	3.40 a.m. light south wind .	761	14
1.17 p.m. strong north wind .	765	25	9.30 p.m. calm . . . : .	761½	14
9.30 p.m. light north wind .	766	13			
May 28.			*June* 8.		
4.45 a.m. strong north wind .	765	14	5.57 a.m. calm	760	15
9.30 p.m. light north wind .	715	17	11.30 a.m. light north wind .	762½	25½
May 29.			9.30 p.m. calm	762½	21
4.25 a.m. light north wind .	764	14	*June* 9.		
1.6 p.m. north storm . . .	765	26	4.45 a.m. calm	761	16½
9.10 p.m. light north wind .	764¼	17	9.45 p.m. light west wind .	759	20
May 30.			*June* 10.		
3.29 a.m. light north wind .	763	16	4 a.m. strong west wind .	758	20
2.45 p.m. north storm . .	763	20½	12.50 noon, strong west wind .	761	25
10.51 p.m. north storm . .	762½	18	10.15 p.m. calm	761	21
May 31.			*June* 11.		
4 a.m. violent north storm .	761¼	15	5.36 a.m. calm	761	19
1.40 p.m. strong north wind .	761	26	12.38 noon, south-west wind .	763½	30
10 p.m. strong north wind .	760½	20	10 p.m. calm	760	21
June 1.			*June* 12.		
3.37 a.m. light north wind .	760	14	3.50 a.m. calm	756	17
1 p.m. light west wind . .	761	28½	2.37 p.m. west wind . . .	760	30
9.45 p.m. calm	761	22	10.8 p.m. north storm . .	761	23
June 2.			*June* 13.		
2.54 a.m. light south wind .	759½	17½	3.55 a.m. strong north storm .	761¼	17
1.20 p.m. strong north wind .	762	25	10 p.m. light north wind .	760¼	20
10 p.m. strong north wind .	762	20			
June 3.			*June* 14.		
3.50 a.m. light north wind .	762½	16	4.30 a.m. calm	758	18
12.5 noon, strong north wind	764	21	12 noon, west wind . . .	760	21
9.25 p.m. calm	763½	15	10 p.m. calm	755	22
June 4.			*June* 15.		
5 a.m. north wind	764	11	5 a.m. most violent north storm	755½	16½
12.20 noon, strong north wind	765	20	10 p.m. calm	760	16
9.57 p.m. calm	764	13			
June 5.			*June* 16.		
4 a.m. light west wind . .	764	9	4.45 a.m. calm	761	15
12 noon, light west wind . .	767	25	3 p.m. strong west wind . .	761½	25
11.5 p.m. light north wind .	765	17	9.55 p.m. calm	760	18

WEATHER AT HISSARLIK. [APP. VII.

	Barometer.	Thermometer, Celsius.		Barometer.	Thermometer, Celsius.
June 17.			**June 28.**		
4.15 a.m. calm	757½	15	4.20 a.m. strong north wind	765¼	17
12.30 noon, violent north wind	759	25	12.10 noon, strong north wind	766½	27¼
9 p.m. calm	759	20	10.5 p.m. light north wind	765	22½
June 18.			**June 29.**		
4 a.m. north storm	759	20	4.50 a.m. light north wind	763	18
1 p.m. most violent north storm	760	14	11.40 a.m. strong north wind	763½	27
10 p.m. calm	761	15	10 p.m. calm	762½	22½
June 19.			**June 30.**		
4.10 a.m. strong north wind	762	19	4.18 a.m. strong north wind	761¼	17
9 p.m. light north wind	762	20	9.50 p.m. light north wind	762	24
June 20.					
6.45 a.m. light south wind	761½	16	**July 1.**		
12.45 noon, light south wind	763½	26	4.25 a.m. light north wind	760	19
10 p.m. calm	762½	19	*at Iné (in the shade).*		
June 21.			2.35 p.m. strong north wind	760	34
2.45 a.m. calm	761½	15	*at Beiramich.*		
2 p.m. north wind	761¼	27			
7 p.m. north wind	763½	22	8.5 p.m. calm	754	29
June 22.			**July 2.**		
6 a.m. light north wind	765	20	*on the bank of the Scamander*		
12.30 noon, strong north wind	764	29	*at the foot of Kurshunlu Tepeh.*		
9 p.m. calm	763½	22	8.15 a.m. calm	751½	19
June 23.			*in our quarters under the trees*		
4.15 a.m. calm	761¼	18½	*of Oba Kioi at the foot of*		
12 noon, strong north wind	763	29½	*Kurshunlu Tepeh.*		
9.45 p.m. calm	760	22½	9.35 a.m. calm	752	36
June 24.			*at Oba Kioi.*		
4.20 a.m. strong north wind	759	18	10.40 a.m. calm	746	32
1 p.m. strong north wind	761	36½	*on the top of Kurshunlu Tepeh.*		
9.30 p.m. light north wind	761	31	2.35 p.m. strong west wind	732½	26
June 25.			*in our quarters as above.*		
5 a.m. light north wind	760½	16	8.10 p.m. calm	743½	26½
9.20 p.m. light north wind	762½	20½			
June 26.			**July 3.**		
4.20 a.m. light north wind	762	16	3.45 a.m. calm	743½	16
2.35 p.m. north storm	761	20	*highest point of the Acropolis of*		
9.25 p.m. light north wind	765	20	*Cebrené.*		
June 27.			10.30 a.m. strong west wind	721	26
3.40 a.m. light north wind	765	16	*lower city of Cebrené.*		
12.45 noon, strong north wind	766½	26	1.40 p.m. strong west wind	716½	27
9.15 p.m. light north wind	767	21	7.45 p.m. calm	719	24

WEATHER AT HISSARLIK

	Barometer.	Thermometer, Celsius.		Barometer.	Thermometer, Celsius.
July 4.			*July 13.*		
lower city of Cebrené.			3.50 a.m. strong north wind	753	18
4 a.m. light north wind	718½	25	12.35 noon, strong south wind	753½	30
at Turkmanli Kïoï.			9 p.m. calm	752½	24
6.30 a.m. calm	753	23	*July 14.*		
halting-place near Iné.			4 a.m. calm	753	21
3 p.m. calm	760	38	3.30 p.m. north storm	755½	26
At Hissarlik.			9 p.m. light north wind	756	22
July 5.			*July 15.*		
12.45 noon, strong west wind	758½	30	4 a.m. calm	755½	16
9.8 p.m. strong north wind	759	20	12 noon, light north wind	757	27
			9.30 p.m. calm	757½	20½
July 6.					
4.30 a.m. strong north wind	760½	16	*July 16.*		
1.35 p.m. strong north wind	762	36	4.30 a.m. calm	757½	19
9.48 p.m. light north wind	761¾	21	1 p.m. west wind	760½	30
July 7.			8.45 p.m. calm	759½	24
3.45 a.m. calm	760¾	16	*July 17.*		
2.40 p.m. north storm	763	30			
9.40 p.m. light north wind	762½	23	4.17 a.m. calm	759	22
			11.30 a.m. west wind	761¼	30¼
July 8.			9.30 p.m. calm	759	24
3.55 a.m. calm	762	20			
1 p.m. light north wind	761	38	*July 18.*		
9.30 p.m. calm	762½	25	3.30 a.m. calm	757½	20
July 9.			12.50 noon, strong north wind	758¼	33
3.47 a.m. light north wind	761	22	8.10 p.m. strong north wind	758¼	26
11.35 a.m. violent north storm	762	31	*July 19.*		
9.30 p.m. light north-east wind	760	26	6.20 a.m. north-east storm	759	23
July 10.			12.20 noon, north-east storm	760	29
4.15 a.m. light north-east wind	758	22	8.45 p.m. north-east storm	758½	24
1.30 p.m. strong north wind	758	34			
9 p.m. calm	756	27	*July 20.*		
July 11.			4.20 a.m. strong north-east wind	758	28
3.20 a.m. calm	752¾	22	12 noon, north storm	758	28
12.30 noon, north-east storm	755¼	34	8 p.m. north wind	758	26
9 p.m. north-east storm	756	27			
July 12.			*July 21.*		
3.30 a.m. north-east storm	757½	22	6.30 a.m. north storm	757½	25
2 p.m. most violent north-east storm	757	30	12 noon, north storm	758	30
9.30 p.m. north-east wind	755½	22½	9 p.m. light north wind	758	26

As will be seen by these tables, we had rain only twice in three months at Hissarlik.

INDEX.

NOTE.—Besides the usual abbreviations, such as Pr. for Promontory, R. for River, &c. ; c. 1, c. 2, &c., stand for the 1st city, 2nd city, &c., *on Hissarlik;* Il. for the Greek and Roman Ilium ; tum. for tumulus.

Names of Places generally refer to the *prehistoric antiquities* found there ; *Museums* to the like objects preserved in them.

Names of Persons generally imply that they are cited as authorities, or their works quoted.

SMALL CAPITALS indicate references to other articles.

To avoid repetition of the word *Acropolis,* all the buildings described belong to the strata on the hill, unless otherwise specified.

The whole Index (like the work itself) must be regarded as supplemental to that of the Author's *Ilios.*

ABRAHAM. | ACROPOLIS.

A.

Abraham; money transactions with Abimelech and the Hittites, 302.
Acanthus-leaf, of capital, 213
Achaeium, Talian Kioi, 311, 312, 342.
Achates, 254.
Achilles; site of combat with Hector, 65 ; helmet crest, 107 ; human sacrifices, 162 ; tent, 284 ; shield, 35, 332.
Achilles, tumulus of, on C. Sigeum ; unanimous tradition for, 17, 27, 242, 243, 343, 344 ; within the ancient Achilleum (*q. v.*), *ib.;* called *Thiol* and *Cuvin, ib.;* conspicuous fr. the sea, as in Homer, 243-4, 250 ; leave obtained, 244 ; work begun, 245 ; dimensions, *ib.;* pretended exploration by a Jew for Count Choiseul-Gouffier, 245 ; his false statements, 246-7 ; succession of strata in shafts, 246 ; no trace of burial, 247 (*see* CENOTAPHS) ; a very ancient arrowhead (*q. v.*) of bronze, *ib.;* archaic Greek wheel-made pottery (*q. v.*), referable to 9th cent. B.C. ; besides some older on the ground, and some later, 248-250 ; one whorl, 250.
Achilleum (Koum Kaleh), on C. Sigeum ; site strewn with architectural fragments and pottery, 243 ; not extant in Pliny's time, 344.
Acropolis of Athens. (*See* ATHENS.)
—— of Second City ; plan of (VII. at end of work), 14 ; site levelled for, and extended to the S. and E., 53, 89, 181 ; foundations of its six great edifices (*q. v.*), 53, 62 ; walls and towers (*q. v.*), 54 ; its three gates (*q. v.*), 62 ; the royal and sacred quarter of Troy, 99. (*See* SECOND CITY ; PERGAMOS ; TROY.)
—— of Ilium, Hellenic well in, 19 ; temples (*q. v.*), 196, f. (*See* ILIUM.)
—— (others in Troad ; *see* arts.) ; Alex. Troas, 341 ; Assos, 316-7 ; Cebrené, 275 ; Eski-Hissarlik, 269 ; Gergis, on Bali Dagh, 264.

Acts of the Apostles, 319.
Ada, scala of, 321.
Adana (cf. ATENA), in Cilicia, 4.
Adramyt Tsai, R., 329.
Adramyttium, ancient; founded by Athenians or Lydians, 328, 329; a flourishing port and *conventus juridicus, ib.;* history, *ib.;* buried under the alluvia, *ib.;* anciently called Pedasus, *ib.;* modern, 303; a flourishing seaport, 328; fountains, *ib.;* rivers bridged with stone steps, 328-9; coins, 339.
—— Gulf of, 316, 319, 333, 347; extent, 320; no port but Assos, nor towns on shore, for fear of pirates; landing-places called *scalas*, 321.
Adultery; punished with death by a king of Tenedos, 224.
Aeanteum, city, at the old tomb of Ajax, 344.
Aegean Sea; 277, 316, 333, 344.
Aegis; tassels of, of gold wire, 107.
Aeneas, 254, his dominion, DARDANIA, cap. DARDANIÉ aft. SCEPSIS, 274, 362; his account of the origin of Troy, 291; tradition of his rule at Troy discussed, 362-3.
Aeolian colonization of Ilium; its date discussed, 237, *Pref.* xv.
Aeschylus; 67, 86.
Agamemnon; cenotaph in Egypt, 253; altar on C. Lectum, 315.
Agil; a poisonous herb on the upper pastures of Ida, 330.
Agora; held by Hector, 283; none among the Cyclops, 290, 331.
Ahrens, on the Cypriote dialect, 159.
Aivali, I., 321.
Ajax; his tumulus at C. Rhoeteum, 262, 343; built by Hadrian, 344; the older sepulchre, *ib.*
A. K.; 'Schliemann's Ilios,' 287.
Akademie der Wissenschaften, 42.
Akerit (Carians), in Egypt. records, 3.
Alampsa; tragical incident at, 311.
Alba Longa, necropolis of, 95.
Albano, necropolis of; hut-urns, 40, 194 (cf. MARINO); resemblance of pottery to the Lydian (c. 6), 238.
Alcaeus, 323.

Alcandra, wife of Polybus, king of Egypt; her gifts to Helen, 296, 298.
Ale, pale, medicinal value of, 6.
Aleisium (or -*us*), 282.
Alexander the Great, 50, 196; descent from Neoptolemus, 290; visit to Ilium; favours to the city, 228, 290; promises only, 370 (cf. ILIUM); political condition of his empire, 228, 319, 342; coin of, 323.
Alexandria Troas, 311; visited (1881), 341; paved road, lined with tombs, *ib.;* walls, like those of Assos, &c., 317, 341 (*see* MASONRY); six miles in circuit, with towers, *ib.;* space covered with ruins, *ib.;* the *Bal Serai* (bath and gymnasium) and other edifices, 342; port and basins, *ib.;* site called *Sigia*, prob. anc. city, *ib.;* history, *ib.;* member of the Ilian union (*q. v.*) of cities, 228; people of Cebrené and Hamaxitus removed, 276, 341; *débris* insignificant, 342; cannon-balls from its columns, *ib.;* excavations of doubtful advantage, 347; coins, 221-3, 339.
Alexandrian, anonymous, on Metrology, 114.
Altar; within S.E. gate of c. 3, 178; signs of exposure to great heat, and inference, 180; of the twelve gods on C. Lectum, 315; of Zeus on Ida, 334; slab discovered, 336.
Altshulduren Tsai, R., 331.
Alyattes; sources of his wealth, 50.
Amber Spindle-Whorls, in Syria, 296.
America, aboriginal; use of ⊔ in, 122, 123.
—— Archaeological Institute of; explorations at Assos, 173, 315, 347.
American Journal of Science, 181.
Amphikypellon (δέπας ἀμφικύπελλον, Hom.); abundant in c. 2-5, and in the Lydian pottery (c. 6), 153; further proofs of its identity, *ib.;* Prof. Maehly on, *ib.;* Prof. Helbig on, 155, f.; Homeric use, 156; various explanations, *ib.;* Dr. Schliemann's approved, 157; Aristotle's discussed, *ib.;* arguments against the double cylindrical vessel, *ib.;*

mode of use at banquets, 158, 160 ;
rationale of the double cups, *ib.;*
synonym of κύπελλον in Homer, also
in Crete and Cyprus ; Homeric testimonies, *ib.;* monumental evidence
at Troy, Mycenae, Camirus, Etruria,
&c., 160 ; its later use in worship,
ib.; attribute of Bacchus, &c., *ib.;*
synonyms, *ib.;* etymology of κύπελλον and ἀμφικύπελλον, 161, 163, f. ;
Homer's use of κύπελλον, 161 ; the
δ. d. of Ulysses, 161 ; light on Homeric society, 161, f. ; the ancestor
of the κάνθαρος and κύλιξ, 163 ; very
large examples (c. 2), 164, 165 ;
nearly always wheel-made, 165.
Analyses of Trojan and Orchomenian
bronze, 104-5.
Anchises, race of ; the Caesars called,
in an Ilian inscr., 232.
Andalusia; caverns of, 36, 39, 42.
Andou; whorls in the Pelew Is., 40.
Andrée, R., ' Ethnographische Parallc-
len u. Vergleiche,' 40, 121, 326.
Andromache; her beauty, 162 ; m. to
Helenus ; queen of Chaonia ; raises
a cenotaph to Hector, 253 ; daughter
of Eëtion of Thebé, 326.
Angelucci, Mr., 111.
Anglo-Saxons; had no swords, armed
with stone-weapons at Hastings, 96.
Anicetus; quoted, 156.
Animal Vases; (c. 2), 130 ; parallels,
131-2 ; others, 139-141 ; still frequent in the Troad, 141.
Animals, rude, on whorls, petroglyphs,
and urns, 121. (Cf. WEIGHTS.)
—— domestic, remains of in c. 1 (*see*
the arts.) ; the *horse, cattle, sheep,
goat, swine, dog;* i e. all usual
among the Aryans, 349 ; *beef* and
pork most used for food, 350.
—— wild, remains of in c. 1 ; only
wild boar and deer ; the people not
dependent on hunting for food, 349.
'*Annals of the Archaeological Institute
of Athens,*' 215.
Antae. (*See* PARASTADES.)
Antandrus (Devrent), 322-3, 329 ;
inscr. of, 323 ; anciently called Edonis and Kimmeris, *ib.;* the people

Leleges, Pelasgians, or Aeolians, *ib.;*
inhabited till Middle Ages, *ib.*
Antenor; saved at Troy through his
feud with Priam, 365.
Anthologia Palatina, 256.
Anthropologische Gesellschaft, 42, 48.
Antigonia; name of Alex. Troas, 342.
Antigonus, King ; his favours to
Ilium, attested by an inscr., 228,
229 ; founds Antigonia (Alex. Troas),
and removes Cebrenians and Ha-
maxitans thither, 276, 341, 342.
Antilochus, tumulus of, at C. Sigeum ;
now first discovered, 17, 242, 243,
344 ; imperfect exploration only al-
lowed, 273 ; same pottery (*q. v.*) as
in tum. of Ach. and Patroclus, *ib.;*
the site confirmed from Strabo, 254.
Antiochus III.; Roman war with,
328 ; gold equestrian statue at Si-
geum, 344.
Antiphon; quoted, 101.
Antiquities found ; division of with
Turkish government, 6 ; objects
parallel to the Trojan : see names
of places and Museums.
Antonia, niece of Augustus and wife of
Drusus, on an Ilian inscr., 232.
Antonines; inscr. of their time, 234.
Apelleies; on an Ilian inscr., 227.
Aphrodité; temple on C. Pyrrha, 320 ;
Livia called, on an Ilian coin, 232.
Apion, ' Gloss. Hom.,' quoted, 83.
Apis, king of Peloponnesus ; myth of
his migration to and worship in
Egypt, discussed, 292 ; true history
of the transport of Apis-worship
from Egypt to Greece, *ib.*
Apollo, beautiful metope of, 18, 202 ;
great wall of Troy ascribed to, 61 ;
temples : at Cilla, 327 ; Thymbra,
345 (cf. TEMPLES) ; on coins of the
Troad, 221, 222, 276, 277, 329.
Apollo Smintheus; temple at Greek
Chrysa (Kulakli Kioi), excavated in
1866, 314 ; size of foundations, *ib.;*
his wooden statue by Scopas, *ib.;*
temple at the Homeric Chrysé, 318.
Apollodorus; the Palladium, 169, 300.
Apollonia; name of Assos ; argument
for identity with Chrysé, 318.

Aqueduct, Roman, of Ilium, from the Thymbrius, 225.
Arabia; gold from, 50.
Arablar Kioi, 316.
Aragonite; eggs of (c. 2), prob. votive offerings, 118, 171.
Arakli, scala of, 321 ; like *Heracleum*, but *that* was on opp. shore, *ib*.
Archaeanax, of Miletus, quoted, 63.
Architects employed in the excavations of 1882 ; 5, 52, 56, 184, 190, 196, 198, 202, 207, 224, 264 ; *Pref*. x.
Ares; his leaps between Callicoloné and Ilium, 281 ; his temple (perhaps) on the hill, 282 ; his huge size, *ib.*
Areté, 161.
Aristarchus, on the δέπας ἀμφ., 156.
Aristotle; his ἀμφικύπελλον discussed, 157-8 ; not the type of Homer's δέπ. ἀμφ., 158, 161 ; quoted, 224, 285 ; at Assos, 319.
Armenia, *Pref*. xi ; gold from, 50.
Armenians, *Pref*. xi ; in the Troad, 340.
Arrian; quoted, 243, 290.
Arrow-heads, bronze or copper (c. 2), 104 ; parallels, *ib.;* with barbs, *ib.;* fastened to shaft by string, as in Homer, 104 ; without barbs, with pins for fastening to shaft (tum. Ach.), 247 ; like Egyptian of 12th dyn., *ib.;* other parallels, *ib.;* barbed, of ivory (c. 2), 117.
Arrow-points of obsidian, made by Californian Indians, 174.
Art, plastic, spirit of, in Homer, 162 ; enthusiasm for physical beauty, *ib.;* types of divinities, 163 ; prototype of the Jove of Phidias, *ib.*
Artaki, G.; advance of the sea in, 283.
Arzruni, A., on jade and jadeite, 42.
Ascherson, Prof. P. ; 334.
Ascidia, 285.
Asi (*Assos, Issa*, or *Issus?*), in Egyptian records, 4.
Asia; 12 cities of, destroyed by an earthquake in time of Tiberius, 26.
Asia Minor; peoples of (about Troy), in Egyptian records, compared with Homer, 3 ; early coinage of, 114.
Assos (cf. ASSI), now Behram ; a Mysian city of the Troad, 4, 315, 316 ; temple in the acropolis, 315 ; American excavations, 173, 315, 347 ; slight *débris*, 315 ; medieval buildings, 317 ; ancient buildings and walls, *ib.;* a quarry for Constantinople, *ib.;* Nymphaeum, *ib.;* walls of lower city, best preserved of any Greek, *ib.;* peculiar masonry (*q. v.*), 271, 317, 341 ; Macedonian and Roman, *ib.;* more ancient walls, of polygonal stones, probably of 6th or 7th cent. B.C., 318 ; paved streets, *ib.;* splendid view, *ib.;* probably Homer's Chrysé, 318, 319 ; also called Apollonia, *ib.;* the only port on the N. shore of the G. of Adramyttium, *ib.;* a member of the Aeolic union, *ib.;* history, *ib.;* bishopric, *ib.;* its strong site, *ib.;* pun on the name, *ib.;* the stone called sarcophagus, 320 ; work of Dr. Joseph Thacher Clarke, *ib.;* inscriptions, *ib.* ; coins, 340.
Assyrian Antiquities; 47, 112, 115, 301.
Astragali (huckle-bones), in all the prehist. c. of Troy, 50 ; (c. 1), 51, 349 ; in the Caucasus, 51 ; (c. 3), 183-4.
Astyra, near Abydos ; gold mines, still visible in Strabo's time, 49 ; reopened by Mr. Calvert, 50.
——, on G. of Adramyttium, buried under alluvia, 328.
Atarneus; gold mine near, 50.
Atena (Adana?), in Egypt. records, 4.
Athenaeus; quoted, 145, 156, 285, 313.
——; on inscription of Antandrus, 323.
Athené; her aegis, 107 ; hall at Pergamum ; helmet covering 100 armies, 283 ; helmeted head in sculptures, 215 ; temples at Ilium, &c. (TEMPLES) ; on coins, with spear, distaff, and spindle, 220, f., 300 ; statue, with distaff and spindle, *ib.* (Cf. PALLADIUM and PALLAS.)
Athené Ergané; the tutelary deity of Troy ; whorls votive offerings to, 106, 300 ; *Pref*. xviii.
Athens; prehist. antiq. of, 39, 44, 136.
'*Athi;* the great goddess of Carchemish, derived from Babylon, probably the original of the Trojan Até and Athené, *Pref*. xviii ; type of the

Trojan idols and owl-vases, and on the cylinders, &c., of Chaldea, Asia Minor, Cyprus, and Mycenae; her image on Sipylus, xviii–xx.
Athos, Mt., distant views of its pyramid, 277, 331, 333; height, 331.
Atshikur, R., 331, 332.
Attalus III., King of Pergamus, 319.
Aufidius, dedicator of a statue, 236.
Augustus, Emp., 229; on Ilian coin and inscription, 220, 232.
Aulé; vestibule of Paris's palace, 86.
Aurelius, M. (on coin), 220.
Auvernier; lake-dwellings of, 110, 171.
Avjilar, village, 323, 329; inscription of Antandrus at, 323, 324; coins, Greek, Roman, and Byz. bought at, 323; inscription and sculpture, 324; Lesbian Greeks at, *ib.;* name corrupted from Evjilar ' hunter,' 325.
Awls, of bone; (c. 1), 50; (c. 3), 184; (c. 4), 188.
Axe, double, of Tenedos, 223, 339.
Axes, stone (cf. BATTLE-AXES); (c. 1), diorite and jade, 41; Fischer on, *ib.* (cf. JADE); Brentano's blunder, *ib. n.;* blunt axe-like implements, 42; parallels, *ib.;* partial perforation and fastening to handle, 43; polished and perforated, 46; (c. 2), polished, of diorite, 119, 172; combined with hammer, partially perforated, 119; (c. 3), 184; (c. 4), 188; double-edged, of green gabbro rock (c. 2), 172; diorite (tum. Protes.), 259.
Aztulan (U. S.); ancient city, with brick walls baked *in situ*, 181,

B.

Baba, on C. *Baba* (LECTUM, PR.); no ancient city; splendid view, 314; 315.
Babies' Feeding-bottles, terra-cotta; (c. 2), 146; parallels, *ib.*
Babylon; copper posts of its gates, 83; relative value of gold and silver at, 101; idols from, 151; *Pref.* xix, xx.
Babylonian Commerce with Western Asia, 302; civilization, the Hittites the medium of, *ib.; Pref.* xvii, xx.
Babylonian-Phoenician weights, 113.

Bacchus; the δέπ. ἀμφ. his attribute, 160; like the κάνθαρος, 161
Bags, leather; for carrying meal, in Homer, 45.
Baikal, Lake; green jade from, 172.
Baking of brick walls in situ. (*See* BRICKS, CRUDE.)
Baking of Trojan pottery; the great dishes and πίθοι the *only articles thoroughly baked*, 150–1.
Bal Serai (honey palace), at Alex. Troas, anc. bath and gymnas. 342.
Bali Dagh, Mt., above Bounarbashi, small city on, excavated, 27; the ancient *Gergis*, wrongly taken for Troy, 264; lower city buried, no wall visible, but house-foundations and Hellenic pottery, *ib.;* two stone circles, 267; the small Acropolis, 264; dimensions of both, *ib.;* excavations by Von Hahn (1864), 265; walls of two epochs, how built, 264–266 (cf. MASONRY); also of small stones, 266; excavations of 1882, *ib.;* likewise two epochs, *ib.;* house-walls of small stones, 266–7; Hellenic and earlier pottery (*q. v.*) 266-7; iron and copper nails in upper stratum, 267; slight separation of the two strata implies close succession of inhabitants, 268; an Hellenic settlement soon after the earlier one, *ib.;* the earlier, probably from 9th to 5th cent. B.C, *ib.;* three plain whorls in the Hellenic stratum, *ib.;* the marble wash-basins (of the Troy Bounarbashi theory) non-existent, *ib.;* only a Doric coronablock brought thither from Ilium, 269; *the Bali Dagh and Eski Hissarlik (q. v.) twin fortresses commanding the road into Asia*, 269–270, 277; its pretensions to be the site of Troy brought to naught, 277, *Pref.* x; "tomb of Priam," 262. (*See* PRIAM.)
Balls; terra-cotta, in temple A (c. 2), 127; patterns, *ib.;* perhaps astronomical, 128; others with parallel lines and zones, *ib.;* do they represent the earth? *ib.;* absurd conclusions of Brentano and Jebb, 128–9; opinion of Dr. Schmidt, 129, 130.

Balls; of serpentine, perforated, in tum. of Protesilaus, 259.
Barometer; metric scale, rule for conversion into inches, 381.
Barrels, terra-cotta; (c. 2), 152; in tomb (Halberstadt), only one found elsewhere than at Troy or Cyprus, *ib.*
Bases for Statues, in lower c., Ilium, 210.
Basket for spinning-work; of silver with a golden orifice, presented to Helen in Egypt, 109, 296, 298-9.
Bastian; his discoveries at Saboya, in Columbia, 110.
Baths modern and Roman, at Ligia Hamam, 309, 310.
Batieia, tomb of, 282.
Batrachomyomachia, the; much later than Homer, 146.
Battle-axes, stone; (c. 1) combined with hammer, 42-3; a parallel, 43.
———, copper or bronze, of usual Trojan form (c. 2), probably after the stone battle-axes, 93; parallels, *ib.;* small perforated (perhaps chisels), 166-7; parallels, 167; large, *ib.*
Battus, king of Cyrené, 298.
Battus, Gustav, overseer, 6.
Βαφή and Βάψις of metals (plunging in water); its meaning and effect, 101; *softening,* not hardening, 102-3; proofs from classic authors, 102; exceptional case of iron and steel, 103-4.
Bazarerek Tsai, R.; 331.
Beauty, physical; Greek sense of, already in Homer, 162-3.
Bede; quoted, 307.
Beder Eddin Effendi, Turkish delegate, 12; his opposition and obstructions, 12, 13; an unmitigated plague, 13.
Bedouins; their dough-cakes, probably like the bread of Homer's time, 45.
Beef; largely eaten at Troy; agreement with Homer, 350; proof that it was boiled, *ib.*
Behram. (See ASSOS.)
Beiramich, town, at foot of Ida; visited (1881), 329, 338; explored (1882), 27, 28; buildings from stones of cities on Kurshunlu Tepeh, 271; site of the later Scepsis, 274; coins, *ib.,* 340; valley of, 273, 277, 331.

Beit Sahour, near Bethlehem, 47.
Belger, C.; on the site of Troy and Count Moltke's services to archaeology, 287.
Belgium, antiquities of, 37.
Beni-hassan; paintings of spinning and weaving at, 294-5.
Bermion, Mt., gold mines, 50.
Besika Tepeh, tumulus explored in 1879; pottery as old as c. 2, but indicates a different people, 260, 261, 345, 347; *Pref.* x.
Berwerth, on jade and jadeite, 42.
Bezzenberger; on the etymology of κύπελλον and ἀμφικύπελλον, 163.
Binder, F.; 'Schliemann und Ilios,' 287.
Birch, Dr. S.; new edition of Wilkinson's 'Ancient Egyptians,' 293, f.
Birds, a few bones of (c. 1), 349.
Birs-i-Nimrûd, 180. *(See* BORSIPPA.)
Bismantova; cemetery, 193, 238.
Bismarck, Prince; 5, 14.
Blind, Karl; on site of Troy, &c., 286-7; review of Prof. Virchow's 'Old Trojan Tombs and Skulls,' in relation to Trojan Ethnology (App. III.), 351, f.; "The Teutonic Kinship of Trojans and Thrakians" (App. IV.), 357, f.
Blovica (Bohemia), tombs; 248.
Boar, wild; bones of (c. 1), 349.
Boeckh, 'Corpus Inscriptionum Graecarum;' 229, 231, 232, 233, 340.
Boetticher, K., 'Die Tektonik der Hellenen;' on *Antae* or *Parastades,* 81, n.
Böttiger; 'Vasengemälde,' 299.
Bohemia; antiquities of, 247-8.
Bologna; antiquities of, 110, 136, 157.
Bolts; bronze, 98; parallels, *ib.*
Bone, objects of. *(See* AWLS, NEEDLES, and KNIFE-HANDLES.)
Bones, found in c. 1; Prof. Virchow on (App. II.), 348; fragments of a human *skeleton (q. v.);* domestic *animals (q.v.)* predominant; few wild, 348-9; *cattle,* 349; *sheep, goats, swine, dogs, birds, fish, ib.;* general results as to stage of *civilization* (cf. the several heads).
Bonpland. (See HUMBOLDT.)

Borax; not used in Trojan gold-soldering, 108.
Borrebey; tumulus at, 94.
Borsippa; brick temple at, built by Nebuchadnezzar; its sixth stage vitrified by burning *in situ,* 180.
Bortolotti, 'Del Talento Omerico,' 114.
Boskisi, village; fragments from ruins of a neighbouring ancient town, 308.
Botti, A. U.; 'La Grotta del Diavolo, Bologna,' 38, 40, 47, 50, 153.
Bottles; gold, for oil, in Homer, 109; etymology of λήκυθος, *ib.*
——, terra-cotta, in form of hunting-bottles; (c. 2), 137-8; parallels, *ib.;* flat tripod, painted, like hunting-bottle (Ilium) 217; similar old Etruscan, plain, no feet, 218.
Bounarbashi; village visited, 27, 345; city on the Bali Dagh excavated, 27; site *invented* for Troy by Lechevalier, 195, 262 (cf. BALI DAGH); Ilian inscription at, 229; springs of, 268; another (*see* BUJUK).
—— *Su,* rivulet, junction with the Scamander, 16.
Bourguignon, A.; his collection of antiquities, 133.
Bovolone (Verona); tombs, 37.
Bowls; (c. 1) fragment of, 31; with tubes for suspension; parallels, 38.
—— (or plates) terra-cotta; polished, one-handled, hand-made (c. 2); at Corneto as covers for funeral urns, 152.
—— bronze or copper; in tomb at Cebrené, 276.
Box, ivory ornament of, 116.
Bracelets, gold; (c. 2) with spectacle-like pattern, 110; copper (c. 2), 166.
Brandis; quoted, 114.
Brazil; antiquities of, 121.
Bread, proper, unknown in prehistoric and Homeric times, 44; probably like the Arab dough-cakes, 45.
Bréal; 'Sur le Déchiffrement des inscriptions cypriotes,' 159.
Brentano, Dr. E.; 'Troia u. Neu Ilion,' 41, 128; blunder about *axes,* 41; his bitter criticisms, *ib.;* takes 卍 and 卐 for *inscriptions, ib.;*

absurd argument from the terra-cotta balls, 128-9; his sad end, 129; 'Ilios im Dumbrekthale,' 288, 306; error about the Simois, 306.
Bricks, Crude; house-walls of, 21; *débris* of, from wall of 2nd city, 22; *walls of, baked in situ;* (c. 2), 52; fortress wall, 59; mode of baking, and marks of the process, 60; *a new discovery,* 61; of the two temples (c. 2), with channels and grooves, described, 76, f.; proofs of the process, 78; the cement also baked, *ib.;* partial action of the fire, *ib.;* house-walls of c. 3, 176; walls of the S.E. gate (c. 3), 180; parallels, temple at Borsippa, *ib.;* Scotch vitrified forts, *ib.;* at *Aztulan (q. v.),* 180-1.
Bricks; colossal masses of burnt (c. 2), left standing by 3rd settlers, 52; partly from houses destroyed in the conflagration, partly from crude brick walls baked *in situ,* 52; difficulty of distinguishing walls and *débris,* 57; brick wall of c. 2, 56 f. (cf. WALLS); of the two temples on stone foundations (c. 2), 76, f. (cf. HOUSES); dimensions of, in temple A, 78; made of clay and straw, 79, 85; numerous shells in, 86; (c. 4), baked and unbaked, of clay and straw; dimensions, 185; vast *débris* from their decay, 186; (c. 5) crude, a few baked, 188; materials and dimensions, *ib.*
Brigands, danger from, 7, 28, 311.
'*British Quart. Review*' on 'Ilios,' 287.
Brizio, Mr.; quoted, 136.
Brockhaus, Mr. F. A.; 303.
Bronze; rare and precious, down to mediæval times, 96; analysis of Trojan, Orchomenian, and Caucasian, 104, 105; utensils in tomb at Cebrené, 276. (Cf. *Pref.* xii.)
Bronze or copper; weapons, instruments, and ornaments (*see* ARROWHEADS, BOLTS, BROOCHES, DAGGERS, GIMLET, KNIVES, LANCEHEADS, NAILS, PINS, PUNCHES, SWORDS); all *cast* not forged (*see* MOULDS), 93, 100; absence of *tools* (c. 2), how explained, 99.

Brooches, bronze or copper ; (c. 1) with spiral or globular heads, 47 ; *no fibula* in c. 1–6, 47 ; frequent in the terramare, 48 ; none in hut-urns of Marino, &c., but fibulae, 48 ; with fibulae in lake-dwellings, and in the Caucasus, *ib.;* one in a tomb in Prussia, 49 ; (c. 2), 105, 138, 139 ; mass of, cemented by carbonate, 106 ; (c. 3), 184 ; (c. 4), 188.
Brugsch-Pasha, Prof. H.; on the peoples of Asia Minor in Egyptian records, 3, 4 ; on the cultus of Apis in Egypt and Greece, 292.
Brun-Rollet; quoted, 326.
Brunck; 'Analecta,' 299.
Buchholz, 'Die Homer. Realien,' 49.
Buckets, terra-cotta ; (c. 2) rude one-handled, 148 ; parallels, *ib.*
Bücking, Prof. H.; on the hardening of iron and steel, 103.
Bugle; vases in shape of, with three feet, characteristic of the Lydian stratum, 194 ; parallels, *ib.*
Buildings; (c. 1), 29 ; (c. 2, &c.), see EDIFICES, GATES, HOUSES, TEMPLES, WALLS.
Bujuk Bounarbashi (large fountain head) ; fountains and pond, 333 ; remains of an ancient building, *ib.;* sculptured marble blocks, 339.
Bullets. (*See* SLING BULLETS.)
Burnouf, E.; collaborator with the author (1879), 1, 52, 76 ; on the 卐, 124, 192 ; 'La Science des Religions,' 192.
Burnt City, of Troy ; the 2nd, not the 3rd, 52 ; causes of the error, *ib.*
Butler, James D.; letter on brick walls baked *in situ*, 180.
Buttmann, 'Lexilogus,' 49, 157.
Button, gold, of a sceptre (c. 2), 106 ; *Pref.* xxii.
Byzantine Church, now a mosque, at Toozla, 313 ; another at Assos, 317.
—— *Coins ;* 323.
—— *Tombs;* in theatre of Ilium, 214.

C.

Cadmus; sources of his wealth, 49.
Caere; antiquities of, 147.

Caesar; gems dedicated by, 219 ; superstition for the number *three*, 289 ; intention of founding a new Troy, 292.
Caesarea. (*See* KAISARIYEH.)
Caïcus, R.; Mysians about, 262, 329.
Caïmacam, Turkish title (mayor), 28.
California, Indians of ; their flint arrows, 174.
Callisthenes, quoted ; 49.
Callicoloné, Mt.; Kara Your, not *Oulou Dagh*, nor *Rhoeteum*, 281–3 ; etymology of the name, 282 ; foundations on, perhaps temple of Ares, *ib.*
Calvert, Mr. Frank; 26, 39, 49, 200, 234, 260, 264, 283, 284, 304, 305, 340, 341, 343, 345 ; 'On the Asiatic coast of the Hellespont,' 283.
Camirus (in Rhodes) ; tomb at, 42, 148 ; the δἱπ. ἀμφ. at, 160.
Camp; Greek, on the left (W.) side of Scamander, 293 ; Trojan, 284.
Campaign, Trojan, of 1882. (*See* EXCAVATIONS.)
Campeggine (Reggio) terramare, 37.
Cana, Mt.; 329.
Canae, 320.
Cannon-balls; cut by Turks from columns of Alex. Troas, 342.
Capitals; Doric, of great temple of Ilium, 197, 202, 203, used for foundations, 224 ; of Roman propylaeum, 209 ; of portico in lower city, 210 ; Corinthian, of theatre, 213.
Cappadocia; early home of Hittites ; sculptures and writing ; 127, *Pref.* xvii, xxv.
Caracalla on coins (Ilium), 221 ; (Alex. Troas), 222.
Carbonate of Copper; cementing action of, 106.
Carchemish (Jerablûs), the Hittite capital on the Euphrates, 4, *Pref.* xvii.
Carians, 3 ; syllabary, *Pref.* xxv.
Carina, 329.
Carpineto, near Cupra-Marittima ; necropolis of, 152, 193.
Carthage; mosaics at, with 卐, 125. (Cf. MUSEUMS.)
Carthaginians; defeated by Sicilian Greeks at Himera, 114 ; present to Damareta, *ib.*

Cassandra, daughter of Priam, 67.
Castello, near Bovolone ; terramare, 37.
Casting of metals ; common in the prehistoric cities of Troy, 100 ; also in Homer, *ib.;* different forms of moulds for, 169-171. (Cf. MOULDS.)
Castorches, Prof. E., 251.
Cat; animal vase like (c. 2) ; if so, probably imported, 141 ; the cat introduced into Egypt fr. Nubia, *ib.,* unknown in Greece till late ; not found at Troy, *ib.*, 349.
Catastrophe, tremendous, of c. 2, evidences of, 90, 182, *et alibi.*
Cato; quoted, 161.
Cattle; the ancient medium of barter, 112 ; hence *pecunia*, 113 ; legal penalties in, *ib.;* numerous bones (c. 1), 349 ; of a smaller breed than the modern German, *ib.; beef* and *pork* most used for food, 350.
Catullus; quoted, 298.
Caucasus; antiquities, 48, 94, 95, 110 ; scene of Greek myths, but no prehistoric antiquities as old as those of Troy, nor stone implements, 280. (*See* KOBAN, SAMTHAWRO.)
—— ' Objets d'Antiquité du Musée de la Société des Amateurs d'Archéologie au Caucase,' 48.
Caunus (cf. KANU), in Caria, 4.
Cavern, on W. side of Hissarlik, with fig-tree, spring, and conduit, excavated in 1879 and 1882, 63, 64.
Caverns; Andalusian, stone period, 39, 42 ; *delle Arene*, near Genoa, 42, 44 ; *of Trou du Frontal-Furfooz*, in Belgium, 37.
Cazazis; rich Greek at Avjilar, 324.
Ceará (Brazil) ; petroglyphs of, 121.
Cebrené, on Mt. Chali Dagh ; visited (1881), 338 ; excavations at, 28, 275 ; position relative to old Scepsis, 274 ; Acropolis on steep rock ; housefoundations and cistern, 275 ; walls not needed, 275, 278 ; lower city, thin *débris*, *ib.;* inexplicable, 276 ; stone house-foundations, 275 ; complete circuit walls, of masonry (*q. v.*) like Assos, 275, 341 ; five gates ; large stone foundations, *ib.;* pottery (*q. v.*) like that of 1st epoch at Bali Dagh, 275, f. ; also like that on Fulu Dagh, and some Macedonian, *ib.;* a very ancient city, 276 ; people moved by Antigonus to Alex. Troas, *ib.;* rock-hewn tombs, with skeletons ; objects found in one, *ib.;* coins of Cebrené and Scepsis, *ib.;* view from the Acropolis, 277.
Cebrenes, the Thracian, perhaps founders of Cebrené, 276.
Ceiling, sculptured, of the Thalamos at Orchomenos, 304.
Cellars, πίθοι used as. (*See* JARS.)
Cement, clay, in brick walls ; of temples (c. 2), 78, 85 ; (c. 4), 185 ; (c. 5), 188.
Cemeteries, Turkish, 307-8 ; sculptured blocks in, 308, *et passim* in Ch. V. and App. I. ; of Kusch Deressi, 312.
Cenotaphs, or memorials ; the tumuli of the Troad proved by the absence of human remains, 252, 263 ; examples in Homer, 252-3.
Chace, the, not a chief subsistence among the primitive Trojans, 349.
Chair, marble, at Kemanli Kioi, like those in theatre of Dionysus at Athens, 341 ; the Hittite 𐋠 127.
Chalcedony; SAWS and KNIVES of (c. 1-5), 46, 173.
Chaldaea, antiq. of, 43, 44, *Pr.* xviii, xx.
Chali Dagh (bush-mountain), site of the ancient CEBRENÉ (*q. v.*).
Chalidagh Kioi; Turkish hospitality at, 338.
Chandler, Dr., 50.
Channels, in brick walls, for burning *in situ*, Co ; their arrangement in the temples (c. 2), 76, f. ; impressions of twigs in them, but no charcoal, 78 ; gen. filled with brick *débris*, from the baking, with some potsherds, *ib.*
Chantre, E.; on site of Troy ; ' L'Age de la Pierre et l'Age du Bronze en Troade et en Grèce,' 286.
Chaonia, 253.
Charcoal; layer of, on S. gate-road, 70, 73 ; *below* floor of temple A, 79.
Chariots, War, (Homeric), used in Cyprus till 5th cent. B.C., 159 ; procession of, fr. temple of Ilium, 205.

Chepuch, scala of, 321.
Chersonese, Thracian, 333; prehistoric settlement on, contemp. with c. 1 of Troy, 260, 304; *Pref.* x, xi.
Chevket Abdoullah, caimacam (mayor) of Iné, 28.
Chiblak; granite columns near, 27; road from Hissarlik to, the ancient road from Troy, 65.
Chierici, Prof. G., keeper of the Museum of Reggio, 37.
Chigri, Mt., fortress on; walls like those of Assos, 317, 341 (*see* MASONRY); prob. NEANDRIA, *ib.*
Chinese; boats, painted eyes on, 32; *daggers*, like the Trojan and Caucasian, 95.
Chipiez, C. (*See* PERROT.)
Chisels (?), bronze; (c. 2), 167.
Choiseul-Gouffier, Count; 'Voyage pittoresque de la Grèce,' 28, 242, 245, 285; full of errors, 252.
Christ, W., 'Die Topographie der Troianischen Ebene,' 61.
Chrysa, the later, 312, 315; at Kulakli Kioi, 314; foundations of temple of Sminthean Apollo, 314; fragments of another edifice, *ib.*
Chrysé, the ancient city (Hom.); prob. Assos, 318, 319; its port, 319.
Chrysippus of Soli, Stoic; 319, 320.
Chthonian god; the δέπας ἀμφικύπελλον his attribute, 160.
Cicero; quoted, 113, 243.
Cilla (Hom.), with temple of Apollo, on R. CILLUS; existed in Strabo's time; buried under the alluvia, 327.
Cillus, R. (Kisillkedjili), 327.
—— hero; tumulus of, 327.
Cimmerians at Troy, 262.
Circles, celestial; supposed, on the Trojan balls, 129.
—— stone; foundations of shepherds' huts, mistaken for cromlechs, 272-3.
Cissophanes; a new name (inscr.), 227.
Cisterns; on Chalidagh (Cebrené), 275.
Civilization; Plato on its three stages after the Deluge, 290.
—— of first settlers on Hissarlik, 349; they possessed all necessary *domestic animals*, except the *cat*, *ib.;* the *chace*

and *fishing* secondary, 349, 350; abundance of *oyster shells*, 350; the broken bones no proof of eating marrow raw, *ib.;* prevalence of *beef* and *pork*, *ib.;* agreement with Homer, *ib.;* of Troy (c. 2), high, denoted by the edifices, 98.
Civita Vecchia; a vase with cow-head handles found at, 193.
Clarke, Dr. E. D., traveller, 271.
—— *Dr. J. T.*, 173; 'Report on the Investigations at Assos,' 320.
Claudian; quoted, 297.
Clay; its use in horizontal roofs of ancient Troy and the modern Troad, 84, 90, 185. (Cf. CEMENT.)
Clay Coating of walls; of S. gate (c. 2), 71; of temple A (c. 2), 79; of temple B, 85; vitrified by conflagration, except in lower part; how explained, 86; of walls (c. 3), 175; of housewalls (c. 4), 185.
Cleanliness, remarkable want of, in the Homeric age, 162.
Cleanthes, Stoic, native of Assos, 319.
Cleinias, in Plato, 290.
Coazze (Verona); terramare, 123, 147.
Coin, origin of. (*See* MONEY.)
Coins of Ilium; chiefly Macedonian and imperial Roman, 219; forty-two found (1882), all bronze, *ib.;* new types, 220; autonomous, *ib.;* Roman imperial, 220-1; others of Asia Minor and Greece found at Ilium, 224; Roman (non-Asiatic), *ib.;* of monasteries, at Ilium, *ib.*
—— of Alex. Troas, 221, f.; Byzantine, 323; Cebrené, beautiful engraving, 276, 277; Larisa, 312; Roman, bought at Iné, 339, 340; of Scepsis, at Beiramich, 274; Sigeum, 223; Tenedos, 224, 339.
Colonae (cf. KELENA), in the Troad, 4; probably at Kestambul, 311.
Colours, artistic, perfectly unknown in all the settlements (1-6) at Troy, below the Hellenic, 239; Virchow, on, as a test of Hellenic or older pottery, 377, 378. (Cf. PAINTING.)
Columbia, antiquities of, 110.
Columella; quoted, 113.

Column, small marble (prob. votive), with an inscription, in the theatre of Ilium, 213.
Columns, Corinthian, discovered on plateau ; 26, 210 (*see* PORTICO) ; semi-cols. of Roman propylaeum, 209.
—— from Ilium, near Chiblak, 27 ; granite ; near Bounarbashi, 27-8 ; near Kestambul, 311 ; others, App. I.
—— Doric, of great TEMPLE of Ilium, 203 ; of Roman PROPYLAEUM, 208-9 ; Doric, Ionic, and Corinthian, of THEATRE, 211.
Commodus ; on coins (Il.), 220, 221.
Conato, Mt., tomb at, 147.
Conduit, primitive, in cavern W. of Hissarlik, like those at Tiryns and Mycenae, 64-5.
Conon ; quoted, 323.
Constantinople ; buildings of, from stones of Assos, 317.
Constantinus Porphyrogennetus, in 10th cent., mentions a bishopric of Ilium, 224.
Contract Tablets, clay, Cappadocian cuneiform, 127 ; *Pref.* xviii.
Copenhagen. (*See* MUSEUMS.)
Copper (cf. BRONZE) ; objects of, found in temple A, 92, f. (see the several heads) ; all at Troy *cast*, not *forged*, 93 ; once valued above gold or silver (Lucret.), 100 ; but the contrary (Hom.), 101 ; relative value 100 : 9 = that of gold to silver in the East, *ib. ;* question of *hardening* or *tempering* by plunging in water, 101 (see the words) ; the idea an error, 102 ; hardened by hammering, 103 ; hardening by rhodium, not proved, 104.
Coracesium (cf. KARKAMASH) in Cilicia, 4.
Corcelettes (Neufchâtel), lake-dwellings, 111, 146, 154, 171.
Corinth, seat of the union (κοινόν) of the Hellenes, 228.
Corinthian order. (*See* CAPITALS, COLUMNS.)
Corn-bruisers ; (c. 3), 184 ; *on* and *in* tum. of Protesilaus, 257.
Corneto (anc. TARQUINII) ; pre-Etruscan tombs, 37, 48, 122, 126, 127, 132, 152, 153. (Cf. FIBULAE, HUT-URNS, MUSEUMS.)
Corridor, narrow, between the two temples (c. 2), 76 ; filled with baked brick débris and scoriae, 85.
Cortaillod ; lake dwellings, 171.
Coryphantis, on S. shore of G. of Adramyttium, 321.
Covers of Vases. (*See* VASE-COVERS.)
Cow-heads ; vase-handles in form of, characteristic of the Lydian settlement, 193 ; parallels at Mycenae and elsewhere, *ib. ;* symbol of, *Pref.* xx.
Craig Phadric ; vitrified fort of, 180.
Cranes ; first passage of, 17.
Crateres. (*See* MIXING VESSELS.)
Crates, of Mallus ; his great terrestrial globe at Pergamum, 128 ; absurd theory of its imitation in the Trojan terra-cotta *balls* (*q. v.*), *ib.*
Crespellani, 'Del Sepolcreto scoperto presso Bassano,' 157.
Crete ; use of κύπελλον in, 159.
Crispina ; on coins of Ilium, 221.
Critics ; 236, 270 ; *Pref.* xiv, xxvii-xxx.
Crocus, on Ida (Hom.), 335.
Croesus ; riches of, 50 ; his gold stater derived from the Homeric talent, 114 ; the Aeolian foundation of Ilium ascribed to his time by Strabo (reading doubtful), 237.
Cromlechs, imaginary, in the Ida region, 272-3.
Crown-shaped handles. (*See* VASE-COVERS.)
Cubit, Trojan ; signs of in the buildings of c. 2 ; probably 0·50 m., 56.
Cuckoo, heard all over the Troad, 337.
Cup, copper, with omphalos (c. 2), 93.
Cups, terra-cotta ; lustrous black (c. 1), 34 ; two or more joined (c. 2), 148 ; parallels, *ib. ;* small, boatshaped (c. 2, 3, 4), prob. used for metallurgy, 153 ; parallels, *ib. ;* (c. 6), one-handled, with hornlike excrescences, 193 ; parallels, 193-4.
Currency, Mercantile ; of silver by weight among the Hittites, 302.
Curtius, G. ; 'Grundzüge d. griechischen Etymologie,' 113, 160 ; etym. of

κύπελλον, 160–1 ; 'Studien zur griech. u. latein. Grammatik,' 159.
Cuvin; Turkish name of tombs of Achilles and Patroclus, 243.
Cyclades, I.; idols of, less rude than the Trojan, 151.
Cyclopean Walls. (See MASONRY.)
Cyclopes; patriarchal government, without an agora or laws, 290, 331.
Cylinders; Chaldean, in Asia Minor, Cyprus, &c., *Pref.* xviii ; at Hissarlik, a test of age, xix, xx ; (c. 2) clay, perforated, prob. weights for weavers' looms, 134–5 ; parallels, *ib.*
Cymatium, of the great temple of Ilium, 203 ; of Macedonian age, *ib.;* of Roman age, 203–4.
Cynossema; tomb of Hecuba, only a natural rock, 304.
Cypriote Character Ko, 146 ; *Dialect;* Homeric peculiarities in, 159 ; alphabet, *Pref.* xxiii.
Cyprus; antiquities, 93, 127, 135, 139, 152 ; use of κύπελλον in, 159 ; Homeric war-chariots, *ib.*
Cyrus the Elder, and the Persian power, 237, 367. (Cf. *Pref.* vi.)

D.

Dagger; original form of the stone age, the type of bronze daggers, lance- and arrow-heads, 95 ; double-edged from Caucasus, like the Trojan lance-heads ; also like the Chinese, Egyptian, and Assyrian, *ib.;* further development to the double-edged sword (*q.v.*), *ib.;* old use of, 96 ; of bronze (c. 2) curled up by the fire, 96–8, 167 ; such at Troy only, 98.
Damareta, wife of Gelon ; her golden wreath, 114.
Danau (Danai?), in Egypt. records, 4.
Dandani. (See DARDANI.)
Danzig; antiquities, 9, 121.
Dardanelles, R., 304. (See RHODIUS.)
Dardanelles, town of ; 7, 304, 339 ; ancient town near, *ib.;* vessels like the old Trojan, but very inferior, in the potters' shops, 141, 142, 188.
Dardani (Dardanians), in Egyptian records, 3 ; a kingdom about 14th cent. B.C., *ib.;* disappear in the list about 1200 B.C., 4 ; *Pref.* xvii.
Dardania, dom. of Aeneas, on slope of Ida, between Scepsis, S., and Zeleia, N., 274.
Dardanié (Hom.) ; site on Kurshunlu Tepeh (*q. v.*), 273 ; at *foot* of Ida, not on *summit, ib.,* 291, 330 ; in Dardania (*q. v.*) ; site unknown to Strabo, 273 ; inhabitants removed to Ilios, *ib.;* succeeded by other colonists, and called SCEPSIS (*q. v.*), *ib.;* position relative to Cebrené, Ida, and the Scamander, *ib.;* destroyed before time of Demetrius, 305 ; confounded with the Greek Dardanus (*q. v.*), *ib.,* 340.
Dardanus, builder of *Dardanié,* 291.
Dardanus; Aeolian city, 305 ; excavations, no result, *ib.*
Darius, his gold stater, 114 ; the *Daricus* half of, or equal to, the Homeric talent, *ib.* (Cf. *Pref.* xi.)
Darzau (Hanover), necropolis of ; 33, 123, 127, 147.
Dead; Turkish respect for the, 307.
Death; for drinking unmixed wine, 145 ; for adultery, at Tenedos, 224.
Débris; vast accumulation on Hissarlik, explained by the structure of the house-*roofs* (*q. v.*), 185 ; insignificant depth of elsewhere, even on the known sites of ancient cities, 278, 347.
Dedeh, Mt. (or FULU DAGH, *q. v.*), city on, excavated, 27, 270.
Deecke; on the Cypriote dialect, 159 ; *Pref.* xxiii–iv.
Deer; bones of (c. 1), 349.
Deluge. (See CIVILIZATION.)
Demeter; Temple of. (See ELEUSIS.)
——— ; temple of (prob.) at foot of Hagios Demetrios Tepeh, 344.
Demetrius; inscr. of Antandrus, 323.
Demetrius, of Scepsis, 49, 66 ; placed Troy at Ἰλιέων κώμη, 274, 345 ; his error about the Erineos, 284 ; discussion of his theory and authority, *ib.,* 362, f.
Demons or *Devils;* the heathen gods regarded as, 289.

Denmark, antiquities of; 43, 94, 248.
Depas. See AMPHIKYPELLON.
Désor ; explorations at Auvernier, 111.
Devaux, C. ; 'Les Kébailes de Djerdjera,' 326.
Devrent, a corruption of ANTANDRUS; pottery and ruins at, 322.
Diavolo, Grotta del. (*See* GROTTA.)
Dictys Cretensis ; quoted, 254.
Diller, J. S. ; on inscriptions at Assos and Lesbos, 320.
Diomedes, 283.
Dion Cassius ; quoted, 219, 243.
Dionysus ; rites of, in an inscription fr. Kurshunlu Tepeh, 235; theatre of, at Athens, 341; on coins of Scepsis, 276, 339; the dimorphous, 224.
Diorite ; axes (c. 1), 41, 43; blunt axe-like implements, 42; parallels, *ib.;* polishers, 47; (c. 2) axes, 119, 172.
Dish, tripod; (c. 2), 136.
Dishes ; huge thick round, slightly curved at rim, peculiar to c. 2, 150; probably for tables, *ib. ;* the only pottery *thoroughly baked* (except the πίθοι), *ib.*
Disks, stone and clay perforated; many in c. 2–5, 171; parallels, *ib.*
Distaff ; use of in spinning, 296, f.; not always essential, *ib. ;* sometimes confused with the *spindle, ib. ;* described, 298; of gold, as divine emblems and presents to great ladies, 298. (Cf. SPINDLE.)
Djemal Pasha, military governor of the Dardanelles; 12, 258, 262, 305.
Dôcos, a new name (inscription), 227.
Dörpfeld, Dr. Wm., architect; assists in the explorations, 5, 12; his Plan of the Acropolis of c. 2, 14; quoted, 40, 43, 75, 98, 101, 112, 113, 130, 281-2, 293; articles on 'Troy and New Ilion,' 288.
Dog ; bones of (c. 1), 349.
Dôma, the dwelling-room in Paris's palace, 86.
Donnar or *Thor*, the ⌐ and ⌐ his symbol, 124.
Doorposts ; of temples and gates, 82–3; of temple A, 84.

Dorian Invasion of the Peloponnesus, 80 years after the taking of Troy, 2.
Doric edifices of Ilium, Greek and Roman. (*See* TEMPLES, PORTICO, PROPYLAEUM, COLUMNS, &c.)
Doric fragments; at springs of Bounarbashi, 269; at Oba Kioi, 271.
Doulton, Mr. ; his experiments on pottery of the 1st city, 33.
Dowth (Ireland), grotto of, 121.
Dress, female, rich and refined, in Homeric age, 162.
Drought, extraordinary in Plain of Troy (1881–2), 15, 16.
Droysen, J. G., 'Geschichte des Hellenismus ;' on Ilium and the union of cities of the Troad, 228.
Drusus, Claudius ; on an inscr., 232.
Ducks, Babylonian weights in the form of, 112, 301.
Duden-Swamp ; 284.
Dumont, A., and Chaplain, J., 'Les Céramiques de la Grèce Propre,' 47, 111, 238, 241; mistake about the fibula, 47, 241; misquoted by Prof. Jebb, 238, 240–1, *Preface* xxix; on the age of the Lydian and other pottery at Hissarlik, 240; particular examples discussed; mistakes corrected, 240–1.
Dyaus. (*See* ZEUS.)

E.

Earrings ; gold, silver, and electrum, of the usual Trojan form (c. 2), 106, 241; silver, flat, crescent-shaped, mistaken by M. Dumont for a fibula, 241; a pair, in tomb at Cebrené, 276.
Earth ; globular form of, first taught by Pythagoras, and proved by Eudoxus of Cnidus, according to Brentano, 128; but doubtless known in the East from a remote antiquity, 130. (Cf. BALLS; CRATES.)
Earthquake, slight shock of, 17; traces of ancient, 26; in time of Tiberius, *ib. n.*
Eckenbrecher, G. von ; 'Ueber die Lage des Hom. Ilion' (1843), 285.

Edifices, six large, on Acropolis of c. 2; 53, 62, 73, 75; the one N.W. of the S.W. gate, 67; described, 89; reconstructed when the gate was enlarged, *ib.*; another demolished when the gate was enlarged, 68; one over N. part of S. gate, 73; described, 87-8; the two *temples* (*q. v.*), 76; one of 1st epoch, built before the two temples, 86-7; construction of all alike, viz., *foundations* of stone cemented with clay, *walls* of brick, terraced *roofs* of wooden beams, rushes, and clay, 90; their grandeur denotes a high civilization, 98.
—— Greek, of Ilium. (*See* ILIUM.)
—— Roman, of Ilium, 207, f.; of white marble on stone foundations, 195: in Acropolis: two Doric (*see* PORTICO and PROPYLAEUM); fragments of others, 210: in Lower City: a Corinthian portico (*q. v.*), 110; small foundations probably for statues, *ib.*; the great theatre (*q. v.*), *ib.*
Edinburgh Review, on '*Ilios*,' 237, 287, 361.
Edonis. (*See* ANTANDRUS.)
Edwin, King of Northumbria, 307.
Eggs; of aragonite (c. 2), prob. votive offerings, 118, 171.
Egypt, invaded by Asiatic confederates about 1200 B.C., 3; testimonies to the existence of Troy and neighbouring peoples, 2-4 (cf. *Pref.* xvi, xvii); use of potter's wheel in, 35; traffic, by weights of gold and silver, 112, 301-2; copper talent, 115.
Egyptian Antiquities, 95, 98, 117, 137, 152, 154, 247, 301.
Elaeus, on the Thracian Chersonese, 254, 256. (*See* PROTESILAUS.)
Electrum; earrings (c. 2), 106.
Eleusis, very ancient pottery and idols found at, 38.
Elm-trees, on tum. of Protesilaus; legend of, 256-7.
Emilia. (*See* TERRAMARE.)
Ephesus, Council of, 319.
Ephron, the Hittite, 302.
Erineos, the; 283, 284.
Eris, sister of Ares, 282.

Erythrae; statue of Athené at, 300.
Eski Hissarlik, ("Old Fortress") an abandoned Turkish fort on the Thracian Chersonese, 254.
—— on the E. bank of the Scamander, opposite the Bali Dagh, near Bounarbashi, excavated, 269, 345; walls of Acropolis well preserved, *ib.*; many house-foundations of lower city, *ib.*; *débris* insignificant, washed off the slope, *ib.*; pottery like that of 1st epoch of Bali Dagh (*q. v.*), *ib.*; hence the two existed simultaneously, *ib.*; they were *twin fortresses*, commanding the road from the Scamander valley into the interior of Asia Minor, 269, 270, 277-8.
Estavayer; lake-dwellings of, 146, 171.
Etruria; traditional colonization of, by the Lydians, 193, 238.
Etruscan and pre-Etruscan Pottery; its resemblance to that below the Greek Ilium on Hissarlik, 193-4, 379.
Etruscan and pre-Etruscan Tombs; 122, 126, 143, 147, 148, 160, 218, 238. (Cf. the several names.)
Etymologicum M.; 83, 113, 115, 156.
Eubulides; monument of, 215.
Eudoxia, empress; her 'Ionia'; lamentation over Ilios; her 'Life of Jesus Christ,' in Homeric verses, 225.
Eudoxus, of Cnidus; proved the globular form of the *Earth* (*q. v.*), and divided it into zones, 128.
Euphorbus, 254.
Euripides (and *Schol. ad*); quoted, 82, 86; (Monk *ad*), 297.
Euryclea, 45.
Eusebius; 'Chronicon,' quoted, 292.
Eustathius, quoted; 115, 150, 155, 156, 254, 283; *Pref.* xi.
Eustratiades, P., 251.
Euthydius, on an inscription, 229.
Evelthon, King of Cyprus, 298.
Evjilar, two Turkish villages (besides AVJILAR), 324: one on the Scamander, near Beiramich, high up on Ida, 274, 324, 329, 330; its wretched

state, 332; primitive agriculture, *ib.;*
ascent of Ida from, 324, 332.
Evjilar, E. of Adramyttium, 325.
Excavations (1879), 303; qualifications
for, and results, *Pref.* viii, f.
—— at Orchomenos (1881), 303.
Excavations and Explorations, new,
for five months in 1882; motives
for undertaking, 1-5; new firmans,
5; architects, *ib.;* overseers, 5, 6;
buildings, 6; provisions, 7; guards,
ib.; majordomo, 8; servants, 9;
instruments, *ib.;* workmen, 10;
begun, March 1st; Turkish delegates, 11, 12; opposition to taking
plans and measurements, 12, 13,
14; first works undertaken, 17;
excavation on north side disap-
pointing, 18; the theatre of Ilium,
18; the great eastern trench, 19;
massive Roman foundations, 20;
fortress-wall of 5th city, *ib.;* peculiarities of stratification, 22; layer
of natural soil below bricks of
2nd city, *ib.;* great earth-blocks, 22,
23; house-walls of 2nd, 3rd, 4th
and 5th cities, *ib.;* chief house of
3rd city, 23; the south-west gate
and road, *ib.;* discovery of a second,
the south gate, 24; a second gate
of the 3rd city, and a third of the
2nd city, *ib.;* Roman gate, *ib.;*
great north trench, *ib.;* walls of the
1st city, *ib.;* on the plateau, east,
south, and west of Hissarlik, *ib.;*
discovery of pottery of 1st and 2nd
cities, 25, 26; of a Corinthian portico
and house-walls of Ilium, 26.
—— in the TROAD, 27; (cf. TUMULI,
&c.); ended in July, 28, great results
and final completion, 277-9.
—— American at Assos, 316; at
Chrysa, by Mr. Pullan, 314; no pro-
spect of further advantage, except at
Assos and (perhaps) Alex. Troas, 347.
Exodus, Book of; 296, 302.
Ex-votos. (See VOTIVE OFFERINGS.)
Eye, the Evil, pictures of eyes to
avert, 32; perhaps meaning of, on
Trojan vases (c. 1), 32.
Eziné. (See INÉ.)

F.

Face Urns of Pommerellen, 121.
Farneto, Grotto of; 39, 135.
Far tostum, roasted spelt, used in
Roman rites, 45.
Fellenberg, M. de; 154.
Fergusson, James; 82.
Festus; quoted, 46, 113.
Fever; the author's suffering from, 28.
Fibula of bronze; never occurs in c.
1-6; invented late, 47; nor in the
terramare, 48; but cf. *n.;* Dumont
corrected, 47-8, *n.;* frequent in hut-
urns of Corneto, Marino, &c., 48,
127; test of comparative antiquity,
48; with brooches in lake dwellings;
and in the Caucasus, *ib.;* engendered from straight brooch, *ib.*
Fick, 'Vergleichendes Wörterbuch der
Indogermanischen Sprachen,' 113.
Fifth City on Hissarlik; extension
eastward beyond the original hill,
20, 62, 188; houses above and beyond old walls, *ib.;* house-walls of
stone and brick; remains, *ib.;* probably new citadel wall of rudely-
wrought stone blocks, 21, 189, 190
(cf. WALL); objects found in, 190-1;
two new types of owl-vases, 191;
curious objects of ivory, 192; Prof.
Jebb's theory that it was Macedonian,
239, 240, *Pref.* xxix-xxxi; Prof.
Virchow on the tests for its age, 376, f.
Fig-tree, triple, above cavern W. of
Hissarlik, 63.
Fimbria; capture of Ilium, and destruction of great temple, 233, 236.
Fire-pans (λαμπτῆρες, Hom.); not
lamps, 146.
First City; characteristic pottery of,
found on plateau, 25, 26; description of, 29, f.; only one or two large
edifices; dimensions; fortification
walls of two epochs; nature of the
masonry; extension to the south;
minor walls; no bricks, 30; slope
of its ground; probably had a lower
city; duration of the settlement; its
stratum 2·5 m. deep; pottery collected, *ib.;* bones, *ib.* and App. II.,

348; evidences of its stage of *civilization* 349; characteristics of its pottery (*q. v.*), 30; stone implements, 41, f.; bronze or copper 47, f.; objects of bone and ivory, 50; huckle-bones, 51; end of the settlement; no signs of a catastrophe, 51; slanting layer of *débris*, succeeded by stratum of earth, proving long desertion, 53.
First City; lower city (prob.) to west, south, and south-east of the hill, indicated by pottery, 30.
Fischer, Prof. H.; 'Nephrit und Jadeit, &c.,' and 'Ueber die Form der Steinbeile, &c.,' 41, *n.*
Fish, vertebrae of (c. 1), 349, 3
Flagons. (*See* OENOCHOAE.)
Flamen Dialis, the, forbidden the use of leavened bread, 46.
Fligier, Dr.; on the site of Troy, 288.
Flint implements; c. 1-4, 46; (c. 2), 173; (c. 3), 184. (Cf. KNIVES, SAWS.)
Floors; of a house, of large pebbles (c. 2), 53; sloping, of temple A, 78; of beaten clay, laid *after* burning the walls, 79; clay of temple B, later than wall-coating, 85; clay, apparently baked, of house (c. 2), 88; of houses of c. 2, of pebbles, clay and pebbles, or beaten clay, vitrified by the conflagration, 90; one only of plates of slate, *ib.*
—— Mosaic; lower c. cı Ilium, 214.
Flowers in the Plain of Troy; none in 1882, 17.
Flute, of pot-stone (*lapis ollaris*), in tum. of Patroclus, like those at Ithaca and Mycenae, 252.
Forchhammer, P. W., 'Topographische und Physiographische Beschreibung der Ebene von Troia,' corrected, 16; site of Troy, 'Der Skamandros,' 285.
Fort, small medieval (prob.) on Acropolis of Ilium, 224.
Forum Palladium, at Rome, 298.
Fountains, ancient; marble, in theatre, 213; at Kestambul, 310; Turkish drinking fountains, 307.
Foundations; massive Roman, 20; Hellenic and Roman, of Ilium, 22;
of 3rd, 4th and 5th cities, *ib.;* of c. 2, large blocks, 52; sunk into the levelled platform, 53; stone, of temples (c. 2), beneath walls of brick, 78, 84; stone, of houses of c. 2, 90; stone, of houses of c. 3, 176.
Foundations of Greek temples at Ilium; position uncertain, 196, 198, 202.
—— Roman, at Ilium; of shelly conglomerate, supporting marble walls, 195-6; of gate and portico, 207. (*See* PORTICO; PROPYLAEUM.)
Fourth City on Hissarlik, 184; built immediately over the 3rd, using and repairing its brick walls; same space, on the hill only, gates in same places, *ib.;* houses, 185; a mere village, *ib.;* end uncertain, perhaps destroyed by enemies; traces of fire, but none of a great conflagration, 186; pottery, 187; whorls and other objects found, 188.
Fowls, domestic; not known in Asia Minor and Greece till the Persian wars, 292.
France; prehistoric pottery of, 37.
Frangioni, A., keeper of museum at Corneto, 122.
Fresdorf (Prussia); Urnenfeld, 135.
Fret or Meander pattern; probable origin from the 卐, 125.
Frieze, Macedonian of great temple of Ilium; sculptures from, 205-6.
Frogs, generally innumerable in Troad, scarcely any in 1882, 17.
Frontal-Furfooz, Trou du, in Belgium; pottery found in, 37.
Frontlet of gold (c. 2), 106.
Fulu Dagh (or *Mt. Dedeh*), ancient settlement on, excavated, 27, 270, 345; double fortification walls, *ib.;* rude unpainted wheel-made pottery like some in c. 7 (Ilium), 270; also some like the coarser pottery of the Bali Dagh; probably therefore of same age, *ib.;* slight depth of *débris*, 278. (Cf. POTTERY.)
Funnels, terra-cotta; (c. 2, 3), 153; parallels, 154; semi-globular, with holes (only in c. 2), *ib.*
Furtwaengler, Dr.; quoted, 147.

G.

Gallienus (coins, Alex. Troas), 223.
Games, at Ilium, before the theatre was built, 212.
Gardner, Prof. Percy; 'The Types of Greek Coins,' 223-4; on the double head in coins of Tenedos, 224.
Gargara, at foot of C. Pyrrha; probable site; column and tumulus, 320; member of the Ilian union, 228.
Gargarus (now Garguissa); highest peak of Ida, 273; about 5806 feet, 334; spring flowers, list of, 334-5; sources of the Scamander, 336; excrescence of rock, like Homer's throne of Zeus, *ib.*
Garguissa and Sarikis; the twin-summits of Ida, 273; *Pref.* ix.
Gates (πύλαι), one gate with folding doors; Homer's 'Scaean' of Troy, 75; of the Parthenon (θύραι), *ib.;* new discoveries of, 24, 25; three of c. 2, two (at least) in use at once; all of the Acropolis, *not named by Homer*, and *not* his *Scaean Gate,* 62.
Gate; the old S.W. of c. 2, 23; road from, sought for, probably on bare rock of plateau, 25; its plan and construction, 67-8; lateral walls, of brick on stone, 67; piers, *ib.;* addition of a second portal, with walls ending in *parastades* (*q. v.*) supporting an upper building, 68, 69; building in front of old gate, 68; demolished, and two erected right and left of new portal, 69; different masonry of the two periods, *ib.;* road-surface of clay, above foundations, approached by paved ramp, 67, 69.
——, *grand S.* of c. 2, discovered, 24, 69; at foot of Acropolis hill, with ascending road, 70; plan and construction, 70, 71; massive lateral stone substruction-walls, well preserved, 70; upper building of brick and wood inferred; effects of conflagration, *ib.;* long gallery up to the Acropolis, *ib.;* its lateral walls of small stones, coated with clay, 71; wooden posts (to support the walls and an upper building) 72; further strengthened by panelling, *ib.;* masonry of entrance, with clay cement, baked *in situ*, *ib.;* paved ramp and road at upper end, 73; road out of it on the rock, 73; this gate burnt before the great catastrophe, *ib.;* replaced by S.E. gate, *ib.*
Gate, S.E. of c. 2, discovered, 24, 73; plan, 179; view, 74; only partly brought to light, because covered by gate of c. 3, *ib.;* its two portals, *ib.;* lateral walls and cross walls, 75; it leads towards the two *temples*, *ib.*
——, *S.W.* of c. 3, discovered, 24; above S.W. gate of c. 2, 177; its road above the old road, 177-8; portals, side walls of brick, and probably an upper building, 178; *débris* covering, *ib.;* impossibility of distinguishing side walls of 2nd and 3rd settlers, *ib.*
——, *S.E.* of c. 3, discovered, 24; above S.E. gate of c. 2, 177, 178; alterations, but by which settlers not known, 178; *altar* (*q. v.*) within it, *ib.; gutter* (*q. v.*), *ib.;* side-walls and tower inferred from fallen bricks and *débris*, 179; walls probably baked *in situ*, 180.
Gates of 4th city, probably of wood, in same places as those of c. 3, but surface of road higher, 184-5.
Gate of Ilium, Roman, discovered, 24. (*See* PROPYLAEUM.)
Gates; in circuit-wall of Cebrené, 275.
Gathón; new name on inscription, 231.
Gauls at Troy, 262.
Gellius, Aulus, quoted, 46.
Gelon, King of Syracuse; golden tripod dedicated by, 114.
Gems; in gold-mines of the Troad, 50; incised, five found at Ilium, 218; explained by Mr. Postolaccas, 219; Pliny on gems at Rome, *ib.;* one in a ring of Pompey, *ib.*
Gendarmes; 7, 27, 28, 304, 330.
Genesis, Book of; 302.
Genoese Ruins in Troad; 322, 326, 329.
Geography, Homeric; problems in, now solved, 303.

George, H. M., King of Greece, 136.
Georgia (Caucasus), antiquities of, 48.
Georgios Paraskevopoulos (named *Laomedon*), overseer, 5; his giant frame and strength, 6.
Gergesh, Kerkesh (*Gergithians*), in Egyptian records, 3.
Gergis (prob.), the city on the BALI DAGH (*q. v.*) above Bounarbashi, 27, 345; coined its own money, 346.
Germanicus Caesar, and *Tib. Claudius*, named on an Ilian inscription, 232.
Gesichtsurnen. (*See* FACE-URNS.)
Gheukli Kioi, village, 308, 342; marble fragments, probably from Alex. Troas, 308.
Gianakis Psochious, peasant at Koum Kioi, 234.
Gibraltar; caverns of, 136.
Gilding; in Homer, 100.
Gimlet; of bronze in temple A (c. 2), a unique prehistoric specimen, 98.
Giuliano, C.; on soldering gold, 108.
Gladstone, W. E.; Pref. to 'Mycenae,' and 'Homeric Synchronism,' 61.
Glass; extreme rarity of, at Ilium, 218; the few fragments, late Roman, *ib.;* a round perforated object of green glass paste, *ib.;* parallels, *ib.*
Glaucus, tripod of; how wrought, 102.
Globe. (*See* BALLS AND CRATES.)
Glykeia, Ilian village, 290.
Goats; bones of, abundant (c. 1), 349.
Goblets, terra-cotta; curious (c. 1), and parallels, 39; double handled (*see* AMPHIKYPELLON).
Gold; whence obtained by the Trojans, 49; principal ancient sources, 50; casting of (Hom.), 100; relative value to copper and silver, 100-101; objects, in and near temple A (c. 2), 106; wire, art of manufacturing, ascribed by Homer to Hephaestus, 107; art of *soldering* (*q. v.*), 108; curious ornament of, frequent at Troy and Mycenae, 110; parallel examples in copper, *ib.;* bracelets, *ib.;* talents of, in Homer, 111, 112; tongue of, at Jericho, 112 (cf. MONEY); votive offerings and presents weighed by the talent, 114;

Damareta's wreath, *ib.;* Gelon's tripod, *ib.;* three cities only called by Homer 'rich in'; Troy, Mycenae, and Orchomenos, 303 (cf. BUTTONS; EARRINGS; FRONTLET); *Pref.* xiii.
Goodwin, Prof. W. W.; 'The Ruins at Hissarlik,' 288.
Gordian III.; coins of, 339.
Gorgon's Head, from frieze, 205.
Gormezano, Jewish agent, 11.
Gout; cured by the sarcophagus, 320.
Gozzadini, on the sepulchres near Bologna, and double cups, 157.
Gozzano (Modena); terramare, 170.
Grain, bruised, not ground, for meal, in prehistoric and Homeric times, 44; toasted, or bruised, or as porridge, in Roman rites, 45; burnt, much, in the two temples (c. 2), 130.
Granite, in pottery of 1st c., 33; grooved piece of, probable weight for net or loom, 172-3.
—— columns, at various places in the Troad, App. I., *passim.*
Grass, abundant in the plain of Troy; scarce in 1882, 17.
Greece, pottery of. (*See* POTTERY.)
——, Proper, coins of (Ilium), 224.
——, king and queen of, 324.
Greek Colonists at Troy, 262; *Pref.* xxviii.
Greeks; their primitive arms, 96.
—— of Asia Minor; their enthusiasm for union with Greece; growing numbers and wealth, 324.
Greg, R. P.; discussion of the ⌊⊓ and ⌊⊐, 124, f.; his Hittite seal, *Pref.* xxi; terra-cotta weight with Trojan inscription, xxv; his scarab with Carian letters, xxvi.
Gregorios Basilopoulos (named *Ilos*), overseer, 5.
Grimm, 'Deutsche Mythologie,' 96.
Grooves, in brick walls, for baking *in situ*, 76, f. (cf. CHANNELS).
Gross, Dr. V.; excavations in Swiss lake-dwellings, 40; on the use of whorls, 41; proof of their use with spindles, 295, 300; 'Les Protohelvètes,' 40, 41, 111, 148, 153, 171;

'Résultat des Recherches exécutées dans les lacs de la Suisse occidentale,' 146; 'Station de Corcelettes,' 146, 154.
Grote, G.; 305, 362; *Pref.* v, vi.
Grotta del Diavolo, Bologna, of first epoch of the rein-deer, 38, 47, 50, 153; whorls, oldest in Italy, 40.
Grottoes in Bologna; 39, 135–6.
Gruter, 'Inscriptions,' 82.
Guben, in Prussia; cemetery, 37, 49.
Guides, at Ilium, 346–7.
Gureliotissa, R.; 327.
Gutter; through S.E. gate of c. 3, like the conduits at Tiryns and Mycenae, 178–9; *not* for blood of sacrifices, but for rain water, 179.
Gygas, Pr.; 305.
Gyges; sources of his wealth, 50.

H.

Hadji Uzin, of Alampsa, 311.
Hadrian; Ilian inscription (probably) of his time, 234.
Haematite. (*See* IRON.)
Hagios Demetrios Tepeh; a natural rock, not a tumulus, 261; ruin of temple close by, 344.
Hahn, J. G. von, excavations in acropolis on Bali Dagh (1864), 265.
Halberstadt; tomb at, 152.
Halil Kioi; Ilian inscriptions found at, 231, 232, 233.
Hallstadt (Austria); necropolis, 280.
Hamar (Old German 'hammer'), an etymological witness to a *stone* weapon, 96.
Hamaxitus, Kemanli Kioi, 341; inhabitants removed to Alex. Troas, *ib.*
Hamid Pasha, civil governor of the Dardanelles, 7, 244, 258.
Hammers; stone, in the Hellenic well, 19; rude (c. 1), 43; parallels, *ib.;* (c. 2) granite, perforated, or partly so, 172; in tum. Protes., 259.
—— stone, and axe combined (c. 1), 42–3; (c. 2), 119; (c. 3), 184; (c. 4), 188; on tum. Protes., 257.
Hanaï Tepeh (*Thymbra*), suspension bowls, 39; perforated vases, 136;

pottery very ancient, but quite different from Trojan; not a tumulus, but a succession of habitations, 260, 345, 347, 349; *Pref.* x.
Handles; how fastened on stone implements, 43; of knives (*see* KNIFE-HANDLES).
Hanover; antiquities of, 123, 127.
Hardening (supposed) of metals by plunging in water (cf. Βαφή, Βάψις), 101; the explanation erroneous, 102–3; copper utensils hardened by hammering, 103; by alloy of copper with rhodium, not proved, 104.
Hardy, E.; 'Schliemann und seine Entdeckungen auf der Baustelle des alten Troja,' 287.
Harper and Brothers, Messrs.; 303.
Hastings, battle of, 96.
Hauterive, lake dwellings of, 148, 153.
Head, double, on coins of Tenedos, 223; different explanations, 224.
Heads, sculptured, lower city of Ilium; small female, helmeted, 214, 215; peculiar treatment of skull, 215; helmeted male, 214; of a horse, 215; terra-cotta, 215.
Heathen Worship; decrees prohibiting, 346.
Hebriones; 285.
Hecamede; 44, 45.
Hecataeus; 344.
Hector, 65, 162, 254, 283, 284; his cenotaph in Chaonia, 253; on coins of Ilium, 220; his name a Greek rendering of the Phrygian Dareios, *Pref.* xi.
Hecuba, tomb of. (*See* CYNOSSEMA.)
Hehn, 'Kulturpflanzen und Hausthiere,' 162.
Heise, K.; 'Map of the Troad' (No. 140), 347.
Helbig, Prof. W.; on the use of whorls, 41; on ancient use of meal, 45; 'Die Italiker in der Po-Ebene,' 41, 45, 95, 96, 162; 'Sopra il Depas Amphikypellon,' 155, f.
Heldreich, Prof. Th. von; 334.
Helen; her silver basket, 109, 296, 299; power of her beauty, 162.
Helenus, King of Chaonia, 253.

Hellanicus; his character and authority discussed, 367, f.
Hellespont; 303, 333, 343, 344, 347; advance of the sea on, 283.
Helmet-crest, of Achilles, 107.
Hephaestus; maker of gold wire (Hom.), 107; of wire net to catch Ares and Aphrodité, 108.
Hera and Hypnos, at Lectum, 313.
Heracleum, on S. shore of G. of Adramyttium, *not* Arakli, 321.
Herakles; representative of the Phoenicians; his expedition to Ilium may point to a Phoenician conquest, 61.
Hercules; Roman statue of, found in lower city of Ilium, 214.
Hermias, a eunuch; ruler at Assos, gives his niece in marriage to Aristotle, 319.
Herodotus; quoted, 4, 82, 96, 100, 159, 162, 193, 196, 238, 254, 294, 298, 323 329, 343, 344, 346; *Pref.* xi, xvii.
Heroic Tombs. (*See* TUMULI.)
Hertz, K., on Schliemann, his life, his excavations, and his literary activity, 287.
Hesychius; quoted, 82, 83; *Pref.* xi
Heth, the sons of. (*See* HITTITES.)
Hierocles; quoted, 340.
Hieroglyphs, Hittite; 𐤉𐤍, perhaps a chair, 127. (Cf. *Pref.* xxiii–xxv.)
Hieronomoi (inscription), the managers of the temple of Athené, 227.
Himera, battle of, 114.
Hippocampus; on coins of Scepsis, 276.
Hirschfeld, Baron von, German Chargé d'Affaires at Constantinople, 13.
Hissarlik; precise and exclusive correspondence with the hill of moderate height, in a large and fair plain, watered by rivers from Ida, on which *sacred Ilios* was built (Plato), 291; viewed from the summit of Ida, 333.
—— excavations on, in 1879, 1, 303; revisited (1881), 306; work resumed in 1882, 5; state of the works since 1879, 5, 306; weather at, 14, 15, and App. VII. 381; the hill extended to the east, after the 4th city, 20, 62; the plateau east, south, and west of the hill, 24; excavations on south-west slope, 25 (cf. EXCAVATIONS); citadel of c. 2 and 7, 62, 343; c. 3 and 4 limited to, 62, 175, 184; c. 5 extended beyond, 62; great depth of *débris* explained, 185, 186; contrasted with the little elsewhere in the Troad, 278, 303, 347; Prof. Jebb's theory of the strata discussed, 236, f.; grand result of discoveries, answering to Homer's Ilios, 277; Prof. Virchow on the age of the strata, 376, f. See *Pref.* xii, f., xv, xvi, xxvi, xxvii.

Hittite use of the 𐤉𐤍, 125–6; probably received from them by the Trojans, 126, *Pref.* xviii, xxi; hieroglyphs, like signs on Trojan whorls, 127; a whorl like the Trojan, *ib.,* *Pref.* xviii.
Hittites (Khita); their empire; capitals Carchemish and Kadesh; war with Ramses II., 3, *Pref.* xvii; allies of, from Asia Minor, *ib.;* link of Babylonian civilization with W. Asia and Europe, 302, *Pref.* xvii; of Palestine, their *silver currency* by weight, 302.
Hoch-Kelpin (Danzig), urn from, 121.
Höfler, Joseph, architect, 5.
Hog; of ivory (c. 2), probably a knifehandle, 115; parallels, *ib.;* vase-head in form of (c. 2), 139, 140.
Holweda; 'Schliemann's Troie,' 287.
Homer: his descriptions of Troy and the Troad, 1, 2; list of Trojan allies, compared with Egyptian records, 3; potter's wheel in, 34; quoted, 44, 45, 49, 57, 61, 65, 66, 75, 96, 100, 101, 102, 104, 107, 108, 109, 111, 112, 114, 116, 118, 123, 145, 146, 149, 150, 155, 157, 162, 163, 244, 253, 254, 273, 274, 281, 282, 283, 284, 290, 297, 303, 312, 315, 318, 319, 326, 327, 328, 332, 334, 335, 337, 346, 350. See *Pref.* xiv, f.
Homeric Age; age, 9th cent. B.C., 278.
—— (*Schol. ad*); quoted, 82, 83, 156.
Hoorn, P. M. van; Schliemann's discoveries and site of Troy, 286.
Horace; prophecy of Juno, Prof. Maehly on, 288; quoted, 297, 298, 325.
Horse, bones of (c. 1), 349; scarcity of at Troy, how explained, *ib.*
Horse's head; tripod vase in form of

(Corneto), 132 ; marble, from lower city of Ilium, 215, 216.
Hostmann, Dr. Chr.; excavations in the necropolis of Darzau, 33 ; on the manufacture of prehistoric pottery, *ib.;* 'Der Urnenfriedhof bei Darzau, 123, 127, 147 ; in 'Zeitschrift für Ethnologie,' 152 ; on hardening and βαφή of metals, 102, 193.
House of Paris, in Homer, has three rooms (like temple B), 86.
Houses (c. 2). (*See* HOUSE-WALLS.)
—— of 3rd city ; probably only one story of brick above substructions of stone, 176 ; plan irregular ; small chambers, *ib.;* the chief one, 23, 57, 58, 176 ; filled with brick *débris* of wall of c. 2, 58.
—— of 4th city ; like those of 3rd ; plan irregular, small chambers, 185 ; of small quarry-stones and clay ; probably only a ground floor, *ib.;* horizontal terrace *roofs* (*q. v.*), *ib.*
——, present, of the Troad, of the same type as in the prehistoric cities of Hissarlik, 84, 185.
House-Walls; of quarry-stones and crude bricks, 21 ; of 2nd, 3rd, 4th, and 5th cities, 22, 23 ; found in shafts on the plateau, 25 ; Hellenic, on plateau, 26.
—— in acropolis of c. 2 (cf. EDIFICES) ; brick, left standing by 3rd settlers, 52 ; beneath the two temples, 86-7 ; over S. gate, 87 ; in N.E. part, 88 ; large, in W. part, *ib.;* walls of two distinct epochs of c. 2, 89.
—— of c. 3 ; built on, and sunk into, calcined *débris* of c. 2, 52-3, 87, 88 ; of small stones and clay, some brick, coated with clay, 175 ; probably crude brick (on stone foundations) baked *in situ,* 176 ; proofs from the fragility of the bricks, *ib.*
—— of c. 4 ; very thin ; some of brick, baked or unbaked ; coated with clay, 185.
—— of c. 5 ; of quarry stones and clay, or bricks with clay cement on stone foundations, 188 ; no tiles (cf. ROOFS), 190.

Huckle-bones. (*See* ASTRAGALI.)
Hultsch, F. ; 'Griechische und Römische Metrologie,' 112.
Human Figures, rude ; on whorls, petroglyphs, and urns, 121-2.
Human Remains. (*See* SKELETONS.)
Human Sacrifices, by Achilles, 162.
Humboldt, A. von ; 'Ansichten der Natur,' 121 ; and *Bonpland,* 'Reise in den Aequinoctial-Gegenden,' 121.
Hunting. (*See* CHACE.)
Hut-urns, funeral, of Marino and Corneto, 48, 122, 126 ; fibulae in, a proof of age later than c. 1-6 of Troy, 48 ; pre-Etruscan, 127 ; peculiar signs on, like Hittite hieroglyphs, 127.
Hyacinth, on Ida (Hom.), 335.
Hyginus, quoted, 254.

I.

Ibrees, in Lycaonia, Hittite sculptures at, 126 ; *Pref.* xxi.
Ida, Mt., snow-clad to March 20, and partially to end of May 15 ; 270, 273, 274, 303, 347 ; meaning of ὑπωρείαι Ἴδης, 273, 291 ; upper ranges uninhabited and pastures unused for six months, 330, 331, 332 ; the eastern pass of, traversed by Xerxes (Herod.), now disused, discovered by author, 329 ; first and second 'gates' (*porta*), 331 ; abundant springs, confirming Homer, *ib.;* descent from second gate to Oba Kioi and Evjilar, *ib. ;* splendid view ; rivers ; vegetation, 331, 332 ; ascent from Evjilar to the twin summits, 324, 325, 332 (*see* GARGARUS, SARIKIS) ; spring flowers, 334 ; altar, shrine, and throne of Zeus, 334, 335, 336 ; no animals, 337.
Idols, female, Trojan, 38 ; terra-cotta (c. 2), one like the stone idols, 141 ; very rude, 142 ; one with great owl-eyes, *ib. ;* of marble or trachyte (c. 2), 151 ; their extreme rudeness, *ib.;* parallels, *ib.;* (c. 2), very remarkable primitive, copper or bronze, probably a PALLADIUM, 169 ; Chal-

dean and Hittite, precisely like the leaden Trojan, a type of the goddess 'ATHI (*q. v.*), *Pref.* xviii.

Idols, found at Eleusis, more primitive than the rudest Trojan, 38.

Iliad. (*See* HOMER.)

Ilians, Village of; its site near Thymbra, 284, 345; why chosen by Demetrius for Troy, 284–5, 362, 363.

Ilios, Sacred; built in the *plain* by people who moved from *Dardanié* (*q. v.*), 274, 291; *decisive testimony of Plato to the identity of its site both with the historic Ilium and with Hissarlik*, 290–1; Homer's description of, realized in the discoveries at Hissarlik, 277; *Pref.* xiv, xv; the name used by the Empress Eudoxia, 225; date of its capture and destruction, *Pref.* xii.

'*Ilios*,' by Dr. Schliemann, quoted *passim*, for the objects described.

Ilium ("Ἴλιον); *Site* and *History;* the *only* classical name of the Greek and Roman city on the site of Troy, with its Acropolis the 7th stratum on Hissarlik, 195; the question of site argued, 291, 361, f.; date of Aeolian colonization, 237, *Pref.* xv; stages of growth, xxvii; a small village before Alexander, 228; his visit, *ib.;* he made it free, &c., *ib.;* his later promises, *ib:;* but *promises only*, performed by Lysimachus and Antigonus, 228, 370–1; alleged decay improbable, 371; head of a federal union, 372; Prof. Jebb's theory discussed, 236, f., 361, f., 376, f., *Pref.* xxix, f.; under the Romans, had 70,000 inhabitants, with sumptuous EDIFICES, 343, 346; visited by pilgrims and tourists in 4th cent., 289; in ruins in time of Eudoxia (unless her lament refers to Homer's *Ilios*), 225; probably a monastery and small medieval fort on the Acropolis, 224; a bishopric mentioned by Constantin. Porphyr., *ib.;* architectural fragments from, in Turkish cemeteries, 308; gems and coins, 218, f.

Ilium, plan of (VIII. at end of volume), 14; search for Greek and Roman foundations and sculptures, 17; its Acropolis on Hissarlik, *ib.;* great corner of wall (probably) of Lysimachus, 195; distinction of Macedonian and Roman MASONRY (*q.v.*), 195–6; great Roman wall, 196; Doric TEMPLES (*q. v.*), 196, f.; the other buildings Roman; their style, 207. (*See* PORTICO, PROPYLAEUM.)

——, Lower City, on the plateau, E., S., and W. of Hissarlik, explored, 24, 62; Macedonian and Roman walls of enclosure, 63; its edifices, 110; a Corinthian PORTICO (*q. v.*), 26, 110; Hellenic house-walls 24; bases for statues; gigantic THEATRE (*q. v.*), 110, f.; tombs, statues, and mosaic floors, found in shafts, 214; other sculptures, 214, 215; terracottas, 216; archaic painted pottery, in the Lower City and in the Acropolis, *ib.*

Iliuna, Iluna, Iriuna, in Egyptian records, perhaps Ilion, 3; capital of Dardanians about 14th cent. B.C., *ib.;* doubt about the reading, *ibid. n.*

Ilus, tumulus of, with its pillar; site further discussed, 283–4; on right bank of the Scamander, 284.

Imbros, I., views of, 277, 331, 333.

Imola, terramare of, 154.

Implements. (*See* BRONZE, COPPER, STONE, and the several objects.)

In Tepeh; three tumuli on the headland above, 27.

In Tepeh Asmak; old bed of the Scamander, 282.

India; whorls found in Buddhist provinces of, 39; gold from, 50.

Indians, N. American; their manufacture of flint implements, 174.

Indra, the rain-god of India; the 卍 and 卐 his symbols. 124.

Iné or Eziné, village on the Scamander; visited, 28, 339; trade of, 339; sellers of ancient coins, *ib.;* scanty *débris*, 340; pottery, *ib.;* probably the ancient SCAMANDRIA, *ib.*

Inscription; from the Parthenon, 75; Puteolanian, 82.
—— (in *Ilios,* pp. 633-5), further discussed by Droysen, 227-8.
Inscriptions, Trojan (c. 2); their relation to the Asianic and Cypriote syllabaries; *Pref.* xxiii-xxv.
——, cuneiform of Van, *Pref.* xi.
—— *of Ilium,* 23 : *Greek,* found in theatre, 211, 213; one on a small column, 213; xxiv. copied and discussed, 226-235; *Latin,* two in cemetery of Koum Kioi, 236.
—— *of the Troad : Greek;* Antandrus, 323; Assos, 320; Avjilar, 243; Kusch Deressi, 312; Lesbos, 320; *Latin ;* Kemanli Kioi, 340; Kestambul, 310.
Ioannes, Philippos, 251
Ireland; prehistoric antiquities of, 121.
Iron ; (*and Steel*), hardening of, by plunging in water, and softening (annealing) by fire, 104; presence in bronze, 104-5; magnetic, slingbullets of, 118.
Iron Age; Caucasian antiquities of, 280.
Issa (cf. ASI); old name of Lesbos, 4.
Issel, ' L' uomo preist. in Italia,' 157.
Issus, in Cilicia, 4.
Italy, prehistoric antiquities of. (*See* ETRUSCAN TOMBS, LAKE DWELLINGS, TERRAMARE, and special names.)
Ithaca; flute found at, 252; pottery of, like some of the pottery on the Fulu Dagh; coin of, at Ilium, 224.
Ivory ; small objects of, (c. 1), 50; (c. 2), 115, 116; ornament of a box, 116; a parallel, *ib.;* probably imported, *ib.;* lamb, 116-7; spoon, 117; arrow-head, *ib.;* (c. 4) two curious objects, 192. (Cf. *Pref.* xiii.)

J.

Jacob and his sons in Egypt, 302.
Jade and *Jadeite,* 41; Prof. Fischer and Prof. Bücking on, 41, 42; mineralogical distinction, *ib.;* investigations of Arzruni and Berwerth, *ib.;* (c. 2) axes of, green and white, 171;

rarity of the white, only *two,* 171-2; (c. 3 and 5), green, 172; jade, neolithic, *ib.; white* from Yarkand, *green* from Lake Baikal, *ib.;* great piece in tomb of Tamerlane, *ib. ;* axes, link between primitive Troy and the furthest East, *Pref.* ix.
Jars, Gigantic (πίθοι), used as cellars, reservoirs, &c.; numerous in c. 2-5, esp. c. 2 and c. 3, 149; how grouped and placed, 150; decorations, 149; in palaces of Zeus and Ulysses, *ib. ;* called κέραμοι, 150; the only *thoroughly baked pottery,* except the huge dishes (*q. v.*), *ib.*
——, large; frag. of on Kurshunlu Tepeh, 273; in Kutchek Tepeh, *ib.*
Jasper, polishers; (c. 1), 47; (c. 2), 172.
Jebb, Prof. *R. C.;* on 'Schliemann's Ilios,' in 'Edinburgh Review,' 287; ' Homeric and Hellenic Ilium,' *ib.;* 'The Ruins at Hissarlik, their relation to the Iliad,' 129, 236, 288; eclectic theory of the topography of the Iliad, 288, *Pref.* xiv; adopts Brentano's absurd theory, *ib. ;* his theory of the strata at Hissarlik and the historic epochs of Ilium, discussed, 236, f. ; character of the Lydian pottery, 238; decisive distinction of Greek pottery, *always painted,* from the pottery of the strata 3, 4, and 5, 239; and of the stone implements, 240; Dumont's views misstated, 240-1; further replies to, App. V., p. 361, f. (Cf. App. VI., 376, f.; *Pref.* p. xxix.)
Jerablûs. (*See* CARCHEMISH.)
Jericho, the spoil of, 112, 302; commerce with Babylon, 302.
Jews, Levantine; Spanish origin; write Spanish with Hebrew characters, 11.
Jocasté, cook, 9.
Jörg, E.; ' Schliemann und Ilios,' 287.
Joseph in Egypt, 302.
Joshua, Book of ; 112, 302.
' *Journal of Hellenic Studies,*' 129, 236, 237, 288, 361, f.
Journey in the Troad (1881), 303 f.; its objects and results, 303, 347; new light on Homeric geography, 303; sites of ancient flourishing cities, but

no considerable prehistoric ruins, except at Hissarlik, 303, 346.
Jugs ; (c. 1) lustrous black, very slight, wheel-made, 34 ; (c. 3) hand-made, 2 spouts, 182-3. Cf. App. VI., 376.
Julia Domna, on coins (Il.), 221.
Julian, Emp. ; letter on his visit to Troy, further discussed, 289, 346.
Julianus, L. Claudius, statue to, 236.
Julius, Dr. ; quoted, 215.
Juno. See HORACE.
Juvenal; quoted, 45.

K.

Kadesh, Hittite city on the Orontes, war of Ramses II. against, 3.
Kadi Kioi, village, 329.
Kaisariyeh (Caesarea), in Cappadocia, antiquities, 127 ; whorl, *Pref.* xviii.
Kalifatli, village, 306.
Kalifatli Asmak, R., the ancient SCAMANDER, 17, 67.
Kanu (Caunus) in Egypt. records, 4.
Kara Agatch Tepeh ("black tree hill "), the tumulus of PROTESILAUS (*q. v.*).
Kara Your, Mt. (*See* CALLICOLONE.)
Karanlik, small gulf of the Hellespont, 8.
Karkamash (Coracesium or *Carchemish*) in Egyptian records, 4 ; Hittite capital, *Pref.* xvii, f.
Karkarideressi, rivulet, 339.
Kattenborn road; cemetery on, 49.
Kazdagh ("geese-mountain "), name of crests of Ida, 331.
Kazmierz-Komorowo, cemetery, 131.
Kelena, Kerena (Colonae), in Egyptian records, 4.
Kemanli Kioi ; site of an ancient city ; Greek pottery, columns, &c. ; sarcophagus; marble slabs ; Latin inscriptions, 340, 341 ; probably HAMAXITUS, 341.
Kerkesh. (*See* GERGESH.)
Kestambul, Turkish village ; ruins, fountain, sarcophagus, inscriptions, pottery, 310 ; prob. COLONAE, 311.
K'hita. (*See* HITTITES.)
Kiln, in theatre of Ilium, for burning marble sculptures to lime, 212.

Kimmeris. (*See* ANTANDRUS.)
Kipes (cupa, hotte); likeness of the Trojan vases to, 38.
Kisillkedjili, R.; contains name of CILLA and CILLUS, 327.
Kluczewo (Posen) ; graveyard of, 122.
Knife-handles; fastened on by pins, 100 ; ivory, in form of a hog (c. 2), 115 ; Assyrian, in form of a lion, *ib.;* bone (c. 2), 117 ; parallels, *ib.*
Knives, bronze or copper ; one of c. 1, 47 ; (c. 2), 100 ; fastened to handles by pins, *ib.;* three small, 167 ; (c. 4), 188 ; *in* tum. Protes., 259.
———, flint or chalcedony ; (c. 3), 184 ; *on* tum. Protes., 257.
Knob, gold, of a sceptre or staff (c. 2), 106 ; Maeonian type, *Pref.* xxii.
Ko, Cypriote character, spiral decoration like, 146. (Cf. SPIRAL.)
Koban, Upper, in the Caucasus, cemetery of, 42 ; its date, 48, 95, 105, 110, 247 ; belongs to beginning of iron age, probably 10th cent. B.C., 280 ; excavations in (*see* VIRCHOW).
Koch Ali Ovassi; anc. quarries, 341.
Koiun Evi, village ; 316.
Koum Kaleh, fortress of, ACHILLEUM ; 12, 13, 16, 243, 257, 262, 344.
Koum Kioi; metopes found at, 199, 200 ; Ilian inscriptions, 234, 236 ; site of POLION or Polisma, 343 ; granite columns and Greek pottery, *ib.*
Korunka (Bohemia) ; tombs of, 248.
Koyunjik (Nineveh) ; palace of Sennacherib, 110, 301.
Krause, Ed., 38, 123, 135.
Kremer, Von; 'Aegypten,' 325, 326.
Kulakli Kioi, site of CHRYSA, 314.
Kurshunlu Tepeh (leaden hill), on right of Scamander, near Ida, 270 ; ruins on, seen by Dr. Clarke, 271 ; a quarry for Beiramich, *ib.;* all gone (1819), *ib.;* visited (1881), 338 ; excavations (1882), 27, 28, 270, f. ; walls of masonry (*q. v.*) like those of Assos, 271, 341 ; probably an oval tower, 271 ; signs of other buildings, 271-2 ; small depth of *débris;* probably washed away, 272, 278 ; pottery, wheel-made, various, 272 ; none

prehistoric or archaic-Hellenic, *ib.;* some like that on Bali Dagh, Eski Hissarlik, and Fulu Dagh, of 9th-5th cent. B.C. ; some like that of Ithaca ; also Macedonian and Roman, *ib.;* rude, strewn on surface, 273 ; beautiful panoramic view from, 273 ; the primitive DARDANIÉ and original Scepsis (PALAESCEPSIS), 273-4 ; habitation impossible higher up Ida, 340 ; Greek inscription of an unknown town, which succeeded Dardanié and Palaescepsis, 234-5.

Kusch Deressi (bird rivulet), 311 ; site of LARISA, 312 ; fragments of marbles and pottery, and coins ; blocks in Turkish cemetery ; inscription, *ib.*

Kutchek Tepeh, tum. (small hill), excavated ; slight results ; enormous stones, probably to consolidate the hillock, as in Ujek Tepeh ; bones, fragment of tiles and jars, 273.

Kutschuk Tsai (little river), 321.

L.

Labionka, R., in N.W. Caucasus, 94.
Laërces; caster of gold (Hom.), 100.
Lagarde, De; quoted, 114.
Lago di Garda; lake dwellings, 57.
Lake dwellings, Italian and Swiss, 42, 44, 48, 95, 111, 146, 148, 153, 154, 171. (Cf. special names and GROSS V.)
Lamb; of ivory (c. 2), 116, 117 ; weights perhaps in the form of, 302.
Lamps; no vestige of in c. 1-6, nor at Mycenae, nor Orchomenos, 145 ; first in 5th cent. B.C., 145-6 ; the Homeric λύχνοι either torches or fire-pans, 146 ; oil lamps in the *Batrachomyomachia,* proof of its late date, *ib.*
Lampsacus; gold-mines, 50 ; a member of the Ilian union, 228.
Lance-heads ; bronze, of common Trojan form (c. 2), 94, 167 ; nearly all *previously* found at Troy *serrated* (a form not found elsewhere), but none of those found in 1882 are serrated, 94 ; *stone serrated* lanceheads in Denmark, &c., of form like the Trojan, 94 ; development of bronze lances, daggers, and swords, from original form of dagger in stone age, 94-5 ; how fastened to shaft, 95.
Lance-heads; of stone and silex, serrated and plain, 94 ; prototypes of the Trojan bronze ones, 94.
Landerer, Prof. X.; quoted, 112.
Lange, 'Römische Alterthümer,' 113.
Larisa (Lares, Larissa in Egyptian records), Pelasgian, city of Troad, 4 ; many others of the name, *ib.;* ruins and coins at Kusch Deressi, 312.
Lava; in the Troad, 315.
Lawton, W. C.; on inscriptions at Assos and Lesbos, 320, 323.
Layard, Sir A. H., 5, 110, 301, *Pref.* vi ; 'Nineveh and its Remains' and 'Nineveh and Babylon,' 301.
Lead; traces of in bronze, 104-5.
Leaven; late use by Romans, 46.
Lechevalier; his *invention* of the Troy-Bounarbashi site, 195 ; he *never visited Hissarlik, ib.;* 242, 285.
Lectum, Pr., 303 ; W. pt. (C. Baba), 314 ; summit, 315 ; ruins of Agamemnon's altar of the twelve gods, *ib.;* enclosures, modern, *ib.;* Macedonian pottery, *ib.;* well, 316 ; neighbouring scenery, 316, 320.
Leleges, in the Troad ; 314, 323.
Lemnos, I., 333.
Lenguas, Indian tribe (Paraguay) ; use of ⌐┌, 122.
Lenormant, Fr.; 3, 4, 224 ; *Pref.* xxiii.
Lenz, 'Die Ebene von Troja nach dem Grafen Choiseul-Gouffier ;' 242, 243, 245, 247, 252.
Lepsius, Prof. G. R.; on the hardening of iron and steel, 103.
Lesbian Greeks; the shrewdest merchants in the world, 324.
Lesbos, I., anciently Issa, belonged to the Troad, 4, 314, 318, 321, 333.
Levelling of hill-top for 2nd city, 22 ; on plateau for wall of lower city, 26.
Lex Aternia Tarpeia, 113.
Libations; unmixed wine used in, 145.
Ligia Hamam; hot springs, 309 ; ruins of Roman baths, *ib.;* of medieval buildings, 310 ; slight *débris, ib.*
Liku (Lycians), in Egyptian records, 3.

Lime; marble sculptures of Ilium burnt to, 212. (Cf. KILN.)
Lions; bronze, series of Assyrian weights in the form of, 301
Lisch, Dr.; on the manufacture of prehistoric pottery, 33.
Livia, the younger, called Aphrodite of the race of Anchises, on an Ilian inscription, 232.
Livonia; antiquities of, 136.
Livy, quoted, 328.
Locrians, in Homer; the sling their only weapon, 96, 119; importance of the statement, 96; of Magna Graecia, laws of Zaleucus, 145.
Locusts, 17; swarms in 1881, 306; their habits, *ib.*
Loitz, vase from, with 𐤇, 123.
Lolling, Dr. H. G., quoted, 215.
Lopöhnen (Prussia), antiquities, 110.
Lotus on Ida (Hom.), 335.
Louvre. (*See* MUSEUMS.)
Lower Cities; (prob.) of c. 1 (*see* FIRST CITY), 30; of ancient Troy (*see* SECOND CITY); of ILIUM (*q. v.*).
Lubbock, Sir J. (*See* PIGORINI.)
Lucan; on the desolation of Troy, an example of poetical disregard of facts, 292.
Lucian; quoted, 243, 254, 289, 343.
Lucius, a Milesian named on an inscr. from Kurshunlu Tepeh, 235.
Lucretius, quoted, 100.
Lugia Hamam; hot mineral baths of, 325; votive offerings, *ib.;* long and high celebrity, 326; medieval ruins, sunk in the swamp, *ib.;* prob. site of Homer's ΘΗΒΗ ΥΠΟΠΛΑΚΙΗ, called from the wooded hill (*Plakos* or *Plax*) of Lugia Tepessi, 326-7; excavations impracticable, 327.
Lugia Tepessi; wooded hill above Lugia Hamam; the only one in the plain of Adramyttium; probably the πλάκος ὑλήεσση of Hom., 326.
Luke, St., at Assos, 319.
Luxury, in the Homeric age, 162.
Lycaonia, Hittite antiquities of, 126.
Lycia; coins with the *triquetrum,* 124.
Lycians, on the R. Zeleia, 3, 274.
Lycophron (*Schol. ad*)*;* quoted, 83.

Lycurgus; on the complete and final desolation of Troy, 225, 291; used as decisive of Greek opinion against the claims of Ilium, *ib.;* reply of Prof. Steitz, *ib.;* follows a poetical tradition, 292; Prof. Mahaffy on, 369, f.; applies only to lower city, *Pref.* xxvi.
Lydia; gold mines of, 50.
Lydian terra-cottas, below Ilium, 22, *Pref.* xxvi. (*See* SIXTH CITY.)
Lydians, 3; their colonization of Etruria, 193; (as rulers) at Troy, 262.
Lyrnesus; buried under alluvia, 328.
Lysanias, an Ilian (inscr.), 227.
Lyseas, stélé of, 160.
Lysimachus; built the city-wall and temples at Ilium, 195, 199, 201, 204; his favours to Ilium, 228, 236; other references, 313, 319, 342.

M.

Macedonian rule at Ilium, 262. (Cf. MASONRY, POTTERY.)
Madsen, 'Antiquités Préhistoriques du Danemark,' 94.
Machly, Prof. J.; quoted, 100; on the δέπας ἀμφικύπελλον, 155; on Juno's prophecy in Horace, 288; 'Schliemann's Troja,' 287.
Maeonian Antiquities, Pref. xviii.
Maeonians, the Lydians, 3; *Pref.* xvii.
Mahaffy, Prof. J. P.; 'The Site and Antiquity of the Hellenic Ilion,' reply to Professor Jebb's papers, 287, and App. V., p. 361, f.; general conclusions, 372-4; balance of the opinions of "intelligent antiquity," 375.
Mahomet; his expedition to Dat-er-Rika, 326.
Mallus, in Cilicia, 4.
Malta, painted eyes on boats of, 32.
Maussen, W. J.; site of Troy; 'Heinrich Schliemann,' 286.
Maps. (*See* TROAD, MAPS OF.)
Marabout Trees; hung with votive offerings, 326.
Marble, white; material of the great Macedonian temple, and of all the Roman edifices, at Ilium, 195;

columns, &c., of Macedonian and Roman buildings, 199, f.; columns and casing of theatre (*q. v.*), 211.
Marcellus; gems dedicated by, 219.
Marino, near Albano; antiquities, 48, 122, 126, 133, 146, 217.
Mariotti, of the Parma Museum, 32.
Marks on Roman blocks of stone at Ilium, 20, 196.
Marmora, Sea of, 333.
Marocco; charm against evil eye, 32.
Marquardt, 'Römische Staatsverwaltung,' 113.
Marrow; (c. I.; oroken bones no proof that it was eaten raw, 350.
Martens, Herr von, on *oysters* or *ascidia* in Homer, 285.
Masistius; 162.
Masitsi, a peasant at Koum Kioi, 234.
Mask, terra-cotta, from lower city of Ilium, 215-16.
Masonry of c. 3, 4, 5, of crude bricks and small stones, 22, 23; of fortress wall ascribed to 5th c., 190.
— *of Ilium;* of the great wall (*q. v.*), 195; the *Macedonian* (except the great temple) of a shelly conglomerate, the *Roman* of marble, on foundations of soft stone, 195-6.
— characteristic, of wedge-shaped blocks, filled in with small stones, at Assos, Alexandria Troas, Kurshunlu Tepeh, Cebrené, and Neandria, 34, 271, 275, 317.
—, *Polygonal;* in the older walls of Assos; not properly Cyclopean, probably of 6th or 7th century B.C., 318; polygonal and regular of two epochs in acropolis on Bali Dagh, 265.
Masu (Mysians), in Egypt. records, 3.
Maulnus or *Mulnus (Mallus ?),* in Egyptian records, 4.
Mauna, Mauon (Mæonians), in Egyptian records, 3.
Maximus, bishop of Assos, 319.
Meal, bruised, used instead of bread, and otherwise, in prehistoric and Homeric times, 44; carried on a journey, 45; used in Roman rites, *ib.;* etymological evidence of a stage in Graeco-Italic civilization, 46.

Meander or *Fret* pattern; probable origin of, from the ⊔, 125.
Measures; all according to the Metric system, 9; notation explained, 59; table of, French and English, xxxiv.
Measurements, difficulties in taking, from the Turkish delegate, 12, 13.
Medallion, Roman, marble, of the shewolf and twins, in theatre, 212.
Medinet-Abou; list of peoples at, 3, 4.
Mehmet, Turk; his curious information about Ida, 329, 330.
Mela, quoted; 320, 343, 344.
Melas Sinus, 333.
Meliteia; a servant of Athené, 227.
Menelaus; his gift to Telemachus, 109; gifts of Polybus to, 111; cenotaph to Agamemnon, 253.
Merum (ἄκρατον), undiluted wine; used only by great drinkers, *ib.;* Zaleucus's penalty of death for drinking it, except by medical order, 145.
Mestorf, Miss J. (See UNDSET.)
Metallurgy, cups for (c. 2, 3, 4), 153.
Metals; no special word in Homer for, 49; etymology of μεταλλάω and μέταλλον, *ib.* (Cf. the several names; HARDENING, TEMPERING.)
Meteorological observations at Hissarlik, 15, and App. VII., 381, f.
Metopes of the great Doric temple (*q. v.* at Ilium; of Apollo and the sun-chariot, 18, 199, 202; another, 198-9, another at Koum Kioi, 199; one at Thymbra, 200-1.
Meuricoffre & Co., of Naples, 133.
Mexico, New, antiquities of, 123.
Mica, in pottery of 1st c., 33.
Michaelis, 'The Parthenon,' 75.
Midas, sources of his wealth, 50.
Milchhoefer, Dr. A.; 'Die Anfänge der Kunst in Griechenland,' 123, *Pref.* xx; on site of Troy, 'Schliemann and his Works,' 287.
Mill for corn (*mola versatilis*) invented by the Volsinians, 46.
Millin; 'Peintures de Vases Ant.' 299.
Milton, quoted, 163.
Minerva, arts of, 298.
Mines (μέταλλα), etymology, 49; of gold, silver, and copper, in the Troad,

49, 346; Phrygia and Mt. Sipylus, *ib.;* Thrace and Mt. Pangaeus, *ib.;* Astyra near Abydos, *ib.;* Lydia, 50; Lampsacus, 50.
Mithridates VI. Eupator, his gem, dedicated by Pompey, 219; Sulla's peace with, 305; Roman wars with, 328.
Mixing Vessels of silver; with gold rims, given by Menelaus to Telemachus, 109; of terra-cotta (c. 2), 145.
Moat (medieval), in Acropolis of Ilium, 224-5; indications of its age, 225.
Mochli Tsai, R., 321.
Moeringen, lake-dwell. of, 111, 154, 171.
Moharrem Effendi, Turkish delegate, 12, 27, 257.
Mola salsa, flour spiced with salt, in Roman rites, 45.
Monastir Tsai, R.; ruins on, 323.
Money; primitive, uncoined, 112; gold and silver estimated by *weights* in the form of animals, *ib.;* 301; in Egypt, silver in form of *rings, ib.;* in Palestine, 302; Abraham's purchase in *a Hittite currency* of silver by weight, *ib.;* Jacob's purchase, *ib.;* both Canaanite and Egyptian during the famine, *ib.;* in the Mosaic law, 302; a *tongue* of gold (at Jericho), like the Trojan blades of silver, *ib.;* cattle the oldest medium of barter, *ib.;* hence the Latin *pecunia,* 113.
——, coined; not older than 7th cent. B.C., 112; the stater coined in Asia Minor, 114; and by Croesus and Darius, *ib.;* in Judea, only after the Captivity, 302.
—— whorls used as, in Pelew Is., 40.
Monk; quoted, 86.
Montélius, 'Congrès International d'Anthropologie Préhistorique,' 95.
Mortillet, G. de; 'Le Signe de la Croix,' 157.
Mosaic Floors; lower c. of Ilium, 214.
Moskonisi, I., 321.
Moulds of mica slate; for weapons, implements, and ornaments, abundant in c. 2; but *none found for* *workmen's tools* (*q. v.*), 100; two sorts of, 169-171; parallels, 170-1; for jewels, found at Koyunjik, 110.
Mouse; of Apollo Smintheus, 314.
Mtskheth, old cap. of Georgia, 48, 110.
Müllenhoff, K. V.; 'Deutsche Altertumskunde,' 61.
Müller, Prof. J., of Geneva, 334.
——, *Dr. K.,* of Halle, 334.
——, *Prof.,* of Berlin, 349.
Mugheir; saws and knives of silex and obsidian from, 47.
Murray, Mr. John; 303.
Museums; objects preserved in, furnishing parallels to those at Troy :—
—— Athens, 39, 136.
—— Berlin, Royal, 38, 110, 121, 147, 148; Ethnological, 122, 123, 135.
—— Bologna, 37, 39, 47, 110, 127, 135, 193.
—— Breslau, 148.
—— British, 47, 98, 133, 134, 139, 167, 217, 218.
—— Brussels, 37.
—— Carthage, 125.
—— Cassel, 36.
—— Castelvetrano, 126.
—— of the Caucasus (Tiflis), 48, 110.
—— Copenhagen, 43.
—— Corneto (Tarquinii), 40, 122, 126, 143, 148, 193, 194.
—— Florence, 137, 143.
—— Geneva, 37, 42, 44.
—— Hanover, 110.
—— Madrid, 36, 39, 42.
—— Mitau, 110.
—— Mycenean, at Athens, 249.
—— Naples, 194.
—— Paris; the Louvre, 39, 42, 44, 115, 117, 143, 144, 147, 148, 151, 152, 194.
—— —— Mus. de Cluny, 93.
—— —— Cabinet des Médailles, 143.
—— Parma, 37, 40, 43, 44, 135, 153, 154, 171, 173.
—— Posen, 131, 148.
—— Prague, 193.
—— Reggio, 37, 40, 43, 44, 153.
—— Rome, Museo Nazionale in the Collegio Romano, 37, 39, 42, 44, 126, 134, 135, 143, 146, 147, 148, 152, 154, 170, 193; the Vatican, 43, 122, 194.

Museums; the Schliemann, at Berlin, 94, 194, 199, 200, 238.
—— South Kensington, Trojan collection formerly at, 237-8, 239, 240.
—— St. Germain-en-Laye, 44, 47.
—— Turin, 93, 98, 137, 148, 152.
Mussels, and other small shells; enormous masses of, 186.
Mussaratli, scala and rivulet, 321.
Mycenae, antiquities; 108, 110, 135, 143, 151; vase-handles in form of cow-heads, 193; its painted pottery, a test of distinction from the Trojan, 239; compared with the very archaic in the tum. Achilles, 248-9; narrow escape of the Mycenean potsherds from destruction, 251; Stephani's absurd theory, 286; Phoen. and Assyr. influence, in contrast with Troy, *Pref.* xvi.
—— Cyclopean water-conduit at, like one outside Troy, 64, and one in the S.E. gate (c. 3), 178; the δέπ. ἀμφ., like the Trojan, 159; pottery, like the Ilian, 216; a flute, 252.
'*Mycenae,*' by Dr. Schliemann; quoted, 61, 64, 110, 135, 151, 178, 193, 252.
Myrina, tomb of, 282.
Mysia, 329; *Pref.* xxv.
Mysians, allies of Hittites, 3; *Pref.* xvii; in Trojan Olympus, driven out by Phrygians from Thrace, settled about sources of the Caïcus, 262.

N.

Naber, S. A.; site of Troy; 'Gladstone and Homer,' 286.
Nails; huge copper, quadrangular, with disk-like heads put on, in beams of temple A. (c. 2), 91, 92; with cast heads, 92; without disks, 166; copper and iron at Bali Dagh, 267.
Naos (sanctuary) of temple A (c. 2), 79; probable dimensions, 2 : 1, 80; doors and posts, 84; raised circles on floor, (altar or base for image?) 84; of temple B, 85; doorways, *ib.*
Naples; antiqq., 111. (Cf. MUSEUMS.)
Narli, scala of, 321.
'*Nation, The*' (New York); 'The True Site of Troy,' 287.

Neandria; the city on Mt. Chigri, 341; coins, 339.
Nebuchadnezzar, 180. (*See* BORSIPPA.)
Needle, curious double - pointed, of Egyptian porcelain (c. 2), 120.
Needles, of bone; (c. 1), 50; parallels, *ib.;* (c. 3), 184; (c. 4), 188.
—— bronze or copper; (c. 2) curiously shaped, probably brooches, 138-9; parallel from Cyprus, *ib.*
Neo Chori. (*See* YENI KIOI.)
Neoptolemus, 290.
Nephrite. (*See* JADE.)
Nestor, 44, 284.
Neufchâtel; lake-dwellings, 146, 154.
Neumark (Prussia), antiqq., 148.
Newton, Prof. C. T., 297.
Nicander of Thyatira, 115.
Nicaragua, antiqq., 121.
Nickam, 326. (*See* SHILLUKS.)
Nicolaos Zaphyros Giannakes, majordomo and purser, 8, 27.
Niké; sculptures of, from frieze of temple, 205-6.
Nikolaides, G., on site of Troy, 285.
Nineveh; daggers from, like the Trojan and Caucasian, 95; weights, 301.
Novum Ilium; the Greek and Roman city on the site of Troy; reasons for rejecting the name, 195.

O.

Oba Kioi, Turkish village, at foot of Kurshunlu Tepeh, marble frag. of Doric architecture, 270, 271, 329.
—— another, higher up on Ida, 274, 329, 331; its wretched state, 332.
Obsidian; saws and knives (*q. v.*), 47; 173; arrow-points still made by Californian Indians, 174.
Odyssey. (*See* HOMER.)
Oedipus Pyromalles; servant, 9.
Oenochoae (flagons), terra-cotta; (c. 2), 132, 133; parallels, 133, 142, 143; curious tripod, 144.
Olga, H. M., Queen of Greece, 135.
Olympia; bronze arrow-heads, 247.
Olympus, Mt. (the Trojan), inhabited by Mysians, 262.
Ophrynium; wrongly identified, 305;

true site at Palaeocastron, 305, 343 ; coined its own money, 346.
Oppidum Nee (Yeni Kioi), 344.
Orchomenos; the Minyan ; Dr. Schliemann's excavations at, 36–7, 303 ; fragments of hand-made vases found at, 36 ; suspension bowls, 39 ; bronze, analysis of, 105 ; 'rich in gold' (Hom.) 123 ; none found, but proof of wealth from the 'treasury' and 'thalamos,' 123, 304 ; the spiral 卐 on ceiling of thalamos, 123.
'*Orchomenos*,' by Dr. Schliemann ; 37, 39, 123.
Ordona; antiquities of, 111.
Orontes, R.; Kadesh on the, 3.
Oulou Dagh, M.; not Callicoloné, 281.
Oumm-esh-sharamat (mother of rags) ; a tamarisk, hung with votive offerings, 326.
Ovens; for Pottery; used in oldest age of Egypt, 35 : *for Bread;* not mentioned by Homer, nor found at Troy, nor in the terramare, 45.
Ovid, quoted ; 254, 297, 298, 299.
Owl; of Pallas on coins, 223, 339.
Owl Vases, with female characteristics ; (c. 1), 31 ; (c. 2–5), 151 ; likeness to the idols of Troy, Mycenae and Tiryns, *ib.;* (c. 4) two remarkable, 187 ; still seen in potters' shops at the Dardanelles, 188 ; (c. 5) two new types, 191 ; the pattern typical of the Babylonian and Hittite goddess 'ATHI, *Pref.* xviii, xix.
Ox, sacrificial, horns of, gilt (Hom.), 100 ; vase in form of (Posen), 131.
Oxen, weights in the form of, 112.
Oysters, in Homer ; meaning of τῆθος, 285 ; shells in c. 1–5, *ib.;* in c. 1, 350.

P.

Paidenli Kioi; 316.
Painting; non-existent on the Trojan pottery of all strata, 1–6 ; and so also that of the terramare, 137 ; a decisive distinction from Greek pottery, *always painted,* 239, 378.
Palaeocastron. (*See* OPHRYNIUM.)
Palaescepsis (the old SCEPSIS (*q.v.*)) ;

site on Kurshunlu Tepeh (*q. v.*), *not* on summit of Ida, 273, 330, 340.
Palau or *Pelew Is.;* whorls like Trojan used as money ; believed to be a gift of the spirits, 40.
Palestine; antiquities of, 47.
Paley, Prof. F. A.; 'Schliemann's Ilios,' in 'Brit. Quart. Review,' 287.
Palladium, the, a bronze copy of (c. 2), 169 ; on coins of Ilium, 220 ; sculptured with distaff and spindle, 300.
Pallas Athené, 281 ; on coins of Ilium, 220, 221 ; of Sigeum, 223 ; implements of spinning dedicated to her, and her emblem on coins, and in the Palladium, 299, 300 (cf. ATHENÉ).
Palm-tree; on coins of Scepsis, 276.
Panelling; walls of S. gate (c. 2), 72.
Pangaeus, Mt. ; gold mines, 49.
Panorama. (*See* VIEWS.)
Panticapaeum, coin of (Ilium), 224.
Papasli, village, 321–2 ; medieval, fortress near, *ib.;* coins Greek, Roman, and Byz., bought at, 323.
Parastades or *Antae;* of wood, on wellwrought base-stones, at front-ends of lateral walls of S.W. gate (c. 2), 68 ; of temple A, 80 ; their artistic purpose in Greek temples, *ib.; their primitive twofold constructive use now first discovered,* viz., to secure the wall-corners and support the beams of the roof, 81, 279 ; note from K. Boetticher on, 81–2, *n.;* classical testimonies, *ib.;* early Greek example in temple at Rhamnus, 83 ; in temple B, 85 ; in houses of c. 2, 87, 89 ; their stone bases *in situ,* 90 ; of Roman propylaeum, 209.
Parion, coin of (Ilium), 224.
Paris; palace of, in Homer, 86 ; at tumulus of Ilus, 283.
Paros; rude idols from, 151.
Parthenon; gate of its *cella,* with folding doors (θύραι), 75.
Patroclus; human sacrifices to his shade, 162 ; his slaughter of the Trojans, indicating the site of the Greek camp, 293.
——, tumulus of, 17, 27 ; the smaller of the two at C. Sigeum ; ancient

tradition uncertain; named by Lechevalier or Choiseul-Gouffier, 242, 243, 344; in Homer perhaps only one for Ach. and Patr.; but this smaller one of like age, 251; excavation by Mr. Calvert (1855); but pottery not then understood, 251; dimensions and *strata*, 252; pottery (*q. v.*) like that in the tumulus of Ach., *ib.*; flute, 252; no trace of burial, 252. (*See* CENOTAPHS.)
Paul, St.; at Assos, 319.
Paulus; quoted, 113.
Pausanias; quoted, 101, 254, 300.
Pavements; of portico of Ilium, 26; stone, of road of S.W. gate (c. 2); covered by road of c. 3, 177–8.
Pebbles; house floors of (c. 2), 53, 90.
Pecunia; etymology of, 112, 113.
Pedasus; city of the Leleges, 314.
Pediment of great temple of Ilium; sculptures from, 204–5, 206–7.
Pelasgians (cf. PULOSATA), 3; at Larisa, 312; at Antandrus, 323.
Pelew Is. (*See* PALAU IS.)
Pelopids, sources of their wealth, 49.
Peltae; named on an inscription of Antandrus, 323; its situation, *ib.*
Penalties, Roman; in cattle, afterwards in money, 113.
Pentaur, Poem of; testimony to Troy and neighbouring peoples, 2, 3.
Percy, Dr. J.; quoted, 153.
Perforated Vases, with holes like sieves (c. 2), 135; parallels, 135–6; use, for cheese-making, improbable, 136; rather for flower-pots, *ib.*
Perforation, imperfect, of stone implements, discussed, 43.
Pergamos, the acropolis of Troy, the SECOND CITY on HISSARLIK (*q. v.*), 14, 20, 70, &c.
Pergamum; gold-mine near, 50; temple of Athené, ⊔⊓ in, 123; globe of Crates at, 128.
Pergamus, coins of, 224, 340.
Perkun or *Perrun,* god of the Slavs; the ⊔⊓ and ⊓⊔ his symbol, 124.
Perrot, G. and *Chipiez, C.,* 'Histoire de l'Art,' 35, 110, 120.

28

Perrot, G.; 'Les Découvertes archéologiques du Dr. H. Schliemann à Troie et à Mycènes,' 287.
Persian supremacy in Asia Minor, 237, 367; rule at Ilium, 262.
Peruvian Antiquities; 135.
Petroglyphs, at Saboya, in Columbia, 110; various, 121.
Petschkendorf (Silesia); antiqq. 148.
Phallus; (c. 2) marble, 172.
Pheretima, queen of Cyrene; 298.
Phidias; his Olympian Jove from the ideal of Homer, 163.
Philemon, comic poet; quoted, 115.
Philios, Dr.; his discovery of very old pottery at Eleusis, 38.
Philip II. of Macedon; coin of, 323.
Philip the Elder (emp.); coin of, 339.
Philistines (cf. PULOSATA), 3.
Philostratus; quoted, 254, 256, 289.
Phocaea; early coinage of, 114.
Phoenician Glass, at Ilium, 218.
Phoenicians; connection with Troy indicated by the legends of Apollo and Herakles, 61–2; traders, 116.
Photius, quoted, 83.
Phrygia; gold-mines of, 49.
Phrygians, from Thrace, captured the ruler and country of Troy, before the Trojan War, 262; affinities with Trojans and Thracians, 357–8; *Pref.* xi.
Phylacé, in Thessaly; warriors of, led by Protesilaus, 254.
Pidasa (Pedasus) in Egypt. records, 3.
Piers; of S.W. gate (c. 2), 67, 68, 69.
Pigorini, L., and *Lubbock, Sir J.*, 'Notes on Hut-Urns and other Objects from Marino, near Albano,' 126, 194, 238.
Pilgrimage to the temple of Athené at Ilium, 289, 346.
Pillar on tomb of *Ilus* (*q. v.*), 283.
Pindar; quoted, 298.
Pins; sticking in bronze knives, for fastening handles on, 100; copper, sticking in a spindle whorl, 107.
Piot, Eugène; his collection at Paris, 93, 144, 194.
Pirates; on S. coast of Troad, 320.
Pitchers; (c. 2) rude one-handled, for use as buckets, 148.

ΠΙΘΟΙ. (*See* JARS.)
Plain of Troy, its usual vegetation; drought in 1882, 17; its soil, 246; Ilium "built in *a large and fair plain* watered by rivers from Ida" (Plato), 291; viewed from side and summit of Ida, 331, 333; best seen from Ujek Tepeh, 343; 8 miles long by less than 4 broad, contained, besides Troy, 2 prehistoric settlements, 11 cities, and 2 villages, 345–6; sources of their wealth, *ib.*; present wretched state, *ib.*
Plans (see VII. and VIII. at end of volume); necessity of new, 13; difficulties by Turkish delegate, *ib.*; made by Dörpfeld and Wolff, 14.
Plants, on summit of Ida, 334–5.
Planum; platform levelled above c. 1, for the Acropolis of c. 2, 53, 181.
Plataeae; 162; bronze arrow-heads found on the battle-field, 247.
Plateau on E., S., and W. of Hissarlik, 24; systematically explored, 25; discovery of pottery of the 1st and 2nd cities, 25, 26. (*See* SECOND CITY, and ILIUM.)
Plates; flat red wheel-made (c. 2), 136; found also on the plateau, 25–6.
——; huge thick, 150 (*see* DISHES); one-handled, 152 (*see* BOWLS); plain wheel-made (c. 2 and 3), 152; parallels, *ib.*
Plato; his testimony for the site of Troy, precisely answering to Hissarlik, and *a decisive proof of Greek opinion for its identity with Ilium*, 290–1.
Pliny (the Elder); 26, 45, 46, 50, 113, 219, 243, 252, 256, 289, 296, 299, 313, 320, 323, 328, 340, 343, 344, 346.
Pliny the Younger; quoted, 230.
Plongeon, 'Fouilles au Yucatan,' 122.
Plough; the present Trojan like that on the shield of Achilles, 332.
Plutarch; quoted, 102, 219.
Polemon (in cent. 3–2, B.C.); 'Description of Ilium,' 289–290; native of Glykeia, *not* of Ilium, 290.
Polion or *Polisma;* site of, at Koum Kioi, 343.

Polishers, stone, for pottery, in the Hellenic well, 19; abundant in c. 1–4 of Troy, 47; (c. 2), porphyry or jasper, 172; see also 377.
Pollio, P. Vedius, friend of Augustus, named on an Ilian inscription, 229.
Pollock, F.; 'The Forms and History of the Sword,' 95.
Pollux; quoted, 82, 101, 115, 299, 313.
Polybus, king of Egypt; his presents to Menelaus, 111, 296.
Pommerellen; Gesichtsurnen of, 121.
Pommern; antiquities of, 123.
Pompeii; the ⌐⌐ frequent at, 123.
Pompey the Great; gems dedicated by, 219; his ring, *ib.*
Poole, Dr. R. S.; quoted, 301, 302.
Porcelain (or rather *Faience*, 120) *Egyptian;* curious ornament of (c. 2), probably imported, 116, *Pref.* xiii; double-pointed needle (c. 2), 120.
Pork; largely eaten at Troy, a point of agreement with Homer, 350.
Porphyry, polishers; 47, 172.
Porridge; used instead of bread, in Homer, 44; by the Romans, 45, 46.
Portico, Corinthian, of lower city of Ilium, discovered, 26, 210.
—— *Roman*, Doric, in Acropolis of Ilium, 207, 209; probable W. boundary of the sanctuary, 210; length unknown, *ib.*; width, *ib.*
Poseidon; great wall of Troy ascribed to, a sign of Phoenician associations, 61; on Saoce, 333.
Posen; antiquities of, 122, 131.
Postolaccas, Achilles; on Trojan soldering of gold, 108; on the Ilian gems, 218, 219; new types of coins described by, 220, f., 340.
Potatoes, not grown in the Troad, 7.
Potstone. (*See* FLUTE.)
Potter's Wheel; Homer's simile from, 35; used in the oldest age of Egypt, *ib.* (Cf. POTTERY, WHEEL-MADE.)
Potters, school of Greek, proved by comparison of examples, 249.
Pottery; archaeological value of, only known of late, 251; example from Mycenae, *ib.*; *Pref.* x, xxvi, xxviii.

Pottery, oldest Egyptian, thoroughly baked in ovens, 35.
—— *Greek ;* its character thoroughly known, 239 ; *always painted*, a decisive distinction from that of strata 3, 4, 5, and 6 on Hissarlik, which differs also in shape, fabric, and clay, 239, 240. *Trojan ;* of all strata below the Hellenic (c. 1–6) ; all *unpainted*, 137, 239 ; persistence of its forms till now, 141–2. (*See* the several arts.)
—— *of First City;* chiefly thick, lustrous black, also red, brown, and yellow, with incised ornamentation filled with chalk, and tubes for suspension, 25, 30 ; found on the plateau, indicating a lower city, 25 ; 30 ; ornamentation, *ib.;* fragments of bowls with owls' eyes on inner side, and tubes for suspension on outside, 31, 32 ; only slightly baked, 33 ; clay containing granite and mica, 33 ; Mr. Doulton's experiments on, *ib.;* Dr. Lisch and Dr. Hostmann on manufacture of, *ib.;* cup and jug, 34 ; few cases of wheel-made pottery, 34 ; thick heavy cups with upright handles, 35 ; unique vessel for drawing water, 35 ; suspension vases, 36 ; parallels, 36 ; hand-made suspension bowls, 38 ; parallels, 38, 39 ; curious goblet, and parallels, 39 ; whorls, 39–41.
—— *of Second City;* dark red, brown, or yellow tripod vases, and flat lustrous red trays or plates ; found on the plateau, 25 ; its character : only slightly baked (except the huge *dishes* and πίθοι), but thoroughly burnt in the catastrophe, 151, 182 ; nearly all *hand-made*, 165 ; various examples, 182 ; in temple A, 130, f. ; in temple B, 135, f.
——, *characteristic of 1st and 2nd Cities*, found on the plateau, proving a lower city, 25, 26, 62 ; also *on* and *in* tum. of PROTESILAUS (*q. v.*), but in no other tumulus, nor elsewhere in the Troad, 257, 259, 260.
—— *of Third City;* but slightly baked, 182–3 ; examples, *ib.*

Pottery of Fourth and Fifth Cities ; no new forms, except some *Owl-Vases* (*q. v.*) 186–8, 190–1.
—— *of the Sixth* (or *Lydian*) *City;* hand-made, with rare exceptions ; its patterns, fabric, and colour, quite different from that of c. 1–5, and of Ilium, and all Greek and Roman pottery, but like that of the hut-urns of Albano, and the pre-Etruscan and archaic-Etruscan tombs, 93, 193, 194, 218, 238, 263 ; its latest date the 10th cent. B.C., 268 ; *Pref.* xxviii.
—— *of the Seventh Stratum, Ilium ;* all *wheel-made*. One sort not prehistoric, nor Lydian, nor Aeolic, prob. of native manufacture ; coarse and heavy, grey or blackish, very slightly baked, but well polished and glazed ; another thoroughly baked, having the red colour of the clay, and either but superficially polished, or not polished at all ; earliest date 9th cent. B.C. to (prob.) 5th cent., 218. The former is found also in the first epoch of the Bali Dagh and at Eski Hissarlik, 267–8, 269 ; also (with the 2nd sort) at Fulu Dagh, Kurshunlu Tepeh, and Cebrené, 270, 272, 275 (*see* the arts.), 378. .(Cf. *Pref.* xxvii.)
—— *Hellenic, of Ilium* (c. 7) ; large mass of archaic painted, 216 ; with spiral ornamentation, like the Mycenean, *ib.;* vase like a turtle, 217 ; flat tripod bottle, *ib.;* found on the plateau, 25 ; Prof. Virchow on the earliest Hellenic pottery with the most primitive form of a real painting, contained in the lowest stratum of the seventh city, and marking earliest possible epoch of Hellenic settlement on Hissarlik (App. VI.).
—— characteristic archaic Greek wheel-made, painted with various colours and bands ; in the tum. of Achilles, 248–250 ; of Patroclus, 252 ; of Antilochus, 253 ; far older than the archaic on the Bali Dagh, 267.
—— Hellenic, older than the Mycenean, very ancient, painted, with suspension system, at Eleusis, 38.

Pottery, Mycenean, 38.
—— monochrome glazed red or black, Macedonian and Roman, found on Kurshunlu Tepeh, 272; Macedonian at Cebrené, 276.
—— Greek and Roman; at various sites in the Troad; App. l., *passim*.
——, *Wheel-made;* usual in Homer's time, 35; rare in all the prehistoric cities (1–6) on Hissarlik, 34, 136, 153, 218; the δέπας ἀμφικύπελλον, with rare exceptions, always wheel-made, 165. (Cf. preceding arts.)
Pozzo, near Chiusi; sepulchre, 147.
Pragatto, Grotto of; 39, 135.
Prehistoric, defined, *Pref.* xv.
Priam, 49, 284, 290, *Pref.* xiii; "tomb" of, on Bali Dagh, explored, 262; fragments of archaic wheel-made pottery, like that in lowest Hellenic stratum (c. 7) at Ilium, 263; no traces of a burial, *ib.;* date probably from 9th to 5th cent. B.C., 267.
Priapus. (*See* PHALLUS.)
Proclus, A. Licinnius (inscr.), 233.
Pronaos, or vestibule, of temple A (c. 2), 79; dimensions, square, 80; end walls faced with *parastades* (*q. v.*), 80; columns between them doubtful, 83.
—— of temple B (c. 2), 85.
Propylaeum, Roman, in Acropolis of Ilium; discovered, 24; stone foundations, 207; sculptured blocks of, 208; restored plan and views, 208, 209, 210; Doric columns, *parastades*, and Corinthian semi-columns, 209; led up to the great temple, *ib.*
Protesilaus, leader of the men of Phylacé, in Thessaly, to Troy; the first Greek who landed and the first killed, 254; his tomb with *heroum* and oracle, on the Thracian Chersonese, near Elaeus, 254; its old pottery tends to confirm the tradition, 260; etymology of the name, 261.
——, tumulus of, on Thracian Chersonese, 27, 254; view, 255; situation and dimensions, 256; plantations on, and legend, *ib.;* hence called *Kara Agatch Tepeh*, 257;

surface strewn with pottery (suspension vases, and bowls), like that of c. 1 of Troy, and stone implements, *ib.;* a brief opportunity seized, 258; results of the partial excavation; pottery inside like that of c. 1 and 2 of Troy; stone implements; a bronze knife; baked bricks, like c. 2 and 3, 259; character of pottery proves an old settlement, contemp. with c. 1 of Troy, 260; the tum. erected with its *débris*, at time of c. 2, *ib.; the only tum. containing Trojan pottery*, 260; prob. contemp. with fall of c. 2, *ib.;* inference that *first settlers of Troy came from Europe, not Asia*, 261; *Pref.* x.
Proverbs, Book of; 296.
Prussia; prehistoric antiquities of, 37, 110, 121, 135.
Pteleos; swamp of, 305.
Pueblos Indians (New Mexico), use of ⊔⊓ among, 123.
Pullan; excavations at Chrysa, 314.
Pulosata, Purosata (Pelasgians, Philistines), in Egyptian records, 3, 4.
Puls. (*See* PORRIDGE.)
Pumpkin Bottle, from Paraguay, with ⊔⊓, 122.
Punch, bronze or copper (c. 1), 47.
Puno (Peru); antiquities of, 135.
Pylos; several, dispute about, 224.
Pyrrha, Pr., 320.
Pythagoras, 128. (*See* EARTH.)

Q.

Quarries; at Koch Ali Ovassi, 341.
Quarry Marks. (*See* MARKS.)
Quarry stones; house-walls of (c. 1), 21; fortress-wall of (c. 2), 54 (cf. FOUNDATIONS); small, of c. 4, 185; and of c. 5, 188.
Quarterly Review; on stone weapons, 174; on 'Ilios,' 287.
Quebrada de las Inscripciones (Nicaragua); petroglyphs, 121.
Quintus Smyrnaeus; quoted, 243.
Quoins, rustic, in walls on the Bali Dagh, 266.

R.

Radowitz, Herr von, German ambassador at Constantinople, 14.
Rain, scarcity of at Hissarlik, 1881-2, 15; effect of, on clay roofs, 185.
Rammelsberg, Prof.; analysis of Trojan and Orchomenian bronze, 104-5.
Ramp, paved, leading up to S.W. gate (c. 2), 67, 70.
Ramsay, W. M.; researches in Cappadocia, 127; *Pref.* xviii, xxi, xxv.
Ramses II., war against Kadesh, 3.
Ramses III., confederacy of Asiatic peoples against, 3, *Pref.* xvii.
Rastellino, Grotto of, 39, 135.
Rattle-boxes, of terra-cotta ; (c. 2), 154; parallels, *ib.*
Reindeer, first epoch of, 38, 40, 50, &c.
Renan, E.; in Phoenicia, 218 ; *Pref.* vi.
Ren Kioi; village and river, absurdly made the Simois by Brentano, 306.
Results of the explorations of 1882 at Hissarlik and other places, confirming the true site of Troy, 277-8; in the heroic *tumuli (q. v.)*, 278 ; architectural discoveries, especially baking of crude brick walls *in situ*, and the original use of *parastades*, 279 ; viewed in the light of the author's original modest expectations, *ib.*
Rhamnus, temple of Themis at, plan of ; an early example of the use of *parastades (q. v.)*, 83.
Rhodes, prehist. antiquities, 39, 42, 148.
Rhodium; hardening of copper by alloy with, not proved, 104.
Rhodius, R. (see DARDANELLES), 304.
Rhoeteum, city, *débris* of, on C. Rhoeteum, *not* at Palaeocastron, 343 ; coined its own money, 346.
———, *Pr.*, 254 ; three nameless tumuli on ; N.E. of tum. of Ajax ; exploration of, stopped, without result, 262 ; the ridge of Rhoeteum *not* Callicoloné, 281-3.
Rings; (c. 2), curious, of bronze or copper, 167 ; (c. 3) clay, well baked, probably stand for vessels, 183 ; silver, used by weight for MONEY, 301.
Rinnekaln (Livonia) ; antiqq., 136.

River-god (probably the Scamander), Roman statue of, 214.
Rivers on S. slope of Ida ; burying of ancient cities by their alluvia, 327-8.
Rivett-Carnac, H., on ' Spindle Whorls and Votive Seals,' 39.
Roads; from S.W. gate, probably on bare rock, 25 ; from Hissarlik to Chiblak, the ἁμαξιτός of Homer, 65 ; of beaten clay of S.W. gate (c. 2), 67, 69 ; another ascending from S. gate to the Pergamos, 70 ; road out of S. gate on the rock, 73 ; paved, of Alexandria Troas, lined with tombs, 341.
Roberts, Prof. W. Chandler; on the hardening and tempering of metals, 101, f., 103-104 ; 153.
Roman Edifices of Ilium, 207 *(see* PORTICO, PROPYLAEUM, THEATRE); MASONRY *(q. v.)* of marble, 196. *(See also* POTTERY and COINS.)
Rome; whorls on the Esquiline, 40.
Romulus and Remus, with she-wolf ; medallion of, in theatre, 212 ; on coins of Ilium, 220, 221 ; on coins of Alex. Troas, 222, 340.
Roof of great temple of Ilium, 203.
Roofs, Trojan ; horizontal, of rafters, rushes, and clay, as still used in the Troad, 84 ; of temple A, inferred from *débris ;* absence of tiles, *ib. ;* of houses (c. 2), 90 ; (c. 4), 185 ; the clay washed down by rain, and always having to be renewed, explains the vast accumulation of *débris* at Hissarlik, 185 ; so in c. 5, 190.
Rossmann, W.; ' Ueber Schliemann's Troja,' 286.
Rovio; cemetery, 193, 238.
Ruins, prehistoric in the plain of Troy; none except at *Besika Tepch, Hanaï Tepch*, and *Hissarlik ;* the last alone considerable, 303, 347 ; *Pref.* x.

S.

Saddle-querns of trachyte ; abundant in cities 1, 2, 3, and 4, of Troy, 44 ; parallels, *ib. ;* (c. 3), 184 ; (c. 4), 188 ; *on* and *in* tum. Protes., 257.

Sagartians, the; had no metal weapons but daggers, 96.
Sahs (O. Germ. 'knife,' 'dagger'), originally *hard stone* (= saxum), 96.
Said Pasha, Grand Master of Artillery at Constantinople, 12.
Sallier Papyrus. (*See* PENTAUR.)
Salzmann, 'Nécropole de Camiros,' 160.
Samarkand; Tamerlane's tomb at, 172.
Samos, I.; coins, 330.
Samothrace, I.; 277, 331, 333.
Samthawro, necropolis of, brooches and fibulae in, 48, 95, 110.
Sankisa, in Behar; whorls and votive seals found at, 39.
Saoce, Mt., in Samothrace; snow-clad to end of March, 15; the seat of Poseidon, 333.
Sarcophagus; inscribed, at Kestambul, 310: a stone near Assos; its consuming power; cure for gout, 320.
Sarikis, Mt.; the second summit of Ida, 273; ascent of, 332; plain at foot, with fountains, *ib.;* the summit, panorama, 333; spring flowers, 334–5; height only 2·5 m. less than GARGARUS (about 5798 ft.), 335; altar and sanctuary of Zeus, 334; discovery of the marble altar-slab, 336.
Sarka, near Prague; vases with cowhead handles, 193.
Satnioïs, R., 314, 318.
Satrius, L.; named on an Ilian inscription, 230; the family, *ib.*
Satyrion; on inscr. of Antandrus, 323.
Sauvastika and Swastika, 卍 and 卐, on the Trojan whorls, and parallels, 122, 124; M. Burnouf's theory of their origin, 124, 192; Mr. R. P. Greg's discussion of, 124; found on Hittite cylinders, and mosaics at Carthage, 125; the Trojan 卍 probably derived from the Hittites, 126; on terra-cotta balls (c. 2), 127–8. (*See* also *Preface* xviii, xxi.)
—— in the *spiral* form, at Troy, Mycenae, and Orchomenos, 123; on Lycian coins, 123–4.
Saws; of flint, chalcedony, and obsidian, abundant in c. 1–4 of Troy, 46; parallels, 47; (c. 3), 184; (c. 5), 173; on tum. Protes., 257; present manuf. of by savage tribes, 173–4.
Sayce, Prof. A. H.; 4, 32, 112, 125, 127, 180, 260, 296; on site of Troy in ' Notes from Journeys in the Troad and Lydia,' 286; *Preface* v, f.
Scaean Gates, of Homer; site, 65; the W. and *only* gate of the *lower city*, leading out to the Plain, 75; why in *pl. ib.;* parallel of the Parthenon, *ib.* (*N.B.*—Homer has no occasion to mention the gates of the acropolis.)
Scalas; landing-places, with stores, on Gulf of Adramyttium, 321.
Scales; Egyptian, for money, 301.
Scamander, R., had no running water in the beginning of July 1882, this generally occurs every three years, 16, 17; its junction with the Bounarbashi Su, 16; Homer's hot and cold springs of, near Troy, 66 (cf. SPRINGS); further proofs of its identity with the Kalifatli Asmak, 66–7; its ancient course to the sea at C. Rhoeteum, 293; see also 273, 274, 282, 283, 284, 306, 332, 333, 339; ford of, 284; its sources on Mt. Gargarus, 336; Roman statue of, at Ilium, 214.
Scamander or *Scamandrius*, named on an Ilian inscription, 234.
Scamandria; probably at *Iné,* 340; inscriptions perhaps referring to, and a bishopric, Σκάμανδρος, 340.
Scaurus, stepson of Sulla, first had gems at Rome, 219.
Scepsis; origin of the name, 274; (1) the original, 273 (*see* PALAESCEPSIS); (2) the new, 60 stadia fr. the old, birthplace of Demetrius, 274; site at BEIRAMICH, *ib.*, 340; coins there, *ib.;* claim to be seat of Aeneas's rule, 363; coins, 276, 339.
Sceptre; gold knob of (c. 2), 107.
Schliemann, Dr. Henry; excavations at Hissarlik in 1879, 1; finished, 303; ' Ilios' published (1880–1), *ib.;* excavations at Orchomenos, *ib.;* journey in the Troad (*g. v.*) 1881, (App. I.), 303, f.; reasons for new

explorations in 1882, 5, f. ; details of the work, 5-27 ; explorations in the Troad, 27, 28 ; suffering from fever, 28 ; the beginning and end of his work at Troy ; original modest expectations ; farewell to readers and critics, 279 ; Trojan collection at Athens, 135, 136, 240 ; Museum at Berlin (MUSEUMS) ; 'Troy and its Remains,' 279 : 'Mycenae,' 'Ilios,' 'Orchomenos.' (*See* the arts.)

Schliemann, Mrs. Sophia; excavation of the Treasury at Mycenae, 135.

Schlosser, F. C.; 'Weltgeschichte ;' emphatic on site of Troy, 285.

Schmidt, Dr. J., astronomer ; on the Trojan terra-cotta balls, 129, f. ; excavations in acropolis on Bali Dagh (1864), 265 ; reduction of the author's observations, 347.

Schöne, Mr., Director-General of the Royal Berlin Museums, 200.

Schröder, Messrs. J. Henry & Co., 6.

Schröter, H. and *Schuchardt, Dr. Th.;* analyses of Trojan bronze, 105.

Schwartz, Prof. F. L. W.; 'Zweiter Nachtrag zu den Materialen zur prachistorischen Kartographie der Provinz Posen,' 131.

Schwarzenberg, Prince Karl von; 'Výlct na Hissarlik,' 288.

Scopas; his Apollo Smintheus, 314.

Scots, armed with stone axes, 96.

Scott, Sir W.; 'The Antiquary,' 300.

Sculptures; Greek and Roman of Ilium, 196 ; of Macedonian age, 18, 214, 215 (cf. HEADS); blocks from the great temple, 198, f. (cf. METOPES, CYMATIUM) ; of the Macedonian and Roman age contrasted, 203-4 ; in the theatre, 212, f. ; broken, and kiln for burning to lime, *ib.;* others in the lower city, 214-216.

Scylax; quoted, 276, 343, 344.

Sea-baths in the Hellespont, 8.

Seals; votive, 39; copper, not engraved, 167 ; inscribed, *Pref.* xxv.

Second City on Hissarlik, the TROY (*q. v.*) of the Homeric Legend, 52 ; plan of its Acropolis (VII. at end of book), 14 ; brick wall of its citadel, 20 ; characteristic pottery of, found on the plateau, 25, 26 ; not rightly distinguished (1879) from the third, *ib.;* not only *the foundation walls*, but the *burnt stratum* belongs to it, *ib.;* causes of the error, 52 ; masses of burnt bricks left by 3rd settlers, even *above* their own foundations, *ib.;* walls of crude bricks burnt *in situ*, *ib.* (cf. BRICKS) ; all its buildings destroyed, *ib.;* stratum often thin, *ib.;* separated by layer of earth from c. 1, 53 ; next, a layer of baked bricks, *ib.;* changes during its duration, *ib.* (cf. GATES) ; *complete levelling of the site*, and extension of acropolis to the S., 52 ; foundations of edifices sunk into this *planum*, *ib.;* old house-floor of white pebbles, 53-4 ; older and later walls (*q. v.*), 54-57 ; towers (*q. v.*), 56-7 ; the treasures (*q. v.*) belonged to it, 57-8 ; *lower city*, 62 (next art.) ; *cavern* and *springs* (*q. v.*) outside on W., 63 ; Scaean gate and road (*q. v.*), 65 ; 3 *gates* (*q. v.*) of acropolis, 67, f. ; edifices, 75, f. ; the 2 *temples* (*q. v.*), 76, f. ; *house-walls* (*q. v.*) of 2 periods, 87, f. ; characteristic mode of building, 90 ; proofs of the catastrophe in which it perished, *ib.;* objects found in, 91,f. (see the several heads) ; high civilization denoted by edifices, 98 ; absence of metal tools explained, 99 ; whorls 105, 119 ; gold, silver, and electrum, 106, f. ; ivory and bone, 115-119 ; eggs of aragonite, 118 ; sling-bullets of magnetic iron or haematite, *ib.;* axes of diorite, 119 ; Egyptian porcelain, 120 ; the 卍 and 卐 and other signs (*q. v.*), 122, f. ; terra-cotta balls (*q. v.*), 127 ; burnt grain, 130 ; pottery in temple A, 130, f. ; in temple B, 136, f. ; objects of bronze or copper, 138, f. ; other pottery, 139, f., 143-8, 151-4 ; πίθοι, 149 ; owl-vases, 151 ; idols, 141-2, 151 ; δέπας ἀμφικύπελλον, 154, f., &c. (see sep. arts.) ; state of ruins after the catastrophe,

175; thin stratum of earth over; probably soon rebuilt, *ib.*; how related to the 3rd city, *ib.*; objects in c. 2 and c. 3 mixed, 182; those of older epoch certain, *ib.*; the rest distinguishable by marks of the great fire, *ib.*; difference of the pottery, *ib.*; marks of agreement with Homer's Troy, *Pref.* xiii, xiv; no trace of Phoenician or Assyrian art, but ancient Babylonian through the Hittites, xvi, xvii; *date* of its destruction doubtful, xv; probably in 12th cent. B.C., xvi, xxii.

Second City; its *Lower City,* on the plateau, 62; proved by its fortress-wall, N.E. of the Acropolis, *ib.*; by prehistoric pottery on the plateau, *ib.*; by the 3 gates of the Acropolis, *ib.*; by the 6 great edifices of the Acropolis, *ib.*; lay long deserted; its materials destroyed, or removed for building elsewhere, as at Sigeum, 63; indications of its extent, *ib.*

Seddul Bahr, Turkish fortress on Thracian Chersonese, 256, 257, 258.

Semper, G.; 'Ueber die Schleudergeschosse der Alten, &c.,' 119.

Sennacherib; his palace at Koyunjik; bronze weights with his name, 301.

Septimius Severus; coins of, 222.

Serpentine; polishers of, 47; balls of, perforated, in tum. Protes., 259.

Servius, ad Vergil., 344.

Sesostris; trophies of (Herod.), near Smyrna, not Egyptian, but memorials of Hittite conquest, *Pref.* xvii.

Severus Alexander; coins of, 222, 339.

Shafts; one sunk in the acropolis to the rock (14 m.), 19; 20 on the plateau in 1873, with little result, 24, 25; new ones to S. and E. of hill, 26; and on N.W. slope, 27; on plateau; tombs, statues, and mosaic floors, found in, 114; in tum. of Achilles and Patroclus, 245, 252; in tum. of Protesilaus, 258; in the three tum. at C. Rhoeteum, 262; in so-called tomb of Priam, *ib.*; on the Bali Dagh, 266; on Fulu Dagh and Kurshunlu Tepeh,

270; on Kutchek Tepeh, 273; at Cebrené, 275-6.

Shafts, of lances, how fastened to the heads, 95; of arrows, fastened by string, as in Homer, 104.

Sheep; six skulls in the Hellenic well, 19; bones abundant in c. 1, 349.

Sheepfolds, Turkish; stone foundations of, mistaken for ancient buildings, 27, 316; on Kurshunlu Tepeh, 272; on top of Ida, 335.

Shekel; Semitic name of the Babylonian-Phoenician weight, probably equal to the Homeric talent, 113, 114; of silver, in patriarchal times, 302; the sacred, *ib.* (Cf. MONEY.)

Shells, in walls of 1st city, 30; abundant in clay of brick walls, 59, 86; signs of the process of burning, 60; enormous masses of small shells in all the strata, 186; of oysters (c. 1), 285, 350.

Shilluks, on White Nile; votive offerings to their ancestor, Nickam, 326.

Sicilian Greeks; their victory over the Carthaginians at Himera, 114.

Sicily; painted eyes on boats of, 32.

Sigeum, C.; tumuli at foot of, 27, 242, 254, .344. (*See* ACHILLES, ANTILOCHUS, PATROCLUS.)

Sigeum (Yeni Shehr), 343, 344; walls of, built from stones of Troy, 63; war with Achilleum, 344; wealth, *ib.*; temple of Athené, *ib.*; coins of, 223.

Sigia; name of Alexandria Troas, probably an older city, 342.

Sigismund, on Cypriote dialect, 159.

Signs, ⊓⊓ and ⊓⊓⊓, on Trojan whorls and pottery, 122, 126, f.; parallels, *ib.*; *in relief* and more ornamented, 𝖄𝖄 and 𝖄𝖄, on Italian hut-urns, *ib.*; and on funeral urn from Darzau, 127; theories of Pigorini, Lubbock, and Virchow, 126; *incised* on Italian whorls, 127; the 𝖄𝖄 a Hittite hieroglyph, perhaps for a *chair, ib.* (Cf. *Pref.* xvii.)

Silesia; antiquities of, 148.

Silex. (*See* FLINT, KNIVES, SAWS.)

Silver; Trojan dagger of, 98; relative value to copper and gold, 100-1; earrings (c. 2), 106; Helen's basket, 109, 296, 299; mixing-vessel, given by Menelaus to Telemachus, 109; the six wedges or *talents* (*q. v.*), 111; primitive use of by weight as MONEY; *Hittite mercantile currency*, 301-2.

Simois, R., dry in spring of 1882; unusual till autumn, 16, 17; three springs N. of Hissarlik, flowing into, 66. *See* also 281, 282, 283, 306, 343.

——, a second, in Chaonia, 253.

Sinai; the Wadi Mokatteb in, 121.

Sinope; Greek traders at, *Pref.* xxv.

Sipylus; gold-mines, 49; the famous 'Niobe' on, an image of the Hittite goddess, of the time of Ramses II.; his cartouche beside it; imitated from the statue of his wife at Abu Simbel; *Pref.* xvii, xxiv.

Sixth or Lydian Settlement on Hissarlik, 193; inferred from its pottery, like the old Etruscan, *ib.;* no walls left, 239; its long duration, 193; vase-handles in forms of snake-heads and cow-heads, *ib.;* other parallels in Etruria and elsewhere, 193-4; characteristic pottery, *ib.;* generally hand-made, 194; colour, fabric, and shape, quite different from the pottery of c. 1-5, and of the Greek Ilium, *ib.* and 238; (*see* POTTERY); Professor Jebb's objection to, answered, 238. (Cf. 379, and *Pref.* xxviii.)

Skeletons, human; one, probably male, (c. 1), teeth and other fragments of, 318; probably brachycephalous, *ib.;* compared with skull of c. 2, *ib.;* two, in tombs at Cebrené, 276.

Skulls, human, found at Troy, 174.

Slate; masses of in c. 2, for flooring, but only one floor *in situ*, 90; their state, evidence of the great conflagration, 90. (*See* WHETSTONES).

Slaves, female Roman, employed in spinning, 299.

Sling, the, of twisted sheep's wool, the only weapon of the Locrians, 119; only twice named by Homer, *ib.*

Sling-bullets, of haematite, 118; G. Semper's work on, 119.

Smith, Philip, 'The Site of Homer's Troy,' in 'Quarterly Review,' 287.

——, *Dr. W.;* 'Dictionary of the Bible, 296, 301; 'Dictionary of Greek and Roman Antiqq.,' 297, 299.

Smithsonian Contributions to Knowledge, 181.

Smyrna; inscription of, compared with an Ilian, 233; (modern), rapid decrease of Turks and increase of Greeks at, 324.

Snake-heads; vase-handles, characteristic of the Lydian settlement, 193.

Snakes, venomous, 18; antidote, 19.

Social State, in the Homeric age, 161, f.; mixture of barbarism with luxury and art, 162; high ideal of plastic beauty, 162-3.

Societies, and their Proceedings.

—— of Antiquaries, 124.

—— Antiquarian of Boston, 316, 318.

—— Archaeol. Inst. of America, 320.

—— Berliner Gesellschaft für Anthropologie, &c., 122, 123.

—— of Dilettanti, 314.

—— Historical of Wisconsin, 180.

Soil, natural; layer of, below bricks of 2nd city, on S. and E. sides of the acropolis, 22; gradually accumulated between c. 3 and c. 4, 184; shewing an interval of time, *Pref.* xvi.

Soldering of gold; universal at Troy, but unknown at Mycenae, 108; done then without silver and borax, 108; a lost art, 109; known to Homer, 109.

Sophocles; quoted, 102, 294.

Sorbet, an antidote for snake-bites, 19.

Spartan relief sculptures; the δέπας ἀμφικύπελλον on, 160.

Spata, tombs of, 111.

Spectacle Pattern; on jewels of Troy and Mycenae, 110; parallels, 110, 111.

Spindles (cf. SPINNING AND WHORLS), found by Dr. V. Gross still sticking in whorls, 41; Egyptian, from Thebes, with whorls, and thread still attached, 295-6; in the O. T., 296; used with or without the distaff (*q. v.*), *ib.;* the Greek and Roman, 297-8; confused with the distaff, *ib.;* golden, of goddesses and great ladies, 298 ; as votive offerings, especially to Pallas, 299, 300 ; her emblem on coins and in the Palladium, 220, 300.

Spindle-whorls, Mr. H. Rivett-Carnac on, 39. (*See* WHORLS.)

Spinning by hand among the ancients, 293, f. ; on the monuments of Egypt, 293-5 ; in the O. T., 296 ; in Homer and later, 296-7 ; the process described, 297, f. ; modern disuse of, 300 ; still used in Greece, *ib.*

Spiral Decoration, like Cypriote *Ko;* on vases (c. 2), 146 ; parallels, 147 ; on archaic Ilian (c. 7) and Mycenean pottery, 216.

Spitting; charm against demons, 289.

Spoons; one of ivory (c. 2), 117 ; rude terra-cotta (c. 2), 153 ; parallels, *ib.*

Spratt; Map of the Troad, 305-6, 343.

Springs; the one nearest to Hissarlik, 10 ; in cavern W. of Hissarlik, 64 ; used for washing in Graeco-Roman time, 65 ; answers to the springs of Homer, *ib.;* the site corresponds to the description, *ib.;* flow into the Scamander, and may have been called its sources, 66 ; no trace of the warm spring, already lost in antiquity, *ib.*:—three, N. of Ilium, flow into the Simois, and may have been called its sources, 66 :—abundant on Ida, 331 ; temperatures of springs in Troad, 347.

Springs of Bounarbashi; no Trojan wash-basins at, 268-9.

Springs, Hot; of Ligia Hamam, 309 ; salt, of Toozla, 312, 313, 314 ; of Lugia Hamam, 325.

Stamatakes, P., delegate at the excavations at Mycenae, 251.

Stater, gold, in the early coinage of Asia Minor, derived from the Homeric talent, 114.

Statue, gold equestrian, of King Antiochus at Sigeum, 344.

Statues; bases for, in lower city of Ilium, 210 ; splinters of white marble, and kiln for burning them to lime, 212 ; in shafts on plateau, 214.

Σταυρός, etymology of, 124.

Steel; how tempered, 101 ; hardened by plunging in water, 102.

Steitz, Prof. A.; 'Die Lage des Homerischen Troia,' 284, 286, 291 ; on the theory of Demetrius, 284 ; on the passage of Lycurgus, 291.

Stephani, L.; on site of Troy, 286 ; his ridiculous theory of the Trojan and Mycenean antiquities, *ib.*

Stephanus Byzantinus; quoted, 224, 276, 313, 323, 328, 343, 344.

Stern, Dr. L.; quoted, 247.

Stone; shelly conglomerate ; material of Macedonian foundations and buildings (except the great temple) at Ilium, 195, f. ; soft limestone, of the Roman foundations, 21, 195-6 ; the stones of Ilium a quarry for later buildings, 21.

Stone Implements (cf. the several heads) ; found in the Hellenic well, 19 ; next below Hellenic stratum, 23 ; abundant in strata 1-5, especially in 4, a decisive proof of *non-Hellenic* character, 240 ; (c. 1) axes, 41 ; blunt axe-like, 42 ; whetstones, 42 ; rude hammers, 43 ; corn bruisers, *ib.;* saddle-querns of trachyte, 44 ; polished and perforated axes, 46 ; saws of flint, &c., *ib.;* parallels, 47 ; polishers for pottery, 47 ; one grooved all round (c. 2), 173 ; parallels, *ib.;* (c. 3), 184 ; (c. 4), 188.

Stone Weapons; late use of, owing to rarity of bronze, 96 ; even by Anglo-Saxons and Scots, *ib.;* confirmed by etymology, *ib.*

Storks, arrival of, 17 ; sacred bird of the Turks, driven off by the Greeks, 306-7, 310, 313.

Strabo; quoted, 49, 50, 63, 66, 196, 201, 204, 228, 242, 243, 254, 262, 274, 276, 281, 283, 284, 304, 305, 312, 313, 314, 315, 319, 320, 323, 326, 327, 328, 341, 342, 343, 344, 346, *Pref.* xi ; his authority discussed, 369.

Stratification, peculiarities of, 22.

Stratonicus, musician, 319.

Streets of Assos, paved with stone blocks, 318.

Suarez, or *Saravita*, *R.*, 110.
Suggenthal (Baden), cheesemaking at, in a perforated bowl, 136.
Suidas; quoted, 285, 290.
Sulla; his seal-ring, 219; peace with Mithridates, at Dardanus, 305.
Surgical Instrument, bronze (c. 1), 105.
Suspension, Tubes for; horizontal and vertical, on vases, 25; abundant fragments of, in c. 1, 30, 32; also on tum. Protes., 257; parallels, 32; vases with foui, 37–8; likeness to kipes, 38; bowls (c. 1), 38; (c. 2), 130, 154; (c. 3), 183.
Swastika. (*See* SAUVASTIKA.)
Swine; bones of, abundant in c. 1, 349; use for food, an agreement with Homer, 350.
Swiss antiquities. (*See* LAKE DWELLINGS.)
Swords, metal; original pattern of, from the primitive dagger, 95; none at Troy, *ib.;* parallels for their absence, *ib.;* Helbig on the difficulty of manufacture and rarity in ancient and medieval times, 96.
Syenite Columns, of portico (lower city of Ilium) with white marble Corinthian caps. and entab., 26, 210.
Syria, Northern; Hittite dominion in, *Pref.* xvii.
Syrian coinage; standard talent of, under the Persians, 114.

T.

Tables (c. 2). (*See* DISHES.)
Tablets; terra-cotta, with winged thunderbolts (Ilium), 216; with Cappadocian characters, *Pref.* xviii.
Tacitus, quoted, 229.
Talents; the six silver (c. 2), 111; further proofs that the Homeric talent was small, *ib.;* Hultsch on, 113; derivation of τάλαντον. *ib.;* prob. identity with the *shekel, ib.;* weight and form of the Homeric, 114; prototype of the gold *stater,* coined in Asia Minor, *ib.;* double or equal of the Daricus, *ib.;* standard of Syrian provincial coinage, *ib.;* another small Asiatic talent, *ib.;* first used by Greeks as a weight for gold, 114; mentioned by Philemon, 115; estimates of its value, *ib.;* called Macedonian, *ib;* Trojan, their form like the *tongue* of gold at Jericho, 302.
Talian Kioi; site of ACHAEIUM; not good for excavations, 342.
Tamerlane; tomb of, 172.
Tangermünde; vase with four double tubes for suspension, found at, 38.
Tantalus; his wealth, 49.
Tarquinii. (*See* CORNETO.)
Tawakli, village, 311.
Taylor, Dr. Isaac; 'The Alphabet,' *Pref.* xxiv.
Teeth, human (c. 1), 348.
Tekri, Tekkari(Teucrians) in Egyptian records, 4; *Pref.* xvii.
Telemachus; 45, 109, 253.
Tempering of metals, is *softening,* not *hardening,* 101; the process explained, *ib.;* confusion with the French *trempe* (i.e. hardening), 102.
Temple of the Seven Lights of Heaven at Borsippa (Birs i Nimrud), 180.
Temples of Troy; two in the Acropolis (c. 2), 75, 76; why so regarded, 76, 86; their deep *débris;* height of standing walls; parallel and close to one another, with narrow corridor between; their walls of brick, baked in *situ,* (v. BRICKS, CRUDE), 76 f.; plans of both, 77; both perished in a fearful catastrophe, 86.
—— (*A*), *the Larger;* brick blocks of, 76; stone foundations of brick walls, 78; how related to the sloping floor, *ib.;* thickness of wall, *ib.;* size and arrangement of bricks, *ib.;* clay coating of walls, 79; clay floor, with charcoal *below,* therefore laid *after* the baking, 79; plan, *ib.;* two compartments (third doubtful), 79; length of naos doubtful, *ib.* (*see* PRONAOS, NAOS, and PARASTADES); base of altar or idol (?), 84; horizontal roof (*q. v.*), *ib.;* area filled with its *débris, ib.;* objects found in, 91–135 (*see* the several heads).
—— (*B*), *the Smaller* (c. 2), parallel to A on N.E. side, 84; narrow passage,

ib.; walls of crude brick, baked *in situ*, on stone foundations, 84; thickness, *ib.;* built after A, proofs, 85; plan, 79, 85; *three* rooms, *ib.; pronaos;* doorways; third room; floor and wall-coating, *ib.;* doorposts, 86; question of a fourth room, *ib.;* resemblance of plan to the palace of Paris in Homer; but still prob. a temple, *ib.;* pottery found in, 135.

Temples, of third city (supposed); scanty remains of, 177.

—— of Athené in the Acropolis of Ilium (1); the original "small and insignificant sanctuary," visited by Alexander, who ordered its adornment (cf. ALEXANDER), 196, 228; no remains of temple visited by Xerxes, 196, 198.

—— —— (2), the small Doric, 196; of 4th cent. B.C., 198; built of shelly limestone, like other Greek temples, 197; architectural details, 197-8; only known by sculptured blocks; foundations and site not found, 198; use of its blocks elsewhere, 199.

—— —— (3), the great Doric, of white marble, Macedonian, 4th cent. B.C., built by Lysimachus, 195, 199, 201, 203, 204; foundations (doubtful) of wrought stone blocks, 202; sculptured blocks on N.E. part of hill, and in Turkish cemeteries, 201, 202, 204; triglyphs and metopes (*q. v.*), 199, f.; restoration of upper part, 202; architectural details, 203; destruction by Fimbria, and restoration by Sulla, confirmed by Roman details, 203-4; final destruction intentional, time doubtful, 204; other sculptures from, 205-206; error respecting corrected, 207; relation of its site to the Roman propylaeum and portico, 209, 210; its custodians (ἱερονόμοι), 227.

—— *in the Troad;* of Apollo Smintheus at Chrysa, 314; Ap. Cillaeus at Cilla, 327; Ap. Thymbrius at Thymbra, 345; Athené at Sigeum, 344; Demeter (on Hag. Dem. Tepeh), 344; of Zeus on Ida, 334.

Temples, Greek; use of PARASTADES or *antae in,* 80-83; of Greece, Italy and Sicily, their materials, 197.

Tenedos, I., 314, 342; coins of, 223; the double head and double axe on, 223-4; *Pref.* xx.

Teos, coin of, found at Ilium, 224.

Terra-cottas, Trojan; all *unpainted;* only the natural colour of the clay; decoration incised, impressed, or in relief; so also those of the terramare, 137-8; also ornamental surface produced with polishing stones, 377-380. (*See* POTTERY, IDOLS, VASES, WHORLS, &c.)

—— of Ilium; heads, 215-6; watch-shaped objects, with two perforations, 216; tablets with thunderbolts, *ib.*

Terramare, Italian, especially of the Emilia; 32, 37, 39, 40, 43, 44, 45, 134, 135, 153, 173; civilization of inhabitants compared with the Graeco-Italic stage, 46, 50; all bronze and copper *cast* (as at Troy), not *forged,* 93; no swords, 95; the ⊢⊣ and ⊔⊓ in, 123; moulds, 170; pottery all *unpainted,* like the Trojan, 137.

Testa, Baron von, German first dragoman at Constantinople, 13, 258.

Teucrians (cf. TEKRI); appear in place of Dardanians; their name equivalent to Trojans, 4; their Thracian affinities, 357, f.; came over from Europe, *Pref.* xi, xii, xvii.

Thalamos, the chamber in Paris's palace, 86; of the Treasury at Orchomenos, 304.

Theatre, at Athens, 341.

—— gigantic, Roman, in lower city of Ilium, 18, 210, f.; white marble casing and columns (Doric, Ionic, and Corinthian), 211; step-seats of calcareous stone, *ib.;* space of the κοιλόν, *ib.;* splendid view from, *ib.;* splinters of marble statues, and kiln for burning them to lime, 212; inscriptions found in, 211, 213: at Assos, 317.

Thebé Hypoplakié (i.e. under a wooded hill, ὑπὸ πλάκῳ ὑληέσσῃ); city of Eëtion and Andromaché; prob. at LUGIA HAMAM, 326-7; plain of, 329.

Thebes, the Egyptian ; inscriptions at, 3 ; spindles from, 295–6 ; the abode of Polybus, 296.
Themis ; temple of, at Rhamnus, 83.
Theocritus ; quoted, 289.
Theodosius II., emp., 225.
Thera, I. ; pottery of, compared with that at Hissarlik, 238–9, 241.
Thermia, I., bronze battle-axes, 167.
Thermometer, Celsius and Fahrenheit ; rule for comparison, 15.
Thessaly ; warriors of, at Troy, 254.
Thetis, 163.
Thiol ; Turkish name of tum. Ach. 243.
Third City on Hissarlik ; formerly confused with c. 2, and taken for the Ilios of Homer, 1 ; reasons for doubting this, 1–2 ; causes of the error, 52 ; its insignificance, 2 ; prob. built soon after end of 2nd, 175 ; the city small and settlers few, on the Pergamos only, 2, 175 ; did not level the ground, 175 ; houses built on or sunk into brick ru. of c. 2, 52, 53, 175 (cf. HOUSE-WALLS) ; thickness, 176 ; no solid foundation, *ib. ;* walls of bricks fr. ruins of c. 2, perhaps temple of c. 3, 176–7 ; repaired and used city walls of c. 2, 57, 177 (*see* WALLS) ; two gates (*q. v.*), *ib. ;* appears a mere village, 185 ; destruction not total, 181 ; some traces of fire, but no great catastrophe, *ib.*, 184 ; portions of walls standing, *ib. ;* objects mixed with those of c. 2, *ib. ;* slight separation from c. 2, 182 ; tests for distinguishing them, *ib. ;* pottery (*q. v.*), 182, f. ; huckle bones, 183 ; whorls, *ib. ;* bronze brooches, 184 ; bone needles, &c., *ib. ;* stone implements, *ib. ;* saws and knives, *ib.* (*See* the headings.)
Thor. (*See* DONNAR.)
Thrace ; gold mines, 49.
Thracians ; their ethnology and affinities with Trojans and other peoples of Asia Minor ; App. III., IV., *passim ; Pref.* xi, xii.
Three, the number as a charm, 289.
Threshold, in house of c. 2, 87.
Throne of Zeus on Ida (Hom.) ; rock like it on summit of Gargarus, 335.

Thryoessa, 282.
Thucydides ; quoted, 2, 323, 343, 344.
Thyatira, coin of (Ilium), 224.
Thymbra, city (Hanaï Tepeh), 200, 284 ; with temple of Apollo, 345.
—— Mr. Calvert's farm ; sites of Thymbra and 'Ιλιέων κώμη, on, 200, 345.
Thymbrius, R., dry in spring of 1882 ; unusual till autumn, 16, 345 ; aqueduct of Ilium from, 224.
Tiberius, emp. ; earthquake in Asia in his time, 26, *n. ;* named on an Ilian inscr., 232.
Tiles, Greek and Roman in well of Acropolis, 19 ; not used in Trojan roofs, 84 ; none found in c. 3, 4 or 5, 185, 190 ; frag. in Kutchek Tepeh, 273.
Tin ; alloying of copper with, 101.
Tiryns, Cyclopean conduit at, like one outside Troy, 64, 178 ; idols, 151.
Tombs ; found in shafts on the plateau, 24 ; impossibility of searching for them at great depth, 25 ; in the theatre, probably Byzantine, 214 ; at Assos, 341 ; rock-hewn with skeletons, at Cebrené, 276.
——, heroic. (*See* TUMULI.)
Tongue, of gold, at Jericho, 112 ; form like the Trojan 'talents,' 112, 302.
Tools, workmen's, of metal, absence of in c. 2 ; how explained, 99 ; the edifices imply their use, but no moulds for them have been found, 100.
Toozla ; hot springs of, 312 ; village, anc. TRAGASAE, 313 ; granite columns, *ib. ;* marble slabs in mosque, *ib.*
Torches (δαΐδες), in Homer ; used for lights till 5th cent. B.C., 145–6 ; still used in the Troad, 337.
Torpedoes in the Hellespont, 258.
Towers, brick, in wall of c. 2, 22, 54, 56 ; like those of Homer's Troy, 57 ; over gates of c. 2 and 3 (*see* GATES) ; in the walls of Assos, 317 ; of Alexandria Troas, 341 ; oval, on Kurshunlu Tepeh, 271.
Tragasae ; ancient salt-works at, 313 ; ruins at Toozla, *ib.*
Trajan, emp. ; 230.
Trays, flat red, of 2nd city, found on the plateau, 25–6.

Treasures; the ten found at Troy, 5, 303; proofs of its wealth and power, *Pref.* xiii; the great one (1873) belonged to c. 2, probably in its brick wall, 57; probably also the others, 58; proofs from the marks of fire on the objects, *ib.*:—one of copper and bronze (c. 2), found near gold treasure of 1878, 165; its contents, 166, f.:—at Mycenae, 303.

Treasury; at Mycenae, 135; at Orchomenos, 304.

Trees; used for votive offerings, 326.

Trenches, the great eastern (SS on Plan VII.), 19; view of, 189; its important results, 20; the great northern, 24, 29; one across the plateau, 25: on north, west, and south of Acropolis, 26; on the Bali Dagh, 266.

Trêres, in the Troad, 262.

Triglyphs; of the great temple (*q. v.*) of Ilium, 197, 202, 203.

Tripods; of gold, dedicated by Gelon at Delphi, 114; of iron, in tomb at Cebrenè, 276; terra-cotta; a dish (c. 2), 136; on surface of tumulus Protes., 257. (*See* next article.)

Tripod Vases; (of c. 2), 130, 131, 144, 154; also on the plateau, 25; flat bottle, painted, of Ilium, 217.

Triquetrum, on Lycian coins, 124.

Troad, the; described by Homer, 1; ancient inhabitants and rulers; the *Mysians,* driven out by the *Phrygians* from Thrace, *before* the Trojan War; *after* it, occupied by Greek colonists, Trêres, Cimmerians, and Lydians, Persians, and Macedonians, finally Gauls, 262; Greek cities in, 227, 343 (cf. UNION, and PLAIN OF TROY); extent, 303; ancient wealth, 49, 50, 346 (cf. MINES).

——, *Journey in* (1881); objects and results, 303, 347; delight in revisiting, 304; equipment, *ib.;* the country unsafe, *ib.;* stages (*see* names); results of the thorough exploration of the Troad, *Pref.* x; *no prehistoric ruins, except at Hissarlik,* Besika Tepeh, *and* Hanaï Tepeh; no further excavations useful, except at Assos and perhaps Alexandria Troas, 347; explorations in, 1882, p. 1, f.; 264, f. (*See* the articles.)

Troad, Maps of; large, at end of vol.; small, No. 140, p. 303, 347, &c.; Spratt's 305, 306; Virchow's, 306.

Troja Vetus; inaccurate name and wrongly placed on maps, 193.

Trojan war (cf. TROY), 80 years after the Dorian invasion, 2; sign of, in Egyptian records, 4.

Trojans, called Teucrians, 4; their ethnology, App. III., IV., p. 351, f.; akin to Thracians and Phrygians, and probably Aryans, *Pref.* x, xi, xii.

Troy, primitive; first settlers of (probably) *from Europe, not Asia* (*see* PROTESILAUS, TUM.); confirmed by traditions of Lydian history, 261-2, *Pref.* x; its Mysian ruler and country captured by Phrygians from Thrace, 262; proofs of its greatness, wealth, and power; two distinct periods of its existence; long duration, *Pref.* xiii. (Cf. SECOND CITY.)

—— (Homeric); doubts about its extent; Homer's descriptions, 1, 2; unanimity of ancient traditions concerning the war, 2; allies of, in Homer, compared with Egyptian records, 3, 4; proofs of its greatness, 5; πολύχρυσος, 5, 303; its towers, 57; legends of building and destruction by Poseidon and Herakles, (*i.e.,* probably by the Phoenicians), 61-2; lower city (*q. v.*), 162; long deserted, 63; story that Sigeum was built from its stones, 63, *Pref.* xiii; result of the discoveries at Hissarlik, answering perfectly to Homer's description of the site, 277; belief of the Greeks in its total and final destruction discussed, 225, 364, f.

——, site of; further lists of advocates of the Bounarbashi theory, 285; of its identity with Ilium and Hissarlik, 285-8; of other theories, 288; 'eclectic' theory of its topography, 288; *Pref.* xiv.

Tsatschenderessi, R., 322.

Tshiisderessi, R., 331.

Tumuli, the so-called heroic; eight explored in 1882, 17, 27, 28, 242, f. (*see* ACHILLES, PATROCLUS, ANTILOCHUS, PROTESILAUS, RHOETEUM C., PRIAM); results, 278; those of *Achilles*, *Patroclus*, and *Antilochus*, probably of 9th cent. B.C. the age of Homer; of *Protesilaus* probably contemporary with c. 2 on Hissarlik, the original Troy, 278; one unexplored on road over heights of Bounarbashi, 28; one unnamed, near Dardanelles, 305; another, the only one on S. shore of the Troad, prob. GARGARA, 320.
Turkoman-Tsesmesi, fountain, 331.
Turks, of the Troad; reverence for storks, 306-7, drinking fountains, *ib.*; respect for the dead, *ib.*; hospitality, 338; rapid decline of, in Asia Minor, 324.
Turtle; archaic painted vase like (Ilium), 217; parallels, *ib.*
Tzetzes, quoted, 254.

U.

Uápes, R.; petroglyphs of, 121.
Ujek Kioi, village, 306.
Ujek Tepeh, 273; revisited (1881), 343, 347; state of shafts and galleries, *ib.*; best view over cities of Troad, 343.
U-lu (Ilium?), in Egyptian records, 4.
Ulysses; talent of gold presented to, 111; great jars (πίθοι) in his palace, 149; his δέπας ἀμφικύπελλον, 161; on coins of Ithaca, 224.
Umbria, pottery from, 37;
Undset, Ingvald, 48; 'Das erste Auftreten des Eisens in Nord Europa,' by Miss J. Mestorf, 110, 121, 148.
Union, federal (κοινόν, συνέδριον) of the Hellenes at Corinth, 228.
—— of *nine* Greek cities of the Troad, attested by inscriptions, 227, 233, 372; Droysen on, 228; Ilium, its centre, *ib.*; proof of its existence before 306 B.C.; founded by Alexander, 228; the cities free, 229; their Aesymnetae, 319.
Urns; with rude drawings of animals, 121, 122; large (c. 2) never found elsewhere, 151; near parallels, *ib.*; human-faced. (*See* FACE-URNS.)

V.

Valerianus, on coins (Alex. Tro.), 223.
Valonea Oaks, in the Troad, 311, 341.
Values, relative, ancient, of gold, silver, and copper, 100, 101.
Van, in Armenia; cuneiform inscriptions at, *Pref.* xi.
Varro; quoted, 45, 46, 113, 219.
Vase-covers; (c. 2), with horns, 147; perforated, for fastening to vase, 144-5; with crown-shaped handles, 147; with plain arched handle, *ib.*; parallels, *ib.*; (c. 4) owl-faced, 187.
Vase-handles; (c. 6) in form of snake-heads and cow-heads, 193; the latter like the Mycenaean, *ib.*; parallels, *ib.*; curious black, in tum. of Protesilaus, 259.
Vase-head (c. 2), unique, 130.
Vases (see POTTERY, and under the several kinds, viz. Animal V., Jugs, Oenochoae, Owl V., Perforated V., Tripod V., Suspension V., &c.); with ⌐⌐, from Corneto, 122; two or more joined (c. 2), 148; lilliputian, in all the prehistoric settlements, *ib.*
Vatican. (*See* MUSEUMS.)
Verona, antiquities of, 147.
Vestibulum of temple A (c. 2), 79.
Views, panoramic; from Kurshunlu Tepeh, 273; from acropolis of Cebrené on the Chalidagh, 277; from eastern pass of Ida, 331; from summit of Ida (Sarikis), 333; from Ujek Tepeh, 343.
Villanova, necropolis of, 157; double cups in, no type of δέπ. ἀμφ., reason for making them, *ib.*, 193, 238.
Virchow, Prof. Rudolf; 1, 94, 95, 104, 105, 110, 123, 136, 174, 280, 281, 285, 329; on bones from c. 1, 30, and App. II., 348; excavations at Upper Koban in the Caucasus, 42, 48; 'Das Gräberfeld von Koban im Lande der Osseten,' 42, 48, 51, 94, 105, 247; admirable character of the work, 280;

'Alttroianische Gräber und Schädel,' 13, 287, 349; reviewed by Karl Blind, 351, f.; 'Verhandlungen der Berliner Gesellschaft für Anthropologie, Ethnologie, und Urgeschichte,' 122, 123, 135; 'Die Hüttenurnen von Marino bei Albano, und von Corneto,' 126; on site of Troy and Schliemann's Discoveries, 287; 'Beiträge zur Landeskunde der Troas,' 306, 349; 'On the Earliest Greek Settlement at Hissarlik,' App. VI., 376.
Virgil; quoted, 101, 253, 320.
Vitrified débris of c. 2, proof of the great conflagration, 90.
Vitrified Forts (Scotland), 180.
Volsinians, invented the corn-mill, 46.
Volterra; cemetery of, 193, 238.
Volusianus (coins, Alex. Tro.), 223.
Votive Offerings; gold, 114; eggs of aragonite, 118; whorls, 105–6; small column for, 213; of implements, as e. g. the distaff and spindle, 299; of garments, &c., for cures, 325.
Votive Seals. (*See* SEALS.)

W.

Wachlin; pre-Slavic tomb at, 123.
Wadi Mokatteb; petroglyphs of, 121.
Wallace, Wm., 96.
Walls of the First City, 24; masonry of fortification and minor walls, 29.
—— *of the Second City;* outer side of east brick wall of citadel, 20; brick wall, with tower of 2nd period, 22; *débris* from the same, *ib.;* great substruction fortress-wall of Acropolis of 1st period, of quarry-stones, described, 54–56; view, 55; towers, 54; its different heights, 61; alterations by 2nd settlers themselves, 54; their new great wall, *ib.;* its purpose, 56; *distinction of old and new walls on Plan VII., ib.;* towers, *ib.;* brick-walls above the stone substructions, 57; repaired by 3rd settlers, *ib.,* 177; *débris* of, in house of c. 3, 58; thickness and height, *ib.;* its construction and material, 59; baked *in situ, ib.* (cf. BRICKS, CRUDE);
imposing aspect on N. when entire, 61; construction ascribed to Poseidon and Apollo, sign of Phoenician associations, *ib.*
Wall of Lower City of Troy (c. 2); search for on plateau, 26; few fragments found, but several traces of the rock having been levelled for, 26, 62, 63.
—— *of Third City;* those of c. 2 repaired, 57, 177; of bricks, baked and unbaked, fr. ruins of c. 2, perhaps temple of c. 3, 176–7; city wall of c. 2 repaired, 177; new one on N.W. side, *ib.;* inferior masonry, *ib.*
—— *of Fourth City;* those of the 3rd used, repaired, and heightened, 184; upper part destroyed, 186.
—— *of Fifth City;* great fortress wall of rudely wrought stones, 21, 190; relative position to citadel walls of Troy and Ilium, 190; view, 189.
—— *of Ilium* (c. 7); *Macedonian,* 63; great city wall, built by Lysimachus, a remarkable corner of, 18, 195; its masonry, *ib.*
—— —— *Roman;* of Acropolis, gigantic, of wrought stones, with stonecutters' marks, 21; well-preserved, 196: of lower city, found in shafts on the plateau, 25.
—— *of Gates, Temples, &c.* (*See* the special headings.)
—— of two epochs at *Bali Dagh,* 265, f.; of *Eski Hissarlik,* 269; on *Fulu Dagh,* 270; on *Kurshunlu Tepeh,* 271; of *Cebrené* on Chalidagh, 275; of *Assos,* of two periods, 318. (*See* the arts. and MASONRY.)
Warka (Chaldea), saws and knives of silex and obsidian from, 47.
Wash-basins; Roman, in front of spring W. of Hissarlik, probably successors to the Trojan ones of Homer, 65; the supposed marble Trojan at the springs of Bounarbashi do not exist, 268; but only a Doric corona-block from Ilium, now used for washing, 269.
Watch-shaped Terracottas, with two holes (Ilium), 216.

Water-pipe, Roman, in cavern W. of Hissarlik, 64, 65.
Weapons, bronze, of c. 2, fused and curled up by the conflagration, 58.
Weather at Hissarlik, 15, 386.
Webb, P. Barker; 'Topographic de la Troade,' 271, 330.
Weights; in the form of animals, for gold and silver, Egyptian and Assyrian, 301, 302; of terra-cotta, inscribed, said to be from Hissarlik, *Pref.* xxv.
——, for looms or nets; (c. 2), 172-3; terra-cotta cylinders, 135; granite, 173.
Welcker, F. G.; 'Ueber die Lage des Homerischen Ilion,' 285.
Wells; Hellenic, in Acropolis, 19, 89; mixture of objects found in it, 19; ancient, at C. Lectum, 316; sulphurous, E. of Assos, 320.
Wheel-made pottery. (*See* POTTERY.)
Whetstones of hardened slate (c. 1), 42; parallels, *ib.;* (c. 2), 172.
Whorls or Whirls, terra-cotta, plain and ornamented; above 22,000 found in c. 1-5, 268; about 4000 found in 1882, 39; their use as votive offerings, *ib.*, 105-6, 300, *Pref.* xviii; in India, with symbols like the Trojan, 39, 40; of terra-cotta or glass, used as money in the Pelew Is., 40; in Italy, 40; in Swiss lake habitations, *ib.;* at Rome and Albano, *ib.;* Helbig and Gross on the use of, 41; found by Gross in Switzerland with spindles still sticking in, *ib.;* so in Egypt, 295; (c. 2), one *with copper pin sticking in it*, indicating its *votive* use, 105-6; many in temple A, 120; appearance of writing on, *ib.* ; other patterns, 71; the sun, animals, manikins, 121; parallels, *ib.* ; the 卍 and 卐, 122, 126, f. ; Hittite and Cypriote, like the Trojan, 127; hundreds of, in c. 3, 183; also in c. 4, 188; vast numbers in c. 1-5, 268; some in c. 6, *ib.* ; a few plain in c. 7 and in the Hellenic layer on Bali Dagh; but none in lowest stratum of the latter, *ib.* ; one in tum. Ach., 250; their use with the *spindle* (*q. v.*), 293, f. ; wood and terra-cotta, on Egyptian spindles, 295; Syrian, of amber, 296; of wood, stone, or metal, on Greek and Roman spindles, 298; found with spindle-sticks and copper nails in, types of their *common* and *sacred* use, 300; carved, with Babylonian symbols, on a Hittite idol, *Pref.* xviii; one from Caesarea in Cappadocia, *ib.*
Wilkinson, Sir G.; 'The Ancient Egyptians,' 293, f.
Winckelmann, 'Geschichte der Kunst des Alterthums,' 156; on the δέπας ἀμφικύπελλον, *ib.*
Wind, North; strong and lasting at Hissarlik, 14, 15.
Wine; of the Troad, excellent, 7; diluted by the Trojans, as in Homer, except for libations; by Greeks and Romans generally, except hard drinkers; severe law of Zaleucus against drinking unmixed, 145.
Winer; engineer, on ancient money, 112; his theory unsound, *ib.*
Wings; of the Trojan owl-vases and idols, significance of, *Preface* xix; seen also on engraved stones of Babylonia, and in the arms of the Mycenean goddess, *ib.*
Wire, gold; made by Hephaestus, 107; net to catch Ares &c., 108.
Witkowsky, N. J., on jade, 172.
Witte, J. de ; on site of Troy, 286.
Wolf's Homeric criticism, *Pref.* xv.
Wolff, J. R., surveyor; his plan of Ilium (VIII. at end of volume), 14.
Workmen, Turkish, Greek, and Jewish, their different characters, 10, 11.
—— Trojan. (*See* TOOLS.)
Worsaae, J. J. A., his 'Nordiske Oldsager i det Kongelige Museum i Kjöbenhavn,' 43, 94, 248; 'Mémoires de la Société Royale des Antiquités du Nord,' 95.
Wreaths of gold, estimated by talents, 114; Damareta's, *ib.*
Written Characters (perhaps) on some

newly found whorls (c. 2), 120; decipherment of those found before, *Pref.* xxv; the Asianic syllabaries of Asia Minor; origin from the Hittite hieroglyphics; difference between the Trojan and Cypriote forms, *Preface* xxiii–xxv.

X.

Xanthus, Lydian historian, on inhabitants and rulers of Troy, 262.
Xenocrates, philosopher, at Assos, 319.
Xenophon; quoted, 276, 323.
Xerxes; his visit to Ilium, 196, 346; march round the E. of IDA, 329.
Xiphion, the sword-lily or sedge-leaf, original pattern of the sword, 95.

Y.

Yarkand; white jade from, 172.
Yates, James; on spinning, 297, f.
Yeni Kioi or *Neo Chori* (new village), 306, 347; site of OPPIDUM NEE, 344.
Yeni Shehr (new town), village, subject to drought, 16; mound near, discovered to be an heroic tomb, 17, 306, 347; site of SIGEUM, 344; unknown ancient town N. of, *ib.*
Yosemite Valley, in California, 174.
Yucatan, pottery with ⌐⌐, 122.

Z.

Z, the letter Zῆτα, probably connected with the 卐, 125.
Zaleucus, legislator, 145.
Zeitounli Kioi, village, 330.
Zeitounli Tsai (river of olives), its ravages, 327, 330, 331.
'*Zeitschrift für Ethnologie*,' 49.
Zeleia; Lycian city, N. limit of *Dardania* (*q. v.*), 274.
Zeno, founder of the Stoics, 319.
Zeus (*Dyaus*); the supreme Aryan god of sky, air, rain, wind, and lightning; the 卐 and 卍 his symbols, 124–5; the πίθοι in his palace (Hom.), 149; the Olympian, of Phidias, 163; his altar, shrine, and throne on Ida, 334, 336; nuptials with Hera, 335. (*See* GARGARUS, SARIKIS.)
—— *Herkeios;* altar of, at Ilium; Priam slain on, 290; sacrifice of Alexander to, *ib.*
Zilenli Kioi, village, 330.
Zilenli Tsai, R., 330.
Ziller, E., architect; excavations in acropolis on Bali Dagh, 265; map of the Troad (No. 140), 347.
Zonaras; quoted, 83.
Zones of the Earth. (*See* BALLS, EARTH, EUDOXUS.)

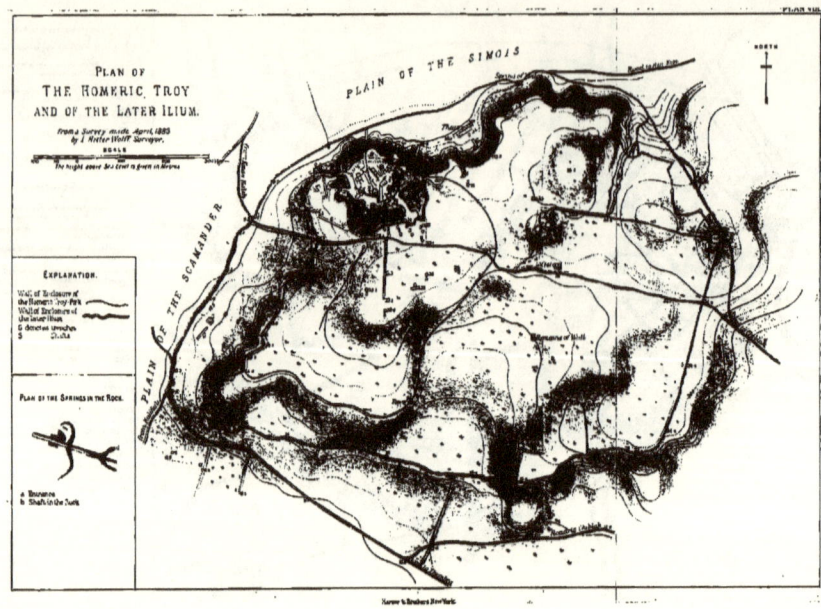

SCHLIEMANN'S ILIOS.

ILIOS, the City and Country of the Trojans. The Results of Researches and Discoveries on the Site of Troy and throughout the Troad in the years 1871–'72–'73–'78–'79; including an Autobiography of the Author. By Dr. HENRY SCHLIEMANN, F.S.A., F.R.I. British Architects; Author of "Troy and its Remains," "Mycenæ," "Troja," &c. With a Preface, Appendices, and Notes by Professors RUDOLF VIRCHOW, MAX MÜLLER, A. H. SAYCE, J. P. MAHAFFY, H. BRUGSCH-BEY, P. ASCHERSON, M. A. POSTOLACCAS, M. E. BURNOUF, Mr. F. CALVERT, and Mr. A. J. DUFFIELD. With Maps, Plans, and about 1800 Illustrations. Imperial 8vo, Cloth, $12 00.

This work is sound and satisfactory in the highest degree. It deals with the varied aspects of a subject of permanent interest with a skill and comprehensiveness that entitle it to a permanent place in the library of all who are interested in the poetical, historical, and physical associations and characteristics of the Troad. * * * The book has claims as genuine on the attention of the admirers of the masterpiece of Greek poetry for its own sake as on the respect of those students who, indifferent to the charms of the noblest of ancient poems, turn eagerly to scrutinize new illustrations of a stage in the struggle of "unaccommodated man" to earn the title of a tool-making animal.—*Athenæum*, London.

His discoveries not only throw a new and copious light on the Homeric controversies, and compel a readjustment of existing notions regarding the geography and history of the Troad, but open vistas in hitherto unknown epochs of its prehistoric civilization.—*N. Y. Sun*.

This new book is profoundly fascinating. * * * This noble book of Dr. Schliemann is a tale of absorbing interest, and has the undoubted merit of being "all true," whatever critics may say of the author's speculations and theories. * * * It is far larger, more minute and copious in details, fuller of autobiographical incidents, and more richly illustrated than any of his previous works. Some of the most learned Orientalists and archæologists of the world have contributed to it. * * * "Ilios" is published in a substantial style of beauty commensurate with the great merits of the work.—*N. Y. Journal of Commerce*.

Few readers of this splendid volume will close its pages without the conviction of intuition that they have been visiting the city of Priam and the scenes of Homer's immortal song. And those who yield only to the conviction of reason will admit that the excavations of Hissarlik would have had an imperishable value even if the "Iliad" had never been sung.—*N. Y. Tribune*.

The importance of this work, and of the wonderful discoveries which are here given to the world can hardly be overrated. Even if Troy were not a classic name, if we had never heard of Achilles, Hector, or Homer, still the discovery of six buried cities on a hill in Asia Minor, piled one upon another, in successive strata to a height of more than fifty feet, one at least being a town of civilization and wealth, and all lying unknown and unsuspected beneath the ruins of a seventh, and this an historic Greek city whose foundation precedes the opening of authentic history, would be an archæological fact of the first magnitude. A mere glance at Schliemann's volume, with its plentiful illustrations, is enough to convince the most sceptical that a new mine of wealth has been opened to archæology. It is time for all scholars to know that a new chapter in the early history of the intercourse of early Greece, as well as Asia Minor, with foreign lands has been opened.—*The Nation*, N.Y.

PUBLISHED BY HARPER & BROTHERS, NEW YORK.

☞ HARPER & BROTHERS *will send the above work by mail, postage prepaid, to any part of the United States, on receipt of the price.*

CESNOLA'S CYPRUS.

CYPRUS: its Ancient Cities, Tombs, and Temples. A Narrative of Researches and Excavations during Ten Years' Residence in that Island. By General LOUIS PALMA DI CESNOLA, Mem. of the Royal Academy of Sciences, Turin; Hon. Mem. of the Royal Society of Literature, London, &c. With Appendix containing a Treatise on "The Rings and Gems in the Treasure of Kurium," by C. W. KING, M.A.; a "List of Engraved Gems found at Different Places in Cyprus;" a Treatise "On the Pottery of Cyprus," by A. S. MURRAY; Lists of "Greek Inscriptions," "Inscriptions in the Cypriote Character," and "Inscriptions in the Phœnician Character." With Portrait, Maps, and 400 Illustrations. Third Edition. 8vo, Cloth, Gilt Tops and Uncut Edges, $7 50.

Cesnola has given us a lively and picturesque narrative. His labors extended over nearly the whole surface of an island one hundred miles in length, by about thirty in greatest breadth, and were continued for nearly ten years. In zeal, patience, and intelligence, therefore—especially when we consider that he was compelled to rely wholly upon his private means—he has proved himself second to no other archæological explorer. * * * He has reaped such a reward as no previous archæologist, working alone and with such restricted means, has ever achieved. His discoveries not only throw an entirely new light upon many centuries of Cypriote civilization, but they also illustrate that of Egypt, Phœnicia, Assyria, and Greece. He has restored, if not the whole, yet a great portion of the "missing link" between the first and the last of these great forces in human history. One would scarcely guess, from his modest, unassuming narrative, the inestimable value of his entire collection of ancient relics.—*N. Y. Tribune.*

The author tells this story in a clear, intelligible, and perfectly straightforward way, and he has brightened it by the introduction of so many anecdotes which serve to illustrate the life of to-day in Turkish countries, so many which give us graphic pictures of his own difficulties, perplexities, and triumphs, that the human interest of the book well-nigh outweighs its archæological interest. It is, in fact, a book which will entertain readers of every class, whether or not they know or care aught for archæology.—*N. Y. Evening Post.*

* * * It must not be supposed that his book is a mere dry catalogue of works of art, discovered and arranged. It is, on the contrary, a most interesting narrative of personal adventure, full of humor, is written in a bright, gossipy vein. * * * The most important discovery made by him was of the golden treasures of Kurium, which he describes in the simple style, absolutely free from egotism or self-laudation, which imparts so much pleasure to the reader. There is nothing in fiction more dazzling than the description he gives of this momentous discovery, no record of exploration so absorbing in interest, so startling in result, as this simple story of the dark passage to the vault, the bursting open of the stone door closed behind some priest twenty-four centuries ago, the removal of the dust, the glitter of the first golden bracelet, and then the heaps of silver plate, the basins filled with exquisite gold jewellery, the delicious gems, the rare alabasters and bronzes which were in the treasure chambers of the old temple. * * * A more interesting and at the same time more valuable work has not been published for a long time.—*Brooklyn Eagle.*

PUBLISHED BY HARPER & BROTHERS, NEW YORK.

☞ HARPER & BROTHERS *will send the above work by mail, postage prepaid, to any part of the United States, on receipt of the price.*

VALUABLE AND INTERESTING WORKS

FOR

STUDENTS OF ANCIENT AND MODERN ART.

☞ HARPER & BROTHERS *will send any of the following works by mail, postage prepaid, to any part of the United States, on receipt of the price.*

☞ *For a full list of works published by* HARPER & BROTHERS, *see* HARPER'S ENLARGED CATALOGUE, *360 pp., 8vo, which will be sent by mail, postage prepaid, on receipt of Nine Cents.*

History of Ancient Art.
By Dr. FRANZ REBER, Director of the Bavarian Royal and State Galleries of Paintings, Professor in the University and Polytechnic of Munich. Revised by the Author, and Translated and Augmented by JOSEPH THACHER CLARKE. With 308 Illustrations, and a Glossary of Technical Terms. 8vo, Cloth, $3 50.

Ilios.
Ilios, the City and Country of the Trojans. The results of Researches and Discoveries on the Site of Troy and Throughout the Troad in the years 1871–'72–'73–'78–'79. Including an Autobiography of the Author. By Dr. HENRY SCHLIEMANN, F.S.A., Author of "Troja," "Mycenæ," &c. With a Preface, Appendices, and Notes by Professors RUDOLF VIRCHOW, MAX MÜLLER, A. H. SAYCE, J. P. MAHAFFY, H. BRUGSCH-BEY, P. ASCHERSON, M. A. POSTOLACCAS, M. E. BURNOUF, Mr. F. CALVERT, and Mr. A. J. DUFFIELD. With Illustrations representing nearly 2000 Types of the Objects found in the Excavations of the Seven Cities on the Site of Ilios. Maps, Plans, and Illustrations. Imperial 8vo, Cloth, $12 00.

Troja:
Results of the Latest Researches and Discoveries on the Site of Homer's Troy, and in the Heroic Tumuli and other Sites, made in the year 1882; and a Narrative of a Journey in the Troad in 1881. By Dr. HENRY SCHLIEMANN, F.S.A., Author of "Ilios," &c. With a Preface by Prof. A. H. SAYCE. With 150 Illustrations and 4 Maps and Plans. Imperial 8vo. (*Just Ready.*)

Pottery and Porcelain of all Times and Nations.
With Tables of Factory and Artists' Marks, for the Use of Collectors. By WILLIAM C. PRIME, LL.D. Illustrated. 8vo, Cloth, Uncut Edges and Gilt Tops, $7 00; Half Calf, $9 25. (In a Box.)

A History of Wood-Engraving.
By G. E. WOODBERRY. Illustrated. 8vo, Ornamental Cloth, $3 50.

South Kensington.
Travels in South Kensington. With Notes on Decorative Art and Architecture in England. By MONCURE DANIEL CONWAY, Author of "The Sacred Anthology," "The Wandering Jew," "Thomas Carlyle," &c. Illustrated. 8vo, Cloth, $2 50.

Contemporary Art in Europe.
By S. G. W. BENJAMIN. Copiously Illustrated. 8vo, Cloth, Illuminated and Gilt, $3 50; Half Calf, $5 75.

Art in America.
By S. G. W. BENJAMIN. Illustrated. 8vo, Cloth, Illuminated and Gilt, $4 00; Half Calf, $6 25.

Cyprus: its Ancient Cities, Tombs, and Temples.
A Narrative of Researches and Excavations during Ten Years' Residence in that Island. By General LOUIS PALMA DI CESNOLA, Mem. of the Royal Academy of Sciences, Turin; Hon. Mem. of the Royal Society of Literature, London, &c. With Appendix containing a Treatise on "The Rings and Gems in the Treasure of Kurium," by C. W. KING, M.A.; a "List of Engraved Gems found at Different Places in Cyprus;" a Treatise "On the Pottery of Cyprus," by A. S. MURRAY; Lists of "Greek Inscriptions," "Inscriptions in the Cypriote Character," and "Inscriptions in the Phœnician Character." With Portrait, Maps, and 400 Illustrations. Third Edition. 8vo, Cloth, Gilt Tops and Uncut Edges, $7 50.

Caricature and other Comic Art,
In all Times and Many Lands. By JAMES PARTON. With 203 Illustrations. 8vo, Cloth, Gilt Tops and Uncut Edges, $5 00.

Ancient Egyptians.
A Popular Account of the Ancient Egyptians. Revised and Abridged from his larger Work. By Sir J. GARDNER WILKINSON, D.C.L., F.R.S., &c. With 500 Illustrations. 2 vols., 12mo, Cloth, $3 50.

Peru.
Incidents of Travel and Exploration in the Land of the Incas. By E. G. SQUIER, M.A., F.S.A., late U. S. Commissioner to Peru; Author of "The States of Central America," "Nicaragua: its People, Scenery, Monuments, Resources, Condition, and Proposed Canal," &c. With Map and 258 Illustrations. 8vo, Cloth, $5 00.

Atlantis:
The Antediluvian World. By IGNATIUS DONNELLY. Ill'd. 12mo, Cloth, $2.

The Mikado's Empire.
Book I. History of Japan, from 660 B.C. to 1872 A.D. Book II. Personal Experiences, Observations, and Studies in Japan, 1870–1874. By WILLIAM ELLIOT GRIFFIS, A.M., late of the Imperial University of Tōkiō, Japan. New Edition. With a Supplementary Chapter on Japan in 1883. Copiously Illustrated. 8vo, Cloth, $4 00.

Bible Lands:
Their Modern Customs and Manners Illustrative of Scripture. By the Rev. HENRY J. VAN-LENNEP, D.D. Illustrated with upward of 350 Wood Engravings and Two Colored Maps. 8vo, Cloth, $5 00; Sheep, $6 00; Half Morocco, $8 00.

Ancient America,
In Notes on American Archæology. By JOHN D. BALDWIN, A.M. With Illustrations. 12mo, Cloth, $2 00.

Fresh Discoveries at Nineveh and Babylon.
Fresh Discoveries at Nineveh and Babylon; with Travels in Armenia, Kurdistan, and the Desert: being the Result of a Second Expedition undertaken for the Trustees of the British Museum. By AUSTEN HENRY LAYARD, M.P. With all the Maps and Illustrations in the English Edition. 8vo, Cloth, $4 00; Half Calf, $6 25.

Nineveh.
A Popular Account of the Discoveries at Nineveh. By AUSTEN HENRY LAYARD, M.P. Abridged by him from his larger Work. Numerous Illustrations. 12mo, Cloth, $1 75.

The North Americans of Antiquity.
Their Origin, Migrations, and Type of Civilization Considered. By JOHN T. SHORT. Illustrated. 8vo, Cloth, $3 00.

The Ceramic Art:
A Compendium of the History and Manufacture of Pottery and Porcelain. By JENNIE J. YOUNG. Illustrated. 8vo, Cloth, $5 00.

Art Decoration Applied to Furniture.
By HARRIET PRESCOTT SPOFFORD. With Illustrations. 8vo, Cloth, $4 00; Half Calf, $6 25.

Historical Studies of Church-Building
In the Middle Ages. Venice, Siena, Florence. By CHARLES ELIOT NORTON. 8vo, Cloth, $3 00.

Sketches and Studies in Southern Europe.
By JOHN ADDINGTON SYMONDS. In 2 vols. Post 8vo, Cloth, $4 00.

The Mythology of Greece and Rome,
With Special Reference to its Use in Art. From the German of O. SEEMANN. Edited by G. H. BIANCHI, B.A., late Scholar of St. Peter's College, Cambridge, Brotherton Sanskrit Prizeman, 1875. With 64 Illustrations. 16mo, Cloth, 60 cents.

The Student's History of Greece.
A History of Greece, from the Earliest Times to the Roman Conquest. With Supplementary Chapters on the History of Literature and Art. By WM. SMITH, D.C.L., LL.D. Illustrated. 12mo, Cloth, $1 25.

The Student's History of Rome.
A History of Rome, from the Earliest Times to the Establishment of the Empire. With Chapters on the History of Literature and Art. By H. G. LIDDELL, D.D., Dean of Christ Church, Oxford. Ill'd. 12mo, Cloth, $1 25.

Carthage and Her Remains:
Being an Account of the Excavations and Researches on the Site of the Phœnician Metropolis, in Africa and other Adjacent Places. Conducted under the Auspices of Her Majesty's Government. By Dr. N. DAVIS, F.R.G.S. Profusely Illustrated with Maps, Woodcuts, Chromo-Lithographs, &c., &c. 8vo, Cloth, $4 00; Half Calf, $6 25.

Art Hints.
Architecture, Sculpture, and Painting. By JAMES JACKSON JARVES. 12mo, Cloth, $1 50.

Life of Benjamin Robert Haydon,
Historical Painter, from his Autobiography and Journals. Edited and Compiled by TOM TAYLOR. 2 vols., 12mo, Cloth, $3 00.

The China Hunters Club.
By the Youngest Member. Illustrated. Post 8vo, Cloth, $1 75.

Art Education Applied to Industry.
By GEO. WARD NICHOLS. Ill'd. 8vo, Cloth, Illuminated and Gilt, $4 00.

www.ingramcontent.com/pod-product-compliance
Lightning Source LLC
Chambersburg PA
CBHW051856300426
44117CB00006B/420